Lecture Notes in Computer Science 7476

Commenced Publication in 1973
Founding and Former Series Editors:
Gerhard Goos, Juris Hartmanis, and Jan van Leeuwen

Editorial Board

David Hutchison
  Lancaster University, UK
Takeo Kanade
  Carnegie Mellon University, Pittsburgh, PA, USA
Josef Kittler
  University of Surrey, Guildford, UK
Jon M. Kleinberg
  Cornell University, Ithaca, NY, USA
Alfred Kobsa
  University of California, Irvine, CA, USA
Friedemann Mattern
  ETH Zurich, Switzerland
John C. Mitchell
  Stanford University, CA, USA
Moni Naor
  Weizmann Institute of Science, Rehovot, Israel
Oscar Nierstrasz
  University of Bern, Switzerland
C. Pandu Rangan
  Indian Institute of Technology, Madras, India
Bernhard Steffen
  TU Dortmund University, Germany
Madhu Sudan
  Microsoft Research, Cambridge, MA, USA
Demetri Terzopoulos
  University of California, Los Angeles, CA, USA
Doug Tygar
  University of California, Berkeley, CA, USA
Gerhard Weikum
  Max Planck Institute for Informatics, Saarbruecken, Germany

T0224195

Axel Pinz   Thomas Pock
Horst Bischof   Franz Leberl (Eds.)

Pattern Recognition

Joint 34th DAGM and 36th OAGM Symposium
Graz, Austria, August 28-31, 2012
Proceedings

 Springer

Volume Editors

Axel Pinz
Graz University of Technology
Electrical Measurement and Measurement Signal Processing
Kronesgasse 5, 8010 Graz, Austria
E-mail: axel.pinz@tugraz.at

Thomas Pock
Horst Bischof
Franz Leberl
Graz University of Technology
Institute for Computer Graphics and Vision
Inffeldgasse 16, 8010 Graz, Austria
E-mail: {pock, bischof, leberl}@icg.tugraz.at

ISSN 0302-9743   e-ISSN 1611-3349
ISBN 978-3-642-32716-2   e-ISBN 978-3-642-32717-9
DOI 10.1007/978-3-642-32717-9
Springer Heidelberg Dordrecht London New York

Library of Congress Control Number: 2012944034

CR Subject Classification (1998): I.5.4, I.5, I.4.6, I.4.8, I.4, I.2.10, I.2.6, I.3.5

LNCS Sublibrary: SL 6 – Image Processing, Computer Vision, Pattern Recognition,
and Graphics

© Springer-Verlag Berlin Heidelberg 2012
This work is subject to copyright. All rights are reserved, whether the whole or part of the material is
concerned, specifically the rights of translation, reprinting, re-use of illustrations, recitation, broadcasting,
reproduction on microfilms or in any other way, and storage in data banks. Duplication of this publication
or parts thereof is permitted only under the provisions of the German Copyright Law of September 9, 1965,
in its current version, and permission for use must always be obtained from Springer. Violations are liable
to prosecution under the German Copyright Law.
The use of general descriptive names, registered names, trademarks, etc. in this publication does not imply,
even in the absence of a specific statement, that such names are exempt from the relevant protective laws
and regulations and therefore free for general use.

Typesetting: Camera-ready by author, data conversion by Scientific Publishing Services, Chennai, India

Printed on acid-free paper

Springer is part of Springer Science+Business Media (www.springer.com)

Preface

On behalf of the Organizing Committee, we would like to welcome you to the proceedings of the joint conference of the DAGM and OAGM that was held in Graz. It was the 34th symposium of the German Association for Pattern Recognition and the 36th OAGM conference. This was, after 1984, 1994, and 2005, already the fourth joint meeting between these two societies, showing their close relationship with each other.

The technical program covered all aspects of computer vision and pattern recognition. The result is reflected in these proceedings, which contain the papers presented at DAGM-OAGM 2012. Our call for papers resulted in 98 submissions from institutions in 19 countries. Each paper underwent a rigorous reviewing process and was assigned to at least three Program Committee members for review. The reviewing phase was followed by a discussion phase among the respective Program Committee members in order to suggest papers for acceptance. The final decision was taken during a Program Committee meeting held in Graz based on all reviews, the discussion results and, if necessary, additional reviewing. This year we introduced a "handling reviewer" for each paper, who summarized the discussion in a consolidation report that was also submitted to the authors. On the basis of this rigorous process we selected a total of 50 papers, corresponding to an acceptance rate of 51%. Out of all accepted papers, 27 were chosen for oral and 23 for poster presentation. Out of the 50 accepted papers, 32 are from Germany, 7 from Austria, 9 from the rest of Europe and 2 from overseas. All accepted papers are published in these proceedings and were given the same number of pages. We would like to thank all members of the Program Committee as well as the external reviewers for their valuable and highly appreciated contribution to the community. We would also like to extend our thanks to all authors of submitted papers; without their contribution we would not have been able to assemble such a strong program.

The technical program was complemented by two workshops: one on "Computer Vision in Applications" and the other on "New Challenges in Neural Computation." The program contained two tutorials: one on "Random Forests in Computer Vision" held by Christian Leistner, the other on "Submodularity in Machine Learning and Computer Vision," held by Andreas Krause and Stefanie Jegelka.

In addition to the presentations from the technical program, we were also proud to have three internationally renowned invited speakers at the conference:

- Francis Bach (INRIA): Large-Scale Convex Optimization for Machine Learning
- Jiri Matas (CTU Prague): Tracking: An Old Dog with Many New Tricks
- Antonio Torralba (MIT): Understanding Visual Scenes

We again organized the Young Researchers Forum at DAGM 2012 to promote scientific interaction between excellent young researchers and our community. This year the contributions of four students were accepted, who presented their bachelor or master thesis work during the conference and interacted with our community. Their participation was kindly supported by Daimler.

We would like to extend our sincere thanks to everyone who helped in making DAGM-OAGM 2012 possible. We are indebted to Renate Hönel and Karin Maier for their help with all organizational matters, and Christian Reinbacher for coordinating the local arrangements.

We would also like to sincerely thank all our sponsors for their financial support, which helped to keep the registration fees as low as possible, especially those of the student attendees. We appreciate their donations to our community, which values and recognizes the importance of these contributions to our field.

It was an honor for us to host the joint DAGM-OAGM meeting this year, and we look forward to next year's DAGM meeting in Saarbrücken.

August 2012   Horst Bischof
                                                      Axel Pinz
                                                    Thomas Pock

Organization

General Chair

Horst Bischof   Graz University of Technology, Austria

Honorary Chair

Franz Leberl   Graz University of Technology, Austria

Local Arrangements

Christian Reinbacher   Graz University of Technology, Austria

Program Committee

Chairs

Axel Pinz   Graz University of Technology, Austria
Thomas Pock   Graz University of Technology, Austria

Members

Csaba Beleznai	Austrian Institute of Technology, Austria
Thomas Brox	University of Freiburg, Germany
Andres Bruhn	University of Stuttgart, Germany
Joachim Buhmann	ETH Zurich, Switzerland
Wilhelm Burger	University of Applied Sciences, Upper Austria
Daniel Cremers	Technische Universität München, Germany
Andreas Dengel	TU Kaiserslautern, Germany
Joachim Denzler	University of Jena, Germany
Michael Felsberg	Linköping University, Sweden
Gernot Fink	TU Dortmund University, Germany
Boris Flach	Czech Technical University, Czech Republic
Uwe Franke	Daimler AG, Germany
Peter Gehler	Max Planck Campus Tübingen, Germany
Margrit Gelautz	Vienna University of Technology, Austria
Michael Goesele	Technische Universität Darmstadt, Germany
Fred Hamprecht	Heidelberg University, Germany
Matthias Hein	Saarland University, Germany
Olaf Hellwich	Technische Universität Berlin, Germany
Vaclav Hlavac	Czech Technical University, Czech Republic
Joachim Hornegger	Universität Erlangen-Nürnberg, Germany

Xiaoyi Jiang	Heidelberg University, Germany
Reinhard Koch	Kiel University, Germany
Arjan Kuijper	Fraunhofer IGD, Germany
Christoph Lampert	Institute of Science and Technology, Austria
Bastian Leibe	RWTH Aachen University, Germany
Helmut Mayer	Universität d. Bundeswehr, München, Germany
Roland Memisevic	Goethe University Frankfurt, Germany
Rudolf Mester	Goethe University Frankfurt, Germany
Sebastian Nowozin	Microsoft Research, Cambridge, UK
Justus Piater	University of Innsbruck, Austria
Gerhard Rigoll	Technische Universität München, Germany
Bernhard Rinner	Alpen-Adria-Universität Klagenfurt, Austria
Bodo Rosenhahn	Leibnitz Universität Hannover, Germany
Stefan Roth	Technische Universität Darmstadt, Germany
Volker Roth	University of Basel, Switzerland
Carsten Rother	Microsoft Research, Cambridge, UK
Bernt Schiele	Max Planck Institut Informatik, Germany
Konrad Schindler	ETH Zurich, Switzerland
Christoph Schnörr	Heidelberg University, Germany
Nicu Sebe	University of Trento, Italy
Siniša Šegvić	University of Zagreb, Croatia
Thomas Vetter	University of Basel, Switzerland
Joachim Weickert	Saarland University, Germany
Martin Welk	UMIT Hall, Austria
Christopher Zach	Microsoft Research, Cambridge, UK

Awards 2011

Deutscher Mustererkennungspreis

The "Deutscher Mustererkennungspreis 2011" was awarded to:

Matthias Hein

for his outstanding work in pattern recognition, especially in the area of *"Graph-based learning methods, in particular manifold learning and nonlinear eigenproblems."*

DAGM Prizes

The main prize for DAGM 2011 was awarded to:

K. Köser, C. Zach, and M. Pollefeys:
"Dense 3D Reconstruction of Symmetric Scenes From a Single Image"

Further DAGM prizes for 2011 were awarded to:

H. C. Burger and S. Harmeling:
"Improving Denoising Algorithms via a Multi-Scale Meta-Procedure"

C. Keller, C. Hermes, and D. M. Gavrila:
"Will the Pedestrian Cross?"

Table of Contents

Segmentation

As Time Goes by—Anytime Semantic Segmentation with Iterative
Context Forests.. 1
  Björn Fröhlich, Erik Rodner, and Joachim Denzler

Interactive Labeling of Image Segmentation Hierarchies............... 11
  Georg Zankl, Yll Haxhimusa, and Adrian Ion

Hierarchy of Localized Random Forests for Video Annotation.......... 21
  Naveen Shankar Nagaraja, Peter Ochs, Kun Liu, and Thomas Brox

Low-Level Vision

A TV-L1 Optical Flow Method with Occlusion Detection 31
  Coloma Ballester, Lluis Garrido, Vanel Lazcano, and Vicent Caselles

Curvature Prior for MRF-Based Segmentation and Shape Inpainting ... 41
  Alexander Shekhovtsov, Pushmeet Kohli, and Carsten Rother

Mean Field for Continuous High-Order MRFs 52
  Kevin Schelten and Stefan Roth

How Well Do Filter-Based MRFs Model Natural Images? 62
  Qi Gao and Stefan Roth

3D Reconstruction

Anisotropic Range Image Integration 73
  Christopher Schroers, Henning Zimmer, Levi Valgaerts,
  Andrés Bruhn, Oliver Demetz, and Joachim Weickert

Modeling of Sparsely Sampled Tubular Surfaces Using Coupled
Curves 83
  Thorsten Schmidt, Margret Keuper, Taras Pasternak,
  Klaus Palme, and Olaf Ronneberger

Shape (Self-)Similarity and Dissimilarity Rating for Segmentation and
Matching 93
  Simon Winkelbach, Jens Spehr, Dirk Buchholz, Markus Rilk, and
  Friedrich M. Wahl

Dense 3D Reconstruction with a Hand-Held Camera 103
  Benjamin Ummenhofer and Thomas Brox

Recognition

OUR-CVFH – Oriented, Unique and Repeatable Clustered Viewpoint
Feature Histogram for Object Recognition and 6DOF Pose
Estimation   113
   Aitor Aldoma, Federico Tombari, Radu Bogdan Rusu, and
   Markus Vincze

3D Object Recognition and Pose Estimation for Multiple Objects Using
Multi-Prioritized RANSAC and Model Updating   123
   Michele Fenzi, Ralf Dragon, Laura Leal-Taixé,
   Bodo Rosenhahn, and Jörn Ostermann

Classification with Global, Local and Shared Features   134
   Hakan Bilen, Vinay P. Namboodiri, and Luc J. Van Gool

Object Detection in Multi-view X-Ray Images   144
   Thorsten Franzel, Uwe Schmidt, and Stefan Roth

Applications

Eye Localization Using the Discriminative Generalized Hough
Transform   155
   Ferdinand Hahmann, Heike Ruppertshofen, Gordon Böer,
   Ralf Stannarius, and Hauke Schramm

Simultaneous Estimation of Material Properties and Pose
for Deformable Objects from Depth and Color Images   165
   Andreas Rune Fugl, Andreas Jordt, Henrik Gordon Petersen,
   Morten Willatzen, and Reinhard Koch

Surface Quality Inspection of Deformable Parts with Variable B-Spline
Surfaces   175
   Sebastian von Enzberg and Bernd Michaelis

Automated Image Forgery Detection through Classification of JPEG
Ghosts   185
   Fabian Zach, Christian Riess, and Elli Angelopoulou

Learning

Synergy-Based Learning of Facial Identity   195
   Martin Köstinger, Peter M. Roth, and Horst Bischof

Information Theoretic Clustering Using Minimum Spanning Trees   205
   Andreas C. Müller, Sebastian Nowozin, and Christoph H. Lampert

Dynamical SVM for Time Series Classification   216
    *Ramón Huerta, Shankar Vembu, Mehmet K. Muezzinoglu, and
    Alexander Vergara*

Trust-Region Algorithm for Nonnegative Matrix Factorization
with Alpha- and Beta-divergences   226
    Rafał Zdunek

Features

Line Matching Using Appearance Similarities and Geometric
Constraints   236
    Lilian Zhang and Reinhard Koch

Salient Pattern Detection Using W_2 on Multivariate Normal
Distributions   246
    Dominik Alexander Klein and Simone Frintrop

A Simple Extension of Stability Feature Selection   256
    A. Beinrucker, Ü. Dogan, and G. Blanchard

Feature-Based Multi-video Synchronization with Subframe Accuracy . . .   266
    A. Elhayek, C. Stoll, K.I. Kim, H.-P. Seidel, and C. Theobalt

Posters

Combination of Sinusoidal and Single Binary Pattern Projection
for Fast 3D Surface Reconstruction   276
    Christian Bräuer-Burchardt, Peter Kühmstedt, and Gunther Notni

Consensus Multi-View Photometric Stereo   287
    Mate Beljan, Jens Ackermann, and Michael Goesele

Automatic Scale Selection of Superimposed Signals   297
    Oliver Fleischmann and Gerald Sommer

Sensitivity/Robustness Flexible Ellipticity Measures   307
    Mehmet Ali Aktaş and Joviša Žunić

Sparse Point Estimation for Bayesian Regression via Simulated
Annealing   317
    Sudhir Raman and Volker Roth

Active Metric Learning for Object Recognition   327
    Sandra Ebert, Mario Fritz, and Bernt Schiele

Accuracy-Efficiency Evaluation of Adaptive Support Weight Techniques
for Local Stereo Matching   337
    Asmaa Hosni, Margrit Gelautz, and Michael Bleyer

Groupwise Shape Registration Based on Entropy Minimization   347
  Youngwook Kee, Daniel Cremers, and Junmo Kim

Adaptive Multi-cue 3D Tracking of Arbitrary Objects   357
  Germán Martín García, Dominik Alexander Klein, Jörg Stückler,
  Simone Frintrop, and Armin B. Cremers

Training of Classifiers for Quality Control of On-Line Laser Brazing
Processes with Highly Imbalanced Datasets   367
  Daniel Fecker, Volker Märgner, and Tim Fingscheidt

PCA-Enhanced Stochastic Optimization Methods   377
  Alina Kuznetsova, Gerard Pons-Moll, and Bodo Rosenhahn

A Real-Time MRF Based Approach for Binary Segmentation   387
  Dmitrij Schlesinger

Pottics – The Potts Topic Model for Semantic Image Segmentation   397
  Christoph Dann, Peter Gehler, Stefan Roth, and Sebastian Nowozin

Decision Tree Ensembles in Biomedical Time-Series Classification   408
  Alan Jović, Karla Brkić, and Nikola Bogunović

Spatio-temporally Coherent Interactive Video Object Segmentation
via Efficient Filtering   418
  Nicole Brosch, Asmaa Hosni, Christoph Rhemann, and
  Margrit Gelautz

Discrepancy Norm as Fitness Function for Defect Detection
on Regularly Textured Surfaces   428
  Gernot Stübl, Jean-Luc Bouchot, Peter Haslinger, and
  Bernhard Moser

Video Compression with 3-D Pose Tracking, PDE-Based Image Coding,
and Electrostatic Halftoning   438
  Christian Schmaltz and Joachim Weickert

Image Completion Optimised for Realistic Simulations of Wound
Development   448
  Michael Schneeberger, Martina Uray, and Heinz Mayer

Automatic Model Selection in Archetype Analysis   458
  Sandhya Prabhakaran, Sudhir Raman, Julia E. Vogt, and Volker Roth

Stereo Fusion from Multiple Viewpoints   468
  Christian Unger, Eric Wahl, Peter Sturm, and Slobodan Ilic

Confidence Measurements for Adaptive Bayes Decision Classifier
Cascades and Their Application to US Speed Limit Detection   478
  Armin Staudenmaier, Ulrich Klauck, Ulrich Kreßel,
  Frank Lindner, and Christian Wöhler

A Bottom-Up Approach for Learning Visual Object Detection Models
from Unreliable Sources... 488
    Fabian Nasse and Gernot A. Fink

Active Learning of Ensemble Classifiers for Gesture Recognition 498
    J. Schumacher, D. Sakič, A. Grumpe, Gernot A. Fink, and
    Christian Wöhler

Author Index.. 509

As Time Goes by—Anytime Semantic Segmentation with Iterative Context Forests

Björn Fröhlich, Erik Rodner, and Joachim Denzler

Computer Vision Group, Friedrich Schiller University of Jena, Germany
http://www.inf-cv.uni-jena.de

Abstract. We present a new approach for contextual semantic segmentation and introduce a new tree-based framework, which combines local information and context knowledge in a single model. The method itself is also suitable for anytime classification scenarios, where the challenge is to estimate a label for each pixel in an image while allowing an interruption of the estimation at any time. This offers the application of the introduced method in time-critical tasks, like automotive applications, with limited computational resources unknown in advance. Label estimation is done in an iterative manner and includes spatial context right from the beginning. Our approach is evaluated in extensive experiments showing its state-of-the-art performance on challenging street scene datasets with anytime classification abilities.

1 Introduction

Semantic labeling or classification is an important task for localizing objects or to perform scene understanding. In a large set of applications, such as road detection [3], street scene analysis [10], and robotics [11], one is often faced with constraints on classification time. Even more severe, those constraints are sometimes a priori unknown and depend on external conditions. For example, the time in which we require road and lane detection depends on the current speed of the car. Machine learning methods that allow for tackling these requirements by providing outputs at different time steps are referred to as anytime classification approaches [5]. The main idea is that output quality increases if more time is provided, while proper results are also available after a short initialization time.

In our paper, we present an anytime semantic segmentation approach, which is able to use contextual cues immediately after the first iteration. The approach is built on a technique, which we call *Iterative Context Forests* (ICF) (Fig. 1). It performs efficient semantic segmentation without explicit need for inference with conditional random field models and without time consuming feature extraction or post-processing steps. Instead of subsequently traversing a decision tree for each pixel until a leaf node is reached, we walk through a tree in a level-based manner for each pixel jointly.

Related Work on Anytime Classification. Anytime classification has been mostly considered for standard machine learning and data mining tasks instead

A. Pinz et al. (Eds.): DAGM/OAGM 2012, LNCS 7476, pp. 1–10, 2012.
© Springer-Verlag Berlin Heidelberg 2012

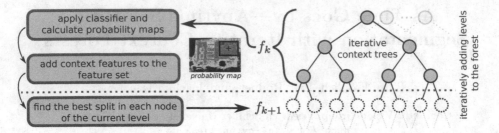

Fig. 1. Learning an Iterative Context Forest: we learn a random decision forest level by level and integrate context cues by always computing features using the previously estimated probability maps. This generates a series of classifiers f_k, which can be used for anytime classification.

of semantic segmentation and visual recognition. In [5], a decision tree classifier is presented, which is able to perform anytime classification and learning. Their paper also gives an introduction into the topic and discriminates between interruptible and contract anytime classifiers. In contrast to interruptible anytime classifiers, which are considered in our paper, contract classifiers are provided with time and memory requirements in advance. The work of [12] considers anytime classification for density estimation. The main idea is to incrementally refine the density estimate by traversing a tree, in which inner nodes store a rough Gaussian approximation of the density and each leaf node is related to a Parzen density estimator. Anytime classification with SVM is studied by [4] using geometric considerations. The authors of [13] use an anytime nearest neighbor classifier and propose methods for scheduling multiple object classification similar to [8]. In contrast to those works, we study anytime classification for visual recognition and show how to perform joint classification of pixels, which incorporates contextual knowledge.

Related Work on Context Modeling. We incorporate context knowledge by using the output of previous levels of a decision tree classifier as features for a new one. This strategy is similar to the one used by [6] for their mutual boosting approach. They train a set of object detectors simultaneously. In each round of the Boosting method, they add features derived from the results of the current classifier. Our work is also related to the approach of [14], where a two stage segmentation technique is proposed. Their idea is to first train a random forest using basic local features and then to train a second random forest using context features calculated using the first forest. In contrast, we learn a single random forest and incrementally add context features derived from coarser levels. This is essential to allow for anytime classification, since the procedure can be stopped at any time and still provides a proper result.

Outline We first give an informal definition of anytime classification and its requirements in Sect. 2. This is followed by describing our approach in Sect. 3.

Experiments in Sect. 4 evaluate our method on street scene analysis tasks and show their advantages as well as anytime properties. A summary of our findings and a discussion of future research directions conclude the paper.

2   Anytime Classification

The goal of standard machine learning methods is to estimate the latent relationship between inputs (feature vectors) and labels from available training data. In most cases, this can be expressed with a function $f : \mathcal{X} \rightarrow \mathcal{Y}$ mapping from the space $\mathcal{X}$ of all inputs to a defined label space $\mathcal{Y}$, such as $\mathcal{Y} \in \{1, \ldots, M\}$ for multi-class classification.

Anytime classification involves some time requirements posed during classification, i.e., the evaluation of the function f. At several time steps t_k, we would like to have a result $f_k(\mathbf{x}_*)$ for a test example $\mathbf{x}_*$. Thus, we have a series $\mathcal{F} = (f_k)_{k=1}^{\infty}$ of functions at certain time steps $(t_k)_{k=1}^{\infty}$. Allowing the system to spend more time during classification, the classification result should be more accurate. In contrast to state estimation in dynamic systems, anytime classification in our case considers the input to be static without any change over time. Thus, we do not get any additional sensor information during classification. The main requirements of anytime classification are given as follows:

1. **Decreasing error rate:** The excepted error ε of the decision functions in $\mathcal{F}$ should be monotonically decreasing, i.e., $\varepsilon(f_k) \geq \varepsilon(f_{k'})$ for $t_k < t_{k'}$.
2. **Flexibility:** The time differences $\triangle_k = t_{k+1} - t_k$ should be small to allow for high flexibility during classification.
3. **Direct availability:** The classification result is directly available in time step t_k and there is no additional time-consuming post-processing required after interrupting the algorithm.

To learn anytime classifiers, it is beneficial to build the series $\mathcal{F}$ of classifiers in an iterative manner, i.e., f_{k+1} is an extension and adaptation of f_k.

For evaluation of anytime classification systems, time/error curves defined by $(t_k, \varepsilon(f_k))_{k=1}^{\infty}$ are an essential tool. The limit of this curve gives us the performance of the classifier disregarding any time constraints. However, in anytime classification scenarios the rate in which the error decreases during the first time steps is often more important than the limit. In the following sections, we show how to develop an anytime classification system using random decision forests, which matches the requirements stated above.

3   Iterative Context Forests (ICF)

Due to the high amount of ambiguities present in recognition tasks, incorporating context knowledge is necessary. A common approach is to utilize a CRF model to combine independent local decisions with global or relative location context. However, those techniques require a large amount of the available classification

time, since they perform optimization with a large number of variables. Iterative Context Forests (ICF) allows for incorporating context knowledge directly during learning of the RDF without CRF modeling. The idea is to train a classifier f_{k+1} for the next time step, $i.e.$, the new level of the random forest, by using the output of the previous classifier f_k to compute additional features introduced in Section 3.3.

3.1   Random Decision Forest

A random decision forest (RDF) is an extension of the well known decision trees. The main disadvantage of decision trees without pruning is the high risk of over-fitting, which [1] try to prevent by different kinds of randomization. RDFs use multiple decision trees in which each tree is trained with a different random subset of the training data. Furthermore, in an inner node of a tree, only a random subset S with τ features is used to find the best binary split of the training data, which is done by maximizing the information gain. A huge benefit of this idea is that not all available features have to be computed in each inner node.

Typically each new example traverses the tree and is classified by using the empirical distribution in the reached leaf node. In contrast, we propose a breadth-first method for classification which enables anytime classification. All new examples traverse the tree jointly in a level-wise manner. In each node, the empirical class distribution estimated during learning can be used as a rough classification result. This offers the possibility to obtain a classification result for all examples at different levels k and time steps t_k. The accuracy depends on the current level reached in the tree and care has to be taken to prevent over-fitting. In our case, over-fitting due to an increasing model complexity is reduced by utilizing the randomization techniques of an RDF classifier. Given multiple trees, all trees are traversed level-wise in a parallel manner. The series of classifiers f_k, as defined in Sect. 2, is thus the learned random forest reduced to a maximum depth of k. Another idea to extend random decision forests towards anytime capability is to traverse one tree after another. However, our approach is more flexible and allows contextual information.

3.2   Color Features

An important requirement for the features is a fast extraction. Therefore, we use basically the same operations as in [14] as an initial feature set with minor modifications:

1. **pixel pair features:** the output of simple operations A, $A - B$, $|A - B|$, $A + B$, with randomly selected pixels A and B in the neighborhood of the current position (Fig. 2a).
2. **Haar like features** [15]: horizontal, vertical, and diagonal differences (Fig. 2b)
3. further **rectangular area features** using integral images to compute the mean values in these area (Fig. 2c-2e)
4. **relative position** in the image (normalized coordinates)

a: pixel pair   b: Haar-like [15]   c: rectangle   d: centered rectangle   e: diff. of two cent. rectangles

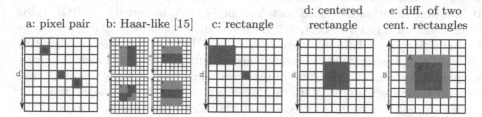

Fig. 2. Features used in our approach for both context and color cues similar to [14]. A window of size d is surrounding the current pixel position (blue pixel). Depending on the type of a feature one or two pixels (a) or one (c and d) or two areas (b and e) are randomly selected. Every parameter is selected randomly (the size of an area, the position of the area etc.) under some constraints, *e.g.*, for image (d) the rectangle is centered. For features utilizing areas, the mean values of the areas is used.

input   iteration f_k probability map for class building   iteration f_{k+1}

Fig. 3. An exemplary scenario: Some windows are wrongly classified as door in iteration f_k. Using the probability map for class building with the rectangle features (see Fig.2c) shown in the third image the wrongly classified windows will be classified correctly in iteration f_{k+1}.

This leads to a large number of possible features computed on RGB or CIELAB color channels. Due to the reason, that only some features are randomly selected as potential split features for a node during training, those feature do not have to be computed in advance. Therefore, we only have to compute a small set of features instead of full feature representation as used in [7].

3.3 Iteratively Extending the Feature Set with Context Features

A standard RDF uses a fixed feature set S during the whole training process. But how is it possible to model important context cues like "window is surrounded by building" and "car stands on road or pavement"? The basic idea of the ICF is to adapt the feature set S during training. For classifying a local image patch, an important context cue is the relative position of other objects. This can be modeled by using the probability for specific classes in an image region with a learned offset (compare Fig. 2c). If we know the probability of each class and each pixel we can utilize the same features used before for the raw image data calculated with these so called probability maps.

This is a typical chicken-egg problem, since an already learned classification model is required. In our case we can use the output of the previous iteration as a rough estimate of the probabilities which automatically improves over time. In the first iteration $k = 1$, $\mathcal{S}$ includes only simple features, *e.g.*, RGB color features as introduced in Sect. 3.2. However, in iteration $k > 1$ the pixel-wise probabilities for each training image estimated by f_{k-1} can be considered to obtain a rough estimate of the position and alignment of other classes. To give a simple example, in the first level of the forest each tree makes a decision based only on the color features. With this the image is very roughly separated in at least two main classes, *e.g.*, "road" and "building". For the next level of the forest we use these rough segmentation as context features. For example, if we want to decide whether the red area is a roof of a building or a car, it might be important if there are some pixel below that area already labeled as building or not. Therefore, we use those pixel-wise probabilities from the previous step to compute semantic context features, which are added to $\mathcal{S}$. In contrast to Shotton [14], we model contextual information with only a single forest, which allows for anytime classification. The training step of an ICF is illustrated in Fig. 1 and an example how context is modeled is shown in Fig. 3.

3.4   Anytime Capability

In Sect. 2, we defined the requirements for anytime classification. Now we show that all of the three points are practically valid for our ICF method. The computational effort for each step is very low, since only one simple decision stump has to be evaluated for each pixel and tree in each level. Consequently, our method is very flexible and allows for decisions in equidistant time steps. Furthermore, we do not need any post-processing steps like an unsupervised segmentation used in previous work [2,7,16,17]. The final labeling is done by assigning the class with the highest probability to each pixel. In our experiments, we show empirically that the first property of decreasing error rates is also satisfied. This is mainly due to the incorporated randomization during learning, which reduces overfitting effects normally appearing when increasing the model complexity of a classifier [1]. However, we are not able to provide a theoretical proof since the characteristics of the test data are not known in advance.

4   Experiments

In the following, we evaluate our method on some datasets related to facade recognition and street scene analysis. time needed for labeling a single image.

Settings. For feature extraction, we use a window with a size of $d = 50$ pixels. The random forest contains five trees with a maximum depth of 15 levels and a random subset of $\tau = 400$ features is used in each node during learning. Computational times are evaluated on a computer with 2.8GHz and four cores. We differentiate between the average recognition rate over all classes and pixel-wise accuracy, which we refer to as overall recognition rate.

Table 1. Recognition rates of our experiments with different classifiers (our approach with (*ICF*) and without context features (*ICFwoC*)) in comparison to previous work (Random Decision Forest (RDF), Sparse Logistic Regression (SLR), Conditional Random Field (CRF) and Hierarchical Conditional Random Field (HCRF)). In contrast to [7], we used random splits of training and testing for the eTRIMS dataset to allow for fair comparison with [16,17].

dataset	approach	average recognition rate	overall recognition rate
eTRIMS	CRF [17]	49.75%	65.80%
	HCRF [16]	61.63%	69.00%
	RDF [7]	62.81% ($\pm$1.58)	64.00% ($\pm$3.28)
	SLR [7]	65.57% ($\pm$2.47)	**71.18%** ($\pm$2.69)
	ICFwoC	64.07% ($\pm$1.72)	61.11% ($\pm$1.59)
	ICF	**68.61%** ($\pm$1.71)	70.81% ($\pm$1.32)
LabelMeF	RDF [7]	44.08% ($\pm$0.45)	49.06% ($\pm$0.52)
	SLR [7]	42.81% ($\pm$0.89)	48.46% ($\pm$1.58)
	ICF	**49.39%** ($\pm$0.48)	**60.68%** ($\pm$0.72)

Facade Recognition. For our experiments, we use the eTRIMS dataset originally introduced by Korč and Förstner [9]. We use ten different random splits of the data into 40 images for training and 20 images for testing similar to [16,17]. Furthermore, the LabelMeFacade dataset introduced in [7], which contains 100 images for training and 845 images for testing, is used as a second dataset being more challenging. Both datasets consists of the eight classes as shown in Fig. 4 and an additional background class named "unlabeled". For trivial decision rules or random guessing the average recognition rate for both datasets is 12.5% and the overall recognition rate is less than 35% (all pixels labeled as building). The results of our method in comparison to other state-of-the-art methods are shown in Table 1. On the eTRIMS dataset, our proposed approach significantly outperform all other methods with respect to average recognition rates. The overall recognition is as good as those of the SLR method introduced in [2,7]. However, the benefits of our approach are more prominent for the challenging LabelMeFacade dataset. ICF outperforms all previous approaches clearly on this dataset. Some sample results are presented in Fig. 4. Please note that rounded corners are somehow characteristic for our approach due to the reason that we do not use an unsupervised segmentation and the usage of rectangle features smooths the result. Furthermore we do not need a time consuming feature extraction step as in all other methods, we are significantly faster. ICF needs $\sim$ 3s for testing compared to $\sim$ 30s for RDF with SIFT feature extraction and unsupervised segmentation, which achieved the fastest classification speed in the evaluation of [7]. Please note that these times include I/O operations. There are also ways to further speed-up our method. The classification step can be highly parallelized using a CUDA implementation. Furthermore, we could apply our method in a coarse to fine manner using image pyramids. The results for anytime classification for eTRIMS are shown in the left image of Fig. 6 and one sample result for

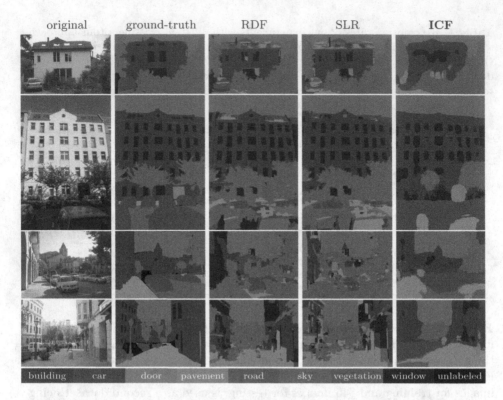

Fig. 4. Example images from eTRIMS (first two rows) and LabelMeFacade database (last two rows). The corresponding results obtained by random decision forest (RDF) [7], sparse logistic regression (SLR) [7], and Iterative Context Forests (ICF) are shown on the right side.

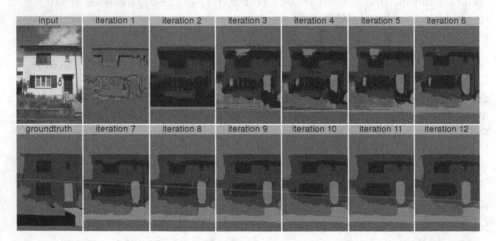

Fig. 5. Sample result for anytime semantic segmentation, input image, ground-truth and segmentation results for 12 time steps

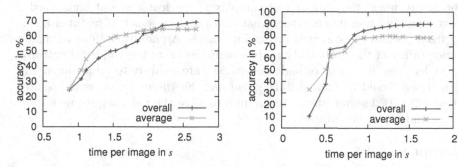

Fig. 6. Recognition performance for different time steps corresponding to the characteristically time/error curve of anytime classifiers for eTRIMS (left) and Leuven street scenes (right). Computational times include I/O operations.

different iterations is presented in Fig. 5. It is obvious that the quality of the result increases with the number of iterations and consequently with time.

Street Scenes for Autonomous Cars. Additionally, we performed experiments on the Leuven street scene database introduced in [10]. This dataset represents a scenario which highly benefits from anytime applications. In the dataset, a car is steered through an urban area. For an autonomous car, it is important to know the exact position of the road and the location of objects and obstacles (like walls or persons). In contrast to [10], we do not use depth information extracted from the stereo images provided in the dataset. Furthermore, neither time context from previous images nor additional adaptations of the settings for this scenario are done. However, our method achieves an overall accuracy of 89.55%. The CRF approach of [10] resulted in 95.7% correctly labeled pixels. The benefit of our method is its speed (1.74s for each image on average) and the ability for interruption. Stopping in a prior iteration speeds up the algorithm and results in near real time capabilities (compare right Fig. 6).

5 Conclusion and Further Work

In this work, we presented a new approach for anytime semantic segmentation, which can be applied in time-critical applications with unknown resource limits. We defined the requirements in those scenarios and showed how to perform semantic segmentation by traversing random decision trees in a level-based manner. This allows for an interruptibility of the algorithm and for including context features iteratively. Context cues are integrated right from the beginning of the algorithm and meaningful classification results are available already after a short time. Evaluation was done on multiple datasets for facade recognition and street scene analysis. For very difficult tasks, our method achieved a superior performance compared to previous approaches in this area and with less computational effort. Furthermore, we have shown that our approach can be used for anytime semantic segmentation with results at several time steps in less than a second.

For future work, we plan to add complex shape features and higher-order context cues. In general, we expect that there is a large set of features benefiting from previously estimated probability maps. An additional cue might be the uncertainty of the probability maps calculated using the empirical entropy. Context features in regions of high uncertainty are unlikely to be a robust cue and their use should be limited during learning. Furthermore, we want to integrate unsupervised segmentation techniques to align the resulting segmentation to edges and object boundaries.

References

1. Breiman, L.: Random forests. Machine Learning 45(1), 5–32 (2001)
2. Csurka, G., Perronnin, F.: An efficient approach to semantic segmentation. IJCV 95(2), 198–212 (2011)
3. Dahlkamp, H., Kaehler, A., Stavens, D., Thrun, S., Bradski, G.: Self-supervised monocular road detection in desert terrain. In: Robotics: Science and Systems (2006)
4. DeCoste, D.: Anytime interval-valued outputs for kernel machines: Fast support vector machine classification via distance geometry. In: Proceedings of the International Conference on Machine Learning (ICML 2002), pp. 99–106 (2002)
5. Esmeir, S., Markovitch, S.: Anytime learning of anycost classifiers. Machine Learning 82(3), 445–473 (2011)
6. Fink, M., Perona, P.: Mutual boosting for contextual inference. In: Advances in Neural Information Processing Systems (NIPS 2003), vol. 16, pp. 1515–1522 (2003)
7. Fröhlich, B., Rodner, E., Denzler, J.: A fast approach for pixelwise labeling of facade images. In: ICPR, pp. 3029–3032 (2010)
8. Hui, B., Yang, Y., Webb, G.: Anytime classification for a pool of instances. Machine Learning 77(1), 61–102 (2009)
9. Korč, F., Förstner, W.: eTRIMS image database for interpreting images of man-made scenes. Tech. Rep. TR-IGG-P-2009-01, University of Bonn (2009)
10. Ladický, Ľ., Sturgess, P., Russell, C., Sengupta, S., Bastanlar, Y., Clocksin, W., Torr, P.: Joint optimisation for object class segmentation and dense stereo reconstruction. In: BMVC, pp. 104.1–104.11 (2010)
11. Rusu, R.B., Holzbach, A., Bradski, G., Beetz, M.: Detecting and segmenting objects for mobile manipulation. In: Proceedings of IEEE Workshop on Search in 3D and Video (S3DV), pp. 47–54 (2009)
12. Seidl, T., Assent, I., Kranen, P., Krieger, R., Herrmann, J.: Indexing density models for incremental learning and anytime classification on data streams. In: Proceedings of the 12th Int. Conference on Extending Database Technology, pp. 311–322 (2009)
13. Shieh, J., Keogh, E.J.: Polishing the right apple: Anytime classification also benefits data streams with constant arrival times. In: Proceedings of the International Conference on Data Mining, pp. 461–470 (2010)
14. Shotton, J., Johnson, M., Cipolla, R.: Semantic texton forests for image categorization and segmentation. In: CVPR, pp. 1–8 (2008)
15. Viola, P., Jones, M.: Robust real-time object detection. IJCV 57, 137–154 (2002)
16. Yang, M.Y., Förstner, W.: A hierarchical conditional random field model for labeling and classifying images of man-made scenes. In: Proceedings of the IEEE Computer Vision Workshops (ICCV Workshops), pp. 196–203 (2011)
17. Yang, M.Y., Förstner, W.: Regionwise Classification of Building Facade Images. In: Stilla, U., Rottensteiner, F., Mayer, H., Jutzi, B., Butenuth, M. (eds.) PIA 2011. LNCS, vol. 6952, pp. 209–220. Springer, Heidelberg (2011)

Interactive Labeling
of Image Segmentation Hierarchies

Georg Zankl[1], Yll Haxhimusa[1], and Adrian Ion[1,2]

[1] Pattern Recognition and Image Processing Group 186/3,
Institute for Computer Aided Automation,
Vienna University of Technology, Austria
[2] Institute of Science and Technology, Austria

Abstract. We study the task of interactive semantic labeling of a segmentation hierarchy. To this end we propose a framework interleaving two components: an automatic labeling step, based on a Conditional Random Field whose dependencies are defined by the inclusion tree of the segmentation hierarchy, and an interaction step that integrates incremental input from a human user. Evaluated on two distinct datasets, the proposed interactive approach efficiently integrates human interventions and illustrates the advantages of structured prediction in an interactive framework.

1 Introduction

Semantic image segmentation is currently considered one of the essential tasks to improve on in computer vision [6]. Its complicacy stems from the fact that success implies both the ability to correctly identify and classify the objects present in an image, as well as to correctly outline the regions that correspond to the projections of these objects in the image – both very hard tasks.

While for some sets of semantic classes the correct result is unambiguous, when considering both compound type objects and their parts as separate classes, this is no longer the case as pixels might belong to multiple classes, e.g. a pixel of class *wheel* may also belong to class *car*. Motivated by this observation and the ill-posedness of the class-independent image segmentation task [13], we consider the task of semantic labeling of a segmentation hierarchy, which offers a way to mitigate both aspects: first, by the presence of an inclusion hierarchy for the image regions, and second, by a semantic label hierarchy corresponding to the composition of parts into objects.

The current performance of automatic semantic-segmentation methods is impressive [5,7,11], yet for many cases the results are not fine enough (e.g. the best results on VOC2011[1] are below 50%). The state-of-the art is dominated by methods that require annotated ground-truth for their supervised training, however, high quality annotations are costly to obtain manually. By including a

---

[1] http://pascallin.ecs.soton.ac.uk/challenges/VOC/voc2011/results/
index.html

A. Pinz et al. (Eds.): DAGM/OAGM 2012, LNCS 7476, pp. 11–20, 2012.
© Springer-Verlag Berlin Heidelberg 2012

feedback-loop based on input from a human user, interactive (semi-automatic) methods effectively address both shortcomings: they improve on the automatic results, and provide a more efficient way to obtain annotated ground-truth than fully manual approaches.

In this paper we study the task of interactive semantic labeling of a given segmentation hierarchy. We propose a framework that integrates a Conditional Random Field (CRF) whose dependencies are defined by the hierarchy, and the feedback provided by a human user (see Fig. 1 for an overview). Promising results are obtained in experiments, e.g. on the Stanford dataset the proposed method requires 25 interactions to raise the classification rate of the initial prediction from 72% to 90%, while our baseline that stands for the scenario of non-interactive labeling and consists of a single prediction followed by fully manual corrections, requires 120 user interactions to reach a classification rate of 90%.

CRF models have been extensively built on for semantic image segmentation [7,12,18]. Nowozin et al. [16] propose a CRF-based model for automatic semantic segmentation, using, like in our case, a dependency graph built from a segmentation hierarchy. Their system is fully automatic and does not integrate human feedback. McAuley et al. [14] also defined a hierarchical classification model, based on a regular pyramid. Mensink et al. [15] propose a CRF-based interactive model for learning annotation hierarchies of images as a whole. Branson et al. [2] use interactive training for deformable part models. The interaction model proposed by them is functionally equivalent to the adjustments of the energy function presented in this paper.

To the best of our knowledge the presented method is the first approach to interactive semantic labeling of a segmentation hierarchy, using a CRF-based statistical model.

The structure of the paper is as follows. Sec. 2 describes the proposed approach and discusses inference and training methodologies. Sec. 3 details the experimental evaluation and results on two datasets. Sec. 4 concludes the paper.

2   Description of the Semantic Labeling Framework

Let $\mathcal{S} = \bigcup_{l=0}^{h} S_l$ be a segmentation hierarchy, where S_l denotes the image segmentation at level l. Every segmentation S_l is coarser than the segmentation S_{l-1} below, s.t. for any segment $s_i \in S_{l-1}$ there exists exactly one segment $s_j \in S_l$ s.t. $s_i \subseteq s_j$. The parent-child mapping $m : \mathcal{S} \to \mathcal{P}(\mathcal{S})$, associates to $s_i \in S_l \subset \mathcal{S}$ a set of segments $\{s_j\} \subseteq S_{l-1}$ s.t. $s_j \subset s_i$, or the empty set if $l = 0$, with $\mathcal{P}(\mathcal{S})$ being the power set of $\mathcal{S}$. Note that this mapping induces the hierarchy among the segments in $\mathcal{S}$.

Given $\mathcal{S}$ and a set of semantic labels $\mathcal{L}$ the output of the system is a labeling that assigns each segment $s_i \in \mathcal{S}$ a semantic label $y_i \in \mathcal{L}$. To predict the labels corresponding to each segment we employ a CRF with the probability distribution over the possible labelings given by:

$$p(y|\mathcal{S}, \theta) = \frac{1}{Z(\mathcal{S}, \theta)} e^{-E(y, \mathcal{S}, \theta)} \tag{1}$$

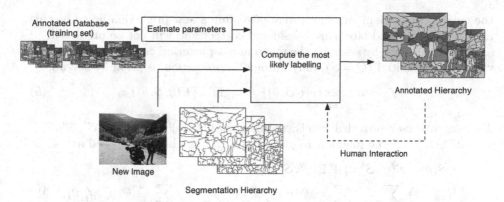

Fig. 1. The proposed framework: in a preliminary step, the parameters of our CRF-based model are trained using ground-truth semantically labeled image segmentation hierarchies; at test time, the system takes as input an image and corresponding segmentation hierarchy. The semantic labeling process alternates between the system predicting labels, and the user correcting a wrongly predicted label.

where $y = (\dots, y_i, \dots)$ is a labeling of all segments $s_i \in \mathcal{S}$, $\theta = (\theta_u, \theta_p)$ is a learned parameter vector containing the unary θ_u and pairwise parameters θ_p, and $Z(\mathcal{S}, \theta) = \sum_{y \in \mathcal{Y}(\mathcal{S})} e^{-E(y, \mathcal{S}, \theta)}$ is the partition function, with $\mathcal{Y}(\mathcal{S})$ the set of all possible labelings of the segments in $\mathcal{S}$. The energy function E for a set of segments $\mathcal{Q} \subseteq \mathcal{S}$ and corresponding labels y is defined as:

$$E(y, \mathcal{Q}, \theta) = \sum_{s_i \in \mathcal{Q}} \Phi(s_i, y_i, \theta_u) + \sum_{s_i \in \mathcal{Q}} \sum_{s_j \in \mathcal{Q} \cap m(s_i)} \Psi(y_i, y_j, \theta_p) \qquad (2)$$

$$\Phi(s_i, y_i, \theta_u) = \theta_u(y_i)^\top \phi(s_i, y_i) \qquad (3)$$

$$\Psi(y_i, y_j, \theta_p) = \theta_p(y_i, y_j)^\top \psi(y_i, y_j) \qquad (4)$$

where ϕ is a unary meta-feature obtained as output of a classifier for each label and ψ is a feature based on the co-occurrence of the labels in the training set (see Sec. 3 for information on how our meta-features are computed). Note that $s_i \notin m(s_i)$ and ψ does not have to be symmetric $\psi(y_i, y_j) \neq \psi(y_j, y_i)$, it is thus explicitly encoded in the features and parameters, which labels correspond to the parent and child segments, respectively. This allows the system to score differently the labeling of a child-segment as e.g. *torso* and the parent *body* compared to labeling the child *body* and the parent *torso*.

2.1   Inference with the Human in the Loop

Given an image and corresponding segmentation hierarchy $\mathcal{S}$ the user is first provided with a prediction of the labels of all segments. Following is an interactive process that alternates between the user adjusting the label of one segment in the current prediction, and the system providing a new prediction based on this input. User provided labels are considered correct and will not be predicted.

Inference is done by selecting the maximum a-posteriori configuration (MAP), which for the initial $(Q = S)$, fully automatic prediction, is given by solving

$$y^* = \underset{y \in \mathcal{Y}(S)}{\operatorname{argmax}} \{p(y|S, \theta)\} = \underset{y \in \mathcal{Y}(S)}{\operatorname{argmin}} \{E(y, S, \theta)\}. \qquad (5)$$

To integrate user provided labels, notice that for disjoint subsets $S', S'' \subseteq S$ with $S' \cup S'' = S$ the function $E(y, S, \theta)$ in Eq. 2 can be decomposed as:

$$
E(y, S, \theta) = E(y', S', \theta) + E(y'', S'', \theta) \\
+ \sum_{s_i \in S'} \sum_{s_j \in S'' \cap m(s_i)} \Psi(y_i', y_j'', \theta) + \sum_{s_i \in S''} \sum_{s_j \in S' \cap m(s_i)} \Psi(y_i'', y_j', \theta), \qquad (6)
$$

where y', y'' are the restrictions of y to the labels corresponding to segments in S', S'', respectively. Starting with $S' = S$ and $S'' = \emptyset$, user interaction is modeled by moving the manually labeled segment s_k from S' to S'' and adding the given corresponding label to y''. Inference is done only over the labels in y' corresponding to the segments in S':

$$y'^* = \underset{y' \in \mathcal{Y}(S')}{\operatorname{argmin}} \left\{ \sum_{s_i \in S'} \Phi'(s_i, y_i', \theta) + \sum_{s_i \in S'} \sum_{s_j \in S' \cap m(s_i)} \Psi(y_i', y_j', \theta_p) \right\}, \qquad (7)$$

where the modified unary potential Φ' is defined as:

$$\Phi'(s_i, y_i', \theta) = \Phi(s_i, y_i', \theta_u) + \sum_{s_j \in S'' \cap m(s_i)} \Psi(y_i', y_j'', \theta_p) + \sum_{s_j \in S'' \cap m'(s_i)} \Psi(y_j'', y_i', \theta_p) \qquad (8)$$

$$\text{with } m'(s_i) = \begin{cases} \{s_j\} & \text{iff } s_j \in m(s_i) \\ \emptyset & \text{otherwise} \end{cases}$$

The pairwise interaction between segments $s_i \in S'$ and $s_j \in S''$ only depends on y_i' and can be included in the unary potential (shown in Eq. 8). During inference y_j'' is fixed. The labels provided by the user change the MAP configuration and if the features are informative enough, other misclassified segments are corrected automatically.

During inference, the labels corresponding to child and parent segments of the user labeled segment s_k, become independent of each other. One can split the segmentation hierarchy at each user labeled segment and obtain a forest where inference is done independently for each tree. Exact inference is done efficiently with the Belief Propagation (BP) algorithm [17].

2.2   Learning

Given N images with corresponding hierarchical segmentations $\{S_k\}$ and ground-truth labelings $\{Y_k\}$, for the k-th image, training is performed by assuming the samples to be i.i.d. and finding the parameters that maximize the probability of the ground-truth under our model (maximizing the likelihood):

$$\theta^* = \underset{\theta}{\operatorname{argmax}} \prod_{k=1}^{N} p(Y_k|\mathcal{S}_k, \theta) = \underset{\theta}{\operatorname{argmin}} \sum_{k=1}^{N} \left[E(Y_k, \mathcal{S}_k, \theta) + \ln Z(\mathcal{S}_k, \theta) \right]. \quad (9)$$

This optimization is done efficiently using a second-order gradient descent with derivatives computed from exact marginals given by inference (in our case BP).

3 Experiments

To the best of our knowledge, open semantic labeling databases provide neither hierarchical ground-truth segmentation, nor hierarchical labeling of segments. For our experiments, we build on two existing datasets: the Stanford Background dataset [8] and the CamVid dataset [3,4], for which we derive ground-truth in the form required by our method. Both datasets provide semantically labeled segmentations on images – a single segmentation, with exclusive labels. The Stanford Background dataset consists of 715 images, and the CamVid dataset of 701 labeled images. In each case 1/4 of the images are randomly selected for testing and the rest 3/4 for training the model. The CamVid dataset consists of several videos with labeled segmentation every 30 frames with a camera mounted to a moving car. Thus, there is no stationary background or motion information.

To compute segmentation hierarchies we use the minimum spanning tree pyramid[9][2] and ground-truth labelings are obtained by determining the occurrence of object classes of the dataset inside the regions of the hierarchy.

McAuley et al. assign a label to a patch if there is an overlap with the original ground-truth segment of at least 25% and extend the initial label set by using *background* (containing no ground-truth classes) and *multiple* (containing more than one ground-truth class) [14].

We extend the label set to contain all combinations $\mathcal{L} = \mathcal{P}(L_B) \setminus \emptyset$ of a set of base labels L_B. The datasets used in our experiments contain full segmentations, so that a *background* has to be defined explicitly as a base label. We start with a small set L_B: the geometric classes of the Stanford Background dataset $\{sky, horizontal, vertical\}$ and $\{car, street, background\}$ of the CamVid dataset (*background* represents the remaining object classes).

The ground-truth labeling is obtained by finding for each segment $s_i \in \mathcal{S}_0$ the base labels that overlap with s_i at least 1/3 of its area. The selected base labels determine the ground-truth label of s_i. The labels of segments in level $l > 0$ are determined by the union of the sets of base labels of its descendants.

We use Geometric Context (GC) features [10]. The meta-feature ϕ is computed from the Mahalanobis distance of the feature vectors to each class (see Features in Sec 3.2, and Table 1 for alternatives). ψ is a function of the co-occurrence of labels in the segmentation hierarchies of the ground-truth and is the same for all edges.

---

[2] In principle, any hierarchical segmentation method can be used, e.g. [1].

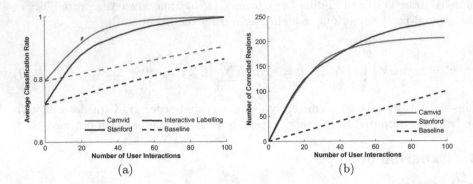

Fig. 2. (a) Average classification rates compared to the baseline on the Camvid and Stanford Background datasets; (b) the average number of corrected regions over the number of user interactions. Evaluation is done with 7 labels.

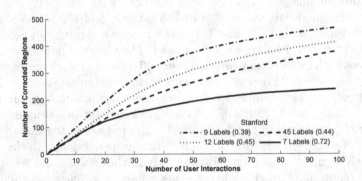

Fig. 3. Interactive improvement depending on the label sets, showing the average number of corrected regions over the number of user interactions on the Stanford Background dataset. Note that the initial handicap still affects this curve. The average classification rate at 0 interactions can be seen in parenthesis of the legend.

Table 1. Classification rates on 20 images of the Stanford Background dataset (and using 20 different images as training set), using geometric labels and all combinations. (LR) is a linear regression to the overlap of image regions; (SVM) measures the distance from the hyperplane of an SVM per class; ($Mahal.$) uses the Mahalanobis distance; ($dSIFT$) uses a Bag of Words histogram of dense SIFT features (extracted at a regular grid of 6 pixels) (GC) uses the Geometric Context features by Hoiem et al. [10].

	LR	SVM	Mahal.
dSIFT	0.448	0.586	0.588
GC	0.384	0.438	**0.732**

3.1   Results of the Proposed System

To evaluate a labeling we measure the classification rate $\frac{|\{y^n=y^*\}|}{|S|}$ and the number of corrected regions $|\{y^n = y^*\}| - |\{y^0 = y^*\}|$, with y^n denoting the inferred labeling after n user interactions. This is done over 100 simulated user interactions and averaged over all images of the test set, using a virtual annotator that always selects the top-most misclassified segment and corrects that prediction.

As baseline we use a system consisting of an initial prediction using the same framework followed by repeated correction of labels performed by a human user. This baseline simulates the scenario of non-interactive labeling and helps illustrate the benefit of the structured model, when it comes to propagating corrections to neighboring regions.

Fig. 2(a) shows that the interactive system outperforms the baseline. An average precision of 90% is reached after 18 user interactions on the CamVid dataset, compared to 97 for the baseline. The same precision is reached on the Stanford Background dataset after 25 user interactions for the full framework and 120 for the baseline. On Fig. 2(b) one sees that after 20 user interactions, while the baseline corrected 20 segment labels, the interactive system corrected an average of 133 labels on the Stanford and 130 labels on the CamVid dataset. If there are less misclassified regions remaining, less regions can be corrected with a single interaction. Thus the slope of all curves decreases until they converge to the point where no misclassified segments are left.

An alternative comparison can be made to fully manual approaches instead of the proposed baseline. A simple comparison is provided by computing the average number of user interactions to reach a precision of 90%. The most basic approach, to label each segment independently, requires 599 and 828 segments to be labeled on the Stanford and CamVid datasets, respectively. A more efficient strategy is to ask the user to label in a top-down order, only the segments that do not have the same label as their parent. This strategy requires 60 and 112 human labeled segments on the Stanford and CamVid datasets, respectively. Both manual approaches require significantly more user interventions than using the proposed interactive method.

In some cases, predictions following human interaction also change the labels of previously correctly classified segments. With a single user interaction, we observe the difference in the number of correctly classified regions ΔR before and after the interaction, with $\min(\Delta R) = -18$ and $\max(\Delta R) = 702$. However, this also depends on the initial handicap, i.e. it is more likely to correct more segments if there are more misclassified segments at the start.

3.2   Components and Alternative Choices

Number of Labels. In order to observe the behavior of the system when increasing the number of base labels, several sets of label combinations, automatically computed and manually selected, are chosen on the Stanford Background dataset. We also compare to the 7 label combinations of the geometric labels used in Fig. 2(b). The label combinations used for 9 labels are the 8 base labels of the semantic classes (sky, tree, road, grass, water, building, mountain and foreground object) and one combined label containing all classes. All combinations containing 1, 2, 7 or 8 base labels are used in order to create 45 label combinations. In the case of 12 labels we manually define the following combined labels: *flora/fauna* = {*tree, grass, fg.obj*}, *nature* = {*tree, grass, water, mountain, fg.obj*}, *city* = {*road, building, fg.obj*}. An example of the generated ground-truth for these 12 labels is illustrated in Fig. 4. Note that these combinations of labels do not consider the foreground-object to be part of a simple scenery, e.g. there is a *fg.obj* on a *road*, a segment containing parts of both objects will be labeled as *city*.

The number of possible label combinations grows exponentially with the number of base labels. Generally the larger the label set, the bigger the classification error. Fig. 3 shows that using 12 semantic labels provides similar classification

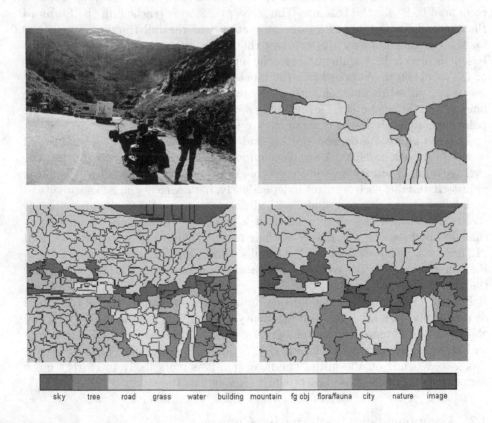

Fig. 4. (*top left*) An example image from the Stanford Background dataset, (*top right*) the associated ground-truth of the dataset and the computed ground-truth of a fine (*bottom left*) and a coarse (*bottom right*) segmentation in the segmentation hierarchy. The illustration uses 8 base labels (semantic labels of the Stanford Background dataset), one label combination containing all labels (*image*) and the following manually defined combinations: *flora/fauna*, *nature* and *city*. (Image best viewed in color).

rates to using most of the combinations of base labels on the Stanford Background dataset (45 labels), but slightly better performance within the interactive framework (i.e. more regions are corrected per interaction).

Features. The feature functions ϕ, ψ and their parameters have been selected on small training and validation sets (20 images each, performed on both data sets). In the described experiments we use $\phi(s_i, y_i) = e^{-0.02d(s_i, y_i)}$, where $d(s_i, y_i)$ is the Mahalanobis distance of the feature vector of segment s_i to the feature distribution of class y_i. We use the GC features from Hoiem et al. [10], apply a principal component analysis and remove all dimensions with eigenvalue $\lambda_i < 10^{-8} \max_j \lambda_j$. The classification rates of the evaluated approaches are shown in Tab. 1 for the Stanford dataset. The classification rates on the CamVid dataset are similar, with a smaller difference (classification rates of 0.646 for Mahalanobis with GC features and 0.617 for all other cases). The pairwise feature is defined as $\psi(y_i, y_j) = e^{-\frac{50}{N}C(y_i, y_j)}$, where $C(y_i, y_j)$ is the co-occurrence of labels in the training set and N is the number of sample images. The contribution of each image to C is L_1-normalized.

Hard Constraints on the Labels. The aggregation of objects from parts induces an ordering of semantic labels, which is implicitly handled by the non-symmetric feature function ψ. An additional choice is to constrain the labels of all descendants of a region labeled by the user based on the ground-truth occurrence of labels (e.g. descendants of a segment labeled *human* should only correspond to body parts). This additional complication only marginally improved results – 1% higher classification rate – and has been intentionally left out of the presented framework.

4   Conclusion

We present a framework for interactive labeling of image segmentation hierarchies and show that it significantly reduces the number of interactions necessary to reach an average classification rate of 90% compared to a baseline, consisting of a single prediction followed by repeated correction of labels by the user. The interactive framework allows a user to create every possible labeling, only restricted by the specified set of labels. Experiments on different label sets also show that using all (or most of the) combinations of base labels is a viable method for evaluation if there is no hierarchy of semantic labels available. A smaller set of manually defined labels with a specific semantic meaning should be preferred.

References

1. Arbelaez, P., Maire, M., Fowlkes, C., Malik, J.: Contour detection and hierarchical image segmentation. PAMI 33(5), 898–916 (2011)
2. Branson, S., Perona, P., Belongie, S.: Strong supervision from weak annotation: Interactive training of deformable part models. In: ICCV, pp. 1832–1839 (2011)

3. Brostow, G.J., Fauqueur, J., Cipolla, R.: Semantic object classes in video: A high-definition ground truth database. PRL 30(2), 88–97 (2009)
4. Brostow, G.J., Shotton, J., Fauqueur, J., Cipolla, R.: Segmentation and Recognition Using Structure from Motion Point Clouds. In: Forsyth, D., Torr, P., Zisserman, A. (eds.) ECCV 2008, Part I. LNCS, vol. 5302, pp. 44–57. Springer, Heidelberg (2008)
5. Carreira, J., Li, F., Sminchisescu, C.: Object Recognition by Sequential Figure-Ground Ranking. IJCV, 1–20 (2011)
6. Everingham, M., Van Gool, L., Williams, C.K.I., Winn, J., Zisserman, A.: The pascal visual object classes (voc) challenge. IJCV 88(2), 303–338 (2010)
7. Gonfaus, J., Boix, X., van de Weijer, J., Bagdanov, A., Serrat, J., Gonzàndlez, J.: Harmony potentials for joint classification and segmentation. In: CVPR, pp. 3280–3287 (2010)
8. Gould, S., Fulton, R., Koller, D.: Decomposing a scene into geometric and semantically consistent regions. In: ICCV, pp. 1–8 (2009)
9. Haxhimusa, Y., Kropatsch, W.: Hierarchy of Partitions with Dual Graph Contraction. In: Michaelis, B., Krell, G. (eds.) DAGM 2003. LNCS, vol. 2781, pp. 338–345. Springer, Heidelberg (2003)
10. Hoiem, D., Efros, A.A., Hebert, M.: Geometric context from a single image. In: ICCV, pp. 654–661 (2005)
11. Ion, A., Carreira, J., Sminchisescu, C.: Probabilistic joint image segmentation and labeling. In: NIPS, pp. 1827–1835 (2011)
12. Ladický, L., Russell, C., Kohli, P., Torr, P.: Associative hierarchical CRFs for object class image segmentation. In: ICCV, pp. 739–746 (2009)
13. Malisiewicz, T., Efros, A.A.: Improving spatial support for objects via multiple segmentations. In: BMVC (2007)
14. McAuley, J., de Campos, T., Csurka, G., Perronnin, F.: Hierarchical image-region labeling via structured learning. In: BMVC (2009)
15. Mensink, T., Verbeek, J., Csurka, G.: Learning structured prediction models for interactive image labeling. In: CVPR, pp. 833–840 (2011)
16. Nowozin, S., Gehler, P.V., Lampert, C.H.: On Parameter Learning in CRF-Based Approaches to Object Class Image Segmentation. In: Daniilidis, K., Maragos, P., Paragios, N. (eds.) ECCV 2010, Part VI. LNCS, vol. 6316, pp. 98–111. Springer, Heidelberg (2010)
17. Pearl, J.: Fusion, propagation, and structuring in belief networks. AI 29(3), 241–288 (1986)
18. Plath, N., Toussaint, M., Nakajima, S.: Multi-class image segmentation using conditional random fields and global classification. In: ICML, pp. 817–824 (2009)

Hierarchy of Localized Random Forests
for Video Annotation

Naveen Shankar Nagaraja, Peter Ochs, Kun Liu, and Thomas Brox

Computer Vision Group
University of Freiburg, Germany
nagaraja@informatik.uni-freiburg.de

Abstract. We address the problem of annotating a video sequence with partial supervision. Given the pixel-wise annotations in the first frame, we aim to propagate these labels ideally throughout the whole video. While some labels can be propagated using optical flow, disocclusion and unreliable flow in some areas require additional cues. To this end, we propose to train localized classifiers on the annotated frame. In contrast to a global classifier, localized classifiers allow to distinguish colors that appear in both the foreground and the background but at very different locations. We design a multi-scale hierarchy of localized random forests, which collectively takes a decision. Cues from optical flow and the classifier are combined in a variational framework. The approach can deal with multiple objects in a video. We present qualitative and quantitative results on the Berkeley Motion Segmentation Dataset.

1 Introduction

An annotated video carries rich information which can be used in many tasks such as improving object classifiers, action recognition and pose estimation. Annotating a video manually is a time consuming task and it comes at a cost. Therefore, researchers have been looking at ways to automate parts of this process [20]. Unsupervised large scale video segmentation in general scenes is currently beyond our abilities. However, making a manual segmentation available in one frame determines the objects we are interested in and tells about their appearance. Automatic segmentation of the rest of the video then becomes a tractable problem, as shown in Fig. 1.

The main challenge in this task is the variation of the considered objects, particularly in combination with disocclusion phenomena. As new parts of an object become visible, there is no direct counterpart in the annotated frame. Consequently, we must learn an object representation from the single annotated frame that generalizes over the typical variations.

For this purpose, we propose the use of a hierarchy of localized random forests trained on the initial frame. In contrast to a global classifier, a localized classifier allows to distinguish objects that have similar global statistics, but differ locally. For instance, some of the glove's dark texture in Fig. 3(a) is similar to parts of the background, but *locally* the textures are never the same. As the optimum scale of localization is not known *a priori*, we suggest combining multiple scales

A. Pinz et al. (Eds.): DAGM/OAGM 2012, LNCS 7476, pp. 21–30, 2012.
© Springer-Verlag Berlin Heidelberg 2012

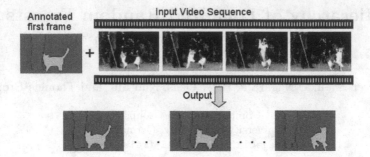

Fig. 1. Given an annotated first frame of a video sequence, we want to achieve a dense labeling of the entire video by propagating the annotations (labels) in the first frame

in a hierarchy of classifiers. Random forests are particularly well suited for this purpose, as they are very efficient and naturally allow combining results from multiple forests.

Pixel classification is only needed in areas that cannot be directly propagated via optical flow. We combine these two complementary cues in a variational framework, where an additional regularizer ensures compact solutions. We show quantitative results on the Berkeley Motion Segmentation Dataset [5], which provides pixel accurate ground truth.

2   Related Work

There are many problem settings of video segmentation in the literature. Interactive video segmentation [14,12] relies on frequent user intervention to prevent the errors from being propagated. It is very accurate and appreciated in video editing, yet the interactive user input prevents its application to large scale video annotation.

Our work is also related to classical tracking methods. Usually a bounding box is propagated to later frames. Boosting based classifiers [17] and random forest classifiers [16] are popular choices for learning and updating the template model. Godec et al. [10] also give a rough segmentation of the object being tracked. Also level set tracking [9] yields rough segmentations, yet with a less sophisticated appearance model. Moreover, these methods are restricted to tracking a single region.

It is also quite common to consider video segmentation as a spatio-temporal MRF optimization problem [2,18,7]. Some of the other methods make use of the superpixels. They connect them spatially and temporally to generate temporally consistent object regions [15,4,19,11]. This approach is often used in an unsupervised setting, which usually leads to severe over-segmentation. As superpixels ignore weak object boundaries, large errors can occur.

In [13] a variant of optical flow is used to propagate labels directly from a training image to a test image. This is similar to how we use optical flow to propagate labels from one frame to the next. Applied over large frame distances,

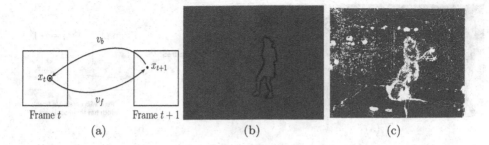

Fig. 2. (a) Forward-backward flow consistency: let a pixel in frame t be denoted by x_t and let the forward flow from frame t to $t+1$ be v_f. Then, $x_{t+1} = x_t + v_f(x_t)$. Let the backward flow be v_b. If there is no occlusion or estimation error then $x_{t+1} + v_b(x_{t+1}) = x_t$. As the optical flow is never perfectly accurate, we allow for a small radius r, in which we consider the flow as reliable: $\| v_f(x_t) + v_b(x_t + v_f(x_t)) \| \leq r$. **(b)** and **(c)** Labels propagated from frame t to $t+1$. The white areas denote pixels with unreliable flow.

this leads to erroneous results due to disocclusion. In contrast, we combine the concept of propagation by optical flow with a localized classifier that is trained to generalize over the object's appearance and can fill disocclusion areas.

3   Optical Flow for Frame-Wise Label Propagation

We start with a user segmented first frame of a given video sequence. Let n different class labels be present. The labels are transferred from a frame at time t to $t+1$ using optical flow from [5]. Optical flow is not reliable near object and motion boundaries, particularly as there may be disocclusions from frame t to $t+1$. It is important to exclude such critical areas from propagation. They are detected by checking the consistency of the forward and the backward flow, as explained in Fig. 2a.

Let x_t denote a pixel in frame t and its corresponding pixel in frame $t + 1$ be x_{t+1}. If the flow passes the consistency check, we assign x_{t+1} the label at x_t. Refer Fig.2(c) for a sample result. Areas that did not pass the consistency check are marked in white. When applying the propagation successively, these areas will get larger and larger, if they are not filled by complementary information.

4   Patch Classification Using Localized Classifiers

For each pixel in frame $t + 1$ which has not been assigned a label by optical flow, we take the features of a patch around it and feed it to a classifier that has been trained on the annotated first frame. We use random forests [3] since they are computationally efficient, have good generalization properties and can be easily applied to multi-class problems. Moreover, results from multiple random forests can be combined in an elegant manner. This property will prove useful in the

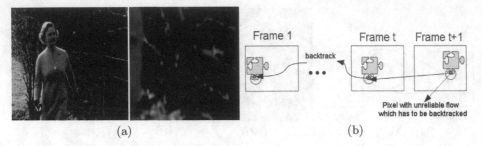

(a)   (b)

Fig. 3. (a) Advantage of localized classifier over a global classifier- the encircled area can be easily misclassified as background by a global classifier whereas a local classifier for an image block can be more discriminative. (b) Coarsely backtracking a pixel with unreliable flow to the annotated Frame 1. A superpixel region around this pixel (shown inside the circle) is backtracked using the average flow within the region.

following combination of multiple local classifiers. As features we use normalized LAB color histograms computed on 15×15 patches. Each channel is treated separately with 32 bins per channel.

4.1   Localization of the Classifier

A single global classifier comes with the problem that overlapping appearance characteristics between the classes lead to misclassifications. We propose the use of localized classifiers based on the observation that the class overlap is less likely to occur with respect to the local appearance distribution; see Fig. 3a. We exploit the 'locality of reference' by dividing the image into non-overlapping spatial blocks and training a separate random forest in each block. At the test time, we run into a technical problem though: as objects move, the location of an area of interest will be different from that in the training image. Consequently, we must model the shift of the location to choose the right local classifier. We take a region around the pixel that should be classified and recursively backtrack it to the annotated frame; see Fig. 3b. Since we cannot backtrack the pixel itself - the optical flow was unreliable at this point - we use the average flow of the reliable flow vectors in a larger neighborhood around that pixel. To avoid neighborhoods that span different objects, the neighborhood is defined by a superpixel computed with the method in [1] using [8]. The size of the superpixel - steerable by choosing the level in the superpixel hierarchy of [1] - is adapted such that it comprises at least one reliable flow vector.

Even though the backtracking is far from being exact, the resulting location (x', y') is accurate enough to choose the right local random forest. To avoid block artifacts, we run bilinear interpolation on the output of the random forests in the vicinity of (x', y'), as shown in Fig. 4(a).

4.2   Hierarchy of Classifiers

An important question is how to choose an optimal block size. Intuitively it makes sense to have a multi-scale model, where random forests are trained for

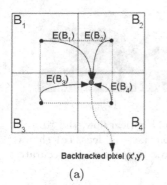 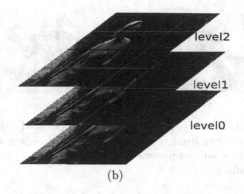

(a)   (b)

Fig. 4. (a) Interpolation of the classification decisions by the participating blocks at a particular hierarchy level. **(b)** Hierarchy of Localized Random Forests- a Random Forest is trained for each block at each hierarchy level.

different block sizes and their decisions are combined to obtain a final score. Apart from the advantage that we avoid a block size parameter, the additional averaging over multiple forests has positive effects on the overall classification performance.

We use a 3-level hierarchy with one random forest trained on the whole image ($level_0$), 2×2 blocks at $level_1$, and 4×4 blocks at $level_2$, as shown in Fig. 4(b). We use 100, 30 and 10 trees for each forest at $level_0$, $level_1$ and $level_2$, respectively.

Instead of giving each level of the hierarchy the same influence, we suggest a weighted average with a weight based on the entropy of the respective random forest. Minimum entropy is already used as a splitting criterion when training a random forest. Now we use the entropy in the opposite way: a high entropy in a block indicates a good mixture of labels from all the classes. Thus the classifier trained in a high entropy block will have better data to make a decision than a classifier that has just seen a single label, i.e., a low entropy block. Let $B^l = \{B_1^l, ..., B_4^l\}$ denote the set of neighboring blocks of (x', y') used for bilinear interpolation at hierarchy level l. We have the frequencies of all the labels in a block B_j^l as $p^1(B_j^l), ..., p^n(B_j^l)$, where n denotes the number of class labels. The entropy of a block is then,

$$h(B_j^l) = - \sum_{i=1}^{n} p^i(B_j^l) \log(p^i(B_j^l)) \tag{1}$$

Let $s^i(B_j^l)$ be the score of label i output by the Random Forest for block B_j^l, then the combined score for label i is,

$$s_i = \sum_{j,l} \alpha_j^l exp(h(B_j^l)) s^i(B_j^l) \tag{2}$$

where α_j^l is the weight due to the bilinear interpolation.

(a)   (b)   (c)

Fig. 5. (a) Frame t. (b) shows labels propagated using only optical flow, the "drag" effect is evident from the segmentation near object motion, i.e., the legs. (c) shows the effect of our framework in addition to the optical flow to get a more accurate segmentation.

5   Integration of the Cues into a Variational Framework

In the previous sections we have described two different sources of information to label each pixel independently by either optical flow based label propagation or a classifier decision. Additionally, we must avoid noisy decisions. Hence, we need a smoothness prior that prefers a homogenous labeling in smooth image areas. All of this can be integrated nicely in a variational approach.

Let L_i be the set of coordinates occupied by label i transferred by optical flow and $\mathbf{u}' := (u'_1, \ldots, u'_n) \colon \Omega \to \{0,1\}^n$, $n \in \mathbb{N}$ be a function indicating the n different labels, i.e.,

$$u'_i(x) := \begin{cases} 1, & \text{if } x \in L_i \\ 0, & \text{else,} \end{cases} \tag{3}$$

where $\Omega \subset \mathbb{R}^2$ denotes the image domain.

We seek a function $\mathbf{u} := (u_1, \ldots, u_n) \colon \Omega \to \{0,1\}^n$ that stays close to the labels propagated from the previous frame using optical flow for points in $L := \bigcup_{i=1}^n L_i$. This is achieved by minimizing the energy

$$E_{\mathrm{OF}}(\mathbf{u}_{t+1}(x)) := \frac{1}{2} \int_\Omega c(x) \sum_{i=1}^n \left(u_{i,t+1}(x) - u'_{i,t}(x + v_b(x)) \right)^2 dx, \tag{4}$$

where v_b is the backward flow from frame $t+1$ to t and and $c \colon \Omega \to \{0,1\}$ is a confidence indicator function with value 1 where the optical flow passes the consistency check and 0 elsewhere.

On points not covered by optical flow based propagation, we make use of the local classifier's output by introducing one more data term which will aid the decision process at these points to take a specific label. We define this part of our energy functional as

$$E_{\mathrm{LC}}(\mathbf{u}_{t+1}(x)) := \int_\Omega (1 - c(x)) \sum_{i=1}^n -s_i(x) u_{i,t+1}(x) dx, \tag{5}$$

where s_i is the score given by the classifier (2) at position x for label i. The advantage of adding (5) over just combining (4) with the smoothness prior is shown in Fig. 5.

A convex combination of the data terms along with a regularizer yields

$$E := \alpha(E_{OF} + E_{LC}) + (1 - \alpha)E_{Reg} \tag{6}$$

s.t. $\sum_i u_{i,t+1}(x) = 1$, $\forall x$ with a model parameter α in $[0, 1)$.
We use a weighted TV based regularizer,

$$E_{Reg}(\mathbf{u}_{t+1}(x)) = \int_\Omega f(x) \sqrt{\left(\sum_{i=1}^{n} |\nabla u_{i,t+1}(x)|^2 + \varepsilon^2 \right)} \, dx, \tag{7}$$

where $f(x) = (|\nabla I(x)|^2 + \varepsilon^2)^{\frac{-1}{2}}$ is a weighting function that reduces smoothing across image edges.
For minimizing (6) we relax the indicator functions u_i to take values in $[0, 1]$. The relaxed problem is convex and we obtain its global optimum by computing the Euler-Lagrange equations and solving the nonlinear system via fixed point iterations and successive over-relaxation (SOR). We obtain the final integer solution by assigning each x the label i with the maximum $u_i(x)$.

6   Experiments and Results

We present quantitative results on the Berkeley Motion Segmentation Dataset (BMS) [6]. BMS has 26 challenging video sequences with varying contrast and illumination and significant motion. For quantitative analysis we have evaluated our output against the ground truth at frame 10, 20, 30, 40 and 50. The evaluation is done by measuring the percentage of pixels that are assigned a different

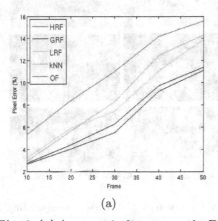

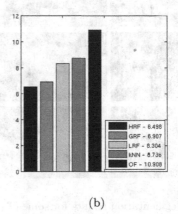

(a)   (b)

Fig. 6. (a) Average pixel error over the BMS sequences after 10,20,30,40 and 50 frames. We compare the proposed hierarchy of random forests (HRF) to a baseline using only optical flow (OF), a k-nearest-neighbor classifier (kNN), a random forest trained on the whole image (GRF) and random forests trained on the lowest level of hierarchy (LRF) i.e. 4×4 blocks. (b) The bar chart shows the average pixel error over all the sequences over all the 50 frames with the exact value in the legend.

Fig. 7. Segmentation results for some of the BMS sequences with their corresponding frame number. The last two rows show typical failure cases, where an object gets fully occluded by another.

label than the ground truth. This pixel error is calculated for only those classes which were present in the annotated first frame, i.e., new objects that appear later in the video are not taken into consideration. We have kept the parameters fixed for all the sequences with $\alpha = 0.6$. Our method takes approximately 75 seconds to segment each frame on a standard computer. The running time includes the optical flow and superpixel computation as well as the SOR solver (which occupies a major percentage of the running time).

Fig. 6 shows the average pixel error across all sequences in BMS. A comparison to the baseline, which uses only optical flow to propagate the labels and fills the unknown areas with the smoothness prior (i.e., setting $E_{LC} = 0$), reveals the importance of adding a classifier that deals with disocclusion areas. In particular when labels are propagated over many frames, a classifier improves results considerably.

The comparison between a global random forest and a k-nearest-neighbor classifier further shows that the discriminative training of random forests clearly outperforms a simple memorization of the patches of the first frame. Apart from the better performance, random forests are also much faster than a k-NN classifier.

Finally, the comparison between the global random forest, the localized random forest on 4×4 blocks, and the proposed hierarchy shows that the hierarchy performs the best. Fig. 7 shows some qualitative results including some typical failure cases.

7   Conclusion

We have presented a method for video segmentation in which we start with a segmented frame and propagate its labels by combining two complementary cues in subsequent frames - one based on optical flow and another based on classification. For the classifier we have proposed a hierarchy of localized random forests, which outperforms the classical global random forests as shown by a quantitative evaluation on a publicly available dataset. The point-wise label predictions are combined with a smoothness prior in a variational setting. The approach can deal with disocclusion and appearance changes as well as multiple objects. It can cover 30-50 frames even on challenging material without introducing large errors. We believe that this tool will help in providing fully segmented video material, which will be useful in many computer vision tasks.

Acknowledgements. We gratefully acknowledge the partial funding by the ERC Starting Grant - VIDEOLEARN.

References

1. Arbelaez, P., Maire, M., Fowlkes, C., Malik, J.: Contour detection and hierarchical image segmentation. IEEE Transactions on Pattern Analysis and Machine Intelligence (2011)

2. Badrinarayanan, V., Galasso, F., Cipolla, R.: Label propagation in video sequences. In: IEEE Conference on Computer Vision and Pattern Recognition, CVPR (2010)
3. Breiman, L.: Random forests. Machine Learning 45, 5–32 (2001)
4. Brendel, W., Todorovic, S.: Video object segmentation by tracking regions. In: IEEE International Conference on Computer Vision, ICCV (2009)
5. Brox, T., Malik, J.: Large displacement optical flow: descriptor matching in variational motion estimation. IEEE Transactions on Pattern Analysis and Machine Intelligence (2010)
6. Brox, T., Malik, J.: Object Segmentation by Long Term Analysis of Point Trajectories. In: Daniilidis, K., Maragos, P., Paragios, N. (eds.) ECCV 2010, Part V. LNCS, vol. 6315, pp. 282–295. Springer, Heidelberg (2010)
7. Budvytis, I., Badrinarayanan, V., Cipolla, R.: Semi-supervised video segmentation using tree structured graphical models. In: IEEE Conference on Computer Vision and Pattern Recognition, CVPR (2011)
8. Catanzaro, B., Su, B., Sundaram, N., Lee, Y., Murphy, M., Keutzer, K.: Efficient, high-quality image contour detection. In: International Conference on Computer Vision, ICCV (2009)
9. Chockalingam, P., Pradeep, N., Birchfield, S.: Adaptive fragments-based tracking of non-rigid objects using level sets. In: IEEE International Conference on Computer Vision, ICCV (2009)
10. Godec, M., Roth, P., Bischof, H.: Hough-based tracking of non-rigid objects. In: IEEE International Conference on Computer Vision, ICCV (2011)
11. Grundmann, M., Kwatra, V., Han, M., Essa, I.: Efficient hierarchical graph-based video segmentation. In: IEEE Conference on Computer Vision and Pattern Recognition, CVPR (2010)
12. Li, Y., Sun, J., Shum, H.Y.: Video object cut and paste. ACM Trans. Graph. (2005)
13. Liu, C., Yuen, J., Torralba, A.: Nonparametric scene parsing- label transfer via dense scene alignment. In: IEEE Conference on Computer Vision and Pattern Recognition, CVPR (2009)
14. Price, B.L., Morse, B.S., Cohen, S.: Livecut: Learning-based interactive video segmentation by evaluation of multiple propagated cues. In: IEEE International Conference on Computer Vision, ICCV (2009)
15. Ren, X., Malik, J.: Tracking as repeated figure/ground segmentation. In: IEEE Conference on Computer Vision and Pattern Recognition, CVPR (2007)
16. Saffari, A., Leistner, C., Santner, J., Godec, M., Bischof, H.: On-line random forests. In: ICCV 2009 Workshop on On-line Computer Vision (2009)
17. Stalder, S., Grabner, H., Van Gool, L.: Beyond semi-supervised tracking: Tracking should be as simple as detection, but not simpler than recognition. In: ICCV 2009 Workshop on On-line Learning for Computer Vision (2009)
18. Tsai, D., Flagg, M., Rehg, J.M.: Motion coherent tracking with multi-label mrf optimization. In: British Machine Vision Conference, BMVC (2010)
19. Vazquez-Reina, A., Avidan, S., Pfister, H., Miller, E.: Multiple Hypothesis Video Segmentation from Superpixel Flows. In: Daniilidis, K., Maragos, P., Paragios, N. (eds.) ECCV 2010, Part V. LNCS, vol. 6315, pp. 268–281. Springer, Heidelberg (2010)
20. Yuen, J., Russell, B., Liu, C., Torralba, A.: Labelme video- building a video database with human annotations. In: IEEE International Conference on Computer Vision, ICCV (2009)

A TV-L1 Optical Flow Method
with Occlusion Detection

Coloma Ballester[1], Lluis Garrido[2], Vanel Lazcano[1], and Vicent Caselles[1]

[1] Dept Information and Communication Technologies, University Pompeu Fabra
[2] Dept Applied Mathematics and Analysis, University Barcelona
{coloma.ballester,vanel.lazcano,vicent.caselles}@upf.edu,
lluis.garrido@ub.edu

Abstract. In this paper we propose a variational model for joint optical flow and occlusion estimation. Our work stems from the optical flow method based on a TV-L^1 approach and incorporates information that allows to detect occlusions. This information is based on the divergence of the flow and the proposed energy favors the location of occlusions on regions where this divergence is negative. Assuming that occluded pixels are visible in the previous frame, the optical flow on non-occluded pixels is forward estimated whereas is backwards estimated on the occluded ones. We display some experiments showing that the proposed model is able to properly estimate both the optical flow and the occluded regions.

1 Introduction

The problem of estimating the motion from a sequence of images is a topic that has received a lot of attention in the computer vision community. The objective of motion estimation methods is to compute a flow field that represents the motion of points in two consecutive frames. Currently the most accurate techniques that address this problem are based on the formulation of the optical flow estimation in a variational setting. In this setting the objective is to minimize an energy function which is a weighted sum of two terms: a data term and a regularization term. The data term is usually based on the conservation of some property during motion. A common data term is based on the brightness constancy assumption, which assumes that the object illumination does not change along its motion trajectory. The regularization term allows to define the structure of the motion field and ensures that the optical flow computation is well posed.

After the initial work in [7], a lot of approaches that focus on accuracy have been developed. These works focus on the use of robust estimators [2], either in the data or smoothness terms, to be able to deal with motion discontinuities generated by occlusions. For the data term, e.g. L^2 or L^1 dissimilarity measures have been used. For the smoothness term, isotropic diffusion, image-adaptive, isotropic diffusion with non-quadratic regularizers [3], or anisotropic diffusion (image or flow-adaptive) [9] have been proposed. We refer to [4] for a detailed account of these possibilities. However, these methods may fail in occlusion areas due to forced, but unreliable, intensity matching. The problem can be further accentuated if the optical flow is smoothed across object boundaries adjacent to occlusion areas.

A. Pinz et al. (Eds.): DAGM/OAGM 2012, LNCS 7476, pp. 31–40, 2012.
© Springer-Verlag Berlin Heidelberg 2012

A step towards taking into account occlusions was done by jointly estimating forward and backwards optical flow in [1]. The authors argue that at non-occluded pixels forward and backward flows are symmetric. Thus, the occlusion is determined by introducing into the formulation an error measure that assesses, for each pixel, the consistency between the forward and backward flows. Intensity matching is still forced at occluded pixels. Optical flow estimation and occlusion detection are decoupled. In [8], the authors propose a formulation that computes optical flow and implicitly detects occlusions, extrapolating optical flow in occluded areas. Occlusions are determined again by assessing the consistency of the forward and backward flows for each pixel. This cue is used to penalize the intensity matching accordingly. Thus, the method does not force matching at occluded pixels. The extrapolation mechanism in the occlusion areas is based on anisotropic diffusion and uses the underlying gradient to preserve optical flow discontinuities. Another joint approach for optical flow and occlusion detection was developed in [18]. This work proposes a two step updating scheme. The first step updates the flow field based only on the data and occlusion cues, given by the mismatch in the intensity value between the two images. The second step performs a flow diffusion process using a bilateral filter that locally adjusts filter strength by means of the occlusion cue.

Layered approaches [16] allow to realistically model occlusion boundaries. In order to do this one has to correctly compute the relative order of the surfaces. Performing inference over the combinatorial range of possible occlusion relationships is challenging. A recent work that explicitly models occlusions and depth ordering can be found in [12]. The authors present a method in which a visibility function is estimated for each layer. Spatial and temporal constraints are imposed to these functions in order to ensure layer consistency. These functions are used to penalize the intensity matching functions correspondingly. The results obtained are very good but the computational load to minimize the associated energy is high.

Other authors try to obtain occlusion boundary information by means of an operator directly applied to the computed motion. In [15], the authors argue that occlusion boundaries can be detected by assessing the points at which the flow changes rapidly. Discontinuities in the optical flow correspond in fact to zeros in the Laplacian fields of each motion component along the direction perpendicular to the occlusion boundary. In [11] video motion is represented as a set of particles. As the authors point out, the divergence of the motion field can be used to distinguish between different types of motion areas. Schematically, the divergence of a flow field is negative for occluded areas, positive for disoccluded, and near zero for the matched areas. Taking this into account, the authors define an intensity matching term that is weighted by a function depending on the divergence of the motion. At each iteration of the optimization procedure, the motion field is filtered, similarly to [18], with a bilateral filter that depends on the divergence of the motion. The latter idea is used in [13] in order to perform a robust median filtering of the motion. In another context, [14] analyzes the problem of estimating the motion of fluids. They use a divergence-curl regularizer to be able to deal with large concentrations of vorticity and divergence.

Our contribution in this paper is a novel joint optical flow and occlusion estimation approach. We build up from the ideas behind the layered approaches and the fact that the divergence of the field can be used to detect occlusion areas. Rather than trying to construct a set of depth ordered layers, we estimate a binary occlusion layer. Our joint optical flow and occlusion estimator is based on the work [17]. The authors present a variational discontinuity preserving formulation based on the total variation regularization of the flow and the L^1 norm of the data fidelity term. Both nonlinearities are decoupled by introducing an auxiliary variable that also represents the flow; then the energy is minimized by means of a numerical scheme based on a dual formulation of the TV energy and an efficient point-wise thresholding step.

The paper is organized as follows: Section 2 presents the model for joint optical flow and occlusion estimation, Section 3 describes its numerical implementation, Section 4 shows some qualitative, and quantitative results and Section 5 presents our conclusions.

2   A Model for Joint Computation of Optical Flow and Occlusions

Assume that two consecutive image frames $I_0, I_1 : \Omega \to \mathbb{R}$ are given. As usual, we assume that the image domain Ω is a rectangle in $\mathbb{R}^2$. Our starting point will be the model introduced in [19]. In order to compute the optical flow $\mathbf{u} = (u_1, u_2) : \Omega \to \mathbb{R}^2$ between I_0 and I_1, the authors propose to minimize the energy

$$E(\mathbf{u}, \chi) = \int_\Omega (\lambda |I_0(\mathbf{x}) - I_1(\mathbf{x} + \mathbf{u}(\mathbf{x}))| + |\nabla u_1| + |\nabla u_2|)\, d\mathbf{x}, \qquad (1)$$

including robust data attachment and regularization terms (namely, the Total Variation of $\mathbf{u}$) with a relative weight given by the parameter $\lambda > 0$.

Following these ideas, we extend the previous model to jointly compute the optical flow and occlusions. Let $\chi : \Omega \to [0,1]$ be the function modeling the occlusion mask, so that $\chi = 1$ identifies the occluded pixels, i.e. pixels that are visible in I_0 but not in I_1. Our model is based on the assumption that pixels that are not visible in frame I_1 are visible in the previous frame of I_0. Let $I_{-1} : \Omega \to \mathbb{R}$ be that frame. Thus, if $\chi(\mathbf{x}) = 0$, then we compare $I_0(\mathbf{x})$ and $I_1(\mathbf{x} + \mathbf{u}(\mathbf{x}))$. If $\chi(\mathbf{x}) = 1$, we compare $I_0(\mathbf{x})$ and $I_{-1}(\mathbf{x} - \mathbf{u}(\mathbf{x}))$. On the other hand, the occluded region given by $\chi = 1$ should be correlated with the region where div$(\mathbf{u})$ is negative. Thus we propose to compute the optical flow by minimizing the energy

$$E(\mathbf{u}, \chi) = E_d(\mathbf{u}, \chi) + E_r(\mathbf{u}, \chi) + \frac{\alpha}{2} \int_\Omega \chi |\mathbf{u}|^2\, d\mathbf{x} + \beta \int_\Omega \chi \text{div}(\mathbf{u})\, d\mathbf{x}, \qquad (2)$$

where

$$E_d(\mathbf{u}, \chi) = \lambda \int_\Omega ((1 - \chi)|I_0(\mathbf{x}) - I_1(\mathbf{x} + \mathbf{u}(\mathbf{x}))| + \chi |I_0(\mathbf{x}) - I_{-1}(\mathbf{x} - \mathbf{u}(\mathbf{x}))|)\, d\mathbf{x}, \qquad (3)$$

$$E_r(\mathbf{u}, \chi) = \int_\Omega g(\mathbf{x})(|\nabla u_1| + |\nabla u_2| + |\nabla\chi|) \, d\mathbf{x}, \qquad (4)$$

and $\alpha \geq 0, \beta > 0$. We can choose $g(\mathbf{x}) = 1$ or $g = (1 + \gamma|\nabla\tilde{I}_0(\mathbf{x})|)^{-1}$, $\mathbf{x} \in \Omega$, where $\tilde{I}_0$ is a smoothed version of I_0 and $\gamma > 0$. We have included a term to penalize large displacements where $\chi = 1$ (with $\alpha > 0$ but small relative to λ). This is motivated by two observations. On one hand, we are assuming that the occluded background area is moving slower than the occluding foreground. On the other, since images have usually self-similarities, a pixel may have several possibilities to match. Based on this, we take $\alpha > 0$ and small (in practice we took $\alpha = 0.01$) to encourage choosing the smallest displacement.

As in [19], in order to cope with the nonlinearities of both $E_d(\mathbf{u}, \chi)$ and $E_r(\mathbf{u}, \chi)$ we introduce an auxiliary variable $\mathbf{v}$ representing the optical flow and we penalize its deviation form $\mathbf{u}$. Thus, we minimize the energy

$$E_\theta = E_d(\mathbf{v}, \chi) + E_r(\mathbf{u}, \chi) + \frac{\alpha}{2} \int_\Omega \chi|\mathbf{v}|^2 \, d\mathbf{x} + \beta \int_\Omega \chi \operatorname{div}(\mathbf{u}) \, d\mathbf{x} + \frac{1}{2\theta} \int_\Omega |\mathbf{u} - \mathbf{v}|^2, \quad (5)$$

depending on the three variables $(\mathbf{u}, \mathbf{v}, \chi)$, where $\theta > 0$. This energy can be minimized by alternatively fixing two variables and minimizing with respect to the third one.

To minimize (5) with respect to $\mathbf{v}$ we linearize each expression $|I_0(\mathbf{x}) - I_i(\mathbf{x} + \epsilon_i\mathbf{u}(\mathbf{x}))|$, $i = -1, 1$ ($\epsilon_{-1} = -1, \epsilon_1 = 1$), around a given vector field $\mathbf{u}_0$ and define the residual

$$\rho_i(\mathbf{v}) := I_i(\mathbf{x} + \epsilon_i\mathbf{u}_0(\mathbf{x})) + \epsilon_i\nabla I_i(\mathbf{x} + \epsilon_i\mathbf{u}_0(\mathbf{x})) \cdot (\mathbf{v}(\mathbf{x}) - \mathbf{u}_0(\mathbf{x})) - I_0(\mathbf{x}). \quad (6)$$

This procedure is applied by iteratively minimizing the energy

$$\widetilde{E}_\theta = \widetilde{E}_d(\mathbf{v}, \chi) + E_r(\mathbf{u}, \chi) + \frac{\alpha}{2} \int_\Omega \chi|\mathbf{v}|^2 \, d\mathbf{x} + \beta \int_\Omega \chi \operatorname{div}(\mathbf{u}) \, d\mathbf{x} + \frac{1}{2\theta} \int_\Omega |\mathbf{u} - \mathbf{v}|^2, \quad (7)$$

where

$$\widetilde{E}_d(\mathbf{v}, \chi) = \lambda \int_\Omega ((1 - \chi)|\rho_1(\mathbf{v})| + \chi|\rho_{-1}(\mathbf{v})|) \, d\mathbf{x}.$$

To minimize $\widetilde{E}_\theta$ we alternate between the minimization with respect to each variable keeping the other two fixed. After iteration of these steps, we proceed to redefine $\rho_i(\mathbf{v})$ (see Algorithm 1). The minimization of $\widetilde{E}_\theta$ with respect to $\mathbf{u}$ is done using Chambolle's algorithm [5].

Proposition 1. *The minimum of $\widetilde{E}_\theta$ with respect to $\mathbf{u} = (u_1, u_2)$ is given by*

$$u_i = v_i + \theta\operatorname{div}(g\xi_i) + \theta\beta\frac{\partial\chi}{\partial x_i}, \quad i = 1, 2, \qquad (8)$$

ξ_1 *and* ξ_2 *are computed using the following iterative scheme*

$$\xi_i^{k+1} = \frac{\xi_i^k + \frac{\tau_u}{\theta}g\nabla(v_i + \theta\operatorname{div}(g\xi_i^k) + \theta\beta\frac{\partial\chi}{\partial x_i})}{1 + \frac{\tau_u}{\theta}|g\nabla(v_i + \theta\operatorname{div}(g\xi_i^k) + \theta\beta\frac{\partial\chi}{\partial x_i})|}, \quad k = 0, 1, 2, \dots \qquad (9)$$

where $\xi_i^0 = 0$ *and* $\tau_u \leq 1/8$.

As in [19], we have:

Proposition 2. *Assume that* $\chi : \Omega \to \{0,1\}$. *The minimum of* $\widetilde{E}_\theta$ *with respect to* $\mathbf{v} = (v_1, v_2)$ *is*

$$
\mathbf{v} = \begin{cases} \alpha_i \mathbf{u} - \mu_i \epsilon_i \nabla I_i(\mathbf{x} + \epsilon_i \mathbf{u_0}) & \text{if } \Lambda_i(\mathbf{u}) > \mu_i |\nabla I_i(\mathbf{x} + \epsilon_i \mathbf{u_0})|^2 \\ \alpha_i \mathbf{u} + \mu_i \epsilon_i \nabla I_i(\mathbf{x} + \epsilon_i \mathbf{u_0}) & \text{if } \Lambda_i(\mathbf{u}) < -\mu_i |\nabla I_i(\mathbf{x} + \epsilon_i \mathbf{u_0})|^2 \\ \mathbf{u} - \epsilon_i \rho_i(\mathbf{u}) \frac{\nabla I_i(\mathbf{x} + \epsilon_i \mathbf{u_0})}{|\nabla I_i(\mathbf{x} + \epsilon_i \mathbf{u_0})|^2} & \text{if } |\Lambda_i(\mathbf{u})| \leq \mu_i |\nabla I_i(\mathbf{x} + \epsilon_i \mathbf{u_0})|^2, \end{cases} \quad (10)
$$

where $i = 1$, $\epsilon_1 = 1$, $\alpha_1 = 1$, $\mu_1 = \lambda\theta$, $\Lambda_1(\mathbf{u}) = \rho_1(\mathbf{u})$ *when* $\chi = 0$, *and* $i = -1$, $\epsilon_{-1} = -1$, $\alpha_{-1} = \frac{1}{1+\alpha\theta}$, $\mu_{-1} = \frac{\lambda\theta}{1+\alpha\theta}$, $\Lambda_{-1}(\mathbf{u}) = \rho_{-1}(\mathbf{u}) + \frac{\alpha\theta}{1+\alpha\theta} \mathbf{u} \cdot \nabla I_{-1}(\mathbf{x} + \epsilon_i \mathbf{u_0})$ *when* $\chi = 1$. *Notice that we omitted the arguments* $\mathbf{x}$ *in* $\mathbf{u}, \mathbf{u_0}$.

Having computed $\mathbf{v}$, let $F = \lambda(|\rho_{-1}(\mathbf{v})| - |\rho_1(\mathbf{v})|)$ and $G = \frac{\alpha}{2}|\mathbf{v}|^2$. As a consequence of [6], we have:

Proposition 3. *Let* $0 < \tau_\eta \tau_\chi < 1/8$. *Given* $\mathbf{u}, \mathbf{v}$, *the minimum* $\bar{\chi}$ *of* $\widetilde{E}_\theta$ *with respect to* χ *can be obtained by the following primal-dual algorithm*

$$
\begin{aligned}
\eta^{n+1} &= P_B(\eta^n + \tau_\eta \, g \, \nabla\chi^n) \\
\chi^{n+1} &= P_{[0,1]} \left(\chi^n + \tau_\chi \left(\mathrm{div}(g\eta^{n+1}) - \beta \, \mathrm{div}\mathbf{u} - F - G \right) \right),
\end{aligned} \quad (11)
$$

where $P_B(\eta)$ *denotes the projection of* η *on the unit ball of* $\mathbb{R}^2$ *and* $P_{[0,1]}(r) = \max(\min(r,1),0)$, $r \in \mathbb{R}$.

Notice that, by the co-area formula, the level sets of χ are also minimizers of $\widetilde{E}_\theta$ ($\mathbf{u}, \mathbf{v}$ being fixed). Thus, before going to next minimization of $\widetilde{E}_\theta$ with respect to $\mathbf{u}$, we redefine $\chi(\mathbf{x}) = T_\delta(\bar{\chi}(\mathbf{x}))$, where $T_\delta(r) = 1$ (resp. 0) if $r \geq \delta$ (resp. $< \delta$). A different relaxation that also produces good results is obtained by replacing $1 - \chi$ and χ by $(1-\chi)^2$ and χ^2, respectively, in all terms of (7) but E_r.

3 Numerical Scheme

The numerical algorithm is summarized in Algorithm 1. The inputs are three consecutive frames I_{-1}, I_0, I_1 of a video sequence and the outputs are the flow field $\mathbf{u}$ and the occlusion layer χ.

The minimization of (2) is embedded into a coarse-to-fine multi-level approach in order to be able to deal with large flow fields. Our code is based on the implementation of [10]. We have also added some of the numerical details of [17]. Image gradient is computed using the filter stencils as proposed in [17]. Warping is performed using bicubic interpolation. Optionally, one can use a structure-texture decomposition of the images, performing the optical flow estimation on the texture part. The use of the texture images allows to improve results for real images, whereas it may degrade performance (with respect to using the original images) on synthetic ones.

Input : Three consecutive frames I_{-1}, I_0, I_1 of a video sequence
Output: Flow field **u** and occlusion layer χ for I_0

Compute down-scaled images I_{-1}^s, I_0^s, I_1^s for $s = 1, \ldots, N_{\text{scales}}$;
Initialize $\mathbf{u}^{N_{\text{scales}}} = \mathbf{v}^{N_{\text{scales}}} = 0$, and $\chi^{N_{\text{scales}}} = 0$;
for $s \leftarrow N_{\text{scales}}$ **to** 1 **do**
    for $w \leftarrow 1$ **to** N_{warps} **do**
        Compute $I_i^s(\mathbf{x} + \epsilon_i \mathbf{u}_0(\mathbf{x}))$, $\nabla I_i^s(\mathbf{x} + \epsilon_i \mathbf{u}_0(\mathbf{x}))$, and ρ_i using (6), $i = -1, 1$;
        $n \leftarrow 0$;
        while $n <$ outer_iterations **do**
            Compute $\mathbf{v}^s$ using (10) (Proposition 2);
            for $k \leftarrow 1$ **to** inner_iterations_u **do**
                Solve for $\xi_i^{k+1,s}$, $i \in \{1, 2\}$, using the fixed point iteration (9);
            end
            Compute $\mathbf{u}^s$ using (8) (Proposition 1);
            for $m \leftarrow 1$ **to** inner_iterations_χ **do**
                Solve for χ^{m+1} using the primal-dual algorithm (11);
            end
        end
    end
    If $s > 1$ **then** scale-up $\mathbf{u}^s, \mathbf{v}^s, \chi^s$ to $\mathbf{u}^{s-1}, \mathbf{v}^{s-1}, \chi^{s-1}$;
end
$u = u^1$ and $\chi = T_\mu(\chi^1)$

Algorithm 1. Algorithm for joint optical flow and occlusion computation

4   Results

In this section we display some experiments done with our occlusion based optical flow algorithm.

Qualitative Results. The first row of Fig. 1 shows three consecutive frames of the Urban2 sequence, publicly available at Middlebury database. They correspond to I_{-1} (frame 9), I_0 (frame 10) and I_1 (frame 11). In this sequence the camera moves to the right. The apparent movement of the buildings produces occlusions between them.

Second row of Fig. 1 shows the optical flow obtained with our algorithm: the optical flow **u** is shown on the left image using the color coding scheme of the gimp color palette, as in [10]. In the middle, the motion compensated image is shown. This image is generated using **u** and backwards compensating from I_1 (resp. I_{-1}) if the corresponding pixel is not occluded (resp. is occluded). Finally, the normalized (to the range $[0, 255]$) absolute value of the difference between I_0 and the motion compensated image is shown on the right.

In Fig. 2 the occlusion layers χ are shown in red superimposed on the frame I_0 of the sequence. On the left (resp. right), the occlusion layer χ with $\alpha > 0$ (resp. $\alpha = 0$) is shown. As it can be seen, our method is able to properly detect the regions of I_0 that get occluded at frame I_1 due to the apparent movement of the buildings.

Fig. 1. *First row*: three consecutive frames I_{-1}, I_0, I_1 of the Urban2 Middlebury video sequence. *Second row*: the optical flow **u**, the backwards motion compensated image using I_1 and I_{-1}, and the normalized absolute value of the difference between the motion compensated image and the original image in the *first row*.

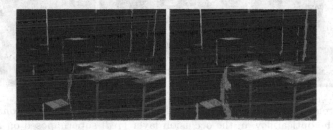

Fig. 2. *Left*: occlusion layer χ (*red*) associated to $\alpha > 0$ superimposed on I_0. *Right*: occlusion layer χ associated to $\alpha = 0$ superimposed on I_0

Fig. 3 shows the interpolation error obtained for the Urban image of the Middlebury evaluation database using our optical flow (left) and the flow of [17] (right). The images shown here have been directly obtained from the Middlebury web evaluation results, with hidden ground-truth flow. As it can be seen, our method behaves better in the occluded regions.

Our next experiment deals with the Backyard sequence, a natural sequence taken with a high-speed camera. The first row of Fig. 4 shows three consecutive frames of this sequence. They correspond to I_{-1} (frame 9), I_0 (frame 10) and I_1 (frame 11). In this sequence the camera pans to the right, in addition the kids move and the ball on the left is falling down. The apparent movement produces different kinds of occlusions.

The second row of Fig. 4 shows the results obtained with our occlusion based optical flow algorithm: the computed optical flow **u**, the occlusion layer (in red) superimposed on I_0, and the normalized absolute value of the difference between

Fig. 3. Interpolation error results obtained from the Middlebury evaluation database for the Urban sequence. *Left*, result of our method. *Right*, result of the method in [17].

Fig. 4. *First row:* three consecutive frames of the Backyard sequence. *Second row: from left to right:* the optical flow **u**, the occlusion layer (*red*) superimposed on I_0, and the normalized absolute difference error between the motion compensated image and I_0.

the motion compensated image and I_0. As can be seen again, our method is able to properly detect occluded pixels around the kids and the ball.

Quantitative Results on the Middlebury test-set. We have used our method on those sequences with at least three frames, using that of [17] if only two frames are available. Table 1 shows the end point error (EPE) and the average angular error (AAE) of the estimated flow fields. These two values are computed using the occlusion layer χ, that is, they are computed only at non-occluded pixels. For this table, we have run the algorithm with the same parameter set: $\lambda = 0.25, \theta = 0.30, \beta = 1, \alpha = 0, g = (1 + \gamma |\nabla \tilde{I}_0(\mathbf{x})|)^{-1}, \mathbf{x} \in \Omega, \gamma = 0.05$, 5 pyramid scales and 10 warpings at each scale. As can be seen in the table, our metod is competitive with the results reported by [17].

The same parameter set has been used to test our method against the Middlebury evaluation test set, see http://vision.middlebury.edu/flow, as well as Fig. 5. At the time of writing this paper (June 2012), our method, called Occlusion-TV-L1 in the Middlebury database, is located at position 24 with respect to the end-point-error, the original TV-L1-improved method being located at position 34.

Table 1. Evaluation results on images of the Middlebury dataset with public ground truth flow. The table shows the end point error (EPE) and the average angular error (AAE) of the estimated flow fields using the same set of parameters for our method and the method presented in [17].

	Grove2	Grove3	Hydra	Rubber	Urban2	Urban3
EPE-TV-L1 improved [17]	0.154	0.665	0.147	0.092	0.319	0.630
Our EPE-Occlusion based	0.121	0.547	0.162	0.093	0.311	0.382
Our AAE-Occlusion based	1.802°	5.400°	1.977°	2.895°	2.497°	3.382°

Average endpoint error	avg. rank	Army (Hidden texture) GT im0 im1 all disc untext	Mequon (Hidden texture) GT im0 im1 all disc untext	Schefflera (Hidden texture) GT im0 im1 all disc untext	Wooden (Hidden texture) GT im0 im1 all disc untext	Grove (Synthetic) GT im0 im1 all disc untext	Urban (Synthetic) GT im0 im1 all disc untext	Yosemite (Synthetic) GT im0 im1 all disc untext	Teddy (Stereo) GT im0 im1 all disc untext
SimpleFlow [52]	22.9	0.09 14 0.24 13 0.08 21	0.24 32 0.78 29 0.20 35	0.43 29 0.96 30 0.21 30	0.16 16 0.77 12 0.09 11	0.71 13 1.04 14 0.55 16	1.47 65 1.56 27 0.76 49	0.13 22 0.12 6 0.22 26	0.50 12 1.04 14 0.72 13
Occlusion-TV-L1 [68]	24.0	0.09 14 0.26 23 0.07 7	0.22 19 0.74 25 0.16 20	0.51 37 1.15 39 0.21 30	0.18 24 0.91 25 0.10 24	0.87 29 1.25 28 0.72 28	0.47 18 1.38 23 0.36 28	0.10 4 0.12 6 0.11 2	0.63 41 1.78 44 0.96 38
Adaptive [20]	25.9	0.09 14 0.26 23 0.06 1	0.23 29 0.78 29 0.16 20	0.54 36 1.19 43 0.21 30	0.18 24 0.91 25 0.10 24	0.88 32 1.25 28 0.73 31	0.50 23 1.28 20 0.31 11	0.14 28 0.16 48 0.22 26	0.65 27 1.37 26 0.79 23
DPOF [18]	27.1	0.12 41 0.33 41 0.08 21	0.26 36 0.80 33 0.20 35	0.24 4 0.49 4 0.20 26	0.19 29 0.83 17 0.13 34	0.66 8 0.98 9 0.40 4	1.11 47 1.41 28 0.57 42	0.25 67 0.14 29 0.55 67	0.51 15 1.02 13 0.54 2
Adapt-Window [34]	27.2	0.10 24 0.24 13 0.09 30	0.19 7 0.59 4 0.15 11	0.27 7 0.64 9 0.17 6	0.18 24 0.82 16 0.11 27	0.74 16 1.07 17 0.56 19	1.78 64 1.73 44 0.95 59	0.22 61 0.16 48 0.45 64	0.70 31 1.28 23 0.88 31
ACK-Prior [27]	28.0	0.11 31 0.25 17 0.09 30	0.18 3 0.59 4 0.13 3	0.27 7 0.64 9 0.16 4	0.15 8 0.78 13 0.09 11	0.82 23 1.14 21 0.71 27	1.90 66 1.90 51 0.99 67	0.23 65 0.17 52 0.49 66	0.77 37 1.44 28 0.91 33
Complementary OF [21]	28.5	0.11 31 0.28 30 0.10 38	0.18 3 0.63 10 0.12 2	0.31 19 0.75 19 0.18 11	0.19 29 0.97 32 0.12 31	0.97 43 1.31 39 1.00 48	1.78 64 1.73 44 0.87 57	0.11 9 0.12 6 0.22 26	0.68 29 1.48 29 0.95 36
ComplOF-FED-GPU [36]	29.6	0.11 31 0.29 33 0.10 39	0.21 16 0.78 29 0.14 7	0.32 21 0.79 23 0.17 6	0.19 29 0.99 33 0.11 27	0.89 33 1.29 34 0.73 31	1.25 49 1.74 46 0.64 46	0.14 28 0.13 17 0.30 51	0.64 25 1.50 31 0.83 26
Classic++ [32]	30.0	0.09 14 0.25 17 0.07 7	0.23 29 0.78 29 0.19 28	0.43 29 1.02 32 0.22 33	0.20 33 1.11 38 0.10 24	0.87 29 1.30 36 0.66 25	0.47 18 1.62 38 0.33 17	0.17 48 0.14 29 0.32 56	0.79 40 1.64 38 0.92 34
Aniso. Huber-L1 [22]	30.3	0.10 24 0.28 30 0.08 21	0.31 43 0.68 38 0.26 48	0.56 42 1.13 37 0.29 48	0.20 33 0.92 26 0.13 34	0.84 26 1.20 24 0.70 26	0.39 5 1.23 18 0.28 5	0.17 48 0.15 39 0.27 41	0.64 25 1.36 25 0.79 23
TriangleFlow [30]	32.8	0.11 31 0.29 33 0.09 30	0.26 36 0.95 42 0.17 17	0.47 36 1.07 35 0.18 11	0.16 15 0.87 23 0.09 11	1.07 50 1.47 55 1.10 51	0.87 41 1.39 25 0.57 42	0.15 36 0.19 62 0.23 30	0.63 24 1.33 20 0.84 27
TV-L1-improved [17]	34.6	0.09 14 0.26 23 0.07 7	0.20 13 0.71 16 0.16 14	0.53 38 1.16 42 0.22 33	0.21 37 1.24 43 0.11 27	0.90 34 1.31 39 0.72 28	1.51 57 1.93 53 0.84 53	0.18 52 0.17 52 0.31 54	0.73 33 1.62 37 0.87 30
LocallyOriented [55]	35.5	0.12 41 0.35 45 0.08 21	0.33 46 1.01 46 0.25 44	0.61 49 1.30 51 0.28 43	0.18 24 0.80 14 0.13 34	0.83 39 1.29 34 0.79 37	0.98 44 1.48 33 0.56 41	0.12 15 0.14 39 0.31 34	0.72 32 1.48 29 0.05 39

Fig. 5. Average end point error on Middlebury flow benchmark (June 22nd 2012)

Our method needs about 538 seconds to compute the optical flow for the "Urban" evaluation sequence using a single CPU. It should be noted that the Teddy sequence has only two images. Thus, for this sequence we used a two frame TV-L1 estimator [17] without occlusion detection using the previously specified parameters for λ and θ, number of pyramid scales, and number of warpings.

5 Conclusions

In this work we presented a variational model for joint optical flow and occlusion estimation. Our work stems from the optical flow method presented in [17] and incorporates information that allows to detect occlusions. This information is based on the divergence of the flow, and the proposed energy contains a term that favors the location of occlusions on regions where this divergence is negative. Based on the mild assumption that, when computing the flow at time t, occluded pixels are visible in the previous frame, the optical flow on non-occluded pixels is forward estimated whereas is backward estimated on the occluded ones.

Our numerical experiments show that the proposed approach is able to properly estimate the optical flow and the occluded regions. It also improves the original method [17].

References

1. Alvarez, L., Deriche, R., Papadopoulo, T., Sanchez, J.: Symmetrical dense optical flow estimation with occlusions detection. International Journal of Computer Vision 75(3), 371–385 (2007)

2. Black, M., Anandan, P.: The robust estimation of multiple motions: Parametric and piecewise-smooth flow fields. Computer Vision and Image Understanding 63(1), 75–104 (1996)
3. Brox, T., Bruhn, A., Papenberg, N., Weickert, J.: High Accuracy Optical Flow Estimation Based on a Theory for Warping. In: Pajdla, T., Matas, J. (eds.) ECCV 2004, Part IV. LNCS, vol. 3024, pp. 25–36. Springer, Heidelberg (2004)
4. Bruhn, A.: Variational optic flow computation: Accurate modeling and efficient numerics. Ph.D. thesis, Department of Mathematics and Computer Science, Saarland University (2006)
5. Chambolle, A.: An algorithm for total variation minimization and applications. Mathematical Imaging and Vision 20(1), 89–97 (2004)
6. Chambolle, A., Pock, T.: A first-order primal-dual algorithm for convex problems with applications to imaging. Journal of Mathematical Imaging and Vision 40(1), 120–145 (2011)
7. Horn, B., Schunk, B.: Determining optical flow. Artificial Intelligence 20 (1981)
8. Ince, S., Konrad, J.: Occlusion-aware optical flow estimation. IEEE Trans. Image Processing 17(8), 1443–1451 (2008)
9. Nagel, H.H., Enkelmann, W.: An investigation of smoothness constraints for the estimation of displacement vector fields from image sequences. IEEE Transactions on Pattern Analysis and Machine Intelligence 8(5), 565–593 (1986)
10. Sánchez, J., Meinhardt-Llopis, E., Facciolo, G.: TV-L^1 optical flow estimation. Image Processing Online (January 2012), http://www.ipol.im
11. Sand, P., Teller, S.: Particle video: Long-range motion estimation using point trajectories. International Journal of Computer Vision 80(1), 72–91 (2008)
12. Sun, D., Sudderth, E.B., Black, M.J.: Layered image motion with explicit occlusions, temporal consistency, and depth ordering. In: Advances in Neural Information Processing Systems, pp. 2226–2234 (2010)
13. Sun, D., Roth, S., Black, M.J.: Secrets of optical flow estimation and their principles. In: CVPR (2010)
14. Corpetti, T., Mémin, E., Pérez, P.: Dense estimation of fluid flows. IEEE Transactions on Pattern Analysis and Machine Intelligence 24(3), 365–380 (2002)
15. Thompson, W.B., Mutch, K.M., Berzins, V.A.: Dynamic occlusion analysis in optical flow fields. IEEE Transactions on Pattern Analysis and Machine Intelligence 7(4), 374–383 (1985)
16. Wang, J.Y.A., Adelson, E.H.: Representing moving images with layers. IEEE Transactions on Image Processing 3(5), 625–638 (1994)
17. Wedel, A., Pock, T., Zach, C., Bischof, H., Cremers, D.: An Improved Algorithm for TV-L1 Optical Flow. In: Cremers, D., Rosenhahn, B., Yuille, A.L., Schmidt, F.R. (eds.) Visual Motion Analysis 2008. LNCS, vol. 5604, pp. 23–45. Springer, Heidelberg (2009)
18. Xiao, J., Cheng, H., Sawhney, H.S., Rao, C., Isnardi, M.: Bilateral Filtering-Based Optical Flow Estimation with Occlusion Detection. In: Leonardis, A., Bischof, H., Pinz, A. (eds.) ECCV 2006, Part I. LNCS, vol. 3951, pp. 211–224. Springer, Heidelberg (2006)
19. Zach, C., Pock, T., Bischof, H.: A Duality Based Approach for Realtime TV-L^1 Optical Flow. In: Hamprecht, F.A., Schnörr, C., Jähne, B. (eds.) DAGM 2007. LNCS, vol. 4713, pp. 214–223. Springer, Heidelberg (2007)

Curvature Prior for MRF-Based Segmentation and Shape Inpainting[*]

Alexander Shekhovtsov[1], Pushmeet Kohli[2], and Carsten Rother[2]

[1] Center for Machine Perception, Czech Technical University
[2] Microsoft Research Cambridge, UK

Abstract. Most image labeling problems such as segmentation and image reconstruction are fundamentally ill-posed and suffer from ambiguities and noise. Higher-order image priors encode high-level structural dependencies between pixels and are key to overcoming these problems. However, in general these priors lead to computationally intractable models. This paper addresses the problem of discovering compact representations of higher-order priors which allow efficient inference. We propose a framework for solving this problem that uses a recently proposed representation of higher-order functions which are encoded as lower envelopes of linear functions. Maximum a Posterior inference on our learned models reduces to minimizing a pairwise function of discrete variables. We show that our framework can learn a compact representation that approximates a low curvature shape prior and demonstrate its effectiveness in solving shape inpainting and image segmentation problems.

1 Introduction

A number of models encoding prior knowledge about scenes have been proposed in computer vision. The most popular ones have been in the form of a Markov Random Field (MRF). An important characteristic of an MRF is the factorization of the distribution into a product of factors. *Pairwise* MRFs can be written as a product of factors defined over two variables at a time. For discrete variables, this enables non-parametric representation of factors and the use of efficient optimization algorithms for approximate inference of the Maximum-a-Posteriori (MAP) solution. However, because of their restricted pairwise form, the model is not able to encode many types of powerful structural properties of images. Curvature is one such property which is known to be extremely helpful for inpainting (see figure 1), segmentation, and many other related problems.

Higher-order Priors. There has been a lot of research into priors based on high-level structural dependencies between pixels such as curvature. These priors can be represented in the probabilistic model using factors which may depend on more than two variables at a time. The largest number of variables in a factor is called the *order* of the model. Higher-order factors defined on discrete variables are computationally expensive to represent. In fact, the memory and time complexity for inferring the MAP solution with general inference algorithms grows exponentially with

---

[*] A. Shekhovtsov was supported by EU project FP7-ICT-247870 NIFTi.

A. Pinz et al. (Eds.): DAGM/OAGM 2012, LNCS 7476, pp. 41–51, 2012.
© Springer-Verlag Berlin Heidelberg 2012

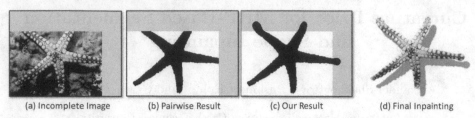

(a) Incomplete Image   (b) Pairwise Result   (c) Our Result   (d) Final Inpainting

Fig. 1. (a) Input image (area for completion of starfish is shown in blue). (b) The starfish was interactively segmented from the image. Then the three arms of the starfish, which touch the image borders, were completed with an 8-connected pairwise MRF which encodes a standard length prior. (c) Completion of the shape with our higher-order curvature prior. (d) Finally, texture was added fully automatically using [2].

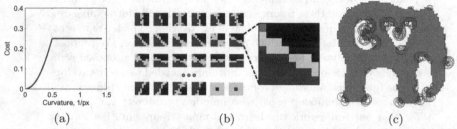

(a)   (b)   (c)

Fig. 2. (a) A given cost function for curvature. (b) "Soft" patterns whose lower envelope approximates the curvature cost of a binary labeling. A pattern fits well (has low cost) if all fore-/background pixels match to blue/red pattern weights, where green pixels can be assigned to both fore- and background. This lower envelope corresponds to a higher-order factor covering 8×8 pixels in every pixel-location in the model. The last two patterns are selected manually such that for interior and exterior pixels the value of the lower envelope is always 0. (c) An example demonstrating the curvature cost computed by our pattern-based approximation at different parts of the object boundary. Circle radius correspond to the assigned cost.

the order, and thus has limited the use of such models. The situation is a bit different for parametric models with continuous variables. Higher-order prior models such as Product of Experts (PoE) [11] or Field of Experts (FoE) [18] are differentiable in both parameters and hidden variables. These models thus enable inference using local gradient descent, and have led to impressive results for problems such as image restoration and optical flow. Recent research on discrete higher-order models has focused on identifying families of higher-order factors which allow efficient inference. The factors can be categorized into 3 broad categories: (a) *Reducable factors*, which allow MAP inference to be reduced to the problem of minimizing a pairwise energy function of discrete variables with the addition of some auxiliary variables [12–14, 17, 19], (b) *Message-enabled factors*, which allow efficient message computation and thus allow inference using message passing methods such as Belief Propagation (BP) and Tree Reweighted message passing (TRW) [10, 15, 25], and (c) *Constraint factors*, which impose global constraints that can be imposed efficiently in a relaxation framework [16, 26].

Pattern-based Representation. Pattern and lower-envelope based representations proposed in [12, 15, 19] can represent some families of *Reducable factors*. The higher-order potentials of [15, 19] are defined by enumerating important configurations (patterns) in a local window. The model of [19] additionally enables deviations from encoded patterns, by using linear weighting functions. The above models are generalized by the representation proposed in [12] which encodes higher-order functions as lower (or upper) envelopes of linear (modular) functions of the variables. The complexity of representing and performing inference depends on the number of linear functions (or patterns) used for representing the higher-order factor. A number of higher-order priors can be encoded using few linear functions (or patterns) and thus allow efficient inference. However, the use of a general higher-order prior would require exponential (in the order of the factor) number of linear functions (or patterns).

Our Contribution. This paper addresses the problem of discovering a compact representation of higher-order factors that encode a curvature prior for labelling problems. Given a set of training examples of labeling and their corresponding desired curvature-based costs, we find parameters of a linear-envelope representation that matches these costs. While the problem is difficult, we propose a simple yet effective algorithm for parameter learning. Figure 2 illustrates our discovered model. We applied the learned prior model to the problems of object segmentation and completion. The experimental results demonstrate that incorporation of this prior leads to much better results than those obtained using low-order (pairwise MRF) based models (see figure 1) and is comparable to other state-of-the-art curvature formulations.

Related work on Curvature. In this work we consider two closely related problems of shape inpainting and image segmentation with curvature prior. Given an image region with a lack of observations, the goal of *shape inpainting* is to complete the region from evidence outside of the region. This problem is related to inpainting of binary images which has been approached in the continuous setting with several curvature-related functionals [3, 6][1]. Image labeling with curvature regularization is an important topic of research, and both continuous and discrete formulations for the problem have been studied. Continuous formulations offer accurate models, however until recently, only local optimization methods were applied. For instance, [8] works with discretized Euler-Lagrange equations of the 4th order. Local optima found by such methods may be of poor quality and several methods solving convex relaxations have already been proposed [5, 9]. Discrete methods for image labeling with curvature regularization build on quantization and enumeration of boundary elements. Until recently, they were applied only in restricted scenarios where it is possible to reduce the problem to a search of the minimal path or minimum ratio cycle [23]. These cases enjoy global optimality, however they do not allow for arbitrary regional terms

---

[1] There is a vast literature on the general image inpainting problem, however these techniques, especially exemplar-based ones, do not extend to image segmentation problem, and are not relevant in the context of this paper.

or impose severe constraints on possible shapes. A series of recent works [20–22, 24] developed a global minimization method for the general discrete setting, where the regions, boundary segments and pairs of adjacent boundary segments can have arbitrary associated costs. The problem is formulated as an ILP and approached by a linear relaxation. It was shown that some image segmentation problems with (approximate) curvature regularization can be solved optimally in this model. For accurate approximation of the curvature, the discretization of the space must form a fine cell complex. Quantization of directions leads to visible artifacts of the segmentation (see section 4). Cell complexes with a finer quantization of directions and adaptive complexes are studied in [24]. A recent work [7] claims to give fast optimal solution for curvature regularization. However, their model is a crude approximation to the curvature functional. Its 4-neighborhood variant essentially penalizes the number of "corners" in the segmentation.

2   Higher-Order Model Representation and Optimization

We consider a set of pixels $\mathcal{V} = \{1 \ldots N_X\} \times \{1 \ldots N_Y\}$ and a binary set of labels $\mathcal{L} = \{0, 1\}$, where 1 means that a pixel belongs to the foreground (shape) and 0 to the background. Let $\mathbf{x} \colon \mathcal{V} \to \mathcal{L}$ be the labeling for all pixels with individual components denoted by x_v, $v \in \mathcal{V}$. Furthermore, let $V(h) \subset \mathcal{V}$ denote a square window of size $K \times K$ at location h, and $\mathcal{U}$ is the set of all window locations. Windows are located densely in all pixels. More precisely, all possible $K \times K$ windows are considered which are fully inside the 2D-grid $\mathcal{V}$ (see fig. 3 for illustration). Let $\mathbf{x}_{V(h)} \colon V(h) \to \mathcal{L}$ denote a restriction of labeling $\mathbf{x}$ to the subset $V(h)$. We consider distribution of the form $p(\mathbf{x}) \propto \exp\{-E(\mathbf{x})\}$ with the following energy function:

$$E(\mathbf{x}) = \sum_{v \in \mathcal{V}} \theta_v(x_v) + \sum_{uv \in \mathcal{E}} \theta_{uv}(x_u, x_v) + \sum_{h \in \mathcal{U}} E_h(\mathbf{x}), \tag{1}$$

where notation uv stands for ordered pair (u, v), $\theta_v \colon \mathcal{L} \to \mathbb{R}$ and $\theta_{uv} \colon \mathcal{L}^2 \to \mathbb{R}$ are unary and pairwise terms, $\mathcal{E} \subset \mathcal{V} \times \mathcal{V}$ is a set of pairwise terms and E_h are higher-order terms. We consider the higher order terms E_h of the following form (equivalent to [19])

$$E_h(\mathbf{x}) = \min_{y \in P} \Big(\langle \mathbf{w}_y, \mathbf{x}_{V(h)} \rangle + c_y \Big). \tag{2}$$

This term is the minimum (lower envelope) of several modular functions of $\mathbf{x}_{V(h)}{}^2$. We refer to individual linear functions $\langle \mathbf{w}_y, \mathbf{x}_{V(h)} \rangle + c_y$ as "soft" patterns. Here $\mathbf{w}_y \in \mathbb{R}^{K^2}$ is a weight vector and $c_y \in \mathbb{R}$ is a constant term for the pattern. Vector $\mathbf{w}_y$ is of the same size as the labeling patch $\mathbf{x}_{V(h)}$ and it can be visualized as an image (see fig. 2(b)). The variable $y \in P$ is called a pattern-switching variable. It is a discrete variable from the set $P = \{0, ..., N_P\}$. We let the pattern which corresponds to $y = 0$ have the associated weights $\mathbf{w}_0 = \mathbf{0}$.

---

[2]   This model has some similarities with a mixture model, as discussed in [1].

This pattern assigns a constant value c_0 to all labellings $\mathbf{x}_{V(h)}$ and it ensures that $E_h(\mathbf{x}) \le c_0$ for all $\mathbf{x}$. (See [1] for detailed relation of this model to [19] and [15]). In our model it is used to represents the maximal cost $f^{\max}$ of the curvature cost function. The minimization problem of energy (1) expresses as

$$\min_{\mathbf{x}} \Big[E_0(\mathbf{x}) + \sum_{h \in \mathcal{U}} \min_{y \in P} \big(\langle \mathbf{w}_y, \mathbf{x}_{V(h)} \rangle + c_y \big) \Big], \tag{3}$$

where unary and pairwise terms are collected into E_0. The problem can also be written as a minimization of a pairwise energy

$$\min_{\substack{\mathbf{x} \in \mathcal{L}^{\mathcal{V}} \\ \mathbf{y} \in P^{\mathcal{U}}}} \Big[E_0(\mathbf{x}) + \sum_{h} \langle \mathbf{w}_{y_h}, \mathbf{x}_{V(h)} \rangle + c_{y_h} \Big], \tag{4}$$

where $\mathbf{y} : \mathcal{U} \to P$ is the concatenated vector of all pattern switching variables[3]. Clearly, problem (4) is a minimization of a pairwise energy function of discrete variables $\mathbf{x}, \mathbf{y}$. The problem is NP-hard in general, however, a number of approximate MAP inference techniques for pairwise energies can be used such as Block-ICM, TRW, BP, or Linear programming based relaxations. Here we report results obtained by the memory-efficient adaptation of TRW-S with post-processing by block-ICM (see details in [1]).

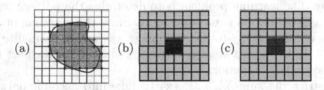

Fig. 3. (a) Continuous shape and its discretization. Filled, small circles show boundary locations. The large blue window illustrates $V(h)$ at location h. (b,c) Fore- and background patterns, which are active at none-boundary locations, with costs: green $w_{y,v} = 0$, red: $w_{y,v} = +B$, blue: $w_{y,v} = -B$, constant c_y is $-4B$ and $+4B$ respectively.

3 Learning a Curvature Cost Model

Suppose we are given a shape $S \subset \mathbb{R}^2$ such that we can calculate the curvature κ at every point of the boundary, ∂S. Let $f(\kappa) \ge 0$ be a curvature cost function, which defines a desired penalty on curvature, in this paper we consider $f(\kappa) = \min(\kappa^2, f^{\max})$. Let the total cost of the shape be $\int_{\partial S} f(\kappa) dl$. Our goal is to approximate this integral by the sum $\sum_{h \in \mathcal{U}} E_h(\mathbf{x})$, where functions E_h operate over a discretized representation of the shape, $\mathbf{x}$, and are of the form (2) with

---

[3] We refer to components of $\mathbf{y}$ by y_h, while y usually denotes an independent bound variable.

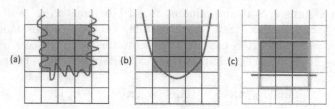

Fig. 4. Problem definition and motivation of large-sized windows. Examples above show discrete labelings on a pixel grid with a corresponding red continuous curve. Note, there are infinitely many continuous curves which give rise to the same discrete labelling - two examples are given in (a) and (b). The red curve in (b) is probably the one with lowest curvature given the discrete labelling. Our goal is to find an energy function which maps every discrete labelling to the corresponding cost of the continuous curvature with *lowest* curvature. (c) makes the important point that larger sized windows have inherently a better chance of predicting well the curvature at the center of the window. In (c) the green window is of size 3x3, while in (b) it is of size 5x5. The underlying discrete labelling is identical in both cases and the red curve is the optimal (lowest curvature) continuous curve given the window. The crucial point is that the curvature of the continuous curve, at the center of the window, is very different in (b) and (c). Note, this problem is to some extend mitigated by the fact that the total cost of segmentation is the sum of costs along the boundary.

weights $\mathbf{w}, \mathbf{c}$. Here $\mathbf{w}$ and $\mathbf{c}$ denote the concatenated vectors of all weights $\mathbf{w}_y$ and c_y, respectively. The learning problem is to determine the pattern weights $\mathbf{w}, \mathbf{c}$ such that the approximation is most accurate. Since the mapping of continuous to discrete curves is a many-to-one mapping, we further formalize our exact goal in figure 4. In the figure we also motivate the important aspect that larger windows are potentially superior.

We first restrict the sum $\sum_{h \in \mathcal{U}} E_h(\mathbf{x})$ to take into account only boundary locations. We call h a *boundary location* for shape $\mathbf{x}$ if the 2×2 window at h contains some pixels which are labeled foreground as well as some pixels which are labeled background, as illustrated in fig. 3. We constrain all soft patterns to be non-negative ($\langle w_y, x \rangle + c_y \geq 0$) and introduce two special patterns (fig. 3b,c), which have cost 0 for locations where the 2×2 window at location h contains only background or foreground pixels. These patterns make $E_h(\mathbf{x})$ vanish over all non-boundary locations, therefore such locations do not contribute to the sum. The learning task is now to determine $E_h(\mathbf{x})$, such that at each boundary location the true cost $f(\kappa)$ is approximated. In this way the discrete sum corresponds to the desired integral if we were to neglect the fact that the number of boundary locations does only approximate the true length of the boundary.

Point-wise learning procedure. Let us assume that in a local $K \times K$ window, shapes of low curvature can be well-approximated by simple quadratic curves[4]. The idea is to take many examples of such shapes and fit $E_h(\mathbf{x})$ to

---

[4] Note, based on our definition in fig. 4 we select curves which are likely to be the ones of lowest curvature (among all curves) for the corresponding discrete labelling.

approximate their cost. We consider many quadratic shapes $(S^i)_{i=1}^N$ in the window $K \times K$ and derive their corresponding discretization on the pixel grid $(\mathbf{x}^i)_{i=1}^N$. Each continuous shape has an associated curvature cost $f^i = f(\kappa^i)$ at the central boundary location. We formulate the learning problem as minimization of the average approximation error:

$$\arg\min_{\mathbf{w},\mathbf{c}} \sum_i |E_h(\mathbf{x}^i) - f^i|, \quad \text{s.t.} \quad \begin{cases} \mathbf{w}_0 = 0, c_0 = f^{\max}; \\ E_h(x) \geq 0 \quad \forall x, \end{cases} \tag{5}$$

where the first constraint represents the special implicit pattern $(w_0, c_0 = f^{\max})$, which ensures that $E_h(\mathbf{x}) \leq f^{\max}$. The second constraint makes sure that cost is non-negative. It is important for the following reason: the formulation of the approximation problem does not explicitly take into account "negative samples", *i.e.* labellings which do not originate from smooth curves, and which must have high cost in the model. However, requiring that all possible negative samples in a $K \times K$ window have high cost would make the problem too constrained. The introduced non-negativity constraint is tractable and not too restrictive. This problem appears difficult, since $E_h(\mathbf{x}^i)$ is itself a concave function in the parameters $\mathbf{w}, \mathbf{c}$. We approach (5) by a k-means like procedure:

Algorithm 1. Iterative Factor Discovery

---

1 **repeat**   /* iteration */
2   **for** $i = 1 \ldots N$ **do**
3       $y^i = \arg\min_y [\langle \mathbf{w}_y, \mathbf{x}^i \rangle + c_y]$;   /* find matching patterns */
4   **for** $y \in 1 \ldots N_P$ **do**   /* refit patterns */
5       $(\mathbf{w}_y, c_y) = \arg\min_{\substack{\mathbf{w}_y, c_y \\ \xi}} \sum_{i|y^i=y} |\langle \mathbf{w}_y, \mathbf{x}^i \rangle + c_y - f^i|$, s.t. $\begin{cases} \xi_v \leq w_{y,v}; \\ \xi_v \leq 0; \\ \sum_v \xi_v + c_y \geq 0. \end{cases}$
6 **until** *convergence or maximum iterations;*

The refitting step 5 is a linear optimization which can be solved exactly. The constraint in step 5 is an equivalent representation of the constraint $\langle \mathbf{w}_y, \mathbf{x} \rangle + c_y \geq 0 \ \forall x$, imposed by (5).

4   Experiments

We applied Algorithm 1 to learn a prior model with 96 patterns of size 8×8 pixels from 10000 randomly, synthetically generated smooth curves and their discretization. We initialize the curvature potential in the learning process by clustering the 10000 patches in 32 groups based on the orientation of the boundary at the patch center. Then each orientation group is further subdivided into 3 bins based on the curvature. To measure the accuracy of our curvature potential approximation, we sampled large shapes for which the true curvature cost can be computed and then compared it with our approximated cost which is obtained by summing the response of our curvature cost potential along the boundary. Further details of the learning procedure are given in [1].

Shape Inpainting. We now demonstrate the learned prior model on the problem of shape inpainting. The goal is to reconstruct the full shape, while only some parts of the shape are visible to the algorithm. This is a useful test to inspect our shape prior. Let $F \subset \mathcal{V}$ be the set of pixels restricted to foreground (shape) and $B \subset \mathcal{V}$ pixels restricted to background. The unary terms of (1), $\theta_v(x_v)$, are set to ∞ if label x_v contradicts with the constrains and 0 otherwise. This ensures that the correct segmentation is inferred in the region $F \cup B$.

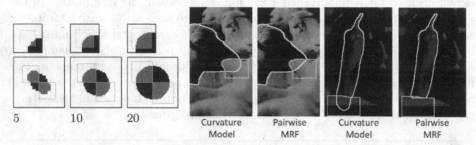

			Curvature	Pairwise	Curvature	Pairwise
5	10	20	Model	MRF	Model	MRF

Fig. 5. Left. Inpainting of a corner and a circle. The green boxes show the area to be inpainted, where the size in pixels of the length of the green boxes is below the images. Pixels in gray show the estimated solution. Note, the boundary conditions are different: right-angle boundary condition (top) and circle boundary condition (bottom). **Right.** Two example for automatic shape completions of an occluded object. In both cases the left result is with a pure curvature prior and the right result with a pure length prior (8-connected). Note, the yellow curve (and a part of the green curve) indicate the original user-defined segmentation. Then the user defines the green area. Inside the green area, the method automatically finds the shape completion (blue curve).

Fig. 6. Combining length and curvature for inpainting: (a) pure curvature, (b) curvature and length, (c) curvature and length (with high weight).

In the unknown region $\mathcal{V} \backslash (F \cup B)$ all unaries are exactly 0. Fig.5(Left) shows examples of inpainting of corners and circles of varying size. Fig.5(Right) demonstrates inpainting with real-world shapes and compares against a naive length regularization. It can be seen that the higher-order model which encodes curvature produces shape completions with smooth boundaries. An example of combining curvature prior with length prior is shown in fig. 6.

Fig. 7. Image segmentation. (a) Image with foreground (green) and background (blue) seeds; (b) Color based unary potential costs (red for foreground, and blue for background). (c) Result from [20] (d) Zoom-in from [20] (top) and our result (e,100). (e) Our model with various strength for curvature prior.

Image Segmentation. We use a simple model for the task of interactive fore- and background segmentation, as in [4]. Based on the user brush strokes (fig. 7(a)) we compute likelihoods using a Gaussian mixture model (GMM) with 10 components. The difference of the unaries $\theta_v(1) - \theta_v(0)$ correspond to the negative log-likelihood ratio of foreground and background. Results for our curvature model for various strengths of the prior are shown in fig.7(e). Increasing the strength of the prior above some limit (1000) has almost no effect on the smoothness of the solution, because each local 8×8 window is already maximally smooth according to the model. Note, that segmentation of this instance with length regularization cannot segment the legs of the giraffe correctly for arbitrary regularization strength (see [1]). Our result is visually superior to [20], see fig. 7(d), despite the fact that we use a grid with much coarser resolution than a fine cell-complex used in [20]. Further results and a detailed comparison to [20] is in [1].

5   Conclusions and Discussion

This paper has shown how to compute compact representations of higher-order priors which enable the use of standard algorithms for MAP inference. We presented results on the problem of learning a curvature-based shape prior for image inpainting and segmentation. Our higher-order shape prior operates on a large set of pixels and is therefore robust to discretization artifacts. In the future, it would be interesting to extend the approach to incorporate other types of local shape properties, not necessarily defined by an analytic function but for instance by exemplars. Such a generalization would likely require a more general learning technique.

References

1. Shekhovtsov, A., Kohli, P., Rother, C.: Curvature prior for MRF-based segmentation and shape inpainting. Tech. rep., research Report CTU–CMP–2011–11, Czech Technical University (2011)
2. Barnes, C., Shechtman, E., Finkelstein, A., Goldman, D.B.: Patchmatch: a randomized correspondence algorithm for structural image editing. ACM Trans. Graph. 28(3) (2009)
3. Bertozzi, A., Esedoglu, S., Gillette, A.: Inpainting of binary images using the Cahn-Hilliard equation. IP 16 (2007)
4. Boykov, Y., Jolly, P.: Interactive graph cuts for optimal boundary & region segmentation of objects in N-D images. In: ICCV (2001)
5. Bredies, K., Pock, T., Wirth, B.: Convex relaxation of a class of vertex penalizing functionals (preprint)
6. Chan, T.F., Shen, J.: Non-texture inpainting by curvature-driven diffusions (CDD). JVCIR 12 (2001)
7. El-Zehiry, N.Y., Grady, L.: Fast global optimization of curvature. In: CVPR (2010)
8. Esedoglu, S., March, R.: Segmentation with depth but without detecting junctions. JMIV 18 (2003)
9. Goldluecke, B., Cremers, D.: Introducing total curvature for image processing. In: ICCV (2011)
10. Gupta, R., Diwan, A.A., Sarawagi, S.: Efficient inference with cardinality-based clique potentials. In: ICML (2007)
11. Hinton, G.E.: Products of experts. In: ICANN (1999)
12. Kohli, P., Kumar, M.: Energy minimization for linear envelope MRFs. In: CVPR (2010)
13. Kohli, P., Ladicky, L., Torr, P.: Robust higher order potentials for enforcing label consistency. IJCV 82 (2009)
14. Kolmogorov, V., Zabin, R.: What energy functions can be minimized via graph cuts? PAMI 26 (2004)
15. Komodakis, N., Paragios, N.: Beyond pairwise energies: Efficient optimization for higher-order MRFs. In: CVPR (2009)
16. Nowozin, S., Lampert, C.: Global connectivity potentials for random field models. In: CVPR (2009)
17. Ramalingam, S., Kohli, P., Alahari, K., Torr, P.: Exact inference in multi-label CRFs with higher order cliques. In: CVPR (2008)
18. Roth, S., Black, M.: Fields of experts. IJCV 82 (2009)
19. Rother, C., Kohli, P., Feng, W., Jia, J.: Minimizing sparse higher order energy functions of discrete variables. In: CVPR (2009)
20. Schoenemann, T., Kahl, F., Cremers, D.: Curvature regularity for region-based image segmentation and inpainting: A linear programming relaxation. In: ICCV (2009)
21. Schoenemann, T., Kahl, F., Masnou, S., Cremers, D.: A linear framework for region-based image segmentation and inpainting involving curvature penalization. CoRR abs/1102.3830 (2011)

22. Schoenemann, T., Kuang, Y., Kahl, F.: Curvature Regularity for Multi-label Problems - Standard and Customized Linear Programming. In: Boykov, Y., Kahl, F., Lempitsky, V., Schmidt, F.R. (eds.) EMMCVPR 2011. LNCS, vol. 6819, pp. 163–176. Springer, Heidelberg (2011)
23. Schoenemann, T., Masnou, S., Cremers, D.: The elastic ratio: Introducing curvature into ratio-based image segmentation. IEEE Transactions on Image Processing 20(9), 2565–2581 (2011)
24. Strandmark, P., Kahl, F.: Curvature Regularization for Curves and Surfaces in a Global Optimization Framework. In: Boykov, Y., Kahl, F., Lempitsky, V., Schmidt, F.R. (eds.) EMMCVPR 2011. LNCS, vol. 6819, pp. 205–218. Springer, Heidelberg (2011)
25. Tarlow, D., Zemel, R., Frey, B.: Flexible priors for exemplar-based clustering. In: UAI (2008)
26. Vicente, S., Kolmogorov, V., Rother, C.: Joint optimization of segmentation and appearance models. In: ICCV (2009)

Mean Field for Continuous High-Order MRFs

Kevin Schelten and Stefan Roth

Department of Computer Science, TU Darmstadt

Abstract. Probabilistic inference beyond MAP estimation is of interest in computer vision, both for learning appropriate models and in applications. Yet, common approximate inference techniques, such as belief propagation, have largely been limited to discrete-valued Markov random fields (MRFs) and models with small cliques. Oftentimes, neither is desirable from an application standpoint. This paper studies mean field inference for continuous-valued MRF models with high-order cliques. Mean field can be applied effectively to such models by exploiting that the factors of certain classes of MRFs can be formulated using Gaussian mixtures, which allows retaining the mixture indicator as a latent variable. We use an image restoration setting to show that resulting mean field updates have a computational complexity quadratic in the clique size, which makes them scale even to large cliques. We contribute an empirical study with four applications: Image denoising, non-blind deblurring, noise estimation, and layer separation from a single image. We find mean field to yield a favorable combination of performance and efficiency, e.g. outperforming MAP estimation in denoising while being competitive with expensive sampling approaches. Novel approaches to noise estimation and layer separation demonstrate the breadth of applicability.

1 Introduction

Probabilistic models have found widespread use in all areas of computer vision. Applying them to a concrete problem entails computing a solution by means of inference. The approach used most widely is maximum a-posteriori (MAP) estimation, which corresponds to a Bayes-optimal prediction under the 0/1-loss (see e.g. [16]). In many applications the 0/1-loss is not appropriate, since it penalizes all incorrect solutions equally. One alternative is to compute the Bayesian minimum mean squared error estimate (MMSE), which amounts to estimating the posterior mean [17]. However, this is challenging in the context of MRF models[1]. Standard approaches to computing the posterior mean are based on sum-product belief propagation (BP) [9,18] or sampling algorithms [22], which often come at a high computational cost.

In this paper we study mean field [4] as efficient alternative for MRFs with continuous variables. To that end we follow Levin et al. [12] to assume that the factors can be represented as Gaussian mixture models, which allows retaining the mixture indices as explicit latent variables. These in turn make it convenient to derive simple update equations. But unlike [12], our focus is on MRFs of high-order, which have found increased adoption in recent years [5,20]. In particular, we argue and show that for a certain class

---

[1] Even though we focus on MRFs, our discussion also applies to conditional random fields.

A. Pinz et al. (Eds.): DAGM/OAGM 2012, LNCS 7476, pp. 52–61, 2012.
© Springer-Verlag Berlin Heidelberg 2012

of problems, one of the key advantages of the mean field method is its computational efficiency even in the presence of high-order factors: The effort of an update cycle scales quadratically in the clique size of the MRF. This is in contrast to the runtime of classical, discrete BP, which scales exponentially in the clique size [18].

To demonstrate the practical benefits of using mean field for inference in continuous high-order MRFs, we study four applications in the context of image restoration, where accurate probabilistic models are available (e.g. [22]). Using image denoising and non-blind deblurring as a testbed, we demonstrate that mean field inference yields a favorable combination of efficiency and performance, outperforming MAP estimation while being much faster than sampling-based inference. We also contribute novel mean field methods for noise estimation and layer separation. Noise es-

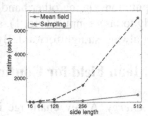

Fig. 1. Empirical runtime comparison of mean field and Gibbs sampling [22] for denoising with an MRF with 3×3 cliques

timates are obtained by maximizing a marginalized density using the Expectation-Maximization (EM) algorithm and mean field to approximate intractable expectations. Layer separation from a single image is a massively inverse problem with a multimodal likelihood. One novelty of our mean field approach is the extraction of an explicit noise layer.

2   Related Work

Geiger and Girosi [4] were among the first to apply mean field to MRFs in vision. In particular, they used formulations based on a line process. Our approach is related in that it also uses discrete latent variables, but employs multinomial rather than binary ones, which correspond to the component indices of a Gaussian mixture. Moreover, [4] is limited to pairwise MRFs, whereas we apply mean field to high-order MRFs.

Although recent work puts forward efficient algorithms for discrete mean field [6], this paper focuses on continuous variables, combined with learned mixture model priors. Mean field has been used for continuous MRFs with mixture model potentials, for example in deblurring [1,12], reflectometry [19], and layer separation of cartoon images [15]. In contrast to previous work, we study the impact of mean field for MMSE estimation in generatively trained, high-order models, derive a polynomial update complexity for a certain class of problems, and develop new methods for noise estimation and natural image layer separation. We also provide a quantitative evaluation of mean field for non-blind deblurring, whereas previous work in deblurring has focused on mean field for kernel estimation in the gradient domain [3,12] instead of image restoration in the spatial domain; Sec. 4 demonstrates the latter.

One advantage of continuous variables and mixture models is that the mean field update scheme scales quadratically in the clique size for typical problems of image restoration. This is notable compared to other approximate inference algorithms that allow moment estimation, such as BP. In the classical, discrete case, the factor-to-variable messages of BP involve a brute-force summation, which incurs an exponential update complexity in the clique size [18]. While BP can be sped up for certain model classes, such techniques have been limited to pairwise potentials [2,9] or graphs with 2×2 cliques [8,18] in practice. Non-parametric BP [23] remains challenging due to the need to approximate a product of Gaussian mixtures of exponential size for every message computation. On the other hand, Gibbs sampling for mixture model priors [22] scales poorly to larger inputs (Fig. 1), and determining convergence of Monte Carlo methods is not always straightforward. By contrast, mean field is guaranteed to converge [14].

3   Mean Field for Continuous High-Order MRFs

Free energy. A key challenge in probabilistic inference is to compute moments or modes of probabilities, whose exact computation is often prohibitive, necessitating approximate inference techniques. The objective of mean field is to approximate an intractable model by a tractable density. The moments of the approximate density then serve as approximations for the true moments. Given a true, intractable posterior $p(\mathbf{x}|\mathbf{y})$ the approximation $q(\mathbf{x})$ is determined by minimizing the Kullback-Leibler divergence $\mathrm{KL}(q(\mathbf{x})\|p(\mathbf{x}|\mathbf{y}))$ [14]. This is equivalent to minimizing the free energy

$$F(q) = -\int q(\mathbf{x}) \log p(\mathbf{x}, \mathbf{y}) d\mathbf{x} + \int q(\mathbf{x}) \log q(\mathbf{x}) d\mathbf{x}. \tag{1}$$

MRFs with mixture potentials. Even though mean field is in principle applicable to arbitrary continuous MRFs where the factors are modeled as Gaussian mixtures, we choose a specific model family for concreteness. We use a variant of Fields of Experts (FoEs) [22,25], a continuous high-order MRF in which the potentials are formulated as a Gaussian scale mixture (GSM) [24]. This not only provides us with a suitable testbed for mean field inference, but after expansion with indicator variables also fulfills the requirement that the potentials are in the exponential family [14]. This class of image priors is based on learned, zero-mean, linear image filters $\mathbf{F}_\gamma$, whose response at factor (clique) $\mathbf{x}_k$ of the image $\mathbf{x}$ is modeled by a learned Gaussian scale mixture expert (potential)

$$\phi_\gamma(\mathbf{F}_\gamma^T \mathbf{x}_k) = \sum_{j=1}^{J} \pi_{\gamma j} \mathcal{N}\left(\mathbf{F}_\gamma^T \mathbf{x}_k | 0, \sigma_{\gamma j}^2\right). \tag{2}$$

The filters $\mathbf{F}_\gamma$ have zero mean in order to be invariant to global gray-level shifts. Multiplying over all filters and cliques, and a broad Gaussian factor ($\epsilon = 10^{-8}$) yields the prior

$$p(\mathbf{x}) \propto e^{-\epsilon \|x\|^2} \prod_k \prod_\gamma \phi_\gamma(\mathbf{F}_\gamma^T \mathbf{x}_k). \tag{3}$$

Following Levin et al. [12], GSMs (and any Gaussian mixture) can be made tractable for mean field inference by expanding with indicator variables, which represent the indices of the mixture components. Each pair of clique and filter (expert) is equipped with a discrete variable $z_{k\gamma} \in \{1, ..., J\}$ such that $p(z_{k\gamma}) = \pi_{\gamma z_{k\gamma}}$. The resulting, fully expanded prior is

$$p(\mathbf{x}, \mathbf{z}) \propto e^{-\epsilon \|x\|^2} \prod_k \prod_\gamma \pi_{\gamma z_{k\gamma}} \mathcal{N}\left(\mathbf{F}_\gamma^T \mathbf{x}_k | 0, \sigma_{\gamma z_{k\gamma}}^2\right), \tag{4}$$

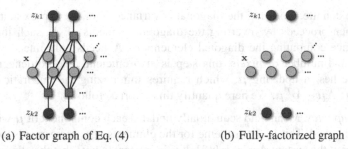

(a) Factor graph of Eq. (4)   (b) Fully-factorized graph

Fig. 2. Illustration of the high-order factor graph representation (a) and the fully factorized approximation (b) for a MRF with 2×2 cliques and 2 filters

with the property that $\sum_{\mathbf{z}} p(\mathbf{x}, \mathbf{z}) = p(\mathbf{x})$. Fig. 2(a) shows an example factor graph for this model. Note that after augmenting with indicator varibles the model continues to be of high order, since the indicators $z_{k\gamma}$ are shared across the whole clique, preventing further factorization. The key benefit is that the prior of Eq. (4) is in the exponential family and thus readily admits mean field inference.

Mean field approximation. As concrete application we consider the problem of Bayesian image restoration $p(\mathbf{x}|\mathbf{y}, \boldsymbol{\theta}) \propto p(\mathbf{y}|\mathbf{x}, \boldsymbol{\theta})p(\mathbf{x})$ of an observed image $\mathbf{y}$, where $p(\mathbf{y}|\mathbf{x}, \boldsymbol{\theta})$ is a likelihood model with parameters $\boldsymbol{\theta}$. For example, $\boldsymbol{\theta}$ may be a blur kernel $\mathbf{K}$ in image deblurring. We make the assumption that the likelihood $p(\mathbf{y}|\mathbf{x}, \boldsymbol{\theta})$ is proportional to a Gaussian in $\mathbf{x}$ with precision matrix $\mathbf{P}$ and mean $\mathbf{P}^{-1}\mathbf{b}$ (see Sec. 4 for concrete examples). Augmented by indicator variables, the Bayesian formulation takes the form $p(\mathbf{x}, \mathbf{z}|\mathbf{y}, \boldsymbol{\theta}) \propto p(\mathbf{y}|\mathbf{x}, \boldsymbol{\theta})p(\mathbf{x}, \mathbf{z})$. The conventional choice of mean field approximation is the fully-factorized model

$$q(\mathbf{x}, \mathbf{z}) = q(\mathbf{x}) \prod_k \prod_\gamma q(z_{k\gamma}), \tag{5}$$

where $q(\mathbf{x}) = \mathcal{N}(\boldsymbol{\mu}, \mathbf{C})$ with a diagonal covariance matrix $\mathbf{C}$. Fig. 2(b) shows the corresponding factor graph. We here follow the fully-factorized approach. Mean field proceeds by updating variables in turn, while holding the others fixed. Detailed update equations arise by inserting $q(\mathbf{x}, \mathbf{z})$ into the free energy from Eq. (1), integrating and differentiating. The updates resemble the case of pairwise MRFs (see [12] for detailed derivations), with the difference being that the filters $\mathbf{F}_\gamma$ cover more than two pixels. The update of the indicator distributions $q(z_{k\gamma})$ has linear complexity in the clique size and number of pixels:

$$q(z_{k\gamma} = j_0) \propto \frac{\pi_{\gamma j_0}}{\sigma_{\gamma j_0}} \exp\left\{ -\frac{E\left[(\mathbf{F}_\gamma^T \mathbf{x}_k)^2\right]}{2\sigma_{\gamma j_0}^2} \right\}. \tag{6}$$

On the other hand, to update $q(\mathbf{x}) = \mathcal{N}(\boldsymbol{\mu}, \mathbf{C})$ we require the matrix

$$\mathbf{A} = \mathbf{P} + \epsilon\mathbf{I} + \sum_\gamma \mathbf{T}_{\mathbf{F}_\gamma}^T \mathbf{W}_\gamma \mathbf{T}_{\mathbf{F}_\gamma}. \tag{7}$$

Here, the $\mathbf{W}_\gamma$ denote diagonal matrices with positive entries [12] whereas the $\mathbf{T}_{\mathbf{F}_\gamma}$ denote convolution matrices, such that $\mathbf{T}_{\mathbf{F}_\gamma}\mathbf{x} \equiv \mathbf{F}_\gamma \otimes \mathbf{x}$. The matrix $\mathbf{A}$ is symmetric and positive definite. Updating the diagonal covariance $\mathbf{C}$ of the approximate $q(\mathbf{x}) = \mathcal{N}(\boldsymbol{\mu}, \mathbf{C})$ then proceeds by inverting the diagonal elements of $\mathbf{A}$, such that $C_{ii} = (A_{ii})^{-1}$. Since computing the diagonal elements of $\mathbf{A}$ needs only linear cost in the clique size and number of pixels, this step is also efficient. The bottleneck of each update cycle lies in updating $\boldsymbol{\mu}$, which requires minimizing the quadratic objective $Q(\boldsymbol{\mu}) = \frac{1}{2}\boldsymbol{\mu}^T \mathbf{A}\boldsymbol{\mu} - \mathbf{b}^T \boldsymbol{\mu}$. We here quantify this effort as follows.

Polynomial updates. Mean field sequentially updates each component of $\boldsymbol{\mu}$ while holding the others fixed. This update scheme for the elements of $\boldsymbol{\mu}$ corresponds to a Gauss-Seidel solver of the system $\mathbf{A}\boldsymbol{\mu} = \mathbf{b}$ [12]. It is important to note that the clique size $\mathcal{C}$ of the MRF $p(\mathbf{x}|\mathbf{y}, \boldsymbol{\theta})$ is given by the size of the largest prior filter among $\{\mathbf{F}_\gamma\}$, whereas the Gaussian likelihood contributes $\mathcal{P}$ pairwise connections to other pixels. The update of μ_i costs $\mathcal{O}(\mathcal{C}^2 + \mathcal{P})$ operations (equating the derivative $\frac{d}{d\mu_i}Q(\boldsymbol{\mu})$ to zero and solving yields the update equation). By contrast, an update of classical, discrete BP in an MRF has *exponential* complexity in the clique size [18], which is prohibitively slow for high-order cliques and large label spaces.

4   Applications and Experiments

To study the application of mean field to continuous high-order MRFs we consider four different applications in image restoration. We use Fields of Experts as image priors, which have served as a testbed for various studies on approximate inference methods [5,8,18]. Specifically, we use the 3×3 FoE and pairwise MRF of [22], which allow to assess efficiency and runtime of inference methods for high-order models.

Image restoration. We consider the following generic formulation for image restoration: Given a blur kernel $\mathbf{K}$ and degraded image $\mathbf{y}$, recover $\mathbf{x}$ such that $\mathbf{y} = \mathbf{K} \otimes \mathbf{x} + \mathbf{n}$. Here, we make the widespread assumption of additive Gaussian noise $\mathbf{n} \sim \mathcal{N}(\mathbf{0}, \sigma^2\mathbf{I})$. It is convenient to represent the blur using a convolution matrix $\mathbf{T_K}$. Denoising is a special case of $\mathbf{T_K} = \mathbf{I}$ being the identity matrix. A Bayesian approach gives rise to $p(\mathbf{x}|\mathbf{y}, \mathbf{T_K}) \propto p(\mathbf{y}|\mathbf{x}, \mathbf{T_K})p(\mathbf{x})$, where the likelihood takes the form $p(\mathbf{y}|\mathbf{x}, \mathbf{T_K}) = \mathcal{N}(\mathbf{y}|\mathbf{T_K}\mathbf{x}, \sigma^2\mathbf{I})$. For non-trivial blur ($\mathbf{T_K} \neq \mathbf{I}$), the posterior is highly connected – hence efficient inference is paramount. For image restoration, Eq. (7) takes the form

$$\mathbf{A} = \sigma^{-2}\mathbf{T_K}^T\mathbf{T_K} + \epsilon\mathbf{I} + \sum_\gamma \mathbf{T}_{\mathbf{F}_\gamma}^T \mathbf{W}_\gamma \mathbf{T}_{\mathbf{F}_\gamma}. \tag{8}$$

To evaluate the applicability of continuous mean field to denoising, we compare to MAP estimation on the one hand, and on the other to MMSE estimation using Gibbs sampling based on the models from [22]. The motivation is twofold: Comparing with MAP estimation in generative models establishes a baseline to be outperformed by MMSE estimation via approximate inference[2]. A comparison with Gibbs sampling allows to assess the potential advantages in terms of efficiency (cf. Fig. 1). Additionally, we also compare with MAP estimation in a standard pairwise MRF with Laplacian

---

[2] We note that it is possible to incorporate the loss function during training of a random field [16], but our focus is on Bayesian prediction with probabilistic models.

Table 1. Denoising results on 10 images [22]. Average PSNR (dB) and runtime for different noise levels. The abbreviation w/ λ denotes usage of a regularization parameter. Average runtime measured on a 2.67GHz Core i7 processor.

		$\sigma = 5$		$\sigma = 10$		$\sigma = 20$	
		PSNR	Runtime	PSNR	Runtime	PSNR	Runtime
pairwise MRF	CG (MAP) w/ λ	35.61	$8m$	30.84	$9m$	26.55	$9m$
	Mean field (MMSE) w/ λ	**36.65**	**8s**	**32.22**	$44s$	28.26	**22s**
	Gibbs sampling (MMSE)	36.41	$57s$	32.09	$2m$	**28.32**	$3m$
pairwise Laplacian	CG (MAP) w/ λ	36.36	**8s**	31.91	**12s**	28.11	$23s$
3×3 FoE	CG (MAP) w/ λ	36.83	$9m$	32.19	$16m$	27.98	$28m$
	Mean field (MMSE) w/ λ	36.83	**89s**	32.36	**63s**	28.40	**72s**
	Gibbs sampling (MMSE)	**37.23**	$8m$	**32.85**	$12m$	**28.91**	$18m$

potentials: $\phi(y) = \exp(-(y^2 + \epsilon)^{\frac{1}{2}})$ for small ϵ. These potentials are in wide use in vision (e.g. [11]) and are also closely related to popular *total variation* (TV) regularizers [21]. This puts the performance of mean field into relation with a model/inference combination standard to vision. For both MAP and mean field, we use a regularization parameter $\lambda \in (0,1)$, such that the influences of prior and likelihood are calibrated via $p(\mathbf{y}|\mathbf{x}, \mathbf{T_K})^\lambda p(\mathbf{x})^{1-\lambda}$. Notably, the parameter λ for mean field is trained on a separate set of images, whereas for the MAP methods, it is *optimized on the test set* to demonstrate the highest achievable performance.

The results are summarized in Tab. 1. Mean field not only outperforms the baseline of MAP estimation in the generative model, but also does better than the (best-case) Laplacian MRF. To compare with Gibbs sampling, we use the publicly available code of [22]. In the pairwise MRF, mean field is competitive with Gibbs sampling, sometimes even outperforming it, while being many times faster. It is interesting to note that the regularization parameter λ helps overcoming some of the deficiencies of the mean field approximation. In case of a 3×3 model, mean field falls somewhat below the performance of Gibbs sampling, most likely due to the full factorization of the approximate distribution being less accurate here. Nonetheless, we find a clear improvement over the pairwise model without incurring a large penalty in terms of computational efficiency; mean field remains many times faster than Gibbs sampling. We also remark that mean field inference even for the *pairwise* MRF outperforms the results obtained for a *high-order* 2×2 FoE model using graph cuts [5] (8–12 minutes on a 2.33GHz Xeon E5345 processor), as well as sum-product [18] (30–60 minutes on a 2.2GHz Opteron 275) and max/sum-product BP [8] (8 hours on a 3GHz Xeon) in terms of image quality and efficiency. Note that the runtime is also competitive with MAP estimation by conjugate gradient descent in the simple pairwise Laplacian model, although specifically tailored optimization techniques may improve the runtime of both methods. As further runtime comparison to Gibbs sampling, we test both methods on a sequence of square images of ascending size $(2^4, 2^5, 2^6 ..., 2^9)$. Fig. 1 demonstrates empirically that mean field scales well to large images, whereas Gibbs sampling quickly incurs high runtime.

With regard to non-blind image deblurring, we use a benchmark of 64 images, each blurred with one of 8 realistic blur kernels [12]. We consider additive noise levels σ corresponding to a range of $1\% - 5\%$ of the maximum gray intensity 255. Tab. 2

summarizes quantitative results over 64 images; MMSE estimation with mean field clearly outperforms standard non-blind MAP methods [7,10] on the majority of noise levels. Moreover, Fig. 3 illustrates a qualitative advantage: mean field yields a deblurring result with both sharp details and fewer ringing artifacts. Previous work in deblurring (e. g. [3]) has largely focused on using mean field for kernel estimation in the gradient domain instead of image restoration in the spatial domain, as we demonstrate here.

Noise estimation. Given an input image $\mathbf{y} = \mathbf{x} + \mathbf{n}$, the task in noise estimation is to determine the standard deviation of (assumed) Gaussian noise $\mathbf{n} \sim \mathcal{N}(\mathbf{0}, \sigma^2\mathbf{I})$ on the latent image $\mathbf{x}$. Much like [12] for kernel estimation, we use the EM algorithm to maximize the incomplete-data likelihood $p(\mathbf{y}|\sigma)$, which under the assumption of a flat prior $p(\sigma) \propto 1$ also maximizes $p(\sigma|\mathbf{y})$. It is convenient to choose the factorization $p(\mathbf{x}, \mathbf{y}, \sigma) = p(\mathbf{y}|\mathbf{x}, \sigma)p(\mathbf{x})$, using the standard likelihood $p(\mathbf{y}|\mathbf{x}, \sigma) = \mathcal{N}(\mathbf{x}, \sigma^2\mathbf{I})$. The E–step requires evaluating the moments of $p(\mathbf{x}|\mathbf{y}, \sigma_{old}) \propto p(\mathbf{y}|\mathbf{x}, \sigma_{old})p(\mathbf{x})$, which is intractable for loopy MRFs. Instead, we leverage mean field to compute an approximation $q(\mathbf{x})$ of $p(\mathbf{x}|\mathbf{y}, \sigma_{old})$. The M–step consists in updating the noise estimate by

$$\sigma_{new} = \underset{\sigma}{\operatorname{argmax}} E_q[\log p(\mathbf{x}, \mathbf{y}|\sigma)] = \sqrt{\frac{E_q[\|\mathbf{x}-\mathbf{y}\|^2]}{N}}, \qquad (9)$$

where N denotes the number of elements in $\mathbf{x}$ and $E_q[\|\mathbf{x} - \mathbf{y}\|^2] = \sum_{i=1}^{N} \mu_i^2 + C_{ii} - 2\mu_i y_i + y_i^2$, for the approximate density $q(\mathbf{x}) = \mathcal{N}(\boldsymbol{\mu}, \mathbf{C})$. We test on a benchmark of 68 images and find superior results on multiple noise levels (Tab. 3) compared to a recent, state of the art method [26], which leverages a connection between white noise and kurtosis values. The results of Tab. 3 are obtained for the high-order 3×3 FoE, and although many EM iterations are required, mean field admits efficient inference.

Layer separation. To show the versatility of mean field as inference algorithm, we lastly consider the problem of recovering two hidden images given their sum $\mathbf{y} = \mathbf{x}_1 + \mathbf{x}_2$, which can occur when light is reflected off glass. This massively inverse problem may be alleviated by user input [11]. Here, the user marks a set of points S_1 and S_2 of the input image $\mathbf{y}$ as edges belonging to layers $\mathbf{x}_1$ and $\mathbf{x}_2$, respectively: Fig. 4 depicts a problem instance. We denote by $\mathbf{S}_1$ and $\mathbf{S}_2$ the diagonal matrices that pick out image elements corresponding to the indices collected in S_1 and S_2, such that e. g., $\|\mathbf{S}_1\mathbf{y}\|^2 = \sum_{k \in S_1} y_k^2$. These matrices allow to encode the user marks into Gaussians: For zero-mean prior filters $\mathbf{F}_\gamma$, we model the user input by

$$p(\mathbf{y}|\mathbf{x}_1, \mathbf{x}_2, S_1, S_2) = \mathcal{N}(\mathbf{x}_1 + \mathbf{x}_2, \sigma^2\mathbf{I}) \prod_{k=1,2} \mathcal{N}(\mathbf{x}_k, \mathbf{M}_k^{-1}), \qquad (10)$$

where the matrices $\mathbf{M}_k = \sum_\gamma (\mathbf{S}_k\mathbf{T}_{\mathbf{F}_\gamma})^T (\mathbf{S}_k\mathbf{T}_{\mathbf{F}_\gamma})$ constrain the filter responses of layer $\mathbf{x}_k$ to be close to those of $\mathbf{y}$ at user marked coordinates. In the case of pairwise derivative filters $\{\mathbf{F}_\gamma\} = \{[1 \; -1], [1 \; -1]^T\}$, this constrains the layer derivatives to be close to those of the input mixture at locations marked by the user. We remark that the likelihood of Eq. (10) is riddled with local optima, and that the problem remains massively inverse even under user input. A Bayesian approach gives rise to $p(\mathbf{x}_1, \mathbf{x}_2|\mathbf{y}, S_1, S_2) \propto p(\mathbf{y}|\mathbf{x}_1, \mathbf{x}_2, S_1, S_2)p(\mathbf{x}_1)p(\mathbf{x}_2)$. Besides introducing a mean

Table 2. Deblurring results on 64 test images and five noise levels corresponding to $1\% - 5\%$ of the highest intensity, 255. PSNR (dB), and SSIM values denote averages over all images. Mean field performs better on the majority of noise levels.

	$\sigma = 2.55$		$\sigma = 5.10$		$\sigma = 7.65$		$\sigma = 10.20$		$\sigma = 12.75$	
	PSNR	SSIM	PSNR	SSIM	PSNR	SSIM	PSNR	SSIM	PSNR	SSIM
Lucy [13]	25.38	.703	23.27	.542	21.85	.423	20.84	.334	19.83	.224
Krishnan & Fergus [7]	26.97	.800	25.69	.724	24.91	.671	24.34	.632	23.93	.608
Levin *et al.* [10]	28.03	.823	26.28	.741	25.36	.689	24.74	**.652**	**24.29**	**.625**
Mean field	**28.20**	**.833**	**26.42**	**.747**	**25.44**	**.692**	**24.77**	.650	24.25	.616

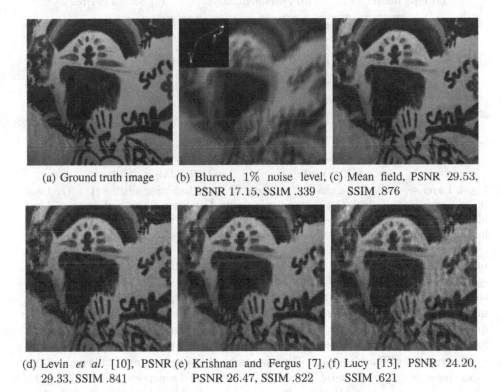

(a) Ground truth image   (b) Blurred, 1% noise level, (c) Mean field, PSNR 29.53,
PSNR 17.15, SSIM .339   SSIM .876

(d) Levin *et al.* [10], PSNR (e) Krishnan and Fergus [7], (f) Lucy [13], PSNR 24.20,
29.33, SSIM .841   PSNR 26.47, SSIM .822   SSIM .621

Fig. 3. Deblurring on a standard image and blur kernel [12] with 1% additive noise ($\sigma = 2.55$). The 27×27 blur kernel is displayed in the upper left corner of the blurry image, enlarged and scaled to full intensity. The result of mean field has sharp details and fewer ringing artifacts.

Table 3. Noise estimation results on 68 test images [20]. Relative absolute error [26] (RAE = $|\sigma_{est} - \sigma|/\sigma$), and relative squared error (RSE = $|\sigma_{est} - \sigma|^2/\sigma^2$) are reported in percent. The entries denote averages over all images.

	$\sigma = 10$		$\sigma = 20$		$\sigma = 30$		$\sigma = 40$		$\sigma = 50$		$\sigma = 60$	
	RAE	RSE	RAE	RSE	RAE	RSE	RAE	RSE	RAE	RSE	RAE	RSE
Zoran & Weiss [26]	**12.58**	**2.41**	9.04	**1.17**	8.98	1.20	10.31	1.51	12.46	2.03	14.96	2.69
EM & mean field	14.34	4.76	**9.00**	1.95	**6.53**	**0.96**	**5.96**	**0.70**	**7.24**	**0.83**	**9.66**	**1.25**

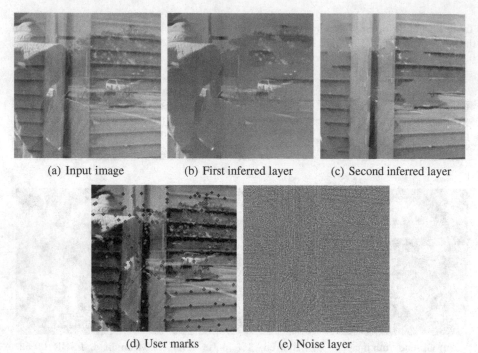

(a) Input image	(b) First inferred layer	(c) Second inferred layer

(d) User marks	(e) Noise layer

Fig. 4. Layer separation by mean field inference of a standard input mixture [11]. The input image is corrupted by additive Gaussian noise of standard deviation 1. Our method recovers two hidden layers and pushes noise into a residual layer by mean field inference. The layers are scaled to the full intensity range for better visualization. *Best viewed on screen.*

field-based technique, the novelty of our formulation lies in the likelihood of Eq. (10), which *allows for slack in the summation*. In contrast, previous work [11] enforces exact summation to the input $y = x_1 + x_2$ by setting $x_2 = y - x_1$. This pushes existing image noise into the recovered layers. Our approach avoids this by separating an additional noise layer. To obtain an MMSE estimate, we infer the hidden layers by mean field. Fig. 4 depicts a result: Hidden image layers are extracted from a user marked mixture corrupted by Gaussian noise. The input image has challenging details and texture exacerbated by the image noise. Nonetheless, our method separates meaningful layers, which gives another example of the efficacy of mean field for generative image models.

5 Conclusion

This paper studied mean field for continuous high-order MRFs, particularly those formulated with Gaussian mixture potentials. We not only addressed an increasing interest in Bayesian estimation beyond the $0/1$-loss, but also computational limitations of existing, largely discrete inference algorithms. In particular, we showed fully-factorized mean field updates to scale quadratically in the clique size of the prior. A broad application study in denoising, deblurring, noise estimation, and layer separation indicated that mean field exhibits a favorable combination of efficiency, versatility, and performance.

References

1. Chantas, G., Galatsanos, N., Likas, A., Saunders, M.: Variational Bayesian image restoration based on a product of t-distributions image prior. IEEE T. Image Process. 17(10), 1795–1805 (2008)
2. Felzenszwalb, P.F., Huttenlocher, D.P.: Efficient belief propagation for early vision. Int. J. Comput. Vision 1(70), 41–54 (2006)
3. Fergus, R., Singh, B., Hertzmann, A., Roweis, S.T., Freeman, W.T.: Removing camera shake from a single photograph. In: SIGGRAPH 2006, pp. 787–794 (2006)
4. Geiger, D., Girosi, F.: Parallel and deterministic algorithms from MRF's: Surface reconstruction. IEEE T. Pattern Anal. Mach. Intell. 13(5), 401–412 (1991)
5. Ishikawa, H.: Higher-order clique reduction in binary graph cut. In: CVPR 2009 (2009)
6. Krähenbühl, P., Koltun, V.: Efficient inference in fully connected CRFs with Gaussian edge potentials. In: NIPS 2011, pp. 109–117 (2011)
7. Krishnan, D., Fergus, R.: Fast image deconvolution using hyper-Laplacian priors. In: NIPS 2009, pp. 1033–1041 (2009)
8. Lan, X., Roth, S., Huttenlocher, D.P., Black, M.J.: Efficient Belief Propagation with Learned Higher-Order Markov Random Fields. In: Leonardis, A., Bischof, H., Pinz, A. (eds.) ECCV 2006, Part II. LNCS, vol. 3952, pp. 269–282. Springer, Heidelberg (2006)
9. Lasowski, R., Tevs, A., Wand, M., Seidel, H.P.: Wavelet belief propagation for large scale inference problems. In: CVPR 2011 (2011)
10. Levin, A., Fergus, R., Durand, F., Freeman, W.T.: Image and depth from a conventional camera with a coded aperture. ACM Transactions on Graphics 26(3), 70:1–70:9 (2007)
11. Levin, A., Weiss, Y.: User assisted separation of reflections from a single image using a sparsity prior. IEEE T. Pattern Anal. Mach. Intell. 29(9), 1647–1654 (2007)
12. Levin, A., Weiss, Y., Durand, F., Freeman, W.T.: Efficient marginal likelihood optimization in blind deconvolution. In: CVPR 2011 (2011)
13. Lucy, L.B.: An iterative technique for the rectification of observed distributions. The Astronomical Journal 79, 745 (1974)
14. Minka, T.: Divergence measures and message passing. Tech. Rep. MSR-TR-2005-173, Microsoft Research, Cambridge, UK (2005)
15. Miskin, J., MacKay, D.J.C.: Ensemble learning for blind image separation and deconvolution. In: Adv. in Ind. Comp. Analysis (2000)
16. Pletscher, P., Nowozin, S., Kohli, P., Rother, C.: Putting MAP Back on the Map. In: Mester, R., Felsberg, M. (eds.) DAGM 2011. LNCS, vol. 6835, pp. 111–121. Springer, Heidelberg (2011)
17. Portilla, J., Strela, V., Wainwright, M.J., Simoncelli, E.P.: Image denoising using scale mixtures of Gaussians in the wavelet domain. IEEE T. Image Process. 12(11), 1338–1351 (2003)
18. Potetz, B.: Efficient belief propagation for vision using linear constraint nodes. In: CVPR 2007 (2007)
19. Romeiro, F., Zickler, T.: Blind Reflectometry. In: Daniilidis, K., Maragos, P., Paragios, N. (eds.) ECCV 2010, Part I. LNCS, vol. 6311, pp. 45–58. Springer, Heidelberg (2010)
20. Roth, S., Black, M.J.: Fields of experts. Int. J. Comput. Vision 82(2), 205–229 (2009)
21. Rudin, L.I., Osher, S., Fatemi, E.: Nonlinear total variation based noise removal algorithms. Physica D 60, 259–268 (1992)
22. Schmidt, U., Gao, Q., Roth, S.: A generative perspective on MRFs in low-level vision. In: CVPR 2010 (2010)
23. Sudderth, E.B., Ihler, A.T., Freeman, W.T., Willsky, A.S.: Nonparametric belief propagation. In: CVPR 2003, vol. 1, pp. 605–612 (2003)
24. Wainwright, M.J., Simoncelli, E.P.: Scale mixtures of Gaussians and the statistics of natural images. In: NIPS 1999, pp. 855–861 (1999)
25. Weiss, Y., Freeman, W.T.: What makes a good model of natural images? In: CVPR 2007 (2007)
26. Zoran, D., Weiss, Y.: Scale invariance and noise in natural images. In: ICCV 2009 (2009)

How Well Do Filter-Based MRFs Model Natural Images?

Qi Gao and Stefan Roth

Department of Computer Science, TU Darmstadt

Abstract. Markov random fields (MRFs) have found widespread use as models of natural image and scene statistics. Despite progress in modeling image properties beyond gradient statistics with high-order cliques, and learning image models from example data, existing MRFs only exhibit a limited ability of actually capturing natural image statistics. In this paper we investigate this limitation of previous filter-based MRF models, which appears in contradiction to their maximum entropy interpretation. We argue that this is due to inadequacies in the leaning procedure and suggest various modifications to address them. We demonstrate that the proposed learning scheme allows training more suitable potential functions, whose shape approaches that of a Dirac-delta function, as well as models with larger and more filters. Our experiments not only indicate a substantial improvement of the models' ability to capture relevant statistical properties of natural images, but also demonstrate a significant performance increase in a denoising application to levels previously unattained by generative approaches.

1 Introduction and Related Work

Both analysis and modeling of the statistics of natural images and scenes have a long history. Statistical analyses have been carried out for natural images, image categories, range images, optical flow, *etc.* [4,13,15]. They have revealed many characteristic properties of natural images and scenes, including power-law frequency spectra, non-Gaussian highly kurtotic marginals, scale-invariant statistics, and non-Gaussian joint statistics of nearby image features [11,15]. These properties have been exploited in various statistical models, local ones that attempt to capture the statistics of one or a few features [11], as well as global models that aim to represent the properties of entire images. Latter often take the form of Markov random fields (MRFs).

MRFs based on linear filter responses, here termed *filter-based MRFs*, are perhaps the most popular form for modeling natural image priors [2,14,19,21]. The design of such models involves various choices, including the size and shape of the cliques, the selection of the image filters, and the shape of the potential functions. Pairwise MRFs are most widely used, for which the filters are simple image derivatives. The FRAME model [21] is an early instance of filter-based, *high-order* MRFs, in which discretized potentials are learned from data, and the filters are automatically chosen from a hand-designed set of candidates. The more recent Fields of Experts (FoEs) [14] use continuous potential functions and additionally learn the filters from training data to achieve better results in practice. Despite success in various applications [9,19], recent work [16] based on drawing samples from FoE priors [14,19] found that they represent

A. Pinz et al. (Eds.): DAGM/OAGM 2012, LNCS 7476, pp. 62–72, 2012.
© Springer-Verlag Berlin Heidelberg 2012

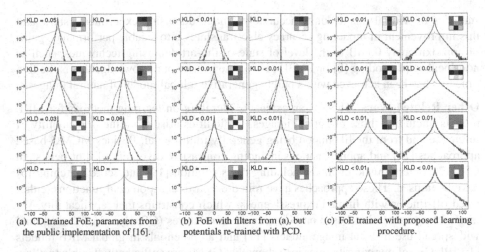

(a) CD-trained FoE; parameters from the public implementation of [16].

(b) FoE with filters from (a), but potentials re-trained with PCD.

(c) FoE trained with proposed learning procedure.

Fig. 1. Filter-based MRFs and image statistics: Image filter (3×3, top right) with corresponding learned potential function (solid, green), marginal histograms of natural images (dash-dotted, red), and model marginals obtained by sampling (dashed, blue). The proposed learning scheme leads to a better match to natural image statistics (top left – marginal KL-divergence).

relevant statistical properties of natural images only quite crudely. This appears in contradiction to the maximum entropy interpretation of filter-based MRFs [21], which suggests that the model should capture the statistics of the in-built features, at least if the potential functions are chosen and learned appropriately. [16] attributed this to previously used potentials not being heavy-tailed enough and suggested learning the shape of a more flexible potential, taken to be a Gaussian scale mixture (GSM) [11]. While this allowed to learn pairwise MRFs that capture derivative statistics correctly, the high-order case was more problematic: Marginal statistics of model samples were found not to be as heavy-tailed as those of natural images (Fig. 1a). Moreover, their study was limited to moderate clique sizes and a comparatively small number of filters.

In this paper we aim to address these issues and explore the limits of how well filter-based MRFs can capture natural image statistics. Motivated by the observation that larger support sizes lead to clearly improved performance bounds for image denoising [6], we also aim to learn models with larger cliques. We propose an improved learning procedure that *(1)* reduces training bias by replacing contrastive divergence (CD) [3] with persistent CD [17] as the learning objective; *(2)* improves robustness by imposing filter normalization and using initializations that allow the model to learn more varied filters; and *(3)* uses a new boundary handling method for sampling, which reduces sampling bias and thus increases both accuracy and efficiency. Our approach has various benefits: It makes learning more robust and consequently enables training models with larger and more filters that exhibit a more structured appearance (Fig. 5). Moreover, it enables learning improved potential functions that are extremely heavy-tailed, almost Dirac-delta like (Fig. 1c), which allow the model to capture the statistics of the model features correctly; the trained models are thus real *maximum entropy models*. More importantly and in contrast to previous approaches, the trained models also represent multi-scale derivative statistics, random filter statistics, as well as joint feature statistics of natural images quite accurately. Image denoising experiments show that this improvement in modeling accuracy also translates into sizable performance gains of approximately 0.3dB to the level of state-of-the-art denoising techniques, such as non-local sparse coding [8] or BM3D [1]. To the best of our knowledge this is the first time this has been achieved with a purely generative, global model of natural images.

Other Related Work. There is an extensive literature on learning methods for MRF models, including those of natural images. Difficulties arise from the intractability of inference and from the likelihood being generally multimodal. Besides MCMC-based approaches [21] and approximations including contrastive divergence [3] or persistent CD [17], deterministic methods including basis rotation [19] and score matching [5] have been used. These approaches have relied on particular potential functions, either fitted off-line or with limited expressiveness, which constrains their applicability. We instead learn potentials based on Gaussian scale mixtures (GSMs), which have found widespread use in local image models [11] and as potentials in global MRF models [16,19]. One of our contributions is to show that GSMs are sufficiently flexible to allow even high-order MRFs to model image statistics to a high degree of accuracy.

2 Basic Model and Learning Procedure

In this paper we explore the capabilities of filter-based, high-order MRFs (*e.g.* [2]). For ease of comparison to previous analyses, we use the particular form of [16]. The prior probability density of a natural image $\mathbf{x}$ under such a model is written as

$$p(\mathbf{x}; \Omega) = \frac{\mathcal{N}_\epsilon(\mathbf{x})}{Z(\Omega)} \prod_{c \in C} \prod_{i=1}^{F} \phi(\mathbf{f}_i^\mathsf{T} \mathbf{x}_{(c)}; \omega_i). \tag{1}$$

The $\mathbf{f}_i$ are the linear filters, and $\phi(\cdot; \omega_i)$ is the respective potential function (or factor/expert) with parameter ω_i. Further, $c \in C$ denote the model cliques, and $Z(\Omega)$ is the partition function that depends on the model parameters $\Omega = \{\mathbf{f}_i, \omega_i | i = 1 \ldots F\}$. A broad (unnormalized) Gaussian $\mathcal{N}_\epsilon(\mathbf{x}) = e^{-\epsilon \|\mathbf{x}\|^2 / 2}$ ensures normalizability (*cf.* [19]).

Due to their flexibility for representing a wide variety of heavy-tailed, highly kurtotic distributions, we follow previous work [7,16,19] and use Gaussian scale mixtures (GSMs) [11] to represent the potentials. In their finite form they can be written as

$$\phi(\mathbf{f}_i^\mathsf{T} \mathbf{x}_{(c)}; \omega_i) = \sum_{k=1}^{K} \omega_{ik} \cdot \mathcal{N}(\mathbf{f}_i^\mathsf{T} \mathbf{x}_{(c)}; 0, z_{ik} \cdot \sigma_i^2), \tag{2}$$

where $\omega_{ik} \geq 0, \sum_k \omega_{ik} = 1$ are the mixture weights of the scales z_{ik}. Note that here we use fixed variances $z_{ik} \cdot \sigma_i^2$ of the Gaussian components.

Basic Learning Strategy. Learning the model parameters Ω from data involves estimating the weights ω_{ik} of the GSM, and in case of Fields of Experts also the filters $\mathbf{f}_i$. The classical learning objective for training models of natural images is maximum likelihood (ML, see Sec. 1 for alternatives). A gradient ascent on the log-likelihood for a parameter Ω_i leads to the update

$$\Omega_i^{(t+1)} = \Omega_i^{(t)} + \eta \left[\left\langle \frac{\partial E}{\partial \Omega_i} \right\rangle_p - \left\langle \frac{\partial E}{\partial \Omega_i} \right\rangle_{\mathbf{x}^\circ} \right], \tag{3}$$

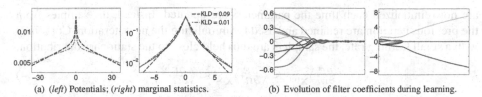

(a) (*left*) Potentials; (*right*) marginal statistics.   (b) Evolution of filter coefficients during learning.

Fig. 2. (*a*) Difference between potentials (for one filter from Fig. 1(a), 2nd row & 2nd column) trained with 1-step CD (dashed, blue) and PCD (dash-dotted, red), as well as resulting model marginals (magnified for display). The marginal KL-divergence is given w.r.t. natural images (solid, black). (*b*) Filter coefficients may decay or disperse without filter normalization.

where E is the unnormalized Gibbs energy according to $p(\mathbf{x}; \Omega) = e^{-E(\mathbf{x};\Omega)}/Z(\Omega)$, η is the learning rate, $\langle \cdot \rangle_{\mathbf{X}^0}$ denotes the average over the training data $\mathbf{X}^0$, and $\langle \cdot \rangle_p$ denotes the expectation value w.r.t. the model distribution $p(\mathbf{x}; \Omega^{(t)})$.

One conceptual advantage is that this minimizes the Kullback-Leibler (KL) divergence between the model and the data distribution and, in principle, makes the model statistics as close to those of natural images as possible. Various difficulties, however, arise in practice. First, there is no closed form expression for the model expectation, and an exact computation is intractable. Approximate inference, *e.g.* using sampling, must thus be used. Markov chain Monte Carlo (MCMC) approximations are historically most common (*e.g.* [21]), but very inefficient. Consequently, ML estimation itself was frequently approximated by contrastive divergence (CD) [3], which avoids costly equilibrium samples: Samplers are initialized at the training data $\mathbf{X}^0$ and only run for n (usually a small number) MCMC iterations to yield the sample set $\mathbf{X}^n$. Then $\langle \partial F/\partial \Omega_i \rangle_{\mathbf{X}^n}$ is used to replace $\langle \partial E/\partial \Omega_i \rangle_p$ in Eq. (3). We here use CD as the basis. A second challenge is the speed of mixing, which is usually addressed with efficient sampling methods, such as hybrid Monte Carlo [20] or auxiliary-variable Gibbs samplers [16]. We employ the latter and use the publicly available implementation of [16].

3 Improved Learning Scheme

The basic learning procedure from Sec. 2 involves a series of approximations. Moreover, the data likelihood is generally multimodal, leading to locally optimal parameters. Since previous filter-based, high-order MRFs failed to capture image statistics accurately (*cf*. Fig. 1a), the shortcomings in learning are a possible cause. We here investigate this issue, show that such a standard learning procedure is insufficient to learn accurate models of natural images, and propose an improved learning scheme.

3.1 PCD *vs*. CD

Although contrastive divergence is a reasonably good and formally justified approximation of maximum likelihood [3], it may still incur a training bias. While using n-step CD (with large n) may reduce the bias, learning becomes much less efficient. Thus previous work typically relied on 1-step CD [20], particularly for high-order models [16]. We instead use *persistent contrastive divergence* (PCD) [17], in which the samplers

are not reinitialized each time the parameters are updated. Instead, the samples from
the previous iteration are retained and used for initializing the next iteration. Combined
with a small learning rate, the samplers are thus held close to the stationary distribution:

$$\left\langle \frac{\partial E}{\partial \Omega_i} \right\rangle_{\mathbf{X}^{\text{PCD}}} \approx \left\langle \frac{\partial E}{\partial \Omega_i} \right\rangle_{\mathbf{X}^{\infty}} \approx \left\langle \frac{\partial E}{\partial \Omega_i} \right\rangle_p. \tag{4}$$

Thus each parameter update closely approximates a true ML update step as in Eq. (3).
Note that even with a small learning rate, PCD has an efficiency comparable to that
of 1-step CD, but substantially reduces bias as the experiments below show. Note that
while PCD has been used to train Restricted Boltzmann Machines [17] and filter-based
MRFs with Student-t potentials [12], this is the first time it has been investigated in
conjunction with more flexible GSM potentials.

Replacing CD with PCD not only reduces training bias, but more importantly improves the models' properties significantly. To demonstrate this, we use the 3×3 FoE
from the public implementation of [16] as a basis and retrain the potentials with PCD,
while keeping the filters fixed. The resulting marginal statistics of the in-built model
features (Fig. 1b) match those of natural images well; all marginal KL-divergences are
below 0.01. Fig. 2(a) shows in detail the parts where PCD affects the potential shape
the most and most improves the resulting model marginal. Another notable benefit of
using PCD is that it enables the following improved boundary handling scheme.

3.2 Boundary Handling for Sampling

Boundary pixels are a common source of problems in MRFs, since they are overlapped
by fewer cliques, making them less constrained than those in the image interior. When
sampling the model, boundary pixels of the samples tend to take extreme values, which
affects both learning and analysis of the model through sampling. Norouzi *et al.* [10]
proposed to use conditional sampling, *i.e.* keeping a small number of pixels around the
boundary fixed and conditionally sampling the interior. The drawback of this scheme
is that the boundary pixels will significantly diffuse into the interior during sampling,
which can be seen from the example in Fig. 3(a,b). To reduce bias in learning and
evaluation of the model, a thick boundary from the samples thus has to be discarded.
The disadvantage is that this lowers the accuracy and the efficiency of learning.

To address this, we instead use *toroidal sampling*, in which the cliques are extended
to also cover the boundary pixels in a wrap-around fashion. The toroidal topology used

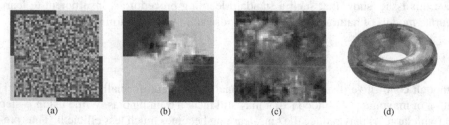

(a)   (b)   (c)   (d)

Fig. 3. Effect of boundary handling on samples: *(a)* Initialization of the sampler; *(b)* typical
sample generated by conditional sampling. Note how the boundaries affect the interior of the
sample; *(c, d)* typical sample and its topology generated by the proposed toroidal sampling.

during sampling is shown in Fig. 3(d). The obvious benefit of using this topology is the absence of any boundary pixels; all pixels are overlapped by the same number of cliques, and there are as many cliques as pixels. Since all pixels are constrained equally, boundary artifacts are avoided, and bias from the boundaries during learning is avoided.

Fig. 3(c) shows how toroidal sampling is less affected by its initialization and can quickly explore a large space. The generated samples will in turn make learning more accurate, while not requiring boundary pixels to be discarded. This increases the learning efficiency, because fewer parallel samplers suffice to estimate the likelihood gradient accurately. It is important to note that while PCD allows using toroidal sampling, the more common CD does not. This is because CD repeatedly initializes the samplers from the training images, which usually do not satisfy periodic boundary conditions.

3.3 Filter Normalization

Some researchers (*e.g.* [5,20]) have suggested to impose constraints on the norms of filters, because filters may otherwise become "inactive", *i.e.* decay to zero during training. As zero filters and the corresponding potentials do not contribute to the model at all, this is an issue, especially when a large number of filters are trained [5,20]. But even with fewer filters as are used here (the flexibility of the GSM potentials imposes limits on the attainable number of filters), we observe that filter coefficients may decay or disperse during learning (Fig. 2b). To address this, we normalize the coefficients of each filter to unit ℓ^2 norm after each parameter update. This incurs no loss of generality due to the redundancy between the GSM scales and the filter coefficient norm: GSM potentials with an infinitely large range of scales can in principle adapt to filters with arbitrary coefficient norm. The necessarily limited range of GSM scales in practice, however, does not allow to properly model the potentials if the filters take extreme values. Moreover, removing the parameter redundancy increases robustness, and in turn enables learning more filters. Fig. 1(c) shows an example in which all 8 filters are "active" and contribute to the model. This is in contrast to the learning approach of [16], for which 3 out of 8 learned filters are effectively inactive (Fig. 1a). Unlike previous uses [5,20], combining filter normalization with more flexible potentials enables learning different, heavy tailed potentials. These notably improve the ability to capture the marginal statistics of the in-built features (Fig. 1c). This also suggests that the learning procedure rather than the representational capabilities of GSMs had been the limiting factor in previous work.

3.4 Initialization of Parameters

The final aspect we address is that of initialization, which is crucial due to the non-convexity of the data likelihood. Specifically, we found that the initialization of the potential shape (GSM weights) can significantly affect learning, including the filters. A uniform initialization of the GSM weights (Fig. 4, red curve) as used, *e.g.*, by [16] is problematic. This overly constrains the pixel values and makes model samples spatially flat. The filter responses on the samples thus fall into a much smaller range than those on training images. The learning algorithm aims to reduce this difference by changing the filters toward patterns that reduce the filter-response range on natural images. The effect is that filters, particularly a Laplacian (Fig. 4, middle), are redundantly learned.

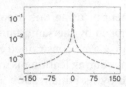

Fig. 4. Typical uniform initialization of GSM weights (dashed, red) leads to filters with fewer patterns (*middle*). Broad (δ-like) initialization (solid, green) leads to more varied filters (*right*).

Fig. 5. 16 learned filters of size 5×5. Note their more structured appearance compared to [14]

We alleviate this by initializing the potentials such that the pixels are initially less constrained than they should be, rather than more. To that end, we initialize the potentials with a broad δ-like shape (Fig. 4, green curve). We found that this improves the robustness of learning and enables training a more varied set of filters that captures different kinds of spatial structures (Fig. 4, right). Our findings indicate that the filters, on the other hand, are best initialized randomly. Initializing them to interpretable filters, such as Gabors, is counterproductive as these are usually not optimal for filter-based MRFs / FoEs, and lead to training becoming stuck in poor local optima.

4   Experiments

Due to the intractability of the partition function, it is not possible to compare models through the likelihood of a test set. We follow [16,21] to evaluate whether other well-known properties of natural image statistics are captured by the learned models. We use a validation set of 1000 non-overlapping images of size 48×48, randomly cropped from a set of natural images. Since computing statistical properties such as marginals exactly is intractable as well, we use model samples from Gibbs sampling.

Evaluated Models. Since the 3×3 FoE of [16] represents image statistics more accurately than pairwise MRFs and, as far as we are aware, also other filter-based, high-order MRFs from the literature, we use it as performance baseline. We train the basic model from Sec. 2 using the improved learning procedure described in Sec. 3 on 1000 randomly cropped 48×48 natural image patches. To facilitate comparison, we trained a model with 8 filters of size 3×3 (Fig. 1c). To showcase the benefits of the improved learning scheme, we also trained 5×5 models with 8 and 16 filters. All models exhibit fully "active" filters and potentials with very broad shoulders and tight peaks. Due to limited space, we only show the learned 16 filters of the 5×5 model in Fig. 5.

4.1   Generative Properties

Model Features. Due to the maximum entropy interpretation of filter-based MRF priors [21], the learned model should perfectly capture its feature statistics if the potential

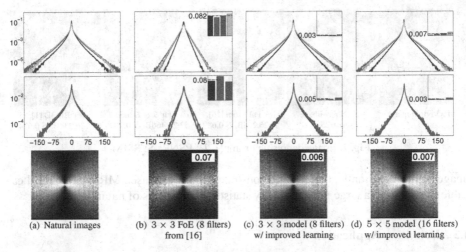

(a) Natural images   (b) 3 × 3 FoE (8 filters)   (c) 3 × 3 model (8 filters)   (d) 5 × 5 model (16 filters)
from [16]   w/ improved learning   w/ improved learning

Fig. 6. Random filter, multiscale derivative and conditional statistics: *(top)* Average marginal histograms of 8 random filters (mean 0, norm 1) of various sizes (3 × 3 – blue, 5 × 5 – green, 7 × 7 – red, 9 × 9 – cyan). *(middle)* Derivative statistics at three spatial scales (0 – blue, 1 – green, 2 – red; scales are powers of 2 with 0 being the original scale). *(bottom)* Conditional histograms of neighboring derivatives. Brightness corresponds to probability. (top right – KL-divergence.)

functions were chosen and learned appropriately. As can be seen from Fig. 1(a), the learning scheme in [16] does not lead to a particularly close match between model marginals and natural image statistics. In contrast, Fig. 1(c) shows that our improved learning procedure allows the identical model design to capture the marginal statistics of the in-built features very well. GSM potentials thus prove to be sufficiently flexible for modeling the potentials in such a filter-based MRF. This is also true for our 5 × 5 model (not shown); all marginal KL-divergences between model and image statistics are < 0.002. The resulting priors are thus real *maximum entropy models*.

Other Important Statistics. Since natural images exhibit heavy-tailed statistics even for the marginals of *random linear filters* [4], we evaluate our models in this regard with random filters of 4 different sizes (8 of each size). Fig. 6 (top) shows the average responses to these random filters for natural images, as well as all models. Moreover, natural images have been found to exhibit *scale invariant derivative statistics* [15]. Hence, we check the marginal statistics of derivatives at 3 image scales (powers of 2), which are shown in Fig. 6 (middle). Natural images have also been found to have characteristic *conditional distributions* of two image features, with a particular bow-tie shape [11]. Fig. 6 (bottom) shows the conditional histograms of neighboring image derivatives. While previous learning approaches come reasonably close regarding all three properties (Fig. 6b), our improved learning procedure reduces the mismatch between model and image statistics by a significant factor of 10, as measured in terms of the marginal KL-divergence (shown at the top-right corner of each plot). The 5 × 5 model improves particularly in terms of (multi-scale) derivative statistics (Fig. 6d). To the best of our knowledge, this is the first time that such close matches between model and natural image statistics have been reported for filter-based MRFs, or any MRF

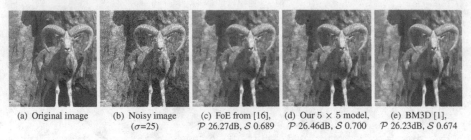

(a) Original image	(b) Noisy image	(c) FoE from [16],	(d) Our 5 × 5 model,	(e) BM3D [1],
	(σ=25)	$\mathcal{P}$ 26.27dB, $\mathcal{S}$ 0.689	$\mathcal{P}$ 26.46dB, $\mathcal{S}$ 0.700	$\mathcal{P}$ 26.23dB, $\mathcal{S}$ 0.674

Fig. 7. Image denoising example. $\mathcal{P}$: PSNR; $\mathcal{S}$: SSIM.

image prior. Importantly, this also demonstrates that filter-based MRFs are indeed capable of capturing a large number of key statistical properties of natural images.

4.2 Denoising Application

To further assess the impact of the proposed learning scheme, we evaluate the learned models using image denoising. Following [16], we estimate the posterior mean (MMSE estimate) using Gibbs sampling and evaluate on the same 68 test images with additive Gaussian noise of known variance. The runtime of our Matlab implementation is on par with [16] for the 3 × 3 model (8 filters), and approximately four times slower for the 5 × 5 one (16 filters). Tab. 1 shows a consistent, substantial boost in denoising performance from our improved learning procedure. Retraining the GSM potentials using PCD yields a gain of 0.15dB; the full learning procedure improves a 3 × 3 model with 8 filters by another 0.08dB. More importantly, the proposed learning scheme also allows training models with larger (*e.g.* 5 × 5) or more (*e.g.* 16) filters, both of which lead to further improvements in terms of denoising performance. In total, we obtain an improvement of 0.3dB over [16], which uses an identical model design but an inferior learning procedure, and even 0.8dB over the 5 × 5 FoE of [14]. This is not only a significant gain in the realm of denoising, but also makes our approach competitive with the latest state of the art in denoising. In particular, it can compete with BM3D (particularly in SSIM [18]) as well as NLSC [8]. As far as we are aware, this is the first time such competitive denoising performance has been achieved with any generative, global model of natural images. An example of denoising is shown in Fig. 7.

Table 1. Denoising results for 68 test images [14] ($\sigma = 25$)

Model/Method	∅ PSNR (dB)	∅ SSIM
5 × 5 FoE [14]	27.44	0.746
3 × 3 FoE [16]	27.95	0.788
8 fixed 3 × 3 filters from [16], learned potentials (proposed proc.)	28.10	0.793
8 learned 3 × 3 filters & learned potentials (proposed procedure)	28.18	0.796
8 learned 5 × 5 filters & learned potentials (proposed procedure)	28.22	0.797
16 learned 5 × 5 filters & learned potentials (proposed procedure)	28.26	0.799
BLS-GSM [11]	28.02	0.789
non-local sparse coding (NLSC) [8]	28.28	0.799
BM3D [1]	28.35	0.797

5 Conclusions

In this paper, we explored the limits of filter-based MRFs for natural image statistics. We identified various shortcomings in previous learning approaches, and proposed several improvements that increase robustness and enable learning larger, more, and more varied image filters. The learned potentials were found having an almost Dirac-delta like shape. Moreover, the proposed learning procedure strongly improves the models' ability of capturing the in-built feature statistics, making them real maximum-entropy models. They also show clear improvements in capturing other important statistical properties of natural images, outlining the capabilities of filter-based MRFs. Denoising experiments demonstrate significant performance gains, bringing the results very close to the state of the art.

Although our procedure allows learning more and larger filters, pushing this even further is currently not practical. Many filters lead to slower mixing, larger ones to less-sparse linear equation systems in sampling. Future work should aim to address this. Nonetheless, the trained models already capture natural image statistics very well, suggesting that further gains are likely challenging and may require new model designs.

References

1. Dabov, K., Foi, A., Katkovnik, V., Egiazarian, K.: Image denoising by sparse 3-D transform-domain collaborative filtering. IEEE T. Image Process. 16(8), 2080–2095 (2007)
2. Geman, D., Reynolds, G.: Constrained restoration and the recovery of discontinuities. IEEE T. Pattern Anal. Mach. Intell. 14(3), 367–383 (1992)
3. Hinton, G.E.: Training products of experts by minimizing contrastive divergence. Neural Comput. 14(8), 1771–1800 (2002)
4. Huang, J.: Statistics of Natural Images and Models. Ph.D. thesis, Brown University (2000)
5. Köster, U., Lindgren, J.T., Hyvärinen, A.: Estimating Markov Random Field Potentials for Natural Images. In: Adali, T., Jutten, C., Romano, J.M.T., Barros, A.K. (eds.) ICA 2009. LNCS, vol. 5441, pp. 515–522. Springer, Heidelberg (2009)
6. Levin, A., Nadler, B.: Natural image denoising: Optimality and inherent bounds. In: CVPR 2011 (2011)
7. Lyu, S., Simoncelli, E.P.: Modeling multiscale subbands of photographic images with fields of Gaussian scale mixtures. IEEE T. Pattern Anal. Mach. Intell. 31(4), 693–706 (2009)
8. Mairal, J., Bach, F., Ponce, J., Sapiro, G., Zisserman, A.: Non-local sparse models for image restoration. In: ICCV 2009 (2009)
9. McAuley, J.J., Caetano, T., Smola, A.J., Franz, M.O.: Learning high-order MRF priors of color images. In: ICML 2006, pp. 617–624 (2006)
10. Norouzi, M., Ranjbar, M., Mori, G.: Stacks of convolutional restricted Boltzmann machines for shift-invariant feature learning. In: CVPR 2009 (2009)
11. Portilla, J., Strela, V., Wainwright, M.J., Simoncelli, E.P.: Image denoising using scale mixtures of Gaussians in the wavelet domain. IEEE T. Image Process. 12(11), 1338–1351 (2003)
12. Ranzato, M., Mnih, V., Hinton, G.E.: Generating more realistic images using gated MRF's. In: NIPS 2010 (2010)
13. Roth, S., Black, M.J.: On the spatial statistics of optical flow. Int. J. Comput. Vision 74(1), 33–50 (2007)
14. Roth, S., Black, M.J.: Fields of experts. Int. J. Comput. Vision 82(2), 205–229 (2009)

15. Ruderman, D.L.: The statistics of natural images. Network: Comp. Neural 5(4), 517–548 (1994)
16. Schmidt, U., Gao, Q., Roth, S.: A generative perspective on MRFs in low-level vision. In: CVPR 2010 (2010)
17. Tieleman, T.: Training restricted boltzmann machines using approximations to the likelihood gradient. In: ICML 2008 (2008)
18. Wang, Z., Bovik, A.C., Sheikh, H.R., Simoncelli, E.P.: Image quality assessment: From error visibility to structural similarity. IEEE T. Image Process. 13(4), 600–612 (2004)
19. Weiss, Y., Freeman, W.T.: What makes a good model of natural images? In: CVPR 2007 (2007)
20. Welling, M., Hinton, G.E., Osindero, S.: Learning sparse topographic representations with products of Student-t distributions. In: NIPS 2002, pp. 1359–1366 (2002)
21. Zhu, S.C., Mumford, D.: Prior learning and Gibbs reaction-diffusion. IEEE T. Pattern Anal. Mach. Intell. 19(11), 1236–1250 (1997)

Anisotropic Range Image Integration

Christopher Schroers[1], Henning Zimmer[2], Levi Valgaerts[3], Andrés Bruhn[4],
Oliver Demetz[1], and Joachim Weickert[1]

[1] Mathematical Image Analysis Group, Faculty of Mathematics and Computer Science,
Campus E1.7, Saarland University, 66041 Saarbrücken, Germany
{schroers,demetz,weickert}@mia.uni-saarland.de
[2] Computer Graphics Laboratory, Department of Computer Science,
ETH Zurich, 8092 Zurich, Switzerland
hzimmer@inf.ethz.ch
[3] Max-Planck-Institut für Informatik,
Campus E1.4, 66123 Saarbrücken, Germany
valgaerts@mpi-inf.mpg.de
[4] Institute for Visualization and Interactive Systems,
Universitätsstraße 38, University of Stuttgart, 70569 Stuttgart, Germany
bruhn@vis.uni-stuttgart.de

Abstract. Obtaining high-quality 3D models of real world objects is an important task in computer vision. A very promising approach to achieve this is given by variational range image integration methods: They are able to deal with a substantial amount of noise and outliers, while regularising and thus creating smooth surfaces at the same time. Our paper extends the state-of-the-art approach of Zach et al. (2007) in several ways: (i) We replace the isotropic space-variant smoothing behaviour by an anisotropic (direction-dependent) one. Due to the directional adaptation, a better control of the smoothing with respect to the local structure of the signed distance field can be achieved. (ii) In order to keep data and smoothness term in balance, a normalisation factor is introduced. As a result, oversmoothing of locations that are seen seldom is prevented. This allows high quality reconstructions in uncontrolled capture setups, where the camera positions are unevenly distributed around an object. (iii) Finally, we use the more accurate closest signed distances instead of directional signed distances when converting range images into 3D signed distance fields. Experiments demonstrate that each of our three contributions leads to clearly visible improvements in the reconstruction quality.

1 Introduction

Range image integration aims at combining multiple range images, also referred to as depth maps, into a single 3D model. During the last few years, the topic of range image integration has attracted an increasing amount of attention because range images are becoming more readily available through devices such as the Kinect or time-of-flight cameras [10]. Furthermore, it is possible to compute depth maps from stereo image pairs using an existing real time or high accuracy stereo method [12]. In this way, one can employ range image integration in a *multi-view stereo* setting [13].

A. Pinz et al. (Eds.): DAGM/OAGM 2012, LNCS 7476, pp. 73–82, 2012.
© Springer-Verlag Berlin Heidelberg 2012

Often intermediate volumetric representations are used to integrate range images because they allow handling meshes of arbitrary genus. Such a volumetric range image integration has first been used to fuse range images captured by active sensors [3,7,16]. In this early work, the range images are converted into 3D signed distance fields and combined into a cumulative signed distance field using an averaging scheme. The 3D model can then be obtained using an isosurface polygonisation method; see e.g. [9].

It is known that averaging without regularisation leads to inconsistent surfaces due to frequent sign changes within the cumulative signed distance field [8]. Zach et al. address this problem in [17] by computing the cumulative signed distance field as the global minimiser of a suitable energy functional that incorporates a total variation (TV) [11] smoothness term along with a robust L^1 data term.

Our Contribution. Our work extends the variational range image integration approach presented by Zach et al. [17] in three aspects. First, the isotropic (space-variant) diffusion term is replaced by an anisotropic (direction-dependent) one, which is designed to smooth along the evolving surface and evolving ridges in the cumulative signed distance field but not across. This way it is possible to obtain very smooth surfaces from noisy range images while preserving ridges and corners. Second, a normalisation is introduced in the data term to maintain balance with the smoothness term. As a result, oversmoothing of locations that are seen seldom is prevented and it is possible to obtain high quality reconstructions of objects that have been captured unevenly often from different sides. Third, compared to Zach et al., we do not use signed distances along the line of sight when converting range images into 3D distance fields. Instead, we compute the closest signed distance to the range surface. We can show for every adjustment that it leads to reconstructions of superior quality.

Organisation of the Paper. In Section 2 we describe how to obtain a more accurate signed distance field from a given range image. Section 3 explains how the signed distance fields are integrated into a globally optimal cumulative signed distance field following the idea of Zach et al. [17]. Moreover, it derives a new anisotropic smoothing behaviour as well as a meaningful normalisation factor for the data term. Subsequently, Section 4 describes implementation aspects before we display experimental results in Section 5. We conclude the paper with a summary in Section 6.

2   Signed Distance Fields

A range image maps each location of the image domain $\Omega_2 \subset \mathbb{R}^2$ to a depth value, which describes the distance from the camera centre to the surface of the scene along the corresponding optical ray. Let us assume that a range image $r : \Omega_2 \to \mathbb{R}_+$ and the corresponding camera projection $\pi : \mathbb{R}^3 \to \Omega_2$ are given.

In volumetric range image integration methods [3,17], a range image r is converted into a 3D signed distance field f by computing the signed distance ℓ of a point $x \in \Omega_3 \subset \mathbb{R}^3$ along the line of sight. Computing this *directional signed distance* is computationally inexpensive because it can directly be evaluated as

$$\ell(x) = r(\pi(x)) - |x - c|, \tag{1}$$

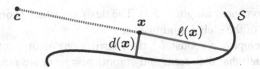

Fig. 1. Generally, the directional signed distance $\ell(\boldsymbol{x})$ overestimates the closest signed distance $d(\boldsymbol{x})$ to the range surface $\mathcal{S}$ and is a less accurate approximation of the true distance to the object

where c corresponds to the camera centre, and locations in front of the surface are arbitrarily given a positive value. However, Figure 1 illustrates that the directional signed distance $\ell(\boldsymbol{x})$ generally overestimates the closest distance. Although directional distance and closest distance can coincide at certain locations, e.g. at the range surface itself, problems occur when averaging and regularising multiple directional signed distance values. Therefore, we propose to use a more accurate approximation of the closest distance to the object by computing the *closest signed distance* to the range surface $\mathcal{S}$:

$$d(\boldsymbol{x}) = \text{sgn}\left(\ell(\boldsymbol{x})\right) \cdot \inf_{y \in \mathcal{S}} |\boldsymbol{x} - \boldsymbol{y}|. \tag{2}$$

Since the range image and its corresponding projection is given, the range surface $\mathcal{S}$ can directly be evaluated. The sign of the closest distance is determined by the sign of the directional signed distance. Alternatively, the sign could also be determined using range surface normals as in [16].

We follow [17] for the remaining part of this section by scaling the signed distance values with a factor of $1/\delta$ and truncating them to the interval $[-1, 1]$:

$$f(\boldsymbol{x}) = \psi\big(d(\boldsymbol{x})\big) \quad \text{with} \quad \psi(d) = \begin{cases} \text{sgn}(d) & \text{if } |d| \geq \delta \\ d/\delta & \text{else.} \end{cases} \tag{3}$$

The parameter δ thus reflects the expected uncertainty of the depth values. We also use a binary weight $w : \Omega_3 \to \{0,1\}$ associated with the signed distance field f in order to assign low confidence to f at locations behind the surface where $d(\boldsymbol{x}) < -\eta$. The parameter $\eta > 0$ thus specifies how much of the occluded region behind a surface is assumed to be solid.

3 Variational Signed Distance Field Integration

The cumulative signed distance function $u : \Omega_3 \to \mathbb{R}$ is computed as the minimiser of an energy functional of type

$$E(u) = \int_{\Omega_3} \left(D(\boldsymbol{f}, \boldsymbol{w}, u) + \alpha\, S(\nabla u) \right) d\boldsymbol{x}, \tag{4}$$

containing n signed distance fields $\boldsymbol{f} = (f_1, \ldots, f_n)^\top$ and the associated weights $\boldsymbol{w} = (w_1, \ldots, w_n)^\top$. The *data term* $D(\boldsymbol{f}, \boldsymbol{w}, u)$ models the assumption that u should be similar to all signed distance fields $\boldsymbol{f}$, while the *smoothness term* or *regulariser* enforces u to be smoothly varying in space by penalising large gradients of u. Its influence is steered by the smoothness weight $\alpha > 0$. The desired surface geometry is then given by the zero level set of the global minimiser u.

Zach et al. [17] employ a robust L^1 data term along with a total variation (TV) smoothness term, such that data term and smoothness term are not continuously differentiable and the resulting energy is not strictly convex. Therefore, they introduce an auxiliary variable and solve a convex approximation of this energy using a numerical scheme that combines the duality principle for the TV term with a point-wise optimisation step.

3.1 Minimisation by Gradient Descent

Alternatively, it is possible to replace the absolute value function by the continuously differentiable and strictly convex approximation $\Psi_D(s^2) = \Psi_S(s^2) = \sqrt{s^2 + \epsilon^2}$ with a small regularisation constant $\epsilon > 0$ yielding the data and the smoothness term

$$D(\boldsymbol{f}, \boldsymbol{w}, u) = \sum_{i=1}^n w_i \Psi_D((u - f_i)^2) \quad \text{and} \quad S(\boldsymbol{\nabla} u) = \Psi_S(|\boldsymbol{\nabla} u|^2), \tag{5}$$

respectively. The resulting energy approximates the TV-L^1 energy by Zach et al. and is strictly convex. Thus, its minimiser can be found as the steady state ($t \to \infty$) of the gradient descent equation

$$\partial_t u = \alpha \operatorname{div}\left(S_{\boldsymbol{\nabla} u}(\boldsymbol{\nabla} u)\right) - D_u(\boldsymbol{f}, \boldsymbol{w}, u). \tag{6}$$

When introducing the abbreviations $\Psi'_{i,D} := \Psi'_D((u - f_i)^2)$ and $\Psi'_S := \Psi'_S(|\boldsymbol{\nabla} u|^2)$, data and smoothness term derivatives are given by

$$D_u(\boldsymbol{f}, \boldsymbol{w}, u) = 2\left(u \sum_{i=1}^n w_i \Psi'_{i,D} - \sum_{i=1}^n w_i \Psi'_{i,D} f_i\right) \quad \text{and} \quad S_{\boldsymbol{\nabla} u}(\boldsymbol{\nabla} u) = 2 \Psi'_S \boldsymbol{\nabla} u. \tag{7}$$

It is known that TV regularisation leads to minimal surfaces because it penalises the perimeter of the level sets of u [2]. Increasing the smoothness weight α thus results in reducing isolated small scale features and generating low-genus isosurfaces instead of an increased smoothing of u. However, the space-variant diffusivity Ψ'_S ignores the surface orientation. Incorporating an orientation dependent behaviour requires anisotropic smoothing [15], which is discussed next.

3.2 Anisotropic Regularisation

In order to obtain an anisotropic smoothing behaviour, we modify the diffusion term in the gradient descent equation (6) by replacing the smoothness term derivative with

$$S_{\boldsymbol{\nabla} u}(\boldsymbol{\nabla} u) = 2 \Psi'_S(\boldsymbol{J}_{\rho,\sigma}) \boldsymbol{\nabla} u. \tag{8}$$

This essentially lifts the idea of Zimmer et al. [19], who modeled an anisotropic disparity-driven stereo vision, to three dimensions. The matrix-valued function Ψ'_S is

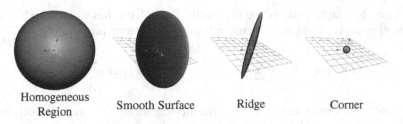

Homogeneous Region   Smooth Surface   Ridge   Corner

Fig. 2. Visualisation of diffusion tensors as ellipsoids for different local structures

an extension of a scalar-valued function that is applied only to the eigenvalues while leaving the eigenvectors unchanged, and

$$J_{\rho,\sigma} := K_\rho * (\nabla u_\sigma \nabla u_\sigma^\top) \tag{9}$$

is the *structure tensor* [4]. Here, $u_\sigma := K_\sigma * u$, where $*$ denotes a convolution with a Gaussian K_σ of standard deviation σ.

Apparently, the structure tensor $J_{\rho,\sigma}$ extends the tensor product $\nabla u \nabla u^\top$ in two aspects: first, u is regularised by a Gaussian convolution with standard deviation σ. In this context, σ can be regarded as a *noise scale* because the low-pass effect of Gaussian convolution attenuates high frequencies. Although ∇u_σ is already useful for edge detection, it is sensitive to noise if σ is chosen too small. On the other hand, cancellation effects are introduced if σ is chosen too large. This is overcome by the second aspect, which is an additional Gaussian convolution of the tensor entries with standard deviation ρ, also referred to as *integration scale*. The integration scale describes the window size over which the orientation is analysed.

Let us now discuss how the anisotropic smoothing behaviour adapts to the local structure by considering the eigenvalues of the diffusion tensor $\Psi_S'(J_{\rho,\sigma})$ for the following four cases: (a) In homogeneous regions, all eigenvalues are equally large, which causes homogeneous smoothing in all three directions. (b) At smooth surfaces, one eigenvalue is close to zero, which leads to anisotropic smoothing along the surface but not across. (c) At ridges, i.e. oriented 1D structures in 3D space, only one eigenvalue is large, resulting in smoothing along the ridge. (d) At corners, all eigenvalues vanish, which prevents smoothing. Figure 2 visualises the diffusion tensors as ellipsoids, where the eigenvectors correspond to the semi-principal axes and the eigenvalues to the respective equatorial radii.

3.3 Data Term Normalisation

The data term is not in balance with the smoothness term because using more range images effectively reduces smoothing as the influence of the data term grows larger. At a first glance it seems that a remedy is given by dividing the data term by the number of cameras used. However, it often happens that different locations are visible unequally often due to the camera positioning and the surface of the object. In this case, locations that have been seen very seldom will be excessively smoothed, whereas locations that have been seen many times only receive very little smoothing. Obviously, this cannot be overcome by adapting the data term globally. Instead, one has to consider how often each location has been observed by normalising the data term accordingly:

$$D(\boldsymbol{f}, \boldsymbol{w}, u) = \Big(\sum_{i=1}^{n} w_i + \gamma \Big)^{-1} \sum_{i=1}^{n} w_i \, \Psi_D\big((u - f_i)^2\big). \qquad (10)$$

If a location has not been seen by any camera, all weights are zero and the small positive constant γ prevents division by zero. In this case, the data term evaluates to zero such that information is filled in solely based on the smoothness term.

4 Implementation

An axis aligned bounding box that contains all range surfaces is chosen as domain of integration Ω_3. It can be discretised by choosing a number of equidistant samples $\boldsymbol{n} = (n_1, n_2, n_3)^\top$ in each direction, resulting in the sampling distances $\boldsymbol{h} = (h_1, h_2, h_3)^\top$.

Efficient Computation and Storage of Signed Distance Fields. In order to set up one of multiple signed distance fields, one has to compute the distance from a point to a triangle $n_1 \cdot n_2 \cdot n_3 \cdot m$ times when assuming that a range surface is discretised by m triangles. This complexity causes severe problems because common resolutions of 200^3 voxels and $6 \cdot 10^5$ triangles require almost $5 \cdot 10^{12}$ computations.

We use two strategies that help to reduce the computational effort when setting up the signed distance fields. First, we accelerate the computation of the closest distance for a single voxel by organising the range surface in a bounding volume hierarchy. Second, we use the directional signed distance as a heuristic for closeness to the surface and only compute the closest distance if $|\ell_i(\boldsymbol{x})| < c \cdot \delta$ for some $c > 1$.

Storing all signed distance fields and their associated weights directly requires a huge amount of memory. In order to reduce the memory requirement, one can either employ a voxelwise runlength encoding [17] or a coarser quantisation of the signed distances leading to a histogram based approach [18]. In some cases, adjusting the data term to enforce similarity to the pointwise weighted median can also yield acceptable results and drastically reduce memory requirement. As the signed distance fields are truncated to the interval $[-1, 1]$, it is possible to implicitly encode a weight of zero by using a value outside this interval.

Numerical Solution of the PDE. We discretise the gradient descent equation (6) on a regular grid using finite differences and solve it efficiently using the recently proposed fast explicit diffusion (FED) [6]. When ignoring the smoothness term, the minimiser u is given by the pointwise weighted median of the signed distance fields. In general, convergence can be strongly accelerated when using this as an initialisation compared to an initialisation with a constant value $z \in [-1, 1]$. If a voxel has never been seen and the bounding box is chosen rather tight, it is most probable that the voxel lies inside the object such that it is reasonable to initialise it with -1. Alternatively, a coarse-to-fine approach can be employed to speed up the convergence. It depends on the input data and the choice of the regularisation paramter α, which strategy yields faster convergence.

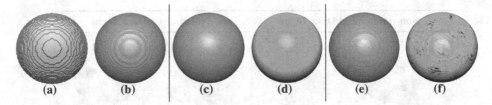

Fig. 3. *From left to right:* **(a)**-**(c)** A sphere was reconstructed from synthetically generated range images with $\delta = 0, |h|/4, |h|$ using closest signed distances. **(d)** Error visualisation for (c). **(e)** Reconstruction using directional signed distances and $\delta = |h|$. **(f)** Error visualisation for (e).

5   Experimental Results

Guidelines for Choosing the Parameters. The parameters δ and η denote the relevant region close to the surface and the occluded region behind the surface, respectively. When choosing $\delta < |h|$, subvoxel accuracy that was originally present in the range image is lost in the signed distance field due to the truncation of distances. Therefore, one can see increasing staircasing artifacts when δ goes from $|h|$ towards zero (see Figure 3 (a)-(c)) and it is advisable to choose $\delta \geq |h|$. Additionally, it makes sense to adapt δ in such a way that it reflects the expected measurement error in the depth maps. Choosing η involves a tradeoff: On the one hand, η should be as small as possible to avoid influencing surfaces on the other side. On the other hand, η has to be large enough to allow for sign changes in the signed distance field.

Directional Distance vs. Closest Distance. In Figure 3 (e) one can see artifacts on a sphere that was reconstructed from 48 ground truth range images using directional signed distance values. Figure 3 (f) shows a visualisation of the error values, where blue corresponds to a negative, red to a positive error value and green corresponds to an error of zero. The error for a vertex is given by its distance to the ground truth according to the error measure for accuracy used in the Middlebury Benchmark [13], and the minimum and maximum error values have been mapped to blue and red, respectively. When using the closest distance to the range surface, one can obtain an accurate reconstruction without artifacts (see Figure 3 (c),(d)).

Non-normalised vs. Normalised Data Term. It is common to downweight the data term by the number of range images used as it is done in the experimental section of [18]. However, depending on the geometry of the object and the camera placement, different locations might not be seen equally often such that a location based normalisation as proposed by us is be required. In order to demonstrate the surface evolution under increasing α, the Stanford bunny taken from the Stanford 3D scanning repository [1] is used to generate 42 range images taken from the front and only 6 from the back. Looking at Figure 4, the experiments verify that using the normalisation smoothes front and back equally as desired. On the other hand, the non-normalised variant excessively smoothes the back while performing almost no smoothing in the front.

Non-normalised Data Term	Normalised Data Term

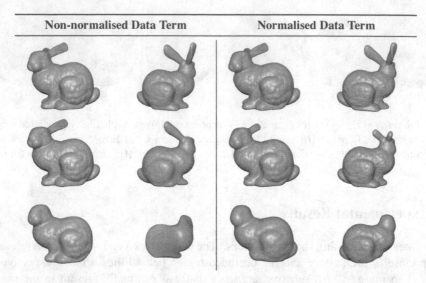

Fig. 4. With α increasing from top to bottom, one can see that the normalisation ensures an equal smoothing of front an back. The variant without normalisation excessively smoothes the back.

Fig. 5. Stairs were reconstructed from 48 synthetically generated range images with a small amount of noise added along the line of sight. *From left to right*: **(a)** One noisy range surface. **(b)** Reconstruction with TV smoothness term. **(c)** Reconstruction with anisotropic diffusion term.

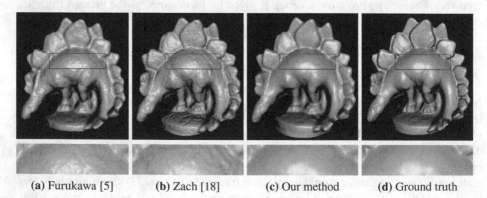

(a) Furukawa [5]	**(b)** Zach [18]	**(c)** Our method	**(d)** Ground truth

Fig. 6. *Top row*: Reconstructions for the dino full dataset from the Middlebury benchmark with the errors 0.32mm, 0.55mm and 0.33mm, respectively. *Bottom row*: Magnification.

Total Variation Vs. Anisotropic Regularisation. A stair like object has been reconstruced from 48 synthetically generated range images. In order to account for measurement errors as they often occur in modern depth cameras, a small amount of noise has been added along the line of sight. Figure 5 shows that the anisotropic diffusion term achieves a superior result when compared to the isotropic one. In the magnification it is clearly visible that the flat parts of the stairs are extremely smooth while the ridges are preserved. The TV smoothness term is also able to preserve the ridges but cannot achieve a comparable smoothness in the flat regions. This also holds for the reconstructions of the full dino dataset from the Middlebury benchmark depicted in Figure 6 (b) and (c). We have used closest distances when converting the range images into signed distance fields, and we have computed depth maps according to the method of Valgaerts et al. [14]. Compared to the method of Zach [18], we are able to significantly improve the accuracy from 0.55mm to 0.33mm. In fact, only Furukawa and Ponce [5] are able to obtain a higher accuracy of 0.32mm at this time. However, the reconstruction of Furukawa is not able to achieve a similar smoothness, such that our reconstruction is visually closer to the ground truth (see Figure 6 (a)). With 4.5 hours, the runtime of our CPU-based implementation lies between those of Furukawa (5.75 h) and Zach (3 min) (see also http://vision.middlebury.edu/mview/). Furthermore, our FED scheme is well suited for parallelisation on GPUs.

6   Conclusions and Future Work

We have extended the variational range image integration method of Zach et al. [17] w.r.t. three aspects. First, an anisotropic smoothing behaviour that outperforms the existing isotropic one has been proposed. It can produce smoother surfaces while preserving ridges and corners. Second, a normalisation of the data term ensures that portions of an object which have only been captured seldom are not overly smoothed. It allows for high quality reconstructions in setups where the camera positions are unevenly distributed. Third, the signed distance fields were generated from range images by computing the closest signed distance to the range surface instead of evaluating the directional signed distance along the line of sight. In the experimental section, we could show that all three modifications were able to improve the reconstruction quality.

Future work could aim at increasing the quality of reconstructions even further by recognising depth discontinuities and treating them in a more sophisticated way.

Acknowledgements. Funding by the Cluster of Excellence *Multimodal Computing and Interaction* is gratefully acknowledged. This work has been performed while all authors were affiliated members of the Mathematical Image Analysis Group.

References

1. The Stanford 3D Scanning Repository,
   http://graphics.stanford.edu/data/3Dscanrep/
2. Chan, T.F., Esedoglu, S.: Aspects of total variation regularized L^1 function approximation. SIAM Journal on Applied Mathematics 65(5), 1817–1837 (2004)

3. Curless, B., Levoy, M.: A volumetric method for building complex models from range images. In: Proceedings of SIGGRAPH 1996, vol. 3, pp. 303–312 (1996)
4. Förstner, W., Gülch, E.: A fast operator for detection and precise location of distinct points, corners and centres of circular features. In: Proc. ISPRS Intercommission Conference on Fast Processing of Photogrammetric Data, Interlaken, Switzerland, pp. 281–305 (June 1987)
5. Furukawa, Y., Ponce, J.: Accurate, dense, and robust multiview stereopsis. IEEE Transactions on Pattern Analysis and Machine Intelligence 32(8), 1362–1376 (2010)
6. Grewenig, S., Weickert, J., Bruhn, A.: From Box Filtering to Fast Explicit Diffusion. In: Goesele, M., Roth, S., Kuijper, A., Schiele, B., Schindler, K. (eds.) DAGM 2010. LNCS, vol. 6376, pp. 533–542. Springer, Heidelberg (2010)
7. Hilton, A., Stoddart, A.J., Illingworth, J., Windeatt, T.: Reliable Surface Reconstruction from Multiple Range Images. In: Buxton, B., Cipolla, R. (eds.) ECCV 1996. LNCS, vol. 1064, pp. 117–126. Springer, Heidelberg (1996)
8. Hornung, A., Kobbelt, L.: Robust reconstruction of watertight 3D models from non-uniformly sampled point clouds without normal information. In: Proc. Fourth Eurographics Symposium on Geometry Processing, pp. 41–50. Eurographics Association (2006)
9. Lorensen, W.E., Cline, H.E.: Marching cubes: A high resolution 3D surface construction algorithm. In: Proceedings of SIGGRAPH 1987, vol. 21, pp. 163–169 (July 1987)
10. Newcombe, R.A., Izadi, S., Hilliges, O., Molyneaux, D., Kim, D., Davison, A.J., Kohli, P., Shotton, J., Hodges, S., Fitzgibbon, A.: Kinectfusion: Real-time dense surface mapping and tracking. In: IEEE International Symposium on Mixed and Augmented Reality, vol. 7(10), pp. 127–136 (2011)
11. Rudin, L.I., Osher, S., Fatemi, E.: Nonlinear total variation based noise removal algorithms. Physica D 60, 259–268 (1992)
12. Scharstein, D., Szeliski, R.: A taxonomy and evaluation of dense two-frame stereo correspondence algorithms. International Journal of Computer Vision 47(1-3), 7–42 (2002)
13. Seitz, S., Curless, B., Diebel, J., Scharstein, D., Szeliski, R.: A comparison and evaluation of multi-view stereo reconstruction algorithms. In: Proc. 2006 IEEE Conference on Computer Vision and Pattern Recognition, pp. I:519–I:528. IEEE Computer Society Press, New York (2006)
14. Valgaerts, L., Bruhn, A., Weickert, J.: A Variational Model for the Joint Recovery of the Fundamental Matrix and the Optical Flow. In: Rigoll, G. (ed.) DAGM 2008. LNCS, vol. 5096, pp. 314–324. Springer, Heidelberg (2008)
15. Weickert, J.: Anisotropic Diffusion in Image Processing. Teubner, Stuttgart (1998)
16. Wheeler, M.D., Sato, Y., Ikeuchi, K.: Consensus surfaces for modeling 3D objects from multiple range images. In: Proc. Sixth International Conference on Computer Vision, pp. 917–924. IEEE Computer Society (1998)
17. Zach, C., Pock, T., Bischof, H.: A globally optimal algorithm for robust TV-L^1 range image integration. In: Proc. Ninth International Conference on Computer Vision, pp. 1–8. IEEE Computer Society Press, Rio de Janeiro (2007)
18. Zach, C.: Fast and high quality fusion of depth maps. In: Proc. Fourth International Symposium on 3D Data Processing, Visualization and Transmission, pp. 1–8 (2008)
19. Zimmer, H., Bruhn, A., Valgaerts, L., Breuß, M., Weickert, J., Rosenhahn, B., Seidel, H.P.: PDE-based anisotropic disparity-driven stereo vision. In: Deussen, O., Keim, D., Saupe, D. (eds.) Proceedings of Vision, Modeling, and Visualization 2008, pp. 263–272. Akademische Verlagsgesellschaft Aka, Konstanz (2008)

Modeling of Sparsely Sampled Tubular Surfaces Using Coupled Curves

Thorsten Schmidt[1,2], Margret Keuper[1,2], Taras Pasternak[3], Klaus Palme[2,3,4], and Olaf Ronneberger[1,2]

[1] Lehrstuhl für Mustererkennung und Bildverabeitung, Institut für Informatik,
[2] Centre of Biological Signalling Studies (BIOSS),
[3] Institut für Biologie II,
[4] Freiburg Inst. for Advanced Studies (FRIAS),
Albert-Ludwigs-Universität Freiburg
tschmidt@informatik.uni-freiburg.de

Abstract. We present a variational approach to simultaneously trace the axis and determine the thickness of 3-D (or 2-D) tubular structures defined by sparsely and unevenly sampled noisy surface points. Many existing approaches try to solve the axis-tracing and the precise fitting in two subsequent steps. In contrast to this our model is initialized with a small cylinder segment and converges to the final tubular structure in a single energy minimization using a gradient descent scheme. The energy is based on the error of fit and simultaneously penalizes strong curvature and thickness variations. We demonstrate the performance of this closed formulation on volumetric microscopic data sets of the *Arabidopsis* root tip, where only the nuclei of the cells are visible.

1 Introduction

The accurate tracing and segmentation of parallel-line (2D) or tubular structures (3D) is an active research topic to solve problems coming from medicine, biology, robotics, or aerial and satellite image analysis. Especially for biological and medical applications, with their wide spectrum of imaging methods this modeling is an important step towards data abstraction and quantification. With the discovery of the green fluorescent protein, and the isolation of its gene, the possibility of imaging organism development in-vivo has led to a revolution in biological research and a tremendous increase in data volume to process.

One popular model organism in plant science is *Arabidopsis thaliana*, due to its simple architecture and comparably small and fully sequenced genome. Especially the stem cell niches in the root and shoot tips (root/shoot apical meristems) are of high interest to understand plant development and signaling within complex organs. The root apical meristem (RAM) consists of a set of tissue layers around the root's axis. Each of these layers can be described using an axis-thickness model, leading to the continuous anatomical model needed to localize events within the root. The simplest and most flexible way of imaging the plant root with cellular resolution is to mark the cell nuclei and relate events

A. Pinz et al. (Eds.): DAGM/OAGM 2012, LNCS 7476, pp. 83–92, 2012.
© Springer-Verlag Berlin Heidelberg 2012

within the organs to a derived overall anatomical model. However, this practical imaging advantage leads to a very sparse representation of the coaxial tubular structures each cell layer represents, posing high demands onto the modeling.

Especially in microscopic data the light is attenuated by the specimen density and scattered at interfaces between regions with different refractive indices leading to a significant loss of signal when imaging through thick tissues. Therefore simple gray-value based approaches like thresholding and/or kernel smoothing to estimate the root axis are biased towards the part of the root close to the objective and tend to fail. We therefore avoid direct use of the image gray values, and instead extract the positions of the nuclei of a selected layer using the detection scheme described in [10]. The detection quality is also biased due to the described effects, and a direct fit to the resulting point cloud using kernel smoothing still shows a systematic fitting error as we will show in the experiments section.

To avoid the described bias we employed a model consisting of a vector-valued function describing the tube's axis and a scalar function describing the variable tube thickness. Both functions are coupled by a common curve parametrization into a combined tubular model which is fit to the data in a robust variational energy minimization scheme. The model is designed to work solely on the sparse point positions, without the need for surface normal estimation. We will show that it leads to very accurate fits even in the case of high noise and missing surface points.

A key benefit of the proposed model is that it "grows" into a large and arbitrarily complex tubular structure from a small local initialization, i.e. it solves the tracing and accurate fitting problem within a single energy minimization.

1.1   Related Work

In medical applications various approaches exist to analyze images of vascular and neuronal networks based on different imaging methods ranging from low resolution CT and MRT, through light microscopy down to electron microscopy [7,3]. All approaches have in common that they rely on densely imaged interfaces between the structures of interest and mainly depend on the gray values and their derivatives to guide the model fitting. One possibility of robustly finding the axis of a tubular structure is a symmetry analysis around the potential axis [8]. Morphology-driven approaches try to find the axis by structure thinning leading to a skeletonization. Filter based approaches first try to emphasize the structures using filter banks or steerable filters and apply thresholding and thinning afterwards. See [4] for an overview comparing the different approaches.

In the field of robotics approaches to fit parametric tubular structures to point cloud data recorded using laser range scanners are of high interest [1]. Most existing approaches exploit the scanned dense mesh structure to estimate local surface normals guiding the model fitting process. These approaches have to cope with noisy data and therefore estimate the normals for each surface position from relatively large neighborhoods. Others try to detect shapes using Hough-like voting based approaches [9]. These are especially suited to detect man-made rigid objects, but don't perform well on deformable objects as they are common in biological and medical applications.

In [5] the coupling of two evolving splines describing the center-lines and thicknesses of roads and rivers in aerial and satellite images was introduced. Although the noise level in images of that kind is very high, the gradients are still a valuable piece of information to guide the snake evolution. A different approach using two coupled splines to describe the outlines of the biologically highly interesting model organism C-Elegans was introduced in [11].

In [6] a non-self-intersecting 1-D line from unstructured and noisy 3D point data was reconstructed using moving least-squares interpolation. For homogeneously distributed tube-surface data around its circumference this approach is also applicable to solve the tube axis fitting task, although it does not determine the tube thickness.

Our setting is different from the above-mentioned, since our approach has to perform the task of simultaneously estimating the axis and variable thickness of a tubular structure based on sparse surface points only. The low point density and high data noise preclude the extraction of reliable surface normals. We formulate the task of fitting the model to a point cloud as one closed energy minimization problem, which incorporates all available points and a set of tubular models to which on demand new tubes can be added.

2 Variational Coupled Curve Fitting

We define a tube as a function mapping a curve parameter $u \in \mathbb{R}$ to the $(D+1)$-dimensional vector $\left(\boldsymbol{a}^\top (u), t (u)\right)^\top$, where $\boldsymbol{a} : \mathbb{R} \to \mathbb{R}^D$ is the tube axis function and $t : \mathbb{R} \to \mathbb{R}$ is the corresponding tube thickness function. Fig. 1 sketches the tube model. To optimally map the model to a set of tube surface points $X = \{\boldsymbol{x}_1, \ldots, \boldsymbol{x}_n\}$, $\boldsymbol{x}_i \in \mathbb{R}^D$ we minimize the energy

$$E_{\text{data}} (\boldsymbol{a}, t) := \sum_{i=1}^n \psi \left(\left(\|\boldsymbol{a} (u_i) - \boldsymbol{x}_i\| - t (u_i)\right)^2\right) \tag{1}$$

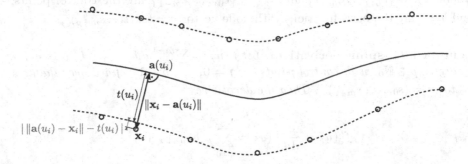

Fig. 1. A 2-D sketch of the tube model fit to a point set depicted as black circles. The axis is shown as blue line, while the dashed lines indicate the estimated tube incorporating the tube thickness. The distance shown in green is minimized during the optimization.

where $u_i := \arg\min_u \|x_i - a(u)\|$ is the curve parameter projection of x_i and $\psi(\rho^2)$ is a robust distance measure.

To cope with sparse surface points and high data noise, we additionally introduce smoothness terms penalizing axis curvature and tube thickness variations

$$E_a(a) = \int_{-\infty}^{\infty} \left\| \frac{d^2}{du^2} a(u) \right\|^2 du \quad \text{and} \quad E_t(t) = \int_{-\infty}^{\infty} \left(\frac{d}{du} t(u) \right)^2 du . \quad (2)$$

For shorter notation we define $\rho_i(u) := (\|a(u) - x_i\| - t(u))$ and get the overall energy functional to minimize

$$E(a,t) := \sum_{i=1}^{n} \psi(\rho^2) + \lambda \int_{-\infty}^{\infty} \left\| \frac{d^2}{du^2} a(u) \right\|^2 du + \mu \int_{-\infty}^{\infty} \left(\frac{d}{du} t(u) \right)^2 du \quad (3)$$

where $\lambda, \mu \in \mathbb{R}^+$ weigh the influence of the smoothness terms.

3   Parametrization Using B-Splines

We approximate the curves with open B-splines of degree p, therefore the nodes at the spline endpoints are repeated $p + 1$ times. W.l.o.g. we will restrict the spline parameter u to the $[0, 1]$-range. We obtain the B-spline approximation of the general functions $a(u)$ and $t(u)$ as follows:

$$a(u) := \sum_{j=0}^{m-1} c_j^a b_{j,p,s}(u) \qquad \text{and} \qquad t(u) := \sum_{j=0}^{m-1} c_j^t b_{j,p,s}(u)$$

where $C^a = \{c_0^a, \ldots, c_{m-1}^a\}$ and $C^t = \{c_0^t, \ldots, c_{m-1}^t\}$ are the control points, and $b_{j,p,s}$ are the basis functions with node-vector $s = (s_0, \ldots, s_{m+p})^\top$.

Lemma 1 (B-spline derivative). *Let $f(u) := \sum_{j=0}^{m-1} c_j b_{j,p,s}(u)$ be a B-spline of degree $p \in \mathbb{N}_0$, with control points c_j, $j = 0, \ldots, m-1$ defined over the knot vector $s = (s_0, \ldots, s_{m+p})^\top$. Then the derivative*

$$f'(u) = \frac{d}{du} f(u) = \sum_{j=0}^{m-2} c_j' b_{j,p-1,s'}(u)$$

is another B-spline of degree $p - 1$ defined over the knot vector $s' = (s_1, \ldots, s_{m+p-1})$ with control points $c_j' = \frac{p}{s_{j+p+1}-s_{j+1}}(c_{j+1} - c_j)$.

More details to splines as well as this Lemma and its proof are detailed in [2].

The general energy from (3) changes to

$$E_{\text{data}}\left(\boldsymbol{a}, t\right) = \sum_{i=1}^{n} \psi\left(\left(\left\|\boldsymbol{a}\left(u_i\right) - \boldsymbol{x}_i\right\| - t\left(u_i\right)\right)^2\right)$$

$$+\lambda \cdot \sum_{d=1}^{D} \int_0^1 \left(\sum_{j=0}^{m-3} c_{j,d}^{\prime a} b_{j,p-2,s'}\left(u\right)\right)^2 du$$

$$+\mu \cdot \int_0^1 \left(\sum_{j=0}^{m-2} c_j^{\prime t} b_{j,p-1,s'}\left(u\right)\right)^2 du. \quad (4)$$

The primed variables are obtained applying Lemma 1 (for the axis twice) to the original splines.

Using the spline parameterization the partial derivatives with respect to the control points c_j^a and c_j^t are needed

$$\frac{\partial}{\partial c_{j,d}^a} E\left(\boldsymbol{a}, t\right) = 2 \sum_{i=1}^{n} \psi'\left(\rho^2\right)\left(1 - \frac{t\left(u_i\right)}{\left\|\boldsymbol{a}\left(u_i\right) - \boldsymbol{x}_i\right\|}\right)\left(a_d\left(u_i\right) - x_{i,d}\right) b_{j,p,s}\left(u_i\right)$$

$$+2\lambda \sum_{j'=0}^{m-1} c_{j',d}^a \int_0^1 \frac{d^2}{du^2} b_{j',p,s}\left(u\right) \frac{d^2}{du^2} b_{j,p,s}\left(u\right) du \quad (5)$$

$$\frac{\partial}{\partial c_j^t} E\left(\boldsymbol{a}, t\right) = -2 \sum_{i=1}^{n} \psi'\left(\rho^2\right)\left(\left\|\boldsymbol{a}\left(u_i\right) - \boldsymbol{x}_i\right\| - t\left(u_i\right)\right) b_{j,p,s}\left(u_i\right)$$

$$+2\mu \sum_{j'=0}^{m-1} c_{j'}^t \int_0^1 \frac{d}{du} b_{j',p,s}\left(u\right) \frac{d}{du} b_{j,p,s}\left(u\right) du, \quad (6)$$

finally leading to the following update rules for moving the control points in a gradient descent manner when introducing an artificial discrete evolution time k with step $\tau \in \mathbb{R}^+$:

$$c_{j,d}^{a\,k+1} = c_{j,d}^{a\,k} - \tau \frac{\partial}{\partial c_{j,d}^a} E\left(\boldsymbol{a}, t\right) \quad \text{and} \quad c_j^{t\,k+1} = c_{j,d}^{t\,k} - \tau \frac{\partial}{\partial c_j^t} E\left(\boldsymbol{a}, t\right). \quad (7)$$

Since all dimensions come into play during the control point updates in each iteration, first the derivatives are computed for each control point, then the update is applied and finally the u_i for each point are recomputed.

We define the outlier-robust distance measure

$$\psi\left(\rho^2\right) := \begin{cases} \rho^2 & \rho < \eta \\ \eta^2 & \rho \geq \eta \end{cases} \quad \text{with derivative} \quad \psi'\left(\rho^2\right) = \begin{cases} 1 & \rho < \eta \\ 0 & \rho \geq \eta \end{cases}$$

and some user-defined threshold $\eta \in \mathbb{R}$ (which should be chosen in the range of the structure radius).

Algorithm 1. The Coupled B-spline fitting algorithm

Require: Point set X, initial cylinder, parameters λ, μ, τ
1: Initialize each model (a, t) with two knots fitting the initial cylinder
2: Compute the initial model energy $E(a, t)$ using (4)
3: **while** not converged **do**
4:     Minimize $E(a, t)$ using (7)
5:     Insert knot and re-parametrize the model
6: **end while**
7: **return** The coupled B-spline model (a, t)

Only points within a certain distance range defined by η will contribute to the derivatives which allows to adapt the model fitting to the surface point density and the data noise. We additionally linearly decrease λ and μ with increasing arc length of the current axis estimate to avoid a bias towards short curves and update the thickness function only with points mapping orthogonally onto the axis to avoid a thickness over-estimation at the tube end points.

We initialize the fit with a manually chosen short cylinder segment represented by a straight B-spline with two knots at the ends with the thickness intialized to the cylinder radius. During the described optimization the number of control points remains constant. Therefore the model will evolve until no more data points can be described by one single degree p polynomial. To allow more complex tube shapes, we alternate between fitting and re-gridding step in which an additional knot is inserted and distribute the knots equidistantly along the curve leading to an intermediate curve length parametrization. The whole fitting process is described in Alg. 1.

3.1 Extension to Multiple Tubes

To simultaneously trace multiple tubular structures, for each a seeding cylinder can be placed. In each iteration step the point set is partitioned into subsets, so that the points in subset X_m are best explained by the mth tubular model according to the data energy term. The evolution of tube m is computed on subset X_m only. The Energy then becomes the sum over all single model Energies.

4   Experiments

4.1   Synthetic Data

We compared the proposed model (using cubic splines) to the axis estimates obtained through Gaussian point cloud kernel smoothing (PKS), which resembles the drawbacks of averaging techniques for curve fitting. For this we synthetically generated data sets consisting of point clouds highlighting specific cases. We used trigonometric functions to model the axis and thickness functions and generated 1000 equally distributed tube surface points around the axis. The point positions were then moved in an arbitrary direction following a Gaussian distribution with standard deviation σ leading to the synthetic ground truth (Fig. 2 left panels). The PKS kernel width was empirically chosen to minimize the fitting error. The error comparison between PKS and the proposed coupled curve model (CCM) is shown in the right panels. For constant tube thickness Fig. 2(a) the axis error of CCM in each direction stays below 20% of the tube thickness whereas PKS already over-smooths the curve leading to undershoots. The thickness is a little over-estimated by on average 5%. Pure thickness variations as in Fig. 2(b) do not influence the axis localization accuracy, but they are reflected in the thickness error, because the model is designed to favor a constant thickness. However, the error stays below 10% for low noise and small μ (here $\mu = 0$). Moderate thickness variations on a bent model as shown in Fig. 2(c) affect the quality of fit only marginally. Finally one of the big strengths of the model is highlighted in

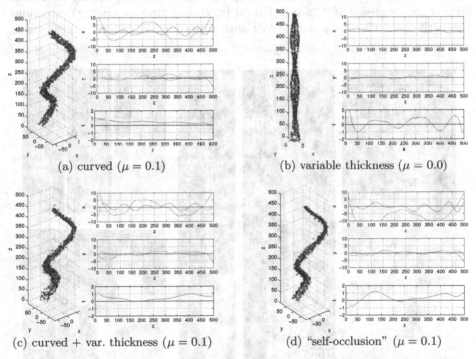

(a) curved ($\mu = 0.1$)   (b) variable thickness ($\mu = 0.0$)

(c) curved + var. thickness ($\mu = 0.1$)   (d) "self-occlusion" ($\mu = 0.1$)

Fig. 2. Sample fits to synthetically generated tubes and the fitting errors for each model dimension ($u = [0, 500]$). The left plots show the generated noisy point clouds (blue crosses) and the axis estimate using the proposed coupled curves model (CCM). The right plots show the axis mismatch in $x-$ and $y-$ direction for point based kernel smoothing (PKS) in green and for the CCM in red. The third plot shows the CCM thickness mismatch. For all experiments we set $\lambda = 0.1$. (a) $a(u) = (50\sin(2\pi u/300), 70\sin(2\pi u/800), u)^{\top}$, $t(u) = 10$, $\sigma = 4$; (b) $a(u) = (0, 0, u)^{\top}$, $t(u) = 20 + 10\sin(2\pi u/200)$, $\sigma = 1$; (c) $a(u) = (50\sin(2\pi u/300), 70\sin(2\pi u/800), u)^{\top}$, $t(u) = 10 + 5\sin(2\pi u/1000)$, $\sigma = 4$; (d) $a(u) = (50\sin(2\pi u/300), 70\sin(2\pi u/800), u)^{\top}$, $t(u) = 10 + 5\sin(2\pi u/1000)$, $\sigma = 4$, with "self-occlusion".

Fig. 2(d), the robustness to biased point cloud distributions on the tube surface. For this all sample points from Fig. 2(c) which are occluded when assuming a solid tube and a fixed view angle were removed from the set. This resulted in an axis position bias for PKS, whereas CCM still reliably estimates tube localization and thickness.

4.2   Microscopic 3D Volumes of the *Arabidopsis* Root Tip

To highlight the practical applicability and robustness of our approach we estimated axis and thickness of *Arabidopsis* root tips using the cell nuclei. The root tips were fixated and DAPI stained to mark the cellular DNA content. After preparation they were recorded using a confocal laser scanning microscope (CLSM) with a 63× water immersion objective. The data volume was reconstructed from a sequence of images using optical sectioning, leading to a final anisotropic voxel-size of $0.2\mu m$ in lateral (x-y) and $1\mu m$ in axial (z) direction. Two orthogonal views of a sample root with superimposed axis fits are shown in

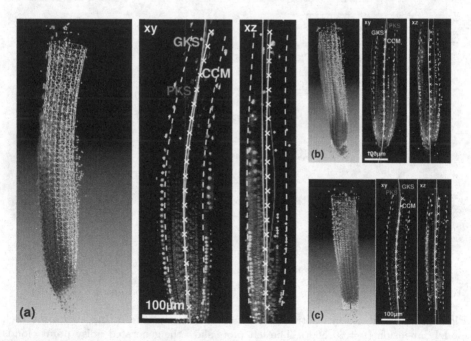

Fig. 3. The Coupled Curves model fit to sample root tip data sets. In gray the gamma corrected DAPI signal is shown, the red line (left panels) depicts the estimated root axis, the yellow mesh the estimated center of the epidermal cell layer and the cyan spheres the noisy epidermis nucleus positions. The right panels show orthogonal cuts through the data sets and the axis fits using gray-value-based kernel smoothing (GKS), point-based kernel smoothing (PKS) and the proposed Coupled Curve Model (CCM). The blue line indicates the cut shown in the different views. One expert annotation is shown as white crosses. The parameters for the CCM model were set to $\lambda = 0.1$, $\mu = 0.1$.

Table 1. Minimum/Maximum/Average root mean squared axis fitting errors between the expert annotations and the fitting approaches on ten sample roots. (GKS = gray-value based kernel smoothing, PKS = surface point based kernel smoothing, CCM = the proposed coupled curve model).

	Expert 2 min/max/avg [μm]	GKS min/max/avg [μm]	PKS min/max/avg [μm]	CCM min/max/avg [μm]
Expert 1	1.78/5.32/3.09	5.52/17.30/10.68	3.69/16.94/8.46	**3.18/11.22/6.07**
Expert 2	N/A	6.38/14.66/11.38	**3.37**/17.36/8.65	4.55/**12.65/7.32**

Fig. 3(a) (panels 2 and 3). Although the images are gamma corrected, the signal attenuation in z direction is still visible.

To evaluate the axis fits, two experts manually annotated axis points of ten root tips. For this the data sets were first rotated to roughly align the root axis with the Euclidean x-axis. This avoids elliptic distortions of the visible root sections during annotation. Both experts picked the root center at every 100th x-section of the data set guided by a circle of appropriate diameter. The average annotation difference between the experts is $3\mu m$, which is in the order of an average nucleus radius.

We detect the nuclear center positions of a selected tissue layer based on rotationally invariant volumetric gray value features, namely the magnitudes of voxelwise solid harmonic spectra [10]. Based on these features a probabilistic SVM model which was trained on two separate datasets is applied and local probability maxima are used as nucleus candidate positions.

We again compared the CCM to Gaussian kernel smoothing approaches, this time incorporating either the gray values directly (GKS) or the positions of the nuclei (PKS). We chose a kernel width of $40\mu m$ to reach a smooth curve, that still shows good localization properties. The estimated axes on sample roots are shown in Fig. 3. Especially in Fig. 3(a) the bias of GKS towards regions with higher gray values is clearly visible. As already seen in the synthetic results PKS relies on homogeneously distributed points, and therefore on the detector quality. In all samples (Fig. 3(a-c)) the detector reported many false positives in low signal parts of the recording, leading to deformations of the PKS axis estimate towards these points. Also CCM was affected by the false positives in the root volume (Fig. 3(b) (xz panel)) resulting in a slight shift of the model axis. In contrast to PKS, in which the points "attracted" the axis, for CCM false detections in the root interior were explained by an erroneous model shift in the opposite direction.

5   Conclusion

We presented a variational approach to robustly model tubular structures defined by their axis and thickness functions based on sparse and noisy surface point samples. The approach is able to follow tubes of very complex bending patterns and also allows for moderate thickness variations. When exchanging the tube thickness constancy penalizer by a penalizer on a higher derivative degree, the approach can be adapted to find the axis of arbitrary objects of revolution.

The possibility to introduce arbitrarily many tube seeds into the model allows to simultaneously match all tubes within a data set. Although branching structures are not yet introduced in the model, its capability to simultaneously model multiple tubes in a data set in one energy minimization allows to trace the single branches up to the branching point.

Acknowledgements. We thank the members of our team for helpful comments on the manuscript. We also gratefully acknowledge the excellent technical support from Roland Nitschke (ZBSA). This work was supported by the DFG, the Excellence Initiative of the German Federal and State Governments (EXC 294), European Space Agency, Bundesministerium für Bildung und Forschung (BMBF) (Fkz 0315329B, 0101-31P5914), Deutsches Zentrum für Luft und Raumfahrt, and the Freiburg Initiative for Systems Biology (FRISYS).

References

1. Bauer, U., Polthier, K.: Generating parametric models of tubes from laser scans. Computer-Aided Design 41(10), 719–729 (2009)
2. de Boor, C.: A practical guide to splines, 3rd edn. Applied Mathematical Sciences, vol. 27. Springer (1978)
3. Friman, O., Hindennach, M., Kühnel, C., Peitgen, H.O.: Multiple hypothesis template tracking of small 3d vessel structures. Med. Image Anal. 14, 160–171 (2010)
4. Kirbas, C., Quek, F.: A review of vessel extraction techniques and algorithms. ACM Comput. Surv. 36(2), 81–121 (2004)
5. Laptev, I., Mayer, H., Lindeberg, T., Eckstein, W., Steger, C., Baumgartner, A.: Automatic extraction of roads from aerial images based on scale space and snakes. In: Machine Vision and Applications, vol. 12, pp. 23–31 (2000)
6. Lee, I.K.: Curve reconstruction from unorganized points. Computer Aided Geometric Design 17(2), 161–177 (2000)
7. Meijering, E., Jacob, M., Sarria, J.C., Steiner, P., Hirling, H., Unser, M.: Design and validation of a tool for neurite tracing and analysis in fluorescence microscopy images. Cytometry Part A 58A(2), 167–176 (2004)
8. Pock, T., Beichel, R., Bischof, H.: A Novel Robust Tube Detection Filter for 3D Centerline Extraction. In: Kalviainen, H., Parkkinen, J., Kaarna, A. (eds.) SCIA 2005. LNCS, vol. 3540, pp. 481–490. Springer, Heidelberg (2005)
9. Schnabel, R., Wahl, R., Klein, R.: Efficient ransac for point-cloud shape detection. Computer Graphics Forum 26(2), 214–226 (2007)
10. Skibbe, H., Reisert, M., Ronneberger, O., Burkhardt, H.: Increasing the Dimension of Creativity in Rotation Invariant Feature Design Using 3D Tensorial Harmonics. In: Denzler, J., Notni, G., Süße, H. (eds.) DAGM 2009. LNCS, vol. 5748, pp. 141–150. Springer, Heidelberg (2009)
11. Wang, Q., Ronneberger, O., Schulze, E., Baumeister, R., Burkhardt, H.: Using Lateral Coupled Snakes for Modeling the Contours of Worms. In: Denzler, J., Notni, G., Süße, H. (eds.) DAGM 2009. LNCS, vol. 5748, pp. 542–551. Springer, Heidelberg (2009)

Shape (Self-)Similarity and Dissimilarity Rating for Segmentation and Matching

Simon Winkelbach[1,2], Jens Spehr[1], Dirk Buchholz[1], Markus Rilk[2], and Friedrich M. Wahl[1]

[1] Institut für Robotik und Prozessinformatik, Technische Universität Braunschweig, Mühlenpfordtstr. 23, 38106 Braunschweig, Germany
{s.winkelbach,j.spehr,d.buchholz,f.wahl}@tu-bs.de
http://www.robotik-bs.de
[2] DAVID 3D Solutions GbR, Beekswiese 29, 38116 Braunschweig, Germany
{s.winkelbach,m.rilk}@david-laserscanner.com
http://www.david-laserscanner.com

Abstract. Similarities and dissimilarities can be found in many natural as well as man-made structures and are an important source of information, e.g., for isolating defects or pathological regions, and for finding unique points and regions of interest on surfaces. This paper introduces a new approach for computing similarity information that can be used, e.g., for surface segmentation or to guide a subsequent registration. The method is based on a probabilistic matching algorithm generating possible partial matches between shapes. For each point of a source surface we analyse the distribution of similar regions on a reference surface. In this way, we obtain a point-wise similarity rating between the source and reference shape. In our experimental evaluation we demonstrate the usability and show some excellent results on several 3D objects, like industrial CAD data sets, bone fractures, and potteries.

1 Introduction

This paper introduces a new surface property characterising shape similarities and dissimilarities. Here, *shape similarity* does not refer to a comparison of different geometries for classification and shape retrieval tasks but is understood as an attribute, which can be computed for every point of a 3D surface data set, such as point clouds or triangle meshes. Such surface attributes build the basis for, e.g., surface segmentation and matching techniques. Our goal is to define an algorithm that assigns a high similarity rating to those surface regions which are very similar to many regions on a given reference shape and a low similarity rating if the region is very dissimilar to others. The similarity/dissimilarity analysis can be performed between two different shapes, or between one shape and itself. The second case is known as self-similarity and self-dissimilarity or symmetry and asymmetry.

A. Pinz et al. (Eds.): DAGM/OAGM 2012, LNCS 7476, pp. 93–102, 2012.
© Springer-Verlag Berlin Heidelberg 2012

1.1   Related Work

Self-similarities and symmetries can be found in many natural structures as well as man-made objects. Therefore, they are subject of many research projects and an essential aspect for numerous applications, including registration and alignment, product inspection, surface reconstruction, segmentation, classification, shape retrieval, and compression. The focus of most publications lies on symmetry detection, more precisely, on approaches that find axes and planes of symmetry or extract symmetric surface parts being invariant under translation, rotation, reflection and uniform scaling. Although there are also important applications for dissimilarities and asymmetries, they attracted less attention in literature. Information about dissimilarities and asymmetries is very useful for isolating shape deviations, defects, pathological regions, and for finding points and regions of interest for registration and matching.

Approaches for detecting symmetries have been extensively discussed in numerous publications in the field of computer vision, robotics, computational geometry, etc. A recent publication of Park et al. [13] evaluates the state-of-the-art algorithms for symmetry detection in 2D images. The goal of many publications, in the context of three-dimensional shapes, is to isolate parts having one or more symmetrical counterparts and are invariant under rotation, translation, scaling and reflection. For Example, [8] and [14] suggest an Hough like approach using local surface descriptors to generate many hypotheses, which form clusters in a high-dimensional transformation space. Such clusters are potential symmetry candidates. In a subsequent step, connected symmetrical surface patches are extracted. Some recent publications propose approaches that are able to detect symmetries being invariant up to isometry or geodesic distance preserving transformations, e.g. [12], [11]. The authors of [7] introduce a framework for detecting and extracting partial intrinsic symmetries. The approach uses a Bayesian belief propagation on a GPU to compute the distribution over all correspondences of a single point, marginalized over all assignments to the other correspondence variables. The approaches have in common that their goal is an extraction of symmetric surface patches. In contrast to that, our work focus on surface attributes for detection and segmentation of dissimilarities, which is different from well-known attributes used in state-of-the-art mesh segmentation approaches [16]. We use a relatively simple approach that can handle objects with imperfect similarities and is robust against surface noise and outliers of varying degrees. The method is based on a probabilistic matching approach generating possible partial matches between two shapes (source and reference shape). For each potential match that meets certain conditions, e.g., a minimal amount of corresponding points, we increase a similarity rating of each source surface point that has a corresponding reference surface point. By this way, we get a point-wise estimate of the number of similar regions between source and reference shape. For analysing self-similarities, the approach is the same, except that source and reference shape refer to the same surface.

2 Similarity and Dissimilarity Rating

The proposed similarity/dissimilarity rating algorithm consists of two steps

1. Generation of potential matches between source and reference shape.
2. For each source surface point, an analysis of the distribution of all match configurations where the point has a corresponding reference surface point.

In the first step, any efficient probabilistic matching approach can be used that generates partial matches uniformly distributed over the space of all possible matches meeting certain predefined constraints. A reasonable matching constraint is, e.g., a minimum number of corresponding points. After the generation of potential matches, we perform a point-wise evaluation of the match distribution, which allows us to determine the type and degree of similarity/dissimilarity at each point.

2.1 Generation of Potential Matches

For the sake of simplicity, we just consider matches that are rigid body transformations (rotation and translation) between two surfaces; but the general idea should also be transferable to other partial mappings between shapes, including scaling and deformable registration. In this work, we choose the fast random sample matching (RANSAM) approach first introduced in [18] because it is very efficient, robust against surface inaccuracies and noise, and has proven to be appropriate for numerous applications (see e.g. [2], [4], [5], [6], [15]). One advantage w.r.t. others is that it does not rely on any surface features (except surface normals). In the following we briefly outline the algorithm that consists of two steps:

1. Generation of a random matching hypothesis (uniform distribution) from the input data set.
2. Evaluation of the quality of the matching hypothesis (i.e. the number of inliers).

These steps are repeated until the matching quality is good enough. The simplicity of the algorithm is also its strength, since thousands of hypothesis can be generated and evaluated in a second. To get such a high performance, the approach exploits the theory of the so-called birthday attack [3], which is an efficient cryptological strategy to generate two different documents with similar digital signatures (hash values). The algorithm repeatedly chooses random dipoles (u, v) (i.e. point pairs) of source and reference shape, and alternately stores them in hash tables using four geometric relations of the dipole as table indices (see Fig. 1). By this, it only needs to process an average of $1.2 \cdot n$ dipoles (where n is the number of points/vertices of the surfaces) until a collision occurs and a matching hypothesis is found. This results in a run-time complexity of $\mathcal{O}(n)$ for the first matching hypothesis and tends to $\mathcal{O}(1)$ for further hypotheses while the relation tables are filled.

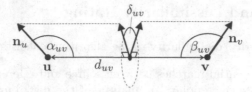

Fig. 1. Four geometrical relations of a dipole invariant under rotation and translation: Euclidean distance d_{uv} between 3D point $\mathbf{u}$ and $\mathbf{v}$, the angles of inclination α_{uv} and β_{uv} between the normals $\mathbf{n}_u$ and $\mathbf{n}_v$ and the line through $\mathbf{u}$ and $\mathbf{v}$, and finally the rotation angle δ_{uv} between the normals around the line through $\mathbf{u}$ and $\mathbf{v}$

Directly after finding a hypothesis, its quality is evaluated by performing a fast Monte Carlo approximation of the contact area (i.e. the number of the source surface points having corresponding reference surface point). If the contact area is less than a predefined Ω_{min}, the hypothesis is dropped early and the algorithm continues to search for a next one.

2.2   Analysis of Matching Distributions

As already mentioned, we assume that a generated matching hypothesis is a rigid body transformation, which can be specified as a homogenous transformation matrix. Let T be the set of transformations representing all matching hypotheses found in the step before. For each source surface point we now analyse the distribution of all transformations $T_i \in T$ where the point is in contact with the reference surface B. The set of all transformations where source point $\boldsymbol{a}$ is in contact with reference surface B is given by

$$T(\boldsymbol{a}) = \left\{ \, T_i \mid \exists \boldsymbol{b} \in B : \|\boldsymbol{a} - T_i \boldsymbol{b}\| < \varepsilon_p \, \wedge \, \left\| 1 - \boldsymbol{n_a}^\top T_i \boldsymbol{n_b} \right\| < \varepsilon_n \right\} , \qquad (1)$$

where ε_p and ε_n are small tolerance values for point distance and surface normal divergence, which should be adapted to the point sampling resolution and surface noise of the data sets. All experimental results in this paper are obtained using an ε_p equal to the average distance of adjacent points (i.e., the mean length of all edges in the mesh) and a constant $\varepsilon_n = 0.2$. Having obtained the set of matches $T(\boldsymbol{a})$, we can derive the proportion of matches where $\boldsymbol{a}$ is involved compared to the total number of matches

$$p(\boldsymbol{a}) = |T(\boldsymbol{a})| \, / \, |T| . \qquad (2)$$

Proportion $p(\boldsymbol{a})$ can also be interpreted as the probability that the probabilistic matching algorithm (of Section 2.1) generates a match where point $\boldsymbol{a}$ has a correspondence on surface B, which implies that $p(\boldsymbol{a})$ represents a quantitative measure of similarity between source and reference shape at point $\boldsymbol{a}$. In our experiments we will show that $p(\boldsymbol{a})$ provides an excellent basis for numerous applications. An example how we can use $p(\boldsymbol{a})$ for surface segmentation is shown in Fig. 2. As it is typical for thrown pottery, most of the broken cup is radial

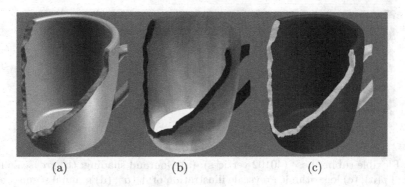

Fig. 2. Broken cup (15743 vertices): (a) Gouraud shading; (b) greyscale illustration of $p(a)$; (e) segmentation result using a threshold on $p(a)$

symmetric on a vertical axis and therefore highly self-similar. We can now easily distinguish between self-similar parts, like the body of the cup, and dissimilar parts, like the area of fracture and the handle by using a simple threshold on $p(a)$ (see Fig. 2(b) and (c)). Particularly remarkable is the fact that the top edge of the cup can be easily distinguished from the fracture area, which cannot be achieved by common thickness-based approaches for segmentation of thin-walled fragments. For a further analysis of the contact distributions we need to change the transformation representation since the space of 4×4 homogeneous transformation matrices is not well-suited for performing linear combinations or Eigendecompositions. Furthermore, the translational part of a relative transformation in homogeneous coordinate notation highly depends on the location of the local coordinate systems of source and reference shape. Fortunately, due to Chasles' theorem (1830), every rigid body displacement can be realized by a screw motion, which is a rotation around an axis combined with a translation along the same axis [1]. Such a screw motion is usually represented as a twist with twist coordinates $\xi = (v, \omega) \in \mathbb{R}^6$. For our goal it is sufficient to know that, in case of a combination of rotation and translation, $\omega \in \mathbb{R}^3$ specifies the orientation of the (screw) axis, $\|\omega\|$ corresponds to the rotation angle, $v \in \mathbb{R}^3$ defines the distance between the axis and the coordinate origin, and $\omega^T v$ corresponds to the translation along ω. We can convert any homogeneous transformation matrix into an equivalent screw motion: $\xi_i = \text{Twist}(T_i)$ (see, e.g., [9] for details). By transforming the set of homogeneous matrices $T(a)$ (defined in Eq. (1)) into their equivalent twist representation we get

$$\xi(a) = \{ \ \xi_i \mid \xi_i = \text{Twist}(T_i) \quad \text{with} \quad T_i \in T(a)\} \ , \tag{3}$$

The sample covariance matrix $C(a)$ of the twist distribution at point a is given by

$$C(a) = \frac{1}{|\xi(a)|} \sum_{\xi_i \in \xi(a)} (\xi_i - \bar{\xi}(a))(\xi_i - \bar{\xi}(a))^\top . \tag{4}$$

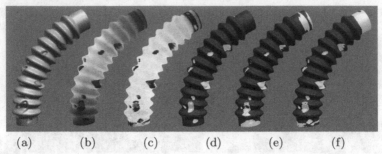

(a)   (b)   (c)   (d)   (e)   (f)

Fig. 3. Flexible rubber hose (40102 vertices): (a) Gouraud shading; (b) greyscale illustration of $p(a)$; (c) logarithmic greyscale illustration of $\Lambda_6(a)$; (d) manual segmentation of the defects; (e) segmentation result using a threshold on $p(a)$; (f) segmentation result using a threshold on $\Lambda_6(a)$

The eigenvectors $x_1(a), ..., x_6(a)$ of $C(a)$, the associated eigenvalues $\lambda_1(a), ..., \lambda_6(a)$, and the products of eigenvalues

$$\Lambda_i(a) = \prod_{k=1}^{i} \lambda_k(a),\tag{5}$$

are other significant attributes of the distribution. The eigenvalues correspond to the variance of the distribution along the eigenvectors and the products of eigenvalues are an indicator for the dimensionality of the distribution. For example, $\Lambda_6(a)$ is equal to the determinant of the covariance matrix and is zero if the dimensionality of the distribution is lower than the dimensions of the random variable. However, due to surface noise and numerical inaccuracies, the determinant is usually not zero but low. An example where $\Lambda_6(a)$ is used for defect segmentation is shown in Fig. 3. The flexible rubber hose is highly self-similar but since it was bended along a free-form curve, the symmetry is imperfect. Therefore, the similarity probability $p(a)$ of Eq. (2) is a good indicator for such defects. However, as can be seen in Fig. 3(b), $p(a)$ tends to decrease towards the hose ends. This can be explained by the fact that the probabilistic matching algorithm finds more matches with a contact area greater than Ω_{min} in the middle of the hose than at the ends. As can be seen in Fig. 3(c), $\Lambda_6(a)$ does not suffer from this problem since the variances of the matching distribution at a surface point are independent from the probability that the point is chosen by the matching algorithm. Fig. 3(d)-(f) show a comparison of segmentation results based on manual segmentation, $p(a)$, and $\Lambda_6(a)$. More examples are given in the following section.

3   Experimental Results

In our experimental evaluation we applied the approach to surfaces of various 3D objects, including industrial CAD data sets, potteries, and many bone fractures. For analysing the matching distributions we generated about 200 potential matches for each object. Depending on the number of points in the data sets, the generation of 200 matches takes between 2 and 10 seconds on an Intel Core 2 Duo CPU with 2.67 GHz. All computations were executed on a single core. The proposed subsequent analysis of the matching distribution is at least one order of magnitude faster than the match generation and can therefore be neglected.

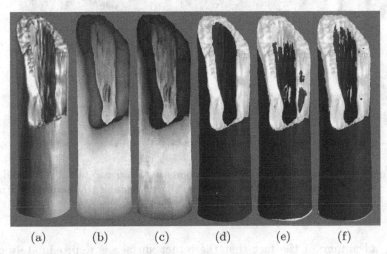

(a)   (b)   (c)   (d)   (e)   (f)

Fig. 4. Distal fragment of a femur shaft fracture (35822 vertices): (a) Gouraud shading; (b) greyscale illustration of $p(a)$; (c) greyscale illustration of $q(a)$; (d) manual segmentation of the fractured surface; (e) segmentation result using a threshold on $p(a)$; (f) segmentation result using a threshold on $q(a)$

In the previous sections we have already shown the dissimilarity segmentation results of a broken cup (Fig. 2) and of a flexible rubber hose (Fig. 3). In the following we will discuss further examples demonstrating the potential and the capabilities of the approach in different applications. Fig. 4 shows the distal fragment of a femur shaft fracture, which was reconstructed from CT data. The segmentation of the fractured surface area is an important preprocessing step before estimating the optimal fragment alignment for fracture reduction in computer and robot assisted surgery (see, e.g., [10], [17]). Of particular interest is those fractured area of the shown fragment, which is parallel to the long axis of the bone. Segmentation approaches using the angle between surface normals and bone axis fail in these areas. In contrast to that, the suggested self-similarity rating is able to identify these parts. As can be seen in Fig. 4(b), the self-similarity probability $p(a)$ results in a significant difference between intact and fractured surface. Figs. 4(d) and (e) show a manual segmentation and a segmentation result obtained by applying a threshold on $p(a)$. As can be seen, most surface parts are classified correctly. However, the approach still has problems to classify some small fracture areas on the right side of the bone, which are almost planar and run parallel to the long axis of the bone , i.e., are very self-similar (i.e., invariant under translation along the axis). In such cases we

(a)   (b)   (c)

Fig. 5. Femur shaft fracture: (a) Distal fragment (left) and two views of a small shaft fragment (right); (b) self-similarity $p(\boldsymbol{a})$ of the shaft fragment; (c) similarity $p(\boldsymbol{a})$ between distal fragment and shaft fragment

can take advantage of the fact that the intact surface is approximately cylindrical and therefore the match distributions of the intact areas offer a higher rotational variance than the fractured area. The rotational variances correspond to the eigenvalues $\lambda_1^{rot}(\boldsymbol{a}), ..., \lambda_3^{rot}(\boldsymbol{a})$ of the lower-right 3x3 submatrix of the covariance matrix (4). The results shown in Fig. 4(c) and (f) were obtained using a product of the major rotational eigenvalue and the similarity probability:

$$q(\boldsymbol{a}) = \lambda_1^{rot}(\boldsymbol{a})p(\boldsymbol{a}).\tag{6}$$

Further experiments on a shaft fragment of the same femur fracture are shown in Fig. 5. Here, the self-similarity probability $p(\boldsymbol{a})$ results in a rather diffuse separation between intact and fractured surface, which is due to the small proportion of intact (and thus self-similar) surface compared to the total size of the shaft fragment (see Fig. 5(b)). For such cases it is much better not to analyse the self-similarity but the similarity between the small fragment and another large fragment. The excellent result of such an inter-fragment similarity rating can be seen in Fig. 5(c), where the whole fractured area of the small fragment gets a very low similarity value whereas the intact parts get a very high similarity rating. This can be explained by the almost perfect geometrical similarity between the intact surface of the shaft fragment and distal fragment. Moreover, every human bone is either mirror-symmetric or has a mirror-symmetric counterpart; therefore the same idea can also be applied to a bone and its mirror-copy or to two mirror-symmetric bones.

Fig. 6 illustrates an industrial example. Like many industrial parts, the shown piston rod has one or more planes of symmetry. But the symmetry is not perfect:

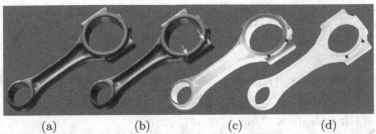

Fig. 6. Piston rod (33487 vertices): (a) Front side; (b) back side with white arrows pointing at tiny bumps; (c) greyscale illustration of $p(a)$; (d) logarithmic greyscale illustration of $\Lambda_1(a)$

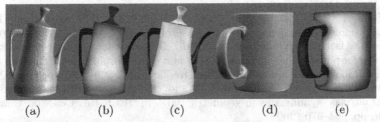

Fig. 7. Pot and cup captured by a 3D laser scanner: (a) 3D scan of the pot (48466 vertices); (b) greyscale illustration of $p(a)$; (c) greyscale illustration of $q(a)$; (d) 3D scan of the cup (132299 vertices); (e) greyscale illustration of $p(a)$

when comparing Fig. 6(a) and (b) one can see two tiny bumps at one side of the rod that can be used to define the correct assembly orientation. Since these bumps violate the self-similarity, they can be easily found automatically using the similarity probability $p(a)$ or the eigenvalue $\Lambda_1(a)$ (see Eq. (5)). The detected irregularities can, for example, be used as interest points/regions for pose estimation and localization approaches where the correct orientation among multiple mirror-symmetric solutions must be found. Approaches that do not focus on these small irregularities, usually produce ambiguous poses, which make them inapplicable for industrial automation.

Last not least we would like to exemplify the usability of our approach for surface registration and matching. Fig. 7 shows our analysis applied to a teapot and a cup, which have been captured by a commercial 3D laser scanner from a single viewing direction. These are two examples of numerous objects with large surfaces that are invariant under rotation or translation. These self-similar regions typically lead to pose ambiguities and misalignments when using matching approaches that maximize the surface overlap. In theses cases, the self-similarity rating can be used to focus on those parts which are geometrically unique and therefore are more important for finding a correct alignment.

In this paper, we focused on presenting the very generic idea how (dis-)similarity information can be used in many different applications. A quantitative analysis of error rates and a comparison with other application dependent approaches would go beyond the scope of this paper and is subject of future research.

Acknowledgement. We acknowledge funding by the German Science Foundation (DFG) WA 848/14-3.

References

1. Ball, R.S.: The theory of screws: A study in the dynamics of a rigid body. Hodges, Foster (1876)
2. Buchholz, D., Wahl, F., Winkelbach, S.: Ransam for industrial bin-picking. In: Proc. of ISR/Robotik 2010, pp. 1317–1322 (2010)
3. Girault, M., Cohen, R., Campana, M.: A Generalized Birthday Attack. In: Günther, C.G. (ed.) EUROCRYPT 1988. LNCS, vol. 330, pp. 129–156. Springer, Heidelberg (1988)
4. Iser, R., Kubus, D., Wahl, F.M.: An efficient parallel approach to random sample matching (pransam). In: Proc. of IEEE Int. Conf. on Robotics and Automation (ICRA), pp. 1199–1206 (2009)
5. Iser, R., Spehr, J., Winkelbach, S., Wahl, F.: Mobile robot localization using the fast random sample matching approach. In: Proc. of Robotik 2008, pp. 163–166 (2008)
6. Kubus, D., Iser, R., Winkelbach, S., Wahl, F.: Efficient parallel random sample matching for pose estimation, localization, and related problems. In: German Workshop on Robotics. Advances in Robotics Research, pp. 239–250. Springer (2009)
7. Lasowski, R., Tevs, A., Seidel, H.P., Wand, M.: A probabilistic framework for partial intrinsic symmetries in geometric data. In: IEEE Int. Conf. on Computer Vision, pp. 963–970 (2009)
8. Mitra, N.J., Guibas, L.J., Pauly, M.: Partial and approximate symmetry detection for 3d geometry. In: ACM SIGGRAPH 2006, pp. 560–568 (2006)
9. Murray, R.M., Li, Z., Sastry, S.S.: A Mathematical Introduction to Robotic Manipulation. CRC Press (1994)
10. Oszwald, M., Westphal, R., Bredow, J., Calafi, A., Hüfner, T., Wahl, F., Krettek, C., Gösling, T.: Robot-assisted fracture reduction using three-dimensional intraoperative fracture visualization - an experimental study on human cadaver femora. Journal of Orthopaedic Research 28(9), 1240–1244 (2010)
11. Ovsjanikov, M., Mérigot, Q., Mémoli, F., Guibas, L.: One point isometric matching with the heat kernel. Computer Graphics Forum 29(5), 1555–1564 (2010)
12. Ovsjanikov, M., Sun, J., Guibas, L.: Global intrinsic symmetries of shapes. Computer Graphics Forum 27(5), 1341–1348 (2008)
13. Park, M., Lee, S., Chen, P.C., Kashyap, S., Butt, A.A., Liu, Y.: Performance evaluation of state-of-the-art discrete symmetry detection algorithms. In: CVPR 2008, pp. 1–8 (2008)
14. Pauly, M., Mitra, N.J., Wallner, J., Pottmann, H., Guibas, L.J.: Discovering structural regularity in 3d geometry. In: ACM SIGGRAPH 2008, pp. 43:1–43:11 (2008)
15. Rilk, M., Kubus, D., Wahl, F., Eichhorn, K., Wagner, I., Bootz, F.: Demonstration of a prototype for robot assisted endoscopic sinus surgery. In: Proc. of IEEE Int. Conf. on Robotics and Automation (ICRA), pp. 1090–1091 (2010)
16. Shamir, A.: A survey on mesh segmentation techniques. Computer Graphics Forum 27(6), 1539–1556 (2008)
17. Westphal, R., Winkelbach, S., Gösling, T., Oszwald, M., Hüfner, T., Krettek, C., Wahl, F.: Robot assisted long bone fracture reduction. Int. Journal of Robotics Research - Special Issue: Medical Robotics, Part II 28(10), 1259–1278 (2009)
18. Winkelbach, S., Molkenstruck, S., Wahl, F.M.: Low-Cost Laser Range Scanner and Fast Surface Registration Approach. In: Franke, K., Müller, K.-R., Nickolay, B., Schäfer, R. (eds.) DAGM 2006. LNCS, vol. 4174, pp. 718–728. Springer, Heidelberg (2006)

Dense 3D Reconstruction
with a Hand-Held Camera

Benjamin Ummenhofer and Thomas Brox

Computer Vision Group
University of Freiburg, Germany
{ummenhof,brox}@informatik.uni-freiburg.de

Abstract. In this paper we present a method for dense 3D reconstruction from videos where object silhouettes are hard to retrieve. We introduce a close coupling between sparse bundle adjustment and dense multi-view reconstruction, which includes surface constraints by the sparse point cloud and an implicit loop closing via the dense surface. The surface is computed in a volumetric framework and guarantees a dense surface without holes. We demonstrate the flexibility of the approach on indoor and outdoor scenes recorded with a commodity hand-held camera.

1 Introduction

Taking a video camera and walking around an object to automatically build a 3D object model has been a long-standing dream in computer vision. What seemed unreachable 20 years ago is now close to our abilities thanks to the many discoveries in 3D geometry and image matching over the years.

What currently seems to hinder the use of more 3D information in other domains is the specialization of 3D reconstruction methods to specific settings. State of the art multi-view stereo methods are able to produce accurate and dense 3D reconstructions. Unfortunately, many of them are tuned to settings like the Middlebury benchmark [15], where the camera poses are known and silhouette information can easily be retrieved. One of these methods is the approach of Kolev et al. [11], which we use as a basis for our approach. On the other hand, structure from motion approaches allow to estimate camera poses and sparse point clouds even from unordered photo collections [16,4].

In this paper we aim to work towards closing the gap between sparse bundle adjustment and dense volumetric reconstruction by proposing a close coupling between the two. We build an initial sparse reconstruction of the scene with incremental bundle adjustment and point correspondences computed with the point tracker by Sundaram et al. [18]. The resulting point cloud is then integrated into an energy functional for dense reconstruction. The point cloud constraints are sufficient to define the coarse object volume. As a consequence, we do not require any silhouette information, which is hard to get in general scenes.

Vice versa, the dense surface is used to improve the camera poses following an idea from Aubry et al. [1]. In our case, this also leads to a refinement of the

A. Pinz et al. (Eds.): DAGM/OAGM 2012, LNCS 7476, pp. 103–112, 2012.
© Springer-Verlag Berlin Heidelberg 2012

point cloud constraints. In contrast to approaches based on depth map fusion, we obtain a fully consistent 3D object reconstruction without holes in the surface. In particular, the coupling between dense and sparse reconstruction leads to an implicit loop closing that corrects the initial errors of bundle adjustment due to drift in the point trajectories.

We show results on an indoor as well as two outdoor videos taken with a consumer camera demonstrating the flexibility of the approach.

2   Related Work

Apart from the above mentioned works and the references within the Middlebury benchmark [15] there are a couple of works, which are closely related to the approach we present in this paper.

Hiep et al. [9] also aims for dense reconstructions and efficiently handles large scenes. The first step in their pipeline is the creation of a point cloud with millions of points. The point cloud is then converted in a visibility consistent triangle mesh. As a last step, a variational method refines the photoconsistency of the mesh. In contrast to our approach, none of these steps uses feedback from the dense reconstruction to improve the initial motion or structure.

A method proposed by Goesele et al. [6] computes depth maps from internet photo collections. As initialization they use the structure from motion approach from [16]. The final dense reconstruction step is based on merging the computed depth maps.

Yezzi and Soatto [21] propose a method where the cameras are refined during the dense reconstruction process. However, their silhouette based approach is not well suited for general image sequences. It works best for textureless scenes where the background can be clearly separated from the object.

Furukawa and Ponce [5] describe an iterative camera calibration and recon- struction approach. A large set of patches is used to refine the camera poses. Vice versa the refined camera poses are used to improve the reconstruction. To compute the dense surface they use the method from Kazhdan et al. [10]. The resulting surface is fitted to the patches by the solution of a Poisson problem. As the spatial Poisson problem does not take photoconsistency into account, results suffer in areas not covered by sufficiently many patches.

Lempitsky and Boykov [12] present a shape fitting approach that maximizes the flux of the surface and a vector field induced by weakly oriented points in the min-cut framework.

Newcombe et al. [14] presented an interactive approach that allows for acqui- sition of dense 3D models in real-time. While [14] is primarily a camera tracker, the underlying dense depth maps can be used also for scene reconstruction. To track the camera, the image is aligned to a 2.5D scene representation based on depth maps. Multiple depth maps are combined to cover the scene. The approach shares the problems of other methods based on depth map fusion. Additionally, since there is no global optimization of the surface, a consistent object reconstruc- tion from all sides currently seems to be out of reach. A similar method has been represented in Graber et al. [7]. Instead of modelling the scene with a collection of depth maps, they fuse generated depth maps into a volumetric grid.

3 Sparse Initialization

This section describes the computation of initial camera poses C and a sparse point cloud P roughly indicating the structure of the scene. As input we assume an image sequence with known camera intrinsics. This is justified if we assume that the camera intrinsics do not change within the sequence, which is true as long as we do not use the zoom function.

To compute the structure of the scene we generate point correspondences using the tracker from Sundaram et al. [18]. The tracker generates point trajectories based on optical flow. Trajectories are generated frame by frame and errors in the optical flow accumulate, leading to significant drift in long trajectories. We will correct the errors due to this drift in Section 4. Short trajectories suffer less from drift but generate only small baseline measurements, which is disadvantageous for bundle adjustment. Therefore, we consider only trajectories with a minimum length of 50 frames

To reconstruct the whole scene we use a hierarchical approach. We divide the sequence into parts with up to 150 frames and perform incremental bundle adjustment on each of the parts. The parts are then recursively merged to obtain the final reconstruction. For bundle adjustment we use the implementation of Wu et al. [20]. After adding a new camera, we generate new points from the trajectories. Among all points we remove those with a reprojection error exceeding 10 pixels on images with a resolution of 1280×720. Fig. 1 shows the sparse reconstruction of a scene with multiple objects.

Fig. 1. Left,Center: Sparse reconstruction of the scene. The scene comprises multiple objects with complex visibility. The reconstruction contains 16125 points and 600 cameras. **Right:** One of the input images used for the sparse reconstruction.

4 Dense Reconstruction

As in [11] we pose the reconstruction problem as a segmentation of a volume into object and empty space. Our energy functional comprises two zero-order terms and one first-order term. The zero-order terms r_1 and r_2 correspond to unary costs in a discrete setting while the first-order term ρ acts as pairwise costs:

$$E(u) = \int \left(\alpha r_1(\mathbf{X}) + r_2(\mathbf{X}) \right) u(\mathbf{X}) + \beta \rho(\mathbf{X}) \|\nabla u\| d\mathbf{X} . \tag{1}$$

The sought binary function $u \in \{0, 1\}$ assigns points to either empty space or object. The function $\rho(\mathbf{X})$ is a photoconsistency measure that indicates the cost when placing the surface at position $\mathbf{X}$. The term involving ρ can be regarded as a weighted Total Variation (TV) norm. Since ρ is positive everywhere, it favors minimal surfaces. The global optimum of the last term alone would be the trivial solution. This is why it must be accompanied by zero-order terms. r_1 imposes constraints based on the sparse reconstruction and is absolutely necessary to kick-start the reconstruction, whereas r_2 is a zero-order representation of the photoconsistency and helps in areas that are not sufficiently covered by initial 3D points. The inclusion of r_2 allows to set $\alpha = 0$ in the last iteration (Sec.4.4) and it yields better results as shown in Fig. 4.

In the two following sections we describe the computation of the functions r_1, r_2 and ρ, which we need to solve (1). In Sec. 4.3 we explain how to update the sparse reconstruction using the dense surface. Our minimization strategy that iteratively refines the sparse and dense reconstruction is described in Sec. 4.4.

4.1   Constraints by the Sparse Point Cloud

In the beginning of the reconstruction process the surface estimation fully relies on the sparse reconstruction. This means that the point set $\mathcal{P}$ together with the last term in (1) with $\rho = 1$ must drive the initial surface. We express the constraints that the surface should be close to the points $\mathcal{P}$ as a voxel-wise cost that can be integrated elegantly in (1).

A point together with a viewing direction clearly indicates the object's interior and exterior in the direct vicinity of the point: the volume in direction of the camera belongs to the exterior while the volume in the opposite direction must belong to the object. We mollify this constraint with anisotropic diffusion [19] where a diffusion tensor emphasizes diffusion in the viewing direction of the camera. Fig. 2 shows the costs generated from a single point-camera pair.

To compute the cost function r_1, all points and all cameras that observe a point are considered and superposed. We use the distinctive region costs shown in Fig. 2 as a lookup-table and superpose all point-camera pairs. This way the cost can be computed voxel-wise and is suitable for implementation on the GPU.

4.2   Photoconsistency Constraints

The photoconsistency function $\rho(\mathbf{X})$ measures the cost of placing the surface at $\mathbf{X}$. If we take a patch in one image and project it to the correct surface, the reprojections of the surface to any camera in which the surface is visible should be identical to the image observed in this camera apart from shading effects. In contrast, the same projection with a badly placed surface will be different to the observed image.

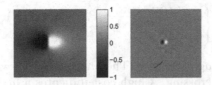

Fig. 2. Left: Central slice of the region cost volume generated by a point-camera pair. The size of the depicted volume is $24 \times 23 \times 23$. **Right:** The seed points with fixed values -1 and 1. The observed point is located between the seed points. The viewing direction of the observing camera is the negative x-axis.

We compute the photoconsistency in the image space for each camera. The photoconsistency P at a pixel $\mathbf{x}$ and depth d is computed with normalized cross correlation in a 7×7 window

$$P_i(\mathbf{x}, d) = \frac{1}{|\mathcal{C}'| - 1} \sum_{j \in \mathcal{C}' \setminus i} \text{NCC}(I_i(\mathbf{x}), R_i^j(\mathbf{x}, d)) , \qquad (2)$$

where I_i is the image of the i-th camera. The corresponding image R_i^j is a rendering of a surface at depth d with the projective texture of camera j. We use normalized cross correlation to be robust to most shading effects.

Computing the photoconsistency is the most expensive part of the dense reconstruction despite the use of the GPU's rendering functions to project each image to the surface and back to each camera. Moreover, since we work with a video, neighboring images are very close together and show very similar content. Hence, we select only a subset $\mathcal{C}' \subset \mathcal{C}$ of about 50 cameras. Additionally, we compute the photoconsistency only near the current surface estimate. In particular, we compute the signed distance function of the surface and generate triangle meshes for the level sets $\{-8, -7, \dots, 8\}$. We render each of these 17 meshes $|\mathcal{C}'|(|\mathcal{C}'| - 1)$ times. We use shadow mapping to mask out those parts of the images that are not visible in the camera providing the texture.

Like in Hernández et al. [8] and Kolev et al. [11], each pixel in each camera casts a vote for the depth with maximal photoconsistency. All votes are accumulated to yield the cost function

$$\rho(\mathbf{X}) = \exp\left(-\lambda \sum_{i \in \mathcal{C}'} \delta(d_i^{\text{max}} = \text{depth}^i(\mathbf{X})) P_i(\pi_i(\mathbf{X}), d_i^{\text{max}})\right) , \qquad (3)$$

where π_i projects to camera i, d_i^{max} is the depth with maximum photoconsistency at $\pi_i(\mathbf{X})$, and the Kronecker δ indicates whether the depth corresponds to the considered voxel $\mathbf{X}$. $\lambda = 0.1$ is a scaling parameter.

To provide a zero-order cost r_2 based on photoconsistency, we search for each voxel parallel to the gradient of the signed distance function for the point with minimum ρ. Let $\mathbf{X}_{\text{min}}$ be the position where ρ is minimal and Φ be the signed distance function, then the term r_2 is defined as

$$r_2(\mathbf{X}) = \begin{cases} \mathrm{erf}\left(\frac{\Phi(\mathbf{X}) - \Phi(\mathbf{X}_{\min})}{\sigma \rho(\mathbf{X}_{\min})}\right), & -8 < \Phi(\mathbf{X}) < 8 \\ 0, & \text{else} \end{cases}, \tag{4}$$

where σ is another scaling parameter. The photoconsistency cost $\rho(\mathbf{X}_{\min})$ steers the slope near the zero-crossing. A high cost indicates a high uncertainty in the position of the surface and r_2 will become flat near the zero-crossing to account for this. Note that we set r_2 to zero in those areas where we did not compute the photoconsistency. This way we make sure not to bias the reconstruction towards the current surface estimate.

4.3   Camera and Points Refinement

The reconstruction quality depends much on the accuracy of the estimated camera poses. The initial camera poses from the sparse reconstruction are subject to the accumulated error in the point trajectories. Fig. 3 shows the influence of the camera poses on the reconstruction quality.

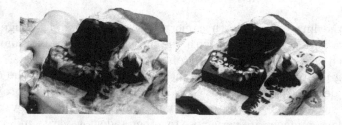

Fig. 3. Left: Dense, textured reconstruction based on the initial camera poses. The objects appear to be molten and the texture is blurred. **Right:** Dense reconstruction after refinement of the cameras.

In classical bundle adjustment, the camera parameters are computed by minimizing the reprojection error of a sparse set of points. Now that we have a dense surface estimate, we can use all points on this surface to minimize a dense reprojection error. Recently, Aubry et al. [1] proposed to estimate this error by means of the optical flow between the textured rendering of the surface and the actual image. We stick to this idea using a GPU implementation of the optical flow from Brox et al. [3]. To generate the texture we simply average the projections from all cameras.

Given the optical flow, we minimize the reprojection error by formulating the problem as a pose estimation problem from 2D-3D point correspondences. The 3D points are generated from the surface estimate such that the projections of the points are evenly distributed in the image. The corresponding 2D points are computed by projecting the 3D points to the image plane and adding the optical flow vector at that position as a correction. The camera pose, minimizing the reprojection error in a least squares sense, is computed using the algorithm by Lu et al. [13].

To account for the uncertainties in the optical flow estimation we verify the consistency between the forward flow $\mathbf{u}_{\mathrm{fwd}}$ and the backward flow $\mathbf{u}_{\mathrm{bwd}}$, and give 2D-3D point correspondences at inconsistent points less weight. The weight w_i for a 3D point $\mathbf{X}_i$ and the corresponding 2D point $\mathbf{x}_i = \pi(\mathbf{X}_i) + \mathbf{u}_{\mathrm{fwd}}(\pi(\mathbf{X}_i))$ is defined as

$$w_i = \frac{1}{1+b} \; ; \quad b = \frac{\|\pi(\mathbf{X}_i) - \mathbf{u}_{\mathrm{bwd}}(\mathbf{x}_i)\|}{\|\mathbf{u}_{\mathrm{fwd}}(\pi(\mathbf{X}_i))\| + \epsilon} \; , \tag{5}$$

where ϵ is a small constant and b is the endpoint error relative to the length of the forward flow vector.

The refined camera poses allow us to update the point cloud $\mathcal{P}$. In contrast to the initial sparse bundle adjustment in Section 3, all cameras are mutually connected via the dense surface. Hence, we can use shorter trajectories, which are less affected by drift, to triangulate the 3D points.

4.4 Minimization

To minimize the energy in (1), we relax the binary function u to take values in the range $[0,1]$. This makes it a convex problem for given camera parameters and photoconsistency ρ. Since the computation of ρ and the refinement of the camera parameters depends non-linearly on u, the overall problem is non-convex. Consequently, it can be optimized only locally by iterating the optimization with respect to u, the camera parameters, and ρ.

To minimize with respect to u we decouple the zero-order terms from the first-order term

$$E(u,v) = \int (\alpha r_1(\mathbf{X}) + r_2(\mathbf{X}))\, v(\mathbf{X}) + \frac{1}{2\theta}(u-v)^2 + \beta\rho(\mathbf{X})\|\nabla u\| \mathrm{d}\mathbf{X} \; . \tag{6}$$

This leads to a simple point-wise optimization problem in v and a standard weighted TV regularization problem in u. The latter can be solved efficiently with the numerical scheme from Bresson et al. [2]. The functions u and v are coupled by the term $\frac{1}{2\theta}(u-v)^2$. This decoupling approach allows for an efficient GPU implementation and has been used in many related problems [22,17,14].

To deal with the non-convexity of the overall problem, we employ a coarse-to-fine approach. For image sequences with a resolution of 1280×720 we suggest three levels with voxel grid resolutions of about 64^3, 192^3 and 320^3. Similarly, we downsample the input images such that the height of the image is twice the largest extent of the grid.

At each level we repeatedly minimize (6) for fixed functions r_1, r_2, and ρ. After each of these inner iterations we refine the cameras $\mathcal{C}'$, the point cloud $\mathcal{P}$, and recompute the terms r_1, r_2, ρ as described in the previous sections. We also linearly decrease the parameter α from $\alpha = 5$ in the first iteration to $\alpha = 0$ in the last iteration. The idea is to give the sparse reconstruction a high weight in the beginning while we solely rely on the photoconsistency in the last iteration. This allows to reintroduce reconstruction details by r_1 that may not have been captured at coarser levels and to avoid reconstruction errors caused by errors in the points $\mathcal{P}$. Fig. 4 shows an example how the coarse-to-fine scheme may lose details when we set $\alpha = 0$ for all iterations on the two finest levels.

Fig. 4. Left: Reconstruction using r_1 and r_2. **Center:** Reconstruction without r_1: the head of the goose is too small to be represented at the coarsest voxel grid and cannot be recovered at finer levels due to local minima in r_2. **Right:** Reconstruction without r_2: the rear part of the shoe has been separated because the point density there is too low.

5   Results

We recorded three sequences in different environments to demonstrate the robustness and usability of our approach. The sequences contain several images affected by motion blur and camera shake. Similar sequences could be captured by any non-expert with their personal camcorder.

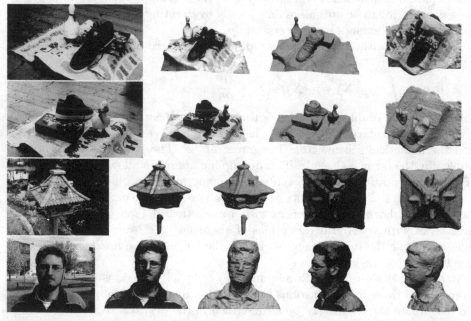

Fig. 5. First, Second Row: Indoor scene *shoe* with many occlusions. Even details such as the shoelaces are reconstructed. Grid size: $[320 \times 199 \times 249]$. **Third Row:** Outdoor scene *bird house*. Green spots on one side of the object in the textured views indicate missing texture, these parts are not seen in any image. The reconstruction of this side is less accurate than the others, but still a consistent reconstruction has been obtained. Grid size: $[320 \times 291 \times 300]$. **Fourth Row:** Outdoor scene *head*. Grid size: $[320 \times 247 \times 266]$.

Fig. 5 shows the recorded scenes and their reconstructions. The *shoe* sequence is an indoor scene with complex visibility as objects mutually occlude each other and some parts are only seen in few frames. The scene also demonstrates the effect of the sparse reconstruction that preserves details like the head of the goose. The *bird house* sequence highlights the importance of camera refinement and the implicit loop closing. While the camera motion for the *shoe* sequence is a complete ring around the object (see Fig. 1), the motion in *bird house* does not describe a closed ring. As a result, the reconstruction on one side is less accurate and the texture cannot be retrieved for the whole object. Another outdoor sequence *head* shows that we can also reconstruct objects that are not perfectly static.

Problematic for our algorithm are small delicate structures. This can be seen in the *shoe* sequence where the beak of the goose is missing or in the *head* sequence where the glasses are missing. In both cases the volume of the missing objects is small and the size of the objects in the images is small which is disadvantegous when computing the photoconsistency.

Table 1. Runtimes on an Intel Xeon X5675@3GHz + GTX580

	Frames	Tracking	Sparse	Dense $\left(\begin{smallmatrix}\text{Iterations}\\\text{per Level}\end{smallmatrix}\right)$	Total
Shoe	600	1h 32m	3m	1h 52m (5)	3h 27m
Bird house	270	0h 56m	2m	1h 59m (5)	2h 57m
Head	251	0h 36m	1m	1h 20m (5)	1h 57m

Table 1 lists the runtimes for the scenes in Fig. 5. All major parts of our algorithm use the GPU. The most time-consuming parts in the dense reconstruction are the photoconsistency computation (ca. 38%), the optical flow (ca. 22%) and minimization of (6) (ca. 10%).

6 Conclusions

We have presented an approach for dense 3D reconstruction from image sequences in the absence of a controlled environment. The approach integrates sparse bundle adjustment into a dense variational formulation to provide an initialization that does not require silhouettes and ensures that important details are not smoothed away. Thanks to the close coupling, both the sparse and the dense parameters benefit from mutual refinement.

Acknowledgement. We gratefully acknowledge partial funding by the ERC Starting Grant VIDEOLEARN.

References

1. Aubry, M., Kolev, K., Goldluecke, B., Cremers, D.: Decoupling photometry and geometry in dense variational camera calibration. In: Proc. ICCV (2011)

2. Bresson, X., Esedoglu, S., Vandergheynst, P., Thiran, J.P., Osher, S.: Fast global minimization of the active Contour/Snake model. Journal of Mathematical Imaging and Vision 28(2), 151–167 (2007)
3. Brox, T., Bruhn, A., Papenberg, N., Weickert, J.: High Accuracy Optical Flow Estimation Based on a Theory for Warping. In: Pajdla, T., Matas, J. (eds.) ECCV 2004, Part IV. LNCS, vol. 3024, pp. 25–36. Springer, Heidelberg (2004)
4. Frahm, J.-M., Fite-Georgel, P., Gallup, D., Johnson, T., Raguram, R., Wu, C., Jen, Y.-H., Dunn, E., Clipp, B., Lazebnik, S., Pollefeys, M.: Building Rome on a Cloudless Day. In: Daniilidis, K., Maragos, P., Paragios, N. (eds.) ECCV 2010, Part IV. LNCS, vol. 6314, pp. 368–381. Springer, Heidelberg (2010)
5. Furukawa, Y., Ponce, J.: Accurate camera calibration from multi-view stereo and bundle adjustment. In: Proc. CVPR (2008)
6. Goesele, M., Snavely, N., Curless, B., Hoppe, H., Seitz, S.M.: Multi-View stereo for community photo collections. In: Proc. ICCV, pp. 1–8 (2007)
7. Graber, G., Pock, T., Bischof, H.: Online 3d reconstruction using convex optimization. In: Computer Vision Workshops (ICCV Workshops). IEEE (2011)
8. Hernández, C., Schmitt, F.: Silhouette and stereo fusion for 3d object modeling. Computer Vision and Image Understanding 96(3), 367–392 (2004)
9. Hiep, V.H., Keriven, R., Labatut, P., Pons, J.P.: Towards high-resolution large-scale multi-view stereo. In: Proc. CVPR (2009)
10. Kazhdan, M., Bolitho, M., Hoppe, H.: Poisson surface reconstruction. In: Symposium on Geometry Processing. Eurographics Association (2006)
11. Kolev, K., Klodt, M., Brox, T., Cremers, D.: Continuous global optimization in multiview 3d reconstruction. Int. Journal of Computer Vision 84(1), 80–96 (2009)
12. Lempitsky, V., Boykov, Y.: Global optimization for shape fitting. In: Proc. CVPR (2007)
13. Lu, C.P., Hager, G.D., Mjolsness, E.: Fast and globally convergent pose estimation from video images. IEEE Trans. Pattern Anal. Mach. Intell. 22(6), 610–622 (2000)
14. Newcombe, R., Lovegrove, S., Davison, A.: DTAM: Dense tracking and mapping in Real-Time. In: Proc. ICCV (2011)
15. Seitz, S.M., Curless, B., Diebel, J., Scharstein, D., Szeliski, R.: A comparison and evaluation of Multi-View stereo reconstruction algorithms. In: Proc. CVPR (2006)
16. Snavely, N., Seitz, S.M., Szeliski, R.: Photo tourism: exploring photo collections in 3D. ACM Transactions on Graphics (TOG) 25, 835–846 (2006)
17. Steinbruecker, F., Pock, T., Cremers, D.: Large displacement optical flow computation without warping. In: Proc. ICCV (2009)
18. Sundaram, N., Brox, T., Keutzer, K.: Dense Point Trajectories by GPU-Accelerated Large Displacement Optical Flow. In: Daniilidis, K., Maragos, P., Paragios, N. (eds.) ECCV 2010, Part I. LNCS, vol. 6311, pp. 438–451. Springer, Heidelberg (2010)
19. Weickert, J.: Anisotropic diffusion in image processing. B.G. Teubner (1998)
20. Wu, C., Agarwal, S., Curless, B., Seitz, S.: Multicore bundle adjustment. In: Proc. CVPR (2011)
21. Yezzi, A.J., Soatto, S.: Structure from motion for scenes without features. In: Proc. CVPR (2003)
22. Zach, C., Pock, T., Bischof, H.: A Duality Based Approach for Realtime TV-L^1 Optical Flow. In: Hamprecht, F.A., Schnörr, C., Jähne, B. (eds.) DAGM 2007. LNCS, vol. 4713, pp. 214–223. Springer, Heidelberg (2007)

OUR-CVFH – Oriented, Unique and Repeatable Clustered Viewpoint Feature Histogram for Object Recognition and 6DOF Pose Estimation

Aitor Aldoma[1], Federico Tombari[2], Radu Bogdan Rusu[3], and Markus Vincze[1]

[1] Vision4Robotics Group, ACIN, Vienna University of Technology
[2] Computer Vision Lab., DEIS - ARCES, University of Bologna
[3] Open Perception Inc.

Abstract. We propose a novel method to estimate a unique and repeatable reference frame in the context of 3D object recognition from a single viewpoint based on global descriptors. We show that the ability of defining a robust reference frame on both model and scene views allows creating descriptive global representations of the object view, with the beneficial effect of enhancing the spatial descriptiveness of the feature and its ability to recognize objects by means of a simple nearest neighbor classifier computed on the descriptor space. Moreover, the definition of repeatable directions can be deployed to efficiently retrieve the 6DOF pose of the objects in a scene. We experimentally demonstrate the effectiveness of the proposed method on a dataset including 23 scenes acquired with the Microsoft Kinect sensor and 25 full-3D models by comparing the proposed approach with state-of-the-art global descriptors. A substantial improvement is presented regarding accuracy in recognition and 6DOF pose estimation, as well as in terms of computational performance.

1 Introduction and Related Work

Recognizing free-form shapes in clutter and occlusion is currently one of the most ambitious and challenging task in the field of 3D computer vision, given the typical distortions which 3D data undergoes due to noisy sensors, viewpoint changes and point density variations. This task, often recalled as *3D object recognition*, is usually carried out together with 3D pose estimation, which requires to compute the 6 degree-of-freedom (DOF) transformation between the current model being recognized and its instance in the scene under analysis. The main advantages of performing object recognition in the 3D space rather than on the image plane are the higher discriminative capabilities towards objects characterized by low informative content in terms of appearance (e.g. low texture), as well as the possibility of directly recovering the full 6DOF pose of the object. 3D object recognition is now a key step for several application scenarios, such as robot grasping and manipulation, scene understanding and place recognition, human-robot interaction.

Recently, research in the field of 3D object recognition has been fostered not only by the development of the aforementioned scenarios, but also by the availability of low-cost, real-time 3D sensors such as the Microsoft Kinect and the

A. Pinz et al. (Eds.): DAGM/OAGM 2012, LNCS 7476, pp. 113–122, 2012.
© Springer-Verlag Berlin Heidelberg 2012

Asus Xtion. Several algorithms have been proposed in literature in the past few years, which can be divided between *local* [5, 6, 8] and *global* approaches [1, 3, 9]. On one side, local algorithms extract repeatable *keypoints* on the 3D surface of models and scene [5], then associating each keypoint with a *description* of its local neighborhood [4, 5, 8], so that, by means of descriptor matching, reliable scene-to-model point correspondences can be determined. This set of correspondences is then usually clustered [5,6] by enforcing geometrical constraints derived from the assumption of rigid transformations between the model and the scene, each correspondence cluster defining a model *hypothesis*, i.e. a subset of correspondences holding consensus for a 6DOF pose of a specific model within the library.

Global approaches compute one single descriptor for each object encompassing the whole object surface. Examples of global descriptors are the Clustered Viewpoint Feature Histogram (CVFH) [1], the Viewpoint Feature Histogram (VFH) [7], Ensemble of Shape Functions (ESF) [9] and the Global Radius-based Surface Descriptors (GRSD) [3]. Obviously, global descriptors can not be directly applied on cluttered scenes, which need to undergo a proper 3D pre-segmentation stage aimed at localizing possible object instances. By means of descriptor matching, each 3D segment extracted on the scene is then associated to a model of the library, yielding model hypotheses. Hence, although less effective in presence of partial object occlusions, the global approach is characterized by a smaller complexity in the description and matching stage with respect to local methods, since each surface is characterized by one single (or a few for multivariate semi-global features [1]) descriptor. Furthermore, this is beneficial also in terms of memory footprint, since a notably reduced amount of information needs to be stored to represent the model library. These properties make global pipelines appealing in scenarios where segmentation is feasible, objects do not present high levels of occlusions and efficiency represents a relevant constraint. Since point-to-point correspondences are not explicitly determined by global algorithms, in order to reconstruct the full 6DOF poses associated with each hypothesis particular expedients have to be deployed. For example, and most notably, in [1] each scene segment is matched to a specific model view, each view retaining its associated yaw and pitch angles of the camera viewpoint. Then, the remaining angle, i.e. the camera roll angle, is retrieved through a specific algorithm known as the Camera Roll Histogram (CRH) [1]. Finally, it is worth noting that both the local and the global pipelines undergo a final stage, known as *Hypothesis Verification, HV*, aimed at pruning inconsistent model hypotheses [6], [4], [5].

In this paper, we aim at 3D object recognition based on the global pipeline, which builds on the proposal in [1] with the aim of improving its capabilities in terms of recognition and pose estimation. The main idea behind this work is to deploy the definition of a *semi-global Reference Frames*, i.e. a repeatable Reference Frame combining local and global aspects of the segmented surface S being recognized, to improve the performance of global descriptors. Note that, conversely to *local Reference Frames* [8], the *semi-global Reference Frame* does not rely on a pre-defined support size, instead its support inherently adapts to the geometric characteristics of S driven by smoothness and continuity.

The contribution of this paper is three-fold. i) a method to estimate Semi-Global Unique Reference Frames (SGURF) computed on the object surface as seen from a single viewpoint. The definition of such reference frame allows avoiding the ambiguity over the camera roll angle, thus eliminating the need for the CRH stage. ii) An efficient 3D semi-global descriptor based on SGURF and CVFH, dubbed OUR-CVFH (Oriented, Unique and Repeatable CVFH), which exploits the orientation provided by the reference frame to efficiently encode the geometrical properties of an object surface. iii) A complete global object recognition pipeline to recognize and estimate the 6DOF pose of objects in scenes obtained with a depth sensor. A main contribution in this aspect is a greedy HV method aimed at selecting the best hypothesis among those directly obtained from the descriptor matching stage. Through an experimental comparison we demonstrate that the proposed reference frame and descriptor allows outperforming the state of the art in terms of recognition and pose estimation while reducing the computational burden.

2   SGURF and OUR-CVFH

In this section, we first describe in detail the CVFH [1] descriptor, then we define the SGURF proposal and show how it can be computed on the visible surface (S) of an object seen from a single viewpoint. Upon the definition of SGURF, we introduce the novel OUR-CVFH descriptor, which relies on SGURF to yield a descriptive and distinctive spatial distribution of S, and finally the complete recognition pipeline is presented.

CVFH. In [1], Aldoma et al. proposed the CVFH descriptor as an extension to the VFH descriptor [7] in order to estimate a more robust coordinate frame that could deal with the different data properties of the models (views obtained by virtually rendering accurate 3D meshes from different viewpoints) and scenes (Kinect data with missing parts due to noise and sensor and segmentation artifacts). The basic idea is to identify smooth and continuous regions C_i – also called CVFH clusters – on the surface S to be described and use only the points in C_i to build a coordinate system while still using all points in S to describe its geometry. Depending on the structure of S, it might be composed of several C_i from which a different coordinate system is obtained and therefore a different CVFH histogram, each one describing the same surface but encoding it differently. Each C_i is paired with a (c_i, n_i), respectively representing the centroid and the average of the normals of C_i. Each pair (c_i, n_i) is then independently deployed as one of the axis of a pointwise reference frame (depending also on $p_j \in S$) from which three angular distributions (each made out of 45 bins) of the normal n_j can be computed and finally added in the corresponding histogram bin. CVFH includes as well a fourth and fifth component (45 and 128 bins respectively) into the histogram, the fourth being based on the $L1$-distribution obtained from c_i

Fig. 1. SGURF and CVFH clusters for different surfaces, left and right respectively. Cloud resolution (r) is 3mm, t_n is 0.15, t_c is 0.015 and $t_d = 2.5 * r$.

and each $p_j \in \mathcal{S}$ and the fifth resulting from yet another angular distribution obtained from each n_j and the central view direction. The total size of a CVFH histogram is 308. CVFH differs as well from other approaches because it explicitly encodes the size of $\mathcal{S}$ by avoiding normalization over the histograms. The assumption is that the spatial sampling resolution of $\mathcal{S}$ in both training and recognition surfaces is equal and therefore the total amount of points in $\mathcal{S}$ is a useful information concerning its size.

CVFH has been shown to deliver good results in the context of 3D recognition as shown in [1]. However, CVFH has two major drawbacks: (i) there is no notion of an aligned Euclidean space causing the feature to miss a proper spatial description and (ii) it is invariant to rotations about the camera's roll angle, addressed in [1] with the CRH as aforementioned in order to yield a full 6DOF pose.

SGURF aims at addressing the limitations of CVFH by defining multiple repeatable coordinate systems on $\mathcal{S}$. These coordinate systems allow, on the one hand, to increase the spatial descriptiveness of the descriptor, on the other to avoid CRH computation and matching by directly obtaining the 6DOF from the alignment of the reference frames.

The first step consists in estimating smooth and continuous clusters $C_i \in \mathcal{S}$ similarly to what CVFH does. First, points whose curvature is higher than a certain t_c threshold are removed from $\mathcal{S}$, yielding $\mathcal{S}^f$. Afterwards, each new cluster is initialized with a random point in $\mathcal{S}^f$ which has not been yet assigned to any cluster. A point p_k with normal n_k is added to a cluster C_i if the cluster contains a point p_j with normal n_j in the direct neighborhood of p_k with a similar normal, i.e. the following constraint is fulfilled:

$$\exists p_j \in C_i : ||p_h - p_j|| < t_d \wedge n_h \cdot n_j > t_n \tag{1}$$

In plain words, the surface $\mathcal{S}^f$ is clustered into smooth and continuous regions, smoothness being controlled by the dot product between the normals of neighboring points while continuity by their Euclidean distance. Differently to CVFH, the points $p_k \in C_i$ are filtered once more by the angle between n_k and n_i (the average normal of the points in C_i). Figure 1 shows the clusters C_i of different surfaces before and after the filtering stage resulting in better shaped clusters for a more robust estimation of the reference frame directions. Each C_i is associated with a pair (c_i, n_i) representing its centroid and average normal. For a specific C_i, the computation of the associated SGURF is as follows:

(i) Compute the eigenvectors of the weighted scatter matrix of the points in C_i, similar to [8]:

$$\mathbf{M} = \frac{1}{\sum_{k \in C_i} (R - d_k)} \sum_{k \in C_i} (R - d_k)(\mathbf{p}_k - \mathbf{c}_i)(\mathbf{p}_k - \mathbf{c}_i)^T \tag{2}$$

where $d_k = \|\mathbf{p}_k - \mathbf{c}_i\|_2$ and R is the maximum euclidean distance between any point in C_i and c_i.

(ii) The sign of the eigenvector related to the smallest eigenvalues, $\mathbf{v_3}$, is disambiguated, differently from [8], by taking the direction yielding a positive dot product with n_i and will represent the z-axis of SGURF. Because the normals of a surface are oriented towards the position of the camera and $\mathbf{v_3}$ is often nearly orthogonal to the surface, the sign disambiguation for this axis is robust.

(iii) At this point, the sign of one axis among the remaining eigenvectors $(\mathbf{v_1}, \mathbf{v_2})$ needs to be disambiguated. Let us recall as $\mathbf{v_1}^-$ and $\mathbf{v_2}^-$ as the opposite vectors to $(\mathbf{v_1}, \mathbf{v_2})$. Disambiguation is carried out by evaluating the difference of point density between the two hemispheres defined by each eigenvector as in [8]. Conversely to [8], though, the disambiguation deploys the whole surface S (and not just those points used for computing the eigenvectors – this characterizing the $global$ aspects of SGURF) and weights each point k according to their distance to c_i. For example, the sign of $\mathbf{v_1}$ is established as follows (analogously for $\mathbf{v_2}$):

$$S_{\mathbf{v_1}}^+ = \sum_{k \in S} \|(\mathbf{p}_k - \mathbf{c}_i) \cdot \mathbf{v_1}\| \cdot ((\mathbf{p}_k - \mathbf{c}_i) \cdot \mathbf{v_1} \geq 0) \tag{3}$$

$$S_{\mathbf{v_1}}^- = \sum_{k \in S} \|(\mathbf{p}_k - \mathbf{c}_i) \cdot \mathbf{v_1}\| \cdot ((\mathbf{p}_k - \mathbf{c}_i) \cdot \mathbf{v_1}^- > 0) \tag{4}$$

$$\mathbf{v_1} = \begin{cases} \mathbf{v_1}, & |S_{\mathbf{v_1}}^+| \geq |S_{\mathbf{v_1}}^-| \\ \mathbf{v_1}^-, & \text{otherwise} \end{cases} \tag{5}$$

For each of the two eigenvectors, we also compute a $disambiguation\ factor$ f_1, f_2:

$$f_i = \frac{min(|S_{\mathbf{v_i}}^-|, |S_{\mathbf{v_i}}^+|)}{max(|S_{\mathbf{v_i}}^-|, |S_{\mathbf{v_i}}^+|)}, \quad i = 1, 2 \tag{6}$$

This factor ranges in $[0, 1]$, 0 representing perfect disambiguation while 1 representing complete ambiguity.

(iv) Among $\mathbf{v_1}, \mathbf{v_2}$, the one with lower disambiguation factor (f_1, f_2) is chosen as the x-axis of SGURF, since the lower this factor, the less ambiguous the choice of the sign of the eigenvector.

(v) The final y-axis is obtained as $x \times z$.

Unfortunately, in some specific situations the disambiguation is not robust. For example, when both eigenvectors report a similar disambiguation factor, we need to generate two RFs, one using $\mathbf{v_1}$ as the x-axis and the other using $\mathbf{v_2}$. The most challenging case occurs when f_1 and f_2 are similar and both close to

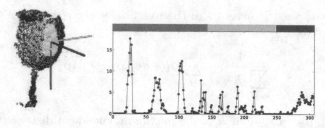

Fig. 2. Left: Point cloud (black) of a wine glass with associated C_i (green) and the SGURF reference frame. Right: The resulting OUR-CVFH histogram. Red and blue bins represent the normal distributions (145 bins) and viewpoint component of CVFH (64 bins). Green bins are the 8 spatial distributions obtained from the points in each octant (104 bins) and the centroid of C_i.

1. In this case, four different reference frames ought to be generated, including both eigenvectors, each encompassing both signs. Figure 2-(a) shows the SGURF associated with a glass of wine. Observe that the x-axis (red) direction is selected along the stem, this helping disambiguation.

The OUR-CVFH Descriptor. So far, for a specific surface S we have computed N triplets (c_i, n_i, RF_i) obtained from the smooth clustering and the SGURF computation. For the surface description we extend CVFH in the following way: first, c_i and n_i are used to compute the first three components of CVFH and the viewpoint component as presented in [1]. The viewpoint component is however encoded using 64 bins instead of the original 128. Since normals are always pointing towards the sensor position, their dot product with the central view direction is ensured to be in the range $[0, 1]$ and therefore there is no need to reserve histogram space for the rest of the range.

The fourth component of CVFH is completely removed and instead the surface S is spatially described by means of the computed RF_i. To perform this, S is rotated and translated so that the RF_i is aligned with the x, y, z axes of the original coordinate system of S and centered in c_i. For future use in Section 2.1, let us refer to such transformation as $\mathcal{T}$. After the transformation, the points in S can be easily divided into the 8 octants naturally defined by the signed axes (x^-, y^-, z^-) ... (x^+, y^-, z^-) ... (x^+, y^+, z^+). Additionally, in order to account for perturbations on RF_i due to noise or partially missing parts, interpolation is performed between neighboring octants by associating to each point p_k eight weights, each referred to one octant. The weights are computed by placing three 1-dimensional Gaussian functions over each axis centered at c_i and with $\sigma = 1$cm, which are combined by means of weight multiplication. Finally, the weights associated with p_k are added to all 8 histograms, its index in each histogram being selected as $\frac{c_i}{R}$, where R is the maximum distance between any point in S and c_i. The total size of the descriptor is $45 * 3 + 8 * 13 + 64 = 303$ bins. In Figure 2-(b) a OUR-CVFH histogram of a wine glass is reported.

2.1   Global Recognition Pipeline

The recognition pipeline presented in Aldoma et al. [1] consists of four steps: (i) segment the scene using a dominant plane assumption and flood-filling to yield possible model hypotheses therein, (ii) describe each model hypothesis using CVFH and retrieve the best N candidates views from the training views (obtained by virtually rendering the training 3D models) (iii) the candidate 6DOF pose is estimated by means of CRH and successively refined via Iterative Closest Point (ICP) (iv) finally, the best hypothesis is selected by counting the number of inliers that a specific candidate presents in the scene. Steps (ii)-(iv) are repeated as many times as model hypotheses are found by step (i).

The proposed object recognition pipeline follows the same guidelines, however, step (iii) is replaced by SGURF alignment and the metric in step (iv) is modified in order to consider not only inliers, but outliers as well. Specifically for step (iii), a surface S – segmented object to be recognized – is matched against a list of candidates $(\mathcal{O}_1, ... , \mathcal{O}_N)$ from the model library. S is associated with a SGURF transformation $\mathcal{T}_S$ (see Section 2) and symmetrically, the candidates are associated with $(\mathcal{T}_{\mathcal{O}_1}, ... , \mathcal{T}_{\mathcal{O}_N})$. Therefore, the 6DOF pose $(\mathcal{P}_{\mathcal{O}_1})$ of $\mathcal{O}_1$ in the scene is given by $\mathcal{P}_{\mathcal{O}_1} = \mathcal{T}_S^{-1} \mathcal{T}_{\mathcal{O}_1}$.

In step (iv), after the pose of all candidates for each segmented object has been computed and refined by ICP ($\mathcal{P}_{\mathcal{O}_i} = \mathcal{P}_{\mathcal{O}_i} \mathcal{P}_{icp}$), we need to select the best candidate, i.e, the one best *explaining* each segmented object. To do so, we compute for each candidate the number of *inliers* and the number of *outliers* based on a distance threshold (t_i). A model point p_j is considered an inlier if, after transformation, its distance to the closest point in S is $\leq t_i$, otherwise it is an outlier. In order for occluded model points not to be considered in the outliers count, a reasoning about occlusions oughts to be made. A model point p_j is considered to be visible if its back-projection on the depth map falls onto a valid pixel (u, v) and its depth d is $\leq$ than the depth at (u, v), meaning that the point lies between the sensor and an actual object. Otherwise, p_j is considered to be occluded and not taken into account for the inliers/outliers count. For each candidate $\mathcal{O}_i$, we compute a metric $\mathcal{M}_{\mathcal{O}_i}$ as follows:

$$\mathcal{M}_{\mathcal{O}_i} = \#inliers - \lambda \#outliers \qquad (7)$$

where λ is a weight for the outliers count. The best candidate is determined as the one maximizing $\mathcal{M}_{\mathcal{O}_i}$.

Moving Least Squares (MLS) Upsampling. We experimentally observed (see Figure 3-(b)) that both CVFH and OUR-CVFH recognition capabilities tends to decrease rapidly as the distance from the camera of the object to be recognized increases. CVFH and OUR-CVFH rely on a common resolution between models and scene data to incorporate the object size in the descriptor. Far away from the camera, the Kinect resolution is lower than 3mm (which is the models' resolution), this violating the aforementioned assumption regarding a common resolution between models and scene. To overcome this issue, we add a preprocessing step during recognition where the segmented object surface is

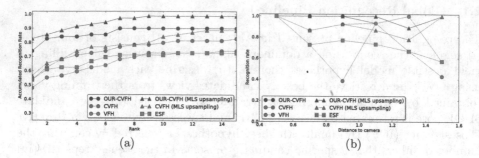

(a)   (b)

Fig. 3. (a) Accumulated Recognition Rate for all scenes in the dataset. (b) Recognition rate relative to sensor distance (computed as the distance from the camera to the centroid of the segmented object). Best viewed in color.

upsampled by means of uniformly sampling the MLS plane computed at each original point [2]. This increases the point density of the surface which afterwards is downsampled to the desired 3mm resolution.

3 Experimental Evaluation

In this Section we demonstrate the applicability of SGURF and OUR-CVFH in the context of 3D object recognition. Specifically, we experimentally evaluate the proposed reference frame, surface description and global pipeline on a test dataset composed of 23 scenes obtained with the Kinect Sensor[1]. The scenes contain a total of 69 instances of 25 models. All scenes have been annotated with the object identifiers composing the scene and their respective 6DOF pose.

Experiment 1. First, we evaluate the performance of the different descriptors regarding object recognition and ignore pose estimation. This experiment allows us to evaluate the distinctiveness of each descriptor independently from the other pipeline stages. One single run is performed over the whole dataset retrieving the first 15 nearest neighbors in the descriptor space. An object is considered to be correctly recognized if the selected id matches that of the ground truth. The rank where the correct id is found is saved and results are presented in Figure 3-(a) in form of accumulated recognition rate vs rank. For CVFH and OUR-CVFH variants, histograms were compared by means of the distance metric presented in [1]. For VFH [7]) and ESF [9] we evaluated different metrics — $L1$, $L2$ and χ^2. VFH performed the best with χ^2 and ESF with $L2$ (both depicted in Figure 3). Figure 3-(a) highlights the importance of an oriented reference frame for a distinctive description of the objects as OUR-CVFH clearly outperforms the compared descriptors (especially when a low number of candidates is retrieved).

Experiment 2. Moreover, we compare the 6DOF pose estimation capabilities of SGURF and CRH within the proposed object recognition pipeline. To this aim,

---

[1] http://users.acin.tuwien.ac.at/aaldoma/datasets/DAGM.zip

Table 1. Results yielded by the proposed pipeline and OUR-CVFH with MLS up-sampling at different ICP iterations (0,10,30), comparing pose estimation yielded by SGURF and by CRH

	#correct_id			#correct_pose			time (s)		
ICP iterations:	0	10	30	0	10	30	0	10	30
SGURF	62	64	66	57	61	63	28.1	48.5	79.2
CRH	49	61	61	35	53	57	42.0	61.3	129.0
Difference:	+13	+3	+5	+22	+8	+6	-13.9	-12.8	-49.8

Table 2. Results in terms of recognition and 6DOF pose estimation comparing OUR-CVFH and the global pipeline with the SHOT [8] descriptor and the local pipeline, both using MLS upsampling

	#correct_id			#correct_pose			time (s)		
ICP iterations:	0	10	30	0	10	30	0	10	30
OUR-CVFH	62	64	66	57	61	63	28.1	48.5	79.2
SHOT	51	61	62	46	60	61	94.4	148.9	229.8
Difference:	+11	+3	+4	+11	+1	+2	-66.3	-100.4	-150.0

we select the best performing descriptor from Figure 3, i.e, *OUR-CVFH MLS upsampling*. The first 10 candidates are retrieved and their pose independently estimated with SGURF and CRH. If an object in the scene has no recognition candidates left after the HV stage ($max(\mathcal{M}_{\mathcal{O}_i}) < 0$), the object is considered to be not recognized. Instead, if the best candidate after HV has the same id as in the annotated data and the RMSE error between ground truth and the aligned model is ≤ 0.005, the object is considered to be correctly recognized and its pose correctly estimated. Results are presented in Table 1 where the candidates' pose is refined with 0, 10 and 30 ICP iterations. Table 1 clearly shows the superiority of SGURF over CRH, this being even more notable when ICP refinement is not performed. SGURF is also superior in terms of efficiency. As explained in [1], CRH is not always resolutive and several roll hypotheses might need to be post-processed in order to select the best one (those within 0.8 of the biggest cross-correlation peak as suggested in [1]). This impacts recognition time since a higher number of hypotheses are generated with respect to SGURF.

Experiment 3. This experiment is similar to experiment 2, but uses as comparison a standard local pipeline (see Section 1) where point-to-point correspondences are established by means of the Signature of Histograms of OrienTations (SHOT [8]) descriptor. Results are presented in Table 2 showing that OUR-CVFH is superior in terms of accuracy (especially when ICP is not deployed) and its computational burden its substantially smaller. For a fair comparison, the local pipeline processes only the segmented surfaces yielded by the initial segmentation stage, and deploys the same HV stage as the global pipeline.

4   Conclusion

We have presented a novel approach to estimate semi-global unique and repeatable reference frames (SGURF) on object surfaces. By combining local and global properties of the surface, SGURF is robust to common artifacts and distortions present in 3D data. SGURF is useful to (i) design a semi-global descriptor, i.e. OUR-CVFH, with spatial awareness resulting in increased distinctiveness and (ii) efficiently estimate the 6DOF pose of an object. The proposed OUR-CVFH descriptor also improves CVFH thanks to an interpolation step conferring improved robustness. Overall, the proposed descriptor and object recognition pipeline are able to correctly recognize and accurately estimate the 6DOF pose of 57 objects out of 69 objects (82%), requiring on the average 0.4s per object. With ICP refinement, the recognition rate increases up to 91% requiring an average of 1s per object. This highlights the importance of faster pose refinement in order to achieve real-time recognition and 6DOF pose estimation.

References

1. Aldoma, A., Blodow, N., Gossow, D., Gedikli, S., Rusu, R.B., Vincze, M., Bradski, G.: CAD-Model Recognition and 6DOF Pose Estimation Using 3D Cues. In: 3DRR Workshop, ICCV (2011)
2. Alexa, M., Behr, J., Cohen-or, D., Fleishman, S., Levin, D., Silva, C.T.: Computing and rendering point set surfaces. IEEE Transactions on VCG 9, 3–15 (2003)
3. Marton, Z., Pangercic, D., Blodow, N., Beetz, M.: Combined 2D-3D categorization and classification for multimodal perception systems. IJRR (2011)
4. Mian, A., Bennamoun, M., Owens, R.: 3D model-based object recognition and segmentation in cluttered scenes. IEEE Trans. PAMI (10) (2006)
5. Mian, A., Bennamoun, M., Owens, R.: On the repeatability and quality of keypoints for local feature-based 3D object retrieval from cluttered scenes. IJCV (2010)
6. Papazov, C., Burschka, D.: An Efficient RANSAC for 3D Object Recognition in Noisy and Occluded Scenes. In: Kimmel, R., Klette, R., Sugimoto, A. (eds.) ACCV 2010, Part I. LNCS, vol. 6492, pp. 135–148. Springer, Heidelberg (2011)
7. Rusu, R.B., Bradski, G., Thibaux, R., Hsu, J.: Fast 3D recognition and pose using the viewpoint feature histogram. In: IROS, Taipei, Taiwan (October 2010)
8. Tombari, F., Salti, S., Di Stefano, L.: Unique Signatures of Histograms for Local Surface Description. In: Daniilidis, K., Maragos, P., Paragios, N. (eds.) ECCV 2010, Part III. LNCS, vol. 6313, pp. 356–369. Springer, Heidelberg (2010)
9. Wohlkinger, W., Vincze, M.: Ensemble of shape functions for 3D object classification. In: ROBIO (2011)

3D Object Recognition and Pose Estimation for Multiple Objects Using Multi-Prioritized RANSAC and Model Updating

Michele Fenzi, Ralf Dragon, Laura Leal-Taixé,
Bodo Rosenhahn, and Jörn Ostermann

Institute for Information Processing (TNT), Leibniz University Hannover, Germany

Abstract. We present a feature-based framework that combines spatial feature clustering, guided sampling for pose generation, and model updating for 3D object recognition and pose estimation. Existing methods fails in case of repeated patterns or multiple instances of the same object, as they rely only on feature discriminability for matching and on the estimator capabilities for outlier rejection. We propose to spatially separate the features before matching to create smaller clusters containing the object. Then, hypothesis generation is guided by exploiting cues collected off- and on-line, such as feature repeatability, 3D geometric constraints, and feature occurrence frequency. Finally, while previous methods overload the model with synthetic features for wide baseline matching, we claim that continuously updating the model representation is a lighter yet reliable strategy. The evaluation of our algorithm on challenging video sequences shows the improvement provided by our contribution.

1 Introduction

3D object recognition is a well established field of research in computer vision, and feature-based approaches have become increasingly popular due to their robustness to clutter, occlusions, changes in scale, rotation and illumination. In the feature-based paradigm, as pioneered in [10,18], a 3D sparse point cloud representing the target object is reconstructed by applying Structure from Motion to features tracked over a set of training images. Once the model is obtained off-line, on-line recognition and pose estimation is performed by matching the image features against the model features and solving the Perspective-n-Point problem for the 2D-3D correspondences. Given a set of correct matches, pose estimation is a well-solved problem, and various solutions have been devised [13,6].

Feature-based methods can be grouped on the basis of the feature used, *e.g.*, edges [7], shape [5], patches [17], interest points [10,18]. We share the same approach of the latter, as we use SIFT features as interest points [15]. Our choice is motivated by SIFT high discriminability and invariance towards rotation, scale and illumination changes, as evaluated in [16].

Recent approaches based on this paradigm rely on feature discriminability for correct matches and on the robust estimator capabilities for outlier rejection [2,11,12]. However, this presents numerous critical issues:

A. Pinz et al. (Eds.): DAGM/OAGM 2012, LNCS 7476, pp. 123–133, 2012.
© Springer-Verlag Berlin Heidelberg 2012

Fig. 1. Performance of our method for challenging scenes with 5 objects (left) and 6 instances of the same object (right). (Figure best viewed in color).

1. Local patterns, although strongly discriminative *per se*, often appear in symmetric and repeated fashion. Feature descriptors at those locations are very similar and thus, the typical image-to-model discriminative matching employed by previous approaches rejects many correct matches. In a domino effect fashion, robust estimators work poorly when the inlier ratio drops, often providing wrong hypotheses if the number of trials is small.
2. Robust estimators, like RANSAC [8], generate pose hypotheses without exploiting any information contained in the model, thus making hypothesis generation prone to the potential inconsistency of the matches. In [11], a simple guided sampling based on co-visibility among correspondences is used, without investigating on other cues. In [14], priority is used in the matching stage by considering only the most recurring features. However, pose estimation still fails if these features cover just a small region of the object.
3. Since features are not perspectively invariant, object recognition fails in case of wide baseline matching. Many approaches handle this by adding synthetic features the training images [12,11]. However, this makes feature matching ambiguous as the number of features grows.

Our contribution is a fully automatic method that individually solves these drawbacks by combining inverse feature matching and spatial feature clustering with multiple instances detection (1), prioritized hypothesis generation (2) and model updating (3). By doing so, our system is able to reliably detect multiple objects and multiple instances of the same object, as shown in Figure 1.

1.1   Our Contribution

We present our contribution by correspondingly addressing the drawbacks given in the previous section.

1. To cope with repeated patterns and image-to-model discriminative matching, we propose to introduce an inverse matching paradigm, *i.e.*, to match the model against the image. Since this approach is still prone to fail when multiple instances of the same object are in the scene, we introduce a spatial feature clustering with multiple instances detection (Sec. 3).

2. As robust estimators rely on a completely random sampling, we propose a consistent guided sampling named Multi-Prioritized RANSAC (Sec. 4). It exploits individual and grouping cues in a probabilistic framework, in contrast to [4], in which samples are simply sorted on the basis of their matching score. In particular, we exploit off- and on-line information on the number of occurrences of each sample, 3D co-visibility among samples and temporal occurrence frequency.
3. To handle wide baseline matching, our solution is to continuously update the model description to adapt it to its on-line appearance (Sec. 5).

In Section 2, an overview of the off-line and on-line stages is given. In the following sections, the contributions outlined above are individually detailed. After experimental evaluation, we give a conclusion.

2   Overview

Off-Line Stage. Firstly, SIFT features are detected from a set of training images covering the object. Each view provides a set of features, $S_{v_i} = \{f_1, \ldots, f_{N_i}\}$, where v_i is the view index. By tracking each feature over the entire set of views, multi-view correspondences are created and input to a Structure from Motion algorithm. The output is a 3D point cloud $\mathcal{M}$. Each point in $\mathcal{M}$ is augmented to take the form of the following 3D feature descriptor

$$\mathbf{X} = \{(x, y, z), \mathcal{F}, \mathcal{V}, l_f\}, \tag{1}$$

where (x, y, z) are the 3D coordinates of the point; $\mathcal{F} - \{f_1, f_2, \ldots, f_n\}$ is the set of 2D feature descriptors located at the 2D positions to which the 3D point projects; $\mathcal{V} = \{v_1, v_2, \ldots, v_n\}$ is the set of view indices where the 2D feature is visible. l_f is the index of the last frame where the 3D feature was detected as inlier during on-line operation; it is initially set to 0. Since 3D feature descriptors are highly redundant in case of long tracks, the point cloud appearance is compressed by using mean-shift clustering in the high-dimensional feature space. The 3D descriptor $\mathbf{X}$ now takes the following compressed form

$$\mathbf{X} = \{(x, y, z), \tilde{f}, \mathcal{V}, l_f\}, \tag{2}$$

where $\tilde{f}$ is the cluster representative.

On-Line Stage. Once the model database is assembled, 3D object recognition can be performed. For each frame t, image features are first detected and clustered on the basis of their location in the image. Each cluster is then verified for the presence of multiple instances of the same object, and possibly split in further clusters (Sec. 3). Then, for each database model $\mathcal{M}_j$, correspondences between its 3D descriptors and each cluster are established by applying SIFT matching. An *inverse matching* approach, *i.e.*, the model is matched against the cluster, is adopted. Once 3D-2D matches are obtained, pose estimation is performed with our novel Multi-Prioritized RANSAC approach (Sec. 4). In case of detection, the model appearance is updated by using the information recovered in the last frames (Sec. 5).

3   Spatial Feature Clustering

Using *inverse matching* against the whole set of image features S is disadvantageous as many false matches arise due to the low inlier ratio. Furthermore, when this strategy is used, multiple instances of the same object interfere with each other's recognition, preventing the system to detect some or even any instance.

The solution we propose is to cluster the image features before matching. Since features tend to naturally group over objects, individual objects can be isolated before matching. We use mean-shift clustering as there is no information on how many objects are in the scene. Therefore, S is spatially split into several clusters $S_1, \ldots, S_q$. Thereby, the inlier ratio increases for the clusters containing target objects, and decreases otherwise. If several instances of the same object are spatially distant in the scene, they are effectively assigned to different clusters.

Nevertheless two drawbacks exist. Firstly, different objects can belong to the same cluster. In this case, the cluster is reconsidered for matching if the number of inliers is too small. Secondly, multiple instances that are spatially close in the image can belong to the same cluster. Our contribution treats the latter as follows.

3.1   Intra-cluster Detection of Multiple Instances

If multiple instances of the same object are grouped together, matching the model against that cluster fails. We propose to detect the instances by treating them as different views of the same object under epipolar geometry constraints.

For each feature, multiple correspondences within the same cluster are created by thresholding on their normalized scalar product. Each match shall identify two instances of the object. Let the matches set be $\mathcal{X} = \{\mathbf{m}_i\}_{i=1}^N$ where $\mathbf{m}_i = (\mathbf{m}_{i_1}, \mathbf{m}_{i_2})$. Given a set of putative hypothesis $\mathbf{F}_1, \ldots, \mathbf{F}_M$, where $\mathbf{F}_j$ is a fundamental matrix, we define a residual vector for each match and hypothesis as

$$\mathbf{r}^i = \begin{bmatrix} r_1^i \ r_2^i \ \ldots \ r_M^i \end{bmatrix}, \quad \text{where } r_j^i = \mathbf{m}_{i_1}^T \mathbf{F}_j \mathbf{m}_{i_2} \text{ and } i = 1, \ldots, N. \tag{3}$$

Let $\tilde{\mathbf{r}}^i$ be $\mathbf{r}^i$ sorted in ascending order, it is possible to rank the M hypothesis according to the *preference* of each match, as described by [3]. Inliers for the same pair of instances are likely to share many common hypotheses at the top of their sorted residual vectors. To quantify the similarity between correspondences, the following measure is used

$$w(\mathbf{m}_i, \mathbf{m}_j) = \frac{1}{h} [\tilde{\mathbf{r}}_{1:h}^i \cap \tilde{\mathbf{r}}_{1:h}^j], \tag{4}$$

where w is the normalized number of hypotheses shared in the first h positions. To choose a minimal subset of size n, the first sample $\mathbf{s}_1$ is randomly selected. Then, to select the k-th sample, the remaining samples are first weighted as follows,

$$w_k(\mathbf{m}_p) = \prod_{i=1}^{k-1} w(\mathbf{m}_p, \mathbf{s}_i), \quad \text{where } k = 2, \ldots, n. \tag{5}$$

Then, the k-th sample is chosen according to $P_k(\mathbf{m}_p) > P_k(\mathbf{m}_q)$ if $w_k(\mathbf{m}_p) > w_k(\mathbf{m}_q)$, where $P_k(\mathbf{m}_p)$ is the probability of $\mathbf{m}_p$ being selected as the k-th sample. Each minimal subset feeds a RANSAC loop and the inlier set is retained if the consensus is large enough.

As a result, the multiple instances can now be isolated by splitting the feature cluster. K-means clustering is used here because the number of instances, provided by the number of inlier sets without repetition, is now known.

4   Object Recognition and Pose Estimation

Once feature clusters are established, object recognition and pose estimation can be performed. Firstly, the 3D descriptors of the model are matched against each feature cluster to produce a set of 3D-2D matches $(\mathbf{X}_i, \mathbf{x}_i)$. A projection matrix $\tilde{\mathbf{P}}$ is computed in order to minimize the sum of the reprojection errors between the 3D points $\{\mathbf{X}_i\}$ and the 2D points $\{\mathbf{x}_i\}$ in the image. Due to the presence of outliers among the putative matches, a robust approach as RANSAC is needed. However, in the basic RANSAC, hypotheses are generated from a minimal subset of randomly selected samples. No additional information regarding the importance of each sample and the relations among the samples is taken into account. We show that exploiting additional information can be highly beneficial.

4.1   Multi-Prioritized RANSAC

As a second contribution, we propose to exploit the information contained in our 3D feature descriptor to drive the minimal subset selection. Firstly, each sample $\mathbf{s} = (\mathbf{X}, \mathbf{x})$, $i.e.$, a 3D-2D match, receives a weight w_1 based on the number of training views n in which the 3D descriptor was visible,

$$w_1(\mathbf{s}) = n. \tag{6}$$

The motivation is that 3D descriptors appearing in many views represent more reliable information on the object appearance.

Secondly, geometrical inconsistency can affect the sample subset if the selected samples belong to 3D points that are not simultaneously visible. This can occur if objects have similar patterns on opposite sides. To avoid this, after the first sample $\mathbf{s}_1$ is chosen, each remaining sample $\mathbf{s}_i$ is further weighted as follows

$$w_2(\mathbf{s}_i, \mathbf{s}_1) = \frac{|\mathcal{V}_1 \cap \mathcal{V}_i|}{|\mathcal{V}_i|}, \tag{7}$$

where the numerator is the number of views shared by the current sample and the first sample, and the denominator is its total number of views. In other words, the co-visibility consistency of the samples is examined, assigning a null weight to samples that do not share any view in common with the first one.

A third weight is given by considering the temporal distance between the current frame t and the last frame l_f where the 3D descriptor was an inlier,

$$w_3(t, \mathbf{s}) = \frac{1}{t - l_f}. \tag{8}$$

Table 1. Mean and std. deviation of the number of iterations for several inlier ratios

Inlier ratio	No weight	w_1	w_2	w_1w_2	$w_1w_2w_3$
60%	39.9 ± 40.6	9.8 ± 9.8	11.9 ± 13.9	6.2 ± 6.77	$\mathbf{5.8 \pm 6.2}$
50%	110.5 ± 113.3	19.2 ± 21.0	28.3 ± 30.4	12.9 ± 13.5	$\mathbf{9.4 \pm 12.6}$
40%	309.0 ± 286.7	46.7 ± 53.9	89.4 ± 101.4	28.3 ± 30.2	$\mathbf{17.4 \pm 19.9}$
30%	627.4 ± 515.0	113.2 ± 128.9	272.6 ± 276.7	71.5 ± 71.5	$\mathbf{19.0 \pm 27.6}$
20%	1428.5 ± 1294.6	411.4 ± 395.2	1047.7 ± 899.8	302.0 ± 317.9	$\mathbf{29.1 \pm 56.1}$

Selecting samples which were inliers in frames close in time to the current one shall increase the inlier ratio of the minimal subset. Thus, minimal sampling is guided by the probability $P(\mathbf{s}) \propto w(\mathbf{s})$, where $w = w_1w_2w_3$, $i.e.$,

$$w(\mathbf{s}_i) \geq w(\mathbf{s}_j) \Rightarrow P(\mathbf{s}_i) \geq P(\mathbf{s}_j). \tag{9}$$

Given the minimal subset, a pose estimation via EPnP [13] and an eventual non-linear minimization is performed in a sample-and-test framework to estimate the pose $\tilde{\mathbf{P}}$ that best fits the matches. In Table 1, each weight is evaluated in terms of the average number of iterations needed to find, for the first time, at least 75% of the inliers and it is averaged over 1000 runs per frame on a sample sequence. Whereas in [11] only w_2 is used, we prove that w_1 is a stronger cue and their combination exceeds both. The best performance is obtained by far with the complete guided sampling, reducing the number of iterations by up to ten times as the inlier ratio decreases. Thus, our method is highly beneficial in applications where the permitted number of iterations is small.

5   Model Updating

To improve recognition performance, our solution is a model updating step where its description is adapted to the current appearance. Given a successful detection, all the inliers $\mathbf{m_i} = (\mathbf{X}_i, \mathbf{x}_i)$ are considered. Each 2D feature $\mathbf{x}_i$ is added to the descriptor set $\mathcal{F}_i$ of $\mathbf{X}_i$. Then, each descriptor set is clustered as in the off-line stage, considering both the training view descriptors and the 2D features collected within the last k frames. By retaining the training views, drift is avoided.

The motivation for this contribution is twofold. Firstly, detection success is dependent on the current object pose as SIFT features are not perspectively invariant. Invariance is indeed rather limited, as its repeatability drops under 80% for an angular difference greater than $20°$[15]. Therefore, object detection fails in case of wide baseline matching. Secondly, by updating the model description the model size remains constant, and it is more efficient than the brute force approach of adding features recovered from synthetic views [12,11]. In the latter, the increase in size and the many wrong matches generated by synthetic views having similar appearance, respectively, need additional countermeasures.

6   Experimental Results

3D object databases are usually composed by small objects on monotone background [9]. When challenging situations are envisaged [11], only recognition methods for still images can be tested. Since our system is designed for videos, we created several 200-frame-long sequences to evaluate the performance of our method. To raise the bar, we assembled a database of 10 household objects, comprising complex items like shoes or toy planes, reflection-prone objects like cups and objects with repetitive structures like milk boxes. The database and the sequences are available at [1]. The experiments focus first on the recognition of a single object in terms of pose accuracy and stability, and then on the recognition of multiple objects and multiple instances of the same object.

6.1   Pose Accuracy and Stability

For each object, we created three frame sequences by freely moving a calibrated camera around the object in challenging scenarios, envisaging occlusion, clutter and a combination of both. Four systems are compared in their performance: the paradigm system proposed in [10] (G&L), where only image-to-model matching and RANSAC is employed, and our system by sequentially adding spatial feature clustering (S.C.), Multi-Prioritized RANSAC (MP-R), and model updating.

The quantitative evaluation is given in terms of the Jaccard index:

$$J = \frac{A \cap A_{gt}}{A \cup A_{gt}}, \tag{10}$$

where A_{gt} is the ground-truth area in the current frame and A is the area of the hull determined by the 3D descriptors re-projected with the recovered pose. We avoided using the mean reprojection error as it can be non-meaningful. Firstly, because arbitrarily small errors can be obtained in RANSAC-like frameworks by tuning the reprojection error and the inlier thresholds. Secondly, because it is not robust to inconsistent poses due to ambiguous configurations. Tab. 2 shows the mean value and the standard deviation of the Jaccard index, as $\mu \pm \sigma$, evaluated over the 200 frames of each sequence. The mean value μ is considered as a measure for pose accuracy and the standard deviation σ for pose stability.

With respect to the state of the art, the combination of feature clustering and MP-RANSAC improves pose accuracy by 20% in terms of correct overlapping. Furthermore, it allows for successful detections over all frames, where the standard method fails in the more complex "Clutter+Occlusion" scenario. Updating the model provides improvement to pose accuracy mostly in the "Clutter+Occlusion" scenario. But its real benefit comes into play for stability, as it is increased by a factor of 2 in all scenarios. To show how pose stability benefits from updating the model, J is shown in Fig. 2 on a frame-by-frame basis for the object "Hexa Tea" in the "Occlusion" scenario. While pose accuracy is slightly improved, pose stability is significantly increased. A comprehensive set of sample pictures regarding the experiments is given in [1].

Table 2. J as $\mu \pm \sigma$ in the "Occlusion", "Clutter", "Occlusion+Clutter" scenarios

Object	G & L	Spat. Clust.	S.C. + MP-RANSAC	S.C. + MP-R + Updating
Hexa Tea	0.47 ± 0.15	0.63 ± 0.15	0.87 ± 0.13	$\mathbf{0.93 \pm 0.02}$
Cube Tea	0.68 ± 0.19	0.81 ± 0.12	0.91 ± 0.10	$\mathbf{0.93 \pm 0.03}$
Coffee	0.73 ± 0.19	0.86 ± 0.09	$\mathbf{0.95 \pm 0.02}$	0.95 ± 0.02
Flower Cup	0.67 ± 0.18	0.75 ± 0.16	0.78 ± 0.11	$\mathbf{0.87 \pm 0.06}$
Bear Cup	0.74 ± 0.21	0.76 ± 0.14	0.88 ± 0.07	$\mathbf{0.94 \pm 0.03}$
City Cup	0.66 ± 0.21	0.79 ± 0.13	0.94 ± 0.05	$\mathbf{0.97 \pm 0.02}$
Toy Plane	0.47 ± 0.16	0.67 ± 0.19	0.70 ± 0.16	$\mathbf{0.83 \pm 0.08}$
Milk	0.63 ± 0.17	0.69 ± 0.16	0.79 ± 0.18	$\mathbf{0.87 \pm 0.09}$
Calippo	0.52 ± 0.19	0.63 ± 0.21	0.75 ± 0.18	$\mathbf{0.85 \pm 0.14}$
Slipper	0.75 ± 0.16	0.78 ± 0.13	0.86 ± 0.11	$\mathbf{0.90 \pm 0.04}$
Average	0.63 ± 0.18	0.74 ± 0.15	0.84 ± 0.11	$\mathbf{0.90 \pm 0.05}$

Object	G & L	Spat. Clust.	S.C. + MP-RANSAC	S.C. + MP-R + Updating
Hexa Tea	0.61 ± 0.23	0.72 ± 0.15	0.92 ± 0.04	$\mathbf{0.93 \pm 0.02}$
Cube Tea	0.79 ± 0.16	0.83 ± 0.13	0.87 ± 0.12	$\mathbf{0.92 \pm 0.05}$
Coffee	0.53 ± 0.25	0.64 ± 0.19	0.83 ± 0.19	$\mathbf{0.91 \pm 0.03}$
Flower Cup	0.63 ± 0.18	0.69 ± 0.14	0.80 ± 0.14	$\mathbf{0.87 \pm 0.06}$
Bear Cup	0.62 ± 0.35	0.71 ± 0.25	0.88 ± 0.13	$\mathbf{0.93 \pm 0.03}$
City Cup	0.64 ± 0.27	0.79 ± 0.16	0.90 ± 0.11	$\mathbf{0.95 \pm 0.04}$
Toy Plane	0.58 ± 0.14	0.55 ± 0.18	0.62 ± 0.21	$\mathbf{0.79 \pm 0.12}$
Milk	0.67 ± 0.24	0.70 ± 0.19	0.88 ± 0.16	$\mathbf{0.90 \pm 0.08}$
Calippo	0.59 ± 0.29	0.77 ± 0.11	0.85 ± 0.06	$\mathbf{0.90 \pm 0.04}$
Slipper	0.72 ± 0.20	0.76 ± 0.17	0.90 ± 0.06	$\mathbf{0.92 \pm 0.03}$
Average	0.58 ± 0.23	0.72 ± 0.17	0.84 ± 0.12	$\mathbf{0.90 \pm 0.05}$

Object	G & L	Spat. Clust.	S.C. + MP-RANSAC	S.C. + MP-R + Updating
Hexa Tea	//	//	0.57 ± 0.29	$\mathbf{0.91 \pm 0.08}$
Cube Tea	//	0.47 ± 0.35	0.70 ± 0.26	$\mathbf{0.91 \pm 0.15}$
Coffee	//	0.65 ± 0.21	0.83 ± 0.16	$\mathbf{0.87 \pm 0.12}$
Flower Cup	//	0.58 ± 0.23	0.78 ± 0.13	$\mathbf{0.81 \pm 0.06}$
Bear Cup	//	0.61 ± 0.35	0.78 ± 0.26	$\mathbf{0.89 \pm 0.09}$
City Cup	//	0.53 ± 0.27	0.77 ± 0.22	$\mathbf{0.89 \pm 0.07}$
Toy Plane	//	//	0.58 ± 0.18	$\mathbf{0.76 \pm 0.10}$
Milk	//	0.51 ± 0.31	0.70 ± 0.22	$\mathbf{0.84 \pm 0.13}$
Calippo	//	0.55 ± 0.27	0.77 ± 0.17	$\mathbf{0.88 \pm 0.06}$
Slipper	//	0.74 ± 0.21	0.87 ± 0.16	$\mathbf{0.91 \pm 0.10}$
Average	//	0.58 ± 0.28	0.73 ± 0.18	$\mathbf{0.87 \pm 0.09}$

6.2 Multiple Object Recognition

To test the performance of our system in recognizing multiple objects and multiple instances of the same object, we have created two different sequences. A calibrated camera moves freely in two scenarios: multiple objects with and without repetition. To evaluate the performance of our system, a recognition is deemed valid if $J > 0.5$, as proposed in [19]. In the first scenario, five different objects are present in the scene, while the second scenario envisages four instances of the same object and two other objects. The performance of our system is shown in Fig. 3 with respect to the ground truth. Sample frames are given in Fig. 4, while a more comprehensive set of sample pictures is given in [1]. The performance regarding false positive and false negatives is remarkable, as no false negatives and very few false positives were found in both sequences.

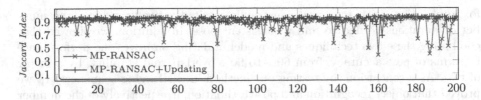

Fig. 2. Frame-by-frame plot of J of the object "Hexa Tea" in the "Occlusion" scenario (cf. Tab. 2) showing the stability improvement given by the model updating

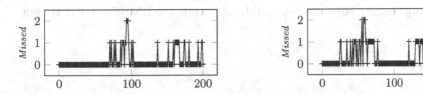

Fig. 3. Missed object detections over different frames (cf. Fig. 4): *Multiple Objects (left)*, and *Multiple Instances (right)*. All objects are detected in 169/200 frames, and in 135/200, respectively. Missed detections are due to heavy blur and occlusion.

Fig. 4. Three frames of the multiple objects (top) and of the multiple instances sequence (bottom). Objects are correctly recognized even in case of heavy clutter and occlusions. (Figure best viewed in color)

7 Conclusions

We showed that for feature-based methods clustering the features before matching makes the system robust in case of multiple patterns. Additionally, multiple object instances belonging to the same cluster can be detected and separated by ordering the features on the basis of their consistency to motion hypotheses. We also proved that our usage of off- and on-line cues for guided sampling, like feature repeatability and temporal occurrence, is highly beneficial for applications with temporal constraints, as it drastically reduces the number of iterations needed to find a consistent pose. In addition, we showed that combining these two techniques and model updating improves the performance in terms of pose accuracy, from 60% to 90% overlap, and stability, by a factor of two. As a conclusion, by testing our method in challenging sequences [1], we proved that object recognition and pose estimation, irrespectively of the number of objects or object instances present in the scene, is significantly improved by our contribution.

Acknowledgement. Research was conducted inside the BMBF-funded project ASEV.

References

1. http://www.tnt.uni-hannover.de/staff/fenzi/
2. Bhat, S., Berger, M.O., Sur, F.: Visual Words for 3D Reconstruction and Pose Computation. In: The First Joint 3DIM/3DPVT Conference (2011)
3. Chin, T.J., Yu, J., Suter, D.: Accelerated Hypothesis Generation for Multistructure Data via Preference Analysis. TPAMI (2012)
4. Chum, O., Matas, J.: Matching with PROSAC Progressive Sample Consensus. In: CVPR (2005)
5. Dambreville, S., Sandhu, R., Yezzi, A.J., Tannenbaum, A.: Robust 3D Pose Estimation and Efficient 2D Region-Based Segmentation from a 3D Shape Prior. In: Forsyth, D., Torr, P., Zisserman, A. (eds.) ECCV 2008, Part II. LNCS, vol. 5303, pp. 169–182. Springer, Heidelberg (2008)
6. DeMenthon, D., Davis, L.: Model-Based Object Pose in 25 Lines of Code. IJCV (1995)
7. Drummond, T., Cipolla, R.: Real-Time Visual Tracking of Complex Structures. TPAMI (2002)
8. Fischler, M., Bolles, R.: Random Sample Consensus: A Paradigm for Model Fitting with Applications to Image Analysis and Automated Cartography. CACM (1981)
9. Geusbroek, J., Burghouts, G., Smeulders, A.: The Amsterdam Library of Object Images. IJCV (2005)
10. Gordon, I., Lowe, D.G.: What and Where: 3D Object Recognition with Accurate Pose. In: Ponce, J., Hebert, M., Schmid, C., Zisserman, A. (eds.) Toward Category-Level Object Recognition. LNCS, vol. 4170, pp. 67–82. Springer, Heidelberg (2006)
11. Hsiao, E., Collet Romea, A., Hebert, M.: Making Specific Features Less Discriminative to Improve Point-based 3D Object Recognition. In: CVPR (2010)
12. Irschara, A., Zach, C., Frahm, J.M., Bischof, H.: From Structure-from-Motion Point Clouds to Fast Location Recognition. In: CVPR (2009)
13. Lepetit, V., Moreno-Noguer, F., Fua, P.: EPnP: An Accurate O(n) Solution to the PnP Problem. IJCV (2009)
14. Li, Y., Snavely, N., Huttenlocher, D.P.: Location Recognition Using Prioritized Feature Matching. In: Daniilidis, K., Maragos, P., Paragios, N. (eds.) ECCV 2010, Part II. LNCS, vol. 6312, pp. 791–804. Springer, Heidelberg (2010)
15. Lowe, D.: Distinctive Image Features from Scale-Invariant Keypoints. IJCV (2004)
16. Mikolajczyk, K., Schmid, C.: A Performance Evaluation of Local Descriptors. TPAMI (2005)

17. Özuysal, M., Fua, P., Lepetit, V.: Fast Keypoint Recognition in Ten Lines of Code. In: CVPR (2007)
18. Rothganger, F., Lazebnik, S., Schmid, C., Ponce, J.: 3D Object Modeling and Recognition Using Local Affine-invariant Image Descriptors and Multi-view Spatial constraints. IJCV (2006)
19. Willems, G., Tuytelaars, T., Van Gool, L.: An Efficient Dense and Scale-Invariant Spatio-Temporal Interest Point Detector. In: Forsyth, D., Torr, P., Zisserman, A. (eds.) ECCV 2008, Part II. LNCS, vol. 5303, pp. 650–663. Springer, Heidelberg (2008)

Classification with Global, Local and Shared Features

Hakan Bilen[1], Vinay P. Namboodiri[2], and Luc J. Van Gool[1,3]

[1] ESAT-PSI/IBBT,VISICS/KU Leuven, Belgium
[2] Alcatel-Lucent Bell Labs, Antwerp, Belgium
[3] Computer Vision Laboratory, BIWI/ETH Zürich, Switzerland

Abstract. We present a framework that jointly learns and then uses multiple image windows for improved classification. Apart from using the entire image content as context, class-specific windows are added, as well as windows that target class pairs. The location and extent of the windows are set automatically by handling the window parameters as latent variables. This framework makes the following contributions: a) the addition of localized information through the class-specific windows improves classification, b) windows introduced for the classification of class pairs further improve the results, c) the windows and classification parameters can be effectively learnt using a discriminative max-margin approach with latent variables, and d) the same framework is suited for multiple visual tasks such as classifying objects, scenes and actions. Experiments demonstrate the aforementioned claims.

1 Introduction

In this paper, we consider the classification problem of deciding whether one of a number of pre-specified object classes, e.g. bicycle, motorbike, or person, is present in an image. We show that also learning pairwise relations between classes improves such classification: when having to tell whether or not a specific *target class* is present, sharing knowledge about other, *auxiliary classes* supports this decision.

Our method stands in contrast to standard classification approaches that only exploit global [11] or local information [15,1] about the target class. In particular, we propose a framework that combines target class-specific global and local information with information learnt for pairs of the target class and each of a number of auxiliary classes. The advantage of adding such pairwise information is that it aids generalization. The common context for a class pair helps it being discriminated against other classes. For instance, similar classes like 'bicycle' and 'motorbike' share features that enable to discriminate both from other classes. The target class-specific parts of the models for 'bicycle' and 'motorbike' rather focus on specific nuances that are needed to discriminate between the pair. Even if in this paper we often formulate the approach in terms of object classification, the very same framework will be demonstrated for scene and action classification just the same.

A. Pinz et al. (Eds.): DAGM/OAGM 2012, LNCS 7476, pp. 134–143, 2012.
© Springer-Verlag Berlin Heidelberg 2012

In summary, our target class model combines information about:

1. global image appearance, using a spatial pyramid over the image, thereby providing context information;
2. local appearance, based on a target class-specific window, loosely corresponding to a bounding box;
3. shared appearances, based on a series of windows, each jointly defined for the target class and one of the auxiliary classes with which there are visual commonalities.

We show that all components of this combined representation can be learnt jointly, with as only supervision the class label for the training images (i.e. which target class appears in the images without any information on its location).

We have evaluated our approach for object, scene and action classification tasks using standard benchmarks, after such joint learning of the global, local, and shared components. We have experimentally evaluated each of these components individually and jointly for solving these various problems. The results show that adding the shared component is beneficial in all cases.

2   Related Work

Object classification is a well studied problem. A detailed survey has been presented by Pinz [20]. One of the more successful techniques is the use of spatial pyramid representations [11] over a bag of visual words [6,27,1,2]. One variation has been the use of multiple feature families [6,26], the organization of the spatial pyramid through sparse representations [27] or joint coding [2]. The above methods all assume a global representation for the whole image. We also integrate locally extracted feature [27] in our work.

The use of local feature representations has recently been considered for the classification of objects [15,1] and actions [7]. Bilen *et al.* [1] consider the localisation – in the form of a window – as a latent variable that is learnt jointly with other classification model parameters. Our framework generalizes feature localization as we show that instead of using one window, using multiple is beneficial for classification.

The use of multiple appearance contexts has been considered for recognizing scenes [21]. However, that work relies on using different features to capture those different appearance contexts. Recent work by Pandey and Lazebnik [18], follows this line of thought and combines global GIST features with local HOG features. Our work is complementary to these ideas. We focus on obtaining different contexts from a single feature type. Yet, our framework is not restricted to a single feature.

The central contribution of this paper is the use of appearance properties that are shared by pairs of classes. The issue of sharing has so far been explored more for object detection [23,5,17] than for object classification, where this is more intricate to implement. In the case of classification we cannot assume that training images come with the locations of objects. Sharing for classification is therefore more challenging. It has been considered in the large margin framework based on a pre-specified hierarchy [3]. We do not rely on such restriction. Sharing has also been implemented by relying on auxiliary information such as text [22] or by constructing hierarchies from WordNet [14]. An interesting recent approach for sharing used other detector information as cues [12]. As a matter of fact, there has also been work that uses the output of classifiers to learn sharing between classes [24]. In contrast to that approach, we learn the sharing together with the classier itself. Moreover, we learn not only to share at the level of a class pair, but also adapt the sharing window to the individual instance of the target class (*i.e.* the window is not at a fixed relative position for the entire class).

3   Model Definition

To build our classifiers, we make use of the structural SVM formulation with latent parameters [28]. In our model, input $x \in \mathcal{X}$, output $y \in \mathcal{Y} = \{c_1, \cdots, c_k\}$ and latent parameters $h \in \mathcal{H}$ correspond to the image, its label, and a set of bounding boxes, respectively. We use discriminant functions of the form $f_\theta : \mathcal{X} \times \mathcal{Y} \times \mathcal{H} \to \mathcal{R}$ which scores triplets of (x, y, h) for a learnt vector θ of the structural SVM model as

$$f_\theta(x, y, h) = \theta^y \cdot \Psi^y(x, y, h) \tag{1}$$

where $\Psi^y(x, y, h)$ is a joint feature vector that describes the relation among x, y and h. In our model, each $\Psi^y(x, y, h)$ concatenates histograms which are obtained from multiple rectangular windows with the bag of words (BoW) representation [27]. We use different windows to encode the 3 information channels, *i.e.* global, local, and shared. We can write our feature vector for class y as $\Psi^y(x, y, h) = \left(\Psi^y_{gl}, \Psi^y_{loc}, \Psi^y_{sh,c_1}, \cdots, \Psi^y_{sh,c_k} \right)$, where the components – again exemplified for object classification – are:

Global Features: $\Psi^y_{gl} = \phi(x)$ is a histogram vector given image x, more specifically a histogram of quantized densely sampled SIFT descriptors [13] over the whole image x by using the spatial pyramid (SP) representation [27]. For the global features, we use three levels $(1 \times 1, 2 \times 2, 4 \times 4)$ for the SP.

Local Features: $\Psi^y_{loc} = \phi(x, h^y_{loc})$ is a histogram over an image part selected with window h^y_{loc}, which roughly corresponds to a bounding box h^y_{loc} around the instance of the target class. We use a two-level SP $(1 \times 1, 2 \times 2)$ over SIFT descriptors for the local feature vector $\phi(x, y, h^y_{loc})$.

Shared Features: $\Psi^y_{sh,\hat{y}} = K_\mathcal{S}(y, \hat{y})\phi(x, h^y_{sh,\hat{y}})$ is a histogram over a window $h^y_{sh,\hat{y}}$. It is a two-level SP over SIFT descriptors. Suppose $\mathcal{S}$ is the set of all class pairs of on the one hand the target class y and on the other hand each one of the auxiliary classes with which the target class is supposed to share information. $K_\mathcal{S}(y, \hat{y})$ is an indicator function that outputs 1, if the label pair $(y, \hat{y}) \in \mathcal{S}$, and else is 0. Note that $K_\mathcal{S}(y, \hat{y}) = K_\mathcal{S}(\hat{y}, y)$. We explain the procedure to obtain $\mathcal{S}$ in section 5.

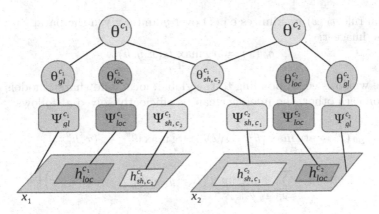

Fig. 1. Graphical illustration of our model for two images containing one target class each. Different types of features are denoted in different colors. Best viewed in color.

We can now rewrite the discriminant function (1) by including these feature vectors:

$$f_\theta(x, y, h) = \theta_{gl}^y \cdot \phi(x) + \theta_{loc}^y \cdot \phi(x, h_{loc}^y) + \sum_{\hat{y} \in \mathcal{Y}} K_S(y, \hat{y}) \theta_{sh,\hat{y}}^y \cdot \phi\left(x, h_{sh,\hat{y}}^y\right) \quad (2)$$

where $\theta_{gl}^y, \theta_{loc}^y, \theta_{sh,\hat{y}}^y$ denote the parts of θ^y that correspond to the global, local, and shared parameter vectors resp, *i.e.* we define $\theta^y = \left(\theta_{gl}^y, \theta_{loc}^y, \theta_{sh,c_1}^y, \cdots, \theta_{sh,c_k}^y\right)$ and $\theta = (\theta^{c_1}, \cdots, \theta^{c_k})^{\mathrm{T}}$. The set of latent parameters can similarly be written as $h^y = \left(h_{loc}^y, h_{sh,c_1}^y, \cdots, h_{sh,c_k}^y\right)$ and $h = (h^{c_1}, \cdots, h^{c_k})^{\mathrm{T}}$.

We use a common or *shared* parameter vector $\theta_{sh,\hat{y}}^y$ to encode the similarity between the labels y and $\hat{y}$. The equality $\theta_{sh,\hat{y}}^y = \theta_{sh,y}^{\hat{y}}$ means that the classes y and $\hat{y}$ share a common parameter vector. Not adopting that equality renders the model heavier while experiments in section 6.4 show a drop in performance. A graphical illustration of our model for a toy object classification task is shown in Fig.1. The images x_1, x_2 are labeled as c_1, c_2 resp. While there are separate class-specific parameter vectors for the global $\theta_{gl}^{c_1}, \theta_{gl}^{c_2}$ and local $\theta_{loc}^{c_1}, \theta_{loc}^{c_2}$ channels, an identical parameter vector $\theta_{sh,c_2}^{c_1}$ is shared between the labels c_1 and c_2. The latent parameters are used to learn instance specific shared, rectangular windows $h_{sh,c_2}^{c_1}$ and $h_{sh,c_1}^{c_2}$ as well as the target class-specific rectangular windows $h_{loc}^{c_1}$ and $h_{loc}^{c_2}$.

4   Inference and Learning

4.1   Inference

The inference problem corresponds to finding a prediction rule that infers a class label and a set of latent parameters for an unseen image. Formally speaking, the prediction rule $g_\theta(x)$ maximizes eq.(1) over y and h given the parameter vector θ and the image x:

$$g_\theta(x) = \arg\max_{y \in \mathcal{Y}, h \in \mathcal{H}} f_\theta(x, y, h) \qquad (3)$$

Since the windows corresponding to the global, local, and shared models do not depend on each other, the inference can be efficiently solved as follows:

$$g_\theta(x) = \arg\max_{y \in \mathcal{Y}} \left[\theta_{gl}^y \cdot \phi(x) + \arg\max_{h_{loc}^y \in \mathcal{H}} [\theta_{loc}^y \cdot \phi(x, h_{loc}^y)] \right.$$

$$\left. + \sum_{\hat{y} \in \mathcal{Y}, \hat{y} \neq y} \arg\max_{h_{sh,\hat{y}}^y \in \mathcal{H}} \left[K_{\mathcal{S}}(y, \hat{y}) \, \theta_{sh,\hat{y}}^y \cdot \phi\left(x, h_{sh,\hat{y}}^y\right) \right] \right] \qquad (4)$$

4.2   Learning

Suppose we are given a set of training samples $\{(x_1, y_1, h_1), \ldots, (x_n, y_n, h_n)\}$ and we want to learn a model θ to predict the class label of an unseen example. Here we assume that each input x_i has only one label y_i. When the set of windows h_i are labeled for the training set, the standard structural SVM [25] solves the following optimization problem:

$$\min_\theta \frac{1}{2} \|\theta\|^2 + C \sum_{i=1}^{n} \left[\max_{y, h^y} \left[\theta^y \cdot \Psi^y(x_i, y, h^y) + \Delta(y_i, y, h_i^{y_i}, h^y) \right] - \theta^{y_i} \cdot \Psi^{y_i}(x_i, y_i, h_i^{y_i}) \right] \quad (5)$$

where C is the penalty parameter and $\Delta(y_i, y, h_i^{y_i}, h^y)$ is the loss function. The loss is taken to be $\Delta(y_i, y, h_i^{y_i}, h^y) = 1$ if $y_i = y$, 0 else. Yet, as the window labels are actually not available for training the classification model, we treat them as latent parameters. To solve the optimization problem in eq.(5) without the labeled windows, we follow the latent SVM formulation of [28]:

$$\min_\theta \frac{1}{2} \|\theta\|^2 + C \sum_{i=1}^{n} \left[\max_{y, h^y} \left[\theta^y \cdot \Psi^y(x_i, y, h^y) + \Delta(y_i, y, h^y) \right] - \max_h \left[\theta \cdot \Psi(x_i, y_i, h^{y_i}) \right] \right] \quad (6)$$

Note that we remove $h_i^{y_i}$ from Δ since it is not given.

The above formulation yields a non-convex problem and can be solved by using the Concave-Convex Procedure (CCCP) [29]. Our problem of learning the target class-specific $\theta_{gl}^y, \theta_{loc}^y$ and shared $\theta_{sh,\hat{y}}^y$ model parameters is compatible with the latent SVM formulation because the class labels and latent parameters can be optimized for each image individually.

5   Choosing Shared Label Pairs

We have introduced the indicator function $K_{\mathcal{S}}(y, \hat{y})$ to allow for sharing only between the class label pairs which are included in the set $\mathcal{S}$, i.e. $K_{\mathcal{S}}(y, \hat{y})$ is 1 if $(y, \hat{y}) \in \mathcal{S}$, else it is 0. $\mathcal{S}$ can be designed in various ways. One can include all class pairs in S and let the learning algorithm determine the weights $\theta^y_{sh,\hat{y}}$. However, this approach may lead to a non-optimal solution since sharing between visually very different classes can degrade the classification performance. Including all the class pairs also leads to a computational complexity that is quadratic in the number of classes. Alternatively, one can introduce additional binary latent variables to learn which class pairs should be included in S. However, naively minimizing the loss in eq. (6) with respect to those latent parameters will always result in including all the pairs.

In our experiments, we assume that the classes that are often confused with the target class in classification share enough visual similarities with the target to turn them into good candidates to build the class pairs. We thus only activate the pairwise features for such pairs. We learn a single threshold to obtain S from the confusion tables of the validation sets. The super-threshold class pairs extracted from the confusion table are symmetric but not necessarily transitive. For example, if the 'bicycle' class shares with 'motorbike' then also vice-versa. However, it may be that 'bicycle' shares with the class 'motorbike' and not 'bus', but 'motorbike' shares with both classes 'bicycle' and 'bus'.

6   Experiments

6.1   Datasets

We evaluate our method on the PASCAL VOC 2006 [4], Oxford Flowers17 [16], Scene15 [11], and TV Human Interactions (Interactions) benchmarks: [19].

VOC2006: This dataset consists of 5,304 images with 10 object categories. We extract dense SIFT features [13] at every fourth pixel at a single scale and quantize them by using a 1024 words dictionary. We use the same training, validation and testing splits as in [1].

Flowers17: The dataset contains 17 flower categories and 80 images from each flower species. We use densely sampled Lab color values and quantize them using an 800 words dictionary. The dataset has three predefined splits including 40/20/20 training-validation-testing images per class. The ground truth pixel-wise segmentation is also available for some images but it is not used in this paper.

Scene15: The dataset contains images from 15 scene categories, covering a wide range, from natural scenes to man-made environments. We extract dense SIFT features [13] at every fourth pixel at a single scale; and quantize them by using a 1024 words dictionary. We apply the same experimental set-up as in [11] and randomly sample 100 images 10 times for training and use the rest for testing. Additionally we randomly pick 30 images for each class from the existing training sets to validate the best threshold for sharing and use the 100 image training splits to train our classifiers.

Interactions: This dataset contains video sequences containing four human inter-action types: hand shakes, high fives, hugs, kisses and an additional background class. The videos are collected from over 20 different TV shows. We describe the videos by a set of HOF and HOG descriptors [10] located at the detected Harris3D interest points [9] and quantize them using a 1024 words vocabulary. We use the same training and testing sets as [19]. We randomly pick 40% of the original training set and use them to validate the selection of the best threshold for sharing and report the performance of our method on the original split.

6.2   Implementation Details

We use a sparse encoding of the BoW feature representation in [27] for all 3 of $\Psi_{gl}^y, \Psi_{loc}^y, \Psi_{sh,\hat{y}}^y$, with 5 nearest neighbors and the respective SPs of $(1 \times 1, 2 \times 2, 4 \times 4), (1 \times 1, 2 \times 2)$ and $(1 \times 1, 2 \times 2)$ in these three cases for the images, and $(1, 2, 4), (1, 2)$ and $(1, 2)$ combinations of frames for the videos. Moreover, we adopt a coarse discretization of the latent space $\mathcal{H}$ by forcing the corners to lie on an 8×8 spatial grid and at the boundaries of 32 equal temporal intervals in the case of videos. Our inference and learning algorithms scale linearly with the number of possible windows, thus this discretization significantly shortens the computation times. As our experiments have shown, defining $\mathcal{H}$ at pixel resolution did not substantially improve the classification performance.

6.3   Baselines

In order to evaluate the contribution of the global (gl), local (loc) and shared (sh) features, we report the classification results for each of these feature types individually, and also for their combinations, *i.e.* gl+loc, gl+sh, loc+sh and gl+loc+sh. We refer to gl and loc as the baselines, corresponding to the work by [27] and [1], resp.

6.4   Results

The results for the baselines and the proposed methods are depicted in Table 1. It shows that the best feature selection always includes the shared features. Some examples of inferred local and shared windows are illustrated in Fig. 2. We provide further details about the selected class pairs and corresponding confusion matrices in the supplementary material.

VOC2006: We can observe from Table 1 that using the shared features is always useful. We obtain the best classification accuracy for the configuration 'gl+sh'. This setting improves the baseline method by 3.39%. We compare our algorithm with three additional baselines as shown in Table 2 with the respective 'gl+asym sh', 'sh with gl' and 'gl+full sh'. For the first one, we do not enforce the symmetry constraint $\theta_{sh,\hat{y}}^y = \theta_{sh,y}^{\hat{y}}$. Although this model has a parameter vector with higher dimension, 'gl+sh' still performs better. For the second baseline, in addition to the global features, we use the whole image for sharing by setting all h_{sh} to

Table 1. Classification results. The results are given as the classification accuracy averaged over the different target classes, in percentages. For the Flowers17 and Scene15 datasets the standard deviation of the accuracy is also given.

		VOC2006 [4]	Flowers17 [16]	Scene15 [11]	Interactions [19]
Baselines	gl[27]	53.83	65.58±4.33	75.93±1.95	34.40
	loc [1]	54.82	63.14±4.01	74.42±1.54	35.20
Ours	gl+loc	54.55	68.72±3.15	77.32±1.92	37.20
	loc+sh	55.16	65.19±5.06	75.16±2.53	37.60
	gl+sh	**58.21**	66.08±3.95	76.47±1.65	**40.00**
	gl+loc+sh	57.59	**71.08±0.68**	**77.45±1.54**	**40.00**

Table 2. The results for three additional baselines

gl+sh	gl+asym sh	sh with gl	gl+full sh
58.21	57.64	49.62	58.06

Fig. 2. Some inferred windows for images from VOC2006. Each row consists of two samples for a 'label 1' and a 'label 2' class. Green and blue windows correspond to h_{loc}^1 and h_{loc}^2 for the labels 1 and 2, resp. Yellow windows indicate those for the shared label pairs $h_{sh,2}^1$.

the entire image size. The result obtained from the second baseline shows that sharing information through smaller learnt windows is beneficial. For the third one, 'gl+full sh', we use all the class pairs to share, i.e. $K_S(y, \hat{y}) = 1$ for all $(y, \hat{y})$ pairs with $\hat{y} \neq y$. The result shows that sharing with all the label pairs results in inferior performance.

Flowers17: We obtain an improvement of 5.5% using the combined configuration of the 'gl+loc+sh' model. This is interesting as the dataset involves difficult, fine-grained (subclass) classification, suggesting that the sharing framework better exploits the subtle differences between classes. Adding the shared part of the model always came out to be beneficial and enhance the classification performance.

Scene15: In this case, we obtain an improvement of 1.52% in the mean classification accuracy. Yet, this improvement is smaller than for object classification. This may be because the classes are rather different from each other and sharing visual features therefore holds less promise.

Interactions: In this dataset we obtain an improvement of 4.8% over the baseline method. Again, the accuracy for classifying actions in these videos was improved by adding shared features. This is interesting as the nature of the dataset is quite different from the image classification datasets. The localization here is purely temporal.

7   Conclusion

This paper provides a method for improved visual classification by sharing localized features between selected pairs of classes. We proposed the combined use of global, local, and shared windows. The experimental evaluation has shown that this framework is applicable to a variety of visual classification tasks such as the classification of objects, scenes and actions. Though we have limited the approach to learning pairwise class relations in this paper, the idea could be extended to sharing among larger class groupings by exploiting hierarchical class taxonomies. In the future, we would like to explore this idea further. We also plan to allow for the presence of multiple target classes by considering the recently proposed multilabel structured output techniques [8].

Acknowledgments. This work was supported by the EU Project FP7 AXES ICT-269980.

References

1. Bilen, H., Namboodiri, V.P., Van Gool, L.J.: Object and Action Classification with Latent Variables. In: BMVC (2011)
2. Boureau, Y., Le Roux, N., Bach, F., Ponce, J., LeCun, Y.: Ask the locals: multi-way local pooling for image recognition. In: ICCV. IEEE (2011)
3. Dekel, O., Keshet, J., Singer, Y.: Large margin hierarchical classification. In: International Conference on Machine Learning (ICML), pp. 27–35 (2004)
4. Everingham, M., Zisserman, A., Williams, C.K.I., Van Gool, L.: The PASCAL Visual Object Classes Challenge 2006 (VOC 2006) Results (2006),
http://www.pascal-network.org/challenges/VOC/voc2006/results.pdf

5. Fergus, R., Bernal, H., Weiss, Y., Torralba, A.: Semantic Label Sharing for Learning with Many Categories. In: Daniilidis, K., Maragos, P., Paragios, N. (eds.) ECCV 2010, Part I. LNCS, vol. 6311, pp. 762–775. Springer, Heidelberg (2010)
6. Gehler, P.V., Nowozin, S.: On feature combination for multiclass object classification. In: ICCV, pp. 221–228 (2009)
7. Hoai, M., Lan, Z.Z., De la Torre, F.: Joint segmentation and classification of human actions in video. In: CVPR (2011)
8. Lampert, C., Austria, I.: Maximum margin multi-label structured prediction (2011)
9. Laptev, I., Lindeberg, T.: Space-time interest points. In: ICCV, pp. 432–439 (2003)
10. Laptev, I., Marszałek, M., Schmid, C., Rozenfeld, B.: Learning realistic human actions from movies. In: CVPR (2008)
11. Lazebnik, S., Schmid, C., Ponce, J.: Beyond bags of features: Spatial pyramid matching for recognizing natural scene categories. In: CVPR, pp. 2169–2178 (2006)
12. Li, L.-J., Su, H., Xing, E.P., Fei-Fei, L.: Object bank: A high-level image representation for scene classification & semantic feature sparsification. In: Advances in Neural Information Processing Systems, NIPS (2010)
13. Lowe, D.: Object recognition from local scale-invariant features. In: ICCV, p. 1150 (1999)
14. Marszałek, M., Schmid, C.: Semantic hierarchies for visual object recognition. In: CVPR (2007)
15. Nguyen, M.H., Torresani, L., De la Torre, F., Rother, C.: Weakly supervised discriminative localization and classification: a joint learning process. In: ICCV (2009)
16. Nilsback, M.E., Zisserman, A.: A visual vocabulary for flower classification. In: CVPR, vol. 2, pp. 1447–1454 (2006)
17. Opelt, A., Pinz, A., Zisserman, A.: Incremental learning of object detectors using a visual shape alphabet. In: CVPR, pp. 3–10 (2006)
18. Pandey, M., Lazebnik, S.: Scene recognition and weakly supervised object localization with deformable part-based models. In: ICCV (2011)
19. Patron, A., Marszalek, M., Zisserman, A., Reid, I.D.: High five: Recognising human interactions in tv shows. In: BMVC, pp. 1–11 (2010)
20. Pinz, A.: Object categorization. Foundations and Trends in Computer Graphics and Vision 1(4) (2005)
21. Quattoni, A., Torralba, A.: Recognizing indoor scenes. In: CVPR (2009)
22. Sadeghi, M.A., Farhadi, A.: Recognition using visual phrases. In: CVPR (2011)
23. Salakhutdinov, R., Torralba, A., Tenenbaum, J.: Learning to share visual appearance for multiclass object detection. In: CVPR (2011)
24. Torresani, L., Szummer, M., Fitzgibbon, A.: Efficient Object Category Recognition Using Classemes. In: Daniilidis, K., Maragos, P., Paragios, N. (eds.) ECCV 2010, Part I. LNCS, vol. 6311, pp. 776–789. Springer, Heidelberg (2010)
25. Tsochantaridis, I., Hofmann, T., Joachims, T., Altun, Y.: Support vector machine learning for interdependent and structured output spaces. In: International Conference on Machine Learning (ICML), pp. 104–112 (2004)
26. Vedaldi, A., Gulshan, V., Varma, M., Zisserman, A.: Multiple kernels for object detection. In: ICCV, pp. 606–613 (2009)
27. Wang, J., Yang, J., Yu, K., Lv, F., Huang, T.S., Gong, Y.: Locality-constrained linear coding for image classification. In: CVPR, pp. 3360–3367 (2010)
28. Yu, C.N.J., Joachims, T.: Learning structural svms with latent variables. In: International Conference on Machine Learning (ICML), pp. 1169–1176. ACM (2009)
29. Yuille, A., Rangarajan, A.: The concave-convex procedure. Neural Computation 15(4), 915–936 (2003)

Object Detection in Multi-view X-Ray Images

Thorsten Franzel, Uwe Schmidt, and Stefan Roth

Department of Computer Science, TU Darmstadt

Abstract. Motivated by aiding human operators in the detection of dangerous objects in passenger luggage, such as in airports, we develop an automatic object detection approach for multi-view X-ray image data. We make three main contributions: First, we systematically analyze the appearance variations of objects in X-ray images from inspection systems. We then address these variations by adapting standard appearance-based object detection approaches to the specifics of dual-energy X-ray data and the inspection scenario itself. To that end we reduce projection distortions, extend the feature representation, and address both in-plane and out-of-plane object rotations, which are a key challenge compared to many detection tasks in photographic images. Finally, we propose a novel multi-view (multi-camera) detection approach that combines single-view detections from multiple views and takes advantage of the mutual reinforcement of geometrically consistent hypotheses. While our multi-view approach can be used atop arbitrary single-view detectors, thus also for multi-camera detection in photographic images, we evaluate our method on detecting handguns in carry-on luggage. Our results show significant performance gains from all components.

1 Introduction

Inspection of passenger luggage for dangerous objects is commonplace to increase security in public transportation, especially at airports all around the world (*cf.* [18]). This task is usually carried out by human operators, who search for forbidden objects using X-ray images of the luggage. However, their detection performance can vary substantially as they get tired or distracted. Therefore, computer-based automatic object detection is a promising approach, since it does not suffer from these human limitations. Even though detection of explosives based on material properties is already used in practice, appearance-based detection of objects in X-ray images is not yet common.

In this work, we employ appearance-based object detection approaches that were developed for photographic images, and adapt them to the specific properties of *dual-energy* image data (*cf.* [18]), as acquired by modern X-ray luggage inspection systems. We analyze different sources of object appearance variations that make detecting objects difficult and show how to address them. Specifically, we reduce distortions from the scanner geometry and adapt the feature representation to the specifics of dual-energy X-ray data. We show that single-view detection is significantly influenced by the applied methods. The key challenge, however, stems from the fact that – unlike many object categories in photographic images – dangerous objects may occur in the luggage

A. Pinz et al. (Eds.): DAGM/OAGM 2012, LNCS 7476, pp. 144–154, 2012.
© Springer-Verlag Berlin Heidelberg 2012

Fig. 1. Multi-view X-ray data example. 4 false color images from dual-energy input.

at any orientation. We first address in-plane rotations using an efficient non-maximum suppression scheme. Moreover, we specifically focus on the challenge of unfavorable viewpoints due to out-of-plane rotations by exploiting multiple views of the passenger luggage, as provided by modern X-ray systems (Fig. 1). Our main contribution is a multi-view (multi-camera) detection approach that combines independent detections from all available views, which we demonstrate to significantly improve detection performance in comparison to single-view detection.

We evaluate our approach on the task of detecting handguns in carry-on luggage using a challenging large-scale dataset of different bags, some of which contain handguns of various types. Although particularly motivated by the task of screening luggage for dangerous objects in the context of airport security, our multi-view detector is not limited to this scenario, and can be used atop arbitrary single-view detectors as long as the imaging geometry of the multi-camera setup is known.

Related Work. It is important to note that our notion of multi-view detection differs from that in the majority of previous work, which aims to detect object classes from arbitrary viewpoints in a given *single input image* [12,14,15]. Our multi-view detector also addresses this challenge, but additionally aims to do so given *multiple input images* (*e.g.*, Fig. 1). To that end we take as input the detections from the individual input images (object location and classifier confidence) and fuse them in a voting-based scheme. There is surprisingly little work that considers object detection from multiple input images – also called multi-camera object detection. Recent exceptions [10,11] consider multi-camera detection and tracking in traffic scenes; they exploit geometric properties of the 3D scene, such as ground plane assumptions, temporal background subtraction *etc.*, which are not appropriate for X-ray inspection.

Most closely related to our application scenario is the work of Mery [6], which uses object detection in multiple X-ray views for luggage screening. Detection (*e.g.*, of razor blades) is conducted by comparing a single SIFT [5] descriptor of a reference object to SIFT descriptors of pre-segmented proposal regions in the image. Detections from different views are combined by tracking sparse SIFT features across images. However, [6] only shows results for simple scenes/bags with little clutter to occlude objects of interest and to interfere with reliable feature extraction (in contrast to our work, *cf*. Fig. 7c); furthermore, it is based on ad-hoc, domain-specific segmentation as a preprocessing step. Unlike Riffo and Mery [9], we are constrained by the geometry of existing X-ray inspection systems and thus assume a fixed number of views beyond our control.

 · Our multi-view fusion/verification approach is related to Ommer and Malik [8], who address object scale as an unknown variable and as a result obtain a line in voting space. They cluster lines to find votes that agree on scales. In the same spirit, we represent

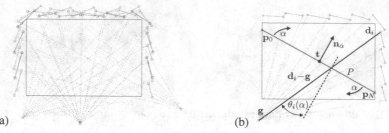

(a)   (b)

Fig. 2. X-ray imaging and preprocessing. *(a)* Arrangement of the four X-ray generators and detectors in the inspection system (color-matched): The detectors are grouped in multiple banks of 64 pixels each. The dotted lines depict the rays between the generators and the first/last pixels in each detector bank. The tunnel is denoted by the black rectangle. *(b)* Illustration of the reprojection approach from individual detector banks to virtual image plane/line (see text); the red line shows the optimized reprojection plane. *Actual geometry differs slightly from this illustration.*

detections from all 2D views with unknown depth to the camera as lines in 3D space; intersecting lines therefore denote detections that agree on 3D object locations.

Although our multi-view approach is not limited to specific single-view detectors to generate detections in each of the input views, we use a standard sliding-window approach with HOG features [1] as the basis. This detector has shown to lead to robust detection results across a wide range of object classes and scenarios, and serves as the backbone of many state-of-the-art systems [4,16]. We here adapt this basic detector to dual-energy X-ray data.

2   Data Acquisition and Preprocessing

The focus of this paper is on detecting dangerous objects in passenger carry-on luggage in the context of airport security check points. Since there is no suitable public dataset available for this task, we recorded one in collaboration with the *German Federal Police* to ensure realism of the data. The recorded X-ray image data contains about 25 different types of real *handguns* placed (randomly and also deliberately concealed) in realistic carry-on luggage. The X-ray inspection system records 4 images of the bag from different viewing angles while it passes through the tunnel (Fig. 2a). Therefore, each *scan* consists of 4 images representing the views of the tunnel (3D scene). The inspection system records with a *dual energy* method: This yields two grayscale X-ray image channels corresponding to a low and a high X-ray energy level, and additional three RGB false-color channels, primarily for visualization, where the colors denote material properties (Fig. 3). In total, we recorded 770 scans of which 652 contain a weapon. All guns in the dataset were annotated with rectangular bounding boxes, which are aligned to the barrel of the gun.

2.1   Image Preprocessing for Distortion Reduction

As can be seen in Fig. 3, the recorded X-ray images appear somewhat distorted (*cf.* the handgun or the bottle opener). This stems from the non-standard imaging process of the

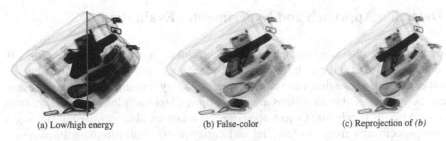

(a) Low/high energy   (b) False-color   (c) Reprojection of *(b)*

Fig. 3. X-ray image example. *(a)* Low and high-energy image pair (high energy left of red line) with associated false-color image *(b)*. The effect of reprojection (view 1) is shown in *(c)*.

X-ray inspection system. While this does not pose a major issue for manual inspection, it may significantly affect appearance-based automatic detection approaches as used here. We thus aim to reduce these effects.

As illustrated in Fig. 2a, each of the four 2D X-ray images that comprise each scan are obtained with a 1D fan-shaped line scanner/camera that captures one image row at a time with a perspective projection, while the belt moves the bag along the inspection tunnel. Furthermore, the pixels of the line scanner are not arranged on a straight line, but around the tunnel in an "L"- or "U"-shaped fashion. The combination of these effects leads to the perceived distortion. To alleviate this, we reproject each image row onto a plane in 3D space, which is chosen to approximate the properties of an orthographic projection as best as possible (*i.e.* an orthogonal intersection of rays with image plane), thus leading to a small amount of distortion no matter where the object is located in the bag. The X-ray inspection system is calibrated ahead of time; we thus assume the belt speed and 3D positions of all X-ray generators and detectors (pixels) to be known.

We define the reprojection plane P as the set of all points $\mathbf{x}$ such that $(\mathbf{x} - \mathbf{t})^{\mathrm{T}} \mathbf{n}_\alpha = 0$, where the normal vector $\mathbf{n}_\alpha = [\sin(\alpha), \cos(\alpha), 0]^{\mathrm{T}}$ is parametrized by the rotation angle α around the center of the scanner tunnel $\mathbf{t}$ (Fig. 2b). The normal vector $\mathbf{n}_\alpha$ is defined as perpendicular to the Z axis, since the individual detector banks for a given view all approximately have the same Z coordinates (up to manufacturing tolerances).

We find the normal vector $\mathbf{n}_{\hat{\alpha}}$ that minimizes the square of the angular deviations

$$\hat{\alpha} = \arg\min_\alpha \sum_i \theta_i(\alpha)^2 \quad \text{with} \quad \theta_i(\alpha) = \arccos\left(\frac{\mathbf{n}_\alpha^{\mathrm{T}}(\mathbf{d}_i - \mathbf{g})}{\|\mathbf{n}_\alpha\|\|\mathbf{d}_i - \mathbf{g}\|}\right) \tag{1}$$

between all X-rays $\mathbf{d}_i - \mathbf{g}$ and the plane normal (Fig. 2b); $\mathbf{d}_i$ is the position of detector pixel i and $\mathbf{g}$ the position of the X-ray generator. The objective in Eq. (1) is periodic (360°) and has a unique minimum in every period, hence a global optimum can be obtained. Subsequently, the image is reprojected onto equidistantly-spaced pixels on the reprojection plane; linear interpolation is used. Note that the four views all have different geometry, hence we require a different reprojection plane P for each of them.

The visual effect of the reprojection can be seen in Fig. 3c; note how the reprojected image looks less distorted with more natural proportions. As we will show in Sec. 3, this reduction in object appearance variation (from distortions) also leads to benefits in terms of detection performance.

3   Detection Approach and Experimental Evaluation

Before explaining our detection approach, it is useful to analyze and separate the object appearance variations that have to be accounted for in our recorded X-ray dataset. As just explained, image distortions inherent to the X-ray imaging process are present, but can be reduced. Other variations are object *intra-class* variations (Intra), *e.g.*, from different types of handguns. Object appearance variations also stem from 3D object rotations, specifically from *in-plane* (In) and *out-of-plane* (Out) rotations. In-plane rotations are object rotations that coincide with the image plane, hence can be undone or accounted for by rotating the 2D image. Out-of-plane rotations correspond to viewpoint changes, which might lead to drastic changes in object appearance. In contrast to in-plane rotations, these cannot be undone by means of a simple image transformation.

To study different kinds of appearance variations individually, and to gain insight to where the challenges are, we create different data subsets. First, we create a hand-selected subset of 300 images that contains handguns viewed from the side, denoted D_{Intra}. Out-of-plane rotations are thus excluded; in-plane rotations are additionally eliminated by *pre-rotating* the images such that the handguns are in a canonical orientation (here possible, since every bag only contains at most one handgun). Hence, the only object variations left are due to intra-class (handgun) variations and from "occlusions" of other unrelated objects (or clutter), which are always present. Next, we use the same subset as described, but do not remove in-plane rotations to gain $D_{Intra+In}$. Then the entire dataset is used, but in-plane rotations are eliminated to yield $D_{Intra+Out}$. Finally, the full dataset without any simplifying alterations or exclusions is referred to as $D_{Intra+In+Out}$.

3.1   Single-View Detection

We now explain our detection approach for a single input image (view). It is important to note that this does not mean that the detector need only detect objects from a single, canonical viewpoint. Due to both its popularity as well as robustness for detecting objects in photographic images, our foundation is a standard sliding-window object detector with a linear SVM classifier and Histogram of Oriented Gradients (HOG) features [1]. We train the SVM with the annotated handgun images as positive training examples, which are brought into a canonical orientation and scaled to the SVM window-size of 128×80 pixels; negative training data is randomly cropped from images that do not contain any weapons. We always use three rounds of bootstrapping for SVM training to make results more stable [16]. The different data subsets are divided into approximately $\frac{2}{3}$ training set and $\frac{1}{3}$ test set; positive and negative training examples are divided in the same manner. We evaluate detection performance on each single image (*i.e.* all 4 views of all scans, but considered independently) with the widely used PASCAL criterion [3]. Thus a detection is regarded as correct if the area of overlap with a ground truth bounding box exceeds 50% (and has not been detected before). Based on this, we calculate precision/recall curves and the average precision (AP).

Out-of-Plane Rotations. Without object out-of-plane rotations in D_{Intra}, we can achieve an average precision (AP) of 88.1% (Fig. 4a). However, with object out-of-plane rotations present in the data ($D_{Intra+Out}$), the performance drops drastically to 26.2% AP.

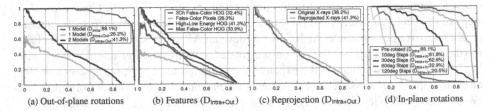

(a) Out-of-plane rotations   (b) Features ($D_{Intra+Out}$)   (c) Reprojection ($D_{Intra+Out}$)   (d) In-plane rotations

Fig. 4. Single-view detection. Effect of different detector configurations and dataset properties on detection performance. Plots show recall (X axis) vs. precision (Y axis). *Best viewed in color.*

Hence, out-of-plane rotations are a major difficulty for detection in the inspection scenario. To alleviate this, we split the positive training data into two sets (aspect ratios) and train an additional detector ("2 models") with a more narrow search window of 128×40 pixels for handguns roughly viewed from the top. Both detectors are applied independently at test time; their detections are simply concatenated. This boosts performance to 41.3% AP on $D_{Intra+Out}$, hence we always use this approach if out-of-plane rotations are present in the data.

Features. As mentioned in Sec. 2, we obtain low and high-energy image channels with a corresponding false-color image from the X-ray inspection system; the false-color image encodes different material properties with colors, *e.g.* blue for metals and orange for organic materials (*cf.* Fig. 3b). Since we have multiple source images, we evaluate (on $D_{Intra+Out}$) which one yields the best results (Fig. 4b). As baseline we use the false-color pixels directly, which achieves 26.3% AP. With HOG computed on the color images, we achieve 33.9% AP (max. gradient response over color channels), and a modest decline to 32.4% AP when computing HOG separately on all color channels and concatenating the descriptor vectors. The best results of 41.3% AP can be obtained when using HOG separately on the low and high-energy channels, again with concatenation of the descriptors. Consequently, we use this feature in all other experiments.

Reprojection. In Sec. 2.1 we showed that the X-ray images are distorted and explained how we reduce these distortions. We evaluate the effect of this on $D_{Intra+Out}$ and find that the influence of our reprojection method is clearly visible (Fig. 4c): Precision is better for almost all recall levels and the maximum recall is slightly increased. Overall, performance increases from 38.2% AP on the original images to 41.3% AP on the reprojected ones. Hence, we use reprojected images in all other experiments.

In-Plane Rotations. So far, we conducted every experiment on pre-rotated images, which serves as an upper bound to the performance on real X-ray data. In-plane rotations can often be ignored when trying to detect object classes in regular photographic images. In pedestrian detection [2], for example, it is safe to assume that people mostly appear in an upright position. However, no such assumptions can be made for the X-ray images, since objects in the passenger luggage may appear at arbitrary 3D rotations.

In a realistic setting, we clearly cannot assume pre-rotated images. At test time we thus search at various orientations, because HOG features are not invariant to rotation (besides searching over multiple scales of the image to account for object size variations). We illustrate the effect of this by comparing the performance on $D_{Intra+In}$ (with several search orientation steps) to the pre-rotated set D_{Intra} (Fig. 4d). Coarse angular steps of 60° and 120° yield poor performance, but further decreasing step sizes successively improves performance. At 10°, we achieve an AP of 81.8%, which is quite close to (the upper bound of) 88.1% AP on pre-rotated images. Smaller angular steps will likely increase performance at the expense of computational effort; we always use 10° angular steps in all subsequent experiments when searching over object orientations. We present single-view detection results for the full dataset $D_{Intra+In+Out}$ (using rotation-search) in Sec. 4, when comparing to our multi-view integration approach (Fig. 6b).

Non-maximum Suppression. After classifying each sliding window (in all scales and rotations) with the linear SVM, we perform non-maximum suppression (NMS) to retain only the local maxima, *i.e.* the most promising object hypotheses with their attached classifier confidence (SVM decision value). One dominant approach for NMS, adopted here, is *pairwise max suppression* (PM) ([2]; *e.g.*, used by [4]), which performs pairwise comparison of all search windows / bounding boxes (BB): If the area of overlap of a pair exceeds a certain threshold, the BB with lower classifier confidence is suppressed. Computing the area of overlap is trivial and computationally efficient if

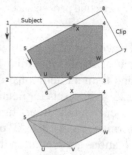

Fig. 5. Weiler-Atherton

bounding boxes are axis-aligned, *i.e.* all line segments are either parallel or orthogonal to each other; however, this no longer applies to arbitrarily rotated BBs, as occur here.

Mittal *et al.* [7] approximate this by simply placing axis-aligned BBs around each rotated BB and then use usual PM, noting (personal communication) that results are very similar as compared to doing accurate calculations. However, this only applies to approximately square BBs, and not to narrow ones as we use to deal with object viewpoint variations. Hence, we are interested in an exact and computationally efficient solution. NMS is performed many times with tens of thousands of BBs, hence naive solutions such as bitmask-based overlap calculations are too inefficient. To perform NMS with rotated BBs efficiently, we propose to use the Weiler-Atherton (WA) algorithm [17], which was originally introduced in computer graphics for polygon clipping. The algorithm efficiently finds the intersection polygon of two input polygons (Fig. 5, top) by alternating between traversing the *subject* and *clip* polygon at every intersection (at U, V, W, and X in Fig. 5); the intersection area is then computed through geometric triangulation (Fig. 5, bottom). The runtime is only dependent on the amount of nodes in both input polygons, hence constant when used with rectangles only. We use the Weiler-Atherton algorithm to perform NMS in all our experiments. Its benefits are that it enables accurate overlap calculations with arbitrarily rotated bounding boxes for PM, yet it is fast enough in practice. As far as we are aware, this is the first time that this algorithm has been used in this context.

4   Multi-view Integration and Experimental Results

The preceding experiments on single input images show that out-of-plane rotations are a major challenge for object detection (Fig. 4a). To improve on this, we exploit the multiple input images available to us from modern X-ray inspection systems (*cf*. Fig. 2a).

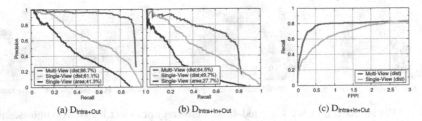

(a) $D_{Intra+Out}$ (b) $D_{Intra+In+Out}$ (c) $D_{Intra+In+Out}$

Fig. 6. Single-view vs. multi-view detection. Results in *(a)* are obtained with pre-rotated images, *i.e.* denote an upper bound on detection performance on real data *(b,c)* without any simplifying assumptions. Results in *(c)* show false positives per image (FPPI) vs. recall. Please see text for further discussion. *Best viewed in color.*

After running single-view detection separately on each of the (in our case 4) input images (views), we fuse their respective detections. The motivation is to suppress false detections, since they are not likely to coincide in different views; similarly, detections that agree on object locations can reinforce each other. Before going into the details of our integration approach, it is important to hightlight its generality; any single-view detection method can be used. We are not even constrained to X-ray image data, as used here. The input to our integration algorithm is a list of object locations (bounding boxes) with corresponding classifier confidences, and the 3D geometry of all cameras.

The main idea of the proposed multi-view integration is that each detection represents a 2D object location with unknown depth/distance w.r.t. the X-ray generator source (*cf*. Fig. 2). Technically, each 2D bounding box (BB) defines a polyhedron of possible object locations in 3D space (a wedge intersected with the cube of the scanner tunnel). Since it is cumbersome to work with this polyhedron, we use the central pixel of each 2D bounding as its proxy and thus obtain a line/ray in 3D space from the X-ray generator source to the detector (pixel) location (*cf*. Fig. 7a and $d_i - g$ in Fig. 2b). In essence, each detection in each view image casts a vote (weighted by the classifier confidence) for the *center* of a particular object location in 3D space with unknown depth. If votes from two or more different views agree, *i.e.* the respective rays intersect in 3D space, we can *(i)* increase our confidence in each of the individual detections, and *(ii)* recover the proposed 3D location of the object's center.

Since detected BBs (and thus their central locations) might be slightly misplaced, we cannot expect perfect intersections from their respective rays and should rather find rays in 3D that come very close to each other. We address this by placing a dense grid of sampling points over the whole 3D volume of the scanner tunnel. Each sampling point is associated with rays in close proximity (*i.e.* below a certain threshold; here less than the distance between sampling points). Confidences of nearby rays are accumulated and finally averaged. To prevent bias from any particular view, we only allow one ray from each view (the one with highest confidence) to contribute to a sampling point.

The result of our integration approach is a 3D confidence map of central object locations (Fig. 7a). We are interested in the most promising locations (local maxima),

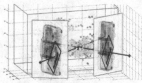

(a) Multi-view integration example   (b) dist criterion example   (c) Single-view vs. multi-view detection example

Fig. 7. *(a)* Partial 3D confidence map (red–high, blue–low) of object locations within scanner tunnel with 2 of 4 views shown to illustrate ray intersections. *(b)* Distance-based evaluation criterion: Only detections within the red circle are considered correct. *(c)* At same recall rate (70%), single-view detection (triangles) produces several false detections (red; correct in green), and multi-view detection none (squares). *Best viewed in color on screen.*

therefore apply (pairwise) non-maximum suppression where each sampling point suppresses all others with lower confidence in a local neighborhood (neighborhood radius based on object class). The obtained local maxima represent our fused detections, which we project back into the original view images to enable comparison with results from single-view detection; however, they also admit 3D object localization.

Evaluation Criterion. The concept of rectangular bounding boxes is lost in our multi-view integration approach. Hence, we evaluate detections with a custom criterion based on relative distance, and not with the usual PASCAL criterion. To that end, we define the relative distance $dist_{rel} = \|center_{gt} - center_{dt}\|/scale_{gt}$, between the ground truth (gt) object location $center_{gt}$ and the detection (dt) location $center_{dt}$, where $scale_{gt}$ is the width of the ground truth bounding box. A detection is considered correct if $dist_{rel}$ is below a threshold (here $\frac{1}{3}$). We do not allow multiple detections of the same object.

Our distance-based evaluation criterion is less restrictive than PASCAL [3], which can be observed in Fig. 6 by comparing single-view detection performance evaluated with both PASCAL (denoted by area) and our criterion (denoted by dist). However, we believe that it is still restrictive enough to provide good object localization in the targeted scenario, as illustrated in Fig. 7.

Experimental Results. We evaluate our multi-view integration approach on the full dataset $D_{Intra+In+Out}$ with our distance-based criterion (Fig. 6b) and find that the average precision (AP) increases substantially from 49.7% in single-view detection to 64.5% with multi-view integration; the difference is also visualized in Fig. 7c. Albeit greatly increased AP, our integration procedure yields lower recall than single-view detection at low precision levels. However, our goal is the detection of dangerous objects in the context of airport security, specifically with the intention of supporting human operators, not replacing them. In this context, we are interested in producing relatively few false alarms/detections per image (FPPI) to only notify operators in case of actual threat items in passenger luggage. We study this effect in Fig. 6c, which shows that on average our multi-view approach is able to detect around 80% of all handguns while producing a single false alarm at every second image; in contrast, single-view detection is able to only find 50% of all handguns at the same false-alarm rate.

5 Summary

In this paper we proposed an approach for object detection in multi-view dual-energy X-ray image data, as it arises for example in luggage inspection systems. We adapted appearance-based object class detection for the specifics of the image data and setting. To that end, we analyzed and addressed several object appearance variations: We reduced distortions in X-ray images, introduced an efficient non-maximum suppression scheme in the context of in-plane rotations, and most importantly introduced a novel multi-view integration approach to deal with out-of-plane object rotations. An experimental evaluation of handgun detection on a challenging dataset of carry-on luggage showed substantial performance improvements from all proposed components of our approach, particularly of our multi-view integration. In the future we plan to further improve the recall at precision levels tolerable for a human operator, in part by closing the gap between performance on pre-rotated (Fig. 6a) and realistic data (Fig. 6b); this may be accomplished by using a rotation-invariant image descriptor (*e.g.* [13]), which has the additional benefit of reducing the computational overhead incurred by searching over many image rotations for single-view detection. Future work may also consider applications of our multi-view integration scheme outside of X-ray imagery.

Acknowledgements. We thank Stefan Walk for helpful discussions. This work is partially funded by the German Federal Ministry of Education and Research project SICURA (BMBF-13N11124).

References

1. Dalal, N., Triggs, B.: Histograms of oriented gradients for human detection. In: CVPR 2005 (2005)
2. Dollár, P., Wojek, C., Schiele, B., Perona, P.: Pedestrian detection: An evaluation of the state of the art. PAMI 34(4) (2012)
3. Everingham, M., Van Gool, L., Williams, C.K.I., Winn, J., Zisserman, A.: The PASCAL Visual Object Classes Challenge 2008 (VOC 2008) Results (2008)
4. Felzenszwalb, P.F., Girshick, R.B., McAllester, D.A., Ramanan, D.: Object detection with discriminatively trained part-based models. PAMI 32(9) (2010)
5. Lowe, D.G.: Distinctive image features from scale-invariant keypoints. IJCV 60(2) (2004)
6. Mery, D.: Automated detection in complex objects using a tracking algorithm in multiple X-ray views. In: OTCBVS 2011 Workshop (in Conj. with CVPR 2011) (2011)
7. Mittal, A., Zisserman, A., Torr, P.: Hand detection using multiple proposals. In: BMVC 2011 (2011)
8. Ommer, B., Malik, J.: Multi-scale object detection by clustering lines. In: ICCV 2009 (2009)
9. Riffo, V., Mery, D.: Active X-ray testing of complex objects. Insight (2011)
10. Roig, G., Boix, X., Shitrit, H.B., Fua, P.: Conditional random fields for multi-camera object detection. In: ICCV 2011 (2011)
11. Sankaranarayanan, A.C., Veeraraghavan, A., Chellappa, R.: Object detection, tracking and recognition for multiple smart cameras. Proc. IEEE 96(10) (2008)
12. Savarese, S., Fei-Fei, L.: 3D generic object categorization, localization and pose estimation. In: ICCV 2007 (2007)
13. Schmidt, U., Roth, S.: Learning rotation-aware features: From invariant priors to equivariant descriptors. In: CVPR 2012 (2012)

14. Thomas, A., Ferrari, V., Leibe, B., Tuytelaars, T., Schiele, B., Van Gool, L.: Towards multi-view object class detection. In: CVPR 2006 (2006)
15. Torralba, A., Murphy, K.P., Freeman, W.T.: Sharing visual features for multiclass and multi-view object detection. PAMI 29(5) (2007)
16. Walk, S., Majer, N., Schindler, K., Schiele, B.: New features and insights for pedestrian detection. In: CVPR 2010 (2010)
17. Weiler, K., Atherton, P.: Hidden surface removal using polygon area sorting. In: SIGGRAPH 1977 (1977)
18. Zentai, G.: X-ray imaging for homeland security. In: IST 2008 Workshop (2008)

Eye Localization Using the Discriminative Generalized Hough Transform

Ferdinand Hahmann[1], Heike Ruppertshofen[2], Gordon Böer[1], Ralf Stannarius[3], and Hauke Schramm[1]

[1] University of Applied Sciences Kiel
[2] Philips Technologie GmbH
[3] Rosemann Software GmbH
{Ferdinand.Hahmann,Gordon.Boeer,Hauke.Schramm}@fh-kiel.de
Heike.Ruppertshofen@philips.com, Ralf.Stannarius@rosemann-software.de

Abstract. The Discriminative Generalized Hough Transform (DGHT) has been successfully introduced as a general method for the localization of arbitrary objects with well-defined shape in medical images. In this contribution, the framework is, for the first time, applied to the localization of eyes in a public face database. Based on a set of training images with annotated target points, the training procedure combines the Hough space votes of individual shape model points into a probability distribution of the maximum-entropy family and optimizes the free parameters of this distribution with respect to the training error rate. This assigns individual positive and negative weights to the shape model points, reflecting important structures of the target object and confusable shapes, respectively. Additionally, the estimated weights allow to determine irrelevant parts in order to eliminate them from the model, making space for the incorporation of new model point candidates. These candidates are in turn identified from training images with remaining high localization error. The whole procedure of weight estimation, point elimination, testing on training images and incorporation of new model point hypotheses is iterated several times until a stopping criterion is met. The method is further enhanced by applying a multi-level approach, in which the searched region is reduced in 6 zooming steps, using individually trained shape models on each level. An evaluation on the PUT face database has shown that the system achieves a state-of-the-art success rate of 99% for iris detection in frontal-view images and 95% if the test set contains the full head pose variability.

1 Introduction

The localization of facial features like the eye is an important prerequisite for a variety of applications in the field of computer vision [3]. Because of its considerable importance, this topic attracted a lot of attention by the scientific community in the past which is reflected in a large variety of different approaches. It is remarkable, that most of the current state-of-the-art systems rely on the usage of a face detector before applying specifically adapted methods for eye localization. The most popular face detection method has been proposed in [17].

A. Pinz et al. (Eds.): DAGM/OAGM 2012, LNCS 7476, pp. 155–164, 2012.
© Springer-Verlag Berlin Heidelberg 2012

This technique uses Haar-Wavelet-Features in a boosted cascade of classifiers to identify regions containing a face. Since the general method can be trained to detect arbitrary objects with well-defined appearance, this face detector has been combined in [12] with a subsequent eye localization, based on the same technique. Although the first step of this procedure substantially reduced the search space, additional knowledge about the specific task had to be incorporated to further restrict the number of hypotheses of the classifier cascade. The usage of task-specific knowledge is prevalent in many state-of-the-art systems published in recent years. In [13], for example, the approximate location of the eye in relation to a given face bounding box is determined and the estimation is refined by searching for a minimum intensity region in a defined neighborhood, which is expected to be the pupil. In [16] the search for a circular, dark structure is performed by means of the orientation of all image gradients, weighted by the gray value, to determine the centers of dark circles (like the pupil).

Further systems determine location hypotheses for both eyes and reject those not meeting the expected eye distance [6] or the allowed in-plane rotation [12]. Only few methods, however, learn these constraints from data, like in [5], where 15 additional facial features are detected together with the eyes and combined with learned feature distance probability distributions.

The usage of expert knowledge can substantially improve the performance of an object localization framework but requires in-depth knowledge about both the task and the system. Yet, such solutions can usually not be generalized to other problems. In addition, the combination of different specialized methodologies into a single framework may lead to complex systems, which are difficult to maintain and advance.

A general and widely used approach of object localization is the Generalized Hough Transform (GHT)[1]. Many extensions to the GHT have been developed in recent years to achieve a reduced processing time and increased robustness, like the Hough Forests [7] or the Discriminative Generalized Hough Transform (DGHT) [15], which has been applied in this work. The DGHT is a general object localization method, initially developed in the field of medical image processing [15], which aims at automatically generating optimal shape models for usage in a standard Generalized Hough Transform. It estimates individual positive and negative model point weights for a given shape model and eliminates irrelevant parts in a subsequent step. In an iterative training procedure, this technique is applied repeatedly to expand the model with image structures of unrecognized targets and confusing objects in the training corpus. In this work, the DGHT method will, for the first time, be applied to an eye localization task. The procedure operates without incorporating additional methods or expert knowledge and achieves state-of-the-art localization rates on a given public database.

Here, section 2 describes the general method, including the GHT (2.1), the discriminative training of GHT models (2.2), and a zooming strategy to improve the robustness and processing time (2.3). Section 3 contains a description of the used database (3.1), the experimental setup (3.2), and lists the achieved results (3.3) followed by a discussion (3.4). Section 4 concludes our contribution.

2   Method

This section presents the Discriminative Generalized Hough Transform (DGHT), a method recently developed in the field of medical image analysis [15]. The technique combines the well-known Generalized Hough Transform (GHT) [1] with a discriminative training technique [2] to generate sparse, efficient and discriminative GHT-models for object detection.

2.1   GHT

The GHT was introduced by Ballard in 1981 [1]. It is a general and well-known model-based method for object localization, widely used for the analysis of 2-D images.

The GHT requires a point model M, representing the structure of the searched-for object in relation to a so-called reference point. This point, usually located in the center of the model, represents the target point of the object detection task in the DGHT framework.

By performing a simple voting procedure, the GHT transforms a feature image X_n into a parameter space H, known as the Hough space. This space consists of accumulator cells, representing possible target point locations and, potentially, model transformations. The amount of votes in an individual cell reflects the degree of matching between the (possibly transformed) GHT model and the feature image. Note that, in this work, no model transformations apart from translations are considered since moderate object variability with respect to shape, rotation and size is learned into the model. In addition, although arbitrary features could be applied in the general GHT framework, the presented system relies on plain edge features, obtained by a standard Canny edge detection [4].

The GHT voting procedure considers all possible combinations of edge points e_i and model points m_j and increments the accumulator cell at the image coordinates x as follows:

$$H(\mathbf{x}) = \sum_{\forall e_i \in X_n} \sum_{\forall m_j \in M} \begin{cases} 1, & \text{if } \mathbf{x} = \mathbf{e}_i - \mathbf{m}_j \text{ and } \arccos(< \varphi_i, \varphi_j >) \leq \vartheta_\varphi \\ 0, & \text{otherwise} \end{cases} \quad (1)$$

Here, φ_i and φ_j denote the gradient direction of e_i and orientation of m_j, respectively. A point pair is allowed to vote if it has a similar direction, meaning that the scalar product must be below the threshold ϑ_φ. In order to speed-up the GHT voting procedure, Ballard introduced the so-called R-table [1]. In this look-up table, each bin is assigned a certain range of angels $\Delta\Phi$ and model points are sorted into the bins according to their orientation. During the voting procedure, an edge point e_i only votes with the model points contained in the bin with the corresponding orientation range.

Obviously, the performance of the GHT-based localization procedure heavily relies on the choice of an appropriate model. In addition to the geometric distribution of the applied point cloud, this may also include a sophisticated weighting scheme of individual points. This is quite reasonable since it can be expected that some parts of a given model are more important than others and should therefore vote with a higher weight. In [15] a novel approach for a discriminative training of GHT model point weights has been presented, including the estimation of both positive and negative weights.

2.2 Discriminative Training of GHT Models

The DGHT framework applies an iterative training procedure [15], which determines the geometric model layout as well as individual weights of the model points in order to take the different importance of model structures into account. To this end, a subset of images from the training corpus with annotated target landmarks is applied to generate an initial GHT model. This is achieved by using the Canny edge points from the selected images as model points and the gradient directions as their orientation. A subsequently performed individual weighting of the model points is achieved by the discriminative training procedure described below. Since model points with a low absolute weight have only a small influence on the resulting Hough space, they are discarded from the model in order to make space for new model point candidates. After that, the model is tested on the whole annotated training dataset to detect images with remaining high localization error. These images are used to learn unknown target object shapes and important rivaling objects which are both incorporated into the model by using the respective edge points as additional model points for the next iteration. The whole procedure, which is described in detail in [15], is iterated until a given stop-criterion is met.

The estimation of individual weights for the J points, contained in a given shape model, is achieved by (1) separating the Hough space votes coming from every single model point, (2) recombining those contributions in a weighted manner and (3) optimizing the introduced weights with respect to an error measure. The theory of this approach is based on describing the GHT as a probabilistic framework in which the Hough space is interpreted as a posterior probability distribution $p(c_i|X_n)$, estimated from the relative frequencies of the model point votes in each Hough cell c_i. The object localization task, performed by the GHT, which searches for the cell with the highest number of votes, can now be formulated as the Bayes classifier $\hat{c} = \arg\max_{c_i} p(c_i|X_n)$. In order to split the total number of votes in a Hough cell c_i into contributions coming from individual model points, we introduce the feature function

$$f_j(c_i, X_n) = v_{i,j},\tag{2}$$

which denotes the number of votes $v_{i,j}$ from model point m_j into cell c_i for a given image X_n. A weighted recombination of those features in a maximum entropy distribution [8]

$$p_\Lambda(c_i|X_n) = \frac{\exp\left(\sum_j \lambda_j \cdot f_j(c_i, X_n)\right)}{\sum_k \exp\left(\sum_j \lambda_j \cdot f_j(c_k, X_n)\right)}\tag{3}$$

preserves objectivity, incorporates the constraints from the GHT voting procedure with the given model and introduces model point specific weights λ_j. The estimation of those free parameters from the side conditions (2) leads to an optimal approximation of the training data distribution. Since this does not necessarily lead to a minimal error rate, we follow an alternative approach, first presented in the field of automatic speech recognition [2]. In our framework, the model point weights λ_j are optimized by using a Minimum Classification Error (MCE) training approach [10], which minimizes a smoothed error measure over the N training images and I Hough cells:

$$E(\Lambda) = \sum_{n=1}^{N} \sum_{i=1}^{I} \varepsilon(c_i, \tilde{c}_n) \cdot \frac{p_\Lambda(c_i|X_n)^\eta}{\sum_k p_\Lambda(c_k|X_n)^\eta}. \tag{4}$$

Here, η in the smoothing term controls the influence of alternative location hypotheses on the error measure and $\varepsilon(c_i, \tilde{c}_n)$ denotes the localization error between the Hough cell c_i and the target Hough cell $\tilde{c}_n$ using the Euclidean distance:

$$\varepsilon(c_i, \tilde{c}_n) = \|c_i, \tilde{c}_n\|_2. \tag{5}$$

In the DGHT framework, the optimization of $E(\Lambda)$ over the model point weights $\Lambda = \{\lambda_1, \lambda_2, ..., \lambda_J\}$ is achieved by applying the method of steepest descent. Although this technique does not assure to find a global minimum, recent experiments in the field of medical image analysis have shown substantial improvement compared to equal weighting strategies or other state-of-the-art methods [15].

The estimated weights of the shape model are directly incorporated into a standard GHT voting procedure by incrementing the value of a Hough cell c_i by $\lambda_j \cdot f_j(c_i, X_n)$ for each model point m_j:

$$H(c_i|X_n) = \sum_{j=1}^{J} \lambda_j \cdot f_j(c_i, X_n). \tag{6}$$

The localization result, i.e., the detected Hough cell $\hat{c}$, is then given by $\hat{c} = \arg\max_{c_i} H(c_i|X_n)$. Note that the usage of this weighting scheme in the localization leads to the same result as applying the maximum entropy distribution (3) used for the optimization. This is, since neither the normalization term in the denominator of (3) nor the exponential function have an influence on the result of the arg max function.

2.3   Multi-level-Approach

In order to speed-up the localization procedure and to increase the robustness of the system, we follow a coarse-to-fine strategy, as described in [14]. A Gaussian image pyramid is created and the localization is performed on each level with a specifically trained shape model. The first resolution level is very coarse and shows little detail but allows for a rough orientation and fast processing since the

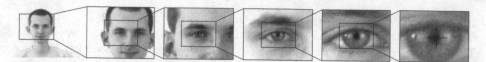

Fig. 1. Image extracts with different resolutions in the multi-level approach

image size is small and the shape model contains only a restricted set of model points with little object detail. The detected point, found with this model, is then used to determine the center of the image extract, used for the next level (see Fig. 1). This extract has half of the size of the original image and a higher resolution than the previous level. The procedure can be repeated several times, each time using a specifically trained and more detailed DGHT model.

Since the image extracts have only a fraction of the original image size, they can be processed quickly, even with the full resolution. In addition, the shape model used in the final level does not need to represent global details since these have already been captured by the previous levels. This specialization of the individual shape models to level-specific details and characteristics aims at reducing the localization error by finding an optimal trade-off between sufficient model accuracy and reduced confusion with concurrent objects.

3   Experiments

3.1   Data

The training and evaluation set used in the experiments is extracted from the publicly available PUT face database [11], which contains 9971 images from 100 subjects. The color images were taken under controlled illumination conditions with a uniform background and have a high resolution of 2048 × 1536 pixels. Manual annotations are provided for various landmarks, e.g., in the center and along the outline of the eyes, nose, face, eyebrows and mouth. Note that those landmarks were only annotated for images where the corresponding facial feature is visible. Despite the uniform background, this database is demanding since it covers a large variation of head poses as shown in Fig. 2, making it an interesting base for localization experiments. In order to study the influence of head pose variations on the localization error rate, a frontal view subset of the data, containing 22 images per subject, was provided as well.

The subjects, contained in the PUT database, were strictly separated during training and evaluation. 60 randomly selected subjects were used for training and the remaining 40 subjects for evaluation. In the experiments reported here, the target point for the localization was always the center of the eye. Since, due to the strong head pose variation, this landmark is not visible in all the images of the database, only a subset with given annotation of this point was used. The training database contains 10 randomly selected images per subject, in total 600 images. The evaluation was done on 3830 images from the 40 test subjects. The frontal view evaluation subset contains 869 images.

Fig. 2. Illustration of the large head pose variability, contained in the PUT database

Table 1. Success rates for DGHT eye localization on the evaluation corpus using error measure (7) and different fault tolerances

	e < 0.1	e < 0.15	e < 0.2	e < 0.25
frontal view subset	99.08%	99.08%	99.31%	99.42%
full head pose variations	95.01%	95.43%	96.01%	96.48%

3.2 System Setup

In all experiments, we used Canny edge detection [4] for the generation of feature images and applied an iterative training [15] and multi-level approach (Section 2.3). In the multi-level framework six zooming levels were used, ranging from the whole image to a small region around the pupil as shown in Fig. 1. In each zooming level, the resolution is 64×48 pixels. The experiments were performed on a 64 bit system with an Intel Xeon W3520 with 2.66 GHz and 24 GB RAM.

To validate the localization success, we use a relative error measure, which was introduced in [9]. It selects the worst of a left and right eye localization and normalizes this error distance to the respective eyes distance:

$$e = \frac{max(||\mathbf{c}_l - \widetilde{\mathbf{c}}_l||, ||\mathbf{c}_r - \widetilde{\mathbf{c}}_r||)}{||\widetilde{\mathbf{c}}_l - \widetilde{\mathbf{c}}_r||}. \tag{7}$$

Here, the vectors $\mathbf{c}_l$ and $\mathbf{c}_r$ are used to denote the localization result for left and right eye localization while $\widetilde{\mathbf{c}}_l$ and $\widetilde{\mathbf{c}}_r$ are the annotated left and right eye positions. Note that, using this measure, an error of less than 0.1 / 0.25 relates to a localization result lying approximately within the iris / eye.

3.3 Results

The iterative training performed 24 iterations on average for the different zooming levels and achieved a final error on training data of 4%. The average number of points in the level-specific shape models is 357, ranging from 180 to 395 points.

The rates for a successful iris localization ($e < 0.1$), shown in Table 1, are competitive with the results reported in [12], where success rates of 99% and 94% were achieved on this database for frontal views and full head pose variations, respectively.

The average processing time measured for a single image was 597 ms, while the GHT voting procedure and identification of the best Hough cell hypothesis took only 1% of the complete runtime.

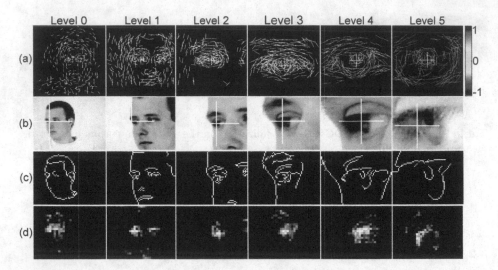

Fig. 3. (a) shows the models for all six zooming levels, (b) - (d) shows a complete example including the result image (b), the feature image (c) and the Hough space (d)

3.4 Discussion

Fig. 3(a) presents the models of all six zoom levels for a right eye localization. The model points are represented as lines, to visualize their orientation. It can be seen that the level of detail increases substantially from the global to the single eye model, similar to the visible structures in the feature images. At level 0, the model contains information about different head sizes and hairstyles, while the eyes and mouth are only coarsely represented. Since global structures like hairs are no longer visible in higher levels, the models may focus on the final target, which leads to a highly detailed iris and pupil modeling.

It is noticeable that in levels 0 to 3 significant differences between the model point weights are visible while the weights in levels 4 and 5 are similar and quite high. This is due to the slightly inaccurate target point annotations (shown in Fig. 4), which, naturally, have the strongest effect on the smallest image extracts. Therefore, the stop criterion in the training procedure was met only after performing a large number of iterations, causing the observed high weights. The random character of these annotation errors also prevents the discrimination of important and irrelevant model points and leads to the more or less equal weighting scheme, visible in Fig. 3.

In the edge image of level 5, it is, furthermore, visible that, in addition to the pupil, also the flash light must be represented by the model. This can indeed be observed on the left and right of the models' pupil structure.

An error analysis unveiled that 61% of the false localizations can be accounted to a confusion of the eyes. In these cases, the independently applied left and right eye detector returned the same result. To this end, it can be assumed that the integration of constraints, like, e.g., a learned eye distance, will result in a higher localization performance.

Fig. 4. Illustration of manual annotations, provided by the PUT face database

It should also be mentioned that first investigations have confirmed, that a substantial runtime improvement can be expected from using faster implementations for the downsampling and feature extraction, since the employed slow procedures require most of the computing performance.

4 Conclusion

In this contribution, we introduced the usage of the Discriminative Generalized Hough Transform (DGHT) for eye localization. The method, which was originally developed in the field of 2-D and 3-D medical image processing, is a general localization technique for arbitrary objects with well-defined shape. Since the iterative training method simply requires a set of images with annotated target points and runs fully automatic without the need of expert knowledge, it can be quickly applied to new tasks.

It should be mentioned that, different to most other state-of-the-art eye localization techniques, no additional method for face localization is required. The first rough orientation step is acquired by the same general approach, simply using a specifically trained model. First experimental results in this new application field show that the DGHT can be successfully applied to eye localization in a controlled environment with a uniform background. Despite substantial head pose variations in the PUT face database, a localization rate of 95% was achieved for iris detection, which is competitive to other methods recently tested on this dataset [12]. This result improves to 99% for a subset of the data containing frontal view images only. An interesting aspect of the presented framework is the possibility of a straightforward interpretation of the resulting models due to their weighted geometric structure. It can be seen that the contour of the head and eyes is of special importance for the coarse localization of the face while the model of the latest zooming level has even learned lighting conditions reflected in the eye. Additionally, it should be stressed that the method operates without incorporation of any task specific constraints, defined, e.g., by an expert. It can, however, be expected that further gains in the success rate could be achieved by exploiting additional knowledge, for example about the expected distance between the target object and other landmarks in the face. The incorporation of this idea into the given framework is quite straightforward and will be investigated in future work.

Acknowledgments. This work is partly funded by the Innovation Foundation Schleswig-Holstein under the grant 2010-90H .

References

1. Ballard, D.: Generalizing the Hough transform to detect arbitrary shapes. Pattern Recognition 13(2), 111–122 (1981)
2. Beyerlein, P.: Discriminative model combination. In: International Conference on Acoustics, Speech and Signal Processing (ICASSP), pp. 481–484 (1998)
3. Böhme, M., Meyer, A., Martinetz, T., Barth, E.: Remote eye tracking: State of the art and directions for future development. In: Conference on Communication by Gaze Interaction (COGAIN), pp. 12–17 (2006)
4. Canny, J.: A computational approach to edge detection. IEEE Transactions on Pattern Analysis and Machine Intelligence 8(6), 679–698 (1986)
5. Cristinacce, D., Cootes, T., Scott, I.: A multi-stage approach to facial feature detection. In: British Machine Vision Conference (BMVC), pp. 277–286 (2004)
6. D'Orazio, T., Leo, M., Cicirelli, G., Distante, A.: An algorithm for real time eye detection in face images. In: International Conference on Pattern Recognition (ICPR), pp. 278–281 (2004)
7. Gall, J., Lempitsky, V.: Class-specific hough forests for object detection. In: Conference on Computer Vision and Pattern Recognition (CVPR), pp. 1022–1029 (2009)
8. Jaynes, E.: Information theory and statistical mechanics. The Physical Review 106(4), 620–630 (1957)
9. Jesorsky, O., Kirchberg, K.J., Frischholz, R.W.: Robust Face Detection Using the Hausdorff Distance. In: Bigun, J., Smeraldi, F. (eds.) AVBPA 2001. LNCS, vol. 2091, pp. 90–95. Springer, Heidelberg (2001)
10. Juang, B., Katagiri, S.: Discriminative learning for minimum error classification. IEEE Transactions on Signal Processing 40(12), 3043–3054 (1992)
11. Kasinski, A., Florek, A., Schmidt, A.: The PUT face database. Image Processing and Communications 13(3-4), 59–64 (2008)
12. Kasinski, A., Schmidt, A.: The architecture and performance of the face and eyes detection system based on the haar cascade classifiers. Pattern Analysis & Applications 13(2), 197–211 (2010)
13. Kroon, B., Hanjalic, A., Maas, S.: Eye localization for face matching: is it always useful and under what conditions? In: International Conference on Content-based Image and Video Retrieval (CIVR), pp. 379–388 (2008)
14. Ruppertshofen, H., Künne, D., Lorenz, C., Schmidt, S., Beyerlein, P., Salah, Z., Rose, G., Schramm, H.: Multi-level approach for the discriminative generalized hough transform. In: Computer- und Roboterassistierte Chirugie (CURAC), pp. 67–70 (2011)
15. Ruppertshofen, H., Lorenz, C., Schmidt, S., Beyerlein, P., Salah, Z., Rose, G., Schramm, H.: Discriminative generalized hough transform for localization of joints in the lower extremities. Computer Science-Research and Development 26(1), 97–105 (2011)
16. Timm, F., Barth, E.: Accurate eye centre localisation by means of gradients. In: Conference on Computer Vision Theory and Applications, VISAPP (2011)
17. Viola, P., Jones, M.: Robust real-time face detection. International Journal of Computer Vision 57(2), 137–154 (2004)

Simultaneous Estimation of Material Properties and Pose for Deformable Objects from Depth and Color Images*

Andreas Rune Fugl[1,2], Andreas Jordt[3], Henrik Gordon Petersen[1],
Morten Willatzen[2], and Reinhard Koch[3]

[1] The Maersk Mc-Kinney Moller Institute, University of Southern Denmark
[2] The Mads Clausen Institute, University of Southern Denmark
[3] Institute of Computer Science, Christian-Albrechts-University of Kiel

Abstract. In this paper we consider the problem of estimating 6D pose, material properties and deformation of an object grasped by a robot gripper. To estimate the parameters we minimize an error function incorporating visual and physical correctness. Through simulated and real-world experiments we demonstrate that we are able to find realistic 6D poses and elasticity parameters like Young's modulus. This makes it possible to perform subsequent manipulation tasks, where accurate modelling of the elastic behaviour is important.

1 Introduction

Accurate grasping and subsequent manipulation of objects is important for many robot application scenarios, where the grasped object must come into contact with or be placed relative to other objects e.g. bin-picking and assembly tasks [12,20]. *Pose estimation*, before and after grasping remains a key component and extensive work has been done for rigid objects [9,8]. Due to the non-constant surfaces of *deformable objects*, it is not straight-forward to apply these methods. A number of methods have been proposed regarding the pre-grasp pose estimation of deformable objects: In [4] Foresti and Pellegrino present a system to recognize, pose estimate and handle deformable objects. It demonstrates good results from the bin-picking of tanned fur. However, the method is only concerned with pre-grasp pose estimation and manipulation.

When performing manipulation tasks with grasped deformable objects they cannot be assumed to rigidly follow the manipulator. A deformation model must be formulated and solved in order to predict the motion of the object. For this, accurate *material properties* must be available particularly the elastic moduli [13]. A task where both elastic behaviour and pose are important is presented in [1]. Bodenhagen et al. used a cantilevered beam model to do off-line learning of the motions to perform Peg-In-Hole actions for deformable objects. However,

---

* This work was co-financed by the INTERREG 4 program Syddanmark-Schleswig-K.E.R.N. by EU funds from the European Regional Development Fund.

A. Pinz et al. (Eds.): DAGM/OAGM 2012, LNCS 7476, pp. 165–174, 2012.
© Springer-Verlag Berlin Heidelberg 2012

the authors relied on tabulated data for material properties and manual measurements of the gripper pose.

There are a wide range of methods for determining the elastic moduli for a
deformable object, but not all are easy to use in a robotics work cell. The most
direct way to measure the elastic moduli is to deform a sample of the object
and measure the resulting force. Given careful control of boundary conditions,
this is an accurate method [3]. For various isotropic metals Oliver et al. [17]
demonstrated that the elastic moduli could be measured by load-displacement
data of an indenter to within an accuracy of 4% and in [15] Meththananda et
al. used indentation tests on soft elastomeric materials. Ultrasound imaging was
used in [2], however large relative errors in estimating Young's modulus were
present.

Few authors have presented work directly relating to robotics work-cells.
Howard and Bekey [10] proposed how to learn parameters for a damped-spring
model and calculate the minimum lifting force required to manipulate deformable
objects. The parameters for the model used are however not easily validated by
experiments nor converted to elastic moduli and they performed no pose estimation of the object after grasping. In [5] Frank et al. used a robot manipulator
equipped with a force-torque sensor and a stereo camera to observe the deformation of flexible objects. By obtaining the deformation by vision along with the
force reading from the sensor when using an indenter, they used a volumetric
model to search for Young's modulus and Poisson's ratio. However no validation
of the elastic moduli was made. In [11] a method for tracking deformable objects in color and depth video was introduced. However, the generic deformation
fitness did not take any physical model into account.

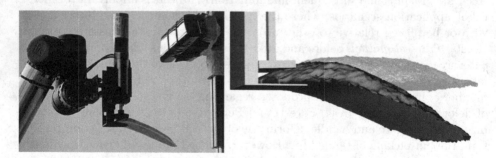

Fig. 1. Left: A deformable object grasped by a robot gripper. Object pose and material
properties are estimated using a 3D data from a Kinect and deformation modeling.
Right: Comparison between undeformed (red) and deformed object

In this paper we propose a system that estimates object pose and material
properties of a deformable object, deforming under gravity (see fig. 1). We combine the deformation tracking concept of [11] with the search for appropriate
material parameters. We search for the best fit to the material parameters for
an underlying physics model while fitting the deformation parameters and object

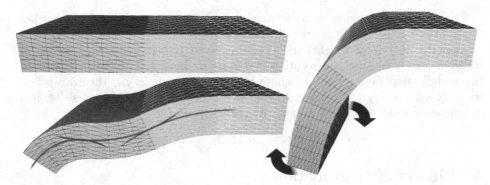

Fig. 2. An example deformation: The box is separated into one section without deflection (white) and several sections of varying curvature (coloured). The undeformed box (upper left corner) is subject to varying deformations. In each section, the applied curvature is constant (lower left). In addition, a global twist of the object can be applied (right)

pose to the input depth and color data. In the following sections we describe the parts of the system. In section 5 test results based on synthetic and real input data are discussed.

2 Parametrization of Deformation

The first step of tracking deformations is to create a deformation model defining the domain of potential deformations along with its parametrization. For gripper based interaction, we are able to reduce the set of generic deformations to deflections typical for this scenario. To do so, the undeformed object model is divided into sections. The first section describes the area in which the gripper directly touches the object surface, the remaining sections are equally distributed over the object part hanging loose under the influence of gravity.

The gripper section is not visible to the optical sensors, but as it is rigidly connected to the robot, the pose of this object part is well known. Outside of the gripper section, the object is subject to gravity and, thus, deflecting. Each of these sections is subject to a constant curvature operator moving the vertices of the section. Each vertex in a section of size x_{size} is manipulated by the mapping

$$\begin{pmatrix} x \\ y \\ z \end{pmatrix} \mapsto \begin{pmatrix} x\cos(\alpha) - (z-r)\sin(\alpha) \\ y \\ (z-r)\cos(\alpha) + x\sin(\alpha) + r \end{pmatrix}, \alpha = \frac{x}{2\pi(r-z)}, r = \frac{x_{size}}{\beta} \quad (1)$$

with a bending angle of $\beta \neq 0$ (see lower left mesh in figure 2) in addition to the affine transformations caused by the bending of preceeding sections.

The number of sections determines how complex the deformations are that can be described by the parametrization. In section 5.1 the necessary number of sections required for good results is discussed.

Preceeding the deflection, a twisting deformation is performed, a rotation around the x-axis (length) of the object by a value linearly depending on the x-value of the vertex (fig. 2 right) and a twisting strength t. In addition, 6 degrees of freedom for translation and rotation in 3D are defined. Let $\beta_1, \beta_2, .., \beta_n$ denote the n deflection parameters, t denote the object twist, x, y, z the translation parameters, and $\gamma_x, \gamma_y, \gamma_z$ the rotation of the object in Euler angles. Then a deformation state can be formulated by the state vector

$$\Theta = (x, y, z, \gamma_x, \gamma_y, \gamma_z, t, \beta_1, \beta_2, ..., \beta_n) \ . \tag{2}$$

3   Physics of Deformation

A *linearly elastic, isotropic material* may be characterised by two position-dependent stiffness parameters: Young's modulus $E(r)$ and Poisson's ratio $\nu(r)$ [13]. When these parameters are known, along with the mass density $\rho(r)$, the geometry of the object and relevant and consistent set of boundary conditions, it is possible to solve for the deformation by the means of analytical or numerical methods.

The full numerical solution of a continuous 3D object is in general a computationally hard problem [5]. Physically discretized models such as mass-spring models are often very fast and efficient, but it can be difficult to relate physical parameters to the stiffness of the springs [16]. In our work we choose a realistic, mathematically discretized model of 1D deformation, namely the static Euler-Bernoulli model [6] formulated for inhomogeneous materials with non-constant cross-sections:

$$\frac{\partial^2}{\partial x^2}\left(E(x)J(x)\frac{\partial^2 w}{\partial x^2}\right) = q(x) \ . \tag{3}$$

where $w(x)$ is the transverse deflection in the z-direction (refer to Fig. 3), $E(x)$ is Young's modulus as previously described, $J(x)$ is the second moment of area and $q(x) = g\rho(x)A(x)$ where g is the gravitational acceleration and ρ and A respectively is the mass density and area for the cross-section. The model accounts for the elastic bending of the neutral axis, whereas stretching and shear effects are ignored [13,14].

In order to find a unique solution $w(x)$, four boundary conditions must be prescribed. To model the situation we use a cantilevered configuration, that is clamped at one end and free to move in the other [14,6].

$$w|_{x=0} = 0 \quad ; \quad \frac{\partial w}{\partial x}\bigg|_{x=0} = m \ . \tag{4}$$

The boundary conditions (4) for the fixed end of the beam are determined by the gripper pose. They prescribe zero deformation and a slope of $m = \Delta w/\Delta x$ of the neutral surface.

$$\frac{\partial^2 w}{\partial x^2}\bigg|_{x=L} = 0 \quad ; \quad \frac{\partial^3 w}{\partial x^3}\bigg|_{x=L} = 0 \ . \tag{5}$$

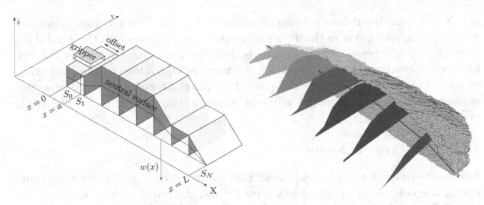

Fig. 3. Left: A gripper grasps a deformable object, with a gripper offset of a. The part from $x = a$ to $x = L$ deforms under its own weight in Z. Right: A triangle mesh as used in the system. At each slice S_i three scalar values are defined: The *cross-sectional area* A, the *z-component of the centroid* C_z and the *second moment of area* J_{C_z} with respect to C_z

The boundary conditions (5) at the free end of the beam correspond to the beam being free to move i.e. no end torque and shear force perpendicular to the beam.

The non-constant material parameters, varying cross section and varying body load in the governing equation, require the usage of a numerical method. (3) has been discretized by means of $O(h^2)$ centered finite differences. The number of discretization points is kept independent of the mesh resolution. The values of J and q are linearly interpolated from the mesh data. Young's modulus E is set by the optimisation. The boundary conditions of (4) and (5) are discretized similarly and used to eliminate the indices of the governing equation which would go beyond the domain. As the derived finite-difference expression is linear in the unknowns $w(x_i)$, we may rewrite it as a sparse, banded coefficient matrix and solve it by direct methods. The output of the numerical method is the deformation $w(x)$ for the neutral surface for each mesh slice. As plane-sections perpendicular to the neutral surfaces stay planar, the surface deformations are recovered by simple trigonometric relations [14].

The physical model is thus able to calculate the deformation curve as a function of Young's modulus E, the mesh geometry and the gripper pose. This is used to evaluate physical correctness for a deformation, formulated by a residual function as described in the next section. In the following we will denote the deformation curve as calculated by the beam-model for a given choice of E by $w_E(x)$.

4   Combining Vision and Physical Correctness

With a parametrizable deformation model at hand and a residual function that provides a measure for physical plausibility for a given deformation Θ and material property E, an overall measure can be defined that also takes the optical depth and color input into account. Similar to [11], an error function is defined which synthesizes a view of the deformed model and compares it to the input data (analysis by synthesis). The synthesis is done by rendering the object subject to the deformation Θ with projection parameters equivalent to the projection of the real camera. To retrieve the projection parameters for the hardware, the system is calibrated beforehand using the algorithm introduced by Schiller et al. in [19].

4.1   Joint Error Function

The joint error value of physical model and camera data is constructed by combining the color error e_c, the depth error e_d and the physical error e_r:
The difference between the simulated color image $\hat{I}_c$ and the input color image I_c is defined as RMS error

$$e_c = \sqrt{\sum_{p \in P_c} \frac{(I_c(p) - \hat{I}_c(p))^2}{|P_c|}} \, , \tag{6}$$

where $P_c = \{p \in \mathbb{N}^2 | \hat{I}(p) > 0\}$ denotes the set of all image pixels nonzero in $\hat{I}_c$. In a similar way, the difference between the simulated depth image $\hat{I}_d$ and the depth input image I_d is defined as

$$e_d = \sqrt{\sum_{p \in P_d} \frac{(I_d(p) - \hat{I}_d(p))^2}{I_d(p)^2 |P_d|}} \, , \tag{7}$$

where $P_d = \{p \in \mathbb{N}^2 | I_d > 0 \wedge \hat{I}(p) > 0\}$ denotes the images pixel that are nonzero in the simulated image and the input image. The distance error is normalized by the measured distance in I_d, so the error remains invariant to the scale with the scene size.

Combining color and depth data in one function is useful, since e.g. the dot based structured light approach of the Kinect causes inaccurate edge information compared to a color image. The joint usage of color and depth data combines the accurate depth (z) information from the depth sensor with the accurate color (x-y) information.

The physical error is the difference between the z-component of the deformation state $w_\Theta(s)$ and the 1D deformation curve calculated by the physical model $w_E(s)$

$$e_r = \frac{1}{|S|} \sum_{s \in S} (w_E(s) - w_\Theta(s))^2 \, , \tag{8}$$

where S is the set of all slices in the mesh (refer to Fig. 3). The error e_r is thus a measure on how well the current guess for a deformation state Θ and material property E match the physical model.

A joint error function mapping a parameter $\Theta' = (\Theta, E)$ to its overall plausibility can now be defined, by the combination of the error values e_r, e_c ,and e_d:

$$f(\Theta') = \sqrt{\lambda_r e_r^2 + \lambda_c e_c^2 + \lambda_d e_d^2} \ . \tag{9}$$

To transfer the error values into a common domain, the weights λ_r, λ_c, and λ_d are chosen according to the scale of the error: Within the deformation model the maximum error value of e_r is given by $e_{r_{max}}$ and λ_r is set to $\frac{1}{e_{r_{max}}^2}$ accordingly. The maximum color error e_c can reach is 255, hence λ_c is set to $\frac{1}{255^2}$. Since e_d is already normalized, λ_d is set to 1.

4.2   Optimization

As in [11], the error function (9) is minimized using CMA-ES (*Covariance Matrix Adaptation - Evolution Strategy* [7]). CMA-ES is a numerical optimization scheme suited for non-separable, non-convex, derivation-free fitness functions. A useful property of CMA-ES is the low number of fitness function evaluations needed, especially in high dimensional search spaces. The resulting parameters $\Theta'_{min} = \text{argmin}_{\Theta'} f(\Theta')$ provide the deformation parameters most suitable to the given input data.

5   Results

To evaluate the algorithm, tests on synthetic data and real data have been performed.

5.1   Experiments on Synthetic Data

The input data for the synthetic test has been generated by the deformation of cuboid shapes, using a Neo-Hookean deformation model [18] as implemented by the Finite-Element modeling software COMSOL[1] 3.5a in MEMS-mode. The simulated material had a size of $140 \times 65 \times 10$ mm. To generate the input image, a high resolution triangle mesh (10000 triangles) was generated from the deflection curve provided by the finite-element software. This model was rendered using the calibration data of the Kinect including lens distortion. A Gaussian distributed noise with a standard deviation of 0.5 mm (1.7% for the object distance of 30 cm) was added to the depth image to simulate the Kinect camera noise.

The tests have been performed on three different, homogeneous materials: Low stiffness ($E = 0.5$ N/mm², $\rho = 1.155 \cdot 10^{-6}$ kg/mm³), medium stiffness ($E = 2.0$ N/mm², $\rho = 1.155 \cdot 10^{-6}$ kg/mm³), and high stiffness ($E = 8.0$ N/mm², $\rho = 1.155 \cdot 10^{-6}$ kg/mm³). Each of the materials has been tested using a varying number of sections of constant curvature (see section 2), to determine the influence of this hyper parameter. Each test result is the average value of 50 test

---

[1] COMSOL Multiphysics, http://www.comsol.com

runs. The following tables show the RMS error from the ground truth data for
the relevant components of Θ'. The position and orientation of the objects have
not been fixed to also test the ability of simultaneous pose estimation:

RMS Error of Parameters on Low Stiffness Object ($E = 0.5$ N/mm^2)

sections	x(mm)	y(mm)	z(mm)	γ_x	γ_y	γ_z	twist	offset(mm)	E
4	0.250	1.386	0.438	0.372°	0.0002°	0.575°	0.013°	5.079	0.060
8	0.267	0.086	0.147	0.056°	0.0001°	0.036°	0.001°	4.945	0.062
12	0.506	0.118	0.122	0.076°	0.0005°	0.052°	0.002°	4.695	0.059

RMS Error of Parameters on Medium Stiffness Object ($E = 2.0$ N/mm^2)

sections	x(mm)	y(mm)	z(mm)	γ_x	γ_y	γ_z	twist	offset(mm)	E
4	0.920	0.127	0.519	0.092°	0.0001°	0.052°	0.003°	2.415	0.103
8	0.726	0.110	0.025	0.078°	0.0002°	0.044°	0.002°	2.638	0.116
12	0.708	0.063	0.034	0.061°	0.001°	0.028°	0.001°	2.766	0.121

RMS Error of Parameters on High Stiffness Object ($E = 8.0$ N/mm^2)

sections	x(mm)	y(mm)	z(mm)	γ_x	γ_y	γ_z	twist	offset(mm)	E
4	0.979	0.083	0.235	0.250°	0.002°	0.030°	0.004°	11.70	2.08
8	0.358	0.115	0.202	0.143°	0.001°	0.043°	0.004°	11.10	1.98
12	1.160	0.245	0.170	0.154°	0.004°	0.080°	0.003°	12.27	2.4

The tests show that the object pose can be retrieved quite accurately, as well
as the material parameters if the object is not too stiff. For very stiff objects,
the RMS of the gripper offset becomes larger which is reasonable (and hence
Young's modulus E), since for completely stiff objects this value is undefined.
Furthermore it shows, that the quality of the results increases considerable for
some values when switching from 4 sections of constant curvature to 8 sections,
while for e.g. 12 section the model tends to overfit in some cases. Therefore we
think 8 sections to be a good compromise between versatility and stability.

5.2   Experiments on Real Data

The real data experiments have been performed using a Microsoft Kinect camera
with a resolution of 640×480 in depth and color images. The distance between
object and camera has been 40 cm. As a consequence of the results discussed in
section 5.1, the number of sections of constant curvature has been set to 8.
To analyze the object material, 3 test objects have been made from the same
material but different thickness, hence different deflection curves. The material is
a Dow Corning Silastic 3481 silicone rubber molded using Silastic 81-R hardener.
The mass density for this is given to $\rho = 1.200 \cdot 10^{-6}$ kg/mm^3. Reference values
for Young's modulus have been estimated by tensile tests using an industrial
robot and a PASCO PS-2189 force sensor. The 7 mm object was estimated to
a value of $E = 0.50$ N/mm^2, while the 10 mm and 13 mm were estimated to
$E = 0.45$ N/mm^2.

Standard Deviation of Parameters on Real Objects

thickn.	x(mm)	y(mm)	z(mm)	γ_x	γ_y	γ_z	twist	offset(mm)	E
7 mm	1.304	1.082	0.705	0.509°	0.002°	1.161°	0.009 °	2.305	0.040
10 mm	1.320	1.722	0.368	0.341°	0.001°	0.707°	0.006 °	1.855	0.029
13 mm	0.162	1.899	0.074	0.058°	0.001°	0.174°	0.001 °	0.367	0.007

The table lists the standard deviation in the optimization results over a sequence of 50 Kinect images. The deviations show a slight increase in comparison
to the synthetic test based on the slightly increased distance between camera
and object and the not Gaussian nature of the noise in the depth values of the
Kinect camera. Especially the higher deviations in γ_z can be explained by the
inaccurate perception of depth discontinuities by the Kinect camera.
The averaged estimate for the 7mm thick object estimated by the algorithm was
$E = 0.40$ N/mm² (0.50 N/mm² in the tensile test), for the 10 mm object it was
$E = 0.47$ N/mm² (0.45 N/mm² in the tensile test), and for the 13 mm object
it was $E = 0.51$ N/mm² (0.45 N/mm² in the tensile test). The real test show
that the actual material parameters have been acquired with an average error
of $E = 0.1$ N/mm² and below.

6   Conclusion

Known elasticity parameters allow a wide range of robot interactions, since any
handling can be simulated and checked for success before it is actually performed
and motions can be planned taking the actual deflection of an object into account. In this article a system to estimate the elasticity parameters, deformation
and 6D pose of an object held by a robot gripper was proposed. The method
was verified by synthetical tests and proofed to be stable when applied to real
data. Furthermore, it was shown that the estimated elasticity parameters correspond to the actual material parameters by comparing the results to tensile test
measurements of the same objects.

References

1. Bodenhagen, L., Fugl, A., Willatzen, M., Gordon, H., Krüger, N.: Learning peg-
   in-hole actions with flexible objects. In: ICAART (2011)
2. Chen, E.J., Novakofski, J., Jenkins, W.K., O'Brien Jr., W.D.: Young's Modulus
   Measurements of Soft Tissues with Application to Elasticity Imaging. IEEE Transactions on Ultrasonics, Ferroelectrics and Frequency Control 43(1) (January 1996)
3. Erkamp, R.Q., Wiggins, P., Skovoroda, A.R., Emelianov, S.Y., O'Donnell, M.:
   Measuring the elastic modulus of small tissue samples. Ultrasonic Imaging 20(1),
   17–28 (1998)
4. Foresti, G., Pellegrino, F.: Automatic visual recognition of deformable objects for
   grasping and manipulation. IEEE Transactions on Systems, Man, and Cybernetics,
   Part C: Applications and Reviews 34(3), 325–333 (2004)

5. Frank, B., Schmedding, R., Stachniss, C., Teschner, M., Burgard, W.: Learning the elasticity parameters of deformable objects with a manipulation robot. In: Proc. of the Int. Conf. on Intelligent Robots and Systems, IROS (2010)

6. Han, S.M., Benaroya, H., Wei, T.: Dynamics of transversely vibrating beams using four engineering theories. Journal of Sound and Vibration 225, 935–988 (1999)

7. Hansen, N.: The CMA Evolution Strategy: A Comparing Review. In: Lozano, J.A., Larrañaga, P., Inza, I., Bengoetxea, E. (eds.) Towards a New Evolutionary Computation. STUDFUZZ, vol. 192, pp. 75–102. Springer, Heidelberg (2006)

8. Holm, P.: Robust Pose Refinement. Ph.D. thesis, University of Southern Denmark (2011)

9. Holm, P., Petersen, H.G.: Refining Visually Detected Object poses (2010)

10. Howard, A., Bekey, G.: Intelligent learning for deformable object manipulation. In: Computational Intelligence in Robotics and Automation, pp. 15–20 (1999)

11. Jordt, A., Koch, R.: Fast tracking of deformable objects in depth and colour video. In: Proceedings of the British Machine Vision Conference, BMVC 2011 (2011)

12. Jorgensen, J.A., Petersen, H.G.: Usage of simulations to plan stable grasping of unknown objects with a 3-fingered Schunk hand. In: IROS (2008)

13. Landau, L.D., Pitaevskii, L.P., Lifshitz, E.M., Kosevich, A.M.: Theory of Elasticity. Butterworth-Heinemann (1986)

14. Love, A.: A treatise on the mathematical theory of elasticity. Courier Dover Publications (1944)

15. Meththananda, I., Parker, S., Patel, M., Braden, M.: The relationship between shore hardness of elastomeric dental materials and young's modulus. Dental Materials 25(8), 956–959 (2009)

16. Mosegaard, J.: Cardiac Surgery Simulation - Graphics Hardware meets Congenital Heart Disease. Ph.D. thesis, Department of Computer Science, University of Aarhus, Denmark (October 2006)

17. Oliver, W.C., Pharr, G.M.: An improved technique for determining hardness and elastic modulus using load and displacement sensing indentation experiments. Journal of Materials Research 7(6), 1564–1583 (1992)

18. Rivlin, R.S.: Large elastic deformations of isotropic materials. i. fundamental concepts. Philosophical Transactions of the Royal Society of London. Series A, Mathematical and Physical Sciences 240(822), 459–490 (1948)

19. Schiller, I., Beder, C., Koch, R.: Calibration of a pmd camera using a planar calibration object together with a multi-camera setup. In: ISPRS, Beijing, China, vol. XXXVII, Part B3a, pp. 297–302 (2008), xXI. ISPRS Congress

20. Schraft, R.D., Ledermann, T.: Intelligent picking of chaotically stored objects. Assembly Automation 23, 38–42 (2003)

Surface Quality Inspection of Deformable Parts with Variable B-Spline Surfaces

Sebastian von Enzberg and Bernd Michaelis

Institute for Electronics, Signal Processing and Communications (IESK)
Otto-von-Guericke-University Magdeburg, Germany
{sebastian.vonenzberg,bernd.michaelis}@ovgu.de

Abstract. High precision range sensors can be used for measuring 3D point clouds of object surfaces for quality inspection in industrial production. It is often difficult to formally describe acceptable tolerance ranges of real surfaces, especially for deformable objects. Instead of a formal definition, the surface and its tolerance range can rather be given by a set of training samples.

In this paper we describe how to apply the Karhunen-Loève-Transform (KLT) on B-spline surfaces. With this transform, a group of similar surfaces can be described with very few characteristic coefficients in the transformed domain, thus allowing the detection of marginal surface deviations on deformable parts.

1 Introduction

Automatic surface quality inspection is an important tool for quality control in industrial manufacturing [12]. Its goal is to find small local defects on a freeform surface. In contrast to geometry inspection ([8], [4]), the global shape is not of importance. Parts made of sheet metal or moulded plastics are deformable before their assembly, and thus have large, variable tolerance ranges. For car body parts, typical defects like dents or bumps may have a lateral spread of several millimeters, but are of very small height (down to 20 μm [12]), which is within tolerance ranges but well visible after polishing or painting. The automatic detection of these defects right after sheet metal forming is a non-trivial task.

In general, high precision 3D measurement of surfaces is possible with high resolution optical sensors and algorithms for dense point cloud acquisition (typically fringe projection, e.g. phase shifting [9]). The acquired data then has to be compared to a model of the surface or a pattern which is adapted to account for the deformation of the measured surface. The difference between model and data yields the undesired surface defects. While this problem is solved for non-deformable parts [2], a formal definition of this model including acceptable tolerance ranges and possible deformation is difficult or in many cases impossible. Methods comparing the data to a low-pass filtered version ([14], [17]) are of limited benefit, since defects with large lateral spread cannot be detected and high-curvature surface areas can be confused for defects.

A. Pinz et al. (Eds.): DAGM/OAGM 2012, LNCS 7476, pp. 175–184, 2012.
© Springer-Verlag Berlin Heidelberg 2012

In [10] a method is proposed which transforms discrete measured data into a variance-based space, whose axes are determined by a set of training data. Rather than a formal definition, several measurements of typical faultless sample surfaces are necessary for describing a defect-free part (see fig. 1). The underlying formalism is commonly known as the Karhunen-Loève transform (KLT). By dimensionality reduction in the transformed domain, "unusual" variances (i.e. defects and measurement noise) are restrained, and can be detected by inverse transformation. A priori information of the average shape and acceptable tolerance ranges and deformations is modeled by the axes of the transformed space and thus allows for high precision defect detection.

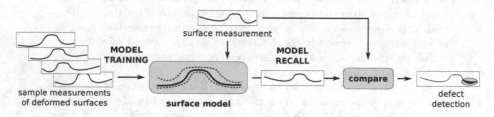

Fig. 1. Surface inspection method with a variable surface model by training with sample measurements, as proposed by [10]

Tensor product B-spline surfaces are a popular way to describe 3D surfaces in computer aided engineering and design. They allow for a parametric description of the surface, thus can be easily evaluated, yet give enough flexibility to describe coarse areas as well as areas with high curvature characterised by the underlying knot vector [5]. By means of surface approximation, 3D point clouds acquired by computer vision methods can be converted to a B-spline surface description. Several efficient algorithms are known which have been developed for reverse engineering (e.g. [7], [13]).

In this paper, the Karhunen-Loève transform is derived for the continous description of a B-spline surface, resulting in a variable B-spline surface model which can be used for high precision surface inspection. The paper is organised as follows: Sections 2.1 and 2.2 give a short review of the Karhunen-Loève-Expansion (KLE) and the basics of B-spline surface description. In section 3, the KLE is applied to B-spline surfaces. An example for a real measurement is given in section 4 and conclusions are given in section 5.

2   Mathematical Tools

2.1   The Continous Karhunen-Loève-Transform

In image processing, mostly the discrete Karhunen-Loève-Expansion is used, which is similar to the Principal Component Expansion (PCA) [6]. It can be generalised for continous functions, if the function can be expressed as a series expansion $z(x)$ [11]:

$$z_k(x) = \sum_{i=1}^{n} c_{ki} \Phi_i(x) \tag{1}$$

The objective is to find a set of optimal base functions $f_i(x)$ of a new series expansion, that approximates a given set of functions $z_k(x)$ with a minimal squared error:

$$R = \sum_k \int_{\Omega_x} \left(z_k(x) - \sum_{i=1}^{\ell} a_{ki} f_i(x) \right)^2 dx \to min! \tag{2}$$

This problem can be solved analytically, if the original base functions $\Phi_i(x)$ are piecewise orthonormal, or if the Gramian matrix is available, allowing for an orthogonalization as described in 2.2. Assuming orthonormal base functions, the inner product of two functions $\langle z_1, z_2 \rangle$, can be computed as the dot product of the vectors of coefficients $\mathbf{c}_k = [c_{k1}, \quad c_{k2}, \quad \ldots]^T$:

$$\langle z_1(x), z_2(x) \rangle = \int_{\Omega_x} z_1(x) z_2(x) dx = \mathbf{c}_1^T \cdot \mathbf{c}_2 \tag{3}$$

So instead of solving integral equations, eq. 2 can be solved entirely by vector and matrix operations. The resulting optimal base $f_i(x)$ is also orthonormal and can be represented in terms of the original function space:

$$f_i(x) = \sum_r e_{ir} \Phi_r(x) \tag{4}$$

By solving eq. 2 it can be shown [11] that vectors $\mathbf{e}_i = [e_{i1}, \quad e_{i2}, \quad \ldots]^T$ describing the optimal base functions $f_i(x)$ are the eigenvectors of the covariance matrix of the original function coefficients $\mathbf{c_k}$:

$$\mathbf{C}\mathbf{e}_i = \lambda_i \mathbf{e}_i \tag{5}$$

$$\text{with} \quad \mathbf{C} = \sum_k \mathbf{c}_k \mathbf{c}_k^T \tag{6}$$

For the approximation of a function $z(x)$ in the optimal function space $f_i(x)$, we first apply the Karhunen-Loève-Transform, then the inverse KLT:

$$a_i = \int_{\Omega_x} f_i(x) z(x) dx = \mathbf{e}_i \mathbf{c}^T \quad \text{(KLT)} \tag{7}$$

$$z(x) \approx z^*(x) = \sum_{i=1}^{r} a_i f_i(x) \quad \text{(KLT)}^{-1} \tag{8}$$

In case of a full transform $r = n$, we get the exact same data after inverse transform. In case of dimension reduction $r < n$, we get an approximation with the most significant statistical properties of the set of functions which are inherent to the covariance matrix C of the eigenvalue problem (5).

2.2   B-Spline Surfaces and Their Orthogonalization

A tensor product B-spline surface is described as the double sum [15]

$$\mathbf{s}(u,v) = \begin{bmatrix} x(u,v) \\ y(u,v) \\ z(u,v) \end{bmatrix} = \sum_{i=1}^{n}\sum_{j=1}^{m}\mathbf{p}_{ij}b_i^k(u)b_j^l(v) \qquad (9)$$

which maps from parametric space $(u,v) \in \mathbb{R}^2$ to a 3d surface $\mathbf{s} = (x,y,z) \in \mathbb{R}^3$. The surface shape is defined by the control points $\mathbf{p}_{ij} \in \mathbb{R}^3$ which are blended using B-spline base functions $b_i^k(u), b_j^l(v)$ of order k, l. They are characterized by knot vectors $\mathbf{U} = [u_0, u_1, ..., u_{(k+n)}], \mathbf{V} = [v_0, v_1, ..., v_{(l+m)}]$, which form a grid.

In order to apply the Karhunen-Loève-Transform to a B-spline surface, orthogonalization of the base functions $b_i^k(u), b_j^l(v)$ is suggested. In general the Gram-Schmidt process [3] can be applied. Its integral equations have to be solved numerically, thus making the computational implementation complicated. In [18] it is shown that orthogonalization of B-spline base functions can also be described as a linear transform with a transformation matrix $\mathbf{\Lambda}$, which results from an arbitrary factorisation $\mathbf{\Lambda}^T\mathbf{\Lambda} = \mathbf{\Sigma}^{-1}$ (e.g. singular value decomposition) of the positive definite Gram-matrix $\mathbf{\Sigma}$:

$$\mathbf{\Sigma_u} = \begin{bmatrix} \int b_1^k(u)b_1^k(u)du & \int b_1^k(u)b_2^k(u)du & \cdots & \int b_1^k(u)b_n^k(u)du \\ \int b_1^k(u)b_2^k(u)du & \int b_2^k(u)b_2^k(u)du & & \vdots \\ \vdots & & \ddots & \\ \int b_1^k(u)b_n^k(u)du & \cdots & & \int b_n^k(u)b_n^k(u)du \end{bmatrix} \qquad (10)$$

Using matrix notation [16] for the B-spline base functions, the Gram-matrices $\mathbf{\Sigma_u}, \mathbf{\Sigma_v}$ can be computed analytically without any complicated integration. Its values are only dependend on the knot vectors $\mathbf{U}, \mathbf{V}$ of the B-spline base $b_i^k(u)$, $b_j^l(v)$. For a given knot configuration (which can be assumed for similar surfaces), the Gram-matrices and the resulting transform matrices $\mathbf{\Lambda_u}, \mathbf{\Lambda_v}$ can be precomputed.

Now, eq. 9 can be written with an orthogonal base in matrix notation. For the x-coordinate of $\mathbf{s}(u,v)$, this is

$$x(u,v) = \mathbf{b^k(u)} \cdot \mathbf{\Lambda_u}^T \cdot \mathbf{P_x^\perp} \cdot \mathbf{\Lambda_v} \cdot \mathbf{b^l(v)}^T \qquad (11)$$

and analogous for $y(u,v)$ and $z(u,v)$, with $\mathbf{b^k(u)} = [b_1^k(u) \quad \cdots \quad b_n^k(u)]$ and $\mathbf{b^l(v)} = [b_1^l(v) \quad \cdots \quad b_m^l(v)]$. The x-, y- and z-components $p_{x,ij}, p_{y,ij}, p_{z,ij}$ of the original surface control points $\mathbf{p}_{ij}$ are ordered into matrices $\mathbf{P_x}, \mathbf{P_y}, \mathbf{P_z}$ and have to be transformed, in order to work with the new orthogonalised base:

$$\mathbf{P_x^\perp} = \left(\mathbf{\Lambda_u}^T\right)^{-1}\mathbf{P_x}\left(\mathbf{\Lambda_v}\right)^{-1} \qquad (12)$$

(and analogous for the y- and z-coordinate of the control points $\mathbf{P_y^\perp}, \mathbf{P_z^\perp}$).

3   Derivation of the KLT for B-Spline Surfaces

With the orthogonalized B-spline base, we can now apply the KLT as described in section 2.1.

After the orthogonal transform (12), the control point matrices $\mathbf{P}^{\perp}_{\mathbf{x}\,k}$, $\mathbf{P}^{\perp}_{\mathbf{y}\,k}$, $\mathbf{P}^{\perp}_{\mathbf{z}\,k}$ have to be vectorised again for all training samples k. We now can solve the eigenvalue problem (5) for the covariance matrix (6) of the orthogonalized control points $\mathbf{p}^{\perp}_{\mathbf{x}\,k}, \mathbf{p}^{\perp}_{\mathbf{y}\,k}, \mathbf{p}^{\perp}_{\mathbf{z}\,k}$:

$$\mathbf{C}_x \mathbf{e}_{x,i} = \lambda_{x,i} \mathbf{e}_{x,i} \tag{13}$$

$$\text{with}\quad \mathbf{C}_x = \sum_k \mathbf{p}^{\perp}_{\mathbf{x}\,k} \left(\mathbf{p}^{\perp}_{\mathbf{x}\,k}\right)^T \tag{14}$$

and similar for dimensions y, z to get eigenvectors $\mathbf{e}_{x,i}, \mathbf{e}_{y,i}, \mathbf{e}_{z,i}$. The eigenvectors describe the statistical properties of the surfaces used for training, and can be put into transform matrices $\mathbf{E_x} = [\mathbf{e}_{x,1} \quad \cdots \quad \mathbf{e}_{x,r}], \mathbf{E_y}, \mathbf{E_z}$.

For the inspection of one surface measurement, we can apply (after orthogonalization) the transforms (7) and (8), which can be written in matrix form:

$$\mathbf{a_x} = \mathbf{E_x} \mathbf{p}^{\perp}_{\mathbf{x}} \qquad \text{(KLT)} \tag{15}$$

$$\mathbf{p}^{\perp *}_{\mathbf{x}} = \mathbf{E_x}^T \mathbf{a_x} \qquad \text{(KLT)}^{-1} \tag{16}$$

The resulting vectors $\mathbf{p}^{\perp *}_{\mathbf{x}}, \mathbf{p}^{\perp *}_{\mathbf{y}}, \mathbf{p}^{\perp *}_{\mathbf{z}}$ represent an approximation of the measured surface in the orthogonalized B-spline space. They can be used as regular B-spline control points after inverse orthogonal transform:

$$\mathbf{P^*_x} = \mathbf{\Lambda_u}^T \left(\mathbf{P}^{\perp *}_{\mathbf{x}}\right) \mathbf{\Lambda_v} \tag{17}$$

Similar to the orthogonalization step (12), control points now have to be in matrix form according to their position in the u-/v-grid of the B-spline representation (9).

In fig. 2, the transformations and different surface representations used for the proposed inspection method are summarized. The necessary steps can be divided in two main steps: In the training phase, the optimal function space is computed from a given set of training samples, giving an implicit surface model. The actual inspection takes place in the recall phase, where a "'defect-free"' surface description is modeled for the measured surface data by dimension reduction in the optimal function space. This can be used for comparison to the measured data (i.e. computation of the orthogonal point distance).

4   Evaluation

4.1   Overview of the Data Set and Its Measurement

The proposed method has been evaluated using a data set consisting of 100 measurements of several car door panels, which have been measured with a photogrammetric multi-camera sensor (4 cameras) and fringe projection (phase shift

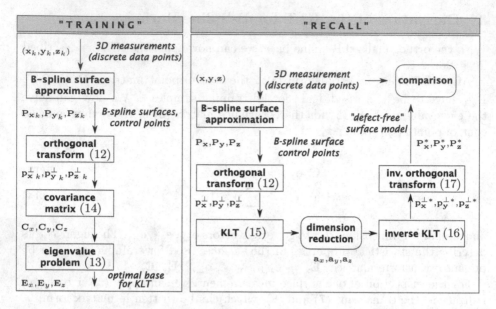

Fig. 2. Summary of surface representations and transforms used. The necessary equation for each transform is referenced in brackets.

method [9]) and have been checked as "defect-free" by a professional auditor. Each measurement consists of 335×354 data points on the same rectangular $1 \times 1mm$-grid in the x/y-plane, and has been converted to a B-spline surface with 172×192 control points with the method recently described in [7]. Though small deviations in positioning can be taken into account by our method, an ICP algorithm [1] has been applied to the 3D points to achieve a comparable coordinate system for each measurement.

In fig. 3, the measured surface is shown as an average of all measurements. Its B-spline representation approximates the point cloud with a standard deviation of $0.001mm$. Since the defects are well below $1mm$, the discrete measured data is visualized as the difference along the z-axis for each point in the x/y-grid compared to another part. Some examples of these difference maps are shown in fig. 4 for typical variations of the part. Especially around the door handle cup, design edges and along the top border the parts may vary by several millimeters, making defect detection difficult.

4.2   Defect Detection

For evaluating our method, 80 of the 100 parts are selected for the training phase, with only the first 20 significant base functions used for further processing. For the recall phase, a gaussian bump with a maximum height of $h = 100\mu m$ and a lateral size of $80 \times 20mm$ is simulated onto the parts not used during training (see fig. 5).

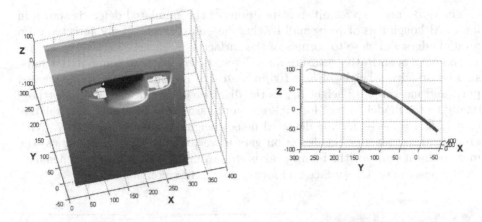

Fig. 3. Surface data of a car door panel, averaged from 100 measurements of several parts

Fig. 4. z-difference maps for 3 parts compared to the average part

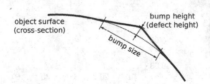

Fig. 5. Simulation of a gaussian-shaped defect onto an object surface. The defect height is usually much smaller compared to its lateral size.

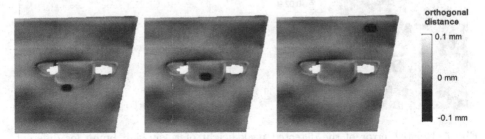

Fig. 6. Map of orthogonal distances of the surface to the measured points with a simulated gaussian bump of $h = 100\mu m$ height and $80 \times 20mm$ spread

The difference map for different positions of the simulated defect is shown in fig. 6. Although it is of very small height, the bump can be easily detected even around edges and close to corners of the surface.

To give a quantitative measure for different defect sizes, we simulated a gaussian bump with a height of $h = 100\mu m$ onto the measured data of one trained part, and measured its height h_m as the distance of the measured data orthogonally to the model surface for different bump sizes and positions. The relative error $\Delta h_{rel} = \frac{h_m - h}{h}$ for the detected defect height can be seen in fig. 7. With growing defect size, defect detection gets more difficult. For large bumps, the measurement error for the bump peak is still around 2%, it is mostly dependend on the position on the surface and local surface characteristics.

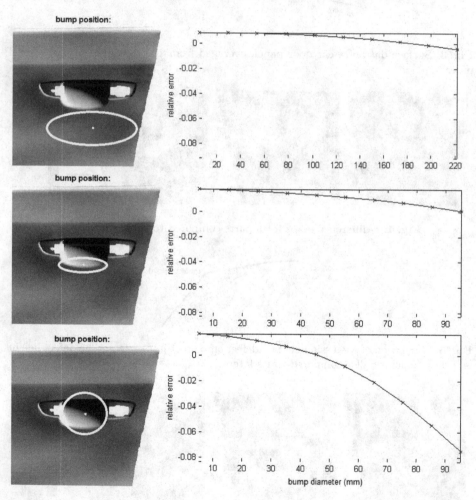

Fig. 7. Relative error of the detected peak height of a gaussian bump for different bump sizes and positions

Since the detection quality is mostly position-dependend, it is useful to have a tool for visualizing the detection quality on the surface. A map $\Delta h_{rel}(u, v)$ can be built by moving the center of a simulated gaussian bump over the whole surface area and selecting the detected height at the bump peak for each position in the map (see fig. 8).

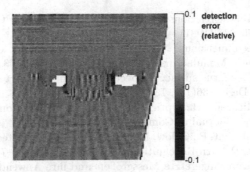

Fig. 8. Map of the position-dependend defect detection quality for a gaussian bump of size $10 \times 10mm$ and $100\mu m$ height

5   Conclusions

In this paper we develop the continous Karhunen-Loève-Transform for B-spline surface descriptions. It can be used for the detection of small defects on digitized surfaces, by modeling the variance of a set of measured sample surfaces as the base of an optimal function space. By selecting only the first significant base functions in the transformed domain, typical surface deviations and tolerance ranges are implied.

We have shown that our method allows the detection of small bumps for deformable parts even on critical areas that contain high curvature and have high tolerance ranges (e.g. edges or design ridges). Also, defects with high lateral spread within tolerance ranges are detected. We have furthermore presented tools for visualising the position dependend detection quality, thus allowing further analysis of our method in future work.

Acknowledgements. This work is part of the project "Oberflaecheninspektion auf Basis angepasster Oberflaechenmodelle" funded by the federal state of Saxony-Anhalt and the "European Regional Developement Fund". 3D data sets have been kindly provided by INB Vision AG.

References

1. Besl, P.J., Mckay, H.D.: A method for registration of 3-D shapes. IEEE Transactions on Pattern Analysis and Machine Intelligence 14(2), 239–256 (1992)
2. Bispo, E.M., Fisher, R.B.: Free-form surface matching for surface inspection. In: Proceedings of the 6th IMA Conference on the Mathematics of Surfaces, pp. 119–136. Clarendon Press (1994)

3. Björck, A.: Numerics of Gram-Schmidt orthogonalization. Linear Algebra and its Applications 197/198, 297–316 (1994)
4. Broggiato, G.B., Campana, F., Gerbino, S.: Shape deviation analysis on sheet-metal parts through reverse engineering techniques. In: ADM International Conference, vol. 12 (2001)
5. Farin, G.: Curves and Surfaces for CAGD - A Practical Guide, 5th edn. Morgan Kaufmann (2002)
6. Gerbrands, J.J.: On the relationships between SVD, KLT and PCA. Pattern Recognition 14(1-6), 375–381 (1981)
7. Koch, K.R.: Three-dimensional NURBS surface estimated by lofting method. Int. Journal of Advanced Manufacturing Technology 49, 1059–1068 (2010)
8. Li, Y., Gu, P.: Free-form surface inspection techniques start of the art review. Computer-Aided Design 36(13), 1395–1417 (2004)
9. Lilienblum, E., Michaelis, B.: Optical 3D surface reconstruction by a multi-period phase shift method. Journal of Computers 2(2) (2007)
10. Lilienblum, T., Albrecht, P., Calow, R., Michaelis, B.: Dent detection in car bodies. In: Proc. 15th Int. Pattern Recognition Conf., vol. 4, pp. 775–778 (2000)
11. Michaelis, B.: Zusammengesetzte Messgrößen und ihre Anwendung. Ph.D. thesis, TH Magdeburg (1980)
12. Özkul, M.: Qualitätsansprüche bezüglich des äußeren Erscheinungsbildes von Automobilen der Premiumklasse. Ph.D. thesis, TU Munich (2009)
13. Park, H., Jung, H., Kim, K.: A new approach for lofted B-spline surface interpolation to serial contours. The International Journal of Advanced Manufacturing Technology 23, 889–895 (2004)
14. Peng, J., Strela, V., Zorin, D.: A simple algorithm for surface denoising. In: VIS 2001: Proceedings of the Conference on Visualization 2001, pp. 107–112. IEEE Computer Society, Washington, DC (2001)
15. Piegl, L., Tiller, W.: The Nurbs Book. Monographs in Visual Communication. Springer (1997)
16. Qin, K.: General matrix representations for B-splines. The Visual Computer 16, 177–186 (2000)
17. Recknagel, R.J.: Defekterkennung an Oberflächen mittels Waveletmethoden. Ph.D. thesis, Universität Jena (2000)
18. Redd, A.: A comment on the orthogonalization of B-spline basis functions and their derivatives. In: Statistics and Computing, pp. 1–7 (2011)

Automated Image Forgery Detection
through Classification of JPEG Ghosts

Fabian Zach, Christian Riess, and Elli Angelopoulou

Pattern Recognition Lab.
University of Erlangen-Nuremberg
{riess,elli}@i5.cs.fau.de

Abstract. We present a method for automating the detection of the so-called JPEG ghosts. JPEG ghosts can be used for discriminating single- and double JPEG compression, which is a common cue for image manipulation detection. The JPEG ghost scheme is particularly well-suited for non-technical experts, but the manual search for such ghosts can be both tedious and error-prone. In this paper, we propose a method that automatically and efficiently discriminates single- and double-compressed regions based on the JPEG ghost principle. Experiments show that the detection results are highly competitive with state-of-the-art methods, for both, aligned and shifted JPEG grids in double-JPEG compression.

1 Introduction

The goal of blind image forensics is to determine the authenticity of an image without using an embedded security scheme. With the broad availability of digital images and tools for image editing, it becomes increasingly important to detect malicious manipulations. Consequently, image forensics has recently gained considerable attention. Most existing methods fall into two categories: a) detecting traces of a particular manipulation operation and b) verifying the "rationality" of expected image artifacts. Good surveys on such methods are [10,4]. For instance, methods for copy-move forgery detection search for duplicated content *within* the same image (see e. g. [3]). However, traces from such a copying operation may be visible to the eye. If a manipulator is careful, he might hide such visible traces using post-processing operations. To counter a careful, yet not technically educated forger, a number of researchers focused on invisible cues for image manipulation. One of the most widely used invisible indicators are JPEG artifacts. Their use in image forgery detection is based on the following key observation: every time that a JPEG image is recompressed, the statistics of its compression coefficients slightly change.

Consider, for example, the case where a manipulator takes a JPEG image, alters part of the image, and saves it again as a JPEG image. Then, the (unaltered) background is compressed twice, while the repainted area appears to be compressed only once in JPEG format — because the JPEG artifacts of the initial compression were destroyed by the painting operation.

A. Pinz et al. (Eds.): DAGM/OAGM 2012, LNCS 7476, pp. 185–194, 2012.
© Springer-Verlag Berlin Heidelberg 2012

Thus, a common goal in JPEG-based forensics is to detect areas with differing numbers of JPEG compression, and report such an irregularity. For instance, Lin et al. [7] showed how the use of different quantization matrices in the first and second compression leads to a telltale high frequency component in the coefficient spectrum. However, their method assumes that the JPEG block grids of the first and second compression are exactly aligned. This holds for image regions in the background, as in the previous example. In more general scenarios, so-called "shifted double-JPEG (SD-JPEG) compression" can be detected. For instance, Qu et al. [8] developed a method for handling arbitrary block grid alignments using independent component analysis. Barni et al. [1] proposed a method that purely relies on non-matching grids. All these methods assume different quantization matrices for the first and second compression. Huang et al. [6] showed how to detect recompression with the same quantization matrices by exploiting numerical imprecisions of the JPEG encoder.

While the majority of the presented approaches rely on statistics, Farid [5] recently presented a perception-oriented SD-JPEG method, called "JPEG ghost" detection. It assumes that the first compression step was conducted on a lower quality level than the second step. Then, it suffices to recompress the image during analysis with various lower quality levels. *Difference images* are subsequently created by subtracting the original image from the recompressed versions (see Sec. 2). For approximately correct recompression parameters, the double compressed region appears as a dark "ghost" in the difference image.

The simplicity of this approach has several advantages: it is easy to implement, its validity can be simply explained, visually verified and demonstrated to non-technical experts. However, an important drawback is the lack of automation for JPEG ghost detection. It is currently infeasible for a human expert to visually examine the difference images for all possible parameters.

The goal of this paper is to address this drawback. We present a method that fully automates the detection of JPEG ghosts. A human expert can still make use of the JPEG ghost scheme, but is relieved from the requirement of manually analyzing hundreds of images. We designed 6 features that operate on the difference images to distinguish between single and double-compressed regions in the JPEG images. A comparison to the method of Lin et al. [7], as well as to results reported by other authors, shows that our JPEG ghost detection has very competitive performance.

2   JPEG Ghost Observation

We briefly restate Farid's ghost observation [5]. Let I_{q_1} be an input image that has been compressed with JPEG quality q_1. Assume that a region of the image has been previously compressed with JPEG quality q_0, where $q_0 < q_1$. To detect this doubly compressed region, define a set of quality factors $Q = \{q_2 | 0 < q_2 < q_1\}$. Recompressing image I_{q_1} with the factors in Q yields a set of test images I_{q_1,q_2}. The difference image D_{q_2} of I_{q_1} and I_{q_1,q_2} is defined as

Fig. 1. Example JPEG ghost. Left: a rectangular region has been double-compressed with primary compression rate $q_0 = 60$. Middle and right: in the difference images Δ_{75} and Δ_{65} a "ghost" gradually appears as a darker region. Note also the noise in Δ_{75} and Δ_{65} due to the image texture.

$$D_{q_2}(x,y) = \frac{1}{3} \sum_{i \in \{R,G,B\}} (I_{q_1}(x,y,i) - I_{q_2}(x,y,i))^2 \ , \tag{1}$$

where x and y denote the pixel coordinates, and $i \in \{R,G,B\}$ the red, green and blue color channels.

If a region of the image has previously been compressed with a compression factor q_0, $q_0 < q_1$, the squared differences become smaller for this part of the image as q_2 approaches q_0. This local region, termed "ghost", appears darker than the remaining image. This comes from the fact that if the coefficients of q_2 become more similar to the coefficients of (the unknown) q_0, similar artifacts are introduced in the image. For robustness to texture, $D_{q_2}(x,y)$ is averaged across small windows of size w. Thus, the differences are computed as

$$\Delta_{q_2}(x,y) = \frac{1}{3w^2} \sum_{i} \sum_{w_x=0}^{w-1} \sum_{w_y=0}^{w-1} (I_{q_1}(x+w_x, y+w_y, i) - I_{q_2}(x+w_x, y+w_y, i))^2 \ , \tag{2}$$

and normalized to lie in the range between 0 and 1.

Fig. 1 shows an example of such a ghost. A rectangular double compressed region has been embedded with $q_0 = 60$ (left). Two difference images Δ_{75} and Δ_{65} are also shown. The resulting ghost can be clearly seen in Δ_{65}. This can directly be forensically exploited by examining a number of difference images Δ_{q_2} for varying q_2. If a dark region appears, it is considered as doubly compressed.

However, in practice, the amount of human interaction is extremely time-consuming for two reasons. First, one has to closely examine every image, as a ghost can be visually hard to distinguish from noise [2]. Second, the number of difference images can become very large: a ghost appears, if the JPEG grid of Δ_{q_2} is exactly aligned with the JPEG grid of the first compression using q_0. Thus, all possible 64 JPEG grid alignments must be visually examined. Ultimately, a human expert has to browse $64 \cdot |Q|$ images, where $|Q|$ is the number of difference images with $q_2 < q_1$. In practice, there are often more than 300 difference images.

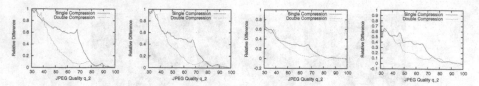

Fig. 2. Difference curves from example JPEG ROIs. The same ROI has been single- and double-compressed and is plotted in a joint diagram. In red, the difference curves for single compression are shown, in green for double compression.

3   Feature Extraction

The information about a JPEG ghost is contained in the differences of a single $w \times w$ window over different quality levels. Consider ROIs which have been single- or double-compressed. Example difference curves for this case are shown in Fig. 2. Here, the differences are computed over four different windows of an image with compression quality $q_1 = 84$, over 70 quality levels $30 \leq q_2 \leq 100$ on a window size $w = 16$. All differences are normalized between 0 and 1. The red curves denote the differences for single compressed windows. The green curves show the same ROIs, but this time double compressed with $q_0 = 69$. The green curve exhibits a second minimum and rapid decay at (the unknown) q_0. Due to differences in image texture, this effect is stronger for the left graphs, than the right graphs.

Our method is based on the analysis of these difference curves. We estimate the quality level q_1 as the global minimum over the curves derived from all windows in the image. We then proceed as follows. Let $c(x)$ be the value of the difference curve for quality level x. We extracted six features that are defined on $c(x)$ for $30 \leq x \leq q_1$. Note that this range implies that we can not detect ghosts with $q_0 < 30$. However, this is mainly an engineering decision, as we considered cases of $q_0 < 30$ as very unlikely. Let, furthermore, $w_1(x) = (x - 30)/(q_1 - 30)$ denote a weighting function that puts more emphasis on high JPEG qualities, and $w_2(x) = 1 - w_1(x)$ a weighting function that emphasizes low JPEG qualities. We employ the following features:

1. The weighted mean value of the curve,

$$f_1 = \frac{1}{\sum_{x=30}^{q_1} w_1(x)} \sum_{x=30}^{q_1} w_1(x) \cdot c(x) \ . \tag{3}$$

2. The median of all values $c(x)$ for $30 \leq x \leq q_1$, i.e. $f_2 = \mu_{1/2}$ where

$$\left(P(c(x) \leq \mu_{1/2}) \geq \frac{1}{2} \right) \wedge \left(P(c(x) \geq \mu_{1/2}) \geq \frac{1}{2} \right) \ , \tag{4}$$

   and $P(c(x) \leq x)$ denotes the cumulative distribution function of $c(x)$.
3. f_3 is the slope of the regression line through $c(x)$ for $30 \leq x \leq q_1$.

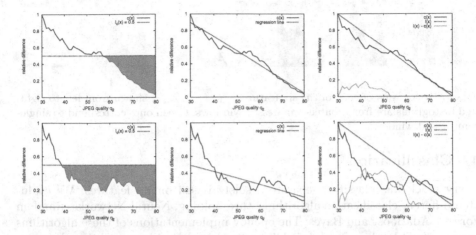

Fig. 3. Visualization of the proposed features. Top: a single-compressed window, bottom: a double-compressed window. Left: area below a normalized error of 0.5. Middle: regression line on the error curve. Right: squared distance of the curve to the line between $(30, 1)$ and $(q_1, 0)$.

4. f_4 is the y-axis intercept of the regression line through $c(x)$ for $30 \le x \le q_1$.

5. The weighted number of points of $c(x)$ with $c(x) < t = 0.5$,

$$f_5 = \Big(\sum_{x-30}^{q_1} w_2(x) \Big)^{-1} \cdot \sum_{x=30}^{q_1} w_2(x) \cdot g_5(x) \ , \text{where } g_5(x) = \begin{cases} 1 & \text{if } c(x) < t \\ 0 & \text{otherwise} \end{cases} \quad (5)$$

6. The average squared distance between the actual curve and the linear function $l(x) = 1 - (x - 30)/(q_1 - 30)$, i.e. the line connecting $(30, 1)$ and $(q_1, 0)$. More formally,

$$f_6 = \sum_{x=30}^{q_1} g_6(x) \ , \text{where } g_6(x) = \begin{cases} (l(x) - c(x))^2 & \text{if } l(x) > c(x) \\ 0 & \text{otherwise} \end{cases} \quad (6)$$

The feature computation is well parallelizable, as every feature depends only on a spatially isolated window. The core idea of this feature set is to identify the steeper decay of the double-compression difference curve (see Fig. 2). Figure 3 illustrates the decision for the feature set on an example window. For each feature, we computed a histogram based on $2.5 \cdot 10^6$ image windows, see Fig. 4. The compression quality levels of these windows were randomly chosen between 50 and 95, with a fixed distance $q_0 - q_1 = 20$. Feature values of single-compressed windows are plotted in green, while features of double-compressed windows are shown in red. From left to right, the distributions for f_1 to f_6 are shown. Although several blocks overlap within a feature, the majority of blocks exhibits good separation between single- and double-compression.

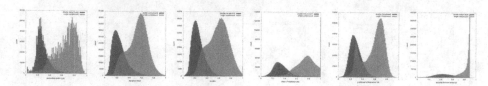

Fig. 4. Histograms of each of the six features, $f_1, f_2, \ldots, f_6$, shown from left to right. Red histograms are from double-compressed windows. Green ones correspond to single-compressed windows.

4 Classification

Every block was classified separately, solely based on its features. We evaluated different classification algorithms: thresholding, Neural Networks, Random Forests, AdaBoost and Bayes. The openCV implementations of these algorithms were used. The values for thresholding were determined by computing the mean values of the feature distributions for single- and double-compressed areas. The actual threshold was then determined as the mean of means for each feature. A block was considered double-compressed, if at least three quarters of the feature values exceeded their respective threshold. The Neural Network was a Multilayer Perceptron with a 10-node hidden layer. The activation function is a sigmoid function with $\alpha = \beta = 1$. For the Random Forests, we used 50 trees for classification, while for Discrete AdaBoost 100 trees. The cost functions of all classifiers were set to a balanced state of false positive and false negative rates.

5 Experiments

We used the Uncompressed Colour Image Database (UCID) [9] for evaluating our method. It consists of 1338 images of size 512×384. For each image, we created a single-compressed version, and two versions with single- and double-compression, where a randomly chosen 192×192 pixels region is differently compressed than the background. In total, this yields twice as many single- as double-compressed pixels. Per image, we randomly selected $q_1 \in [50; 95]$, and set $q_0 = q_1 - \delta$, where $5 \leq \delta \leq 20$. We varied the length w of a window between 8 and 64 pixels. Following [5], we excluded very smooth image regions, i.e. windows with an intensity variance below 5 points. For the training of the classifiers, we used 10% of the images from all three classes. Note that the test- and training sets are still weakly correlated due to the high variability of the dataset.

As a quality measure, we used specificity and sensitivity. Let sc and dc denote "single-compressed" and "double-compressed", respectively. Then, let

$$\text{TP} = P(\text{dc}|\text{dc}) , \quad \text{TN} = P(\text{sc}|\text{sc}) , \quad \text{FP} = P(\text{dc}|\text{sc}) , \quad \text{FN} = P(\text{sc}|\text{dc}) \quad (7)$$

be the true positives, true negatives, false positives and false negatives, respectively. Then, specificity and sensitivity are defined as

$$\text{specificity} = \frac{\text{TN}}{\text{TN} + \text{FN}} , \quad \text{sensitivity} = \frac{\text{TP}}{\text{TP} + \text{FN}} . \quad (8)$$

Table 1. Experiments on the UCID database for shifted ghost detection on misaligned DCT grids at a per-window level

δ	w	Thresh.	MLP	RF	Boost.	Bayes
5	8	0.798/0.702	0.866/0.826	0.804/0.889	0.834/0.886	0.469/0.984
	16	0.805/0.704	0.855/0.880	0.811/0.901	0.841/0.893	0.483/0.983
	32	0.816/0.717	0.865/0.891	0.838/0.925	0.847/0.919	0.505/0.981
	64	0.840/0.596	0.897/0.833	0.889/0.890	0.907/0.870	0.562/0.976
10	8	0.815/0.728	0.865/0.864	0.831/0.901	0.852/0.896	0.479/0.986
	16	0.821/0.730	0.869/0.873	0.834/0.914	0.858/0.910	0.497/0.984
	32	0.833/0.745	0.835/0.935	0.850/0.941	0.865/0.934	0.520/0.983
	64	0.837/0.755	0.917/0.847	0.908/0.893	0.924/0.869	0.579/0.979
20	8	0.844/0.778	0.888/0.910	0.865/0.938	0.895/0.934	0.506/0.985
	16	0.849/0.783	0.895/0.906	0.864/0.937	0.902/0.938	0.520/0.984
	32	0.857/0.796	0.865/0.935	0.879/0.935	*0.912/0.957*	0.553/0.983
	64	*0.861/0.804*	*0.925/0.892*	*0.931/0.913*	0.938/0.916	*0.622/0.977*

Note that two other popular measures, the false positive rate and the false negative rate, additively complement specificity and sensitivity to 1. All results in the tables are presented as specificity/sensitivity pairs.

5.1 Experiments on Individual Image Windows

Tab. 1 shows the results for the evaluation per $w \times w$ window. Here, "Thresh.", "MLP", "RF", "Boost." and "Bayes" denote classification by thresholding, multilayer perceptron, random forests, discrete AdaBoost and the Bayesian classifier, respectively. The difference in the quality levels of primary and secondary compression is denoted as $\delta = q_1 - q_0$. In order to have a relatively balanced number of single and double compressed pixels, we only evaluated the performance on the correct shift of the doubly-compressed region. However, when we evaluated the whole pipeline, we tested all 64 shifts of the JPEG grid.

The best performance per classifer (considering the sum of specificity and sensitivity) on all combinations of δ and the region size is printed in italics. As expected, typically the highest tested compression distance of $\delta = 20$, together with the largest examined window size 64×64 yields best results. Note that AdaBoost performed best below the maximum windows size. Note also that for $\delta = 10$ and $\delta = 5$, boosting, followed by neural networks (MLP) and random forests (RF) all provide very strong results. Furthermore, the performance of these three methods degrades gracefully for smaller windows. Thus, as a pre-processing step for guiding a human expert towards a JPEG ghost location, we consider these three classifiers highly suitable. Additionally, the good discrimination for small values of δ improves over the results reported in [5], which reports $\delta \geq 20$ as a good quality distance for detection. In [7], detection rates for $\delta \leq 10$ vary between 50% and 70%.

Table 2. Experiments on the UCID database for ghost detection on aligned DCT grids at image level

δ	w	Lin et al.	Thresh.	MLP	RF	Boost.	Bayes
5	8	0.583/0.640	0.806/0.766	0.783/0.870	0.756/0.929	0.823/0.867	0.576/0.846
	16	-	0.816/0.760	0.783/0.871	0.762/0.934	0.832/0.867	0.646/0.841
	32	-	0.812/0.755	0.749/0.889	0.726/0.949	0.811/0.883	0.742/0.822
	64	-	0.830/0.481	0.963/0.355	0.978/0.375	0.982/0.378	0.882/0.606
10	8	0.658/0.597	0.820/0.759	0.774/0.874	0.913/0.857	0.918/0.880	0.594/0.892
	16	-	0.827/0.758	0.777/0.870	0.897/0.873	0.916/0.899	0.772/0.815
	32	-	0.830/0.737	0.776/0.857	0.882/0.883	0.916/0.895	0.840/0.845
	64	-	0.852/0.439	0.946/0.377	0.968/0.416	0.989/0.412	0.938/0.684
20	8	*0.705/0.605*	0.832/0.880	0.864/0.941	0.905/0.960	0.997/0.939	0.533/0.997
	16	-	*0.858/0.883*	*0.892/0.957*	0.904/0.973	0.996/0.956	0.647/0.997
	32	-	0.867/0.868	0.865/0.947	*0.908/0.972*	*0.993/0.960*	0.839/0.988
	64	-	0.933/0.484	0.866/0.517	0.959/0.519	0.997/0.507	*0.960/0.955*

5.2 Experiments on Automated Tampered Image Detection

For comparison to other methods, we implemented a straightforward tampered image classifier based on the recognition of partially double-compressed JPEG images. To remove outliers on the marked windows from the previous section, we applied a 3×3 pixels morphological opening with a cross-topology on these markings. We considered an image tampered, if 10% of the windows are marked. Note that an embedded foreground-ghost contains about 20% double-compressed pixels, a background-ghost about $100\% - 20\% = 80\%$. As before, we created three images from every UCID image. Once completely single-compressed, once with an embedded foreground-ghost, and once with an embedded background-ghost. Tab. 2 shows the result for JPEG ghosts that were exactly aligned with the JPEG grid. We used the same notation as in the previous Subsection.

For comparison, we evaluated the method of Lin et al. [7] on our test set. As this method operates on 8×8 windows, only these results are presented. The approach of Lin et al. is more general, in the sense that it can also detect double-compression where $q_0 > q_1$. However, this comes at the expense of the accuracy in the presence of very small differences in the compression parameters. Thus, if the initial assumption $q_0 < q_1$ for JPEG ghosts is fulfilled, the proposed method provides much higher specificity and sensitivity rates.

The best success rates do not occur at the larger window sizes. This is due to the fact that the embedded foreground ghosts of 192×192 pixels are comparably small. When applying morphological opening on the windows that have been marked as double-compressed, more accurate detectors lose too many windows on the boundary of the marked region. This renders very large window sizes less successful. One notable exception is the Bayesian classifier. As can be seen from Tab. 1, Bayesian classification exhibits very low specificity, i.e. creates many erroneously marked regions. The morphological operator removes a large

Table 3. Experiments on UCID database for shifted ghost detection on misaligned DCT grids on image level

δ	w	Thresh.	MLP	RF	Boost.	Bayes
5	8	0.742/0.772	0.982/0.904	0.923/0.960	0.990/0.955	0.907/0.981
	16	0.755/0.708	0.993/0.934	0.940/0.952	0.987/0.944	0.919/0.982
	32	0.750/0.698	0.973/0.915	0.969/0.952	0.984/0.947	0.923/0.983
	64	0.763/0.468	0.967/0.765	0.992/0.843	1.000/0.809	0.951/0.983
10	8	0.762/0.794	0.978/0.932	0.938/0.957	0.978/0.951	0.923/0.983
	16	0.779/0.733	0.975/0.913	0.955/0.954	0.984/0.948	0.945/0.983
	32	0.791/0.728	*0.981/0.968*	0.961/0.957	0.986/0.950	0.951/0.983
	64	0.795/0.646	0.984/0.755	0.993/0.803	0.998/0.775	0.966/0.986
20	8	0.784/0.836	0.977/0.955	0.969/0.972	0.993/0.971	0.987/0.985
	16	*0.802/0.795*	0.963/0.939	*0.978/0.972*	0.995/0.969	0.993/0.987
	32	0.806/0.786	0.862/0.953	0.948/0.963	*0.995/0.971*	0.995/0.988
	64	0.810/0.659	0.988/0.833	0.994/0.806	0.999/0.818	*0.997/0.988*

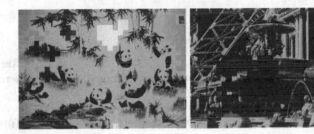

Fig. 5. Two example markings on individual windows. Green and red are single- and double compressed, respectively. Gray denotes low contrast regions. Left: the rectangular double compression region could only in the high-contrast windows be recovered. Right: the double compression region is clearly visible. In a classification on image level, the left example is a false negative case, the right example true positive.

number of these false positive markings, and makes detection with larger window sizes possible. In comparison, the remaining classifiers exhibit their peak performance at window sizes around 16×16 pixels. Again, discrete Adaboost clearly outperforms the other methods.

In shifted double-compression, the grid of the inserted region is not required to properly align with the JPEG grid of the background. To detect such tampered images, we computed all 64 shifts and selected the one with the highest response of double-compressed blocks (see Tab. 3 for the results). A surprising result is that shifted double JPEG compression can be slightly better discriminated than the non-shifted version: while the overall best result in Tab. 2 is 0.997/0.939, several results in Tab. 3 perform better, e.g. the Bayesian classifier on a 64×64 grid for $\delta = 20$ with 0.997/0.988. During shifted double-compression, $q_1 = 100$ is often (wrongly) estimated. Interestingly, the increased gap between q_0 and q_1 improves classification. Based on our results, we recommend the use of AdaBoost for JPEG ghost detection. Its reliability on small window sizes yields in many cases a high level of detail in the marked blocks (see Fig. 5). The quality difference δ can be decreased to an empirical minimum of 5 points. In such cases, other methods often exhibit difficulties; e.g. [5] and [7] reported increased error rates for $\delta < 20$ and $\delta < 10$, respectively.

6   Conclusions

We proposed a JPEG-based forensic algorithm to automatically distinguish single-compressed and double-compressed image regions. We presented a classification scheme that exploits the JPEG-ghost effect, but completely removes the requirement of browsing the images. Best results were achieved by training a boosted classifier on 6 specially designed features. The classification performance is encouraging. The best specificity and sensitivity are 0.912 and 0.957, respectively. For tampering detection, the difference in primary and secondary compression may be as small as $\delta = 5$.

References

1. Barni, M., Costanzo, A., Sabatini, L.: Identification of Cut & Paste Tampering by Means of Double-JPEG Detection and Image Segmentation. In: International Symposium on Circuits and Systems, pp. 1687–1690 (May 2010)
2. Battiato, S., Messina, G.: Digital Forgery Estimation into DCT Domain – A Critical Analysis. In: Multimedia in Forensics, Security and Intelligence, pp. 37–42 (October 2009)
3. Bayram, S., Sencar, H.T., Memon, N.: A survey of copy-move forgery detection techniques. In: IEEE Western New York Image Processing Workshop (2009)
4. Farid, H.: A Survey of Image Forgery Detection. Signal Processing Magazine 26(2), 16–25 (2009)
5. Farid, H.: Exposing Digital Forgeries from JPEG Ghosts. IEEE Transactions on Information Forensics and Security 1(4), 154–160 (2009)
6. Huang, F., Huang, J., Shi, Y.Q.: Detecting Double JPEG Compression With the Same Quantization Matrix. IEEE Transactions on Information Forensics and Security 5(4), 848–856 (2010)
7. Lin, Z., He, J., Tang, X., Tang, C.K.: Fast, Automatic and Fine-grained Tampered JPEG Image Detection via DCT Coefficient Analysis. Pattern Recognition 52(11), 2492–2501 (2009)
8. Qu, Z., Luo, W., Huang, J.: A Convolutive Mixing Model for Shifted Double JPEG Compression with Application to Passive Image Authentication. In: International Conference on Acoustics, Speech and Signal Processing, pp. 1661–1664 (March 2008)
9. Schaefer, G., Stich, M.: UCID - An Uncompressed Colour Image Database. In: SPIE Storage and Retrieval Methods and Applications for Multimedia, pp. 472–480 (January 2004)
10. Sencar, H., Memon, N.: Overview of State-of-the-art in Digital Image Forensics. In: Algorithms, Architectures and Information Systems Security, pp. 325–344 (2008)

Synergy-Based Learning of Facial Identity

Martin Köstinger, Peter M. Roth, and Horst Bischof

Institute for Computer Graphics and Vision
Graz University of Technology, Austria
{koestinger,pmroth,bischof}@icg.tugraz.at

Abstract. In this paper we address the problem that most face recognition approaches neglect that faces share strong visual similarities, which can be exploited when learning discriminative models. Hence, we propose to model face recognition as multi-task learning problem. This enables us to exploit both, shared common information and also individual characteristics of faces. In particular, we build on Mahalanobis metric learning, which has recently shown good performance for many computer vision problems. Our main contribution is twofold. First, we extend a recent efficient metric learning algorithm to multi-task learning. The resulting algorithm supports label-incompatible learning which allows us to tap the rather large pool of anonymously labeled face pairs also for face identification. Second, we show how to learn and combine person specific metrics for face identification improving the classification power. We demonstrate the method for different face recognition tasks where we are able to match or slightly outperform state-of-the-art multi-task learning approaches.

1 Introduction

For humans the recognition of familiar faces is straight forward. Computational face recognition matches the performance of humans in controlled environments, however, often fails under unconstrained real-world conditions (e.g., diversity in viewpoint, lighting, clutter, or occlusions). This can be explained by essential differences in human and machine learning. Typically when machine learning techniques learn a specific visual model they focus on individual characteristics and neglect general concepts or visual commonalities of similar objects. In contrast, the human visual system learns in a more synergistic way that benefits from commonalities and takes into account prior knowledge. Hence, for computational recognition systems it would be beneficial also to exploit such information.

One popular concept that addresses this demand is transfer learning, which aims at improving the performance of a target learning task by also exploiting collected knowledge of different sources [1]. Two related aspects are domain adaptation and multi-task learning. Domain adaptation tries to bridge the gap between a source domain with sufficient labeled data to a specific target domain with little or no labels [1]. In contrast, multi-task learning (MTL) [2] approaches a cluster of similar tasks in parallel. Each task describes a target learning problem

A. Pinz et al. (Eds.): DAGM/OAGM 2012, LNCS 7476, pp. 195–204, 2012.
© Springer-Verlag Berlin Heidelberg 2012

and contributes labeled data. The knowledge transfer between the tasks is then established through a shared intermediate representation. The basic assumption is that it is easier to learn several hard tasks simultaneously than to learn those isolated. In this way underrepresented tasks that have only a limited number of labeled samples can be handled. Prominent approaches rely on neural nets [3,4] (sharing layers) or support vector machines [5] (sharing weight vectors).

In this paper, we adapt multi-task learning for real-world, large-scale face recognition. In order to cope with the real-world challenges we want to incorporate as much relevant information as possible. In particular, given by similar/dissimilar labeled face pairs, where we have no access to the actual class labels. These labeled pairs are mainly used for face verification (deciding if two faces match) and are rather easy to obtain also on a large scale. For face identification it is not immediately obvious how to make use of this anonymous information. But these additional face pairs allow us to learn a more robust measure of face similarity. Multi-task learning then spreads this knowledge between the tasks. Hereby, to enable meaningful transfer of knowledge, multi-task learning faces the problem of different label sets. On the one hand side for face identification the label set consists of class labels while on the other hand side we have only equivalence labels. Thus, one important aspect of multi-task learning is label-incompatible learning, the support of different label sets for different learning tasks. Particularly, the successful multi-task adaptation of support vector machines [5] lacks this feature.

Recently, Mahalanobis metric learning [6,7] showed favorable performance for various computer vision tasks including face verification [8]. The goal is to find a global linear transformation of the feature space such that relevant dimensions for classification or ranking are emphasized while irrelevant ones are discarded. One particular advantage is that Mahalanobis metric learning methods usually operate on the space of pairwise differences, thus enabling label-incompatible learning. The method of Parameswaran and Weinberger [9] extends Mahalanobis metric learning to the multi-task paradigm. Nevertheless, due to the particular optimization it relies on labeled triplets and can thus not benefit from data just labeled with equivalence constraints. Further, it requires computationally expensive iterations making it impractical for large-scale applications. Hence, to capitalize on multi-task learning for face recognition, one faces the additional challenges of scalability and the ability to deal just with equivalence labels.

To meet these requirements, we extend a recent efficient metric learning algorithm [10] to the multi-task paradigm. The resulting algorithm enables label-incompatible learning as it only relies on pairwise equivalence labels. These are considered as natural inputs to distance metric learning algorithms as similarity functions basically establish a relation between pairs of points. In particular, we want to learn specific Mahalanobis distance metrics for each person. This is inspired by the recent finding of Weinberger and Saul [11] that especially for large-scale applications better results can be obtained by learning multiple distance metrics. Also many other learning algorithms cast a complex multi-class problem in series of simpler, often two class, problems, followed by a voting rule to form the final decision [12]. Thus, inspired by the successful strategy applied for multi-class support vector machines we intend to learn individual distance metrics. Our method is scalable to large datasets and not prone to over-fitting. To demonstrate the merits of our method we compare it to recent multi-task and metric learning approaches on the challenging PubFig [13] face recognition benchmark.

2   Multi-task Metric Learning for Face Recognition

In the following, we introduce our new multi-task metric learning approach for face recognition. First, in Section 2.1 we briefly describe the metric learning approach introduced in [10], which is very efficient in training as it avoids complex iterative computations and is thus scalable to large datasets. Next, in Section 2.2, we extend this approach for the multi-task domain. Finally, in Section 2.3 we introduce a voting scheme that allows for classification using multiple metrics. The overall goal is to combine several person specific metrics to a multi-class decision which should lead to lower error rates.

2.1   Mahalanobis Metric Learning

One prominent approach for metric learning is to learn a Mahalanobis distance d_{M}^2, which measures the squared distance between two data points $\mathbf{x}_i, \mathbf{x}_j \in \mathbb{R}^d$:

$$d_{\mathrm{M}}^2(\mathbf{x}_i, \mathbf{x}_j) = (\mathbf{x}_i - \mathbf{x}_j)^\top \mathbf{M}(\mathbf{x}_i - \mathbf{x}_j) . \tag{1}$$

The only requirement to induce a valid (pseudo) metric is that $\mathbf{M}$ is a symmetric positive semi-definite matrix. Several different approaches (e.g., [11], [7], or [8]) have been proposed that address different loss functions or regularizations to optimize such a metric for specific problems. However, such approaches typically require complex iterative, computationally expensive optimization schemes and fully labeled data. Instead, *KISS metric* learning (KISSME) [10] overcomes these limitations by introducing an efficient statistical motivated formulation that allows to learn just from equivalence constraints. Analog to the KISS principle (*keep it simple and straightforward!*) the method is conceptually simple and efficient per design.

For the following discussion let $\mathbf{x}_i, \mathbf{x}_j \in \mathbb{R}^d$ be a pair of samples and $y_i, y_j \in \{1, 2, \ldots, c\}$ the according labels. Further we define a set of similar pairs $\mathcal{S} = \{(i, j) \,|\, y_i = y_j\}$ and a set of dissimilar pairs $\mathcal{D} = \{(i, j) \,|\, y_i \neq y_j\}$. The goal of KISSME is to decide whether a pair (i, j) is similar or not. From a statistical inference point of view the optimal statistical decision can be obtained by a likelihood ratio test. Hereby, the hypothesis H_0 that the pair is dissimilar is tested against H_1 that the pair is similar:

$$\delta(\mathbf{x}_{ij}) = \log\left(\frac{p(\mathbf{x}_{ij}|H_0)}{p(\mathbf{x}_{ij}|H_1)}\right) = \log\left(\frac{f(\mathbf{x}_{ij}|\theta_0)}{f(\mathbf{x}_{ij}|\theta_1)}\right) , \tag{2}$$

where δ is the log-likelihood ratio, $f(\mathbf{x}_{ij}|\theta)$ is a pdf with parameters θ and $\mathbf{x}_{ij} = \mathbf{x}_i - \mathbf{x}_j$. Thus, KISSME casts the metric learning problem into the space of pairwise differences, as also the similarity Eq. (1) is defined via pairwise differences. This space has zero-mean and is invariant to the actual locality of the samples in the feature space. Assuming zero-mean Gaussian distributions within the difference space Eq. (2) can be re-written to

$$\delta(\mathbf{x}_{ij}) = \log \left(\frac{\frac{1}{\sqrt{2\pi|\Sigma_D|}} \exp(-1/2\, \mathbf{x}_{ij}^T\, \Sigma_D^{-1}\, \mathbf{x}_{ij})}{\frac{1}{\sqrt{2\pi|\Sigma_S|}} \exp(-1/2\, \mathbf{x}_{ij}^T\, \Sigma_S^{-1}\, \mathbf{x}_{ij})} \right), \tag{3}$$

where Σ_S and Σ_D are the covariance matrices of S and D, respectively. Let $\mathbf{C}_{ij} = (\mathbf{x}_i - \mathbf{x}_j)(\mathbf{x}_i - \mathbf{x}_j)^T$ be the outer product of the pairwise differences of $\mathbf{x}_i$ and $\mathbf{x}_j$, the covariance matrices can be written as

$$\Sigma_S = \frac{1}{|S|} \sum_{(i,j)\,\in\,S} \mathbf{C}_{ij}\,, \quad \Sigma_D = \frac{1}{|D|} \sum_{(i,j)\,\in\,D} \mathbf{C}_{ij}\,. \tag{4}$$

The maximum likelihood estimate of the Gaussian is equivalent to minimize the distances from the mean in a least squares manner. This allows KISSME to find respective relevant directions for S and D. By taking the log and discarding the constant terms we can simplify Eq. (3) to

$$\delta(\mathbf{x}_{ij}) = \mathbf{x}_{ij}^T\, \Sigma_S^{-1}\, \mathbf{x}_{ij} - \mathbf{x}_{ij}^T\, \Sigma_D^{-1}\, \mathbf{x}_{ij} = \mathbf{x}_{ij}^T(\Sigma_S^{-1} - \Sigma_D^{-1})\mathbf{x}_{ij}\,. \tag{5}$$

Finally, the Mahalanobis distance matrix $\mathbf{M}$ is obtained by

$$\mathbf{M} = \left(\Sigma_S^{-1} - \Sigma_D^{-1}\right)\,. \tag{6}$$

2.2   Multi-task Metric Learning

Now having introduced KISSME, we can extend formulation Eq. (6) to the multi-task learning paradigm. The general idea of multi-task learning is to consider T different, but related learning tasks in parallel. In our case a task is to learn a face verification model for a specific person, and the relation is intuitively given via the shared visual properties of faces. There are different concepts to realize such a setting. In particular, we adopt the formulation of Parameswaran and Weinberger [9]. We model the individual metric for each task $t \in \{1, 2, \ldots, T\}$ as combination of a shared metric $\mathbf{M}_0$ and a task-specific metric $\mathbf{M}_t$:

$$d_t^2(\mathbf{x}_i, \mathbf{x}_j) = (\mathbf{x}_i - \mathbf{x}_j)^T(\mathbf{M}_0 + \mathbf{M}_t)(\mathbf{x}_i - \mathbf{x}_j)\,. \tag{7}$$

Each task defines a subset of task specific samples given by the index set $\mathcal{I}_t$. Hence, to adopt the formulation Eq. (7) for the KISS metric, we have to define a task-specific subset of similar and dissimilar sample pairs: $\mathcal{S}_t = \{(i,j) \in \mathcal{I}_t | y_i = y_j\}$ and $\mathcal{D}_t = \{(i,j) \in \mathcal{I}_t | y_i \neq y_j\}$. In cases where $\mathcal{S}_t$ and $\mathcal{D}_t$ is not given, these sets can be sampled randomly of the actual class labels. Hence, according to Eq. (6) we can estimate task specific metrics by

$$\mathbf{M}_t = \left(\frac{1}{|\mathcal{S}_t|} \sum_{(i,j) \in \mathcal{S}_t} \mathbf{C}_{ij} \right)^{-1} - \left(\frac{1}{|\mathcal{D}_t|} \sum_{(i,j) \in \mathcal{D}_t} \mathbf{C}_{ij} \right)^{-1} . \tag{8}$$

Similarly, by estimating the weighted sum over the individual task specific characteristic we get the shared or common metric

$$\mathbf{M}_0 = \left(\frac{1}{T} \sum_{t=1}^{T} \frac{1}{|\mathcal{S}_t|} \sum_{(i,j) \in \mathcal{S}_t} \mathbf{C}_{ij} \right)^{-1} - \left(\frac{1}{T} \sum_{t=1}^{T} \frac{1}{|\mathcal{D}_t|} \sum_{(i,j) \in \mathcal{D}_t} \mathbf{C}_{ij} \right)^{-1} . \tag{9}$$

Then, the final individual Mahalanobis distance metric is given by

$$\hat{\mathbf{M}}_t = \mathbf{M}_0 + \mu \, \mathbf{M}_t . \tag{10}$$

Intuitively, $\mathbf{M}_0$ picks up general trends across all tasks and thus models commonalities. In contrast, $\mathbf{M}_t$ models task-specific characteristics. As only free parameter we retain a balancing factor μ between the task specific metric $\mathbf{M}_t$ and the shared metric $\mathbf{M}_0$. Intuitively, the more samples a task contributes the more focus lies on its specific metric.

2.3   Multi-task Voting

To fully exploit the power of our multi-task metric learning method for face recognition, we combine multiple, person specific, metrics into a multi-class decision. However, the outputs of the different metrics are not necessarily compatible and cannot be compared directly. A prominent strategy to reconcile classifier outputs is to calibrate them by fitting a sigmoid curve to a held-out set [14]. Nevertheless, since such an approach requires a large amount of labeled data, it is inapplicable for our purpose. Another successful strategy is to assign the class that wins most pairwise comparisons [15], also referred as *max-wins* rule.

To adapt this strategy for multi-task metric learning, we assume that the positive samples for task t coincidence with the class label $\mathbf{x}_i : y_i = t$. Then the combination rule

$$\arg\max_t(\mathbf{x}_i) =$$

$$\arg\max_t \sum_{u \neq t} \left[\mathrm{I}\left(\min_{j \in \mathcal{I}_t \wedge y_j = t} d_t^2(\mathbf{x}_i, \mathbf{x}_j) \leq \min_{k \in \mathcal{I}_u \wedge y_k = u} d_t^2(\mathbf{x}_i, \mathbf{x}_k) \right) \right.$$

$$\left. + \mathrm{I}\left(\min_{j \in \mathcal{I}_t \wedge y_j = t} d_u^2(\mathbf{x}_i, \mathbf{x}_j) \leq \min_{k \in \mathcal{I}_u \wedge y_k = u} d_u^2(\mathbf{x}_i, \mathbf{x}_k) \right) \right] \tag{11}$$

checks if the minimum distance of a given test sample $\mathbf{x}_i$ to class t is smaller than to class u. The indicator function

$$I(x) = \begin{cases} 1 \text{ if } x \text{ is true} \\ 0 \text{ otherwise} \end{cases} \tag{12}$$

scores for class t if this is true. This comparison is done with the individual distance metric of task t. Further, we also compare the distances under the complementary distance metric of task u. The basic idea is that if class t scores even under that metric it is an indicator for class t. Intuitively, the final decision is for the class that wins most pairwise comparisons.

3 Experiments and Evaluations

In the following, we demonstrate the performance of our method on the Public Figures Face Database (PubFig) [13]. The dataset can be considered as very challenging as it exhibits huge variations in pose, lighting, facial expression and general imaging and environmental conditions. As features we use the "high-level" description of visual face traits [13], which describes the presence or absence of 73 visual attributes, such as gender, race, hair color etc. For the intended face identification benchmark we organize the data similar to the existing verification protocol in 10 folds for cross-validation. Therefore, we split the images of each individual into 10 disjoint sets. The goals of our experiments are twofold. First, in Section 3.1 we show that multi-task learning allows us to successfully exploit additional data with anonymous pairwise labels for face identification. Next, in Section 3.2 we show that multi-task learning of person specific metrics boosts the performance for face identification. In particular, we show that the power lies in the combination of multi-task learning and the person specific metrics, as it is not sufficient to learn them off-the-shelf. Further, we compare our results to standard metric learning and related multi-task learning approaches.

Fig. 1. PubFig database [13]: The evaluation set contains 42,461 images of 140 individuals. The number of images (i.e., numbers below the images) per individuals ranges from 63 (Dave Chappelle) to 1536 (Lindsay Lohan). We split the images in 10 non-overlapping folds for cross-validation.

3.1   Inducing Knowledge from Anonymous Face Pairs to Face Identification

First, we show that multi-task learning allows us to transfer general knowledge about face similarity from anonymous face pairs to face identification. In order to enable a meaningful transfer of knowledge hereby multi-task learning faces the problem of different label sets. We test a multi-task learning scenario with two learning tasks, one with pairwise equivalence labels for the face pairs and one with class labels for face identification. The goal is to show that the additional anonymous face pairs help to improve the face identification performance. We sample the pairs randomly of the predefined development split of the dataset, containing 60 people. For the identification task we use the evaluation set, containing 140 people (Fig. 1). Thus, we ensure that the subjects for the tasks are mutually exclusive. For a given test sample we perform k-NN classification using a single metric to the 140 classes. Using different values for k revealed that there is no significant performance change, although simple nearest neighbor assignment leads to the best performance. Thus, we stick to a simple nearest neighbor assignment.

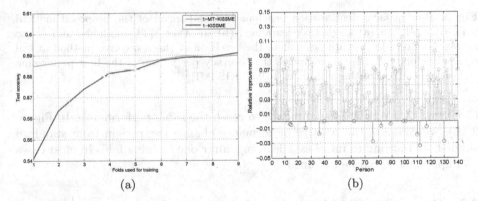

(a)   (b)

Fig. 2. Benefiting from additional pairwise labels for face identification on the Pub-Fig dataset: (a) k-NN classification accuracy of KISSME multi-task vs. standard single-task learning in relation to the amount of training data; (b) relative performance change per person from single-task to multi-task learning after using one fold for training. Green indicates positive induction while red indicates a negative induction.

In Figure 2 (a) we plot the face identification performance in relation to amount of data used to train the metric. Testing is done on a held-out set via 10 fold cross-validation. In each step we increase the number of folds used to train the identification task by one. As expected, the distance metric trained via multi-task learning (1-MT-KISSME) yields reasonable results right from the beginning. Obviously, it is able to reuse knowledge of the anonymous face pairs. In contrast, the distance metric trained without the additional pairwise labels

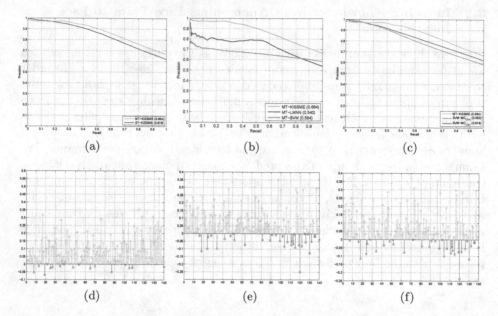

Fig. 3. PubFig face identification benchmark. Comparison of the proposed method (MT-KISSME) to (a) single-task learning , (b) to other MTL methods, and (c) to SVMs. Numbers in parentheses denote the precision of the respective method at full recall. Bottom row, (d)-(f), compares the accuracy per person of the best performing competing method of the plot above to MT-KISSME.

(1-KISSME) needs by far more data to reach the same performance. In Figure 2 (b), we compare the relative performance change per person from standard single-task learning to multi-task learning, after one training fold. In most cases an improvement can be obtained.

3.2 Person Specific Metric Learning

Second, we demonstrate the performance of our MTL method to learn person specific distance metrics. To show the merit of our method we compare it to recent MTL methods [5,9] and also benchmark to multi-class support vector machines [16,17]. We report the face identification performance in a refusal to predict style. Therefore, we rank and threshold the classifier scores. In that sense, recall means the percentage of samples which have a higher score than the current threshold and thus are labeled. Precision means the ratio of correctly labeled samples.

In Figure 3 (a) we compare, as a sanity check, the performance of estimating person specific metrics via multi-task vs. single-task learning. The MTL method outperforms the single-task learning over most levels of recall. At full recall the performance difference is about 4.5%. The main advantage of our MTL method s revealed if we compare the recognition accuracy per person. With multi-task learning we reach a person accuracy of 63.10% while single-task reaches only 54.08%. Thus, it is favorable to learn person specific metrics multi-task. In Figure 3 (d) we compare the relative performance change per person. Only for a small number of classes the performance drops slightly while for the vast number the performance increases.

Next, in Figure 3 (b) we benchmark to recent MTL methods, MT-LMNN [9] and MT-SVM [5]. Both methods are not really able to capitalize on the synergies of the face identification task. Both methods are outperformed by MT-KISSME over all levels of recall. At full recall the respective performance gain compared to MT-LMNN is 12.4%, compared to MT-SVM 8%. In Figure 3 (e) we plot the relative performance change on person level compared to MT-SVM. Hence, our method is able also to compete with two recent MTL approaches. Compared to the MT-SVM one advantage may be that MT-KISSME operates in the space of pairwise differences, which eases meaningful transfer of knowledge between the learning tasks. Further, compared to both competing MTL methods MT-KISSME is able to gain information from pairwise labels.

Finally, in Figure 3 (c) we benchmark our method to multi-class support vector machines. Particularly, the method of Crammer and Singer [16] has shown recent success also compared to metric learning methods [6]. The standard multi-class one-vs-all SVM reaches with 58.4% at full recall about the same performance as the MT-SVM. The method of Crammer and Singer [16] beats this by 3.7%. This may be accounted to the fact that it attempts to solve a single multi-class optimization problem that is better suited for unbalanced datasets. Nevertheless, MT-KISSME outperforms the one-vs-all method by 8.5% and the method of Crammer and Singer by 4.5%.

4 Conclusion

In this work we presented a synergistic approach to exploit shared common as well as person specific information for face recognition. By extending KISSME [10] metric learning we developed a multi-task learning method that is able to learn from just equivalence constraints, thus, enabling label-incompatible learning. Overall, we get a conceptually simple but very effective model, which is scalable to large datasets. Further, we showed that learning person specific metrics boosts the performance for face identification. In particular, we revealed that the power lies in the combination of multi-task learning and person specific metrics, as it is not sufficient to learn the metrics decoupled. To show the merits of our method we conducted two experiments on the challenging large-scale PubFig face benchmark. We are able to match or slightly outperform recent multi-task learning methods and also multi-class support vector machines.

Acknowledgments. The work was supported by the Austrian Science Foundation (FWF) project Advanced Learning for Tracking and Detection in Medical Workflow Analysis (I535-N23) and by the Austrian Research Promotion Agency (FFG) project SHARE in the IV2Splus program.

References

1. Pan, S.J., Yang, Q.: A survey on transfer learning. IEEE Trans. on Knowledge and Data Engineering 22, 1345–1359 (2010)
2. Caruana, R.: Multitask learning: A knowledge-based source of inductive bias. In: Proc. IEEE Intern. Conf. on Machine Learning (1993)
3. Caruana, R.: Multitask learning. Machine Learning 28, 41–75 (1997)
4. Collobert, R., Weston, J.: A unified architecture for natural language processing: deep neural networks with multitask learning. In: Proc. IEEE Intern. Conf. on Machine Learning (2008)
5. Evgeniou, T., Pontil, M.: Regularized multi-task learning. In: Proc. Intern. Conf. on Knowledge Discovery and Data Mining (2004)
6. Weinberger, K.Q., Blitzer, J., Saul, L.K.: Distance metric learning for large margin nearest neighbor classification. In: Advances in Neural Information Processing Systems (2006)
7. Davis, J.V., Kulis, B., Jain, P., Sra, S., Dhillon, I.S.: Information-theoretic metric learning. In: Proc. IEEE Intern. Conf. on Machine Learning (2007)
8. Guillaumin, M., Verbeek, J., Schmid, C.: Is that you? Metric learning approaches for face identification. In: Proc. IEEE Intern. Conf. on Computer Vision (2009)
9. Parameswaran, S., Weinberger, K.: Large margin multi-task metric learning. In: Advances in Neural Information Processing Systems (2010)
10. Köstinger, M., Hirzer, M., Wohlhart, P., Roth, P.M., Bischof, H.: Large scale metric learning from equivalence constraints. In: Proc. IEEE Intern. Conf. on Computer Vision and Pattern Recognition (2012)
11. Weinberger, K.Q., Saul, L.K.: Fast solvers and efficient implementations for distance metric learning. In: Proc. IEEE Intern. Conf. on Machine Learning (2008)
12. Rifkin, R., Klautau, A.: In defense of one-vs-all classification. Journal of Machine Learning Research 5, 101–141 (2004)
13. Kumar, N., Berg, A.C., Belhumeur, P.N., Nayar, S.K.: Attribute and Simile Classifiers for Face Verification. In: Proc. IEEE Intern. Conf. on Computer Vision (2009)
14. Platt, J.C.: Probabilistic outputs for support vector machines and comparisons to regularized likelihood methods. In: Advances in Large-Margin Classifiers. MIT Press (1999)
15. Friedman, J.H.: Another approach to polychotomous classification. Technical report, Department of Statistics, Stanford University (1996)
16. Crammer, K., Singer, Y., Cristianini, N., Shawe-taylor, J., Williamson, B.: On the algorithmic implementation of multiclass kernel-based vector machines. Journal of Machine Learning Research 2, 265–292 (2001)
17. Chang, C.C., Lin, C.J.: LIBSVM: A library for support vector machines. ACM Trans. on Intelligent Systems and Technology 2, 27:1–27:27 (2011)

Information Theoretic Clustering
Using Minimum Spanning Trees

Andreas C. Müller[1,*], Sebastian Nowozin[2], and Christoph H. Lampert[3]

[1] University of Bonn, Germany
[2] Microsoft Research, Cambridge, UK
[3] IST Austria, Klosterneuburg, Austria

Abstract. In this work we propose a new information-theoretic clustering algorithm that infers cluster memberships by direct optimization of a non-parametric mutual information estimate between data distribution and cluster assignment. Although the optimization objective has a solid theoretical foundation it is hard to optimize. We propose an approximate optimization formulation that leads to an efficient algorithm with low runtime complexity. The algorithm has a single free parameter, the number of clusters to find. We demonstrate superior performance on several synthetic and real datasets.

1 Introduction

Clustering data is one of the fundamental problems in machine learning. In clustering, the goal is to divide data points into homogeneous subsets, called clusters. Many different formulations of the clustering problem are given in the literature. Most algorithms are based on ad-hoc criteria such as intra-cluster similarity and inter-cluster dissimilarity. An alternative approach is to formalize clustering using an information theoretic framework, where one considers inputs as well as cluster assignments as random variables. The goal is then to find an assignment of data points to clusters that maximizes the mutual information between the assignments and the observations.

In this work, we rely on a non-parametric estimator of the data entropy to find clusterings of maximum mutual information. The use of non-parametric estimates allows a data-driven approach, without making strong assumptions on the form of the data distribution. As a consequence, we obtain a very flexible model that, e.g., allows non-convex clusters. The resulting objective is easy to evaluate, but difficult to optimize over. We overcome this by proposing an efficient approximate optimization based on the Euclidean minimum spanning tree algorithm. Because the estimator and the optimization are both parameter-free, the only free parameter of the algorithm is the number of clusters, which makes it very easy to use in practice. The contributions of this work are:

- Proposing the use of a MST-based entropy estimator in information theoretic clustering.

---

* This work was founded by the B-IT research school.

A. Pinz et al. (Eds.): DAGM/OAGM 2012, LNCS 7476, pp. 205–215, 2012.
© Springer-Verlag Berlin Heidelberg 2012

- Give a fast algorithm for a relaxed version of the resulting problem.
- Show the practicality on a number of synthetic and real datasets.

2   Related Work

The most commonly used clustering algorithm is the k-Means algorithm, also known as Lloyd's algorithm [14, 13]. While k-Means often works well in practice, one of its main drawbacks is the restriction in cluster shape. They are given by the Voronoi tessellation of the cluster means and therefore always convex.

Another widely used method is spectral clustering [20, 16], which solves a graph partitioning problem on a similarity graph constructed from the data. While spectral clustering is much more flexible than k-Means it is quite sensitive to the particular choice of graph construction and similarity measure. It is also computationally expensive to compute, because clustering n points requires computing the eigenvalues and -vectors of an $n \times n$ matrix.

Information theoretic approaches to clustering were first investigated in the context of document classification. In this setting, training examples are described by a discrete distribution over words, leading to the task of *distributional clustering*, which was later related to the Information Bottleneck method by [21]. This setting was described in detail by [4]. In distributional clustering, it is assumed that the distribution of the data is known explicitly (for example as word counts), which is not the case in our setting.

Later, Banerjee et al. [1] introduced the concept of Bregman Information, generalizing mutual information of distributions, and showed how this leads to a natural formulation of several clustering algorithms. Barber [2] construct a soft clustering by using a parametric model of $p(Y \mid X)$. The framework of mutual information based clustering was extended to non-parametric entropy estimates by Faivishevsky and Goldberger [5]. They use a nearest neighbor based estimator of the mutual information, called MeanNN, that takes into account all possible neighborhoods, therefore combining global and local influences. The approximate mutual information is maximized using local search over labels.

Clustering algorithms based on minimum spanning trees have been studied early on in the statistics community, due to their efficiency. One of the earliest methods is single-link agglomerative clustering [8]. Single-link agglomerative clustering can be understood as a minimum spanning tree-based approach in which the largest edge is removed until the desired number of components is reached. Zahn [23] refines this criterion by cutting edges that are longer than other edges in the vicinity. This approach requires tuning several constants by hand. More recently, Grygorash et al. [9] proposed a hierarchical MST-based clustering approach that iteratively cuts edges, merges points in the resulting components, and rebuilds the spanning tree. We will limit our discussion to the most widely used algorithm from [8].

3   Information Theoretic Clustering Using Nonparametric Entropy-Estimates

In general, the goal of clustering can be formulated as follows: given a finite collection of samples $\mathbf{x} = (x_1, \ldots, x_n)$, we want to assign cluster-memberships $\mathbf{y} = (y_1, \ldots, y_n), y_i \in \{1, \ldots k\}$ to these samples. We adopt the viewpoint of information theoretic clustering of Gokcay and Principe [6], where the x_i are considered i.i.d. samples from a distribution $p(X)$, and the y_i are found such that the mutual information $I(X, Y)$ between the distribution $p(X)$ and the assigned labels $p(Y)$ is maximized. We can rewrite this objective as

$$I(X, Y) = D_{\mathrm{KL}}(p(X, y) \parallel p(X)p(Y)) = H(X) - \sum_{y=1}^{k} p(Y{=}y)H(X \mid Y{=}y) \quad (1)$$

where

- $D_{\mathrm{KL}} = \int_{\mathcal{X}} p(X) \ln(\frac{p(X)}{q(X)})dX$ is the Kullback-Leibler divergence,
- $H(X) = \int_{\mathcal{X}} p(X) \ln(p(X))dX$ is the differential entropy, and
- $H(X \mid Y{=}y) = \int_{\mathcal{X}} p(X \mid Y{=}y) \ln(p(X \mid Y{-}y))dX$ is the conditional differential entropy.

Expressing the mutual information in terms of the entropy is convenient, since the objective then decomposes over the values of Y. Additionally, $H(X)$ is independent of the distribution of Y and therefore does not influence the search over $\mathbf{y}$.

Because we are given only a finite sample from $p(X)$, there is no way to exactly compute $I(X, Y)$, and this is still true if we fix a set of cluster indicators y_i Possible ways to overcome this are:

1. Fit a parametric model $\hat{p}(X, Y \mid \theta)$ to the observations.
2. Use a non-parametric model $\hat{x}$ to approximate $p(X, Y)$.
3. Estimate $H(X \mid Y)$ directly using a non-parametric estimate.

We choose the third option, as it is the most flexible while avoiding the curse of dimensionality that comes with using non-parametric density estimates.

Let $\mathbf{x}_y$ be the set of x_i with label y. Given a non-parametric density estimator H_{est} we have $H_{est}(\mathbf{x}_y) \approx H(X \mid Y{=}y)$, leading to the clustering problem

$$\max_{\mathbf{y}} \quad - \sum_{y=1}^{k} p(Y{=}y)H_{\mathrm{est}}(\mathbf{x}_y), \quad (2)$$

where the probability $p(Y{=}y)$ is given by the empirical frequency of y, $p(Y = y) = \frac{n_y}{n}$ for $n_y = \frac{|\{i|y_i=y\}|}{n}$.

3.1   Minimum Spanning Tree Based Entropy Estimation

From now on, we assume that $\mathcal{X} = \mathbb{R}^d$ and $p(X)$ is absolute continuous. This setting allows the use of the non-parametric entropy estimate of Hero III and Michel [10], that constructs a minimum spanning tree of the data and obtains an estimate of the data entropy from the logarithm of the length of the spanning tree. More precisely, the entropy estimate of a dataset $\mathbf{x} = (x_1, \ldots, x_n)$ is given by

$$H_{mst}(\mathbf{x}) = d\log(L) - (d-1)\log(n) + \log(\beta_d). \tag{3}$$

where L is the length of a minimum spanning tree $T(\mathbf{x})$ of $\mathbf{x}$ and β_d is an unknown, but data-independent constant. The estimator H_{mst} is consistent in the sense that $H_{mst}(\mathbf{x}) \to H(X)$ for $n \to \infty$ [10]. Using Equation (3) as a non-parametric entropy estimate in Equation (2) yields the problem to maximize $\hat{I}(\mathbf{x}, \mathbf{y})$ with

$$\hat{I}(\mathbf{x}, \mathbf{y}) := -\sum_{y=0}^{k} p(y)\Big[d\log(L_y) - (d-1)\log n_y\Big] + C, \tag{4}$$

$$= -\sum_{y=0}^{k} p(y)\Big[d\log(\bar{L}_y) + \log n_y\Big] + C' \tag{5}$$

$$= -d\sum_{y=0}^{k} p(y)\log(\bar{L}_y) - \sum_{y=0}^{k} p(y)\log p(y) + C'' \tag{6}$$

where n_y is the cardinality of $\mathbf{x}_y$, L_y is the length of the minimum spanning tree $T(\mathbf{x}_y)$ and C, C' and C'' are constants independent of $\mathbf{y}$. We defined $\bar{L}_y := \frac{L_y}{n_y}$, the mean edge length per node in $T(\mathbf{x}_y)$.

Equation (6) has a natural interpretation: The first term penalizes long spanning trees, weighted by the size of the cluster. The second term favors a high entropy of $p(y)$, leading to balanced clusters. Note that there is a natural trade-off between enforcing intra-cluster similarity, expressed through L and the balancing of cluster sizes. This trade-off is similar to formulating an objective in terms of a loss and a regularizer. In contrast to the "loss+regularizer" setup, where the trade-off needs to be specified by the user, the trade-off in Equation (6), given by the factor d, is a direct consequence of the entropy estimator.

The reliance on the dimensionality of the ambient space $\mathbb{R}^d$ can be seen as the requirement that d is actually the intrinsic dimensionality of the data. This requirement is made explicit in our assumptions of an absolute continuous data density: If the support of $p(X)$ was a lower-dimensional sub-manifold of $\mathbb{R}^d$, $p(X)$ could not be absolute continuous.

3.2   Finding Euclidean Minimum Spanning Tree Clusterings

The objective given by Equation (4) is a non-linear combinatorial optimization problem. It has two properties that make it hard to optimize:

Algorithm 1. Information Theoretic MST-based Clustering

Input: Points $\mathbf{x}$, desired number of clusters k.
Output: Clustering $\mathbf{y}$ of $\mathbf{x}$

$\quad G \leftarrow T(\mathbf{x})$
$\quad$ **for** $i = 0, \ldots, k-1$ **do**
$\qquad$ **for** $G_j, j = 0, \ldots, i$ connected components of G **do**
$\qquad\quad e_j \leftarrow \text{SplitCluster}(G_j)$
$\qquad l \leftarrow \arg\max_j \hat{I}(G_j \setminus e_j)$
$\qquad G \leftarrow G \setminus e_l$

$\quad$ **function** SPLITCLUSTER(G)
$\qquad$ Pick arbitrary root x_0 of G.
$\qquad$ **for** node x starting from leaves **do**
$$w_x \leftarrow \sum_{c \in \text{children}(x)} w_c + d(x, c)$$
$$n_x \leftarrow 1 + \sum_{c \in \text{children}(x)} n_c$$
$\qquad$ **for** node x starting from root **do**
$$w'_x \leftarrow w'_{\text{par}(x)} + w_{\text{par}(x)} - w_x - d(x, \text{par}(x))$$
$\qquad$ **for** $e \in E(G), e = (c, p)$, p parent of c **do**
$$v_c \leftarrow w'_p + w_p - w_c - d(p, c)$$
$$m_c \leftarrow n - n_c$$
$$\text{objective}(e) \leftarrow dm_c \ln(m_c) - (d-1)m_c \ln(v_c) + dn_c \ln(n_c) - (d-1)n_c \ln(w_c)$$
$\qquad e^* \leftarrow \arg\max_{e \in E(G)} \text{objective}(e)$

---

1. The objective depends in a non-linear way on L_y. This makes linear programming techniques, that proved successful for other combinatorial task, not directly applicable.
2. L_y is defined in terms of minimum spanning trees. This set is hard to characterize, as changing the cluster membership of a single node may change the two minimum spanning trees involved completely.

For the above reasons, we propose a simple procedure to approximately solve Equation (4). Consider a graph G with nodes $\mathbf{x}$ and edge weights given by the Euclidean distances between points. The connected components of G induce a clustering $\mathbf{y}(G)$ of $\mathbf{x}$, by assigning x_i and x_j the same cluster if and only if they are in the same connected component of G. Define

$$\hat{I}(G) := -\sum_{y=0}^{k} p(y)\Big[d \log(L_{G,y}) - (d-1)\log n_y\Big], \qquad (7)$$

where y enumerates the connected components $G_0, \ldots, G_k$ of G, $n_y = |V(G_y)|$ is the number of nodes in G_y and $L_{G,y} = \sum_{e \in E(G_y)} w(e)$ is the sum of the weights of all edges in the connected component G_y. Then $\hat{I}(G) \geq \hat{I}(\mathbf{x}, \mathbf{y}(G))$, by the definition of the minimum spanning tree, and equality holds if and only if G_y is

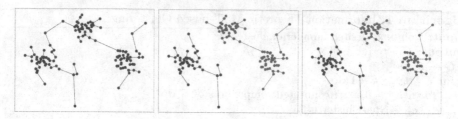

Fig. 1. Illustration of the optimization algorithm for $k = 3$ on synthetic dataset. *Left*: Euclidean minimum spanning tree of the data. *Center*: The edge that yields the best two-cluster partition in terms of Equation (4) was removed, yielding two connected components. *Right*: Another edge from the forest was removed, resulting in the desired number of three components. Note that the edge that are removed are not the longest edges but form a trade-off between edge length and cluster size.

the minimum spanning tree of its nodes for all y. We try to find a graph G with k components, such that $\hat{I}(G)$ is maximal. We can restrict ourself to optimizing over the set $\mathcal{F}$ of forests over $\mathbf{x}$ with k components, as adding edges inside connected components will only decrease the objective. Thus we can formulate the clustering problem equivalently as $\max_{G \in \mathcal{F}} \hat{I}(G)$.

Optimization over forests remains hard, and we further restrict ourself to solutions from $\mathcal{G} := \{F \in \mathcal{F} \mid F$ subgraph of $T(\mathbf{x})\}$ for a given minimum spanning tree $T(\mathbf{x})$, leading to the problem $\max_{G \in \mathcal{G}} \hat{I}(G)$. This restriction allows for a very fast, combinatorial optimization procedure.

For the two class case, optimization of the above objective can be solved exactly and efficiently by searching over all of $\mathcal{G}$. This amounts to searching for the edge e that maximizes $\hat{I}(T(\mathbf{x}) \setminus e)$. The naive algorithm that computes the objective for each edge separately has run time that is quadratic in the number of data points. To improve upon this, we use a dynamic programming approach as described in Algorithm 1, in function SplitCluster, which has only linear complexity. Using this algorithm, run time in the two cluster case is dominated by computing $T(\mathbf{x})$. We extend this algorithm to the case of more than two clusters in a greedy way: Starting with the full spanning tree of $\mathbf{x}$, we remove the edge yielding the lowest value of Equation (7) until the number of components equals the number of desired clusters. The overall procedure is summarized in Algorithm 1, an illustration can be found in Figure 1. We refer to Algorithm 1 as *Information Theoretic MST-based (ITM) clustering*.

We use the dual-tree Boruvka algorithm [15] to compute the minimum spanning tree, which has runtime close to $O(n \log(n)\alpha(n))$. Here α is the inverse of the Ackerman function, which grows so slowly as to be considered constant in practice. The dynamic programming solution of Algorithm 1 has a run time of $O(n)$ per removed edge, leading to an overall run time of $O(n \log(n)\alpha(n) + nk)$. The $O(nk)$ comes from a worst case scenario, in which each step in the hierarchical clustering procedure only splits off a constant number of points. In a more realistic setting, we expect that the individual clusters are much smaller than the original dataset. In this case, the $O(nk)$ factor would improve to $O(n \log(k))$.

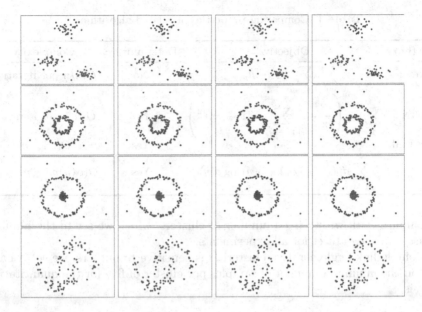

Fig. 2. Comparison of k-Means (left), MeanNN (center left), single link (center right) and ITM (right) on four synthetic datasets. Without the need to tune parameters, ITM can adjust to different cluster shapes. MeanNN is able to recover non-convex clusters (third row) but often produces similar results to k-Means (second and last row). Single link clustering is very sensitive to noise, as it does not take cluster size into account.

4   Experiments

We compared ITM to the popular k-Means algorithm [14, 13], to the MeanNN algorithm of Faivishevsky and Goldberger [5] and to single-link agglomerative clustering [8]. The similarities between single-link agglomerative clustering and the proposed MST-based optimization make it a good baseline for tree-based clustering approaches.

A comparison of ITM, MeanNN and the baseline methods, k-Means and single link agglomerative clustering, in terms of their objective, optimization and complexity can be found in Table 1. We implemented the ITM clustering procedure as well as MeanNN in Python. We used the k-Means implementation available in the scikit-learn library [17]. We use the dual tree Boruvka algorithm implemented in the mlpack machine learning library [3]. The source code is available online[1].

4.1   Experimental Setup

For both k-Means and MeanNN, we restart the algorithm ten times using different random initializations, keeping the result with the best objective value. As ITM is deterministic there is no need for random restarts. All of the algorithms

---

[1] https://github.com/amueller/information-theoretic-mst

Table 1. Comparing properties of related algorithms

Algorithm	Objective	Deterministic	Complexity
k-Means	$\sum_{y}\sum_{i,y_i=y}\|x_i-\mu_y\|^2$	No	$O(nk)$ per iteration
MeanNN	$\sum_{y}\log\left(\frac{1}{|\mathbf{x}_y|}\sum_{i,j,y_i=y_j=y}\|x_i-x_j\|^2\right)$	No	$O(n^2)$ per iteration
Single Link	$-$	Yes	$O(n\log n)$
ITM	$\sum_{y=0}^{k}dp(y)\log(\bar{L}_y)+p(y)\log p(y)$	Yes	$O(\alpha(n)n\log n+nk)$

we compare work with a fixed number of clusters, which we set to the number of classes in the dataset for all experiments.

As single link agglomerative clustering is sensitive to outliers, we set a hard limit on the minimum number of samples per cluster of five for the quantitative analysis.

4.2 Qualitative Results

Figure 2 shows qualitative results on three synthetic datasets. For well separated, convex clusters, all four algorithms produce the same clustering (see top row). If the structure of the data is more complex, the advantage of the proposed method is apparent. Note that there was no need to specify any other parameters than the number of clusters to produce these results. It is also noteworthy that the results of MeanNN are very close to those produces by k-Means in most cases. This similarity can be explained by the close relation of the objective functions, listed in Table 1.

4.3 Quantitative Results

We present results on several standard datasets from the UCI repository, selecting datasets that span a wide range of combinations of number of samples, features and clusters. To satisfy the assumption of absolute continuity of the data distribution, we restrict ourself to data with continuous features.

We evaluated the experiments using the *adjusted Rand index (ARI)* [11] and *normalized mutual information (NMI)* [22], two popular measures of cluster quality [7, 12]. The Rand index [19] between two clusterings counts on how many pairs of points two clusterings agree. The adjusted Rand index contains a calibration against chance performance.

Table 2 summarizes the results. The two entropy-based methods (MeanNN, ITM) have a clear advantage of the other methods, with ITM finding better clusterings than MeanNN in the majority of cases. The single link agglomerative clustering procedure produces reasonable results on datasets with little noise and well-separated clusters, but fails otherwise. When inspecting the results, we

Table 2. Scores (ARI/NMI) of k-Means, MeanNN, single link agglomerative clustering and ITM on several benchmark datasets (higher is better). The best score for each dataset is printed in bold.

Dataset			Results			
Description	n	d	k	k-Means	MeanNN	SL	ITM
digits	1797	64	10	0.62 / 0.71	0.67 / 0.76	0.10 / 0.50	**0.85 / 0.89**
faces	400	4096	40	0.41 / 0.76	**0.49 / 0.80**	0.08 / 0.69	0.02 / 0.49
iris	150	4	3	0.72 / 0.76	0.75 / 0.78	0.55 / 0.72	**0.88 / 0.87**
usps	9298	256	10	0.52 / 0.61	**0.54 / 0.65**	0.00 / 0.04	0.44 / 0.58
vehicle	846	18	4	0.10 / 0.15	0.09 / 0.11	0.00 / 0.04	**0.10 / 0.14**
vowel	990	10	11	0.17 / 0.37	0.19 / **0.40**	0.00 / 0.16	**0.20** / 0.39
waveform	5000	21	2	**0.37** / 0.35	0.30 / **0.38**	0.00 / 0.00	0.23 / 0.22

observed that ITM produced several very small clusters on the *faces* dataset. Indeed, increasing the minimum cluster size to 6 or more improved the results to 0.59/0.84. A possible explanation for this is that very small clusters make the entropy estimate less reliable. The single-link method also benefited from this, improving its results to 0.42/0.82. The run time of computing the ITM clustering was dominated by the computation of the MST of the data. The implementation in mlpack took 60 seconds on a desktop computer for *usps*, the largest dataset in our experiments. The other methods had run times in the order of seconds, but given the different implementations we used, this should not be interpreted as a general statement about the speed of the individual methods.

5 Conclusions

In this work we proposed the use of a minimum spanning tree based, non-parametric entropy estimator in information theoretic clustering, ITM. Thereby we extended the work of Faivishevsky and Goldberger [5] to a more flexible and efficient entropy estimate. We proposed an approximate optimization method by formulating the clustering problem as a search over graphs. The resulting algorithm is deterministic has sub-quadratic run time. Empirical comparisons showed that the proposed method outperforms standard algorithms and the non-parametric entropy based clustering of [5] on multiple benchmark datasets. We demonstrated that ITM is able to detect non-convex clusters, even in the presence of noise. In contrast to other algorithms that can handle non-convex clusters, ITM has no tuning parameters, as the objective presents a natural trade-off between balancing cluster sizes and enforcing intra-cluster similarity.

A limitation of the proposed algorithm is that it is based on the assumption of an absolute continuous data distribution. This assumption eliminates the possibility of using categorical variables and data that lies on a submanifold of the input space. In future work we plan to investigate a way to overcome this limitation, for example by estimating the intrinsic dimensionality of the data [18].

We will also investigate optimizations of the objective Equation (7) that go beyond the proposed method. Move-making algorithms seem a promising way to refine solutions found by Algorithm 1. Branch and bound techniques could provide an alternative approach.

References

[1] Banerjee, A., Merugu, S., Dhillon, I., Ghosh, J.: Clustering with Bregman divergences. Journal of Machine Learning Research 6 (2005)

[2] Barber, F.: Kernelized infomax clustering. In: Neural Information Processing Systems (2006)

[3] Curtin, R.R., Cline, J.R., Slagle, N.P., Amidon, M.L., Gray, A.G.: MLPACK: A scalable C++ machine learning library. In: BigLearning: Algorithms, Systems, and Tools for Learning at Scale (2011)

[4] Dhillon, I., Mallela, S., Kumar, R.: A divisive information theoretic feature clustering algorithm for text classification. Journal of Machine Learning Research 3 (2003)

[5] Faivishevsky, L., Goldberger, J.: A nonparametric information theoretic clustering algorithm. In: International Conference on Machine Learning (2010)

[6] Gokcay, E., Principe, J.: Information theoretic clustering. Pattern Analysis and Machine Intelligence 24 (2002)

[7] Gomes, R., Krause, A., Perona, P.: Discriminative clustering by regularized information maximization. In: Neural Information Processing Systems (2010)

[8] Gower, J., Ross, G.: Minimum spanning trees and single linkage cluster analysis. Applied Statistics (1969)

[9] Grygorash, O., Zhou, Y., Jorgensen, Z.: Minimum spanning tree based clustering algorithms. In: International Conference on Tools with Artificial Intelligence (2006)

[10] Hero III, A., Michel, O.: Asymptotic theory of greedy approximations to minimal k-point random graphs. Information Theory 45 (1999)

[11] Hubert, L., Arabie, P.: Comparing partitions. Journal of Classification 2 (1985)

[12] Kamvar, K., Sepandar, S., Klein, K., Dan, D., Manning, M., Christopher, C.: Spectral learning. In: International Joint Conference of Artificial Intelligence (2003)

[13] Lloyd, S.: Least squares quantization in PCM. Information Theory 28 (1982)

[14] MacQueen, J.: Some methods for classification and analysis of multivariate observations. In: Berkeley Symposium on Mathematical Statistics and Probability (1967)

[15] March, W.B., Ram, P., Gray, A.G.: Fast Euclidean minimum spanning tree: algorithm, analysis, applications. In: International Conference on Knowledge Discovery and Data Mining (2010)

[16] Ng, A., Jordan, M., Weiss, Y.: On spectral clustering: analysis and an algorithm. In: Neural Information Processing Systems (2002)

[17] Pedregosa, F., Varoquaux, G., Gramfort, A., Michel, V., Thirion, B., Grisel, O., Blondel, M., Prettenhofer, P., Weiss, R., Dubourg, V., et al.: Scikit-learn: Machine learning in python. Journal of Machine Learning Research 12 (2011)

[18] Pettis, K., Bailey, T., Jain, A., Dubes, R.: An intrinsic dimensionality estimator from near-neighbor information. Pattern Analysis and Machine Intelligence 1 (1979)

[19] Rand, W.: Objective criteria for the evaluation of clustering methods. Journal of the American Statistical Association (1971)

[20] Shi, J., Malik, J.: Normalized cuts and image segmentation. Pattern Analysis and Machine Intelligence 22 (2000)

[21] Slonim, N., Tishby, N.: Agglomerative information bottleneck. In: Neural Information Processing Systems (1999)

[22] Strehl, A., Ghosh, J.: Cluster ensembles–a knowledge reuse framework for combining multiple partitions. Journal of Machine Learning Research 3 (2003)

[23] Zahn, C.: Graph-theoretical methods for detecting and describing gestalt clusters. IEEE Transactions on Computers 100 (1971)

Dynamical SVM for Time Series Classification

Ramón Huerta[1], Shankar Vembu[2,*], Mehmet K. Muezzinoglu[1],
and Alexander Vergara[1]

[1] BioCircuits Institute, University of California, San Diego, USA
{rhuerta,vergara}@ucsd.edu, kerem.muezzinoglu@gmail.com
[2] Donnelly Centre for Cellular and Biomolecular Research,
University of Toronto, Canada
shankar.vembu@utoronto.ca

Abstract. We present a method for classifying multidimensional time series using concepts from nonlinear dynamical systems theory. Our contribution is an extension of support vector machines (SVM) that controls a nonlinear dynamical system. We use a chain of coupled Rössler oscillators with diffusive coupling to model highly nonlinear and chaotic time series. The optimization procedure involves alternating between using the sequential minimal optimization algorithm to solve the standard SVM dual problem and computing the solution of the ordinary differential equations defining the dynamical system. Empirical comparisons with kernel-based methods for time series classification on real data sets demonstrate the effectiveness of our approach.

1 Introduction

We consider the problem of classifying multidimensional time series. One of the popular approaches to solving this problem involves defining distance measures and kernels on time series [1,15,5,3] using dynamic time warping [14]. These distance measures and kernels can then be used in distance based classifiers such as k nearest neighbor algorithm or support vector machine. Another class of approaches involves designing kernels by making probabilistic assumptions on the underlying mechanism that generated the time series, for instance by assuming that each time series was generated by a linear dynamical system [17] or a linear vector autoregressive model [4]. These methods can be seen as combining generative models with a discriminative classifier.

We propose a solution using concepts from nonlinear dynamical systems theory that should provide another avenue alongside existing approaches. While there has been extensive progress in modeling nonlinear dynamics in the physics and applied mathematics communities [16,10,7], to the best of our knowledge, these ideas have not made their way into mainstream machine learning. Our main contribution is the design of a discriminative method for multidimensional time series classification called *dynamical SVM* by unifying nonlinear dynamical

---

* Most of the work was carried out while Shankar Vembu was at UCSD.

A. Pinz et al. (Eds.): DAGM/OAGM 2012, LNCS 7476, pp. 216–225, 2012.
© Springer-Verlag Berlin Heidelberg 2012

systems and the classical SVM. We provide an algorithm that iteratively modifies the control parameters of the dynamical system to improve the classification performance on stationary or non-stationary multidimensional signals.

We compare the performance of dynamical SVM against SVMs trained with state-of-the-art kernels for time series based on autoregressive models [4] and dynamic time warping [3]. On several benchmark data sets and on a real data set collected in our lab, we found that dynamical SVMs perform better than the competing methods in most of the cases.

2 Nonlinear Dynamical Systems

We begin with a brief introduction to nonlinear dynamical systems. The interested reader is referred to [6,16,10] for an in-depth treatment of this subject area. A nonlinear dynamical system is a time evolution defined by a set of nonlinear ordinary differential equations (ODE):

$$\frac{d\mathbf{x}}{dt} = \mathbf{F}(\mathbf{x}, \mu) \ , \tag{1}$$

where $\mathbf{x} \in \Re^M$ are the system variables that define the *phase space* of the system, M is the dimensionality of the dynamical system, μ are the control parameters of the system and $\mathbf{F}(\cdot)$ is a differentiable function. In this paper, we will consider one of the most popular and simple nonlinear dynamical system capable of generating chaotic behavior, namely the Rössler attractor [13]. The Rössler system is a three-dimensional dynamical system governed by the following system of equations:

$$\frac{d\,x^1}{dt} = -x^2 - x^3,$$
$$\frac{d\,x^2}{dt} = x^1 + 0.1\,x^2,$$
$$\frac{d\,x^3}{dt} = 0.1 + x^3(x^1 - \mu).$$

By varying the control parameter μ, the system can exhibit a wide range of dynamical behavior. Figure 1 illustrates this behavior of the Rössler system for several values of the control parameter μ while undergoing a *period-doubling* bifurcation that leads to chaotic behavior. When $\mu = 4$, we observe what is known as the *limit cycle*, a closed trajectory in the phase space. When $\mu = 6$, the limit cycle undergoes a period-doubling such that the period of the new limit cycle is twice that of the old one, and similarly when $\mu = 8$. Finally, when $\mu = 18$ we see the typical form of chaotic attractor with a dense population of infinitely many unstable limit cycles coexisting in the same phase space.

The Rössler system is an example of an autonomous, dissipative nonlinear dynamical system. In a dissipative system, the volume in the phase space is not conserved and is usually contracted by the time evolution unlike in conservative

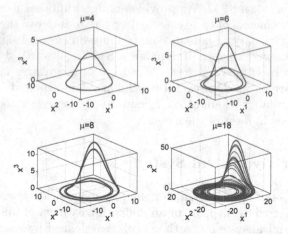

Fig. 1. Trajectories in the phase space of the Rössler system for four different values of the control parameter $\mu = 4, 6, 8, 18$

systems where the volume is conserved. Dissipative systems can form complex trajectories beyond simple stable fixed points like limit cycles, heteroclinic and homoclinic orbits, and strange attractors [6,10]. These systems are also deterministic in the sense that the state space $\mathbf{x}(t + \delta t)$ at time $t + \delta t$ is uniquely determined by the state $\mathbf{x}(t)$. One of the most important properties of nonlinear dissipative dynamical systems is that despite having low number of dimensions (three for the Rössler system) and being deterministic, they are unpredictable since they can be placed in a *chaotic* state. A dynamical system is chaotic if two close initial trajectories get separated exponentially from each other as time goes to infinity. Since the system is dissipative the separating trajectories are bound and return to the attractor set[1] [6]. Dissipative dynamical systems can thus represent a rich variety of trajectories and time series in a small number of dimensions.

3 Dynamical SVM

3.1 Model Description

The dissipative dynamical system that we are going to use for time series classification is *non-autonomous*. Non-autonomous dynamical systems receive inputs from an external force unlike autonomous dynamical systems. These external inputs are the time series signals that we wish to classify. Consider a non-autonomous dynamical system whose time evolution is governed by the following set of ordinary differential equations:

---

[1] An attractor set is a subset of the phase space toward which a dynamical system evolves over time.

$$\frac{d\mathbf{x}}{dt} = \mathbf{F}(\mathbf{x}, \mu, \sigma \mathbf{I}(t)) ,$$

where $\mathbf{x} \in \Re^M$ are the system variables, μ are the control parameters of the system and $\mathbf{I}(t)$ is the multidimensional time series with dimension M'. Note that the main difference between this system and the one introduced in the previous section (1) is the dependence of the function $\mathbf{F}(\cdot)$ on the time series signal $\mathbf{I}(t)$. Let the solution of this ordinary differential equation be denoted by $\phi(\sigma \mathbf{I}(t), \mathbf{x}_0, t, \mu)$ where $\mathbf{x}_0$ are the initial conditions, and σ is a small parameter that scales the strength of the input. Intuitively, the dynamical system can be seen as extracting features $\phi(\cdot)$ from the time series input $\mathbf{I}(t)$. To allow flexibility we assume that the dynamical system is made of dynamical elements or oscillators coupled to each other with each oscillator receiving one of the channels (dimensions) of the multidimensional time series such that $M \geq M'$. We explore one of the most popular network constructions in coupled oscillators [16], namely, chains of diffusively coupled oscillators, since many physical interactions are modeled using nearest neighbors. They can be written as an oscillator j that integrates the activity of its two closest neighbors, $j - 1$ and $j + 1$, as

$$\frac{d\mathbf{x}_j}{dt} = \mathbf{F}_j(\mathbf{x}_j, \mu, \sigma \, I_j(t)) - \Gamma \left[\left(2\mathbf{x}_j - \mathbf{x}_{(j \bmod M')+1} - \mathbf{x}_{((j+M'-2) \bmod M')+1} \right) \right] ,$$

where $\mathbf{x}_j \in \Re^{M/M'}$, $j = 1, \ldots, M'$ is the oscillator index, and $\Gamma[\cdot]$ is a connection operator that defines the nature and the strength of coupling. Note that while this representation is popular due to its simplicity, there are several other ways to connect the oscillators using, for instance, nonlinear interactions.

We now proceed with solving the supervised learning problem of classifying multidimensional time series. We are given a training set consisting of (time series, label) pairs, $\{(\mathbf{I}_i(t), y_i)\}$ for $i = 1, \ldots, N$ and each $y_i \in \{+1, -1\}$. Each input time series induces a set of solutions $\phi(\sigma \, \mathbf{I}_i, \mathbf{x}_0, t, \mu)$ that we will denote by $\phi_i(t, \mu)$ because, for simplicity, in this paper, we set the same initial conditions $\mathbf{x}_0 = \mathbf{0}$. We will also use the same control parameters μ such that it becomes the same scalar for all the oscillators.

To encode each dimension j of the input time series we use one Rössler system. The Rössler systems will be coupled by dissipation in a similar manner as in [11] that simplifies the problem as

$$\frac{dx_j^1}{dt} = -x_j^2 - x_j^3 + \sigma \, I_{ji}(t),$$

$$\frac{dx_j^2}{dt} = x_j^1 + 0.1 \, x_j^2 - \epsilon(2 \, x_j^2 - x_{(j \bmod M')+1}^2 - x_{((j-2+M') \bmod M')+1}^2),$$

$$\frac{dx_j^3}{dt} = 0.1 + x_j^3(x_j^1 - \mu)$$

where ϵ is a scalar that represents the strength of coupling, $j = 1, \ldots, M'$ such that there is one Rössler oscillator for every dimension of the multidimensional time series, and $M = 3M'$. Note that in $I_{ji}(t)$ the index j is used for the oscillator number from 1 to M' and i is used to index the training examples from 1 to N.

The classifier function is

$$f(\mathbf{I}_i(t)) = \langle \mathbf{w}(t, \mu), \phi_i(t, \mu) \rangle - b \ ,$$

where $\mathbf{w}(t, \mu)$ is the separating trajectory that plays the same role as the separating hyperplane in standard SVMs, and b is the bias. To address the temporal nature of the dynamical system, we express the inner product in the classifier function as

$$\langle \mathbf{w}(t, \mu), \phi_i(t, \mu) \rangle = \sum_{j=1}^{M'} \int_0^T \phi_{ij}(t, \mu) w_j(t, \mu) dt \ ,$$

where T is the integration window, i.e., the length of the time series. Note that this functional form allows the classifier to handle variable-length time series. To simplify the notation we use $\mathbf{w}$ instead of $\mathbf{w}(t, \mu)$ keeping in mind that $\mathbf{w}$ depends on μ and t. The learning problem consists of finding $\mathbf{w}$, b, and μ such that $y_i(\langle \mathbf{w}, \phi_i(t, \mu) \rangle - b) \geq 1$. The regularized risk minimization problem is

$$\min_{\mathbf{w}, b, \mu} E = \tfrac{1}{2} \langle \mathbf{w}, \mathbf{w} \rangle + C \sum_{i=1}^{N} [1 - y_i(\langle \mathbf{w}, \phi_i(t, \mu) \rangle - b)]_+ \ , \tag{2}$$

where $C > 0$ is the regularization parameter and $[k]_+ = \max(k, 0)$. Introducing slack variables η leads us to the following optimization problem:

$$\min_{\mathbf{w}, b, \mu, \eta} \ \tfrac{1}{2} \langle \mathbf{w}, \mathbf{w} \rangle + C \sum_{i=1}^{N} \eta_i$$

$$\text{s.t. } y_i(\langle \mathbf{w}, \phi_i(t, \mu) \rangle - b) \geq 1 - \eta_i, \quad \eta_i \geq 0, \ \forall i \in \{1, \dots, N\} \tag{3}$$

Introducing Lagrange multipliers for the constraints, we get

$$L = \frac{1}{2} \langle \mathbf{w}, \mathbf{w} \rangle + C \sum_{i=1}^{N} \eta_i - \sum_{i=1}^{N} \zeta_i \eta_i - \sum_{i=1}^{N} \alpha_i [y_i(\langle \mathbf{w}, \phi_i(t, \mu) \rangle - b) - 1 + \eta_i] \tag{4}$$

with $\alpha_i \geq 0$ and $\zeta_i \geq 0$. Taking partial derivatives: $\frac{\partial L}{\partial \mathbf{w}}$, $\frac{\partial L}{\partial b}$, and $\frac{\partial L}{\partial \eta}$ and setting them to 0, we get

$$\mathbf{w} = \sum_{i=1}^{N} \alpha_i y_i \phi_i(t, \mu) \ ; \quad 0 = \sum_{i=1}^{N} \alpha_i y_i \ ; \quad \alpha_i = C - \zeta_i \ , \tag{5}$$

which means that the separating trajectory $\mathbf{w}$ is a linear combination of the ODE solutions that depend on the initial conditions $\mathbf{x}_0$ and the control parameter μ. The classifier function can thus be written as

$$f(\mathbf{I}_i(t)) = \sum_{j=1}^{N} \alpha_j y_j \langle \phi_j(t, \mu), \phi_i(t, \mu) \rangle - b \ .$$

3.2 Parameter Estimation

Since we are going to use the same initial conditions, we are left with a separating trajectory that depends only on the control parameter. The approach we propose to solve the optimization problem (3) is, first, to solve the standard SVM quadratic optimization problem by having a fixed μ because, in this form, there is only one single solution, and, second, to calculate the subgradient of the cost function (2) w.r.t. the control parameter μ because it can be directly co-integrated into the ODEs of the dynamical system.

Thus, by having the same initial conditions and by fixing μ, we insert the conditions (5) into the Lagrangian (4) to obtain the following dual program:

$$\max_{\alpha} \left\{ \sum_{i=1}^{N} \alpha_i - \frac{1}{2} \sum_{i,j=1}^{N} \alpha_i y_i \alpha_j y_j \left\langle \phi_i(t,\mu), \phi_j(t,\mu) \right\rangle \right\}, \tag{6}$$

with constraints $\sum_{i=1}^{N} \alpha_i y_i = 0$ and $0 \leq \alpha_i \leq C$. To solve this problem we use the sequential minimal optimization (SMO) algorithm [12,8]. Once the optimal separating trajectory $\mathbf{w}$ and the bias b are found, we compute the subgradient of the cost function E w.r.t. μ, knowing that $\mathbf{w}$ is a function of μ. The subgradient can be expressed as follows:

$$\frac{\partial E}{\partial \mu} = \langle \mathbf{w}, \partial_\mu \mathbf{w} \rangle - C \sum_{i=1}^{N} y_i \Theta \left(1 - y_i(\langle \mathbf{w}, \phi_i(t,\mu) \rangle - b) \right)$$

$$[\langle \mathbf{w}, \partial_\mu \phi_i(t,\mu) \rangle + \langle \partial_\mu \mathbf{w}, \phi_i(t,\mu) \rangle - \partial_\mu b] ,$$

where $\partial_\mu \mathbf{w} = \sum_{i=1}^{N} \left(\partial_\mu \alpha_i y_i \phi_i(t,\mu) + \alpha_i y_i \partial_\mu \phi_i(t,\mu) \right)$ and $\Theta(\cdot)$ is the Heaviside step function. The calculation of $\partial_\mu \phi_i(t,\mu)$ can be directly obtained from the integration of the dynamical system as will be shown below. The partial derivative of the Lagrange multipliers $\partial_\mu \alpha_i$ requires some elaboration. The solution of the optimization problem (6) verifies the Karush-Kuhn-Tucker (KKT) conditions which are

$$\alpha_i = 0 \Rightarrow y_i (G_i - b) \geq 0$$
$$0 < \alpha_i < C \Rightarrow y_i (G_i - b) = 0$$
$$\alpha_i = C \Rightarrow y_i (G_i - b) \leq 0$$

where $G_i = \sum_{j=1}^{N} \alpha_j y_j K_{ij} - y_i$ with K being the kernel matrix, and the condition $\sum_i \alpha_i y_i = 0$. To facilitate the calculation of the solution changes with respect to the parameter μ, the solutions can be expressed in a linear form as

$$\mathcal{K} \cdot \begin{pmatrix} \alpha \\ b \end{pmatrix} = \mathbf{u}, \tag{7}$$

where α is the column vector of α_i, $i = 1, \ldots, N$. $\mathcal{K}$ is an $(N+1) \times (N+1)$ matrix whose i-th row is

$$\mathbf{k}_i^T = \begin{cases} [\, y_1 K_{1i} \cdots y_N K_{Ni} \ -1], & \text{if } 0 < \alpha_i < C \\ [\qquad \mathbf{e}_i^T \qquad\quad 0], & \alpha_i = 0 \text{ or } \alpha_i = C \\ [\, y_1 \qquad \cdots \ y_N \qquad 0], & \text{if } i = N+1 \end{cases}$$

with $\mathbf{e}_i^T$ being the i-th unit (row) vector of dimension N, whose i-th entry is 1 and all others are zero. The inequalities are encoded as the exact KKT solutions because the infinitesimal changes with respect to μ will not change the inequalities. The N-dimensional column vector $\mathbf{u}$ has the following entries for $i = 1, \ldots, N$

$$u_i = \begin{cases} y_i \text{ , if } 0 < \alpha_i < C \\ 0 \text{ , if } \alpha_i = 0 \\ C \text{ , if } \alpha_i = C. \end{cases}$$

with the last coordinate $u_{N+1} = 0$. Taking the derivative of equation (7) on both sides with respect to μ, we obtain

$$\frac{\partial \mathcal{K}}{\partial \mu} \cdot \begin{pmatrix} \alpha \\ b \end{pmatrix} + \mathcal{K} \cdot \partial_\mu \begin{pmatrix} \alpha \\ b \end{pmatrix} = \frac{\partial \mathbf{u}}{\partial \mu},$$

which can be expressed as

$$\partial_\mu \begin{pmatrix} \alpha \\ b \end{pmatrix} = -\mathcal{K}^{-1} \left[\frac{\partial \mathcal{K}}{\partial \mu} \cdot \begin{pmatrix} \alpha \\ b \end{pmatrix} \right].$$

The partial derivative of $\partial_\mu \mathcal{K}$ can be calculated from

$$\frac{\partial K_{uv}}{\partial \mu} = \left\langle \frac{\partial \phi_u(\cdot)}{\partial \mu}, \phi_v(\cdot) \right\rangle + \left\langle \phi_u(\cdot), \frac{\partial \phi_v(\cdot)}{\partial \mu} \right\rangle,$$

where $\frac{\partial \phi_u(\cdot)}{\partial \mu}$ is obtained from the numerical integration of the ODEs as

$$\frac{d\mathbf{x}}{dt} = \mathbf{F}(\mathbf{x}, \mu, \sigma \mathbf{I}(t)) \text{ , } \frac{d\mathbf{x}'}{dt} = \mathbf{F}(\mathbf{x}', \mu + \delta\mu, \sigma \mathbf{I}(t)) \text{ ,}$$

and calculating $(\mathbf{x}'(t) - \mathbf{x}(t))/\delta\mu$.

Note that the partial derivatives of the αs at $\alpha_i = 0$ and $\alpha_i = C$ are 0 because infinitesimal changes of the kernel values on μ do not nullify the KKT conditions, $\alpha_i = 0 \Rightarrow y_i(G_i - b) \geq 0$ and $\alpha_i = C \Rightarrow y_i(G_i - b) \leq 0$ due to the presence of the inequalities. $y_i(G_i - b) = 0$, on the other hand, has zero measure and, then, any infinitesimal changes on the kernel evaluation K_{ij} can break the equality. Thus the gradient estimation can, in principle, be simplified further by only concentrating on the Lagrange multipliers $0 < \alpha_i < C$ because the rest are $\partial_\mu \alpha_i = 0$.

To summarize, we first use the SMO algorithm as in [8] to solve the SVM dual (6) for a fixed μ starting from initial conditions $\mathbf{x}_0 = \mathbf{0}$ and reach a unique solution for the Lagrange multipliers. We then calculate the subgradient of the cost function (2) w.r.t μ, $\partial_\mu E$, as described above. Then at every iteration, τ, the control parameter is modified as $\mu(\tau + 1) = \mu(\tau) - \lambda \partial_\mu E$, where λ is the learning rate. Such an optimization strategy where we alternate between optimizing the SVM dual and a subgradient computation is similar to the one described in [2]. However, the subgradient computation is problem-specific and in our case it involves numerical integration of the ODE of the dynamical system amongst other computations described above. The software can be found at http://biocircuits.ucsd.edu/huerta/DSVMpublic.tar.gz.

4   Experiments

We report results on the binary classification problems of the benchmark UCR time series data sets [2] [9] and on a real data set collected in our lab (Table 1). The

Table 1. Details of the UCR two-class time series [9] and the wind tunnel data sets

Data set	Training set	Test set	Dimension (M')	Length (T)
Coffee	28	28	1	286
Lightning-2	60	61	1	637
Gun-Point	50	150	1	150
ECG	100	100	1	96
Yoga	300	3000	1	426
Wafer	1000	6174	1	152
Wind Tunnel	90	90	8	1800

real data set (named "wind tunnel" in the table) consists of 180 three-minute responses of a portable sensor array endowed with eight metal-oxide based carbon monoxide (CO) sensors located at two fixed locations in a CO plume. The plume was created in a wind tunnel where the chemical analyte source was fixed. The measurements were recorded from six fixed locations in the plume, where three of them were located on the left side and three on the right side of the test bed. The binary classification problem is to detect whether the recordings originated from the sensor arrays located on the left or the right side of the wind tunnel, also known as the chemical source localization problem in chemical sensing and robotics. We compared the performance of dynamical SVM with (i) an SVM trained with autoregressive kernel (AR kernel) [4], (ii) an SVM trained with global alignment kernel (GA kernel) based on dynamic time warping [3], and (iii) baseline SVM with RBF kernel trained directly on the time series by treating them as "features" and thus disregarding temporal information. We tuned the regularization parameter C using cross-validation ($C = 1, 10, 100$) for all the experiments with dynamical SVM and fixed the coupling parameter at high dissipation $\epsilon = 5$ chosen from $\epsilon = -0.01, 0, 1, 5$ for the experiments with multidimensional time series (wind tunnel data set). For the SVMs trained with time series kernels, we tuned the regularization parameter and the kernel parameters using cross-validation. For the GA kernel, we set the bandwidth parameter according to the guidelines given in [3]. For the AR kernel, the order P of the autoregressive model was chosen from a wide range of values using cross-validation. The test set performance of all the methods is shown in Table 2.

On all the UCR data sets except *Coffee*, dynamical SVM outperforms the competing methods. The SVM trained with AR kernel was found to perform better than the one trained with GA kernel on all but the *Yoga* data set. The *Wafer* data set was too big to experiment with precomputed AR and GA kernels with proper tuning of kernel parameters; therefore we excluded comparisons

---

[2] We use the version *data1* available at
http://www.cs.ucr.edu/~eamonn/time_series_data/dataset.zip

Table 2. Test set error rates (in %) of dynamical SVM (DSVM) and SVMs trained with AR kernel (AR) and global alignment kernel (GA) on the binary classification problems from the UCR time series data sets and the wind tunnel data set.

Data set	DSVM	SVM	AR	GA
Coffee	3.57	10.8	**0**	**0**
Lightning-2	**0**	26.4	24.6	29.5
Gun-Point	**0**	5.4	2.7	7.3
ECG	**5**	11	11	12
Yoga	**4.27**	19.6	30.4	15.3
Wafer	**0.24**	0.6	-	-
Wind tunnel	16.5	25.8	**12.22**	20.12

with these kernels on this particular data set. Nevertheless, the dynamical SVM performed better than the baseline SVM. We also performed experiments on a modified UCR data set where we converted the one-dimensional time series data to a three-dimensional data set[3]. Interestingly, we found that the performance of dynamical SVM dropped to 0% on *Coffee* with this modification and outperformed the competing methods again on all the other data sets. Also, we found the performance of SVM trained with AR kernel to improve on this modified data set, in particular for *Lightning-2* and *Yoga* where the error rates obtained were 3.3% and 13.67% respectively.

Finally, we performed the experiments on the wind tunnel data set. Although the dynamical SVM performed better than the baseline SVM and the GA kernel, we found that the SVM trained with AR kernel performed best on this data set. We would like to emphasize that an SVM trained with AR kernel is a strong baseline for multidimensional time series classification. Although the AR kernel uses an autoregressive model, the model parameters are never inferred explicitly; instead the kernel computation uses a Bayesian approach that involves an integration over the entire parameter space thereby generating an infinite family of features [4] and thus making it a very powerful method.

5   Conclusion

The main contribution of this paper is to use concepts from nonlinear dynamical systems theory to extend SVMs for multidimensional time series classification. Most of the existing approaches to solve this problem use linear models such as autoregressive models or linear dynamical systems to capture the temporal structure in the time series. While there has been a lot of fundamental progress in modeling nonlinear dynamics in the fields of physics and applied mathematics, these ideas have not made their way into mainstream machine learning. We believe the techniques presented in this paper is an interesting step toward bridging this gap and will foster further research in this direction.

---

[3] To convert the one-dimensional time series $s(t)$ with $t = 0, \ldots, T-1$, we form $I_j(t') = s(t'M' + j)$ with $t' = 0, \ldots, \lfloor T/M' \rfloor - 1$ and $j = 0, \ldots, M'-1$, and M' is the dimensionality of the multidimensional time series.

The performance of dynamical SVM introduced in this paper is on par with and in several instances better than state-of-the-art kernel-based approaches for multidimensional time series classification. The Rössler oscillator used in this paper was chosen because it is one of the most popular dynamical systems capable of exhibiting complex dynamics. The identification of the best nonlinear dynamical system to solve the discrimination problem remains an open question.

References

1. Bahlmann, C., Haasdonk, B., Burkhardt, H.: On-line handwriting recognition with support vector machines - A kernel approach. In: Proceedings of the 8th International Workshop on Frontiers in Handwriting Recognition (2002)
2. Chapelle, O., Vapnik, V., Bousquet, O., Mukherjee, S.: Choosing multiple parameters for support vector machines. Machine Learning 46(1-3), 131–159 (2002)
3. Cuturi, M.: Fast global alignment kernels. In: Proceedings of the International Conference on Machine Learning (2011)
4. Cuturi, M., Doucet, A.: Autoregressive kernels for time series (2011), http://arxiv.org/abs/1101.0673
5. Cuturi, M., Vert, J.P., Birkenes, O., Matsui, T.: A kernel for time series based on global alignments. In: Proceedings of the IEEE International Conference on Acoustics, Speech and Signal Processing (2007)
6. Eckmann, J.P., Ruelle, D.: Ergodic theory of chaos and strange attractors. Reviews of Modern Physics 57, 617–656 (1985)
7. Kantz, H., Schreiber, T.: Nonlinear Time Series Analysis, 2nd edn. Cambridge University Press (2004)
8. Keerthi, S.S., Shevade, S.K., Bhattacharyya, C., Murthy, K.: Improvements to Platt's SMO algorithm for SVM classifier design. Neural Computation 13(3), 637–649 (2001)
9. Keogh, E.J., Xi, X., Wei, L., Ratanamahatana, C.A.: The UCR Time Series Classification/Clustering Homepage (2006), http://www.cs.ucr.edu/~eamonn/time_series_data/
10. Ott, E.: Chaos in Dynamical Systems. Cambridge University Press (2002)
11. Parlitz, U., Junge, L., Lauterborn, W., Kocarev, L.: Experimental observation of phase synchronization. Physical Review E 54(2), 2115–2117 (1996)
12. Platt, J.C.: Fast training of support vector machines using sequential minimal optimization, pp. 185–208. MIT Press, Cambridge (1999)
13. Rössler, O.E.: An equation for continuous chaos. Physics Letters A 57(5), 397–398 (1976)
14. Sakoe, H., Chiba, S.: Dynamic programming algorithm optimization for spoken word recognition. IEEE Transactions on Acoustics, Speech, and Signal Processing 26(1), 43–49 (1978)
15. Shimodaira, H., Noma, K., Nakai, M., Sagayama, S.: Dynamic time-alignment kernel in support vector machine. In: Advances in Neural Information Processing Systems 14 (2001)
16. Strogatz, S.H.: Nonlinear Dynamics and Chaos: With Applications to Physics, Biology, Chemistry, and Engineering, 1st edn. Westview Press (2001)
17. Vishwanathan, S., Smola, A.J., Vidal, R.: Binet-cauchy kernels on dynamical systems and its application to the analysis of dynamic scenes. International Journal of Computer Vision 73(1), 95–119 (2007)

Trust-Region Algorithm for Nonnegative Matrix Factorization with Alpha- and Beta-divergences

Rafał Zdunek

Institute of Telecommunications, Teleinformatics and Acoustics,
Wroclaw University of Technology, Wybrzeze Wyspianskiego 27,
50-370 Wroclaw, Poland
rafal.zdunek@pwr.wroc.pl

Abstract. Nonnegative Matrix Factorization (NMF) is a dimensionality reduction method for representing nonnegative data in a low-dimensional nonnegative space. NMF problems are usually solved with an alternating minimization of a given objective function, using nonnegativity constrained optimization algorithms. This paper is concerned with the projected trust-region algorithm that is adapted to minimize a family of divergences or statistical distances, such as α- or β-divergences that are efficient for solving NMF problems. Using the Cauchy point estimate for the quadratic approximation model, a radius of the trust-region can be estimated efficiently for a symmetric and block-diagonal structure of the corresponding Hessian matrices. The experiments demonstrate a high efficiency of the proposed approach.

1 Introduction

NMF [9] is an unsupervised learning technique that has found many applications in machine learning, pattern recognition and computer vision [2, 6–8, 10, 12, 15, 17].

It learns nonnegative low-rank part-based representations from high dimensional nonnegative data using alternating minimization of an objective function. Many objective functions used for NMF can be derived from two basic families: α- and β-divergences [4]. In particular, the Euclidean distance, generalized Kullback-Leibler (KL) divergence or Itakura-Saito (IS) distance are special cases of these functions.

Several attempts [4, 5] have been done to minimize the generalized objective functions for NMF. They are mostly concerned with the use of multiplicative algorithms which are characterized by a low computational complexity but also a very slow convergence. To tackle the convergence problem, the second-order algorithms (quasi-Newton, GPCG) [4, 18] have been applied to minimize the α- and β-divergences subject to nonnegativity constraints. This approach considerably improves a convergence behavior but also increases a computational complexity since these methods compute the Newton search direction by solving a matrix equation with an explicitly derived Hessian matrix. For a large dataset, Hessian matrices for updating the NMF factors can be very large. Despite a block-diagonal structure of the Hessians, the computation of the Newton search directions with

A. Pinz et al. (Eds.): DAGM/OAGM 2012, LNCS 7476, pp. 226–235, 2012.
© Springer-Verlag Berlin Heidelberg 2012

such huge Hessians is still computationally expensive. Moreover, a control over positive-definiteness of the Hessians is also very difficult. In [18], the Hessians are regularized using the Levenberg-Marquardt approach with a gradually deceasing regularization parameter. The decay of this parameter is set up heuristically.

Positive-definiteness of a Hessian can be controlled with the Trust-Region (TR) optimization framework [1, 14, 16] if a radius of the trust-region is selected carefully. NMF based on the Interior-Point TR algorithm [16] have been proposed in [19] but only to the Euclidean distance. In that approach, the least-squares problems, penalized with barrier functions to enforce nonnegativity, are approximated with the quadratic model within a given trust-region. To estimate search directions, the TR subproblems are transformed to vectorized QP problems. In consequence, this approach is efficient only for updating small-scale factors.

To relax these problems, we propose to use the Trust-Region (TR) algorithm with the Cauchy point estimate that involves the Hessian matrix only to compute the second-order term of the Taylor series approximation model. Considering a symmetric block-diagonal structure of the Hessian for the α- and β-divergences, this term can be computed with a computational effort substantially lower than an exact estimate of the Newton search direction. The computations of this term can be also simplified for a Tikhonov regularized objective functions.

The paper is organized as follows: Section 2 discusses the selected objective functions for NMF. The proposed TR-based algorithm is presented in Section 3. The experiments are described in Section 4. Finally, the conclusions are drawn in Section 5.

2 Nonnegative Matrix Factorization

The aim of NMF is to find such lower-rank nonnegative matrices $A = [a_{ij}] \in \mathbb{R}_+^{I \times J}$ and $X = [x_{jt}] \in \mathbb{R}_+^{J \times T}$ that $Y = [y_{it}] \cong AX \in \mathbb{R}_+^{I \times T}$, given the data matrix Y, the lower rank J, and possibly some prior knowledge on the matrices A or X. The orthant of nonnegative real numbers is denoted by $\mathbb{R}_+$. Typically we have high redundancy, i.e. $J << \frac{IT}{I+T}$ but in our considerations we assume $J \leq \min\{I, T\}$ and $T >> I$.

To estimate the nonnegative factors A and X, an objective function $D(Y\|AX)$, which measures misfitting between Y and AX, is minimized with the following alternating optimization strategy:

Initialize $A^{(0)} \in \mathbb{R}^{I \times J}$ and $X^{(0)} \in \mathbb{R}^{J \times T}$, for $s = 1, 2, \ldots$ do

$$X^{(s)} = \arg\min_{X \geq 0} D(Y\|A^{(s-1)}X), \qquad A^{(s)} = \arg\min_{A \geq 0} D(Y\|AX^{(s)}), \quad (1)$$

until some stopping criterion is satisfied.

The choice of the objective function $D(Y\|AX)$ should be motivated by an underlying statistical model for the observations in Y. The α- and β-divergences [4, 13] unify many well-known statistical measures that are efficient for NMF problems. The α-divergence is given by the following function:

$$D_A(Y\|AX) = \sum_{i,t} \left(y_{it} \frac{(y_{it}/q_{it})^{\alpha-1} - 1}{\alpha(\alpha-1)} + \frac{q_{it} - y_{it}}{\alpha} \right), \quad (2)$$

where $y_{it} = [\boldsymbol{Y}]_{it}$, $q_{it} = [\boldsymbol{AX}]_{it}$. As reported in [4],

$$\lim_{\alpha \to 1} D_A(\boldsymbol{Y} \| \boldsymbol{AX}) = D_{KL}(\boldsymbol{Y} \| \boldsymbol{AX}) = \sum_{i,t} \left(y_{it} \ln \frac{y_{it}}{q_{it}} + q_{it} - y_{it} \right), \qquad (3)$$

where $D_{KL}(\boldsymbol{Y} \| \boldsymbol{AX})$ is the KL divergence. When $\alpha \to 0$: $\lim_{\alpha \to 0} D_A(\boldsymbol{Y} \| \boldsymbol{AX}) = D_{KL2}(\boldsymbol{Y} \| \boldsymbol{AX}) = D_{KL}(\boldsymbol{Y} \| \boldsymbol{XA})$, where $D_{KL2}(\boldsymbol{Y} \| \boldsymbol{AX})$ is the dual KL divergence. For $\alpha = 2, 0.5, -1$, the Pearson's, Hellinger's and Neyman's χ-square distances can be obtained, respectively.

The β-divergence [4] can be expressed as:

$$D_B(\boldsymbol{Y} \| \boldsymbol{AX}) = \sum_{i,t} \left(y_{it} \frac{y_{it}^{\beta} - q_{it}^{\beta}}{\beta} + \frac{q_{it}^{\beta+1} - y_{it}^{\beta+1}}{\beta + 1} \right). \qquad (4)$$

When $\beta \to 0$: $\lim_{\beta \to 0} D_B(\boldsymbol{Y} \| \boldsymbol{AX}) = D_{KL}(\boldsymbol{Y} \| \boldsymbol{AX})$, and for $\beta \to -1$, the IS distance can be obtained: $D_{IS}(\boldsymbol{Y} \| \boldsymbol{AX}) = \sum_{i,t} \left(\ln \left(\frac{q_{it}}{y_{it}} \right) + \frac{y_{it}}{q_{it}} - 1 \right)$. For $\beta = 1$, the function (4) simplifies to the standard squared Euclidean distance.

3   Algorithm

Since the subproblems (1) are symmetric with respect to the factors $\boldsymbol{A}$ and $\boldsymbol{X}$, we discuss the TR algorithm only for updating $\boldsymbol{X}$, assuming the factor $\boldsymbol{A}$ can be estimated by solving the transposed system $\boldsymbol{X}^T \boldsymbol{A}^T = \boldsymbol{Y}^T$.

The idea of the TR algorithm is to approximate the objective function $D(\boldsymbol{y}_t \| \boldsymbol{Ax}_t)$ for $t = 1, \ldots, T$ in the k-th iteration with the second-order Taylor-series expansion of $D(\boldsymbol{y}_t \| \boldsymbol{Ax}_t)$ within a ball of the radius $\Delta_t^{(k)}$ around $\boldsymbol{x}_t^{(k)}$. Thus $D(\boldsymbol{y}_t \| \boldsymbol{Ax}_t) \cong m_k(\bar{\boldsymbol{x}}_t^{(k)})$, where

$$m_k(\bar{\boldsymbol{x}}_t^{(k)}) = D(\boldsymbol{y}_t \| \boldsymbol{Ax}_t^{(k)}) + (\boldsymbol{g}_t^{(k)})^T \bar{\boldsymbol{x}}_t^{(k)} + \frac{1}{2} (\bar{\boldsymbol{x}}_t^{(k)})^T \boldsymbol{H}_t^{(k)} \bar{\boldsymbol{x}}_t^{(k)}, \qquad (5)$$

$\bar{\boldsymbol{x}}_t^{(k)} = \boldsymbol{x}_t - \boldsymbol{x}_t^{(k)}$ is the search direction that satisfies the condition $\|\bar{\boldsymbol{x}}_t^{(k)}\|_2 \leq \Delta_t^{(k)}$, $\boldsymbol{g}_t^{(k)} = \nabla_{\boldsymbol{x}_t} D(\boldsymbol{y}_t \| \boldsymbol{Ax}_t^{(k)}) \in \mathbb{R}^J$ and $\boldsymbol{H}_t^{(k)} = \nabla_{\boldsymbol{x}_t}^2 D(\boldsymbol{y}_t \| \boldsymbol{Ax}_t^{(k)}) \in \mathbb{R}^{J \times J}$ are the gradient and Hessian of $D(\boldsymbol{y}_t \| \boldsymbol{Ax}_t)$ at $\boldsymbol{x}_t^{(k)}$, respectively. The ball $\mathcal{B} = \{\boldsymbol{x} : \|\boldsymbol{x} - \boldsymbol{x}_t^{(k)}\|_2 \leq \Delta_t^{(k)}\}$ is called the trust-region. The radius $\Delta_t^{(k)}$ determines the region around $\boldsymbol{x}_t^{(k)}$ in which the quadratic model (5) can be trusted to accurately represent the function $D(\boldsymbol{y}_t \| \boldsymbol{Ax}_t)$.

The search direction $\tilde{\boldsymbol{x}}_t^{(k)}$, which is referred to as the trial step, is estimated by solving the constrained subproblem:

$$\tilde{\boldsymbol{x}}_t^{(k)} = \arg\min_{\bar{\boldsymbol{x}}_t^{(k)}} m_k(\bar{\boldsymbol{x}}_t^{(k)}) \qquad \text{s.t.} \qquad \|\bar{\boldsymbol{x}}_t^{(k)}\|_2 \leq \Delta_t^{(k)}. \qquad (6)$$

Then, the step $\tilde{\boldsymbol{x}}_t^{(k)}$ is tested by evaluating the goodness of fitting the quadratic model (5) to the objective function $D(\boldsymbol{y}_t \| \boldsymbol{Ax}_t)$. The quality of fitting is measured with the gain ratio $\rho_t^{(k)}$ that expresses a ratio between the actual and predicted decrease in a function value:

$$\rho_t^{(k)} = \frac{D(\boldsymbol{y}_t \| \boldsymbol{A} \boldsymbol{x}_t^{(k)}) - D(\boldsymbol{y}_t \| \boldsymbol{A}(\boldsymbol{x}_t^{(k)} + \tilde{\boldsymbol{x}}_t^{(k)}))}{m_k(\boldsymbol{0}) - m_k(\tilde{\boldsymbol{x}}_t^{(k)})}. \tag{7}$$

If $\rho_t^{(k)} < 0$, there is an increase in the objective function $D(\boldsymbol{y}_t \| \boldsymbol{A}(\boldsymbol{x}_t^{(k)} + \tilde{\boldsymbol{x}}_t^{(k)}))$. Hence the step $\tilde{\boldsymbol{x}}_t^{(k)}$ must be rejected and the radius $\Delta_t^{(k)}$ reduced. If $\rho_t^{(k)} = 1$, the fitting is perfect, and this case suggests that the trust region may be expanded. The expansion of the TR is governed by the rule $\Delta_t^{(k+1)} = \min(2\Delta_t^{(k)}, \bar{\Delta})$, where $\bar{\Delta}$ is the maximum allowed radius. When $\rho_t^{(k)} \in [0.25\ 0.75]$, the radius $\Delta_t^{(k)}$ remains unchanged for the next iteration.

3.1   Cauchy Point

The problem (6) can be solved with many methods, e.g. the Cauchy point, Dogleg, two-dimensional subspace minimization, or CG-Steihaug algorithm [14]. We selected the Cauchy point method due to a symmetric block-diagonal structure of the Hessians for the α- and β-divergence. This method is related to the line search by estimating along the steepest direction, i.e. $\tilde{\boldsymbol{x}}_t^{(k)} = \tau_t^{(k)} \hat{\boldsymbol{x}}_t^{(k)}$, where $\hat{\boldsymbol{x}}_t^{(k)}$ is an estimate to the problem:

$$\hat{\boldsymbol{x}}_t^{(k)} = \arg\min_{\hat{\boldsymbol{x}}_t^{(k)}} \left\{ D(\boldsymbol{y}_t \| \boldsymbol{A} \boldsymbol{x}_t^{(k)}) + (\boldsymbol{g}_t^{(k)})^T \hat{\boldsymbol{x}}_t^{(k)} \right\} \text{ s.t. } \|\bar{\boldsymbol{x}}_t^{(k)}\|_2 \le \Delta_t^{(k)}, \tag{8}$$

which is a linear approximation to (6). The scalar $\tau_t^{(k)} > 0$ determines the maximum steplength along $\hat{\boldsymbol{x}}_t^{(k)}$ to satisfy the TR bound. Thus:

$$\tau_t^{(k)} = \arg\min_{\tau > 0} m_k(\tau \hat{\boldsymbol{x}}_t^{(k)}) \quad \text{s.t.} \quad \|\tau \hat{\boldsymbol{x}}_t^{(k)}\|_2 \le \Delta_t^{(k)}. \tag{9}$$

Note that the solution to (8) can be presented in the closed-form:

$$\hat{\boldsymbol{x}}_t^{(k)} = -\frac{\Delta_t^{(k)}}{\|\boldsymbol{g}_t^{(k)}\|_2} \boldsymbol{g}_t^{(k)}. \tag{10}$$

Thus the Cauchy point has only a linear rate of convergence. When $\hat{\boldsymbol{x}}_t^{(k)}$ is a descent direction, we have:

$$(\hat{\boldsymbol{x}}_t^{(k)})^T \boldsymbol{g}_t^{(k)} = -\xi (\boldsymbol{g}_t^{(k)})^T \boldsymbol{g}_t^{(k)} < 0,$$

where $\xi = \frac{\Delta_t^{(k)}}{\|\boldsymbol{g}_t^{(k)}\|_2} > 0$. From (9) and (5), one obtains:

$$m_k(\tau \hat{\boldsymbol{x}}_t^{(k)}) = D(\boldsymbol{y}_t \| \boldsymbol{A} \boldsymbol{x}_t^{(k)}) + \tau (\boldsymbol{g}_t^{(k)})^T \hat{\boldsymbol{x}}_t^{(k)} + \frac{\tau^2}{2} (\hat{\boldsymbol{x}}_t^{(k)})^T \boldsymbol{H}_t^{(k)} \hat{\boldsymbol{x}}_t^{(k)}. \tag{11}$$

Considering (10) and from $\frac{\partial}{\partial \tau} m_k(\tau \hat{x}_t^{(k)}) \triangleq 0$, we have:

$$\hat{\tau}_t^{(k)} = -\frac{(g_t^{(k)})^T \hat{x}_t^{(k)}}{(\hat{x}_t^{(k)})^T H_t^{(k)} \hat{x}_t^{(k)}} = \frac{\|g_t^{(k)}\|_2^3}{\Delta_t^{(k)} \left(g_t^{(k)}\right)^T H_t^{(k)} g_t^{(k)}}. \tag{12}$$

Note that for $\tau_t^{(k)} = 1$, $\|\hat{x}_t^{(k)}\|_2 = \Delta_t^{(k)}$, that is, the point $\hat{x}_t^{(k)}$ is located on the boundary of the TR. When $(g_t^{(k)})^T H_t^{(k)} g_t^{(k)} \leq 0$, the point $\hat{x}_t^{(k)}$ is inside the TR, which leads to $\tau_t^{(k)} = 1$. Finally, we have:

$$\tau_t^{(k)} = \begin{cases} 1 & \text{if} \quad (g_t^{(k)})^T H_t^{(k)} g_t^{(k)} \leq 0, \\ \min\left(1, \hat{\tau}_t^{(k)}\right) & \text{otherwise} \end{cases} \tag{13}$$

3.2   Simplification of Cauchy Point for α- and β-divergences

For the α-divergence given by (2), the gradient $g_t = \nabla_{x_t} D_A \in \mathbb{R}^J$ with respect to x_t can be written as:

$$g_t = \begin{cases} \alpha^{-1} A^T \left(1 - (y_t \oslash q_t)^\alpha\right) & \text{for} \quad \alpha \neq 0, \\ A^T \ln\left(q_t \oslash y_t\right) & \text{for} \quad \alpha = 0, \end{cases} \tag{14}$$

where $q_t = A x_t$ and $\oslash$ means an element-wise division. The Hessian has the form:

$$H_t = A^T \operatorname{diag}(h_t) A \in \mathbb{R}^{J \times J}, \tag{15}$$

where:

$$h_t = \frac{y_t^\alpha}{\alpha q_t^{\alpha+1}} \in \mathbb{R}^J \text{ for } \alpha \neq 0, \quad \text{and} \quad h_t = \frac{1}{q_t} \in \mathbb{R}^J \text{ for } \alpha = 0. \tag{16}$$

The gradient for the β-divergence (4) with respect to x_t can be written as:

$$g_t = \nabla_{x_t} D_B = A^T \left[(q_t - y_t) \odot (q_t)^{\beta-1}\right] \in \mathbb{R}^J, \tag{17}$$

where $\odot$ stands for the Hadamard product. The Hessian has also a block-diagonal structure as in (15), where

$$h_t = (\beta q_t - (\beta - 1) y_t) \odot q_t^{\beta-2} \in \mathbb{R}^J. \tag{18}$$

Taking into account a symmetric block-diagonal structure of the Hessian (15), the term $(g_t^{(k)})^T H_t^{(k)} g_t^{(k)}$ in (12) and (13) can be rewritten as:

$$(g_t^{(k)})^T H_t^{(k)} g_t^{(k)} = (g_t^{(k)})^T A^T \operatorname{diag}(h_t^{(k)}) A g_t^{(k)} = e_J^T \left(h_t^{(k)} \odot (A g_t^{(k)})^2\right),$$
$$= \left[e_J^T \left(\check{H}^{(k)} \odot (A G^{(k)})^2\right)\right]_t \tag{19}$$

where $\breve{H}^{(k)} = \left[h_1^{(k)}, \ldots, h_T^{(k)} \right] \in \mathbb{R}^{J \times T}$, $G^{(k)} = \left[g_1^{(k)}, \ldots, g_T^{(k)} \right] \in \mathbb{R}^{J \times T}$, and $e_J = [1, \ldots, 1]^T \in \mathbb{R}^J$. A rise to the power two denotes an element-wise power.

Using the formula (19), the steplength (12) can be expressed as:

$$\hat{\tau}_t^{(k)} = \frac{\left[e_J^T (G^{(k)})^3 \right]_t}{\Delta_t^{(k)} \left[e_J^T \left(\breve{H}^{(k)} \odot (AG^{(k)})^2 \right) \right]_t}. \tag{20}$$

The expression (10) can be also simplified to the form:

$$\hat{X}^{(k)} = -e_J \left(\frac{\Delta^{(k)}}{e_J^T (G^{(k)})^2} \right) \odot G^{(k)}, \tag{21}$$

where $\Delta^{(k)} = [\Delta_1^{(k)}, \ldots, \Delta_T^{(k)}] \in \mathbb{R}^{1 \times T}$. The Cauchy point is given by:

$$\tilde{X}^{(k)} = e_J \tau^{(k)} \odot \hat{X}^{(k)}, \tag{22}$$

where $\tau^{(k)} \in \mathbb{R}^{1 \times T}$ is obtained from (13) and (20). Thus $e_J \tau^{(k)} \in \mathbb{R}^{J \times T}$.

Note that the computation of the Cauchy point in this approach uses the second-order term information represented by the matrix $\breve{H}^{(k)} \in \mathbb{R}^{J \times T}$ that is considerably smaller than the Hessian matrix $\nabla_X^2 D(Y \| AX) \in \mathbb{R}^{JT \times JT}$.

3.3 TR-NMF Algorithm for α- and β-divergences

The TR algorithm for updating the matrix X is given by Algorithm 1. The operation $[\xi]_+ = \max(0, \xi)$ performs a simple projection of ξ onto the nonnegative orthant $\mathbb{R}_+$. The complete NMF algorithm based on the TR optimization is represented by Algorithm 2. Note that the radii $\Delta_X^{(0)}$ and $\Delta_A^{(0)}$ in Algorithm 1 are determined by the whole alternating optimization process, e.g. the last update for Δ_X and Δ_A in the k-th alternating step of Algorithm 2 becomes an initializer for $(k+1)$-th alternating step. Starting from small radii $\Delta_X^{(0)} \geq 0$ and $\Delta_A^{(0)} \geq 0$, the initial alternating optimization steps update the factor in the close vicinity (a small ball) of the initializers $A^{(0)}$ and $X^{(0)}$. Then, the search regions (TR radii) gradually expand if a decrease in an objective function value is observed. This approach is motivated by the TR method given in [19], and aims at avoiding a convergence to some undesirable local minima. In [19], the convergence is controlled by a gradually decreasing regularization parameter but this control is enforced by the schedule defined in advance. Here the TR radii are data-driven by the gain ratio $\rho^{(k)}$ in each k-th iteration. Both algorithms 1 and 2 can be terminated by the stopping criteria given in [11] or [4] (Ch. 5).

4   Experiments

The experiments are carried out for some Blind Source Separation (BSS) problem, using the benchmark of 7 synthetic sparse nonnegative signals (the file

---

Algorithm 1. TR algorithm

Input : $Y \in \mathbb{R}_+^{I \times T}$, $A \in \mathbb{R}_+^{I \times J}$, $X^{(0)} \in \mathbb{R}_+^{J \times T}$ - initial factor, k_{TR} - number of

TR iterations, $\Delta^{(0)} \in (0, \bar{\Delta}) \in \mathbb{R}^T$ - initial TR radii,

Output: $X \in \mathbb{R}_+^{J \times T}$ - estimated factor

1 **for** $k = 0, 1, \ldots, k_{TR}$ **do**

2   Estimate the Cauchy point $\tilde{X}^{(k)} = [\tilde{x}_1^{(k)}, \ldots, \tilde{x}_T^{(k)}]$ according to (22);

3   Evaluate the gain ratios $\rho_t^{(k)}$ with (7);

4 **if** $\rho_t^{(k)} > \frac{3}{4}$ and $\|\tilde{x}_t^{(k)}\|_2 = \Delta_t^{(k)}$ **then**

5   $\Delta_t^{(k+1)} = \min(2\Delta_t^{(k)}, \bar{\Delta})$;   // Expansion of TR

6   $X^{(k+1)} = \left[X^{(k)} + \tilde{X}^{(k)} \right]_+$;

7 **else if** $\frac{3}{4} \geq \rho_t^{(k)} \geq \frac{1}{4}$ **then**

8   $\Delta_t^{(k+1)} = \Delta_t^{(k)}$;

9   $X^{(k+1)} = \left[X^{(k)} + \tilde{X}^{(k)} \right]_+$;

10 **else**

11   $\Delta_t^{(k+1)} = \frac{1}{4} \|\tilde{x}_t^{(k)}\|_2$;   // Reduction of TR

12   $X^{(k+1)} = X^{(k)}$;

AC-7_2noi.mat) taken from the Matlab toolbox *NMFLAB for Signal Process-ing*[1] [3]. Thus $X \in \mathbb{R}_+^{7 \times 1000}$. The entries of the mixing matrix $A \in \mathbb{R}_+^{70 \times 7}$ are generated from an uniform distribution $\mathcal{U}(0, 1)$.

The estimates for the matrices A and X are obtained with the selected NMF algorithms. The standard multiplicative Lee-Seung algorithms [9] for minimizing the Euclidean distance and the KL divergence are denoted by the MUE and MKL, respectively. The LPG stands for the projected gradient NMF proposed by C. Lin [11]. The Alpha-QN refers to the projected Quasi-Newton (QN) algorithm for minimizing the α-divergence [18]. We used the unregularized version with $\alpha = 1$, which corresponds to the KL divergence.

To test the efficiency of the discussed algorithms, 100 Monte Carlo (MC) runs of the NMF algorithms are performed, each time the initial matrices A and X are generated randomly from an uniform distribution. The algorithms are terminated after 200 and 100 iterations for noise-free and noisy data, respectively. The results are evaluated in terms of the Signal-to-Interference Ratio (SIR) [4] between the true matrix A and estimated one. In the TR-NMF given by Algorithm 2, we set $\Delta_A^{(0)} = \Delta_X^{(0)} = 10^{-3}$, $\bar{\Delta} = 10^6$, $k_{TR} = 5$, and we used the β-divergence with $\beta = 0$. This corresponds to the KL divergence.

Fig. 1 shows the SIR statistics for estimating the mixing matrix A from noise-free and noisy observations. The additive noise is generated from a zero-mean Gaussian distribution with the variance adopted to $SNR = 20[dB]$. The KL divergence averaged over 100 MC runs versus alternating steps is plotted in Fig. 2 for noise-free and noisy data.

---

[1] http://www.bsp.brain.riken.jp

Algorithm 2. NMF Algorithm

Input : $Y \in \mathbb{R}^{I \times T}$, J - lower rank, Δ - initial TR radius, $\bar{\Delta}$ - maximum TR radius

Output: Factors $A \in \mathbb{R}_+^{I \times J}$ and $X \in \mathbb{R}_+^{J \times T}$

1 $k = 0$; $\Delta_X^{(0)} = \Delta e_T^T$, $\Delta_A^{(0)} = \Delta e_I^T$;

2 **Initialize:** A and X with nonnegative random numbers;

3 Replace negative entries (if any) in Y with zero-value;

4 **repeat**

5    $\left[X^{(k+1)}, \Delta_X^{(k+1)} \right] = \texttt{TR\_algorithm}(Y, A^{(k)}, X^{(k)}, \Delta_X^{(k)})$;

6    $\bar{d}_j^{(k+1)} = \sum_{t=1}^{T} x_{jt}^{(k+1)}$,
     $X^{(k+1)} \leftarrow \operatorname{diag}\left\{ \left(\bar{d}_j^{(k+1)} \right)^{-1} \right\} X^{(k+1)}$, $A^{(k)} \leftarrow A^{(k)} \operatorname{diag}\left\{ \bar{d}_j^{(k+1)} \right\}$;

7    $\left[\bar{A}^{(k+1)}, \Delta_A^{(k+1)} \right] = \texttt{TR\_algorithm}(Y^T, (X^{(k+1)})^T, (A^{(k)})^T, \Delta_A^{(k)})$;

8    $A^{(k+1)} = (\bar{A}^{(k+1)})^T$;

9    $\bar{\bar{d}}_j^{(k+1)} = \sum_{i=1}^{I} a_{ij}^{(k+1)}$,
     $X^{(k+1)} \leftarrow \operatorname{diag}\left\{ \bar{\bar{d}}_j^{(k+1)} \right\} X^{(k+1)}$, $A^{(k+1)} \leftarrow A^{(k+1)} \operatorname{diag}\left\{ \left(\bar{\bar{d}}_j^{(k+1)} \right)^{-1} \right\}$;

10   $k \leftarrow k + 1$;

11 **until Stop criterion** is satisfied ;

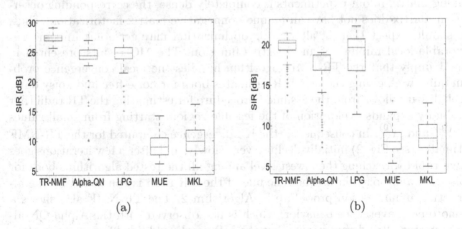

(a)   (b)

Fig. 1. SIR statistics for estimating the mixing matrix A from: (a) noise-free observations; (b) noisy observations with $SNR = 20[dB]$

The averaged elapsed time for the TR-NMF, Alpha-QN, LPG, MUE, and MKL, measured in Matlab 2008a for 100 iterations, executed on the 64 bit Intel Quad Core CPU 3GHz, 8GB RAM is as follows: 31.3, 221.3, 4.44, 0.81, and 3.12 seconds, respectively. Moreover, the TR-NMF algorithm implemented without the simplifications given in Section 3.2 needs 1346 seconds for the same dataset.

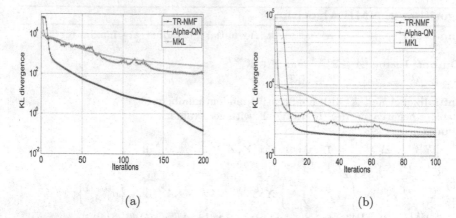

(a)   (b)

Fig. 2. KL divergence versus iterations for: (a) noise-free observations; (b) noisy observations with $SNR = 20[dB]$

5 Conclusions

The tests demonstrate that the proposed TR-NMF algorithm may be useful for solving some NMF problems, in particular for BSS applications. Since the mixing matrix in our experiments is completely dense, the corresponding observation matrix does not have an unique nonnegative matrix factorization. Thus, we should expect that an alternating optimization may get stuck in some unfavorable local minima of an objective function. The MC results presented in Fig. 1 imply that the TR-NMF algorithm handles the local convergence problem quite well, giving the best SIR estimates both for noise-free and noisy data. Probably it follows from the assumed procedure for estimating the TR radii that gradually expands exploration of the feasible region, starting from small values of $\Delta_A^{(0)}$ and $\Delta_X^{(0)}$. In consequence, the KL divergence computed for the TR-NMF estimates (see Fig. 2) initially declines very slowly, and after a few iterations goes down rapidly, reaching the lowest level among all the tested algorithms both for noise-free and noisy data. The schedule of the TR radii is controlled by the alternating minimization procedure in Algorithm 2. The TR-NMF also shows a monotonic convergence behavior, which is not observed with the Alpha-QN algorithm. Fig. 2(a) demonstrates that the SIR results obtained for noise-free data may be still improved by using more iterations with the TR-NMF. In contrary, Fig. 2(b) informs us that we may still shorten the computational time for noisy-data by using the appropriate stopping criterion. The running time proves that the simplifications discussed in Section 3.2 accelerate the TR-NMF algorithm more than 40 times.

Summing up, the proposed TR-NMF algorithm seems to be suitable for solving some NMF problems, especially when the metrics are given by the α- or β-divergence.

Reference

1. Bardsley, J.M.: A nonnegatively constrained trust region algorithm for the restoration of images with an unknown blur. Electronic Transactions on Numerical Analysis 20, 139–153 (2005)
2. Berry, M., Browne, M., Langville, A.N., Pauca, P., Plemmons, R.J.: Algorithms and applications for approximate nonnegative matrix factorization. Computational Statistics and Data Analysis 52(1), 155–173 (2007)
3. Cichocki, A., Zdunek, R.: NMFLAB for Signal and Image Processing. Tech. rep., Laboratory for Advanced Brain Signal Processing, BSI, RIKEN, Saitama, Japan (2006), http://www.bsp.brain.riken.jp
4. Cichocki, A., Zdunek, R., Phan, A.H., Amari, S.I.: Nonnegative Matrix and Tensor Factorizations: Applications to Exploratory Multi-way Data Analysis and Blind Source Separation. Wiley and Sons (2009)
5. Févotte, C., Bertin, N., Durrieu, J.L.: Nonnegative matrix factorization with the Itakura-Saito divergence: With application to music analysis. Neural Computation 21(3), 793–830 (2009)
6. Févotte, C., Idier, J.: Algorithms for nonnegative matrix factorization with the beta-divergence. Neural Computation 13(3), 1–24 (2010)
7. Guillamet, D., Vitrià, J., Schiele, B.: Introducing a weighted nonnegative matrix factorization for image classification. Pattern Recognition Letters 24(14), 2447–2454 (2003)
8. Heiler, M., Schnoerr, C.: Learning sparse representations by non-negative matrix factorization and sequential cone programming. Journal of Machine Learning Research 7, 1385–1407 (2006)
9. Lee, D.D., Seung, H.S.: Learning the parts of objects by non-negative matrix factorization. Nature 401, 788–791 (1999)
10. Li, S.Z., Hou, X.W., Zhang, H.J., Cheng, Q.S.: Learning spatially localized, parts-based representation. In: Proc. of the IEEE Computer Society Conference on Computer Vision and Pattern Recognition (CVPR 2001), vol. 1, pp. I-207–I-212 (2001)
11. Lin, C.J.: Projected gradient methods for non-negative matrix factorization. Neural Computation 19(10), 2756–2779 (2007)
12. Mauthner, T., Roth, P.M., Bischof, H.: Instant Action Recognition. In: Salberg, A.-B., Hardeberg, J.Y., Jenssen, R. (eds.) SCIA 2009. LNCS, vol. 5575, pp. 1–10. Springer, Heidelberg (2009)
13. Minka, T.: Divergence measures and message passing. Tech. Rep. MSR-TR-2005-173, Microsoft Research (2005)
14. Nocedal, J., Wright, S.J.: Numerical Optimization. Springer Series in Operations Research. Springer, New York (1999)
15. Qin, L., Zheng, Q., Jiang, S., Huang, Q., Gao, W.: Unsupervised texture classification: Automatically discover and classify texture patterns. Image and Vision Computing 26(5), 647–656 (2008)
16. Rojas, M., Steihaug, T.: An interior-point trust-region-based method for large-scale non-negative regularization. Inverse Problems 18, 1291–1307 (2002)
17. Wang, F.Y., Chi, C.Y., Chan, T.H., Wang, Y.: Nonnegative least-correlated component analysis for separation of dependent sources by volume maximization. IEEE Transactions Pattern Analysis and Machine Intelligence 32(5), 875–888 (2010)
18. Zdunek, R., Cichocki, A.: Nonnegative matrix factorization with constrained second-order optimization. Signal Processing 87, 1904–1916 (2007)
19. Zdunek, R., Cichocki, A.: Nonnegative matrix factorization with quadratic programming. Neurocomputing 71(10-12), 2309–2320 (2008)

Line Matching Using Appearance Similarities and Geometric Constraints

Lilian Zhang* and Reinhard Koch

Institute of Computer Science, University of Kiel, Germany
{lz,rk}@mip.informatik.uni-kiel.de

Abstract. Line matching for image pairs under various transformations is a challenging task. In this paper, we present a line matching algorithm which considers both the local appearance of lines and their geometric attributes. A relational graph is built for candidate matches and a spectral technique is employed to solve this matching problem efficiently. Extensive experiments on a dataset which includes various image transformations validate the matching performance and the efficiency of the proposed line matching algorithm.

1 Introduction

One of the challenging areas in computer vision is feature matching which is a basic tool for applications in scene reconstruction, pattern recognition and retrieval, motion estimation, and so on. Most of the existing matching methods in the literature are based on local point or region features [1] which are deficient for low-texture scenes [2]. On the contrary, line features are often abundant in these situations. Moreover, line features and other local features provide complementary information about the scenes. Therefore line matching is both desirable and indispensable in many applications. Although some progress was achieved recently for the line matching problem [2,3], they are quite computationally expensive, prohibiting their usage in many applications. This paper addresses the problem of robust and efficient line feature matching.

Several reasons make line matching a difficult problem, including: inaccurate locations of line endpoints, fragmentation of lines, lack of strongly disambiguating geometric constraints, and lack of distinctive appearance in low-texture scenes [3,4]. To deal with these challenges, the approach in this paper is built on three strategies. The first is to extract lines in the scale space making the matching algorithm robust to the image scale changes. The second is to check the consistency of line pairs in a loose way which combines the appearance similarities and geometric constraints. The third novel part is to solve the matching problem by a spectral method [5] which avoids the combinatorial explosion inherent to the graph matching problem. The geometric relationship of corresponding line pairs in two images may be not exactly affine invariant

---

* This work was supported by China Scholarship Council (No.2009611008). Special thanks to Markus Franke whose work was valuable in improving this paper.

A. Pinz et al. (Eds.): DAGM/OAGM 2012, LNCS 7476, pp. 236–245, 2012.
© Springer-Verlag Berlin Heidelberg 2012

because they are often not coplanar. However, for images without strong view point changes, most of the correctly corresponding line pairs tend to establish strong agreement links among each other while the incorrect assignments have weak links in the graph and few of them have strong links by accident. This property makes the spectral technique a promising strategy to efficiently solve the matching problem.

Compared to state-of-the-art methods, experiments validate that the proposed line matching approach is faster to generate the matching results. It's also robust against various image transformations including occlusion, rotation, blurring, illumination changes, scale changes, and moderate view point changes even for non-planar scenes or low-texture scenes.

2 Related Work

Existing approaches to match lines are of three types: those that match individual line segments, those that match groups of line segments and those that perform line matching by employing point correspondences.

For matching lines in image sequences or small baseline stereo where extracted corresponding segments are similar, approaches based on matching individual lines are suitable [6,7] because of their better computational performance. Among the first group, Wang et al. [8] propose a descriptor named Mean-Standard deviation Line Descriptor (MSLD) for line matching based on the appearance of the pixel support region. This approach achieves good matching results for moderate image variations in textured scenes.

Generally, approaches which match groups of line segments have the advantage that more geometric information is available for disambiguation [9,10,11]. Bay et al. [12] present a wide baseline stereo line matching method which compares the histograms of neighboring color profiles and iteratively eliminates mismatches by a topological filter. The results shown in their work are for structured scenes with small number of lines, thus the performance on images featuring a larger range of conditions is not clear. Wang et al. [2] use line signatures to match lines between wide baseline images. To overcome the unreliable line detection problem, a multi-scale line extraction strategy is employed which significantly improves the repeatability of line signatures and therefore has a good matching performance. However, this method is quite computationally expensive.

Given a set of point correspondences, Schmid and Zisserman [4] take the epipolar constraint of line endpoints for short baseline matching and present a plane sweep algorithm for wide baseline matching. More recently, Fan et al. [3] explore an affine invariant from two points and one line. They utilize this affine invariant to match lines with known point correspondences. The main drawback of these approaches is the requirement of known epipolar geometry or point correspondences. Besides, their performance in low texture scenes is limited because of the lack of good point correspondences.

The rest of this paper is organized as follows. Sec.3 presents the way to extract lines in the scale space and generate the candidate matched pairs. Sec.4

Fig. 1. Illustration of line direction histograms. The first two images show the reference and query images with detected lines and the plot shows their direction histograms. The resolution of each bin is 20 degrees, so there are 18 bins for each histogram.

introduces the process to build the relational graph and the spectral technique to solve the graph matching problem. The experimental results are reported in Sec.5. Finally, we draw the conclusion in the last section.

3   Generating the Candidate Matching Pairs

3.1   Detecting Lines in the Scale Space

To overcome the fragmentation problem of line detection and improve the performance for large scale changes, in our line detection framework, we employ a scale-space pyramid consisting of n octave images which are generated by down-sampling the original image with a set of scale factors and Gaussian blurring. There is no intra-layer between two consecutive octaves. We first apply the ED-Line [13] algorithm to each octave producing a set of lines in the scale space. Then we re-organize them by finding corresponding lines in the scale space. For all lines extracted in the scale space, they will be assigned a unique ID and stored into a vector called LineVec if they are related to the same event in the image (i.e. the same region of the image with the same direction). The final extracted results are a set of LineVecs. The line detecting approach is different from Wang's [2] by reorganizing all line segments detected in the scale-space to form LineVecs which reduce the dimension of the graph matching problem.

3.2   Unary Geometric Attribute

The unary geometric attribute considered in our work is the direction of lines. At first glance, this attribute is ambiguous and unreliable as image pairs can have arbitrary rotation changes. Though this is exactly true, there is often an approximate global rotation angle between image pairs. We could employ this attribute whenever it is available to reduce the number of candidate matches.

In [3], the approximate rotation relationship between the reference and query images are calculated from the point feature correspondences. Inspired by this, although we don't have such point correspondence information, we can directly compute the line direction histograms of the reference and query images. Here, the line direction is given by making the gradients of most edge pixels pointing from its left side to its right side. Note that, lines in the same LineVec have the same direction, so each LineVec has a unique direction. We first calculate the two direction histograms of LineVecs from two images, then normalize them to get $(\mathbf{h}_r, \mathbf{h}_q)$ in which the subscript r denotes the reference image and q denotes the query image. Then we shift $\mathbf{h}_q$ by a angle θ varying from 0 to 2π and search for the approximate global rotation angle θ_g. By taking the angle as index in the histogram for simplicity, θ_g is estimated as:

$$\theta_g = \operatorname*{argmin}_{0 \leq \theta \leq 2\pi} \|\mathbf{h}_r(x) - \mathbf{h}_q(x - \theta)\|. \tag{1}$$

Since it's not always suitable to approximate the perspective transformation of images by a global rotation change, we have to check whether the estimated rotation angle is genuine. In practice, if the perspective transformation can be approximated by a rotation, then the shifted histogram distance $\|\mathbf{h}_r(x) - \mathbf{h}_q(x - \theta_g)\|$ is small. Fig.1 gives an example of line direction histograms of an image pair. The estimated θ_g is 0.349 rad and the shifted histogram distance is 0.243. In our implementation, we accept the estimated global rotation angle when the shifted histogram distance is smaller than 0.5. Once θ_g is accepted, for a pair of LineVecs to be matched, if $|\alpha - \theta_g| > t_\theta$ in which α is the angle between their directions, they are considered to be a non-match without further checking their appearance similarities. If there is no accepted rotation angle between two images, then only the appearance similarities are applied.

3.3   Local Appearance Similarity

There are few robust line descriptors based on the local appearance of a line in the literature. Two of them have remarkable performance: one takes the mean and standard deviation of the pixel gradients in a region centered at a line as its descriptor [8] and the other computes the line band descriptor (LBD) based on the band representation of lines [14]. As LBD is computationally more efficient and has better performance for most of image transformations, in our work we choose it to measure the appearance similarity of a pair of LineVecs.

Each LineVec may include more than one line in the scale space. For each line in the LineVec, we will generate a LBD1 descriptor [14] from the octave image where the line is extracted. In our work, for a line we use 9 bands each with width of 7 pixels, resulting in a 72-dimensional LBD1 descriptor vector V. When matching two sets of LineVecs extracted from an image pairs, the distances between all descriptors of a reference LineVec and a test LineVec are evaluated, and the minimal descriptor distance is used to measure the LineVec appearance similarity s. If $s > t_s$ in which t_s is the local appearance dissimilarity tolerance, then the corresponding two LineVecs won't be considered further.

After checking the unary geometric attribute of LineVecs and their local appearance similarities, the pairs passing the test are taken as candidate matches. A set of loose thresholds should be chosen, otherwise there will be a larger chance of missing correct matches. In our implementation, the thresholds are set as $t_\theta = \pi/4$, and $t_s = 0.35$. The number of candidate matches is quite larger

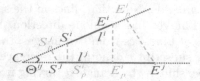

Fig. 2. Illustration of the pairwise geometric attributes. C is the intersection of two lines. (S^i, E^i) are endpoints of the line l^i and (S_p^i, E_p^i) are their projections onto the line l^j. Similarly, (S^j, E^j) are endpoints of the line l^j and (S_p^j, E_p^j) are their projections onto the line l^i.

than the number of real matches because one can not only rely on the aforementioned verifications to decide the final matching results. However, the checking still significantly reduces the dimension of the following graph matching problem compared with direct combinations.

4   Graph Matching Using Spectral Technique

For a given set of candidate matches, we build the relational graph whose nodes represent the potential correspondences and the weights on the links represent pairwise consistencies between them. Then recover the correct matches by using the spectral technique and imposing the mapping constraints.

4.1   Building the Relational Graph

Given a set of n candidate matches, the relational graph is represented by an adjacency matrix M with a size of $n \times n$ following the terminology in [5]. The value of the element in row i and column j of M is the consistent score of candidate LineVec matches (L_r^i, L_q^i) and (L_r^j, L_q^j) where L_r^i, L_r^j are LineVecs in the reference image and L_q^i, L_q^j are LineVecs in the query image. The consistent score is computed from the pairwise geometric attributes and appearance similarities of the candidate matched pairs.

For describing the pairwise geometric attributes of two LineVecs (L^i, L^j), we choose two lines (l^i, l^j) which lead to the minimal descriptor distance between these two LineVecs. Then referring to the work in [2], we describe the geometric attributes of (l^i, l^j) by their intersection ratios (I^i, I^j), projection ratios (P^i, P^j) and relative angle Θ^{ij} as shown in Fig.2. I^i and P^i are computed as:

$$I^i = \frac{\overrightarrow{S^iC} \cdot \overrightarrow{S^iE^i}}{|\overrightarrow{S^iE^i}|^2}, \quad P^i = \frac{|\overrightarrow{S^iS_p^i}| + |\overrightarrow{E^iE_p^i}|}{|\overrightarrow{S^iE^i}|}. \tag{2}$$

I^j and P^j can be calculated in the same way. The relative angle Θ^{ij} is easily calculated from the line directions. These three attributes are invariant to changes of translation, rotation, and scale.

As introduced in Sec.3.3, we use the LBD1 descriptor vector V to represent the local appearance of a line. We now get two sets of pairwise geometric attributes and local appearances for two candidate matches (L_r^i, L_q^i) and (L_r^j, L_q^j)

as: $\{I_r^i, I_r^j, P_r^i, P_r^j, \Theta_r^{ij}, V_r^i, V_r^j\}$ and $\{I_q^i, I_q^j, P_q^i, P_q^j, \Theta_q^{ij}, V_q^i, V_q^j\}$. Then the consistent score M^{ij} is computed as:

$$M^{ij} = \begin{cases} 5 - d_I - d_P - d_\Theta - s_V^i - s_V^j, & if \quad \Gamma = true; \\ 0, & else. \end{cases} \tag{3}$$

where d_I, d_P and d_Θ are the geometric similarities and s_V^i, s_V^j are the local appearance similarities. They are defined as:

$$\begin{cases} d_I = min(\frac{|I_r^i - I_q^i|}{t_I}, \frac{|I_r^j - I_q^j|}{t_I}); d_P = min(\frac{|P_r^i - P_q^i|}{t_P}, \frac{|P_r^j - P_q^j|}{t_P}); d_\Theta = \frac{|\Theta_r^{ij} - \Theta_q^{ij}|}{t_\Theta}; \\ s_V^i = \frac{\|V_r^i - V_q^i\|}{t_s}; \quad s_V^j = \frac{\|V_r^j - V_q^j\|}{t_s}; \quad \Gamma \equiv \{d_I, d_P, d_\Theta, s_V^i, s_V^j\} \leq 1. \end{cases} \tag{4}$$

Where $\Gamma \leq 1$ means each element in Γ is less than 1. Compared with [2], the definition of d_I in our work is more robust against the fragmentation problem of line detection because only if one pair of matched lines in the reference and query images is well extracted, then d_I could be very small no matter how bad the other pair is extracted. The definition of d_P shares the same advantage. t_I, t_P, t_Θ and t_s are thresholds. In our implementation, they are set as $t_I = 1$, $t_P = 1$, $t_\Theta = \pi/4$ and $t_s = 0.35$. The five terms in the consistent score equation (3) are given the same weights while [15] introduces a method to learn weights of these terms which will be part of our future considerations. For all the candidate matches, we compute the consistent score among them and obtain the adjacency matrix M. The diagonal elements of M equal zero as suggested by [15] for better results and let $M^{ji} = M^{ij}$ to keep the symmetry.

4.2 Generating the Final Matching Results

The matching problem is now reduced to finding the cluster of matches $\mathcal{LM}$ that maximizes the total consistent scores $\sum_{(L_r^i, L_q^i), (L_r^j, L_q^j) \in \mathcal{LM}} M^{ij}$ such that the mapping constraints are met. We use an indicator vector x to represent the cluster such that $x(i) = 1$ if $(L_r^i, L_q^i) \in \mathcal{LM}$ and zero otherwise. Thus, the problem is formulated as [5]:

$$x^* = argmax(x^T M x) \tag{5}$$

where x is subject to the mapping constraints. The general quadratic programming techniques are too computationally expensive to solve this problem. We employ the spectral technique which relaxes both the mapping constraints and the integral constraints on x such that its elements can take real values in $[0, 1]$.

By the Raleigh's ratio theorem [5], the x^* that will maximize $x^T M x$ is the principal eigenvector of M. What still remains is to binarize the eigenvector using mapping constraints and obtain a robust approximation of the optimal solution. The mapping constraints applied here are the sidedness constraint [12,9] and the one-to-one constraint. Details of the algorithm are as follows:

1. Extract LineVecs from the reference and query images by EDLine [13] in the scale space to obtain two sets of LineVecs $\mathcal{L}_r$ and $\mathcal{L}_q$;
2. Estimate the global rotation angle θ_g of the image pair from the direction histograms of $\mathcal{L}_r$ and $\mathcal{L}_q$;
3. Compute the LBD1 descriptors [14] of LineVecs in $\mathcal{L}_r$ and $\mathcal{L}_q$;
4. Generate a set of candidate matches $\mathcal{CM} = \{(L_r^1, L_q^1), (L_r^2, L_q^2), \ldots, (L_r^n, L_q^n)\}$ by checking the unary geometric attribute and local appearance similarities of LineVecs in $\mathcal{L}_r$ and $\mathcal{L}_q$;
5. Build the adjacency matrix M with a size of $n \times n$ according to the consistence scores of pairs in $\mathcal{CM}$;
6. Get the principal eigenvector x^* of M by using ARPACK[16];
7. Initialize the matching result: $\mathcal{LM} \leftarrow \oslash$;
8. Find $a = \mathrm{argmax}(x^*(i))$, $i = 1, \cdots, n$. If $x^*(a) = 0$, then stop and return the matching result $\mathcal{LM}$. Otherwise, set $\mathcal{LM} = \mathcal{LM} \cup \{(L_r^a, L_q^a)\}$, $\mathcal{CM} = \mathcal{CM} - \{(L_r^a, L_q^a)\}$ and $x^*(a) = 0$.
9. Check all the candidates in $\mathcal{CM}$. If (L_r^j, L_q^j) conflicts with (L_r^a, L_q^a), then set $\mathcal{CM} = \mathcal{CM} - \{(L_r^j, L_q^j)\}$ and $x^*(j) = 0$.
10. If $\mathcal{CM}$ is empty, then return $\mathcal{LM}$. Otherwise go back to Step 8.

5   Experiments

To evaluate the performance of the proposed line matching algorithm, we conduct a set of experiments for image pairs under various transformations. We also compare our results to state-of-the-art methods. The following experiments are performed on a 3.4GHz Intel(R) Core 2 processor with 8 GB of RAM.

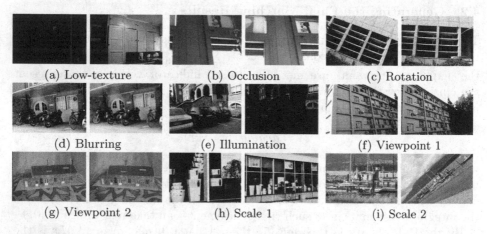

(a) Low-texture   (b) Occlusion   (c) Rotation

(d) Blurring   (e) Illumination   (f) Viewpoint 1

(g) Viewpoint 2   (h) Scale 1   (i) Scale 2

Fig. 3. Dataset for experiments

• **Line Matching Results:** We present the results of our line matching algorithm on nine image pairs as shown in Fig.3. The occlusion images are captured

Fig. 4. Illustration of the line matching results

in our office and the others are from some publicly available dataset[2,3]. The matching results in three challenging scenes are shown in Fig.4 (The rest of matching results are presented in the supplementary materials because of the space limitation). The matched lines in each pair are assigned the same color and one of their endpoints are connected to illustrate their correspondences. These figures are better viewed in color. The first image pair in Fig.4 is low-texture planar scene with illumination and view point changes. The second image pair in Fig.4 is non-planar scene with moderate view point changes. The last image pair in Fig.4 is textured scene with strong scale and rotation variations. The matching algorithm is less performing for these three image pairs than for the rest of image pairs. Nevertheless, the results shown in Fig.4 are still quite acceptable and establish many matched lines with few mismatches.

It's worth to note that similar to the parameter detection methods adopted in [2] and [3], it's quite empirical to find the good parameter settings. However, these parameter settings are fixed as presented in Sec.3 and Sec.4 for all the experiments. The results show that the algorithm works well for a large range of image variations as illustrated in Fig.3.

Table 1. Comparison of our approach (AG) with three other line matching algorithms (MSLD [8], LP [3], LS [2]). For each image pair, the following results are reported: the number of total matches, the matching precision and the computational time.

	Img	AG	MSLD	LP	LS		Img	AG	MSLD	LP	LS		Img	AG	MSLD	LP	LS
	a	54	20	5	54		a	94	60	60	96		a	0.11	0.30	5	8
	b	54	42	37	76		b	100	95	100	100		b	0.04	0.24	6.5	1
Total Matches	c	263	238	230	188	Matching Precision (%)	c	100	92	100	100	Time(s)	c	0.38	0.42	14	26
	d	106	96	58	43		d	100	92	100	100		d	0.55	0.54	35	5
	e	245	245	211	241		e	100	98	100	100		e	0.59	0.50	25	8
	f	446	568	364	281		f	100	96	100	100		f	1.75	0.61	29	10
	g	87	82	80	151		g	100	73	86	98		g	0.20	0.24	20	8
	h	19	18	30	37		h	95	67	95	97		h	0.17	0.32	13	9
	i	44	30	48	14		i	95	33	88	29		i	0.51	0.42	72	8

- **Comparison with State-of-the-art Methods:** We compare our matching results with some state-of-the-art methods to further show its performance. As introduced in Sec.2, the existing approaches to match lines are mainly of three types. We choose three representatives from the three groups which are recently reported to feature highly remarkable performance: the Mean-Standard deviation Line Descriptor (MSLD) [8], the Line Signature (LS) [2] and the Line matching leveraged by Point correspondences (LP) [3]. As our method combines the Appearance and Geometric constraints together, it's called AG here. The implementations of LS and LP are supplied by their authors while MSLD is implemented by ourselves. In our implementation of MSLD, the parameters are chosen as recommended by its authors.

The test dataset used in the comparison is the same as in Fig.3. The comparison results are given in Tab.1. All the matched lines are checked one by one manually to test whether a matched line pair is correct or not. The input lines for different matching methods are not exactly the same except for AG and MSLD, because the binary codes of these algorithms have their default line detection methods embedded. However, the results shown in Tab.1 represent their performance for the nine image pairs. It's clear that MSLD and LP are less performing for the low-texture scene, because the local appearances of lines are indistinguishable and the images lack of stable point correspondences. The results also show that AG achieves higher accuracy than MSLD which proves that the graph matching process using spectral technique is necessary especially for these challenging situations. Surprisingly, LS has a bad matching result for image pair (i) which is inconsistent with the result presented in [2]. If we change the role of reference and query images, then we can get the same good result. This illustrates that the matching results of LS are depending on the order of images in a pair. Compared to LP and LS, the most superior feature of AG is its time performance. Here, the time of LP given in Tab.1 is its complete processing time which includes generating point correspondences and matching lines.

6   Conclusion

We address the problem of line matching for image pairs under various situations: low-texture scenes, partial occlusion, rotation changes, blurred images, illumination changes, moderate viewpoint changes, and scale changes. We show the robustness and the efficiency of our graph matching process. The good performance achieved by the proposed algorithm is mainly because we detect lines in the scale space and combine the local appearance and geometric constraints together which eliminates lots of mismatches. The geometric constraints are enforced globally in this paper by using the spectral technique. For images undergoing a moderate transformation, the global geometric constraints are maintained well. For strong wide baseline images of the non-planar scenes, the global constraints may be violated, then it's better to enforce the local geometric constraints like the approach in [2] although it is more time consuming.

References

1. Mikolajczyk, K., Schmid, C.: A performance evaluation of local descriptors. PAMI 27, 1615–1630 (2005)
2. Wang, L., Neumann, U., You, S.: Wide-baseline image matching using line signatures. In: ICCV, pp. 1311–1318 (2009)
3. Fan, B., Wu, F., Hu, Z.: Line matching leveraged by point correspondences. In: CVPR, pp. 390–397 (2010)
4. Schmid, C., Zisserman, A.: Automatic line matching across views. In: CVPR, pp. 666–671 (1997)
5. Leordeanu, M., Hebert, M.: A spectral technique for correspondence problems using pairwise constraints. In: ICCV, pp. 1482–1489 (2005)
6. Neubert, P., Protzel, P., Vidal-Calleja, T., Lacroix, S.: A fast visual line segment tracker. In: ETFA, pp. 353–360 (2008)
7. Woo, D.M., Park, D.C., Han, S.S., Beack, S.: 2d line matching using geometric and intensity data. In: AICI, pp. 99–103 (2009)
8. Wang, Z., Wu, F., Hu, Z.: Msld: A robust descriptor for line matching. PR 42, 941–953 (2009)
9. Horaud, R., Skordas, T.: Stereo correspondence through feature grouping and maximal cliques. PAMI 11, 1168–1180 (1989)
10. Christmas, W., Kittler, J., Petrou, M.: Structural matching in computer vision using probabilistic relaxation. PAMI 17, 749–764 (1995)
11. Wilson, R.C., Hancock, E.R.: Structural matching by discrete relaxation. PAMI 19, 634–648 (1997)
12. Bay, H., Ferrari, V., Van Gool, L.: Wide-baseline stereo matching with line segments. In: CVPR, pp. 329–336 (2005)
13. Akinlar, C., Topal, C.: Edlines: A real-time line segment detector with a false detection control. Pattern Recognition Letters 32, 1633–1642 (2011)
14. Zhang, L., Koch, R.: Lbd: A fast and robust line descriptor based on line band representation. Technical Report (2012), http://www.mip.informatik.uni-kiel.de
15. Leordeanu, M., Sukthankar, R., Hebert, M.: Unsupervised learning for graph matching. IJCV, 1–18 (2011)
16. http://www.caam.rice.edu/software/ARPACK/

Salient Pattern Detection Using W_2 on Multivariate Normal Distributions

Dominik Alexander Klein and Simone Frintrop

Department of Computer Science III, University of Bonn, Germany

Abstract. Saliency is an attribute that is not included in an object itself, but arises from complex relations to the scene. Common belief in neuroscience is that objects are eye-catching if they exhibit an anomaly in some basic feature of human perception. This enables detection of object-like structures without prior knowledge. In this paper, we introduce an approach that models these object-to-scene relations based on probability theory. We rely on the conventional structure of cognitive visual attention systems, measuring saliency by local center to surround differences on several basic feature cues and multiple scales, but innovate how to model appearance and to quantify differences. Therefore, we propose an efficient procedure to compute ML-estimates for (multivariate) normal distributions of local feature statistics. Reducing feature statistics to Gaussians facilitates a closed-form solution for the W_2-distance (Wasserstein metric based on the Euclidean norm) between a center and a surround distribution. On a widely used benchmark for salient object detection, our approach, named CoDi-Saliency (for Continuous Distributions), outperformed nine state-of-the-art saliency detectors in terms of precision and recall.

1 Introduction

The detection of salient objects that visually stand out from their surrounding and automatically attract attention has been intensely investigated during the last decade. It is of interest not only from a psychological perspective, but also from a computational one. Finding salient regions in images supports applications such as general object detection and segmentation in web images [1,15], or steering a robots eyes and head [18,19]. The proposed algorithm not only convincingly fulfills its main purpose to quantify saliency, but does this at low computational costs. We integrated efficient and innovative solutions for the most critical parts of saliency systems based on feature statistics: local estimation of distributions and calculation of their contrast. Therefore, CoDi-Saliency is especially suited for such large scale offline application or online usage on restricted mobile platforms.

Many computational approaches have been presented during the last two decades that compute visual saliency, ranging from the well-known Itti-Koch model [11] to approaches that learn optimal feature combinations with machine learning techniques [15]. A survey on computational attention systems that determine saliency can be found in [5].

A. Pinz et al. (Eds.): DAGM/OAGM 2012, LNCS 7476, pp. 246–255, 2012.
© Springer-Verlag Berlin Heidelberg 2012

Since saliency is intrinsically based on the difference of a region with respect to its surround, it is clear that the computation of a feature (e.g. colors, gradients, entropy, etc.) is per se not sufficient to determine saliency. An example is a single bird that is salient in front of a blue sky but not among a swarm of other birds. Instead, computing the difference of some feature qualities in a region and in its surround is essential [3,14,12]. Most approaches determine the center-surround contrast by DoG-filters or approximations of these [11,4]. Recently, some groups have represented the center and surround area by feature distributions to capture more information about the area [3,6,14,12]. These approaches use discrete distributions in the form of histograms to represent the occurrences of features in an image patch. In contrast to this, we represent feature statistics by multivariate normal distributions that are compared with the Wasserstein distance based on the Euclidean norm. This metric is a well-known method to compare probability distributions and, in contrast to methods such as KLD, considers also the distance of feature entries. This is especially useful for computing saliency since there the similarity of feature values is an essential aspect.

This mathematically well-founded way to compute the saliency of a feature dimension is integrated into a complete framework that is based on findings from neuroscience and psychophysics. It computes several feature cues on multiple scales and finally fuses their conspicuities into a single saliency map. In contrast to most other saliency computation methods, our approach outputs fine-grained saliency maps in which the complete salient objects stand out. We show that our approach outperforms nine state-of-the-art saliency detectors in a segmentation task on the MSRA salient object database [15]. In addition, we show the biological validity of our approach on psychophysical test patterns.

2   The Saliency Model

The structure of our saliency system complies with the architecture of approved psychological visual attention models like those of Treisman and Gelade [20] or Wolfe [22]. Basic features of the human attention system [23] are processed independently from each other. Anomalous appearances of a feature with respect to surroundings are emphasized, resulting in one map of perceptional conspicuity per basic feature. Then, individual conspicuities are fused into a conjoint saliency map.

In CoDi, basic features are investigated in a multi-scale approach, utilizing a difference-of-Gaussian pyramid representation of the input image constructed as in [16]. We implemented the basic features of intensity and color, nevertheless it is possible to adopt the computational methods presented in this paper to further basic features as well. We express local feature occurrences by means of normal distributions. For each point in the image (scale-)space, two normal distributions are estimated: one characterizing the feature appearance closely centered around the point, the other incorporating appearance of a wider surround. Then, the W_2-distance between those distributions is used as conspicuity measure determining the local center-surround contrasts. Figure 1 shows a flowchart of our system.

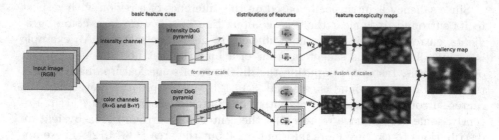

Fig. 1. Schematic intra-system view of the CoDi-Saliency computation

2.1 Basic Feature Cues

In a first step, the input image is transformed from RGB into a simple, but more psychologically motivated color space following the opponent-process theory [10]. From every pixel, the intensity and color features are computed as

$$I(x,y) = \left(\frac{R+G+B}{3} \right)_{(x,y)} \quad \text{and} \quad C(x,y) = \binom{c_1}{c_2} = \binom{R-G}{B - \frac{R+G}{2}}_{(x,y)} . \quad (1)$$

From this image in opponent color space, a difference-of-Gaussian pyramid is computed. That way, we achieve a scale-separated representation $I(x,y;t)$ of one-dimensional intensity feature and $C(x,y;t)$ of two-dimensional color feature consisting of a red-green and blue-yellow contrast dimension. In theory, it would be best to use a perceptually normalized color space like CIELAB[1], but this requires additional knowledge about the illuminant, which is not given but varies heavily in image collections from unknown sources. Constant use of D_{65} standard illuminant factors for midday sunlight would probably introduce similar inaccuracies as using the proposed, efficiently computable space.

2.2 Local Feature Statistics

In our framework, local feature statistics are summarized by one-dimensional normal distributions for intensity, respectively two-dimensional distributions for color. To facilitate an efficient maximum likelihood estimation of the normal distribution parameters, supplementing layers are added to the feature maps, resulting in

$$I_+(x,y;t) = \binom{i}{i^2}_{(x,y;t)} \quad \text{and} \quad C_+(x,y;t) = (c_1, c_2, c_1^2, c_2^2, c_1 c_2)^T_{(x,y;t)}. \quad (2)$$

Local occurrences of a feature are treated as weighted samples for the estimation process. The weights are determined by a Gaussian integration window (cf. Fig. 2), implemented by discrete convolution of the feature maps

---

[1] http://www.hunterlab.com/appnotes/an07_96a.pdf

$$\bar{I}_+(x,y;t) = \left(g\left(\sigma^2\right) * I_+(t)\right)(x,y)$$
$$\bar{C}_+(x,y;t) = \left(g\left(\sigma^2\right) * C_+(t)\right)(x,y). \tag{3}$$

Sophisticated optimizations and approximations are essential to be applied in this step to achieve competitive performance: For Gaussians of a small standard deviation, separability of the Gaussian kernel in x- and y-dimension is exploited, resulting in run-time complexity $\mathcal{O}(\sigma n)$. For those of bigger σ, based on the central limit theorem, a Gaussian filter is approximated by repeated smoothing with b box-filters, choosing their width and height so that the result is a bth-order approximation of a Gaussian of slightly smaller σ_{box}, inspired by [13]. The standard deviation of a box filter of extent w equals $\sqrt{(w^2-1)/12}$. Thus, applying b iterations, a filter of size $w_{\text{ideal}} = \sqrt{(12\sigma^2)/b + 1}$ would provide the best approximation of this Gaussian. However, since $w \in \mathbb{N}$, we choose the next smaller and larger odd filter sizes

$$w_1 = 2\left\lceil 0.5\sqrt{(12\sigma^2)/b + 1}\right\rceil - 1 \quad \text{and} \quad w_2 = w_1 + 2 \tag{4}$$

instead. The closest approximation we can get showing a standard deviation lower than σ, is achieved by

$$m_1 = \left\lceil \frac{12\sigma^2 - bw_1^2 - 4bw_1 - 3b}{-4w_1 - 4}\right\rceil \quad \text{and} \quad m_2 = b - m_1 \tag{5}$$

repeated rounds of box-filtering with extents w_1 and w_2, respectively. This process results in an overall standard deviation of

$$\sigma_{\text{box}} = \sqrt{(m_1 w_1^2 + m_2 w_2^2 - b)/12}. \tag{6}$$

The small defect of $\sigma_\Delta = \sqrt{\sigma^2 - \sigma_{\text{box}}^2}$ is then smoothed as described before, resulting in overall run-time complexity of $\mathcal{O}(\sigma_\Delta n + bn)$. Furthermore, one can apply stepwise smoothing when computing center ($\bullet$) and surround ($\odot$) statistics, since w.l.o.g. for $\sigma_s \geq \sigma_c$

$$\bar{I}_{+,\odot} = g\left(\sigma_s^2\right) * I_+ = g\left(\sigma_s^2 - \sigma_c^2\right) * g\left(\sigma_c^2\right) * I_+ = g\left(\sigma_s^2 - \sigma_c^2\right) * \bar{I}_{+,\bullet} \tag{7}$$

and the same holds true for color.

After applying this local weighting of feature samples by means of smoothing the annotated feature maps, one can easily compute a center and a surround ML-estimate of normal distribution parameters with help of the images $\bar{I}_{+,\{\bullet,\odot\}}$ and $\bar{C}_{+,\{\bullet,\odot\}}$ utilizing the relations

$$\hat{\mu}_I = \bar{i}, \hat{\sigma}_I = \overline{i^2} - \bar{i}^2, \hat{\mu}_C = \begin{pmatrix} \bar{c}_1 \\ \bar{c}_2 \end{pmatrix}, \quad \text{and} \quad \hat{\Sigma}_C = \begin{pmatrix} \overline{c_1^2} - \bar{c}_1^2 & \overline{c_1 c_2} - \bar{c}_1 \bar{c}_2 \\ \overline{c_1 c_2} - \bar{c}_1 \bar{c}_2 & \overline{c_2^2} - \bar{c}_2^2 \end{pmatrix} \tag{8}$$

for every pixel and scale. Note that this computation scheme could also be applied in a similar way for multivariate normal distributions of more than two dimensions.

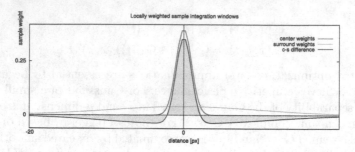

Fig. 2. Center and surround integration windows of feature samples are Gaussians of different standard deviations. Especially the large surround integration window requires fast approximation algorithms.

2.3   Center-Surround Difference of Feature Statistics

In the last section, we explained how to efficiently compute (multivariate) normal distributions of local, basic feature occurrences, so we can assume a center $P_\bullet$ and a surround distribution $P_\odot$ to be given for every pixel and scale. The next step is to determine how much the center appearance sticks out of the surround, in other words how different those two distributions are. Here, a plausible distance measure should not only score the similarity of probabilities between same feature manifestations, but also take into account the visual difference between manifestations. A white region within a black image is clearly more conspicuous than a gray one. The W_2-distance on the Euclidean norm, which is defined as

$$W_2(P_\bullet, P_\odot) = \left[\inf_{\gamma \in \Gamma(P_\bullet, P_\odot)} \int_{\mathbb{R}^n \times \mathbb{R}^n} \|x - y\|_2 \, d\gamma(x, y) \right]^{\frac{1}{2}} \tag{9}$$

with $\Gamma(P_\bullet, P_\odot)$ denoting the set of all couplings of $P_\bullet$ and $P_\odot$, meets this requirements, if the underlying feature space is defined reasonably. Most often it is imagined as a transport of mass problem: how much (probability) mass needs to be moved how far (wrt. Euclidean distance) to transform one probability density function into the other. For example, in computer vision the W_1-distance on discrete random variables is also referred to as earth mover's distance (EMD).

It would be intractable to evaluate the integral in equation 9 in case of arbitrary distributions. Thankfully, it can be solved algebraically for multivariate normal distributions, as established by Givens and Shortt [7], resulting in the closed form expression

$$W_2(P_\bullet, P_\odot) = \left[\|\mu_\bullet - \mu_\odot\|_2^2 + \mathrm{tr}\left(\Sigma_\bullet\right) + \mathrm{tr}\left(\Sigma_\odot\right) - 2\,\mathrm{tr}\left(\sqrt{\Sigma_\bullet^{\frac{1}{2}} \Sigma_\odot \Sigma_\bullet^{\frac{1}{2}}}\right) \right]^{\frac{1}{2}}. \tag{10}$$

Applying equations 8 and 10 to our basic features $\bar{I}_{+,\{\bullet,\odot\}}(x, y; t)$ and $\bar{C}_{+,\{\bullet,\odot\}}(x, y; t)$ yields pyramids of intensity $\mathcal{I}(x, y; t)$ as well as color $\mathcal{C}(x, y; t)$ conspicuities.

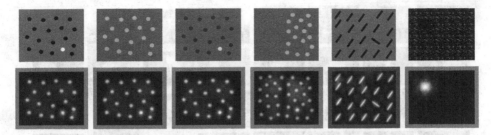

Fig. 3. Saliency maps of our system on psychophysical test patterns provided by Klein and Frintrop [12]

2.4   Fusion of Scales and Feature Modalities

For every feature, the arithmetic mean over normalized scales is calculated as

$$\mathcal{I}(x,y) = \frac{1}{s} \bigoplus_{t=1}^{s} \sqrt{t}\, \mathcal{I}(x,y;t) \quad \text{and} \quad \mathcal{C}(x,y) = \frac{1}{s} \bigoplus_{t=1}^{s} \sqrt{t}\, \mathcal{C}(x,y;t) \tag{11}$$

with $\oplus$ denoting a rescale and add-per-pixel operator. Finally, the saliency map is given by the arithmetic mean across feature modalities

$$\mathcal{S}(x,y) = \frac{1}{2}\left(\mathcal{I}(x,y) + \mathcal{C}(x,y) \right). \tag{12}$$

3   Evaluation

We compared our saliency model, CoDi, with nine state-of-the-art saliency models: the iNVT by Itti et al. [11], the Saliency Toolbox (ST) [21], two systems of Hou and Zhang (HZ07,HZ08) [8,9], the AIM model of Bruce and Tsotsos [3], the system of Ma and Zhang (MZ) [17], two versions of Achanta et al. (AC09,AC10) [1,2], and the BITS system of Klein and Frintrop [12].

The evaluation was done first on the psychophysical test patterns used in [12] (Sec. 3.1) and second on the MSRA database of salient objects [1] (Sec. 3.2).

3.1   Psychophysical Soundness

The purpose of a saliency model usually is to mimic human behavior, thus it is crucial to obey the findings of neuroscience about the human attention mechanism. There, attention was studied testing the human ability to immediately detect outliers in so called "pop-out" images. A conform computational saliency model should likewise output the maximum saliency at the positions of such pop-outs.

Klein and Frintrop [12] introduced suitable test patterns and compared several approaches. Only the BITS system successfully passed all tests, the others ([11,21,1,2,9,3]) each failed in at least two of the patterns. The CoDi-Saliency detector passes every pattern but the orientation (cf. Fig. 3), since this basic feature is not integrated. However, since the proposed framework is very generic, it should be possible to add further feature cues to our system.

Fig. 4. Comparison of saliency maps on natural images from the MSRA dataset [15]. First row shows the original images, second row the corresponding ground truth. Next, results of the following saliency methods are listed from top to bottom: our approach CoDi, BITS [12], AC10 [2], ST [21], AIM [3], iNVT [11], HZ08 [9].

3.2   Salient Object Detection

A quantitative performance analysis of our algorithm was done on the subset of 1000 images out of the MSRA salient object database [15] that was first used in [1]. The images contain objects that have been consistently marked as salient by several subjects. Pixel-precise binary maps are available that contain the ground truth shapes of the objects. Figure 4 shows exemplary results of the saliency maps of different saliency detectors with available source code.

The quantitative experiments were conducted as in [1]: all saliency maps are binarized by thresholding the intensity values between $[0, 255]$. Thereby, one achieves 256 possible segmentations for the dataset. Then, each is matched against the ground truth binary masks to obtain precision and recall. Finally, results are plotted together in the graph depicted in Figure 5. It can be seen that our approach outperforms the others. The second best, BITS, is also based on local distributions of basic features, but seems to be inferior because of two major points: first, the Kullback-Leibler divergence as a distance between distributions

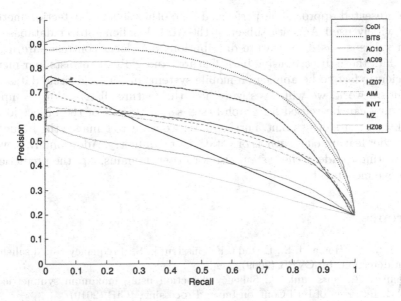

Fig. 5. Precision-recall curves for the salient object dataset of 1000 images from [1]. We compared our system CoDi against nine other saliency detectors.

does not consider distances in the feature domain like the Wasserstein metric. Second, feature space discretization in histograms can be problematic, especially for 2D features such as color. Instead, our algorithm works on continuous distributions. The precision value for threshold 255 using our approach is ≈ 0.01 (cf. left boundary of Fig. 5), stating that in more than 9 out of 10 cases the most salient point was located on the object of interest. Thus, it should serve as a good starting point for a subsequent object segmentation algorithm.

With parameters chosen as used for this evaluation, the computation time per image executed by an Intel Core i7-2600 CPU is 82ms on average. It mainly depends on the number and resolution of evaluated scales. If necessary, it can be tuned to even less computation time without disproportionally downgrading the results. Besides that, the framework is well suited for parallelization and should benefit much if one makes use of a modern GPU.

4   Conclusion

We introduced CoDi-Saliency, a new method to compute visual saliency in a probabilistic fashion. The overall framework follows the conventional structure of cognitive visual attention systems, computing the conspicuity for each basic feature cue individually before fusing them to a common saliency map. Local normal distributions of basic features were aggregated and estimated employing an efficient approximation algorithm for Gaussian image convolution on intelligently supplemented feature maps. This enabled the computation of W_2-distance in constant time per pixel.

The presented approach outperformed nine other saliency detection methods on the widely used Achanta subset of the MSRA salient object database. Although systems based on feature distributions and local contrasts are usually slower than those directly using basic features and global contrasts, our method is sufficiently fast to be applied on mobile systems or for large scale datasets.

In future work, we will investigate how the feature distributions computed for saliency can be reused for graph-based segmentation of the object located around the most salient point. Furthermore, we want to enhance the framework with further feature cues such as orientation or symmetry. Additionally, it would be interesting to adopt the system also for other domains, e.g. the prediction of human eye movements.

References

1. Achanta, R., Hemami, S., Estrada, F., Süsstrunk, S.: Frequency-tuned salient region detection. In: CVPR (2009)
2. Achanta, R., Süsstrunk, S.: Saliency detection using maximum symmetric surround. In: Proc. of Int'l Conf. on Image Processing, ICIP (2010)
3. Bruce, N., Tsotsos, J.: Saliency, attention, and visual search: An information theoretic approach. Journal of Vision 9(3), 1–24 (2009)
4. Frintrop, S.: VOCUS: A Visual Attention System for Object Detection and Goal-Directed Search. LNCS (LNAI), vol. 3899. Springer, Heidelberg (2006)
5. Frintrop, S., Rome, E., Christensen, H.I.: Computational visual attention systems and their cognitive foundation: A survey. ACM Trans. on Applied Perception 7(1) (2010)
6. Gao, D., Vasconcelos, N.: Bottom-up saliency is a discriminant process. In: Proc. of ICCV (2007)
7. Givens, C.R., Shortt, R.M.: A class of wasserstein metrics for probability distributions. Michigan Math. J. 31(2) (1984)
8. Hou, X., Zhang, L.: Saliency detection: a spectral residual approach. In: Proc. of CVPR (2007)
9. Hou, X., Zhang, L.: Dynamic visual attention: Searching for coding length increments. In: Advances in Neural Information Processing Systems (2008)
10. Hurvich, L., Jameson, D.: An opponent-process theory of color vision. Psychological Review 64(6) (1957)
11. Itti, L., Koch, C., Niebur, E.: A model of saliency-based visual attention for rapid scene analysis. IEEE Trans. on PAMI 20(11) (1998)
12. Klein, D.A., Frintrop, S.: Center-surround divergence of feature statistics for salient object detection. In: Proc. of Int'l Conf. on Computer Vision, ICCV (2011)
13. Kovesi, P.: Arbitrary gaussian filtering with 25 additions and 5 multiplications per pixel. Tech. Rep. UWA-CSSE-09-002, School of Computer Science, University of Western Australia (2009)
14. Lin, Y., Fang, B., Tang, Y.: A computational model for saliency maps by using local entropy. In: Proc. of AAAI (2010)
15. Liu, T., Yuan, Z., Sun, J., Wang, J., Zheng, N., Tang, X., Shum, H.Y.: Learning to detect a salient object. IEEE Trans. on PAMI (2009)
16. Lowe, D.G.: Distinctive image features from scale-invariant keypoints. Int'l J. of Computer Vision (IJCV) 60(2), 91–110 (2004)

17. Ma, Y.F., Zhang, H.J.: Contrast-based image attention analysis by using fuzzy growing. In: ACM Int'l Conf. on Multimedia (2003)
18. Ruesch, J., Lopes, M., Bernardino, A., Hörnstein, J., Santos-Victor, J., Pfeifer, R.: Multimodal saliency-based bottom-up attention: A framework for the humanoid robot icub. In: Proc. of Int'l Conf. on Robotics and Automation, ICRA (2008)
19. Schauerte, B., Kühn, B., Kroschel, K., Stiefelhagen, R.: Multimodal saliency-based attention for object-based scene analysis. In: Proc. of Int'l Conf. on Intelligent Robots and Systems, IROS (2011)
20. Treisman, A.M., Gelade, G.: A feature integration theory of attention. Cognitive Psychology 12, 97–136 (1980)
21. Walther, D., Koch, C.: Modeling attention to salient proto-objects. Neural Networks (2006)
22. Wolfe, J.M.: Guided search 2.0: A revised model of visual search. Psychonomic Bulletin and Review 1(2) (1994)
23. Wolfe, J.M., Horowitz, T.S.: What attributes guide the deployment of visual attention and how do they do it? Nature Reviews Neuroscience 5, 1–7 (2004)

A Simple Extension
of Stability Feature Selection

A. Beinrucker, Ü. Dogan, and G. Blanchard

University of Potsdam, Institute of Mathematics

Abstract. *Stability selection* [9] is a general principle for performing feature selection. It functions as a meta-layer on top of a "baseline" feature selection method, and consists in repeatedly applying the baseline to random data subsamples of half-size, and finally outputting the features with selection frequency larger than a fixed threshold. In the present work, we suggest and study a simple extension of the original stability selection. It consists in applying the baseline method to random submatrices of the data matrix $\mathbf{X}$ of a given size and returning those features having the largest selection frequency. We analyze from a theoretical point of view the effect of this subsampling on the selected variables, in particular the influence of the data subsample size. We report experimental results on large-dimension artificial and real data and identify in which settings stability selection is to be recommended.

1 Introduction

1.1 Stability Selection

Let $(X_i, Y_i)_{1 \leq i \leq n}$ be a data sample where the goal is to predict $Y \in \mathbb{R}$ from $X \in \mathbb{R}^d$. Feature (or variable) selection methods aim at finding a (data-dependent) subset of the coordinate indices $\mathcal{F} = \{1, \ldots, d\}$ so that the corresponding coordinates of X are the most relevant for prediction of Y. Feature selection is useful both as a data analysis tool (find out which features are informative about the target) as well as a preprocessing step (reducing significantly the dimensionality of the data before applying a computation-intensive learning algorithm).

Stability (feature) selection [9] (herafter abbreviated as SFS) is a general principle for performing feature selection. It functions as a meta-layer on top of a "baseline" feature selection method which we will denote `BaselineFS`. The baseline feature selection takes as an input a training sample S and returns a subset $F = \texttt{BaselineFS}(S)$ of selected features out of the initial pool of candidates $\mathcal{F}$. SFS consists in repeatedly applying `BaselineFS` to random subsamples of size $\lfloor n/2 \rfloor$ of a given training sample, and finally outputting the features with selection frequency larger than a fixed threshold τ. Its underlying subsampling principle in order to achieve stabilization is reminiscent of subagging [4]. Due to its reported significant improvements over the baseline, SFS has given rise to significant attention and follow-up works recently [11].

A. Pinz et al. (Eds.): DAGM/OAGM 2012, LNCS 7476, pp. 256–265, 2012.
© Springer-Verlag Berlin Heidelberg 2012

1.2   Overview and Contributions

We suggest and study two simple extensions of the original SFS. First, we propose to subsample the original sample into subsamples of possibly smaller size. Secondly, we propose to consider simultaneously random subsampling of the set of candidate features themselves, so that the baseline feature selection is repeatedly applied on a random subsets of the initial feature set $\mathcal{F}$. In other words, if $\mathbf{X}$ denotes the $n \times d$ design matrix, extended stability selection consists in applying the baseline method to random submatrices of $\mathbf{X}$ of size $\lfloor n/L \rfloor \times \lfloor d/V \rfloor$, and returning those features having the largest selection frequency. We abbreviate hereafter this method as $SFS(L, V)$ (the original method being therefore $SFS(2, 1)$). A precise pseudo-code description of the method is available in the supplementary material.[1]

While a subsample of size $\lfloor n/2 \rfloor$ is less biased with respect to the original sample size n, smaller subsamples lead to more independence between different subsamples and thus to variance reduction. This assertion is supported theoretically in Section 2.1 where we derive a bound on the proportion of noise variables selected in error. This result generalizes previous ones obtained in the case $L = 2$ and highlights some points that were not immediately apparent in that case, namely an exponential concentration in the integer L (variance reduction) which is to be balanced against a bias increase for individual subsamples for larger L. The effect of random feature sampling is more difficult to analyze in all generality, but we argue in Section 2.2 that it is expected to be beneficial when there are significant correlations between the relevant variable that can lead to a "mutual masking" effect.

The effect of both of these extensions is studied on controlled experiments in Section 3. We first report that (on artificial small-size datasets), the standard SFS(2,1) does not always improve over the standalone baseline feature selection. Importantly however, in the studied datasets our proposed extensions $SFS(L, V)$ improve over the standard SFS(2,1) *whenever the latter itself improves over the baseline feature selector*. To put it briefly, whenever standard SFS is advisable, then it is also avisable to consider the extensions proposed here to yield further improvements. Furthermore, on a real high-dimensional classification dataset, the proposed extensions led to a significant performance improvement. In addition, we underline that the proposed method also offers a noticeable *computational advantage*, in that the `BaselineFS` method only has to be applied on smaller (by a factor LV) chunks of data. This can help significantly with parallelization and memory constraints, particularly if the `BaselineFS` implementation requires the processed data to be loaded in memory in its entirety. This is a significant advantage for large-scale, high-dimensional applications.

1.3   Comparison to Previous Work

The early reference [2] applied linear SVMs to bootstrap subsamples of the data to select a stable set of variables. The idea of additional subsampling of *features*

---

[1] http://users.math.uni-potsdam.de/~blanchard/publi/BeiDogBla12aSupp.pdf

appeared under various forms in past literature, one prominent example being Random Forests [3]. The original work [9] proposed "randomizing"; it consists in reweighing each feature in the Lasso ℓ_1 penalty by a random factor w_i^{-1}, where $w_i \in [\alpha, 1]$. Feature subsampling can be intuitively seen as a crude version of this where instead of reweighting, we simply drop out randomly a large part of the features. The first advantage is that this principle is applicable to any baseline and not specifically designed for the Lasso. A second advantage is a reduction in computational complexity (and memory requirements) by effectively considering smaller dimensional data when repeatedly running the baseline.

A recent method having some similarity with the present work is Random Lasso [12]. Lasso is used as a baseline and run repeatedly on bootstrap samples of the data and random subsets of the features. In a second phase, Lasso is run again repeatedly but this time features are drawn randomly with probability proportional to their importance as estimated in the first phase. The final regression coefficient of a variable is the average of its obtained coefficients over this second phase. Extensive experimental results are provided in [12] but no theoretical analysis.

In the present paper, we consider subsampling rather than bootstrap for the data samples and provide a theoretical analysis of subsample size, showing that it has an important effect on variance reduction. We consider selection of variables following the original stability selection ansatz and are interested in quality of feature recovery as well as in prediction accuracy using only the effectively selected variables (while [12] use a weighted randomized ensemble method). We also present applications to methods other than Lasso. Concerning the theoretical results, we note the related reference [13] studying the effect of subsample size in the context of subagging for ensemble methods.

2   Analysis

2.1   Effect of the Subsample Size

In this section we assume only subsampling of the data, not of the features. The goal of this section is to relate the set of features selected by stability selection to a target set of features having probability of selection larger than θ for the baseline method. In this we extend the theoretical results obtained in [9] and [11] for the case $L = 2$ to the more general situation considered here.

Let S_L^{Base} denote the output of `BaselineFS` with a single random sample of size $\lfloor n/L \rfloor$, and $S_{L,\tau}^{SFS}$ the output of the stability selection algorithm with subsamples of size $\lfloor n/L \rfloor$ and selection frequency threshold τ. That is, $S_{L,\tau}^{SFS}$ is the set of features whose overall selection frequency over the data subsampling repetitions is larger than τ. Let $p_{k,L} = \mathbb{P}\left[k \in S_L^{Base}\right]$ denote the probability for feature number k to be selected by `BaselineFS` using a random data sample of size $\lfloor n/L \rfloor$. Let $\theta \in (0, 1)$ a number and $A_{\theta,L} := \{k : p_{k,L} \leq \theta\}$. The latter set will be interpreted as the set of unwanted features having low (below θ) selection probability under the baseline, and we regard each selected feature belonging to

$A_{\theta,L}$ as an "error". We follow in this the formalism proposed in [11] for the case $L = 2$.

Theorem 1. *Let τ be the selection frequency threshold used in the procedure and $\theta < \tau$ a positive number. For any integer $\ell_0 \in \{1,\ldots,L\}$ such that $\lceil L\theta \rceil \leq \ell_0 \leq \lceil L\tau \rceil$, denoting $p_0 := \frac{\ell_0}{L}$, it holds that*

$$\frac{\mathbb{E}\left[|S_{L,\tau}^{SFS} \cap A_{\theta,L}|\right]}{|A_{\theta,L}|} \leq C(p_0,\tau,L)\exp\left(-LD\left(p_0,\theta\right)\right), \qquad (1)$$

where $D(p,q) := p\log\frac{p}{q} + (1-p)\log\frac{1-p}{1-q}$ and $C(p_0,\tau,L) := \left(\frac{1-p_0+\frac{1}{L}}{\tau-p_0+\frac{1}{L}}\right)$. If we require the slightly stronger condition $\ell_0 \geq \lceil L\theta \rceil + 1$, it holds

$$\frac{\mathbb{E}\left[|S_{L,\tau}^{SFS} \cap A_{\theta,L}|\right]}{\mathbb{E}\left[|S_L^{Base} \cap A_{\theta,L}|\right]} \leq C(p_0,\tau,L)\frac{\exp\left(-LD\left(p_0,\theta\right)\right)}{\theta}. \qquad (2)$$

Similarly, if $\theta > \tau$, for any integer $\ell_0 \in \{1,\ldots,L\}$ such that $\lfloor L\tau \rfloor \leq \ell_0 \leq \lfloor L\theta \rfloor$, We have

$$\frac{\mathbb{E}\left[|(S_{L,\tau}^{SFS})^c \cap (A_{\theta,L})^c|\right]}{|(A_{\theta,L})^c|} \leq C'(p_0,\tau,L)\exp\left(-LD\left(p_0,\theta\right)\right), \qquad (3)$$

where $C'(p_0,\tau,L) := \left(\frac{1-p_0+\frac{1}{L}}{p_0-\tau+\frac{1}{L}}\right)$; and if $\ell_0 \leq \lfloor L\theta \rfloor - 1$,

$$\frac{\mathbb{E}\left[|(S_{L,\tau}^{SFS})^c \cap (A_{\theta,L})^c|\right]}{|(S_L^{Base})^c \cap (A_{\theta,L})^c|} \leq C'(p_0,\tau,\ell)\frac{\exp\left(-LD\left(p_0,\theta\right)\right)}{1 \quad \theta}. \qquad (4)$$

These inequalities give upper bounds on the averaged number of "selection errors" $|S_{L,\tau}^{SFS} \cap A_{\theta,L}|$ (features which are selected but were unwanted, because they have low average selection frequency under the baseline), reported to the total number of unwanted features (1) or to the average number of selection errors of the baseline (2). Conversely, inequalities (3)-(4) give upper bounds on the number of missed features that were considered desirable for selection.

As a corollary, we give a consequence of this general result under the assumptions considered in the original SFS work [9]. Assume that the features are divided into a set N of "noise" features and S of "signal" features, and that the goal is to recover the set S as good as possible. Furthermore, assume the following, denoted below as assumption **(A)**:

- the noise features are exchangeable, that is, the data distribution is invariant under arbitrary permutation of the set N;
- the baseline feature selection has probability better than pure random of selecting any given signal variable.

Corollary 1. *Suppose assumption* **(A)** *holds, and put $q = \mathbb{E}\left[|S_L^{Base}|\right]$. Then for any $\tau \geq q/d$:*

$$\frac{\mathbb{E}\left[|S_{L,\tau}^{SFS} \cap N|\right]}{|N|} \leq \min_{\lceil \frac{qL}{d}\rceil \leq \ell_0 \leq \lceil \tau L \rceil} \left(\frac{1-\frac{\ell_0-1}{L}}{\tau-\frac{\ell_0-1}{L}}\right)\exp\left(-LD\left(\frac{\ell_0}{L},\frac{q}{d}\right)\right). \qquad (5)$$

Inequalities (2) and (4) imply the result of [11] (Theorem 1) for the special case $L = 2$. Similarly, (5) implies the error control in the original paper [9] (Theorem 1). Namely, take $\ell_0 = L = 2$, then $\exp(-2D(1,\theta)) = \theta^2$, recovering the previous bounds in $O(q^2/d)$, as well as the constraint $\tau > \frac{1}{2}$.

Our extension illustrates some important points that were not immediately apparent from previous analyses in the case $L = 2$. First, it allows to obtain a meaningful bound for $\tau \leq \frac{1}{2}$ when $L > 2$, whereas the rather large selection threshold $\tau > \frac{1}{2}$ was assumed in previous work. Secondly, there is an exponential decay of the error as a function of the number of splits L. This implies that, as intended, the effect of subsampling is to "stabilize" selection, that is to say, reduce the variance of the set of selected features. Of course, there is a tradeoff with the fact that the theorem considers the set of unwanted features $A_{\theta,L}$ whereas we would be ideally interested in $A_{\theta,1}$. There is obviously a form of bias/variance tradeoff here: as L increases, the variance is reduced, but on the other hand we expect that the selection probabilities $p_{k,L}$ of relevant and noisy features become more similar (and thus more difficult to separate) since the subsample size is smaller. However, our analysis explains in principle why it can be of advantage to split the sample more, provided the gain in variance outbalances the loss in bias.

2.2   Feature Subsampling

Feature subsampling is delicate to analyze in all generality. A first observation is that we can consider feature subsampling as an integral part of the baseline procedure. This means that `BaselineFS` is formally replaced by `BaselineFS`$_{fsub}$, which consists in dividing the feature set in L random non-overlapping blocks and apply the baseline on these blocks, then return the set union of the features selected on each block. In this sense, feature subsampling formally results in replacing the probability of individual feature selection of the baseline $p_{k,L}$ by a modification $\widetilde{p}_{k,L}$; up to this modification, the analysis of data subsampling as presented in the previous section applies unchanged. In other words, while we demonstrated in the previous section that data subsampling tends to reduce variance, feature subsampling will have an effect on the bias of the baseline.

The difficulty of providing a fairly general analysis is two-fold: the features have in general a complex dependence structure; and the exact effect of feature subsampling depends on the baseline procedure used. We think that feature subsampling can help in particular with the problem of "mutual masking" of relevant features, a problem that occurs when relevant features are intercorrelated, and that was pointed out by some authors in a discussion [7] of the original SFS paper. In the supplementary material, we argue in this direction through a heuristic analysis on a simplified example. We note that [7] proposed the use of elastic net regularization instead of Lasso as the baseline to counteract the masking effect. Here, our aim is to suggest instead a general-purpose approach that can potentially be applied to any baseline. In particular, the masking effect is likely to occur with many other popular feature selection methods that work in a greedy-iterative fashion (such as CMIM, considered below in the experiments).

3   Experimental Results

3.1   Relevant Feature Identification

We first report experimental results on datasets with known ground truth that were used in [9]. In each case, we consider $n = 500$ i.i.d. realizations of the couple (X, Y) where the output variable Y follows a generating sparse linear model $Y = \sum_{i \in I} \beta_i X_i$, with $|I| = 20$ relevant variables out of a total of $d = 1000$ (except for data 'Vitamin', where we have 4088 variables in 115 samples from a real dataset). In this section, the goal is to identify as well as possible the set of relevant features, i.e., the set I. As in [9], the Lasso is used as the baseline selection procedure. We follow the following evaluation protocol iterated over the integer parameter N_{Base}:

- on each data (or subsampling) realization, the Lasso regularization constant is taken as the smallest one such that at most N_{Base} features are selected.
- for standalone Lasso, the scores of the features are taken to be their estimated regression coefficients $\widehat{\beta}_i$ (of which only N_{Base} are non-zero by construction).
- for stability selection methods, the score of the features are their selection frequency over the subsample repetitions.
  for each method, we consider the 20 top score features (excluding zero scores, i.e. for standalone Lasso we consider $\max(20, N_{Base})$ features) and report how many of them, on average, are indeed relevant.
- finally, we report this number of correct features for N_{Base} ranging over $\{1, \ldots, 100\}$, averaged over 50 independent realization of the data.

Dataset description. We used four artificial datasets and a real dataset which were used in the original paper [9] (except '4 Blocks' below). The design matrices of the artificial datasets are generated as follows:

- 10 Blocks: The vector of covariates follows a $\mathcal{N}_d(0, \Sigma)$ distribution, where $\Sigma_{i,j} = 0.5 * \mathbf{1}\{i = j \bmod 10\}$
- 4 Blocks: The vector of covariates follows a $\mathcal{N}_d(0, \Sigma)$ distribution, where $\Sigma_{i,j} = 0.8 * \mathbf{1}\{i = j \bmod 4\}$
- Toeplitz: The vector of covariates follows a $\mathcal{N}_d(0, \Sigma)$ distribution, where $\Sigma_{i,j} = 0.99^{|i-j|}$
- Latent Factors: each covariate X_k is generated as $X_k = \sum_{i=1}^{10} f_{k,i}\Phi_i + \nu_k \forall k = 1 \ldots d$ where the latent factors Φ_i, and noise ν_k follow a standard normal distribution. The factor loading coefficients $f_{k,i}$ are fixed for any given realization of the dataset and are drawn beforehand from a $\mathcal{N}(0, 1)$ distribution.
- 'Vitamin' data: real dataset used in [9].

In each case, the 20 relevant indices were drawn uniformly at random among the available dimensions except for the following settings:

- "Toeplitz, grouped predictors": the relevant variables were drawn in 5 groups of 4 variables each uniformly drawn in the interval $[100g-20, 100g+20]$ where g is the group number. In this sense the predictor variables exhibit a cluster structure.

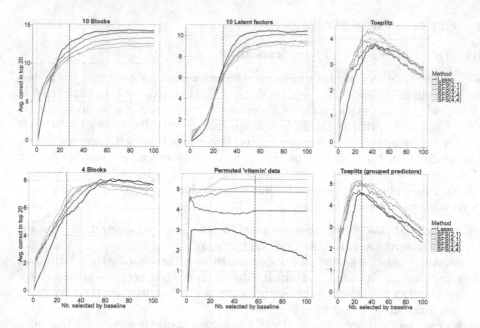

Fig. 1. Reported is the averaged (over 50 random data realizations) number of correct features (higher is better) among the top 20 ranked features for each method, as a function of the number of features selected by the Lasso baseline. "Lasso" is standalone Lasso; SFS(L,V) denotes (extended) stability selection based on L data slices and V feature slices. SFS(2,1) is the original stability selection method. The dashed line indicates the rule $k \simeq \sqrt{0.8d}$ suggested in [9].

– For the 'Vitamin' data, we did not use the linear generating model for Y stated above, but used the Y values given in the dataset. Following [9], we permuted all except six X coordinates across the samples to generate noise variables. For each sample we used the same permutation to conserve the dependencies between the noise variables. The six signal variables were choosen among the ones with high correlation with the target.

Discussion. *Stability selection vs. standalone Lasso.* One surprising outcome of our simulation results is that, although we used the same datasets and a setting very similar to [9], it turned out that the original stability selection algorithm did not always improve over standalone Lasso, although a systematic improvement was reported in [9] accross the board. To the best of our understanding, the difference in the reported results is due to the differing criteria for performance evaluation. In [9], authors reported the successful retrieval of $\lceil 0.4s \rceil$ relevant features (where $s = 20$ here is the number of informative features and $\gamma \in \{0.1; 0.4\}$). A "successful retrieval" for the SFS method meant that the top ranked $\lceil 0.4s \rceil$ are indeed relevant features. However, for standalone Lasso, the criterion for a "sucessful retrieval" used there was more stringent, namely, that at least $\lceil 0.4s \rceil$ relevant features get a nonzero coefficient $\widehat{\beta}_i$, and that *none of the* *irrelevant features get a nonzero coefficient.* We believe however that it is fairer and more intuitive to interpret the estimated Lasso coefficients as providing themselves a ranking of the selected features (this is meaningful if the features are assumed to be scaled), which is what we did here. In this sense, it is meaningful to consider the top 20 ranked features picked by one run of Lasso, even if Lasso selected a larger number of features. Also, we noticed that the probability of successfull retrieval was not a very stable measure, often lying very close to 0 or 1. For this reason we preferred the criterion used here (nb. of correct out of the top 20), which we think is meaningful in relation to practice.

Extended versus original stability selection. We come to the conclusion that our proposed extentions of stability selection are generally likely to yield an improvement over the original method *whenever the latter itself improves over standalone Lasso.* This is positive news for our proposed extensions as one can say that they tend to *enhance* the effect of the original stability selection, which was in part suggested by our theory.

Role of the number of features selected in the baseline. It appears that the number k of features selected by the baseline Lasso plays an important role in the performance of the method. A general message is that for all methods, the peak in performance is attained when the number of selected features is significantly larger than the number of relevant feautures. As a rule of thumb, we recommend that 2-3 times more features should be selected by the baseline as the final targeted number of selected features. In particular, on the examples studied we note that the rule suggested in [9] to take $k \simeq \sqrt{0.8d}$ (dashed line on Figure 1) generally seems smaller than the optimal k.

When should stability selection be used? The most delicate problem remains to determine when (extended) stability selection is to be recommended in practice, since we have observed that it is in fact detrimental in some cases studied here – including for the original stability selection, provided the comparative performance of Lasso is determined as described above. We observe that the common characteristics of the datasets where stability selection results in an improvement in the following situations:

- noise variables are possibly correlated to predictor variables, but only "localy" (see datasets Toeplitz design, and Vitamin – in the latter case noise and irrelevant variables are actually independent by construction).
- feature subsampling seems to be more effective when there is some significant dependencies between some of the relevant predictor variables (see datasets Vitamin and Toeplitz design with grouped predictors). This confirms our heuristic analysis (see Section 2.2 and the supplementary material).

In practice, since the true relevant variables are unknown, our recommendation is to use cross-validated predition error as a surrogate to determine if (extended) SFS methods improve over the Lasso. For this, on each cross-validation slice one can apply an ordinary least squares estimator using only selected features. If one sees an improvement for cross-validated prediction error, it is plausible that (extended) SFS improves over the baseline for finding the relevant features.

3.2 Classification Accuracy after Feature Selection (Filtering)

Dataset Description. We used a subset of the MNIST [8] dataset which contains grayscale images of hand-written digits (10 classes) and all images have a size of 28×28 pixels. Training and test dataset contains 6000 examples from the original MNIST dataset. We used a library of 40 different image feature extractors (developed by various contributors in the framework of the MASH project [1]), and concatenated their responses to one large feature vector of dimension 48416. There are three important aspects of this feature space. First, it is not sparse (in the sense that most features are generally nonzero). Second, the feature space is known to be redundant because many feature extractors are similar. Third, a large proportion of features contain at least some information (i.e. have significant correlation with the class label). In this situation, we are interested in variable selection not because of any assumed inherent sparsity of the underlying solution, but rather in order to reduce data complexity before applying a learning method. The application of such a method to the full dimensional data would be much more costly, both in terms of memory and computation.

Experimental Setup and Results. As the baseline feature selection method, we used Conditional Mutual Information Maximization ([6], hereafter abbreviated CMIM). In order to reduce computation load, we used early stopping by limiting the number of CMIM iterations where feature scores get updated to $k_0 \in \{10, 100\}$. After k_0 iterations, the set of selected features is given by the k_0 features selected during the iterations, together with the $(k - k_0)$ remaining features having top CMIM scores at this point, where k is the total number of features to be selected. The subscript of each method shows the value of k_0 used, e.g. SFS$_{10}$ stability selection is used based on CMIM stopped after $k_0 = 10$ iterations.

The following parameters were used. For standard stability selection SFS$(2, 1)$ we used $R_{rs} = 100$ repeated sample splits. For extended stability selection, we used SFS$(2, 10)$, i.e. we split the training examples into 2 disjoint sets ($L = 2$), and the features into 10 disjoint sets ($V = 10$). We used $R_{rs} = 10$ repeated sample splits and $R_{rf} = 10$ repeated feature splits. Since $R_{rs} \times R_{rf} = 100$, the number of calls to the baseline procedure are comparable (but the dimension of the projected data is 10 times smaller for extended stability selection). For the number of features to be finally selected before applying the learning algorithm, we considered the two different values 100 and 1000, corresponding to 0.21%, resp 2.1% of the initial number of features. After feature selection we used AdaBoost.MH [5,10] as a classifier, and varied the number of boosting iterations. Results are reported in Table 1.

Conclusions. Feature subsampling improved significantly classification performance, while data subsampling did not (see the supplementary material for additional empirical results to this regard). Both of these results are in favor of the proposed methodology, as we are able to improve performance over the baseline while simultaneously reducing significantly the size of data chunks on which the baseline FS has to be applied. In particular, splitting the data matrix into small submatrices can lead easily to parallelization.

Table 1. Adaboost.MH classification accuracies (and standard deviations), averaged over 10 train/test subsamples from the original MNIST dataset, after selecting 100, resp. 1000, features for different numbers of boosting iterations and feature selection methods. Bold results show the best result in the corresponding half-row.

# iter.	CMIM$_{10}$	SFS$_{10}$(2,1)	SFS$_{10}$(2,10)	CMIM$_{100}$	SFS$_{100}$(2,1)	SFS$_{100}$(2,10)
100 selected features						
100	7.4 (0.5)	**6.7 (0.2)**	7.7 (0.2)	7.2 (0.5)	**6.3 (0.2)**	7.5 (0.3)
400	4.5 (0.2)	4.4 (0.2)	**4.1 (0.2)**	4.1 (0.1)	4.0 (0.1)	**3.9 (0.1)**
1600	3.6 (0.1)	3.4 (0.2)	**3.1 (0.2)**	3.5 (0.1)	3.2 (0.1)	**2.9 (0.1)**
1000 selected features						
100	5.5 (0.2)	5.0 (0.2)	**4.5 (0.3)**	5.3 (0.3)	4.9 (0.2)	**3.0 (0.2)**
400	2.8 (0.2)	2.8 (0.1)	**2.4 (0.2)**	2.7 (0.2)	3.0 (0.2)	**2.2 (0.1)**
1600	2.1 (0.1)	2.0 (0.1)	**1.8 (0.1)**	2.0 (0.1)	2.1 (0.2)	**1.6 (0.1)**

Acknowledgements. This work was supported by the European Community's Seventh Framework Programme FP7 - Challenge 2 - Cognitive Systems, Inter-action, Robotics - under grant agreement No 247022 - MASH. We express our greatest gratitude to N. Meinhausen and P. Bühlmann for providing the code of their original algorithm, which was used as a basis for this work.

References

1. MASH project, http://www.mash-project.eu
2. Bi, J., Bennett, K., Embrechts, M., Breneman, C., Song, M.: Dimensionality reduction via sparse support vector machines. JMLR 3, 1229–1243 (2003)
3. Breiman, L.: Random forests. Machine Learning 45, 5–32 (2001)
4. Bühlmann, P., Yu, B.: Analyzing Bagging. The Annals of Statistics 30(4), 927–961 (2002)
5. Escudero, G., Màrquez, L., Rigau, G.: Boosting Applied to Word Sense Disambiguation. In: Lopez de Mantaras, R., Plaza, E. (eds.) ECML 2000. LNCS (LNAI), vol. 1810, pp. 129–141. Springer, Heidelberg (2000)
6. Fleuret, F.: Fast binary feature selection with conditional mutual information. JMLR 5, 1531–1555 (2004)
7. Kirk, P., Lewin, A., Stumpf, M.: Discussion of "Stability Selection" by Meinshausen and Bühlmann. J. Roy. Statist. Soc., Ser. B 72(4), 456–458 (2010)
8. LeCun, Y., Bottou, L., Bengio, Y., Haffner, P.: Gradient-based learning applied to document recognition. Proceedings of the IEEE 86(11), 2278–2324 (1998)
9. Meinshausen, N., Bühlmann, P.: Stability selection. J. Roy. Statist. Soc., Ser. B 72(4), 417–448 (2010)
10. Schapire, R., Singer, Y.: Improved boosting algorithms using confidence-rated predictions. Machine Learning 37(3), 297–336 (1999)
11. Shah, R., Samworth, R.: Variable selection with error control: Another look at stability selection. J. Roy. Statist. Soc., Ser. B (to appear, 2012)
12. Wang, S., Nan, B., Rosset, S., Zhu, J.: Random Lasso. The Annals of Applied Statistics 5(1), 468–485 (2011)
13. Zaman, F., Hirose, H.: Effect of Subsampling Rate on Subbagging and Related Ensembles of Stable Classifiers. In: Chaudhury, S., Mitra, S., Murthy, C.A., Sastry, P.S., Pal, S.K. (eds.) PReMI 2009. LNCS, vol. 5909, pp. 44–49. Springer, Heidelberg (2009)

Feature-Based Multi-video Synchronization
with Subframe Accuracy

A. Elhayek, C. Stoll, K. I. Kim, H.-P. Seidel, and C. Theobalt

MPI Informatik
{elhayek,stoll,kkim,hpseidel,theobalt}@mpi-inf.mpg.de

Abstract. We present a novel algorithm for temporally synchronizing multiple videos capturing the same dynamic scene. Our algorithm relies on general image features and it does not require explicitly tracking any specific object, making it applicable to general scenes with complex motion. This is facilitated by our new trajectory filtering and matching schemes that correctly identifies matching pairs of trajectories (inliers) from a large set of potential candidate matches, of which many are outliers. We find globally optimal synchronization parameters by using a stable RANSAC-based optimization approach. For multi-video synchronization, the algorithm identifies an informative subset of video pairs which prevents the RANSAC algorithm from being biased by outliers. Experiments on two-camera and multi-camera synchronization demonstrate the performance of our algorithm.

1 Introduction

The last ten years have observed significant advances in mobile camera technology. The widespread use of smart-phones facilitated casually capturing and sharing any scenes of interest. The abundance of these data resulted in new opportunities and challenges in computer vision and computer graphics. For instance, there are more chances than ever to capture the same scene with multiple cameras: e.g., street performance captured by several spectators. This can significantly broaden the domain of multiple-camera computer vision and graphics applications (e.g., markerless motion capture and video-based rendering [1]). However, it should be noted that these algorithms typically assume that the cameras are synchronized, i.e., the ratio between the frame rates and the relative offsets are known. In general uncontrolled settings, this may not be true: the camera hardwares maybe heterogeneous and accordingly the recorded sequences (videos) have different frame rates. Sometimes, we only have the sequences with unknown source cameras. Furthermore, it is unlikely that the recorded sequences have the same offset. Accordingly, automatic synchronization is required.

There exist several synchronization algorithms. However, these algorithms are limited to specific scenes where it is possible to track the objects of interest, or to scenes where the objects show specific motions such as ballistic motion [2], or to synchronizing two sequences only.

As a step towards the general case of uncontrolled video synchronization problem, we propose a multi-video synchronization algorithm which works for objects exhibiting any type of motion. In particular, we do not assume that the objects of interest are

A. Pinz et al. (Eds.): DAGM/OAGM 2012, LNCS 7476, pp. 266–275, 2012.
© Springer-Verlag Berlin Heidelberg 2012

explicitly tracked. This is facilitated by feature-based matching: we extract a set of features and track them in each video, which constitute a set of feature trajectories. Then, the problem of synchronization is cast into spatio-temporally matching the trajectories across different sequences. Since such general features usually exist in any video, our algorithm is applicable to general scenes with any number of objects therein. Moreover, the dynamic properties of these trajectories enable the algorithm to achieve sub-frame accuracy of the synchronization parameters.

The technical challenges lie in the fact that the tracked trajectories are in general very noisy, *e.g.*, the tracked location of detected feature points are not precisely aligned in a video and tracking could fail. Furthermore, since there can be many trajectories in a given set of videos, identifying correctly matching pairs of trajectories across different videos is challenging. One of our main contributions is a method for resolving these problems. We propose a set of criteria to filter out noisy and uninformative trajectories and pairs of trajectories (details will be discussed in Sec. 3). As a result, a set of tentative trajectory pairs are generated. Among them, the correct subset (inliers) is identified by minimizing a global energy based on RANSAC-type optimization. Since the energy is defined for any number of sequences, our algorithm can be consistently applied to the multi-video case as well as to the two-video case. However, in this case, additional robustness is achieved by identifying weakly coupled pairs of cameras and removing them from the evaluation of energy. This leads to an automatic generation of a graph representing the cameras and their connectivity. In the experiments, we demonstrate the effectiveness of our algorithm with datasets that are difficult to synchronize with the existing object tracking based synchronization techniques.

Related Work. One of the first video synchronization algorithms is described in [3] where the algorithm detects static features and tracks moving objects. Based on these detected and tracked features, it estimates the planar alignment as well as the epipolar geometry. This algorithm permits for synchronizing videos which show significantly different view points. However, its usage is limited by the fact that it requires explicitly tracking objects and is applicable only to a pair of videos. One or both of these limitations are shared by most existing algorithms. For instance, the algorithms of Dai et al.[4] and Caspi et al. [5] are designed specifically for the two-video case. On the other hand, Sinha and Pollefeys' silhouettes-based algorithm [6] and Meyer et al.'s algorithm for moving cameras [7] can synchronize multiple cameras, which are based on explicit feature tracking or on the (often violated) assumption of the existence and detection of reliable (long and clean) trajectories.

Most strongly related to the proposed algorithm is [5], where the concept of feature trajectory matching was introduced for video synchronization. Our algorithm extends this algorithm and explicitly overcomes the two main limitations of [5]: 1) our algorithm is applicable when there is arbitrary time shift and frame rate differences, 2) our algorithm enables multi-camera synchronization. Neither of this is directly feasible using Caspi et al.'s algorithm [5] since they use grid search of parameters, which is applicable when only one or few parameters need to be estimated. An alternative to video-based synchronization is to exploit additional data, e.g., audio [8] or still images obtained with controlled flashes [9].

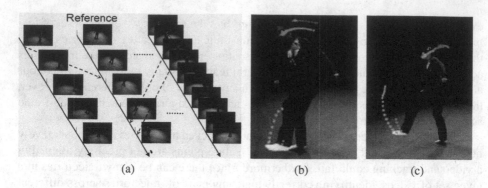

(a)   (b)   (c)

Fig. 1. (a) Schematic diagram of multi-video synchronization. Time lines of different sequences with different frame rates are mapped to non-integer points along a single reference time line, as indicated by the arrows. (b) and (c) show two temporally corresponding frames from two different video sequences with some corresponding space-time trajectories resulting from the actor's motion in the previous frames.

2 Problem Formulation

Similar to other synchronization methods [5,10], we assume that each video is recorded by a camera which has a constant frame rate. In this case, the temporal misalignment between a set of videos occurs if they have a time-shifts (offsets) between their start times, and/or when they have different frame rates (Fig. 1(a)). Accordingly, there is an affine relationship between the time lines (time coordinate values) of each pair of sequences.

For the two-video case, synchronization can be performed by firstly setting one sequence as a reference (denoted as S_r) and estimating the relative offset θ_i and the frame rate R_i of the other sequence (denoted as S_i) with respect to the reference time line t_r of S_r:

$$t_r = R_i * t_i + \theta_i, \tag{1}$$

where t_i is the time line of S_i. For general multi-video synchronization, consistent comparison of multiple sequences can be facilitated by establishing a global reference time line. While any global parametrization should work, for a given set of input unsynchronized sequences $\mathcal{S} = \{S_0, \ldots, S_N\}$, we simply set the time line of the first sequence S_0 as the reference. This sequence and the corresponding time line will henceforth be denoted as S_r and t_r, respectively. With this representation, our algorithm produces an estimate of synchronization parameters $\{\theta_i, R_i\}$ (with respect to t_r) for each sequence $S_i \in \mathcal{S} \setminus S_r$.

Since the sequences in $\mathcal{S}$ capture the same scene, there is a geometrical relationship between the appearances of the scene components in each pair of sequences: Let $\mathbf{x}_r = (x_r, y_r, t_r)$ be a space-time point in the reference sequence S_r and $\mathbf{x}_i = (x_i, y_i, t_i)$ be the corresponding points in $S_i \in \mathcal{S} \setminus S_r$ (i.e., t_r and t_i are related based on Eq. 1). Then, they should satisfy the below given fundamental geometrical relationship:

$$p_r(t_r)^\top F_i(t_i) p_i(t_i) = 0 \tag{2}$$

where, $p_r(t_r)$ is a vector consisting of the spatial coordinate values (i.e., $\{x_r, y_r, 1\}$) of $\mathbf{x}_r$ and F_i is the fundamental matrix relating the reference camera and the i-th camera.[1]

3   General Synchronization Algorithm

This section presents our synchronization algorithm. We first discuss the two-video synchronization setting and illustrate the essential idea. Then, we discuss how this framework can be applied to multi-video data sets.

3.1   Two-Video Synchronization

Our algorithm is based on matching trajectories of features appearing in a pair of videos. First, a set of features (SIFT features) are extracted from each frame of a sequence. Then, we use Best-Bin-First (BBF)-based feature matching to establish correspondences between features appearing in each pair of consecutive frames; see [11] for details. If the features corresponding to a single 3D-point are matched across more than two consecutive frames, the corresponding trajectory is constructed. Each trajectory is represented based on spatial coordinates of the corresponding feature points, each of which is assigned with the corresponding frame index. For instance, a trajectory in S_r can be represented as

$$T_r = \{p_r(t), p_r(t+1), p_r(t+2), ..., p_r(t+k)\},$$

where $k + 1$ is the length of the trajectory (i.e., tracking is successful for $k + 1$ consecutive frames).

Matching a pair of trajectories implies establishing the correspondence between two sets of points contained in the two trajectories, respectively. Precisely matching a pair of *non-trivial* trajectories (details will be discussed shortly), uniquely defines the spatial parameters (i.e. fundamental matrix; cf. Eq. 2), and since each point is assigned with the time index, the corresponding temporal parameters (offset and frame rate ratio).

In general, the construction of trajectories is noisy. For example, usually the locations of detected features do not precisely correspond to each other across the consecutive frames and the tracking can be erroneous. Accordingly, the constraint (2) might not be exactly satisfied. Alternatively, one could minimize the following residual error with respect to those parameters [5]:

$$E(F_i, \theta_i, R_i) = \sum_{t_i \in support(T_i)} d_{F_i}\left(p_r(R_i \cdot t_i + \theta_i), p_i(t_i)\right), \tag{3}$$

where $d_F(A, B)$ is the Euclidean distance between a feature A and the epipolar line corresponding to a feature B mapped based on F (see Fig. 2(c)).

The above-described strategy is applicable only when a correct pair of trajectories (each from a single sequence) is identified. In general, there are multiple trajectories

---

[1] Throughout the current paper, we assume that the cameras are static. For the general moving camera case, F has to be defined for each pair of corresponding frames as in [8].

constructed in each sequence and the correspondences between them are not known *a priori*. Suppose that m and n trajectories are constructed from S_r and S_i, respectively. Then there are $m \times n$ potential matching pairs of trajectories, only a few of which are correct. Our approach is to use RANSAC which can effectively filter out the outliers matches. However, naively feeding all potential matches into a RANSAC step does not yield a proper parameters estimate: there exist several *trivial* trajectories which geometrically match many other trajectories. Moreover, the large number of trivial trajectories decreases the computational efficiency of the method. Therefore, we introduce three trajectory filtering steps. Firstly, we remove very short trajectories which are shorter than a specific number of frames (5 frames in our experiments). The second filter removes trajectories corresponding to static feature points: a trajectory is removed if the variance of its spatial coordinate values is small (i.e. less than 15 pixels in our experiments). Finally, we remove all trajectories which may generate ambiguous matches. This happens when the tangents of trajector points are nearly parallel to the points epipolar line defined by the fundamental matrix of the camera pair. We cannot distinguish any motion along that line in the other camera. This may lead to the feature match being classified as an inlier with low energy even for wrong matches. To find these trajectories, for each point in the trajectory, we check the angles between the tangent and the epipolar line of the point in its own camera. If the sum of these angles is too small, the corresponding trajectory may erroneously match many trajectories in the other sequence. We reject a trajectory if the score $\sum_{t_i \in sup(T_i)} 1 - cos(angle)$ is less than 0.32 (see supplementary material for more details).

Even after the trajectory filtering stage, eroneous candidate trajectory pairs may remain. These may negatively influence the run-time of a RANSAC optimization, and for a prescribed finite run-time, can bias RANSAC toward a unreliable solution. It should be noted that in order for a pair of trajectories to match, they have to overlap with each other in space and in time. Checking this can quickly filter out most wrong matches: Given a candidate match, we intersect the epipolar line corresponding to each feature point in the shorter trajectory with the longer trajectory (Fig. 2(a)). Since the frame rates of corresponding source videos are fixed, the consecutive epipolar lines should intersect with the longer trajectory such that the points of intersection are roughly equally spaced.[2] To check this, we first calculate the hypothetical frame rate ratios of two videos (denoted as R_T) based on the entire interval of intersection. For instance, in Fig. 2(a), R_T is calculated by dividing the number of feature points lying between $F_i \cdot p_1$ and $F_i \cdot p_7$ on the longer trajectory with 7 which is the number of intersecting epipolar lines. In the same way, we calculate hypothetical frame rate ratios from each consecutive interval on the trajectory (e.g., $[F_i p_1, F_i p_2]$). All of these estimated frame rate ratios should agree roughly with R_T: we decide that a new hypothetical frame rate ratio R_N agrees with R_T if $|R_T - R_N| < 0.5 R_T$.

Then, the degree of overlap between two trajectories is measured based on the number of consecutive epipolar lines (P_{min}) which satisfies the above described condition. When, P_{min} is smaller than 5 (threshold found by experimental validation), the corresponding trajectory pair is rejected. It should be noted that in general, an epipolar line

---

[2] Note that in case of corresponding trajectories from identical cameras (i.e. equal frame rates) the distances between consecutive points of intersection along the time dimension must be 1.

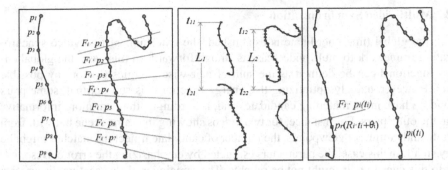

Fig. 2. (a) Left: Epipolar trajectory matching test. (b) Center: Estimation of synchronization parameters based on two distant pairs of matching trajectories. (c) Right: Trajectory point residual error measure as the distance between the point $p_r(R_i \cdot t_i + \theta_i)$ and the epipolar line $F_i \cdot p_i(t_i)$.

can intersect with a trajectory more than once (Fig. 2(a)). This case can be dealt with by retaining multiple hypothetical framerate ratios (R_T) accordingly. The result of this step is a table of tentative matching trajectories.

The extension of the energy functional (3) for multiple trajectory case, given a precomputed fundamental matrix F_i for static cameras, is as folows:

$$E(\theta_i, R_i) = \sum_{T_i \in \Gamma_i} \sum_{t_i \in support(T_i)} d_{F_i}(p_r(R_i \cdot t_i + \theta_i), p_i(t_i)), \qquad (4)$$

where Γ_i is the set of trajectories for the i-th video, minimizing it with the tentative matches does not correctly estimate the synchronization parameters since the tentative matches still contain a lot of outliers. Accordingly, we apply the RANSAC algorithm instead. It should be noted that each iteration of RANSAC requires generating hypothetical synchronization parameters. This can be determined from two pairs of corresponding feature points. These can be sampled from a single pair of matching trajectories, but we select them from two distinct candidate matches. This turned out to be more robust; see Fig. 2(b). Then, the hypothetical parameters are computed by solving the following equations for the two unknowns:

$$t_{11} = R_i * t_{12} + \theta_i,$$
$$t_{21} = R_i * t_{22} + \theta_i$$

and the corresponding residual error is used to classify the tentative matches into inliers and outliers; see Fig. 2(c). The number of iterations of RANSAC adaptively changes based on the number of inliers [12]. At the end of the RANSAC loop, the parameters with the highest number of inliers are selected. The estimated parameters are further refined by continuously optimizing (4) with only inliers: We first render the problem into continuous optimization by interpolating each trajectory with cubic-splines. Then a standard gradient descent is performed. However, our preliminary experiments revealed that the continuous optimization step does not significantly improve the result over the initial RANSAC estimate. Further detail of the algorithm can be found in the supplementary material.

3.2   Multi-video Synchronization

Once the global time coordinate is established, the extension of two-video synchronization framework to multi-video case is straightforward. In this case, the global energy functional can be defined as the sum of pair-wise energies (4) for any possible pairs. However, naively optimizing this energy functional is sub-optimal: some pairs of videos have more matching candidates and, accordingly, they are more informative than the other pairs. For instance, for two videos showing the same scene but with from significantly different viewpoints, the number of candidate trajectory matches might be very small. In this case, the parameters estimated by emphasizing the error corresponding to this camera pair might not be reliable. The remainder of this section discusses a strategy for solving this problem.

The relationships between a set of videos (or cameras) can be represented as a graph (see Fig. 3) in which a node corresponds to a sequence and an edge represents a set of tentative matching pairs of trajectories plus the corresponding synchronization parameters (of one node, with the other node treated as a reference). In this case, there are as many sets of parameters as the number of edges (i.e. local edge parameters), while the actual number of sets of parameters should correspond to the number of nodes (i.e. global parameters related to reference time line).

To ensure that a consistent global parametrization can be recovered from a set of local edge parameterizations, in each RANSAC step, we remove any cycle in the graph. This can be done, in principle, by randomly building a spanning tree. However, we have empirically observed that the accuracy of the estimated synchronization parameters between a pair of videos decreases with increasing distance between the cameras. Specifically, the lower the number of tentative matches between a pair of sequences, the less accurate the resulting estimation of synchronization parameters becomes. We exploit this observation by pre-filtering edges between distant pairs of cameras based on the number of tentative matches (35 in our experiments). An example of the resulting *connectivity graph* is shown in Fig. 3.

Figure 3 exemplifies a single step of RANSAC iteration. The global parameters R_2 and θ_2 (with respect to the reference sequence S_0) can be estimated based on the edges e_{21}, e_{10} and e_{20}. In general, the pairwise estimates of local parameters for each of these edges conflict with each other. To rule this out, in the RANSAC step, we construct a random spanning-tree, e.g., by removing edges E_{20} and E_{10}.

The estimated local edge parameters are converted to the global parameters using the relations

$$R_{xy} = \frac{R_x}{R_y}, \quad and \quad \theta_{xy} = \frac{\theta_x - \theta_y}{R_y}, \tag{5}$$

where R_{xy} and θ_{xy} are the parameters of the edge between any two nodes x and y. Once the global synchronization parameters are constructed, they are evaluated based on the number of inliers using every edge in the graph, i.e, the trajectory pairs which are not contained in the spanning tree are used as well. After the RANSAC iteration, the set of global parameters corresponding to the highest number of inliers is selected.

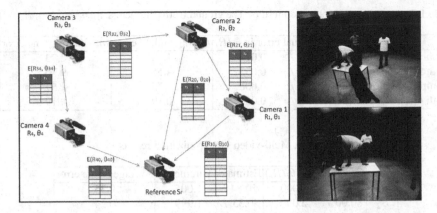

Fig. 3. (a) Left: An example of multi-video connectivity graph constructed by our algorithm. **(b) Right:** An example frames (1296 x 968) from the videos S_r^2 and S_1^2 (250 and 300 frames respectively).

4   Experimental Evaluation

In this section, we evaluate our algorithm based on two sets of unsynchronized videos capturing different scenes with different number of moving persons. To facilitate quantitative evaluation, we set the cameras up such that accurate timestamps for each frame can be obtained, which provide the corresponding ground-truth synchronization parameters for each set of videos. Once features are extracted, our algorithm took on average 20 seconds and 3.5 minutes for two-video and four-video synchronization, respectively.

In our evaluation, we show the *residual error* of the parameters as well as the average and maximum *frame errors*, that are computed by aligning each frame of the synchronized video to the reference time line and by computing the deviations of the corresponding frame numbers from the ground-truth.

In the first set of experiments, we evaluated the performance of our algorithm for the two-video case. To gain an insight into the role of individual filtering steps (Sec. 3.1), we constructed two different versions of our algorithm - one of them is constructed by removing the static filtering, the other one by removing the epipolar filtering stage from the original algorithm. We have also performed experiments with known framerates, which are assumed to be known for most existing synchronization algorithms. Table 1 shows the results for a dataset consisting of two videos.[3] Additional results (with another set of videos) are provided in the accompanying supplementary material. The results suggest that both filtering stages, most notably the epipolar filtering, are critical to the performance of our algorithm; and that if once the frame rates are known, significant improvement can be gained.

Table 2 summarizes the result of multi-video synchronization experiments for two sets of videos, which show two different scenes containing four ($\mathcal{S}^1 = \{S_r^1, S_1^1, S_2^1, S_3^1\}$)

---

[3] The continuous optimization step improved the average error by only 0.01 from the RANSAC results with significant additional computation. Accordingly, for the rest of the experiments, we do not adopt this stage.

Table 1. Two-video synchronization results. The ground truth parameters are $\theta_i = -50, R_i = 1$.

	Residual error in θ_i/R_i		Average frame error	Maximum frame error
Without static filtering	2.74 /	0.014	1.32	2.73
Without epipolar filtering	9.70 /	0.052	4.55	9.70
Complete algorithm	1.57 /	0.008	0.75	1.57
With given R_i	0.19 /	0.000	0.19	0.19

Table 2. Multi-video synchronization results

Video	Ground truth (θ_i/R_i)		Estimated parameters		Average frame error
S_1^1	-50.00 /	1.000	-50.84 /	1.005	0.35
S_2^1	80.00 /	2.000	80.35 /	1.999	0.24
S_3^1	-30.00 /	1.000	-23.85 /	0.969	2.61
S_1^2	79.20 /	1.000	78.41 /	1.027	1.67
S_2^2	50.12 /	1.000	51.06 /	1.001	1.01

and three ($S^2 = \{S_r^2, S_1^2, S_2^2\}$) video-sequences, respectively. This result demonstrates the effectiveness of our multi-video synchronization algorithm. The average frame error is less that two frames except for one pair of cameras: the average error for the sequence S_3^1 is rather high, which is most likely caused by the significantly different viewpoint from the rest of the videos in S^1.

Our algorithm is capable of exploiting relationship among more than two video streams, and accordingly, it is naturally suited for multi-video applications. However, it should be noted that it is always possible to decompose a given multi-video synchronization problem into a set of two-video problems: one could first build a spanning tree and estimate the local pairwise synchronization parameters for each edge. Then, a globally consistent set of synchronization parameters can be estimated based on Eq. (5).[4] In general, the performance of multi-video synchronization should be better than this two-video synchronization-based approach, since the former can exploit all the available pairwise relationships, most of which are discarded when building a spanning tree. To exemplify this, we have selected three pairs of videos (namely $\{S_r^1, S_1^1\}$, $\{S_r^1, S_2^1\}$ and $\{S_r^1, S_3^1\}$), estimated pair-wise synchronization parameters, and obtained the global synchronization parameters based on (5). The performance of this algorithm is significantly worse than of our original multi-video synchronization algorithm: the average frame errors for S_1^1, S_2^1 and S_3^1 were $0.753, 0.298$ and 37.5, respectively. Especially, the two-video algorithm completely failed for S_3^1 since, as mentioned above, the camera's viewpoint is very different from the rest of the cameras; only one edge in the graph is not sufficient to compute reasonable estimate of the parameters.

In a final experiment, we evaluated the performance of a variant of our algorithm which determines the parameters based on grid search: each parameter is sampled at regular grid and the parameter set corresponding to the largest number of inlier is selected for multi-video synchronization. This can be regarded as an instantiation of Caspi el al.'s algorithm [5] in our feature-based setting. We found out that the grid

---

[4] This corresponds to a single step of our multi-video RANSAC iteration.

search algorithm needs much longer computation times to yield results of comparable accuracy than our method because of the high dimensionality of the parameter space. For instance, for four videos in $\mathcal{S}^1$, to achieve a comparable runtime efficiency to our original algorithm, we had to choose very coarse grid spacings of more than 50 and 0.5 for θ_i and R_i, respectively (with reasonable search ranges of parameters $[-150, 150]$ and $[0.1, 2]$ for θ_i and R_i, respectively). The parameters S_1^1, S_2^1 and S_3^1 optimized in this way are $-150/1.6$, $-150/0.1$ and $-50/1.1$, respectively, which are considerably worse than the results of our original algorithm.

5 Conclusion and Future Work

We have presented a multi-video synchronization algorithm that succeeds on multi-video sets comprising two or more views of general scenes. It does not require tracking of a specific object but utilizes feature trajectories tracked in individual cameras that are matched across views. To enable this, we contributed a robust trajectory filtering and energy minimization framework based on RANSAC for the multi-camera case. In the future, we plan to extend our approach to moving cameras, in order to pave the way for handling general outdoor videos.

References

1. Ballan, L., Brostow, G.J., Puwein, J., Pollefeys, M.: Unstructured video-based rendering: interactive exploration of casually captured videos. In: ACM SIGGRAPH (2010)
2. Wedge, D., Huynh, D.Q., Kovesi, P.: Motion Guided Video Sequence Synchronization. In: Narayanan, P.J., Nayar, S.K., Shum, H.-Y. (eds.) ACCV 2006, Part II. LNCS, vol. 3852, pp. 832–841. Springer, Heidelberg (2006)
3. Stein, G.P.: Tracking from multiple view points: Self-calibration of space and time. In: DARPA IU Workshop, pp. 521–527 (1998)
4. Dai, C., Zheng, Y., Li, X.: Subframe video synchronization via 3d phase correlation. In: IEEE International Conference on Image Processing (2006)
5. Caspi, Y., Simakov, D., Irani, M.: Feature-based sequence-to-sequence matching. Int. J. Comput. Vision 68, 53–64 (2006)
6. Sinha, S.N., Pollefeys, M.: Synchronization and calibration of camera networks from silhouettes. In: ICPR (2004)
7. Meyer, B., Stich, T., Pollefeys, M.: Subframe temporal alignment of non-stationary cameras. In: BMVC (2008)
8. Hasler, N., Rosenhahn, B., Thormählen, T., Wand, M., Gall, J., Seidel, H.P.: Markerless motion capture with unsynchronized moving cameras. In: CVPR (2009)
9. Shrestha, P., Weda, H., Barbieri, M., Sekulovski, D.: Synchronization of multiple video recordings based on still camera flashes. ACM Multimedia (2006)
10. Pádua, F.L.C., Carceroni, R.L., Santos, G.A.M.R., Kutulakos, K.N.: Linear sequence-to-sequence alignment. IEEE Trans. Pattern Anal. Mach. Intell. 32, 304–320 (2010)
11. Lowe, D.G.: Distinctive image features from scale-invariant keypoints. Int. J. Comput. Vision 60, 91–110 (2004)
12. Hartley, R., Zisserman, A.: Multiple View Geometry in Computer Vision, 2nd edn. Cambridge University Press (2004)

Combination of Sinusoidal and Single Binary Pattern Projection for Fast 3D Surface Reconstruction

Christian Bräuer-Burchardt, Peter Kühmstedt, and Gunther Notni

Fraunhofer IOF Jena, Albert-Einstein-Str. 7, D-07745 Jena, Germany
{christian.braeuer-burchardt,peter.kuehmstedt,
gunther.notni}@iof.fraunhofer.de

Abstract. A new method for 3D surface reconstruction is introduced combining classical fringe projection technique and binary single pattern projection. The new technique allows keeping the high accuracy obtained by phase shifting but solves the additional necessary period identification by replacing the extensive Gray-code sequence by a single image of a certain binary pattern. The core of the new method is an algorithm which realizes the assignment of corresponding image regions using epipolar constraint and image correlation. An algorithm is introduced generating a single binary pattern which is optimized concerning image correlation. The results of first measurements show the high robustness of the new method and advantages of the optimized patterns compared to the use of conventional random patterns.

1 Introduction

High precision measurement systems based on active light projection are increasingly used in the industrial quality management, scientific research, medicine, architecture, archaeology, and cultural heritage preservation. Whereas the demands concerning accuracy and robustness constantly increase, the measurements should always become faster and more data should be produced and processed. These requirements lead to a revision of the classical active light projection techniques.

Many applications require faster but constantly accurate and robust measurements. In industry, the quality control should usually be integrated into the production process in order to spend no additional time on the quality control. Moreover, often moving objects are observed. That means the optical sensors for 3D reconstruction either have to be used in the moving state or have to realize ultra-fast measurement cycles. Nevertheless, in both cases they should operate vibration-free.

The fringe projection technique is an established method for contactless 3D surface reconstruction with a high accuracy and robustness. The basic principles are described e.g. by Chen and Brown [1] or Schreiber and Notni [2]. Recently some work has been published on 3D measurements using fringe projection, e.g. by Kühmstedt et al. [3] or Wang et al. [4]. Zhang [5] gives an overview of fringe projection techniques for 3D surface measurement.

Optical 3D sensors based on classical fringe projection technique may be very accurate. The main disadvantage is the relatively long image recording and

A. Pinz et al. (Eds.): DAGM/OAGM 2012, LNCS 7476, pp. 276–286, 2012.
© Springer-Verlag Berlin Heidelberg 2012

subsequently measurement time. Recently some work on ultra-fast solutions using a reduced number of fringe images has been pblished. Another possibility to improve the speed is to use fast projection and image recording. This, however, requires short exposure times and does not reduce the calculation effort. Zhang [6] suggests a technique with ultrafast projection (1000 Hz) of a one bit fringe pattern which becomes sinusoidal by defocusing.

Speed profit can be obtained typically by the reduction of the number of projected patterns. For example, by using only three sinusoidal fringe patterns, phase images can be computed (see e.g. [7] for description of phase measurement techniques). However, code reduction often leads to a loss of precision or robustness. An interesting alternative to the fringe projection technique provides the use of stochastic patterns for point correspondence finding and 3D reconstruction algorithms (see e.g. D'Apuzzo [8] and Shi and Zhang [9]). These patterns may be conventionally produced by a digital projector or by laser speckle technique as used by Dekiff et al. [10], which usually allows a faster projection rate. A more deterministic structure have the so called random band-limited patterns as e.g. used by Wiegmann et al. [11].

Additionally, some other projected patterns have been proposed for 3D surface measurement techniques, e.g. by Zhou and Fraser [12]. An overview of existing methods is given by Salvi et al. [13, 14]. There are also techniques using color images for pseudo-random pattern coding as proposed by Dejardins and Payeur [15].

Recently, Xu et al. [16] presented a smart approach for fast surface measurement using two-level fringe patterns. Pribanic et al. [17] suggest an interesting method combining passive stereo matching and structured illumination using fringe projection.

The objective of this work was to develop a robust method for code reduction of the classical fringe sequence in order to achieve shorter image recording time and subsequently to obtain the 3D measurement result faster. This code reduction will be obtained by replacement of the classical Gray-code by a special binary pattern which can be realized as stochastic pattern or barcode-pattern or optimized binary pattern.

2   Fringe Projection and Random Pattern Projection

The principle of fringe projection technique is explained in the following. The measurement object is illuminated using a fringe projection unit and observed with one or more cameras. Corresponding points have to be identified either between two camera images (stereo pair), between one camera and the projector (origin of the ray of the object point), or multiple projector or camera images. The reconstruction of the observed points will be obtained by triangulation between two or bundle adjustment of multiple rays from the image points through the optical centers of the cameras or projectors, respectively. For a more detailed description see e.g. [1, 2, 18].

The technique to obtain 3D measurement points by fringe projection is denoted by phasogrammetry representing the mathematical combination of fringe projection and photogrammetry [2, 3]. The projection unit produces sequences of phase shifted sinusoidal patterns which are observed by the cameras. Every image point (pixel) gets a so called raw (or wrapped) phase value obtained by phase shifting algorithms (see [7]). This technique makes the position unique within one fringe period. The global uniqueness will be obtained by additional projected and observed patterns, usually a Gray-code sequence. One or two sequences are usually projected. If two sequences are projected the second sequence of fringes is directed perpendicular to the first one [2]. If only one direction is used, epipolar geometry [18] of the system should be used. Figure 1 shows a Gray-code sequence and a sequence of sinusoidal patterns.

The main advantage of the fringe projection technique is the high accuracy which can be obtained. Usually, every phase value can be localized with a precision of about 0.02 to 0.03 pixels, which can be obtained using simply one intensity image only in the case of sharp edges (as done by photogrammetry). This accuracy allows high-precision measurements which are necessary e.g. in the industrial quality control. However, the price for the high accuracy is the large number of fringe images per sequence which leads to long measurement times.

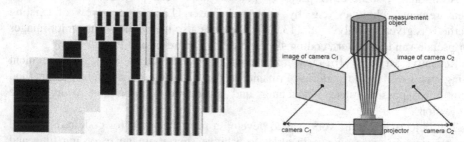

Fig. 1. Gray-code sequence (five images) and four image sinusoidal fringe sequence (left) and typical arrangement of projector and two cameras (right)

Another approach to obtain corresponding points for triangulation is to use stochastic or pseudo-stochastic patterns as e.g. speckle patterns or band-limited patterns (BLP). This technique is denoted in the following by random pattern projection (RPP). Sequences of these patterns are used for both global and local point correspondence finding. The advantage is that point correspondences can be obtained from about six images (see [19]). Both robustness and accuracy strongly depend on the number of images per sequence. However, the actual number of patterns per sequence is arbitrary, which makes RPP quite flexible. For example, the accuracy can be adaptively controlled by the number of random patterns. Additionally, RPP can be done without using a special display, e.g. by using speckle technique ([see [19]) which allows a much faster projection frequency (up to 1000 Hz, see [10]) compared to fringe projection.

Contrary, in fringe projection the precision depends on the number of sinusoidal patterns and the period length, whereas robustness depends on the additional pattern, e.g. the Gray-code sequence.

3   Approach of the New Method

As mentioned before both fringe projection and random pattern technique have their advantages and limitations. However, a combination may ensure the advantages of both techniques: high precision and short sequences as described in the following.

Our approach pursues the idea to replace the Gray-code sequence which is typically used by fringe projection technique by a single pattern. This single image may contain a stochastic pattern as used by RPP or, as we will see later, a special binary or bar-code pattern. As the information about the order of the fringe period is coded in every pixel of the period by using Gray-code, we will use this overdeterminacy in order to reduce the number of necessary images.

Briefly, the idea of the new method can be outlined as follows. Details of this method will be described in the following section. See Fig.1 for illustration.

- Perform calibration of the stereo system consisting of cameras C_1 and C_2
- Project a sequence of sinusoidal fringe patterns and one additional binary pattern and record with C_1 and C_2
- Determine raw phase values at every image point of C_1 and C_2
- Select bundles of pairs of corresponding epipolar lines (ELs) covering the image areas of interest, apply distortion correction, select points
- Divide ELs into segments according to the projected fringe periods (FPs)
- Assign corresponding segments (by special new algorithms)
- Assign corresponding image points
- Perform triangulation and obtain resulting 3D points

3.1   The New Method in Detail

Let us assume without loss of generality the following situation. Let a 3D scanner consisting of a stereo camera pair and a projection unit producing arbitrary monochrome digital patterns be given. Let the intrinsic and extrinsic parameters (only relative orientation between the two cameras is necessary) of the two cameras be given obtained by a camera calibration procedure including distortion determination. In order to obtain 3D point coordinates we have to perform triangulation (see [18]) between corresponding image points (CPs). Hence, the search of the corresponding image points is the tasks to be solved here.

In order to restrict the area of potential CPs we use epipolar geometry (see [18]). We define a bundle of corresponding epipolar lines by use of every central point of each pixel line in the image of camera C_1. This may be done because every point p in the image I_1 of camera C_1 defines a corresponding straight line h_2 (epipolar line) in the image I_2 of the second camera C_2. Additionally, every point q on h_2 defines a straight line h_1 (epipolar line) in the image I_1 of the first camera C_1. Epipolar lines h_1 and h_2 are called corresponding epipolar lines (see Fig. 2).

Now, we select points p_i and q_i on the straight lines h_1 and h_2, respectively, e.g. by choosing all points with integer x-coordinates. The raw phase values of these points are determined by analysis of the sequences of sinusoidal fringe images for both cameras. See Fig. 2 for illustration. There are shown two corresponding ELs and the raw phase values of the selected points p_i and q_i. The phase shifts define the borders of the periods. Note, that the points p_i and q_i are transformed yet to p'_i and q'_i in order to compensate distortion effects. The distortion correction operators DC_1 and DC_2 are obtained within the process of camera calibration. Actually, DC_1 and DC_2 transform the epipolar lines h_1 and h_2 into epipolar curves h'_1 and h'_2, respectively. However, we will nevertheless identify h'_1 by h_1 and h'_2 by h_2 and use the denotation epipolar line (EL) instead of epipolar curve.

In result of this procedure we obtain an ordered sequence of points on every EL. Each point is assigned to a relative indenture number describing the order of periods along the epipolar line. Let φ_i be the observed raw phase value at point p_i. Let there be m periods on h_1, k periods on h_2, and n the number of projected periods. It does not necessarily hold $n = m = k$ because there may be different fields of observation, occlusions, shadowing, and image disturbances leading to missing periods, or double numbering of shortened periods.

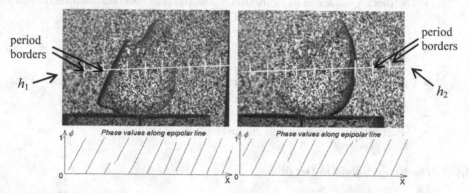

Fig. 2. Corresponding epipolar lines with period borders (above) and phase profiles (below)

Corresponding fringe periods (i.e. sections on the ELs h_1 and h_2) have to be identified. Let two sequences of determined periods on two corresponding ELs be denoted by $S^1=(FP^1_1, FP^1_2,..., FP^1_m)$ and $S^2=(FP^2_1, FP^2_2,..., FP^2_k)$. Let $FP^1_i \sim FP^2_j$ indicate that FP^1_i corresponds with FP^2_j. Note that the relation $FP^1_i \sim FP^2_j$ is not necessarily bijective. The task is to find a certain assignment A which realizes an unambiguous assignment between S^1 and S^2.

3.2   Period Assignment Procedure

In the following we describe the procedure of period assignment between the sections of two corresponding ELs. The correlation is determined for all pairs of potentially corresponding image sections. The end points of these sections are defined by the phase period borders (see Fig. 2).

Let λ be the number of pixels of one projected fringe period on the projector chip. Usually λ equals a power of 2. Let $p_0=(x_0,y_0)$ and $p_\lambda=(x_\lambda,y_\lambda)$ be the point coordinates of the end points of the considered segment seg with sub-pixel accuracy and let

$p_k=(x_k,y_k)$ be the selected points on this segment with normalized raw phase values φ_k in the interval [0 ... 1].

Let $p_i = (x_i,y_i)$ with $i=0,...,\lambda$ be the points on *seg* where it holds $\varphi_i =\varphi(x_i, y_i)=i/\lambda$. We define the period representation matrix M by a $\lambda \times l$ matrix with odd l and elements m_{ij} representing the image content of $\lambda \times l$ projected pixels observed by the cameras (see Fig. 3). Along the ELs the elements m_{ic} of the central row of M are calculated by:

$$m_{ic} = \frac{1}{\displaystyle\sum_{k=1}^{z} w_k}\sum_{k=1}^{n} w_k g(x_k,y_k); \quad w_k = \begin{cases} 1; & x_{i-1} \le x_k \le x_i \\ 0; & else \end{cases}; \quad i=1,..,\lambda \tag{1}$$

where $g(x_k,y_k)$ are the grey values at positions $p_k=(x_k,y_k)$ and z the number of selected points on the segment. For the rows of M not being central the calculation of the m_{ij} are performed analogously considering selected neighboring ELs.

Correlation will always be determined between two matrices M_1 and M_2 representing potential corresponding periods in the two camera images. If the periods do coincide, corresponding elements m_{ij} of M_1 and M_2 represent regions in the images which are illuminated by the same projector chip element.

See the example of an 8 x 3 matrix in Fig. 3. The image sections (synthetically produced) show a strongly curved surface (e.g. a sphere or cylinder with small radius). Note that although the corresponding camera images are different, the matrices M_1 and M_2 strongly correlate, and, if they are binarized, are even identical.

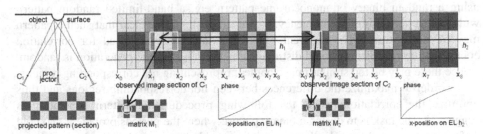

Fig. 3. Sketch of recording situation of a strongly curved object – view from above with rays (left), assignment of pixels along corresponding ELs for image region correlation ($\lambda = 8, l = 3$) of cameras C_1 (middle) and C_2 (right) with raw phase behavior and binarized matrices M_1 and M_2. The arrows refer to corresponding regions (white rectangles), i.e. identic projection pixels.

In case of the ELs intersecting the centers of the projected pixels, the m_{ij} would represent exactly the pixels of the projected image. However, pixel border localization is achieved only in the direction of the ELs using the raw phase information. In the perpendicular direction, the projected pixels are usually observed as interpolation of two projected pixels. However, this typically occurs similarly in M_1 and M_2.

After having determined the matrices M_1 and M_2 representing certain image regions the correlation $corr(M_1, M_2)$ between M_1 and M_2 can be commonly defined, e.g. as proposed by Schaffer [19]. Alternatively, other parameters to evaluate similarity may be chosen. The correlation values $corr_{ij}(FP^1_i, FP^2_j)$ for all pairs (i,j), $i=1,\ldots,m$; $j=1,\ldots,k$ of periods from sequences S^1 and S^2 are determined and stored producing a matrix $CORR$ of correlation values $corr_{ij}$.

After initial correspondence finding, which is obtained by selection of the maximal correlation values, a resolution of ambiguities is achieved by enforced monotony and closure of gaps until the final correspondence finding is achieved.

3.3   The Complete Correspondence Finding Algorithm and 3D Reconstruction

The complete algorithm regarding one pair of corresponding ELs may be outlined as:

- Construct normalized image section representation matrices using ELs h_1 and h_2 and raw phase values for every considered period segment on h_1 and h_2
- Perform correlation between all pairs (FP^1_i, FP^2_j) and store correlation values
- Construct initial period correspondence as described
- Resolve ambiguities until a complete period correspondence is achieved

3D reconstruction will be obtained by triangulation between the corresponding points obtained by raw phase comparison in the corresponding periods for all selected corresponding ELs including distortion correction by DC_1 and DC_2.

4   Pattern Optimization

In the following we describe which pattern should be applied. We initially suggest using a random binary or monochrome pattern e.g. a band-limited random pattern with a meaningful limiting frequency. However, it should be clear that such a pattern may be not optimal. The different image regions which are used for correlation coefficient determination should distinguish maximally, but the generation is random. Hence there may be too similar image content representing not corresponding regions.

In order to maximize the differences between not corresponding regions and thus optimize the correlation results the following procedure of pattern generation is suggested. The task is to design a binary pattern where the periods provide a maximal difference compared to each other, especially neighboring periods. In order to prevent unfavorable grey value interpolation perpendicular to the ELs we suggest varying the projected pattern only in the direction mainly corresponding to the direction of the ELs. This leads to a bar-code pattern and means that all lines of the projected pattern are equal. Each column has the same (binary) value.

Let our projected fringe period be of the length λ. Then we may produce 2^λ different binary basic patterns B_i of the length λ. Note that the binary pattern should be well resolved in the camera image. Usually at least two to three pixels should map the same projected binary pixel. This may motivate the fixing of the length len of the binary basic pattern to $len = \lambda$, $len = \lambda/2$ or $len = \lambda/4$, respectively.

For projection we have $z = dx/len$ periods of sinusoidal fringe patterns where dx is the number of pixels of the projected pattern in X-direction. Hence we want to produce an image which consists of a sequence S of z periods of λ binary elements.

Let i be the indenture number in S ($i=1,\ldots, z$). The optimization criterion should be the following. The closer two periods in the sequence are, the larger the difference of the binary basic patterns B_i should be. Let the difference $diff(i,j)$ be defined as

$$diff(i, j) = \frac{1}{\lambda}\sum_{k=1}^{len}\left|b_k^i - b_k^j\right| \qquad (2)$$

where b_k is the kth bit of the pattern B. Then we formulate a distinguishing function $dis(S)$ for the whole sequence S by weighting the distances of two patterns B in S by

$$dis(S) = \sum_{i=1}^{dstmx} w_i \cdot \sum_{k=1}^{z-i} diff(k, k+i) \rightarrow max \qquad (3)$$

for given weights w_i which should be maximized. It should hold $w_i > w_j$ for $i < j$. The number $dstmx$ gives the maximum distance of the influence of the difference between the basic patterns.

Let us consider the following example. Assume a projector image size of 1024 x 768 pixels and a camera image size of 2452 x 2054 pixels. We generate 128 fringes with the length $\lambda=8$. Hence our binary pattern has a length of $len=8$. We obtain $2^8=256$ different binary basic patterns B_i and a sequence S consisting of 128 of the B_i.

We choose $dstmx = 4$ and $w_1=0.4$, $w_2=0.3$, $w_3=0.2$, and $w_4=0.1$. Now we can produce all possible sequences S and choose one with maximum value of $dis(S)$. Alternatively, we randomly produce a number of sequences and save the sequence S with the maximum value of $dis(S)$ over a given threshold. The selected pattern is extended to a whole bar-code image (see Fig. 4).

The use of this pattern allows the determination of the indenture number directly from the elements m_{ij} of the matrices M according to equation (1) by binarization and comparison with the projected pattern. Together with the exploitation of additional features like monotony the robustness of the identification is improved.

Fig. 4. Section of an optimized bar-code pattern for projection consisting of 32 consecutive basic binary patterns with period enumeration

5   Experiments and Results

In order to evaluate the new method we performed the following experiments. Some measurement objects (plane, sphere, machine tool – see Fig. 5) were selected. We used a 3D stereo sensor developed at our institute with the properties:

- Camera resolution 2452 x 2054, projector resolution 1024 x 768 pixels,
- Camera pixel size: 3.45 µm,
- Measurement volume: 80 mm diameter x 25 mm height.

Four different additional patterns were used for measurement defining the modes m1 to m4, but all use sinusoidal fringe sequence for the raw phase calculation. For phase unwrapping we used a Gray-code sequence (m1), one random BLP (m2), one binary pattern (m3), and one optimized bar-code pattern (m4). The characteristic quantities for the evaluation of the new method are measurement accuracy and robustness. Measurement accuracy is represented by the standard deviation σ of the 3D points concerning fitted planes or spheres, respectively. Completeness is represented by the percentage of true point assignments concerning the reference measurement m1. We used an eight-phase algorithm (see [7]) for phase calculation and a period length of $\lambda = 8$.

Table 1 shows the first results. It should be noticed that the accuracy is equal in all modes (m1 to m4). Best completeness is achieved using optimized the bar-code pattern. Table 2 shows the reduction of the data recording time concerning to the reference method assuming different typical numbers of fringe images (between four and sixteen). It can be seen that a recording time reduction by up to 58% without loss of measurement accuracy and robustness can be achieved.

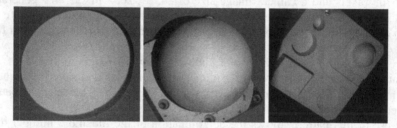

Fig. 5. Different measurement objects: plane disc, sphere, machine tool

Table 1. Accuracy and completeness of various methods using different measurement objects

quantity	object mode	disc	sphere	tool
accuracy	m1	16.7	13.1	17.1
(standard deviation fit in μm)	m2	16.8	13.2	17.0
	m3	16.8	13.1	17.2
	m4	16.7	13.1	17.1
completeness	m1	100	100	100
(% correct correspondences)	m2	99.5	97.5	95.0
	m3	99.0	98.0	94.2
	m4	100	99.9	98.6

Table 2. Number of patterns and reduction for single pattern against Gray-code use (8 images)

algorithm (see [7])	mode m1	m2 / m3/ m4	reduction [%]
4-phase	12	5	58
6-phase	14	7	50
8-phase	16	9	44
16-phase	24	17	29

6   Summary, Discussion, and Outlook

We presented a new method for 3D surface reconstruction combining classical fringe projection technique with optimized binary single pattern projection. The optimized pattern replaces the Gray-code sequence and thus leads to code reduction. Hence recording time reduction by up to 58% can be achieved.

The longer the fringe periods are (and therefore less periods are present) the better is the correlation and the more robust is the use of only one additional pattern. This should be also confirmed by further experiments. However, if the fringe period is short (e.g. eight projected pixels) random patterns (m2 and m3) are no more sufficient to obtain the same completeness as when using the optimized pattern (m4) which has advantages compared to conventional stochastic patterns.

It is assumed by the authors that pattern optimization can still be improved. Depending on the observed object and the measurement conditions further additional information, e.g. according to the maximum possible period shift in the valid measurement volume should be used in order to improve the optimization procedure. This will be one of the next future tasks. Future work should also include more sophisticated measurement objects with more occluded image parts and shadows.

References

1. Chen, F., Brown, G.M.: Overview of three-dimensional shape measurement using optical methods. Opt. Eng. 39, 10–22 (2000)
2. Schreiber, W., Notni, G.: Theory and arrangements of self-calibrating whole-body three-dimensional measurement systems using fringe projection techniques. Opt. Eng. 39, 159–169 (2000)
3. Kühmstedt, P., Munkelt, C., Heinze, M., Himmelreich, M., Bräuer-Burchardt, C., Notni, G.: 3D shape measurement with phase correlation based fringe projection. In: Proc. SPIE, vol. 6616, 66160B-1–66160B-9 (2007)
4. Wang, Z., Nguyen, D.A., Barnes, J.C.: Some practical considerations in fringe projection profilometry. Optics and Lasers in Engineering 48, 218–225 (2010)
5. Zhang, S.: Recent progresses on real-time 3D shape measurement using digital fringe projection techniques. Optics and Lasers in Engineering 48, 149–158 (2010)
6. Zhang, S., Van Der Weide, D., Oliver, J.: Superfast phase-shifting method for 3-D shape measurement. Optics Express 18(9), 9684–9689 (2010)
7. Creath, K.: Temporal Phase Measurement Methods. In: Interferogram Analysis - Digital Fringe Pattern Measurement Techniques, pp. 94–140. Inst. of Physics Publ., London (1993)
8. D'Apuzzo, N.: Surface measurement and tracking of human body parts from multi-image video sequences. ISPRS Journal 56, 360–375 (2002)
9. Shi, C.Q., Zhang, L.Y.: A 3D Shape Measurement System Based on Random Pattern Projection. In: Proc. Fifth Int. Conf. on Frontier of Computer Science and Technology, pp. 147–153 (2010)
10. Dekiff, M., Bersenbrügge, P., Kemper, B., Denz, C., Dirksen, D.: Three-dimensional data acquisition by digital correlation of projected speckle patterns. Appl. Phys. B 99, 449–456 (2010)

11. Wiegmann, A., Wagner, H., Kowarschik, R.: Human face measurement by projecting bandlimited random patterns. Optics Express 14(17), 7692–7698 (2006)
12. Zhou, M., Fraser, C.S.: Automated extraction in real time photogrammetry. In: International Archives of Photogrammetry and Remote Sensing, IAPRS, vol. XXXIII, Part B5, pp. 943–950 (2000)
13. Salvi, J., Pages, J., Batlle, J.: Pattern codification strategies in structured light systems. Pattern Recognition 37, 827–849 (2004)
14. Salvi, J., Fernandez, S., Pribanic, T., Llado, X.: A state of the art in structured light patterns for surface profilometry. Pattern Recognition 43, 2666–2680 (2010)
15. Dejardins, D., Payeur, D.: Dense Stereo Range Sensing with Marching Pseudo-Random Patterns. In: Fourth Canadian Conference on Computer and Robot Vision (2007)
16. Xu, J., Ning, X., Zhao, Z., Gao, B., Shi, Q.: Rapid 3D surface profile measurement of industrial parts using two-level structured light patterns. Optics and Lasers in Engineering 49, 907–914 (2011)
17. Pribanic, T., Obradovic, N., Salvi, J.: Stereo computation combining structured light and passive stereo matching. Optics Communications 285, 1017–1022 (2012)
18. Luhmann, T., Robson, S., Kyle, S., Harley, I.: Close range photogrammetry. Wiley Whittles Publishing (2006)
19. Schaffer, M., Grosse, S., Kowarschik, R.: High-speed pattern projection for three-dimensional shape measurement using laser speckles. Applied Optics 49(18), 3622–3629 (2010)

Consensus Multi-View Photometric Stereo

Mate Beljan, Jens Ackermann, and Michael Goesele

TU Darmstadt

Abstract. We propose a multi-view photometric stereo technique that uses photometric normal consistency to jointly estimate surface position and orientation. The underlying scene representation is based on oriented points, yielding more flexibility compared to smoothly varying surfaces. We demonstrate that the often employed least squares error of the Lambertian image formation model fails for wide-baseline settings without known visibility information. We then introduce a multi-view normal consistency approach and demonstrate its efficiency on synthetic and real data. In particular, our approach is able to handle occlusion, shadows, and other sources of outliers.

1 Introduction

Recently, several multi-view photometric stereo techniques have been proposed that use some kind of global surface smoothness or similar assumptions [4,9,12]. In contrast, classical single-view photometric stereo is a very local technique allowing to recover even fine variations of the surface normals. In this paper, we analyze to what extent a multi-view reconstruction of surface orientation is possible if surface points are considered to be totally independent. We propose to move to a different scene representation consisting of surface points with normal information. Such a representation is especially suited for cluttered, real-world scenes with multiple, arbitrary objects.

One could argue that real-world objects typically show some kind of connectivity that should be exploited. However, the validity of any assumption on surface point interdependence is subject to the scale at which we observe the surface. For example, any approximation with linear or even curved patches only makes sense for a sufficiently low-frequent surface compared to the patch size. On the other hand, complete independence of surface points is a much more flexible paradigm. If we know that the data fulfills certain assumptions, such as smoothness, then it of course makes sense to exploit those. But if such properties are not known *a priori* it makes more sense to employ a general algorithm than to work with a method whose prerequisites are not met.

Similar arguments hold for explicit outlier removal: Modeling each error source individually, e.g., by shadow detection or special treatment of non-Lambertian points, can only address limited types of outliers. In contrast, the proposed hypotheses concept allows us to treat all outliers uniformly and to automatically select suitable subsets of observations that lead to consistent normals.

A. Pinz et al. (Eds.): DAGM/OAGM 2012, LNCS 7476, pp. 287–296, 2012.
© Springer-Verlag Berlin Heidelberg 2012

Our contribution lies in deriving a consistency measure that incorporates both position and surface orientation and does not rely on assumptions concerning surface smoothness. This new measure is based on the consistency of normal hypotheses that are generated from different subsets of all available views. In particular, we present a reconstruction approach that operates without an initial segmentation of object and background. It can handle scenes with an unknown number of objects, and is robust against shadows and occlusions by treating both uniformly as outliers.

1.1 Related Work

Multi-view stereo techniques [5,14,16] reconstruct a surface by comparing the texture of small patches. They typically fail on uniformly colored objects [15]. In contrast, photometric methods use shading information, e.g., based on the Lambertian image formation model to estimate the surface orientation. This is only possible if pixel correspondences in different views are known. In the single-view case these correspondences are given inherently. But for a multi-view data set this poses a fundamental challenge since knowing the pixel correspondences is equivalent to knowing the actual 3D position of the respective surface point.

As observed by Zhang et al. [19], most multi-view reconstruction techniques do not explicitly compute surface normals or even consider them in their matching cost. A notable exception are techniques that reconstruct specular surfaces [1,13]. One of the first approaches was proposed by Coleman and Jain [3] who also introduced the concept of normal hypotheses. They propose to extend classical photometric stereo by taking four images from a fixed view-point under varying illumination, therefore generating four albedo and normal hypotheses per pixel. Only those hypotheses observing the surface under Lambertian conditions are correct and mutually consistent. Maki and Cipolla [10] extend this later to five images. We use the idea of hypothetical normals and extend it to the multi-view setting. This increases the number of hypotheses tremendously and introduces new challenges including computational complexity and occlusion handling.

Similar to us, Higo et al. [6] determine several normals at a single point from different sets of lighting directions, but for a single-view setting. They restrict the solution space to a cone spanned by these normals whereas we use them to find a maximal inlier set and then perform regular photometric stereo. Another line of research related to our work is the reconstruction of moving, diffuse objects. Maki et al. [11] present the theory and analyze the least squares intensity constraint. Their ideas use intensity subspaces and assume that the light source illuminates all points on the object, avoiding shadows and occlusions. Simakov et al. [15] also use the least squares error of the Lambertian image formation model as their consistency measure. The maximal rotation in their experiments is 50 degrees between a pair of views, but the whole set of views actually spans only a limited range of angles. Almost all surface points are seen in every view and therefore there are no outliers due to occlusion that would bias the least squares error. Lim et al. [9] investigate the question whether inaccurate initial pixel correspondences, e.g., from a rough, piecewise planar approximation, can be improved by photometric stereo. They assume an evolving surface that arises from an integrable normal field and minimizes the least squares error of the Lambertian model. Similarly, Joshi and Kriegman [7] use a cost function based on the error of a rank three approximation of the observed image intensities to get an initial, smoothed surface. The main difference that separates our work from these approaches is that they all cannot handle occlusions, shadows, or other sources of outliers. This becomes, however, a necessity if we consider wide baseline scenarios with complex scenes.

Several methods try to circumvent the problem of unknown occlusions or visibility with a proxy object that is refined iteratively. Weber *et al.* [17] apply a voxel-based approach. It relies on object silhouettes and iteratively carves away voxels outside the *consistency hull*. Due to visibility information from the evolving surface, their technique can also handle wide baseline scenarios. Similarly, Hernandez *et al.* [4] use a triangle mesh as proxy geometry and iteratively refine vertex positions and face normals. Again, the initialization and the illumination estimation rely on the visual hull being extracted from object silhouettes. Moses and Shimshoni [12] reconstruct a smooth 3D model from several calibrated images of a featureless Lambertian object under known point light illumination. Starting at an initial depth, the algorithm estimates neighbouring positions guided by the recovered normal at that point and then grows the surface by iterating this procedure. Yoshiyasu and Yamazaki [18] also use silhouettes and a mesh deformation approach. Their iterative optimization alternates between a mesh-based representation and oriented points to handle topology changes. In our work, we directly recover oriented points and do not assume an evolving surface. This is especially challenging since it implies that visibility information is not available, but allows us to reconstruct scenes even with multiple objects. Another distinguishing feature is that we are independent of object silhouettes and visual hulls which are difficult to recover in some scenes.

2   Multi-view Photometric Stereo

Outlier-free settings with a narrow baseline between views have been studied repeatedly and with good results [7,15]. We assume that we have N images taken from known camera positions $\mathbf{C_i}$ under a point light source with constant intensity d and changing but known light position $\mathbf{L_i}$. In this case, for any voxel $\mathbf{p}$, we can find a normal $\tilde{\mathbf{n}}$ which minimizes the least squares error

$$e(\mathbf{p}) = \min_{\tilde{\mathbf{n}}} \frac{1}{N} \sum_{i=1}^{N} (I_{p,i} - d_{p,i}\mathbf{L}_{p,i} \cdot \tilde{\mathbf{n}})^2 \qquad (1)$$

defined by the corresponding pixel intensities $I_{p,i}$, light directions $\mathbf{L}_{p,i} = (\mathbf{L}_i - \mathbf{p})/\|\mathbf{L}_i - \mathbf{p}\|$ and light intensities $d_{p,i} = d/\|\mathbf{L}_i - \mathbf{p}\|^2$ in each of the N images. For large $e(\mathbf{p})$ we can be sure that the voxel is not on the surface S, since for $\mathbf{p} \in S$ the corresponding normal would explain all observations with a small error. For small $e(\mathbf{p})$, however, we cannot conclude the inverse since the error can be small for certain $\mathbf{p} \notin S$. This occurs, e.g., if the true surface points observed through

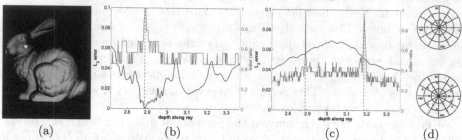

Fig. 1. Error measures along a viewing ray (*blue:* L_2-error, *green:* inlier ratio for normal consistency). (a) The ray marked in the input image. (b) For narrow baseline (9 views) both measures indicate the correct depth (ground truth in *red*). (c) For 62 views (wide baseline) the inlier ratio detects even the intersection at the back whereas the L_2-error is not discriminant. (d) Upper and lower hemisphere with selected views for the front (*red*) and back (*blue*) intersections.

p have the same normal (e.g., for a planar target). The blue curve in Fig. 1(b) shows this L_2-error for voxels along a ray from the camera center of the reference view in Fig. 1(a). The ground truth depth of the surface point is indicated by the red line and we observe that the L_2-error is a useful indicator of the surface. This example was computed from nine synthetic images of the *bunny* (see Section 3) with camera positions from the same octant.

The illustration in Fig. 1(c), however, clearly shows that this error measure is not suitable for wide-baseline datasets. In this example, the same object is rendered from 62 views that are uniformly distributed on a sphere. There is no minimum at the ground truth location and the curve gives no indication of the true surface. In contrast our proposed technique (in green) which we will discuss in detail in the next section finds both front and back surface points reliably.

2.1   Consistency of Normal Hypotheses

The problem with the least squares error is that it treats all occurring errors equally and is thus not robust against outliers. In real scenarios with multiple views and wide baselines, an observed intensity might be an outlier due to occlusion, shadows, or for various other reasons. Since we have no visibility information available, it is important to robustly select a subset of suitable observations. We therefore introduce the concept of normal hypotheses that allows for a more fine-grained selection of reasonable observations and fits well into a RANSAC framework.

For a single voxel **p** and each possible triplet of intensities **I** arising from linearly independent light directions $\mathbf{L}_{p,i}$ we can solve the illumination equation

$$\mathbf{I} = \begin{pmatrix} d_{p,1}\mathbf{L}_{p,1}^{T} \\ d_{p,2}\mathbf{L}_{p,2}^{T} \\ d_{p,3}\mathbf{L}_{p,3}^{T} \end{pmatrix} \cdot \mathbf{n} \tag{2}$$

for **n**. This yields a hypothesis for the albedo $\beta = \|\mathbf{n}\|$ and for the normal $\tilde{\mathbf{n}} = \mathbf{n}/\beta$. The case $N = 4$ with a fixed camera has been discussed by Coleman *et al.* [3] in the context of specularities. We consider arbitrary N and make use of the fact that the concept is independent of the fixed view-point assumption. Because we do not allow repetitions this results in $\binom{N}{3}/3!$ distinct possibilities. The similarity of these hypotheses can now provide an important clue. For $\mathbf{p} \notin S$ the actually observed surface points differ and thus the computed normal hypotheses will differ considerably. For points on the surface, most hypotheses will coincide except those obtained from false observations.

We propose to look at the set of supporting observations for each hypothesis. That means we build an inlier set $\mathcal{I}$ of views that are consistent with the normal $\tilde{\mathbf{n}}$ we estimated from views i_1, i_2 and i_3 by applying an angular threshold t_{ang}:

$$\left| \cos^{-1}\left(\frac{I_i}{\beta d_{p,i}} \right) - \cos^{-1}(\mathbf{L}_{p,i} \cdot \tilde{\mathbf{n}}) \right| < t_{\mathrm{ang}}, \quad \forall i \in \mathcal{I}. \tag{3}$$

Instead of evaluating all triplets which becomes infeasible with an increasing number of images we use a RANSAC algorithm at each $\mathbf{p}$ to select the best supported hypothesis. We found, however, the above criterion alone to be ambiguous in some cases. If view i has actually observed the occluding surface point $\bar{\mathbf{p}}$ with normal $\bar{\mathbf{n}}$ and this normal is by chance in the cone defined by $\mathbf{L}_{p,i}$ and the hypothesis $\tilde{\mathbf{n}}$, then i will be included as inlier. For this reason we introduce an additional check for views in $\mathcal{I}$. We require all hypotheses $\tilde{\mathbf{h}} \in \{\tilde{\mathbf{n}}_{i_1,i_2,i}, \tilde{\mathbf{n}}_{i_1,i,i_3}, \tilde{\mathbf{n}}_{i,i_2,i_3}\}$ to deviate at most t_{ang} degrees from the candidate $\tilde{\mathbf{n}}$ before including i in $\mathcal{I}$:

$$\cos^{-1}(\tilde{\mathbf{h}} \cdot \tilde{\mathbf{n}}) \leq t_{\mathrm{ang}}. \tag{4}$$

With the triplet approach we can also easily perform further analysis on views. In particular, we check for 'front-facing' cameras and lights by evaluating the corresponding dot product before assigning them to the inlier set.

Fig. 1 shows our error measure along a ray from the reference camera: For each voxel the size $\#\mathcal{I}$ of the largest inlier set over all hypotheses is computed and then normalized with the maximal number of inliers encountered along the ray. From the ground truth overlay we conclude that this is a good indicator for whether or not a point is part of the surface. The maximum is attained at the correct position for both the narrow- and wide-baseline settings. We observe a second maximum in the wide-baseline case which is due to the back of the object. The inlier set in Fig. 1(d) is comprised of different views for each maximum. Finally, from the observations in the inlier set we can robustly re-estimate the normal at each voxel using least squares. So we not only obtain an indicator for the position of the surface but also its orientation.

3   Results

In this section, we present results for the consistency measure, recovered inlier views, surface orientation, and final 3D models. For these datasets, we determine the largest inlier set for all voxels in a regular 256^3 grid that we manually position in the scene. We found 500 RANSAC iterations at each point and $t_{\mathrm{ang}} = 5°$

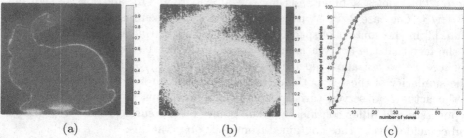

(a)	(b)	(c)

Fig. 2. *Analysis:* (a) 2D slice showing the inlier ratio for the *bunny* data set normalized over the maximum inlier set of the slice (b) L_2-error for the same slice is not discriminant at all. The error is normalized over the maximum L_2-error of the slice. (c) Cumulative percentage of surface points plotted over the number of missed (*blue*) and erroneous (*green*) views.

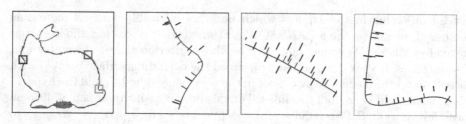

Fig. 3. *Normal Comparison:* Three surface regions with different curvature and visibility. The normals computed by our method (*black*) for the most consistent grid points ($\#\mathcal{I} > 15$) are close to the ground truth (*blue ticks*).

to yield good results — often fewer iterations suffice. Furthermore, we discard image triples with over- or underexposed pixels ($I_i < 0.05$ or $I_i > 0.95$).

Rendered Input Images. To separately study the impact of various effects on the consistency measure, we first evaluate the performance of our technique on ray traced images with available ground truth data. We choose 62 light and coinciding camera positions uniformly distributed around the observed object. The 256^3 volume was computed in 11 hours on an Intel quad-core i7 960. Given the totally independent voxels further parallelization is trivial.

Extending Fig. 1, we now show a complete slice through the 3D volume in Fig. 2(a). Again, the size of the largest inlier set is a good surface indicator. The consistency is smeared out in regions with planar surfaces (e.g., the bottom of the bunny). This shading ambiguity is expected in the planar case. Nevertheless, the normals estimated for voxels in that region still yield the correct orientation. Fig. 3 shows the normals corresponding to the most consistent points in the grid together with the ground truth normals. Note that both the 3D points and the estimated surface orientation match the ground truth quite accurately.

We also investigated whether the least squares error for the normal estimated from the inlier set could be used as a discriminant error measure. Fig. 2(b) shows that this is not the case: RANSAC works so well that the inlier set leads to a small

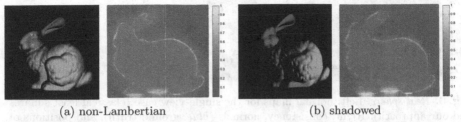

(a) non-Lambertian   (b) shadowed

Fig. 4. *Robustness through outlier handling:* Input image and a 2D slice of the consistency measure for (a) an object deviating from the Lambertian assumption and (b) a data set showing strong shadows.

Fig. 5. *Multiple object scene.* Left to right: One of the input images. Visualisation of the selected 2D slice. Consistency in the 2D slice for a complete scene. Closeup of the spiral with ground truth overlaid in *blue*.

error for almost all voxels. The ability of RANSAC to select the correct subset of views at each voxel is illustrated in Fig. 2(c). For each point on the ground truth surface, we determine the views $\mathcal{I}_{GT}$ that actually observe it. We then compute the number of missed views $\#(\mathcal{I}_{GT} \setminus \mathcal{I})$ and the number of erroneously included views $\#(\mathcal{I} \setminus \mathcal{I}_{GT})$. The cumulative histogram (blue) indicates that for about 50% of the surface points, we miss at most 7 views. The green curve shows that we select less than 5 erroneous views in 70% of the cases.

Our approach is also robust against different non-ideal conditions. Fig. 4(a) uses a plastic material with specular highlights in the reflection direction. In Fig. 4(b), we move the light sources away from the camera positions to add cast shadows to the images. Even the shiny material which violates the Lambertian assumption underlying photometric stereo has no apparent effect on the quality of the surface contour. The consensus-based reconstruction automatically discards those views as outliers that do not exhibit sufficiently diffuse behaviour. A similar argument holds for self-shadowing as in Fig. 4(b).

Finally, the flexibility of the consensus-based approach becomes most apparent when considering scenes with multiple surfaces instead of a single object. Fig. 5 shows our technique on such a challenging data set that we rendered with 89 views distributed on a hemisphere. The two arms of the spiral to the left are only partially recovered (see closeup). The missing parts are due to the surface facing downwards and are thus not seen by most of the views. The bunny is well reconstructed and for the flower on the right we recover even the sharply twirled edges.

Fig. 6. *Real sphere.* Left: normal maps for the single-view case (classical least squares and our approach). Right: consistency, normals (*blue:* ground truth), and positions of camera (*top*) and light source (*bottom*) in the multi-view setting.

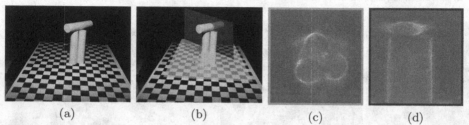

    (a)   (b)   (c)   (d)

Fig. 7. *Chalk dataset:* (a) Input image. (b) Visualisation of two slices. (c-d) Consistency measure for the horizontal and vertical slice.

Results on Real Images. We spray-painted a sphere with chalk and took several linear 14 bit images with a Canon EOS 5D after calibrating its intrinsic parameters. Computing the point light source positions from the reflections on five shiny spheres while keeping the camera fixed allows us to estimate the surface orientation using classical least squares as in Eq. (1). A multi-view photometric reconstruction technique should ideally fall back to the classical photometric stereo method if the camera positions $\mathbf{C}_i$ all coincide. The comparison in Fig. 6 proves that our algorithm recovers the correct surface normals in the single-view case. We also used the same setup to capture a wide-baseline multi-view dataset. In this case it is hard to determine the correct surface position from the smeared-out consistency in Fig. 6. The recovered normals, however, still follow the curvature even at voxels that are slightly off the surface.

To evaluate another multi-view reconstruction, we placed four pieces of chalk on a turnable checkerboard. 84 images were taken from different heights with a flash attached to the camera and pointing at the scene. We determine the extrinsic camera parameters with the camera calibration toolbox [2]. The light directions are then given by the fixed distance between flash and the optical axis of the camera (which we measured as 175 mm). In Fig. 7 we show the results for the *Chalk* dataset. Note that we do not compute an object mask or any occluding contours. With the proposed measure, the overall shape of the surface is clearly visible in the individual slices. We capture the smoothly curving parts as well as the sharp edge at the end of the sticks in Fig. 7(d). We observe, however, that a lot of voxels inside the object have quite high consistency scores. There is still a difference between the consistency scores for on and off the surfaces but it is

Fig. 8. *Rendering novel views:* Smooth surface extraction can be applied as an additional step if required, e.g. for rendering. (Thresholds used: $t_{cs} = 15/15/25$).

less pronounced than in the synthetic test cases. Some problems occur in surface regions with low local visibility, e.g., where the sticks touch in Fig. 7(c).

3.1 Surface Extraction

The aim of our work is to analyze to which extend the reconstruction of possibly disconnected, oriented points is possible for uniformly colored objects. But if required, the flexibility of our scene representation fits almost any surface extraction method as an additional step to create a triangle mesh or introduce regularization. We show this in Fig. 8 for a basic scheme of running Poisson surface reconstruction [8] on all points with $\#\mathcal{I} > t_{cs}$.

The reconstruction of the *bunny* appears slightly smoothed compared to the ground-truth. This is due to the regular grid and its limited resolution which prevent a faithful reconstruction of the high-frequency details. In future work, this could be addressed by an adaptive sampling since the measure itself does not rely on the uniform grid structure. For the *chalk* dataset, the regularization removes some of the sharp edges that were recognizable in the voxel-based reconstruction, see Fig. 7(d). Again the single pieces of chalk are easily discernible.

4   Discussion and Future Work

Abandoning almost all possible assumptions, e.g., baseline sizes, surface smoothness, visibility data, or object segmentation leads to a very challenging reconstruction problem. We have shown that reconstructions for narrow- and wide-baseline settings are possible even for scenes with multiple, discontinuous surfaces, but the lack of a per-voxel normalization limits the current approach. If we knew $\mathcal{I}_{GT}(\mathbf{p})$, it would make sense to rather consider $\#(\mathcal{I} \cap \mathcal{I}_{GT})$. Currently, if $\#\mathcal{I}_{GT}(\mathbf{p}_1) \ll \#\mathcal{I}_{GT}(\mathbf{p}_2)$ for two surface points, then usually $\#\mathcal{I}(\mathbf{p}_1) \ll \#\mathcal{I}(\mathbf{p}_2)$. That means that $\mathbf{p}_1$ will get a much lower score than $\mathbf{p}_2$ even if all non-occluded views are consistent. For example, the back of the bunny in Fig. 2 shows large consensus sizes while the paws are only seen in few views and have lower consistency values. Thus, we observe a certain dependency on the view distribution that we would like to investigate further. Another issue is, that the quality of the real world results is not as good as we expected after experiencing the robustness on synthetic data. While the normals can be recovered quite accurately, the depth reconstruction merits further inspection. Finally, we would like to remark that the approach we presented will not outperform more specialized solutions if their respective prerequisites are met. But it is more flexible and we believe that this aspect will become even more important in the future.

Acknowledgments. This work was supported in part by the DFG Emmy Noether fellowship GO 1752/3-1.

References

1. Bonfort, T., Sturm, P.F.: Voxel carving for specular surfaces. In: ICCV (2003)
2. Bouguet, J.Y.: Camera calibration toolbox for matlab (2012), http://www.vision.caltech.edu/bouguetj/calib_doc/
3. Coleman, E.N., Jain, R.: Obtaining 3-dimensional shape of textured and specular surfaces using four-source photometry. Computer Graphics and Image Processing 18, 309–328 (1982)
4. Esteban, C.H., Vogiatzis, G., Cipolla, R.: Multiview photometric stereo. PAMI 30(3), 548–554 (2008)
5. Goesele, M., Snavely, N., Curless, B., Hoppe, H., Seitz, S.M.: Multi-view stereo for community photo collections. In: ICCV (2007)
6. Higo, T., Matsushita, Y., Ikeuchi, K.: Consensus photometric stereo. In: CVPR (2010)
7. Joshi, N., Kriegman, D.: Shape from varying illumination and viewpoint. In: ICCV (2007)
8. Kazhdan, M., Bolitho, M., Hoppe, H.: Poisson surface reconstruction and its applications. In: Eurographics Symposium on Geometry Processing (2006)
9. Lim, J., Ho, J., Yang, M.H., Kriegman, D.J.: Passive photometric stereo from motion. In: ICCV (2005)
10. Maki, A., Cipolla, R.: Obtaining the shape of a moving object with a specular surface. In: BMVC (2009)
11. Maki, A., Watanabe, M., Wiles, C.: Geotensity: Combining motion and lighting for 3D surface reconstruction. IJCV 48(2), 75–90 (2002)
12. Moses, Y., Shimshoni, I.: 3D shape recovery of smooth surfaces: Dropping the fixed-viewpoint assumption. PAMI 31(7), 1310–1324 (2009)
13. Nehab, D., Weyrich, T., Rusinkiewicz, S.: Dense 3D reconstruction from specularity consistency. In: CVPR (2008)
14. Seitz, S.M., Curless, B., Diebel, J., Scharstein, D., Szeliski, R.: A comparison and evaluation of multi-view stereo reconstruction algorithms. In: CVPR (2006)
15. Simakov, D., Frolova, D., Basri, R.: Dense shape reconstruction of a moving object under arbitrary, unknown lighting. In: ICCV (2003)
16. Slabaugh, G.G., Culbertson, W.B., Malzbender, T., Stevens, M.R., Schafer, R.W.: Methods for volumetric reconstruction of visual scenes. IJCV 57(3), 179–199 (2004)
17. Weber, M., Blake, A., Cipolla, R.: Towards a complete dense geometric and photometric reconstruction under varying pose and illumination. In: BMVC (2002)
18. Yoshiyasu, Y., Yamazaki, N.: Topology-adaptive multi-view photometric stereo. In: CVPR (2011)
19. Zhang, L., Curless, B., Hertzmann, A., Seitz, S.M.: Shape and motion under varying illumination: Unifying structure from motion, photometric stereo, and multi-view stereo. In: ICCV (2003)

Automatic Scale Selection
of Superimposed Signals

Oliver Fleischmann and Gerald Sommer

Cognitive Systems Group, Department of Computer Science
Kiel University

Abstract. This work introduces a novel method to estimate the characteristic scale of low-level image structures, which can be modeled as superpositions of intrinsically one-dimensional signals. Rather than being a single scalar quantity, the characteristic scale of the superimposed signal model is an affine equivariant regional feature. The estimation of the characteristic scale is based on an accurate estimation scheme for the orientations of the intrinsically one-dimensional signals. Using the orientation estimations, the characteristic scales of the single intrinsically one-dimensional signals are obtained. The single orientations and scales are combined into a single affine equivariant regional feature describing the characteristic scale of the superimposed signal model. Being based on convolutions with linear shift invariant filters and one-dimensional extremum searches it yields an efficient implementation.

1 Introduction

One of the most important and desirable properties of low-level image features is their equivariance with respect to certain geometric transformations acting on the input images. The property of equivariance states, that under certain transformations of the input image, the detected feature transforms accordingly. In the case of purely point based spatial features or interest points a simple example are features obtained from the responses from linear shift invariant filters such as the Harris corner detector [5]. These features are equivariant with respect to translations of the input. In addition to purely point based features, it is often desirable to describe local neighborhoods of spatial interest points, resulting in regional features. If these regional features are equivariant with respect to a group of transformations, they can always be normalized. This corresponds to a transformation back to an identity element, such that so called feature descriptors, e.g. SIFT [8], are able to describe and summarize the content of the image within the local neighborhood specified by the regional feature. We will introduce a method to obtain a regional feature which is affine equivariant, including non-uniform changes in scale. In contrast to existing attempts such as the Harris-affine or Hessian-affine detectors [9], [7], our method follows a non-iterative strategy which allows for an efficient implementation. We use a model based approach, assuming that the neighborhoods around interest points can be described as superpositions of intrinsically one-dimensional signals.

A. Pinz et al. (Eds.): DAGM/OAGM 2012, LNCS 7476, pp. 297–306, 2012.
© Springer-Verlag Berlin Heidelberg 2012

The scale selection for the superimposed signal model relies on an accurate orientation estimation for the intrinsically one-dimensional signals. Our approach for the orientation estimation, which is described in section 2, follows the concept introduced in [1]. We will extend the approach and simplify the estimation of the single orientations. In section 3 we will use the orientations to estimate the characteristic scales of the single intrinsically one-dimensional signals. Based on the single orientations and scales we introduce our affine equivariant regional feature, the *affine characteristic scale*. Section 4 finally provides examples of the method for synthetic and real-world images.

2   Orientation Estimation

In the following we will study superpositions of *intrinsically one-dimensional* (i1D) signals. We call a signal $f : \mathbb{R}^2 \to \mathbb{R}$ intrinsically one-dimensional with orientation $\theta \in [0, \pi[$, if f is non-constant and there exists a $\tilde{f} : \mathbb{R} \to \mathbb{R}$ with $f(\boldsymbol{x}) = \tilde{f}(k\langle \boldsymbol{x}, \boldsymbol{n} \rangle)$ for all $\boldsymbol{x} \in \mathbb{R}^2$ where $\boldsymbol{n} = (\cos(\theta), \sin(\theta))^T$ is the orientation vector, $k \in \mathbb{R}$ is a constant and $\langle \cdot, \cdot \rangle$ denotes the standard Euclidean inner product. Given n intrinsically one dimensional signals $f_0, \dots, f_{n-1}$, we call

$$f(\boldsymbol{x}) = \sum_{i=0}^{n-1} f_i(\boldsymbol{x}) = \sum_{i=0}^{n-1} \tilde{f}_i(k_i \langle \boldsymbol{x}, \boldsymbol{n}_i \rangle) \tag{1}$$

a superposition of intrinsically one-dimensional signals. Such superpositions will constitute the signal model. Figure 1 shows three examples of superimposed signals. We will assume that certain image structures can locally be described by superimposed intrinsically one-dimensional signals. Let $I : \mathbb{R}^2 \to \mathbb{R}$ be a two-dimensional signal which we will also refer to as an image. We say the model (1) holds *locally* in a neighborhood Ω around $\boldsymbol{x}_0 \in \mathbb{R}^2$, if for all $\boldsymbol{x} \in \Omega(\boldsymbol{x}_0)$

$$I(\boldsymbol{x}) \approx f(\boldsymbol{x}). \tag{2}$$

Suppose an intrinsically one-dimensional signal f_i is given. From its definition it follows, that f_i is constant along all lines perpendicular to its orientation vector $\boldsymbol{n}_i$ and consequently its gradient vanishes along these lines yielding

$$\mathcal{D}_i f_i(\boldsymbol{x}) = \langle \nabla f_i(\boldsymbol{x}), \bar{\boldsymbol{n}}_i \rangle = 0 \quad \text{for all } \boldsymbol{x} \in \mathbb{R}^2 \text{ with } \langle \boldsymbol{n}_i, \bar{\boldsymbol{n}}_i \rangle = 0. \tag{3}$$

The differential operators $\mathcal{D}_i$ are commuting first order differential operators such that for any $\mathcal{D}_i, \mathcal{D}_j$ it holds that $\mathcal{D}_i \mathcal{D}_j f = \mathcal{D}_j \mathcal{D}_i f$ with $i, j \in \{0, \dots, n-1\}$. For a superposition f of n intrinsically one-dimensional signals the commutation relation especially implies, that the composition of the operators $\mathcal{D}_0, \dots, \mathcal{D}_{n-1}$ applied to f is zero, i.e.

$$\mathcal{D}_0 \mathcal{D}_1 \dots \mathcal{D}_{n-1} f(\boldsymbol{x}) = 0 \quad \text{for all } \boldsymbol{x} \in \mathbb{R}^2. \tag{4}$$

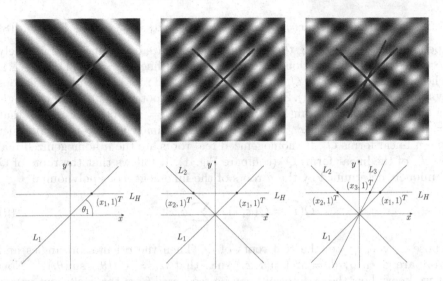

Fig. 1. Top row: Superpositions of 1,2 and 3 intrinsically one dimensional signals and the estimated orientations depicted in blue color. Bottom row: Geometric illustration of the homogenized roots of the polynomials Q and the roots of the inhomogeneous polynomials $\bar{Q}$ for each signal..

Recalling that the operators $\mathcal{D}_i$ are the inner products of the perpendicular orientation vectors and the gradient of f, that is $\mathcal{D}_i f = \langle \nabla f, \bar{n}_i \rangle$, equation (4) can be rewritten as

$$\mathcal{D}_0 \mathcal{D}_1 \ldots \mathcal{D}_{n-1} f(x) = \sum_{i=0}^{n} a_i \frac{\partial^n}{\partial x^{n-i} \partial y^i} f(x) = 0 \quad \text{for all } x \in \mathbb{R}^2 \quad (5)$$

where $a = (a_0, \ldots, a_n)^T$ is a vector of coefficients of the polynomial

$$Q(x,y) = \prod_{i=0}^{n-1} Q_i(x,y) = \prod_{i=0}^{n-1} (\bar{n}_{i,1} x + \bar{n}_{i,2} y) = \sum_{i=0}^{n} a_i x^{n-i} y^i. \quad (6)$$

Identifying the partial derivatives

$$v(x) = (\frac{\partial^n}{\partial x^n} f(x), \frac{\partial^n}{\partial x^{n-1} \partial y} f(x), \ldots, \frac{\partial^n}{\partial y^n} f(x))^T \quad (7)$$

with points in $\mathbb{R}^{n+1}$, the relationship (5) geometrically states that the partial derivatives evaluated at the points $x \in \mathbb{R}^2$ lie in a n-dimensional linear subspace in $\mathbb{R}^{n+1}$ perpendicular to the vector a. We will show, how the orientation vectors n_i can be recovered from the coefficient vector a. $Q(x,y)$ is homogeneous polynomial of degree n, also known as a *binary form* of degree n, which is factorable into n linear binary forms Q_i. Of special interest are the roots of the binary form Q. We will first consider the homogenized real roots of the linear binary forms Q_i. The homogenized real roots of the forms Q_i are the lines

$$L_i = \{(x,y) : Q_i(x,y) = (\bar{n}_{i,1}x + \bar{n}_{i,2}y) = 0\} = \{\lambda \, n_i, \lambda \in \mathbb{R}\} \qquad (8)$$

perpendicular to $\bar{n}_i$ passing through the origin. Since every line L_i is uniquely determined by its intersection with the horizontal line $L_H = \{(x,1)^T, x \in \mathbb{R}\}$, the homogenized root L_i of Q_i intersects L_H in a real root of the inhomogeneous polynomial $\tilde{Q}_i(x) = Q_i(x,1)$. Suppose x_i is the real root of $\tilde{Q}_i(x)$. Then the angle θ_i is obtained as $\theta_i = \arctan(1/x_i)$ if $x_i \neq 0$ and $\theta_i = \pi/2$ otherwise, such that $n_i = (\cos(\theta_i), \sin(\theta_i))^T = (x_i, 1)^T / \|(x_i,1)^T\|$. The binary form Q is the product of the n linear forms Q_i. Its homogenized real roots are the n homogenized real roots L_i of the linear forms Q_i (compare Fig. 1). It follows that the roots of Q are uniquely determined by the n roots of the inhomogeneous polynomial

$$\tilde{Q}(x) = Q(x,1) = \sum_{i=0}^{n} a_i x^{n-i}. \qquad (9)$$

Suppose $x_1, \ldots, x_n$ are the real roots of $\tilde{Q}$. Then the orientation angles and vectors are given by $\theta_i = \arctan(1, x_i)$ such that $n_i = \cos((\theta_i), \sin(\theta_i))^T$. Now that we know, how the orientations can be recovered from the coefficient vector a, it is left to show how a is estimated from an image I. Suppose that in a local neighborhood $\Omega(x_0)$ around a point $x_0 \in \mathbb{R}^2$ the image I can be modeled as a superposition f of n i1D signals. As already mentioned above, the coefficient vector a is perpendicular to the hyperplane in $\mathbb{R}^{n+1}$ spanned by the partial derivatives of order n, interpreted as points in $\mathbb{R}^{n+1}$. The coefficient vector a is then found by a classical least squares fit of an n-dimensional hyperplane to the partial derivatives, leading to the optimization problem

$$\min_{a} \int_{\Omega(x_0)} \langle v(x), a \rangle^2 \, dx \quad \text{s.t.} \, \|a\| = 1 \qquad (10)$$

where $v(x)$ are the n-th order partial derivatives of f at x according to (7). The solution to the least squares problem above is obtained as the eigenvector corresponding to the smallest eigenvalue of the matrix (see e.g.[6])

$$S(x_0) = \begin{bmatrix} S_{0,0}(x_0) & \cdots & S_{0,n}(x_0) \\ \vdots & \ddots & \vdots \\ S_{n,0}(x_0) & \cdots & S_{n,n}(x_0) \end{bmatrix} \qquad (11)$$

with

$$S_{ij}(x_0) = \int_{\Omega(x_0)} \frac{\partial^n}{\partial x^{n-i} \partial y^i} f(x) \frac{\partial^n}{\partial x^{n-j} \partial y^j} f(x) dx. \qquad (12)$$

In the case of $n = 1$ the matrix S corresponds to the classical *structure tensor* introduced in [5] and [3].

3   Automatic Scale Selection

3.1   Affine Characteristic Scale

The previous section introduced a method to estimate the orientations of n superimposed intrinsically one-dimensional signals. The orientations are equivariant with respect to rotations in the plane. As the transformations acting on images usually do not only consist of pure rotations but also changes in scale, it is mandatory to achieve scale equivariance of the underlying model. The scale changes we will consider are not restricted to uniform scale changes. Instead we focus on scale changes along arbitrary orthogonal axes in conjunction with rotations described by actions of

$$G = \left\{ \boldsymbol{U}\boldsymbol{D}\boldsymbol{V}^T : \boldsymbol{U}\boldsymbol{U}^T = \boldsymbol{I}, \boldsymbol{V}\boldsymbol{V}^T = \boldsymbol{I}, \boldsymbol{D} = \begin{bmatrix} s_1 & 0 \\ 0 & s_2 \end{bmatrix} \right\} \tag{13}$$

where all the matrices are real-valued and $s_1, s_2 \in \mathbb{R}^+$. It is convenient to illustrate our scale selection method for the superimposed signal model in the frequency domain. We consider the ideal case of n superimposed cosine waves

$$f(\boldsymbol{x}) = \sum_{i=0}^{n-1} A_i \cos(k_i \langle \boldsymbol{x}, \boldsymbol{n}_i \rangle - \varphi_i). \tag{14}$$

whose two-dimensional Fourier transform in the sense of distributions is the superposition of $2n$ Dirac delta impulses

$$\mathcal{F}f(\boldsymbol{u}) = \sum_{i=0}^{n-1} \frac{A_i}{2} e^{-\imath \varphi_i (u+v)} (\delta(\boldsymbol{u} - k_i \boldsymbol{n}_i) + \delta(\boldsymbol{u} + k_i \boldsymbol{n}_i)). \tag{15}$$

Let $P = \{k_i \boldsymbol{n}_i\} \cup \{-k_i \boldsymbol{n}_i\}$ denote the $2n$ points which coincide with the locations of the delta impulses in the frequency domain. Let

$$\boldsymbol{M}_F = \frac{1}{2n} \sum_{p \in P} \begin{bmatrix} p_1^2 & p_1 p_2 \\ p_1 p_2 & p_2^2 \end{bmatrix} \tag{16}$$

denote the second moment matrix of the points P in the frequency domain. The matrix $\boldsymbol{M}_F$ is symmetric and positive-definite, describing an ellipse in the frequency domain whose axes point along the eigenvectors and whose axes lengths are given by the square-roots of the eigenvalues of $\boldsymbol{M}_F$. Figure 2 shows two superimposed signals for $n = 2$ and $n = 3$ and the corresponding idealized Dirac impulses in the frequency domain. Further it illustrates the ellipse described by $\boldsymbol{M}_F$ obtained from the locations of the Dirac impulses.

Definition 1 (Affine characteristic scale). *Suppose we decompose $\boldsymbol{M}_F$ by its singular value decomposition as $\boldsymbol{M}_F = \boldsymbol{U}_M \boldsymbol{\Sigma}^{-1} \boldsymbol{V}_M^T$. We define the matrix $\boldsymbol{M}_S = \boldsymbol{U}_M \boldsymbol{\Sigma} \boldsymbol{V}_M^T$ describing an ellipse with the same axes directions as $\boldsymbol{M}_F$, but reciprocal axes lengths. We call the matrix $\boldsymbol{M}_S$ the affine characteristic scale of f.*

Suppose G acts on f in the spatial domain as f as $(g \circ f)(\boldsymbol{x}) = f(g^{-1}\boldsymbol{x}) = f(\boldsymbol{A}\boldsymbol{x})$ with $\boldsymbol{A} = \boldsymbol{U}\boldsymbol{D}\boldsymbol{V}^T$. Due to the affine theorem of the Fourier transform (see e.g. [2]), the induced action on the Fourier transform of f is given by

$$\mathcal{F}(g \circ f)(\boldsymbol{u}) = \frac{1}{|det(\widetilde{\boldsymbol{A}})|} \mathcal{F}f(\widetilde{\boldsymbol{A}}\boldsymbol{u}) \tag{17}$$

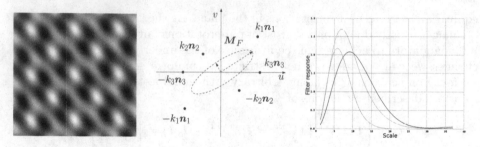

Fig. 2. Left : Superimposed signal consisting of $n = 3$ i1D signals. Middle : Schematic illustration of the Dirac delta impulses in the Fourier domain and the corresponding ellipse described by the second moment matrix M_F Right : Filter responses of the steered Gaussian derivatives.

with $\widetilde{A} = U D^{-1} V^T$. While the rotations by U, V^T are the same as in the spatial domain, the scale changes along the rotated axes act reciprocally. It follows that the induced action on the locations of the delta impulses and therefore the second moment matrix M_F is given by $\widetilde{M}_F = \widetilde{A} M_F \widetilde{A}^T$.

Proposition 1 (Affine equivariance). *The affine characteristic scale M_S is equivariant with respect to the group G where G acts on M_S as $\widetilde{M}_S = A M_S A^T$.*

We conclude that the knowledge of the orientations n_i and frequencies k_i allows the construction of a regional feature which is equivariant with respect to the group G.

3.2   Estimation of the Single Scales

Although a method to estimate the orientations n_i of the signal model from an input signal has already been introduced in the previous section, we still have to estimate the frequencies k_i in order to construct the affine characteristic scale M_S. Rather than estimating the frequencies directly we will follow a slightly different approach. Suppose f is the superposition of n intrinsically one-dimensional signals f_i, not necessarily cosine waves. Further suppose that we have estimated the orientations n_i using the method introduced in section 2. Using the estimated orientations, we will estimate the characteristic scales of the intrinsically one-dimensional signals separately. To obtain the characteristic scales, a family of steerable wavelets parameterized by scale $s \in \mathbb{R}^+$ is chosen. The wavelets are supposed to act as bandpass filters along the orientations n_i. We will use the scale-normalized second order Gaussian derivatives ([4])

$$\phi(\boldsymbol{x}; s) = s^2 \left(\frac{\partial^2}{\partial x^2} g(\boldsymbol{x}; s), \frac{\partial^2}{\partial x \partial y} g(\boldsymbol{x}; s), \frac{\partial^2}{\partial y^2} g(\boldsymbol{x}; s) \right)^T \qquad (18)$$

with $g(\boldsymbol{x};s) = \frac{1}{2\pi s}e^{-(x_1^2+x_2^2)/(2s)}$ to construct the bandpass filters steered along the orientations θ_i

$$\psi_i(\boldsymbol{x};s) = \langle \boldsymbol{c}(\theta_i), \boldsymbol{\phi}(\boldsymbol{x};s) \rangle \tag{19}$$

using the steering coefficients $\boldsymbol{c}(\theta_i) = (\cos^2(\theta_i), 2\cos(\theta_i)\sin(\theta_i), \sin^2(\theta_i))^T$. The signal f is projected to the steered filters $\psi_i(\boldsymbol{x},s)$ as

$$E_i(s) = \int_{\mathbb{R}^2} \psi_i(\boldsymbol{x};s)f(\boldsymbol{x})d\boldsymbol{x}. \tag{20}$$

The characteristic scales s_i are then chosen as the extrema of the functions $E_i(s)$ maximizing the modulus $|E_i(s)|$. If no extrema exist, the interest point is discarded. Figure 2 shows the functions $E_i(s)$ for two example signals, each having a unique extremum which is chosen as the characteristic scale s_i. Suppose that the n characteristic scales s_i of the intrinsically one-dimensional signals f_i have been estimated. Then $|E_i(s)|$ is maximal at s_i. If we consider the Fourier transform $\mathcal{F}\psi_i(\boldsymbol{u};s_i)$ of the filter $\psi_i(\boldsymbol{x};s_i)$, there exist two points $\boldsymbol{p}_{i,1}, \boldsymbol{p}_{i,2} = \pm(c/s_i)\boldsymbol{n}_i$, where c is a constant, for which the amplitude $|\mathcal{F}\psi_i(\boldsymbol{u};s_i)|$ in the frequency domain attains its maximum. If the filter ψ_i is scaled along the orientation $\boldsymbol{n}_i$ as $\psi_i(\boldsymbol{x};r\,s_i), r \in \mathbb{R}^+$, the points of the maximal energy change reciprocally as to $\tilde{\boldsymbol{p}}_{i,1}, \tilde{\boldsymbol{p}}_{i,2} = \pm(c/(r\,s_i))\boldsymbol{n}_i$ according to the similarity theorem of the Fourier transform. Thus from the scales s_i and the orientations $\boldsymbol{n}_i$ we obtain an estimate for the locations of maximal amplitude along the orientations $\boldsymbol{n}_i$ in the frequency domain, which have been idealized by Dirac delta impulses in the previous section. Let $P = \{(c/s_i)\boldsymbol{n}_i\} \cup \{-(c/s_i)\boldsymbol{n}_i\}$ for $i \in \{0, \dots, n-1\}$ denote these estimated locations. The location estimates yield the second moment matrix $\boldsymbol{M}_F$

$$\boldsymbol{M}_F = \frac{1}{2n}\sum_{\boldsymbol{p}\in P} \begin{bmatrix} p_1^2 & p_1\,p_2 \\ p_1\,p_2 & p_2^2 \end{bmatrix} = \boldsymbol{U}_M\boldsymbol{\Sigma}^{-1}\boldsymbol{V}_M^T \tag{21}$$

such that final affine characteristic scale reads $\boldsymbol{M}_S = \boldsymbol{U}_M\boldsymbol{\Sigma}\boldsymbol{V}_M^T$.

4 Application Examples

We have tested the proposed method with synthetic and real world images. In practice, the number of superpositions n is unknown. Nonetheless, we may choose a maximum number n of superpositions such that $\boldsymbol{S}$ will be a $(n+1) \times (n+1)$ matrix consisting of the outer product of the n-th order partial derivatives. The rank of $\boldsymbol{S}$ is then equal to the number of underlying superimposed signals such that it is possible to decide, if the underlying signal consists of less than n superimposed i1D signals. In the case of our affine equivariant regional features a maximum of $n = 3$ turned out to be sufficient to describe the transformation properties of the region. Figure 3 shows the estimation of the affine characteristic scale for interest points in synthetic and real world images. The real world

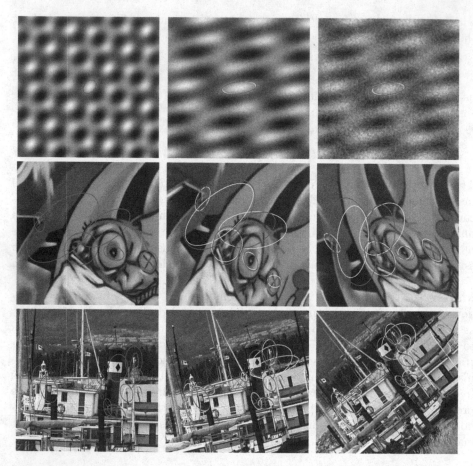

Fig. 3. Left column: Reference frames with estimated affine characteristic scales. Middle and right column: Estimated affine characteristic scales (yellow) and affine characteristics scales mapped by ground truth homographies (red).

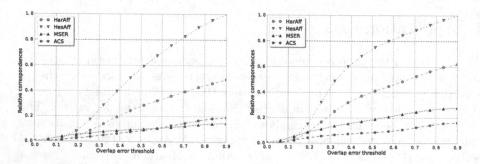

Fig. 4. Relative correspondences of the graffiti (left) and boat sequence (right) with respect to the tolerated overlap threshold

images are part of the *graffiti* and *boat* sequences[1] which have also been used in e.g. [9]. The red ellipses in the left column show the affine characteristic scales for a few manually selected interest points for illustration purposes. They act as the reference ellipses. The remaining two columns consist of images transformed by affine transformations. The synthetic test image has additionally been perturbed by Gaussian white noise with SNR of 10dB and 2dB. Using the ground truth homographies provided by the authors, the ellipses from the reference frames are mapped to the new frames and plotted in red color. In the case of the graffiti sequence, which is subject to a projective transformation, the homography is linearized by an affine transformation. The estimated ellipses, assuming a model of $n = 3$ superimposed signals in a local neighborhood of each interest point, are depicted in yellow color. Figure 4 provides an impression of the performance of the method applied to the boat and graffiti sequences in terms of the relative correspondences between frames with respect to the overlap error of the elliptical regions introduced in [9]. To evaluate our Affine Characteristic Scale (ACS) method, initial keypoints are detected as Difference-of-Gaussian extrema as in [8]. Afterwards, at each extremum the proposed method is applied, to compute the affine equivariant regional features. The method is compared to the Harris-Affine, Hessian-Affine and MSER detector. While it is outperformed by the MSER method, our method is comparable to the Harris- and Hessian-affine methods.

5 Conclusion

We have presented a method to obtain the characteristic scale of superimposed signals, leading to an affine equivariant regional feature. In contrast to the Harris-affine and Hessian-affine region detectors, the estimation procedure is of non-iterative nature in the sense that the orientations are obtained in closed form, depending only on convolutions with Gaussian derivative filters followed by n one-dimensional exhaustive extremum searches for the steered filter responses, whose complexity depends linearly on the number of sampled scales. Consequently no scale re-estimation, as it is the case of the Harris- and Hessian-affine detectors has to be performed. Further, the filter responses for the steered band-pass filters can be pre-calculated, such that only linear combinations of the pre-calculated basis filter responses are necessary. It turned out that the estimation is accurate even under noisy conditions. The proposed regional feature can be integrated into existing algorithms or coupled with existing feature descriptors to achieve equivariance for non-uniform scale changes. Future work will include in-depth performance tests and comparisons to existing affine equivariant approaches.

References

1. Aach, T., Mota, C., Stuke, I., Mühlich, M., Barth, E.: Analysis of Superimposed Oriented Patterns. IEEE Transactions on Image Processing 15(12), 3690–3700 (2006)

---

[1] http://www.robots.ox.ac.uk/~vgg/research/affine/

2. Bracewell, R.: The Fourier Transform and its Applications. McGraw-Hill (1978)
3. Förstner, W., Gülch, E.: A Fast Operator for Detection and Precise Location of Distinct Points, Corners and Centres of Circular Features. In: Proc. Intercommission Conference on Fast Processing of Photogrammetric Data (ISPRS), pp. 281–305 (1987)
4. Freeman, W., Adelson, E.: The Design and Use of Steerable Filters. IEEE Transactions on Pattern Analysis and Machine Intelligence 13(9), 891–906 (1991)
5. Harris, C., Stephens, M.: A Combined Corner and Edge Detector. In: Alvey Vision Conference, pp. 147–152 (1988)
6. Kanatani, K.: Statistical Optimization for Geometric Computation: Theory and Practice. Elsevier Science Inc., New York (1996)
7. Lindeberg, T.: Feature Detection with Automatic Scale Selection. International Journal of Computer Vision 30(2), 79–116 (1998)
8. Lowe, D.G.: Distinctive Image Features from Scale-Invariant Keypoints. International Journal of Computer Vision 60, 91–110 (2004)
9. Mikolajczyk, K., Schmid, C.: Scale & Affine Invariant Interest Point Detectors. International Journal of Computer Vision 60(1), 63–86 (2004)

Sensitivity/Robustness Flexible Ellipticity Measures

Mehmet Ali Aktaş[1] and Joviša Žunić[1,2]

[1] University of Exeter, Computer Science
Exeter EX4 4QF, U.K.
[2] Mathematical Institute of Serbian Academy of Science and Arts, Belgrade
{M.A.Aktas,J.Zunic}@ex.ac.uk

Abstract. Ellipse is one of basic shapes used frequently for modeling in different domains. Fitting an ellipse to the certain data set is a well-studied problem. In addition the question how to measure the shape ellipticity has also been studied. The existing methods to estimate how much a given shape differs from a perfect ellipse are area based. Because of this, these methods are robust (e.g. with respect to noise or to image resolution applied). This is a desirable property when working with a low quality data, but there are also situations where methods sensitive to the presence of noise or to small object deformations, are more preferred. (e.g. in high precision inspection tasks.)

In this paper we propose a new family of ellipticity measure. The ellipticity measures are dependent on a single parameter and by varying this parameter the sensitivity/robustness properties of the related ellipticity measures, vary as well.

Independently on the parameter choice, all the new ellipticity measures are invariant with respect to the translation, scaling, and rotation transformation, they all range over $(0; 1]$ and pick 1 if and only if the shape considered is an ellipse. New measures are theoretically well founded. Because of this their behavior in particular applications is well understood and can be predicted to some extent, which is always an advantage.

Several experiments are provided illustrate the behavior and performance of the new measures.

Keywords: Shape, shape descriptors, shape ellipticity, early vision.

1 Introduction

Feature extraction and classification of objects based on their appearance is an important task in image analysis. As information objects are digitized, more and more digital images have been generated. There is a strong demand for effective tools to facilitate a fast and efficient analysis of images and object appearing on them. Several methods have been applied and used to extract feature for

A. Pinz et al. (Eds.): DAGM/OAGM 2012, LNCS 7476, pp. 307–316, 2012.
© Springer-Verlag Berlin Heidelberg 2012

analyzing objects, such as texture, colour. Shape is also an important visual feature and it is one of the basic features used to describe image content. Moreover, shape representation compared to other features, like texture and colour, is much more effective in semantically characterizing the content of an image [1]. However, the fundamental problem of shape descriptors is the accurate extraction and representation of shape characteristics of objects regardless their size and orientation. Various shape descriptors exist in the literature, mainly categorized into two groups: contour-based shape descriptors and region-based shape descriptors. Contour-based methods only exploit shape boundary information which in some cases may not be available completely. Region-based methods, however, do not rely on shape boundary information, but they take into account all the pixels within the shape region. Contour-based shape descriptors includes Fourier descriptor [4,5], wavelet descriptors [6] and curvature scale space (CSS)[7]. Region-based shape descriptors includes moment invariants [11] and Zernike moments [8]. Alternatively, there are shape descriptors which use a single characteristic of shapes: Circularity [21], sigmoidality [17], symmetry [19], etc. In this paper we deal with another region based global shape descriptor: *shape ellipticity*. We define a family of new ellipticity measures with a clear motivation: The presented technique enable us to independently control the sensitivity and robustness properties of the ellipticity measures. The new ellipticity measures are theoretically well founded, have a clear geometric meaning and have several desirable properties. Measures, from the new family, are compared with several existing ellipticity measures, on small shape ranking, shape matching and shape classification tasks, in order to illustrate their behaviour and effectiveness.

The paper is organized as follows. Section 2 gives a brief review of the existing ellipticity measures used for the comparison with the new measure. The new measure is defined in Section 3. Experimental results are presented in Section 4. The conclusions are provided in Section 5.

2   Related Work

Measuring shape properties is an important area of computer vision systems and widely applied to a vast range of image processing tasks. Application areas are identifying certain grains, onions, watermelons, cells, human faces and it is also used to ensure the quality of steel coils before they are shipped out [2,3]. A number of ellipticity measures have been proposed in the literature [9,13,14,15,18]. Different techniques were employed - e.g. Discrete Fourier Transform [14], or affine moment invariants [15].

As expected, each of these techniques has its advantages and disadvantages, and it is not easy to establish a strict ranking among them. Methods performances can vary depend on the application. In this paper, we introduce and analyze an infinite family of new shape measures, which estimate a single shape characteristic: *Ellipticity*.

We begin a short overview, of the existing ellipticity measures, with a recent measure $\mathcal{E}_I(S)$ defined in [15]. The measure $\mathcal{E}_I(S)$ varies through the interval

$[0, 1]$ and picks the value 1 when the considered shape S is an ellipse. A problem could be that $\mathcal{E}_I(S) = 1$ does not guarantee (or at least this has not been proven) that the measured shape S is a perfect ellipse. Also, since $\mathcal{E}_I(S)$ is defined by using a projective invariant [10], it does not change the assigned ellipticity measure under affine transformations applied to the shape S. Of course, there are applications where such a property can be an advantage, but in some other applications it can be a disadvantage. $\mathcal{E}_I(S)$ uses the following affine moment invariant [10]:

$$I(S) = \frac{\mu_{20}(S) \cdot \mu_{02}(S) - \mu_{11}^2(S)}{\mu_{00}^4(S)} \tag{1}$$

and is defined as follows:

$$\mathcal{E}_I(S) = \begin{cases} 16 \cdot \pi^2 \cdot I(S) & \text{if } I(S) \leq \dfrac{1}{16\pi^2} \\ \dfrac{1}{16 \cdot \pi^2 \cdot I(S)} & \text{otherwise.} \end{cases} \tag{2}$$

The quantities $\mu_{p,q}(S) = \iint_S \left(x - \frac{\iint_S x\, dx\, dy}{\iint_S dx\, dy} \right)^p \left(y - \frac{\iint_S y\, dx\, dy}{\iint_S dx\, dy} \right)^q dx\, dy$, appearing in (1), are well known as the centralized moments [18].

There are also some standard approaches which can be used to define an ellipticity measure. For example, the most common method [18] to determine an ellipse $E_f(S)$ which fits with a given shape S, also uses the moments for the computation. The major axis and minor axis of $E_f(S)$ are [18]:

$$major\ axis = \sqrt{\mu_{2,0}(S) + \mu_{0,2}(S) + \sqrt{4 \cdot (\mu_{1,1}(S))^2 + (\mu_{2,0}(S) - \mu_{0,2}(S))^2}} \tag{3}$$

$$minor\ axis = \sqrt{\mu_{2,0}(S) + \mu_{0,2}(S) - \sqrt{4 \cdot (\mu_{1,1}(S))^2 + (\mu_{2,0}(S) - \mu_{0,2}(S))^2}}, \tag{4}$$

respectively. Notice that the ratio between the major axis and minor axis well known as *the shape elongation* measure.

The angle φ between the major axis of $E_f(S)$ and the x-axis is computed from

$$\tan(2 \cdot \varphi) = \frac{2\mu_{11}(S)}{\mu_{20}(S) - \mu_{02}(S)}. \tag{5}$$

Now, we can define an ellipticity measure $\mathcal{E}_f(S)$ by comparing a given shape S and the ellipse $SE_f(S)$, which is actually the ellipse $E_f(S)$ scaled such that the area of S and the area of $E_f(S)$ coincide, and translated such that the centroids of $E_f(S)$ coincides with the centroid of S. A possible definition is:

$$\mathcal{E}_f(S) = \frac{Area(S \cap SE_f(S))}{Area(S \cup SE_f(S))}. \tag{6}$$

The angle φ, defined as in (5), is very often used to define the shape orientation [18]. The problem is that this method for the computation of the shape orientation fails in many situations, but also can be very unreliable [20]. Because of that, we modify the $\mathcal{E}_f(S)$ measure by replacing $SE_f(S)$ in (6) by rotating $SE_f(S)$

around the centroid for an angle θ which maximizes the area of $S \cap SE_f(S)$. If such a rotated ellipse $SE_f(S)$ is denoted by $SE_f(S(\theta))$ then we define a new ellipticity measure $\mathcal{E}_{fm}(S)$ as:

$$\mathcal{E}_{fm}(S) = \frac{Area(S \cap SE_f(S(\theta)))}{Area(S \cup SE_f(S(\theta)))}. \tag{7}$$

All three measures $\mathcal{E}_I(S)$, $\mathcal{E}_f(S)$, and $\mathcal{E}_{fm}(S)$, mentioned above, as well as ellipticity measures defined in the next section, are area based. This means that all the interior points are used for their computation. This enables us to say that all the shapes whose mutual set differences have the area equal to zero, are equal. For example, the shape of an open circular disc $\{(x,y) \mid x^2 + y^2 < 1\}$ and the shape of the closed one $\{(x,y) \mid x^2 + y^2 \le 1\}$ will be considered as equal shapes. Obviously, this is not a restriction in image processing tasks, but will simplify our proofs.

3   Methodology

In this section we introduce a family of ellipticity measures and give some desirable properties of them.

For our derivation we need an auxiliary ellipse $\mathbf{E}(S)$, defined for a given shape S, in the following way

$$\mathbf{E}(S) = \left\{ (x,y) \mid \frac{\pi}{\rho(S)} \cdot x^2 + (\pi \cdot \rho(S)) \cdot y^2 \le 1 \right\}. \tag{8}$$

In the above equation $\rho(S)$ is the ratio between the major-axis and the minor-axis of S, defined as in (3) and (4). Notice that the area of $\mathbf{E}(S)$ is 1.

The ellipse $\mathbf{E}(S)$ can be expressed in many different ways. Indeed, let $\lambda > 0$ and let the function $\Phi_\lambda(x,y)$ be defined as

$$\Phi_\lambda(x,y) = \left(\frac{\pi}{\rho(S)} \cdot x^2 + (\pi \cdot \rho(S)) \cdot y^2 \right)^\lambda, \tag{9}$$

then

$$\mathbf{E}(S) = \{(x,y) \mid \Phi_\lambda(x,y) \le 1\} \qquad \text{for all } \lambda > 0. \tag{10}$$

It is easy to see that regions on the right side of (8) and (10) are both bounded by the same curve given by the equation $\Phi_\lambda(x,y) = 1$, which does not depend on λ. I.e. the equations $\Phi_\lambda(x,y) = 1$ and $\Phi_\gamma(x,y) = 1$ are equivalent for all $\lambda, \gamma > 0$.

Now, we give the theorem which gives the theoretical foundations for our definition of the new ellipcity measures.

Theorem 1. *Let a given shape S whose area is 1 and whose centroid coincides with the origin. Let $S(\alpha)$ be the shape S rotated around the origin for an angle α, and let fix $\lambda > 0$. Then:*

(a) $\displaystyle\iint_S \Phi_\lambda(x,y)\ dx\ dy = \iint_{\mathbf{E}(S)} \Phi_\lambda(x,y)\ dx\ dy \quad \Rightarrow \quad S = \mathbf{E}(S);$

(b) $\displaystyle\min_{\alpha\in(0,2\pi]}\iint_{S(\alpha)} \Phi_\lambda(x,y)\ dx\ dy = \frac{1}{1+\lambda} \quad \Leftrightarrow \quad S \text{ is an ellipse.}$

Proof. (a) Fix $\lambda > 0$. Since all the points (x,y) satisfying $\Phi_\lambda(x,y) \le 1$ are inside the ellipse $\mathbf{E}(S)$ (see (10)) we deduce

$$(x,y) \in \mathbf{E}(S) \quad \text{and} \quad (u,v) \notin \mathbf{E}(S) \quad \Rightarrow \quad \Phi_\lambda(x,y) \le 1 < \Phi_\lambda(u,v). \qquad (11)$$

Let us assume that the shapes S and $\mathbf{E}(S)$ are different, i.e.

$$\Delta = Area(S \setminus \mathbf{E}(S)) = Area(\mathbf{E}(S) \setminus S) > 0. \qquad (12)$$

The above implication (11) gives

$$\iint_{S\setminus\mathbf{E}(S)} \Phi_\lambda(x,y)\ dx\ dy \ge \iint_{\mathbf{E}(S)\setminus S} \Phi_\lambda(x,y)\ dx\ dy \qquad (13)$$

and further

$$\iint_S \Phi_\lambda(x,y)\ dx\ dy \ge \iint_{\mathbf{E}(S)} \Phi_\lambda(x,y)\ dx\ dy. \qquad (14)$$

Finally, the required implication (in *(a)*) follows from the fact that the equality $\iint_S \phi_\lambda(x,y)dxdy = \iint_{\mathbf{E}(S)} \Phi_\lambda(x,y)dxdy$ holds if and only if

$$\iint_{S\setminus\mathbf{E}(S)} \Phi_\lambda(x,y)\ dx\ dy = \iint_{\mathbf{E}(S)\setminus S} \Phi_\lambda(x,y)\ dx\ dy = 0$$

(a direct consequence of (11) and (14)) – i.e., if the shapes S and $\mathbf{E}(S)$ are equal.

(b) This item follows from *(a)*, which actually says that $\iint_{S(\alpha)}\Phi_\lambda(x,y)dxdy$ reaches the minimum possible value $\dfrac{1}{1+\lambda}$ (notice $\dfrac{1}{1+\lambda} = \iint_{\mathbf{E}(S)} \Phi_\lambda(x,y)dxdy$ and see (14)) if there is an angle α such that $S(\alpha) = \mathbf{E}(S)$. $\qquad\square$

By the arguments of Theorem 1 we define the following ellipticity measure.

Definition 1. *Let a given shape S and let $\lambda > 0$. The ellipticity $\mathcal{E}_\lambda(S)$ of S is defined as*

$$\mathcal{E}_\lambda(S) = \frac{1}{1+\lambda} \cdot \frac{Area(S)^{1+\lambda}}{\min_{\alpha\in[0,2\pi]} \iint_{S(\alpha)} \Phi_\lambda(x,y)\ dx\ dy} \qquad (15)$$

where $\Phi_\lambda(x,y)$ is defined as in (9) and $S(\alpha)$ denotes the shape S rotated around the origin for an angle α.

Now, we summarize desirable properties of $\mathcal{E}(S)$.

Theorem 2. *All ellipticity measures $\mathcal{E}_\lambda(S)$, $\lambda > 0$, have the following properties:*

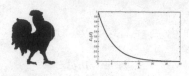

Fig. 1. Two shapes and their corresponding graphs $\mathcal{E}_\lambda(S)$, for $\lambda \in [0.1, 30]$

(a) $\mathcal{E}_\lambda(S) \in (0, 1]$;
(b) $\mathcal{E}_\lambda(S) = 1$ *if and only if S is an ellipse;*
(c) $\mathcal{E}_\lambda(S)$ *is invariant with respect translation, rotation and scaling transformations.*

Proof. The proof of *(a)* and *(b)* follows from Theorem 1. $\mathcal{E}_\lambda(S)$ is translation and rotation invariant from the definition. Basic calculus is sufficient to prove the scaling invariance of $\mathcal{E}_\lambda(S)$. □

Fig. 3 shows how $\mathcal{E}_\lambda(S)$ changes if S is fixed and λ varies. Two shapes and their corresponding graphs $\mathcal{E}_\lambda(S)$ for λ varing through the interval $\in [0.1, 30]$ are displayed.

4   Evaluation

In this section we give several experimental results which illustrate the behavior of $\mathcal{E}_\lambda(S)$ measures and compare them with the behavior of related measures $\mathcal{E}_f(S)$, $\mathcal{E}_{fm}(S)$, and $\mathcal{E}_I(S)$.

First Experiment. In this experiment we illustrate how the sensitivity of the ellipcity measures $\mathcal{E}_\lambda$ vary if λ varies. The shape in Fig.2(a) is an ellipse with noise added. As expected, $\mathcal{E}_f$, $\mathcal{E}_{fm}$, and $\mathcal{E}_I$, being area based measures, assign a very high ellipticity, close to 1, and do not make much difference between this "noise shape" and a perfect ellipse. As intended, new measures assign ellipcity values from a wider interval, and depending on our preference may ignore the presence of noise (e.g. by setting $\lambda = 0.5$) or strongly penalize such a presence (e.g. by setting $\lambda = 20$ when the ellipticity assigned becomes less than 0.7). Similar comments hold for the next two shapes. Shape in Fig.2(b) is bounded by a polygonal approximation of an ellipse, and the shape in Fig.2(c) is an ellipse with noise added to its boundary.

Second Experiment. Ten arbitrary shapes are in Fig.3. They are listed in accordance with the increasing $\mathcal{E}_{\lambda=2}(S)$ measure. The computed measures $\mathcal{E}_{\lambda=2}(S)$, $\mathcal{E}_f(S)$, $\mathcal{E}_{fm}(S)$, and $\mathcal{E}_I(S)$ are in the table below the shapes.

First. This experiment illustrates that the measures $\mathcal{E}_\lambda(S)$ essentially differs from $\mathcal{E}_f(S)$, $\mathcal{E}_{fm}(S)$, and $\mathcal{E}_I(S)$. Indeed, if we consider the rankings

$$\mathcal{E}_{\lambda=2} : (b)(c)(d)(e)(f)(g)(h)(i)(j); \quad \mathcal{E}_f : (b)(d)(e)(c)(f)(g)(j)(i)(h);$$
$$\mathcal{E}_{fm} : (b)(d)(e)(c)(f)(g)(j)(h)(i); \quad \mathcal{E}_I : (c)(b)(d)(e)(g)(f)(i)(j)(h);$$

obtained by these 4 measures, we see that the ranking obtained $\mathcal{E}_{\lambda=2}(S)$ differs from the rankings obtained by $\mathcal{E}_f(S)$, $\mathcal{E}_{fm}(S)$, and $\mathcal{E}_I(S)$. Thus, they might be

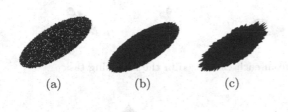

	(a)	(b)	(c)
$\mathcal{E}_{\lambda=0.5}$	0.9915	0.9971	0.9957
$\mathcal{E}_{\lambda=1}$	0.9830	0.9943	0.9914
$\mathcal{E}_{\lambda=4.5}$	0.9256	0.9745	0.9619
$\mathcal{E}_{\lambda=10}$	0.8422	0.9442	0.9172
$\mathcal{E}_{\lambda=20}$	0.6832	0.8915	0.8413
$\mathcal{E}_f$	0.9667	0.9449	0.9276
$\mathcal{E}_{fm}$	0.9796	0.9462	0.9322
$\mathcal{E}_I$	0.9676	0.9922	0.9849

Fig. 2. Shapes similar to a perfect ellipse are is measured with $\mathcal{E}_\lambda$, for $\lambda \in$ $\{0.5, 1, 4.5, 10, 20\}$, and with $\mathcal{E}_f$, $\mathcal{E}_{fm}$, and $\mathcal{E}_I$

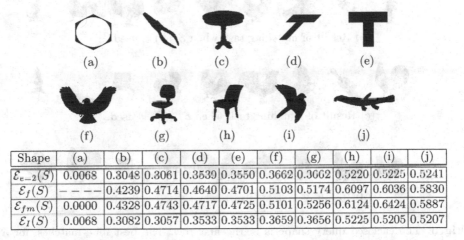

Shape	(a)	(b)	(c)	(d)	(e)	(f)	(g)	(h)	(i)	(j)
$\mathcal{E}_{e-2}(S)$	0.0068	0.3048	0.3061	0.3539	0.3550	0.3662	0.3662	0.5220	0.5225	0.5241
$\mathcal{E}_f(S)$	$----$	0.4239	0.4714	0.4640	0.4701	0.5103	0.5174	0.6097	0.6036	0.5830
$\mathcal{E}_{fm}(S)$	0.0000	0.4328	0.4743	0.4717	0.4725	0.5101	0.5256	0.6124	0.6424	0.5887
$\mathcal{E}_I(S)$	0.0068	0.3082	0.3057	0.3533	0.3533	0.3659	0.3656	0.5225	0.5205	0.5207

Fig. 3. Shapes are displayed in accordance with their increased $\mathcal{E}_{\lambda=2}(S)$ measure

considered as essentially different and can be combined in some classification, matching or recognition tasks.

Second. Fig.3(a) illustrates that the new measure can be applied to the shapes which are N-fold rotationally symmetric or which have big holes, without any restriction. This is not true for $\mathcal{E}_f(S)$ (cannot be applied to rotationally symmetric shapes [20]), and for $\mathcal{E}_{fm}(S) = 0$ (gives the ellipticity value 0 for shapes with big holes which do not intersects with $SE_f(S)$)).

Third Experiment. In this experiment a shape matching task was performed. For this experiment the MPEG7 CE Shape-1 Part-B database was used. 140 images were chosen from 7 different classes: chicken, lizzard, lmfish, rat, ray, tree, turtle – for some examples see Fig.4 . The image "chicken-14" was selected as the query image (the enclosed shape in Fig.5).

A very good matching result was obtained for a new ellipticity measure and for $\lambda = 2.5$. If $\mathcal{E}_{\lambda=2.5}(S)$ is used for the matching 6 out of 9 best matches were chicken. These shapes are displayed in the first row in Fig.5). The experiment

Fig. 4. Example images from each class used in the matching task

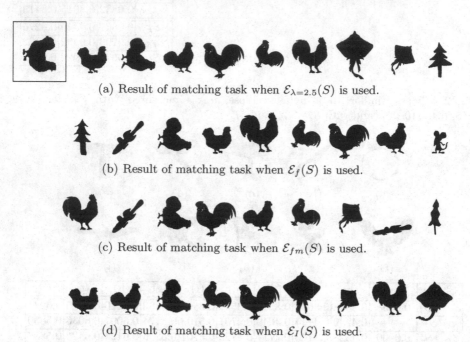

(a) Result of matching task when $\mathcal{E}_{\lambda=2.5}(S)$ is used.

(b) Result of matching task when $\mathcal{E}_f(S)$ is used.

(c) Result of matching task when $\mathcal{E}_{fm}(S)$ is used.

(d) Result of matching task when $\mathcal{E}_I(S)$ is used.

Fig. 5. The enclosed query shape is in the first row. The best nine matches, for a different choice of ellipticity measures used, are displayed in the corresponding rows.

was repeated by using the measure form the set $\{\mathcal{E}_f(S),\ \mathcal{E}_{fm}(S),\ \mathcal{E}_I(S)\}$ and the best 9 matches are displayed in the corresponding rows.

Fourth Experiment. This experiment is a classification task. The well known [12] data set consists of 112 galaxy images (100×100 pixels). The corresponding galaxies belong to three groups: spiral,lenticular and elliptical. We have used binary images (i.e. images are thresholded [16] before the classification, as shown in Fig.6) for the classification.

Five classification tasks by using a single ellipticity measure from $\{\mathcal{E}_{\lambda=1}(S),$ $\{\mathcal{E}_{\lambda=5}(S),\ \mathcal{E}_f(S),\ \mathcal{E}_{fm}(S),\ \mathcal{E}_I(S)\}$ were performed. k-NN classifier, with $k = 5$ was used and $\approx 30\%$ of galaxy-images, from each classes were used for the training while the remaining images were used for testing. The classification rates obtained are displayed in the table in Fig.6. It can be seen that $\mathcal{E}_{\lambda=1}(S)$ (74.22% classification rate achieved) has performed better than the measures $\mathcal{E}_f(S)$ (70.10%), $\mathcal{E}_{fm}(S)$ (69.07%), and $\mathcal{E}_I(S)$ (72.16%).

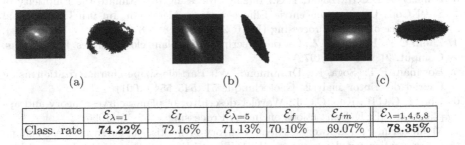

(a)   (b)   (c)

	$\mathcal{E}_{\lambda=1}$	$\mathcal{E}_I$	$\mathcal{E}_{\lambda=5}$	$\mathcal{E}_f$	$\mathcal{E}_{fm}$	$\mathcal{E}_{\lambda=1,4,5,8}$
Class. rate	**74.22%**	72.16%	71.13%	70.10%	69.07%	**78.35%**

Fig. 6. Sample galaxy images with their shapes extracted by thresholding [16]. The galaxy on the left (a) is spiral, the galaxy in (b) is lenticular and the galaxy in (c) is elliptical. The classification rate obtained are in the table.

Finally, since a family of ellipcity measures was obtained, we have used the opportunity to combine several of them to increase the classification accuracy. An increase of classification accuracy to 78.35% was obtained by using four dimensional feature vectors for the classification. The feature vector components were the following ellipticity measures: $\mathcal{E}_{\lambda=1}(S)$, $\mathcal{E}_{\lambda=4}(S)$, $\mathcal{E}_{\lambda=5}(S)$, and $\mathcal{E}_{\lambda=8}(S)$). The same 5-NN classifier and the same split 70%/30% of training/test images were used.

5 Conclusion

This paper introduces a family of ellipticity measures $\mathcal{E}_\lambda(S)$, where λ is a positive number. The robustness/sensitivity of measures from the family can be controlled by a suitable choice of the parameter λ. All measures from the family range over $(0, 1]$ and give 1 if and only if the measured shape is an ellipse. Also, they are invariant with respect to translation, rotation and scaling transformations.

All the measures from the family are well motivated and theoretically well founded. They have a clear geometric interpretation which enables a better understanding of their behavior and an appriory prediction (to some extent) how well they suit a certain application.

Several experimental results are provided to illustrate the behavior of the new measures and to demonstrate their applicability in different tasks.

References

1. Persoon, E., Fu, K.: Shape discrimination using Fourier descriptors. IEEE Trans. Systems, Man and Cybernetics 7, 170–179 (1977)
2. Stojmenovic, M., Nayak, A.: Direct Ellipse Fitting and Measuring Based on Shape Boundaries. In: Mery, D., Rueda, L. (eds.) PSIVT 2007. LNCS, vol. 4872, pp. 221–235. Springer, Heidelberg (2007)

3. Schleicher, D.C.H., Zagar, B.G.: Image Processing to Estimate the Ellipticity of Steel Coils Using a Concentric Ellipse Fitting Algorithm. In: 9th International Conference on Signal Processing (ICSP 2008), pp. 884–890 (2008)
4. Zahn, C.T., Roskies, R.Z.: Fourier descriptors for plane closed curves. IEEE Trans. Comput. 21, 269–281 (1972)
5. Bowman, E.T., Soga, K., Drummond, W.: Particle shape characterization using Fourier descriptor analysis. Geotechnique 51, 545–554 (2001)
6. Chang, G.C.H., Kuo, C.C.J.: Wavelet descriptor of planer curves: theory and applications. IEEE Transactions on Image Processing 5, 56–70 (1996)
7. Mokhtarian, F., Mackworth, A.K.: A theory of multiscale, curvature-based shape representation for planer curves. IEEE Transactions on Pattern Analysis and Machine Intelligence 14, 789–805 (1992)
8. Khotanzad, A., Hong, Y.H.: Invariant image recognition by Zernike moments. IEEE Transactions on Pattern Analysis and Machine Intelligence 12, 489–498 (1990)
9. Fitzgibbon, A.M., Pilu, M., Fisher, R.B.: Direct least square fitting of ellipses. IEEE Transaction on Pattern Analysis and Machine Intelligence 21, 476–480 (1999)
10. Flusser, J., Suk, T.: Pattern recognition by affine moment invariants. Pattern Recognition 26, 167–174 (1993)
11. Hu, M.: Visual Pattern recognition by moment invariants. IRE Trans. Inf. Theory 8, 179–187 (1962)
12. Lekshmi, S., Revathy, K., Prabhakaran Nayar, S.R.: Galaxy classification using fractal signature. Astronomy and Astrophysics 405, 1163–1167 (2003)
13. Peura, M., Iivarinen, J.: Efficiency of simple shape descriptors. In: Arcelli, C., Cordella, L.P., Sanniti di Baja, G. (eds.) Aspects of Visual Form Processing, pp. 443–451. World Scientific, Singapore (1997)
14. Proffitt, D.: The measurement of circularity and ellipticity on a digital grid. Pattern Recognition 15, 383–387 (1982)
15. Rosin, P.L.: Measuring shape: ellipticity, rectangularity, and triangularity. Machine Vision and Applications 14, 172–184 (2003)
16. Otsu, N.: A threshold selection method from gray level histograms. IEEE Trans. Systems, Man and Cybernetics 9, 62–66 (1979)
17. Rosin, P.L.: Measuring sigmoidality. Pattern Recognition 37, 1735–1744 (2004)
18. Sonka, M., Hlavac, V., Boyle, R.: Image Processing, Analysis, and Machine Vision. Thomson-Engineering (2007)
19. Zabrodsky, H., Peleg, S., Avnir, D.: Symmetry as a continuous feature. IEEE Transactions on Pattern Analysis and Machine Intelligence 17, 1154–1166 (1995)
20. Žunić, J., Kopanja, L., Fieldsend, J.E.: Notes on shape orientation where the standard method does not work. Pattern Recognition 39, 856–865 (2006)
21. Žunić, J., Hirota, K., Rosin, P.L.: A Hu moment invariant as a shape circularity measure. Pattern Recognition 43, 47–57 (2010)

Sparse Point Estimation for Bayesian Regression via Simulated Annealing

Sudhir Raman and Volker Roth

Department of Mathematics and Computer Science, University of Basel,
Bernoullistr. 16, CH-4056 Basel, Switzerland
{sudhir.raman,volker.roth}@unibas.ch

Abstract. In the context of variable selection in a regression model, the classical Lasso based optimization approach provides a sparse estimate with respect to regression coefficients but is unable to provide more information regarding the distribution of regression coefficients. Alternatively, using a Bayesian approach is more advantageous since it gives direct access to the distribution which is usually summarized by estimating the expectation (not sparse) and variance. Additionally, to support frequent application requirements, heuristics like thresholding are generally used to produce sparse estimates for variable selection purposes. In this paper, we provide a more principled approach for generating a sparse point estimate in a Bayesian framework. We extend an existing Bayesian framework for sparse regression to generate a MAP estimate by using simulated annealing. We then justify this extension by showing that this MAP estimate is also sparse in the regression coefficients. Experiments on real world applications like the splice site detection and diabetes progression demonstrate the usefulness of the extension.

1 Introduction

One of the frequently encountered modeling scenarios in various application domains like image, text and biological data analysis involves high-dimensional data with small number of measurements. In such situations, finding meaningful explanations to data through simpler models is often desired. We now relate this modeling scenario to a standard linear regression model which explains real-valued observations $y = (y_1, \ldots, y_n)^t$ as products of input vectors $x_i \in \mathbb{R}^d$ and regression coefficients $\beta = (\beta_1, \ldots, \beta_d)^t$, with additional additive noise:

$$y_i = x_i^t \beta + \epsilon_i \Leftrightarrow y = X\beta + \epsilon, \quad \text{where} \ \epsilon_i \sim N(0, \sigma^2) \tag{1}$$

where X is the $n \times d$ design matrix containing the vectors of input variables as rows and the noise terms ϵ_i's are uncorrelated. In many practical applications of regression, we are not only interested in estimating coefficients β which are good for predicting the target variable y, but also in identifying significant factors through models which are sparse in β. These significant factors may correspond to individual input variables and higher-order interactions (like pair-wise and

A. Pinz et al. (Eds.): DAGM/OAGM 2012, LNCS 7476, pp. 317–326, 2012.
© Springer-Verlag Berlin Heidelberg 2012

triplet interactions), and sparsity in this context interprets to a classical variable selection problem. The Lasso (ℓ_1-norm) constraint on β as introduced in [16] has been a popular choice for imposing sparsity with respect to regression coefficients. Solving this optimization problem results in estimates which are *sparse* in β. From an application perspective, variable selection via these sparse estimates is often useful in deciding a future course of action. Various efficient algorithms exist for solving this problem (see [3] for example). However, they fail to provide more detailed information regarding the posterior distribution over the regression coefficients. To address this shortcoming, a Bayesian formulation of the Lasso has been introduced in [11] and generalized to varying sparsity levels in [2]. These models have been extended to handle sparsity on grouped variables in [12] and [5], which is a probabilistic counterpart for the Group-Lasso defined in [19]. A common feature of these models is the introduction of *auxiliary variables*, which makes inference feasible through MCMC sampling and these variables are later integrated out stochastically during the process of inference. The generated samples can be used to summarize the posterior distribution over regression coefficients in traditional ways like estimates for the expectation and variances. Since the estimate of the first moment is not sparse, variable selection is usually carried out using heuristics like thresholding (see [12]).

In this work, we define a more principled approach for sparse point estimation in a Bayesian framework. As a result, we obtain an omnibus framework which is capable of producing different estimates based on varying application requirements. We extend an existing Bayesian framework for sparse regression defined in [13] to additionally generate a MAP estimate. This extension is based on simulated annealing (SA) (as defined in [8] and [17]) and is achieved by introducing a computational temperature parameter to the existing framework. Since all annealed conditional posterior distributions are of standard form, the annealing is carried out using Gibbs sampling. It is, however, non-trivial to assume that the MAP estimate produced by annealing will also be sparse in β. An important part of this work involves showing that inspite of this change, the joint MAP estimate is sparse in the regression coefficients, with an adjusted value of the sparsity parameter in the model. As a result, we derive the upper bound of this parameter through a special case of the Lasso to ensure that solutions produced below such a threshold value of this parameter are guaranteed to be sparse.

2   Method

2.1   Existing Bayesian Framework Description

We begin by describing the classical Lasso with respect to a standard regression problem given by eqn. (1):

$$\min \|\boldsymbol{y} - X\boldsymbol{\beta}\|_2^2 \text{ subject to } \|\boldsymbol{\beta}\|_1 \leq \kappa. \tag{2}$$

By translating the Lasso constraint to a suitable prior over the regression coefficients, a Bayesian view of the same problem is expressed as:

$$p(\boldsymbol{\beta}|X, \boldsymbol{y}, \sigma^2) \propto N(\boldsymbol{y}|X\boldsymbol{\beta}, \sigma^2)\, p(\boldsymbol{\beta}), \tag{3}$$

We use the prior defined in [13] since it caters to generalized linear models and grouped variable selection and has an extra parameter for tuning the prior to achieve varying levels of sparsity. The prior over β is expressed as a two-level hierarchical model, by introducing auxiliary variables Λ:

$$p(\beta, \Lambda | \mathbf{X}, \sigma^2, \alpha, \rho) \propto \prod_{g=1}^{d} N(\beta_g | 0, \lambda_g^2 \sigma^2 I) \prod_{g=1}^{d} \text{Gamma}\left(\lambda_g^2 | \alpha, \frac{\rho}{2}\right), \qquad (4)$$

where Λ is a $(d \times d)$ diagonal matrix consisting of λ_g^2's as diagonal elements. We denote the marginal prior $p(\beta | \alpha, \sigma^2, \rho)$ (after integrating out Λ) as P_M. The parameter α controls the nature of sparsity inducing properties of P_M. Particularly, $\alpha = 1$ is the Bayesian Lasso case with P_M as a product of Laplacian distributions Here, $\alpha = 1$ forms an upper bound below which P_M is sparsity inducing. The key advantage of this parameter is that sparser solutions can be generated by decreasing this parameter without resulting in excessive global shrinkage of the regression coefficients. The parameters ρ and σ play the role of the Lagrangian parameter $\left(= \sqrt{\rho \sigma^2}\right)$ in the classical Lasso. Further, standard conjugate hyperpriors are introduced for ρ and σ^2. The complete hierarchical model including all the hyperpriors is given in Figure 1. The introduction of Λ makes all the

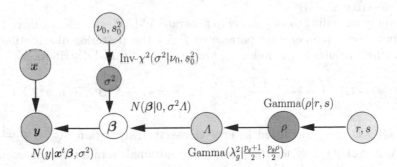

Fig. 1. The full hierarchical model for the Bayesian Group-Lasso - The different colors indicate different roles of the variables in the model. Green - given observations, cyan - auxiliary variable, brownish - model selection parameters, blue - fixed hyperparameters.

posterior conditional distributions of standard form. Hence, it is straightforward to apply Gibbs sampling to generate samples from the posterior distribution over the parameters and then summarize the distribution using these samples. The summary usually includes estimates of the expectation and variance of the regression coefficients as shown in [12]. Also, the geometric ergodicity of the Gibbs sampler for the Lasso (see [9]) indicates rapid convergence of the sampler.

A shortcoming of the model discussed so far is that the estimate of expectation thus obtained is not sparse in β. To obtain a truly sparse β estimate for variable selection, we extend this model to generate a MAP estimate over the parameters and justify that this MAP estimate is non-trivially sparse in β. As mentioned earlier, σ^2 and ρ together form the Lagrange parameter in the regularized regression framework and can be viewed as model selection parameters. Hence, we estimate the expected values of σ^2 and ρ from the samples generated so far and use it to find the MAP over the remaining variables β and Λ.

2.2   Extension - MAP Estimate via Simulated Annealing

An annealing procedure involves generating samples from a posterior distribution parameterized by an extra computational temperature parameter T. Samples are generated from this parameterized distribution, starting with the original distribution ($T = 1$), and slowly reducing T based on a cooling schedule. Although standard results exist for asymptotic convergence of this procedure to the mode for discrete domains, it is much harder to prove convergence for continuous spaces in general. However, convergence results do exist for specific cases. For example, convergence in continuous domains for a specific version of the Metropolis sampler is shown in [4]. [1] uses Foster-Lyapanov criteria for proving convergence for non-compact spaces under specific conditions. Other results involve proving convergence under suitable hypothesis for diffusion processes (see [15];[6]) and analyzing their discretized versions [14]. Although not formally shown here, empirical observations support the assumption of convergence for Gibbs sampling in our case (see also [7]).

We apply annealing to our model to generate a MAP estimate, by introducing a computational temperature parameter T for the posterior distribution over (β, Λ), which results in the following posterior conditional distributions:

$$p(\lambda_g^2|\bullet) \sim \text{GIG}\left(\frac{\alpha - 1.5 + T}{T}, \frac{\rho}{T}, \frac{b_g}{T}\right), \quad p(\beta|\bullet) \sim N(\beta|\widetilde{\Sigma}X^t y, \sigma^2 T \widetilde{\Sigma}), \quad (5)$$

where GIG is the generalized inverse Gaussian distribution, $b_g = \frac{\|\beta_g\|_2^2}{\sigma^2}$ and $\widetilde{\Sigma} = (X^t X + \Lambda^{-1})^{-1}$. Since the posterior conditionals retain the same standard forms as in the original problem with only a change in the parameters, we again use Gibbs sampling. The detailed sampling steps are described in Algorithm 1. Next, we discuss the properties of this joint MAP estimate with respect to sparsity of β and justify that it serves our initial goal of finding a sparse estimate of β.

2.3   Sparsity Properties of the Joint MAP Estimate

We define two MAP estimation problems related to this model. The first one is the joint MAP estimate of the regression coefficients and the auxiliary variables on which the annealing algorithm in the previous section is based:

Definition 1 MAP_1: $\arg\max\limits_{\beta, \Lambda} p(\beta, \Lambda|\bullet)$.

The second MAP estimate is obtained from the classical Lasso:

Algorithm 1. Gibbs Sampling for Simulated Annealing

1: **Initialize:** Parameters $\beta, \sigma^2, \rho, \Lambda$.
2: T = 1
3: **for** $m = 1$ to BayesIter **do**
4:     Sample $\rho|\beta, \sigma^2, \Lambda, y, \alpha, D$ - from a gamma distribution.
5:     Sample $\Lambda |\beta, \sigma^2, \rho, y, \alpha, D$ - from a generalized inverse Gaussian distribution.
6:     Sample $\beta, \sigma^2 |\rho, \Lambda, y, \alpha, D$ - σ^2 is sampled from an inverse-chi square distribution
         and β conditioned on σ^2 from a multivariate normal distribution.
7: **end for**
8: Fix (σ^2, ρ) to the expected values based on posterior samples.
9: Repeat steps 3 to 7 with the annealed posterior conditionals reducing T based on
    a cooling function.

Definition 2 MAP_2: $\arg \max\limits_{\beta,\alpha=1} \int p(\beta|\Lambda, \bullet)p(\Lambda|\bullet)d\Lambda,$

where the auxiliary variable Λ is integrated out. As is evident from the classical
Lasso, MAP_2 will result in a sparse estimate of β. Also, MAP_2 defines a threshold
$\hat{\alpha} = 1$ below which the solutions will tend to be sparse. Our goal is to show that
MAP_1 is also sparse with an adjusted threshold value of α below which the
sparsity of solutions is guaranteed.

Proposition 1. *The solution of MAP_1 for $\alpha = 1.5$, and the solution of MAP_2
for $\alpha = 1$ coincide with respect to β and hence is sparse in β.*

The detailed proof of this proposition based on variational formulation is given
in Appendix A. Having shown the sparsity of MAP_1 for $\alpha = 1.5$, the next step
is to show that this value of α is an upper bound, below which the solutions for
MAP_1 are guaranteed to be sparse in β. We proceed as in proposition 1 and details are shown in Appendix B. In summary, we have shown that the joint MAP
estimate produced by SA is *sparse* in the regression coefficients for $\alpha \leq 1.5$ and
hence can be used, in addition to the estimates of the first and second moments,
to summarize the posterior over the regression coefficients. As a result, it offers
a more principled approach to variable selection in the Bayesian regime.

Other Extensions. The annealing extension can also be generalized to grouped-
variable selection and to specific generalized linear models using the model defined in [13]. For generalized linear models the only addition to the algorithm
is the sampling of an extra auxiliary variable η. Before the annealing step, it
is fixed to its expected value, as was done for ρ and σ^2, in order to avoid an
undesirable mixing problem in the sampler. The annealing part of the algorithm
remains the same. The sparsity properties for these extended models can be
derived in the same way as before. For grouped variable selection, β is divided
into G groups/sub-vectors each group g of size p_g. Derived in a similar way, the
final threshold value for $\alpha = \min\limits_{g} \left(\frac{p_g+2}{p_g+1} \right)$. Since $\alpha \geq 1$, setting $\alpha = 1$ guarantees
a sparse solution.

3   Real World Applications

3.1   Variable Selection for Disease Progression in Diabetes

Our first application involves variable selection in the context of disease progression for diabetes patients (see [3]). The data consists of $n = 442$ diabetes patients and $d = 10$ variables measured for each patient and is available as a part of the LARS R package. The response is a measure of disease progression. The inference was first carried out using the optimization based algorithm in the LARS package. The solution paths of all the coefficients produced by the LARS package are shown in Figure 2 top-left panel. But the optimization based framework does not provide any further information regarding the posterior distribution over the regression coefficients as opposed to the Bayesian framework. To obtain more posterior information for the same dataset, we ran the Gibbs sampling steps without annealing (i.e. till step 7 in the algorithm) for 5000 iterations. A box plot of the samples is shown in Figure 2 top-right panel. It provides more detailed information about the variances of the regression coefficients. As mentioned earlier, the estimated mean is not sparse in β. In Figure 2 bottom-left

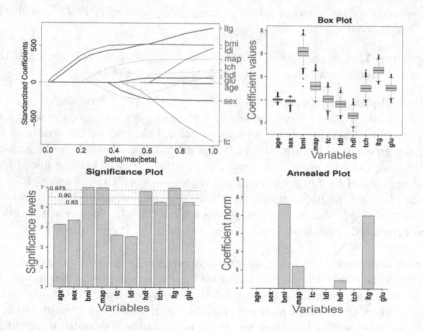

Fig. 2. TopLeft: Plot of the LASSO solution path generated from the LARS R package which contains a standard LASSO implementation. **TopRight:** A box plot of the coefficient values calculated from the samples generated from the un-annealed part of the algorithm. **BottomLeft:** A significance plot for the regression coefficients. **BottomRight:** The plot of the norms of the coefficient values after annealing resulting a truly sparse estimate.

panel, we plot the significance levels of the regression coefficient values. Variable selection can be performed by thresholding at a particular level. The plot shows three such possible thresholds, which can result in different number of variables selected and it is unclear which threshold is better. To have a more principled approach to variable selection, we execute our proposed SA part of Algorithm 1 for about 10, 000 iterations to produce a truly sparse estimate of the regression coefficients which automates the variable selection step. The cooling function that we use is geometric in nature. The final sparse output is shown in the bottom-right panel of Figure 2. Based on the above plots, we observe the advantages of the Bayesian framework which clearly provides more information regarding the posterior distribution of the regression coefficients. Additionally, our proposed extension provides a principled approach to variable selection in the Bayesian regime as opposed to heuristics like thresholding.

3.2   Analysis of Donor Splice Sites in Human DNA

The analysis of DNA sequences to locate genes is an important task in genomics. Genes, however, do not necessarily occur as a continuous sequence in the DNA, but are separated by non-coding regions known as introns. Splice sites are regions in the DNA which separate the coding regions (exons) from introns. In this paper, we focus our attention on the donor splice site, which is marked by the 5' end or the starting point of an intron. We use the MEMset Donor dataset (available at http://genes.mit.edu/burgelab/maxent/ssdata/) which is balanced (see [10]) to contain an equal number of true and false human donor sites. The data consists of a sequence of DNA of size 7 which has the last 3 positions before the splice site and first 4 positions after it. The positions are numbered as (-3,-2,-1,2,3,4,5) where positions (0,1) consist of the splice site ([18]). Following the work in [13], pairwise interactions are included and dummy variables are introduced using polynomial contrast coding. The goal of the analysis is to identify the significant interaction patterns with respect to the classification of true vs false splice sites

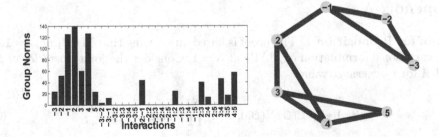

Fig. 3. Left panel: A bar graph representing the result of variable selection via simulated annealing. **Right panel:** An alternate graphical representation of the selected interactions based on the non-zero group norms. The circles indicate the individual variables and the lines indicate first-order (pairwise) interactions.

for which we use a binomial probit model. The results are described in Figure 3 which shows the interactions which were selected as a result of annealing. Most of the significant interactions are similar to the ones identified in [13] which is plausible since the model is essentially the same with the difference being the manner in which the significant interactions are obtained. An additional interaction identified by SA is the strong pairwise interaction between positions (-1:2). This observation is interesting from a biological viewpoint since it favors the role of inter-region interactions for the identification of true splice sites.

4   Conclusion

In the context of variable selection, a Bayesian framework is useful in summarizing information regarding the distribution over regression coefficients in various ways like the first and second moments. However, a truly sparse estimate in β is still missing since the expectation is not sparse. We have extended an existing Bayesian framework for sparse regression by adding a simulated annealing component in order to produce a joint MAP estimate in (β, Λ). A key part of our analysis is the justification that the joint MAP estimate over the regression coefficients and the auxiliary variables will be sparse in the regression coefficients below a threshold value of 1.5 for the sparsity parameter α. Hence, this sparse MAP estimate is useful as another form of summary of the posterior distribution over the regression coefficients. We have also extended our model to grouped variable selection and some generalized linear models.

Using applications from biology, we have shown how variable selection performed via annealing is more principled than heuristics, like thresholding, which suffer from interpretability issues. In conclusion, we have extended a Bayesian framework for sparse regression to create an omnibus framework, which can be used for summarizing the posterior over the regression coefficients through various estimates like first and second moments, and now additionally with a sparse point estimate to serve different application requirements.

Appendix A

Proof for Proposition 1. The proof is based on showing that MAP$_1$ at $\alpha = 1.5$ is a variational formulation of MAP$_2$ at $\alpha = 1$. Consider the joint posterior of β and Λ for a generic α value:

$$p(\beta, \Lambda|\bullet) \propto \mathcal{L}(\beta)N(\beta|0, \sigma^2\Lambda)\prod_{g=1}^{d}\text{Gamma}(\lambda_g^2|\alpha, \frac{\rho}{2}), \qquad (6)$$

where $\mathcal{L}()$ is the likelihood function. Setting $\alpha = 1.5$ and taking -ve log likelihood:

$$C(\beta, \Lambda) = 0.5\sum_{g=1}^{d}(\frac{\beta_g^2}{\sigma^2\lambda_g^2} + \lambda_g^2\rho) - \ln \mathcal{L}(\beta), \qquad (7)$$

where $C(\beta, \Lambda)$ is the resulting cost function which needs to be minimized (equivalent to $p(\beta, \Lambda)$ being maximized) ignoring the constant terms. First consider fixing β and finding the optimal Λ for a fixed β. Minimizing $C(\beta, \Lambda)$ for a fixed β, we obtain the optimal value of each $\lambda_g \; \forall g$ as $\hat{\lambda}_g^2 = \sqrt{\frac{\beta_g^2}{\sigma^2 \rho}}$. Hence this implies that the function $C(\beta, \Lambda)$ is an enveloping function for $C(\beta, \hat{\Lambda})$ at every β where $\hat{\Lambda} = \{\lambda_g^2\}_{g=1}^d$. Replacing $\hat{\Lambda}$ in $C(\beta, \Lambda)$ we get $C(\beta) = -\ln \mathcal{L}(\beta) + \sqrt{\frac{\rho}{\sigma^2}} \sum_{g=1}^d |\beta_g|$, where minimizing $C(\beta)$ is exactly the Lasso optimization problem or MAP_2. Solving for the optimal value for this function gives us sparse MAP estimate of β. Hence, at $\alpha = 1.5$, MAP_1 is a variational formulation of MAP_2 at $\alpha = 1$ and solving for β in either case results in a sparse point estimate.

Appendix B

Upper bound for α. As before we derive the expression for $C(\beta, \Lambda)$ and find the optimal value of λ_g for a fixed β_g. This gives us $\hat{\lambda}_g^2 = \frac{(\alpha - 1.5) + \sqrt{(\alpha - 1.5)^2 + b_g \rho}}{\rho}$. Similar to Appendix A we derive a more complicated expression for $C(\beta)$. To analyze the properties of this function, we reformulate $C(\beta)$ in probabilistic terms by considering $\exp(-C(\beta))$. This gives us back a probability expression in the form of a product of the likelihood and a prior term $\mathrm{P}_C = p(\beta | \Lambda, \alpha, \sigma^2, \rho)$, conditioned on the auxiliary variables Λ, which is clearly different from P_M where Λ was integrated out. We plotted the prior P_C in two dimensions and for

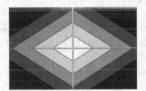

Fig. 4. Left: Plot of P_C for $\alpha = 1.5$ which resembles the Lasso constraint. **Center:** Plot of P_C for $\alpha = 1.0$ which is also observed to be a sparsity inducing prior. **Right:** Plot of P_C for $\alpha = 2.0$ which resembles a normal distribution.

three different α values (1, 1.5 and 2), giving us the resulting plots in Figure 4. At value 1.5, P_C takes the form of a product of Laplace distributions (left panel of Figure 4), which is a sparsity inducing prior. For $\alpha = 1$ P_C is still a sparsity inducing prior (right panel of Figure 4) and this is observed in general for values ≤ 1.5. Further, for $\alpha > 1.5$, P_C becomes a non-sparsity inducing prior and resembles the Gaussian distribution (see bottom panel of Figure 4). Hence $\alpha = 1.5$ becomes the adjusted threshold below which MAP_1 is sparse in β.

References

1. Andrieu, C., Breyer, L.A., Doucet, A.: Convergence of simulated annealing using Foster-Lyapunov criteria. J. Appl. Probab. 38(4), 975–994 (2001)
2. Caron, F., Doucet, A.: Sparse Bayesian nonparametric regression. In: ICML 2008, pp. 88–95. ACM (2008)
3. Efron, B., Hastie, T., Johnstone, I., Tibshirani, R.: Least angle regression. The Annals of Statistics 32(2), 407–499 (2004)
4. Gelfand, S.B., Mitter, S.K.: Metropolis-type annealing algorithms for global optimization in Rd. SIAM J. Control Optim. 31, 111–131 (1993)
5. van Gerven, M., Cseke, B., Oostenveld, R., Heskes, T.: Bayesian source localization with the multivariate laplace prior. In: Advances in Neural Information Processing Systems 22, pp. 1901–1909 (2009)
6. Goldstein, L.: Mean square rates of convergence in the continuous time simulated annealing algorithm on Rd. Adv. Appl. Math. 9, 35–39 (1988)
7. Gramacy, R.B., Polson, N.G.: Simulation-based Regularized Logistic Regression. ArXiv e-prints (May 2010)
8. Kirkpatrick, S., Gelatt, C.D., Vecchi, M.P.: Optimization by simulated annealing. Science 220(4598), 671–680 (1983)
9. Kyung, M., Gill, J., Ghosh, M., Casella, G.: Penalized regression, standard errors, and Bayesian Lassos. Bayesian Analysis 5(2), 369–412 (2010)
10. Meier, L., van de Geer, S., Bühlmann, P.: The Group Lasso for logistic regression. J. Roy. Stat. Soc. B 70(1), 53–71 (2008)
11. Park, T., Casella, G.: The Bayesian Lasso. Journal of the American Statistical Association 103, 681–686 (2008)
12. Raman, S., Fuchs, T., Wild, P., Dahl, E., Roth, V.: The Bayesian Group-Lasso for analyzing contingency tables. In: Proceedings of the 26th International Conference on Machine Learning, pp. 881–888 (June 2009)
13. Raman, S., Roth, V.: Sparse Bayesian Regression for Grouped Variables in Generalized Linear Models. In: Denzler, J., Notni, G., Süße, H. (eds.) DAGM 2009. LNCS, vol. 5748, pp. 242–251. Springer, Heidelberg (2009)
14. Roberts, G.O., Stramer, O.: Langevin diffusions and Metropolis-Hastings algorithms. Methodology and Computing in Applied Probability 4, 337–357 (2002)
15. Royer, G.: A remark on simulated annealing of diffusion processes. SIAM Journal on Control and Optimization 27(6), 1403–1408 (1989)
16. Tibshirani, R.: Regression shrinkage and selection via the Lasso. J. Roy. Stat. Soc. B 58(1), 267–288 (1996)
17. Černý, V.: Thermodynamical approach to the traveling salesman problem: An efficient simulation algorithm. Journal of Optimization Theory and Applications 45(1), 41–51 (1985)
18. Yeo, G., Burge, C.: Maximum entropy modeling of short sequence motifs with applications to RNA splicing signals. J. Comp. Biology 11, 377–394 (2004)
19. Yuan, M., Lin, Y.: Model selection and estimation in regression with grouped variables. J. Roy. Stat. Soc. B, 49–67 (2006)

Active Metric Learning for Object Recognition

Sandra Ebert, Mario Fritz, and Bernt Schiele

Max Planck Institute for Informatics
Saarbrucken, Germany

Abstract. Popular visual representations like SIFT have shown broad
applicability across many task. This great generality comes naturally
with a lack of specificity when focusing on a particular task or a set of
classes. Metric learning approaches have been proposed to tailor general purpose representations to the needs of more specific tasks and have
shown strong improvements on visual matching and recognition benchmarks. However, the performance of metric learning depends strongly on
the labels that are used for learning. Therefore, we propose to combine
metric learning with an active sample selection strategy in order to find
labels that are representative for each class as well as improve the class
separation of the learnt metric. We analyze several active sample selection strategies in terms of exploration and exploitation trade-offs. Our
novel scheme achieves on three different datasets up to 10% improvement of the learned metric. We compare a batch version of our scheme
to an interleaved execution of sample selection and metric learning which
leads to an overall improvement of up to 23% on challenging datasets for
object class recognition.

1 Introduction

Similarity metrics are a core building block of many computer vision methods e.g. for object detection [12] or human pose estimation [15]. Consequently,
their performance critically depends on the underlying metric and the resulting
neighborhood structure. The ideal metric should produce small intra-class distances and large inter-class distances. But standard metrics often have problems
with high dimensional features due to their equal weighting of dimensions. This
problem is particularly prominent in computer vision where different feature dimensions are differently affected by noise e.g. due to signal noise, background
clutter, or lighting conditions.

A promising direction to address this issue is metric learning [6,11,9]. E.g.,
pairwise constraints from labeled data are used to enforce smaller intra-class distances. But this strategy can be problematic [18,2] if only few labels are available
that might be not informative enough to learn a better metric. For example, outliers may completely distort the metric while redundant samples may have little
effect on metric learning. In this paper, we combine active sampling of labels
with metric learning to address these problems.

In general, active learning methods [3,8] use sample selection strategies to
request uncertain as well as representative samples so that a higher classification

A. Pinz et al. (Eds.): DAGM/OAGM 2012, LNCS 7476, pp. 327–336, 2012.
© Springer-Verlag Berlin Heidelberg 2012

performance can be achieved with only a small fraction of labeled training data. However, the success of active learning critically depends on the choice of the sample selection strategy. Therefore the first main contribution of this paper is to analyze which sampling strategy is best suited to improve metric learning. The analysis is done for three different datasets and in particular for settings where only a small number of labels is available. The second main contribution is to propose two methods that combine active sampling with metric learning leading to a performance improvements of up to 23%.

2   Related Work

Supervised metric learning is a promising direction to improve the neighborhood quality of representations for computer vision. Frequently used are methods that learn a global Mahalanobis distance [6,11,9] based on pairwise constraints. One advantage of these methods is the kernelized optimization so that multiple kernels can be optimized at the same time [11] and the run time depends only on the number of labels instead of the dimensions. However, a large number of labeled pairs is required to learn a good Mahalanobis distance [10].

In contrast, active learning is a successful strategy to reduce the amount of labels by preserving the overall performance. Methods of active learning can be divided into exploration-driven (density-based), exploitation-driven (uncertainty-based), or a combination of both. Exploitative strategies focus mainly on uncertain regions [14,16] while explorative methods sample more representative labels by considering the underlying data distribution [13,5]. But it turns out that a combination of both strategies leads often to a better solution [3,8].

But there are only few methods that try to reduce the number of required labels [2,18]. In [18], the authors improve a Bayesian framework for metric learning by a pure exploitation-driven criteria. [2] refines a pairwise constrained clustering by incorporating a pure exploration-driven criteria. However, the previous work lacks an analysis of active sampling methods and there is no attempt to combine active sampling with metric learning in an interleaved framework.

3   Methods

In this section, we introduce the employed metric learning algorithm [6] as well as our active sampling procedure [8] including several criteria for exploration and exploitation. These criteria can be used either separately or in combination within our framework. Finally, we briefly introduce three different classification algorithms that are used with our active metric learning, i.e., k nearest neighbor classifier (KNN), SVM, and the semi-supervised label propagation (LP) [19].

3.1   Metric Learning

We use the information-theoretic metric learning (ITML) proposed by [6]. ITML learns a global metric by optimizing the Mahalanobis distance,

$$d_A(x_i, x_j) = (x_i - x_j)^T A(x_i - x_j), \tag{1}$$

between two labeled points $x_i, x_j \in \mathbb{R}$ with a Mahalanobis matrix A such that intra-class distances are small and inter-class distances are large, i.e.,

$$\min D_{ld}(A, A_0)$$
$$s.t. \ d_A(x_i, x_j) \le u \quad (i, j) \in \mathcal{S} \tag{2}$$
$$d_A(x_i, x_j) \ge l \quad (i, j) \in \mathcal{D}$$

with LogDet loss D_{ld} and the original data space A_0. u and l are upper and lower bounds of similarity and dissimilarity constraints. $\mathcal{S}$ and $\mathcal{D}$ are sets of similarity and dissimilarity constraints based on the labeled data. This linear optimization can be easily transformed into a kernelized optimization by $K = X^T A X$ to speed up the learning.

3.2 Active Sample Selection

In this work, we explore two exploration and two exploitation criteria. Let us assume, we have $n = l + u$ data points with l labeled examples $L = \{(x_1, \hat{y}_1), ..., (x_l, \hat{y}_l)\}$ and u unlabeled examples $U = \{x_{l+1}, ..., x_n\}$ with $x_i \in \mathbb{R}^d$. We denote $\hat{y} \in \mathcal{L} = \{1, ..., c\}$ the labels with c the number of classes.

Exploitation. *Entropy* (Ent) is the most common criteria for exploitation [1] that uses the class posterior:

$$Ent(x_i) = \sum_{j=1}^{c} P(y_{ij}|x_i) \log P(y_{ij}|x_i) \tag{3}$$

where $\sum_j P(y_{ij}|x_i) = 1$ are predictions of a classifier. This criteria focuses more on examples that have a high overall class confusion.

Margin (Mar) computes the difference between best versus second best class prediction [14]:

$$Mar(x_i) = P(y_{ik_1}|x_i) - P(y_{ik_2}|x_i) \tag{4}$$

such that $P(y_{ik_1}|x_i) \ge P(y_{ik_2}|x_i) \ge ... \ge P(y_{ik_c}|x_i)$. In each iteration, label $x^* = \operatorname{argmin}_{x_i \in U} Mar(x_i)$ is queried. In contrast to Ent, this criteria concentrates more on the decision boundaries between two classes.

Exploration. These criteria are often used in combination with exploitation criteria as they do not get any feedback about the uncertainty during the active sample selection so that more labels are required to obtain good performance.

Kernel farthest first (Ker) captures the entire data space by looking for the most unexplored regions given the current labels [1,2] by computing the minimum distance from each unlabeled sample to all labels

$$Ker(x_i) = \min_{x_j \in L} d(x_i, x_j), \tag{5}$$

and then requesting the label for the farthest sample $x^* = \operatorname{argmax}_i Ker(x_i)$. This criteria samples evenly the entire data space but often selects many outliers.

Graph density (Gra) [8] is a sampling criteria that uses a k-nearest neighbor graph structure to find highly connected nodes, i.e.,

$$Gra(x_i) = \frac{\sum_i W_{ij}}{\sum_i P_{ij}}. \tag{6}$$

with the similarity matrix $W_{ij} = P_{ij} \exp\left(\frac{-d(x_i, x_j)}{2\sigma^2}\right)$ and the adjacency matrix P_{ij}. After each sampling step, the weights of direct neighbors of sample x_i are reduced by $Gra(x_j) = Gra(x_j) - Gra(x_i)P_{ij}$ to avoid oversampling of a region.

Active Sampling. We use our time-varying combination of exploration and exploitation introduced in [8], i.e.,

$$H(x_i) = \beta(t)r(U(x_i)) + (1 - \beta(t))r(D(x_i)) \tag{7}$$

with $U \in \{Ent, Mar\}$, $D \in \{Ker, Gra\}$, $\beta(t) : \{1, ..., T\} \to [0, 1]$, and a ranking function $r : \mathbb{R} \to \{1, ..., u\}$ that uses the ordering of both criteria instead of the values itself. We set $\beta(t) = log(t)$ that means more exploration at the beginning followed by exploitation at the end of the sampling process. Finally, we request the label for the sample with the minimal score $\operatorname{argmin}_{x_i \in U} H(x_i)$.

3.3   Classification Algorithms

In the following, we explain the use of three different classifier in our active sampling framework because not all classifier provide a class posterior that can be immediately used for *Ent* or *Mar*.

1) KNN. Similar to [11], we show results for the k nearest neighbor classifier with $k = 1$ because it shows consistently best performance. For the class posterior $p(y_{ij}|x_i)$, we use the confusion of the 10 nearest labels for each unlabeled data point weighted by their similarity and finally normalized by the overall sum.

2) SVM. We apply libSVM [4] with our own kernels in a one-vs-one classification scheme. The accumulated and normalized decision values are used as the class posterior. Parameter C is empirically determined but is quite robust.

3) Label propagation (LP). For semi-supervised learning, we use [19] that propagates labels through a k nearest neighbor structure, i.e.,

$$Y_j^{(t+1)} = \alpha S Y_j^{(t)} + (1 - \alpha)Y_j^{(0)} \tag{8}$$

with $1 \leq j \leq c$, the symmetric graph Laplacian $S = D^{-1/2}WD^{-1/2}$ based on the similarity matrix W from above, the diagonal matrix $D_{ii} = \sum_j W_{ij}$, the original label vector $Y_j^{(0)}$ consisting of $1, -1$ for labeled data and 0 for the unlabeled data. Parameter $\alpha \in (0, 1]$ that controls the overwriting of the original labels. The final prediction is obtained by $\hat{Y} = \operatorname{argmax}_{j \leq c} Y_j^{(t+1)}$. For the class posterior, we use the normalized class predictions $P(y_{ij}|x_i) = \frac{y_{ij}^{(t+1)}}{\sum_{j=1}^c y_{ij}^{(t+1)}}$.

4   Active Metric Learning

By requesting more informative and representative training examples, we expect that metric learning achieves better performance given the same amount of training data or – respectively – achieve equal performance already with significantly less annotated data. Therefore, we explore two different ways to combine active sampling with metric learning.

4.1   Batch Active Metric Learning (BAML)

Our first approach starts by querying the desired number of labeled data points according to the chosen sample selection strategy and learns a metric based on this labeled data. As the metric is learnt only once across the whole pool of labeled data points, we call this approach *batch active metric learning (BAML)*. While this method obtains good performance, it does not get any direct feedback involving the learnt metric during sampling. To improve the coupling between the two processes we propose a second version of our method which interleaves active sampling and metric learning.

4.2   Interleaved Active Metric Learning (IAML)

The second active metric learning approach alternates between active sampling and metric learning. We start with active sampling in order to have a minimum of similarity constraints for metric learning. In our experiments, we apply metric learning each m iterations with $2 \leq m \leq |L|$, c the number of classes, and $|L|$ the average number of requested labels per class. After metric learning we use the learned kernel to request the next batch of labels with active sampling. In each iteration we learn the metric based on the original feature space with the current available labels and all pairwise constraints. We found experimentally that using the original feature space is less susceptible to drift than incrementally updating the learnt metric.

5   Datasets and Representation

In our experiments, we analyze three different datasets for image classification with increasing number of classes and difficulty. Fig. 1 shows sample images.

ETH-80 consists of 8 classes (*apple*, *car*, *cow*, *cup*, *dog*, *horse*, *pear*, and *tomato*) photographed from different viewpoints in front of a uniform background. This dataset contains $3,280$ images.

C-PASCAL is subset of the PASCAL VOC challenge 2008 data used in [7] in a multi-class setting. Single objects are extracted by bounding box annotations. The resulting dataset consists of $4,450$ images of aligned objects from 20 classes but with varying object poses, background clutter, and truncations.

IM100 is a subset ImageNet 2010 that consists of 100 classes similar to Caltech 101. IM100 contains 100 images per class resulting in a dataset with $10,000$

ETH   C-PASCAL   IM100

Fig. 1. Sample images for ETH (left), C-PASCAL (middle), and IM100 (right)

images. Objects can be anywhere in an image and images often contain background clutter, occlusions, or truncations.

Representation. In the experiments, we show results for a dense SIFT Bag-of-Words representation. SIFT-features are extracted using the implementation by [17], sampled on a regular grid, and quantized into $1,000$ visual words.

6   Experiments

In our experimental section, we first analyze in Sec. 6.1 different sampling criteria and their combinations in terms of representativeness for metric learning. We focus on the 1-NN classification performance as it reflects the change of the underlying metric. Then, we explore in Sec. 6.2 if these insights transfer also to other algorithms. Finally in Sec. 6.3, we show further improvements by applying our interleaved active metric learning (IAML) framework.

6.1   Different Sampling Criteria for Metric Learning

In this subsection, we analyze several sampling criteria and mixtures of those in comparison to random sampling and their influence on the entire metric. For this purpose, we look at the 1-NN accuracy as this measure gives a good intuition about the learned neighborhood structure. Tab. 1 shows results before and after metric learning for different average number of labels per class $|L|$. We request at most 10% labels, i.e., for ETH we vary $|L|$ from 5 to 25 and for IM100 from 3 to 10. *Rand* is our baseline using random sampling where we draw exactly $|L|$ labels per class with a uniform distribution. Last line in each table is the average performance over the whole column. All results are averaged over 5 runs.

Before metric learning (Tab. 1, top), we notice large differences between several sampling criteria. In average, we observe a performance of 29.7% for random sampling while for single active sampling criteria the accuracy vary from 26.2% for *Ker* to 31.4% for *Mar*. Both *Mar* and *Gra* are better than *Rand*. *Ent* and *Ker* are worse than *Rand* due to their tendency to focus more on low density regions. Then we look at each specific dataset, *Mar* performs best for ETH that contains a smooth manifold structure. In contrast, *Gra* tends to oversample dense regions, e.g., *pear*, leading to worse performance in comparison to *Ker*. On more complex datasets such as C-PASCAL or IM100, *Gra* clearly outperforms all other single criteria. For C-PASCAL with 25 labels per class we achieve a performance of 27.5%

Table 1. 1-NN accuracy before (1st table) and after (2nd table) metric learning for single criteria and the mixtures Ent+Gra (E+G), Ent+Ker (E+K), Mar+Gra (M+G), and Mar+Ker (M+K)

		Accuracy before metric learning							
		Single criteria				Mixture of two criteria			
$\|L\|$	Rand	Ent	Mar	Gra	Ker	M+G	M+K	E+G	E+K
				ETH					
5	50.6	45.9	57.0	51.1	46.0	**59.8**	43.3	55.0	49.1
15	69.1	59.7	69.7	62.6	64.0	**71.0**	65.1	62.0	60.5
25	74.2	62.7	74.4	69.8	72.4	**77.3**	72.1	66.2	66.4
				C-PASCAL					
5	12.6	11.3	16.1	17.8	9.8	19.1	11.1	17.1	10.3
15	17.5	19.8	21.0	**24.1**	12.4	23.2	14.9	21.8	17.5
25	19.3	21.8	23.4	**27.5**	13.9	24.8	17.7	24.5	19.7
				IM100					
3	6.3	5.1	5.6	**8.2**	5.1	**8.2**	5.4	7.2	5.2
5	7.6	6.0	6.8	**9.3**	5.6	**9.3**	6.2	8.1	5.9
10	9.8	7.3	8.6	10.5	7.0	**10.6**	7.9	9.0	7.0
				Overall average					
	29.7	26.6	31.4	31.2	26.2	**33.7**	27.1	30.1	26.8

		Accuracy after metric learning							
		Single criteria				Mixture of two criteria			
$\|L\|$	Rand	Ent	Mar	Gra	Ker	M+G	M+K	E+G	E+K
				ETH					
5	61.6	59.3	67.7	52.7	67.5	**70.0**	63.3	62.7	65.8
15	79.8	67.9	82.2	69.1	80.0	**83.0**	82.0	70.7	76.3
25	82.8	74.6	84.5	78.1	83.5	**86.3**	86.1	73.3	79.4
				C-PASCAL					
5	16.9	19.4	22.4	23.5	17.1	25.7	20.0	**26.2**	18.9
15	25.2	32.5	32.6	34.4	18.5	**34.5**	22.4	33.2	29.1
25	28.8	37.9	**39.0**	36.9	22.5	38.4	29.6	38.4	36.6
				IM100					
3	6.7	6.4	7.4	9.3	6.8	**10.6**	7.0	9.6	6.8
5	11.4	8.6	9.6	10.7	8.0	**13.0**	9.2	11.7	8.6
10	15.9	12.6	14.6	12.5	11.1	**16.3**	14.6	15.3	12.4
				Overall average					
	36.6	35.5	40.0	36.4	35.0	**42.0**	37.1	37.9	37.1

for *Gra* while *Mar* shows a performance of 23.4% and *Ker* achieves only 13.9% accuracy. Finally, the combination *Mar+Gra* outperforms with 33.7% in average the best single criteria with 31.2%. All other combinations are strongly limited to the power of the combined criteria that means using *Gra* shows better performance than using *Ker*, and mixtures with *Mar* are in average better than mixtures with *Ent*.

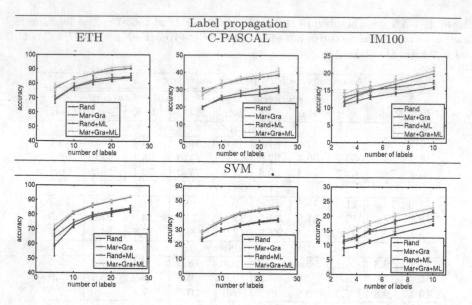

Fig. 2. LP and SVM accuracy of all three datasets and different number of labels for random sampling and the mixture Mar+Gra with and without metric learning

After metric learning (Tab. 1, bottom), we observe a consistent improvement to the previous table that means metric learning always helps. For example, *Rand* is overall improved by 6.9% from 29.7% without metric learning to 36.6% with metric learning and our best combination *Mar+Gra* is increased in average by 8.3% from 33.7% to 42.0%. From these improvements we see also that there is a larger benefit when using our BAML in comparison to *Rand* with metric learning. This observation also holds true for most other active sampling selection methods, e.g., *Ent+Ker* is improved by 10.3% from 26.8% to 37.1% that is better than *Rand* after metric learning. Another important insight results from the comparison of the influence of active sample selection on metric learning. Obviously, metric learning has a larger impact on the overall performance than active sample selection that means *Rand* is improved from 29.7% to 33.7% with *Mar+Gra* and to 36.6% with metric learning alone. But if we combine both strategies we achieve a final performance of 42.0% that corresponds to an overall increase of 12.3% across three datasets.

To conclude this subsection, metric learning benefits significantly from labels that are more representative. In average, *Mar+Gra* is the best sampling strategy for our BAML. Finally, metric learning combined with active sample selection achieves consistent improvements over random sampling of up to 12.3%.

6.2   BAML on LP and SVM

In this subsection, we explore if our insights from the previous subsection translate to more complex classification schemes such as label propagation (LP) or

Table 2. Interleaved active metric learning (IAML) in comparison to the batch active metric learning (BAML) both for Mar+Gra sampling

$\|L\|$	ETH			C-PASCAL			IM100		
	BAML	IAML	diff	BAML	IAML	diff	BAML	IAML	diff
5	70.0	68.0	-2.0	25.7	23.3	-2.4	10.6	10.5	-0.1
10	77.4	79.8	+2.4	30.6	32.1	+1.5	11.5	12.0	+0.5
15	83.0	82.6	-0.4	34.5	40.7	+6.2	13.0	13.0	0.0
20	85.1	87.2	+2.1	36.7	41.7	+5.0	14.2	14.9	+0.7
25	86.3	90.3	+4.0	38.4	43.5	+5.1	16.3	17.1	+0.8

SVM. Fig. 2 shows accuracy for random sampling (*Rand*) and *Mar+Gra* – the best sampling strategy from Sec. 6.1 – before and after metric learning. The first row contains results of LP and the second row for SVM. Again, we show the average over 5 runs including standard deviation for different number of labels.

We also observe a consistent improvement for LP and SVM when applying BAML. For IM100 with 10 labels per class, we increase our performance with LP from 15.9% (*Rand*) to 17.5% (*Mar+Gra*) to 19.9% (*Rand+ML*) to 20.7% (*Mar+Gra*), and with SVM from 17.1% (*Rand*) to 19.2% (*Mar+Gra*) to 21.7% (*Rand+ML*) to 23.3% (*Mar+Gra+ML*). For datasets with a small number of classes, i.e., ETH and C-PASCAL, active sampling is more important than metric learning that is contrary to the previous subsection. The reason is that these methods benefit from their regularization during the learning while the KNN performance is directly connected to the neighborhood structure. But for datasets with a large number of classes like IM100, metric learning is still more important because there are more constraints to fulfill. Another interesting point turns out when looking at the SVM results. For a small number of labels, SVM benefits more from metric learning although this algorithm learns a metric by itself. This can be seen in particular for ETH and IM100.

6.3 Interleaved Active Metric Learning (IAML)

In this subsection, we show 1-NN results in Tab. 2 for the interleaved active metric learning (IAML) when using our best active sampling strategy *Mar+Gra*. In average, we observe an additional improvement that tends to be higher the more labels we use. For example, C-PASCAL with 15 labels is increased by 6.2% from 34.5% (BAML) to 40.7% (IAML). In few cases, we also observe a decrease in performance in particular for a small number of labels that can be explained by a drifting effect. In all experiments we recover from these issues for $|L| > 15$.

7   Conclusion

We present an active metric learning approach that combines active sampling strategies with metric learning. While a first version (BAML) of the approach operates in batch mode and already allows to learn better metrics from fewer training examples, our second version (IAML) interleaves active sampling and metric learning even more tightly which leads to further performance improvements by providing better feedback to the active sampling strategy. Our analysis of different sampling criteria and their influence on the KNN performance shows the importance of choosing an appropriate sampling scheme for metric learning. While we show consistent improvements over a random sample selection baseline, a combination of density and uncertainty-based criteria performs best on average. Finally, we improve also results for different supervised as well as semi-supervised classification algorithms. All our experiments are carried out on three challenging object class recognition benchmarks, where our new approaches consistently outperform random sample selection strategies for metric learning leading to improvements of up to 23% for KNN.

References

1. Baram, Y., El-Yaniv, R., Luz, K.: Online Choice of Active Learning Algorithms. JMLR 5, 255–291 (2004)
2. Basu, S., Banerjee, A., Mooney, R.: Active Semi-Supervision for Pairwise Constrained Clustering. SIAM (2004)
3. Cebron, N., Berthold, M.R.: Active learning for object classification: from exploration to exploitation. DMKD 18(2), 283–299 (2009)
4. Chang, C.C., Lin, C.J.: LIBSVM: A library for support vector machines. ACM Transactions on Intelligent Systems and Technology 2(3), 1–27 (2011)
5. Dasgupta, S., Hsu, D.: Hierarchical sampling for active learning. In: ICML (2008)
6. Davis, J., Kulis, B., Jain, P., Sra, S., Dhillon, I.: Information-theoretic metric learning. In: ICML (2007)
7. Ebert, S., Fritz, M., Schiele, B.: Pick Your Neighborhood – Improving Labels and Neighborhood Structure for Label Propagation. In: Mester, R., Felsberg, M. (eds.) DAGM 2011. LNCS, vol. 6835, pp. 152–162. Springer, Heidelberg (2011)
8. Ebert, S., Fritz, M., Schiele, B.: RALF: A Reinforced Active Learning Formulation for Object Class Recognition. In: CVPR (2012)
9. Goldberger, J., Roweis, S., Hinton, G., Salakhutdinov, R.: Neighbourhood Components Analysis. In: NIPS (2005)
10. Guillaumin, M., Verbeek, J., Schmid, C.: Multiple Instance Metric Learning from Automatically Labeled Bags of Faces. In: Daniilidis, K., Maragos, P., Paragios, N. (eds.) ECCV 2010, Part I. LNCS, vol. 6311, pp. 634–647. Springer, Heidelberg (2010)
11. Kulis, B., Jain, P., Grauman, K.: Fast Similarity Search for Learned Metrics. PAMI 31(12), 2143–2157 (2009)
12. Malisiewicz, T., Gupta, A., Efros, A.: Ensemble of Exemplar-SVMs for Object Detection and Beyond. In: ICCV (2011)
13. Nguyen, H.T., Smeulders, A.: Active learning using pre-clustering. In: ICML (2004)
14. Settles, B., Craven, M.: An analysis of active learning strategies for sequence labeling tasks. In: Emp. Meth. in NLP (2008)
15. Straka, M., Hauswiesner, S., Ruether, M., Bischof, H.: Skeletal Graph Based Human Pose Estimation in Real-Time. In: BMVC (2011)
16. Tong, S., Koller, D.: Support Vector Machine Active Learning with Applications to Text Classification. JMLR 2, 45–66 (2001)
17. Vedaldi, A., Fulkerson, B.: VLFEAT: An Open and Portable Library of Computer Vision Algorithms (2008), http://www.vlfeat.org/
18. Yang, L., Jin, R., et al.: Bayesian active distance metric learning. In: UAI (2007)
19. Zhou, D., Bousquet, O., Lal, T.N., Weston, J., Schölkopf, B.: Learning with Local and Global Consistency. In: NIPS (2004)

Accuracy-Efficiency Evaluation
of Adaptive Support Weight Techniques
for Local Stereo Matching

Asmaa Hosni*, Margrit Gelautz, and Michael Bleyer**

Institute for Software Technology and Interactive Systems
Vienna University of Technology, Vienna, Austria
http://www.ims.tuwien.ac.at

Abstract. Adaptive support weight (ASW) strategies in local stereo matching have recently attracted many researchers due to their compelling results. In this paper, we present an evaluation study that focuses on weight computation methods that have been suggested in the most recent literature. We implemented 9 ASW stereo methods and tested them on all (35) ground truth test stereo image pairs of the Middlebury benchmark. Our evaluation considers both the accuracy of the matching process and the computational efficiency of its GPU implementation. According to our results, high-quality matching results at real-time processing speeds can be achieved by using the guided image filter weights.

1 Introduction

The idea of adaptive support weights (ASW) in local matching was first introduced in [15], where the weight for each pixel inside the support window was computed as proportional to both the color similarity and spatial proximity to the window's central pixel. Since then, several alternatives for computing the support weights have been introduced. Researchers in this field typically have to compromise between two main aspects of stereo matching, i.e, the matching *accuracy* and matching *efficiency*. According to the Middlebury on-line evaluation table [11], efficient ASW methods achieve high processing speed with relatively low-quality disparity maps, e.g. [10], while accurate ASW methods [15] , [6] are usually time-consuming[1].

In the context of improving the accuracy, the work of [12] suggests using a pre-computed mean shift-based color segmentation for the input stereo images. In this case, the segmentation information is deployed within the weight function to increase the reliability of the matching. More recently, [6] have proposed a weights computation method in which the *connectivity* property is taken into

* Supported by the Vienna PhD School of Informatics.
** Has been funded by the Vienna Science and Technology Fund (WWTF) through project ICT08-019.

[1] To the best of our knowledge, the only ASW method which is fast and lies at the top quarter of the Middlebury on-line ranking table is [9].

A. Pinz et al. (Eds.): DAGM/OAGM 2012, LNCS 7476, pp. 337–346, 2012.
© Springer-Verlag Berlin Heidelberg 2012

consideration via a geodesic distance transform. This *connectivity* property leads to a more meaningful color segmentation inside the support window and, consequently, improved disparity maps.

In order to speed up ASW methods, many researchers have realized *constant-time, i.e. O(1)*, algorithms, in which the matching process is independent of the chosen support window size. The main idea behind achieving such constant run time is that the weighted costs aggregation step can be considered as equivalent to *smoothing* (*filtering*) the costs computed between left and right images at each disparity hypothesis (disparity space image, DSI) by an edge-preserving filter. Some authors have achieved fast run times relying on reformulations of the joint bilateral weights. An example is given in [10], where the joint bilateral filter is approximated based on the bilateral grid of [8]. Recently, [9] has presented an algorithm that exploits the recently proposed guided image filter [4] to smooth the cost volume (DSI). Analogous to the bilateral filter, the guided image filter has edge-preserving properties, with the additional advantage that it can be implemented in a non-approximate manner in a very fast way.

The goal of our work lies in a systematic evaluation study on ASW local stereo methods, with a focus on recently suggested support aggregation schemes. In the context of prior work, evaluation surveys can be found in [3] , [5] , [13]. The study in [3] is restricted to stereo matching approaches that are suitable for real-time systems, whereas the work in [5] concentrates on radiometrically invariant dissimilarity cost measurements. The work closest to ours is [13] where the authors run an experimental comparison among different local methods. There is overlap with our study in that the ASW methods of [15] and [12] are investigated. The main differences are: (1) We evaluate a large set of ASW strategies, which also includes very recent ones (e.g., [9] and [6]). (2) We evaluate over a large set of ground truth test images, i.e., we use 35 pairs in comparison to four pairs used in [13]. (3) We have implemented all approaches on the GPU to bring these approaches to maximum speed. This allows for a fair run time comparison, as we run all algorithms on the same hardware platform and have spent considerable engineering effort to optimize the runtime behavior of *all* approaches.

2   Stereo Algorithm

Every ASW stereo algorithm is composed of three main steps: (1) Costs Generation. (2) Weighted Costs Aggregation. (3) Disparity Assignment. Our tested algorithms differ in the way of applying step (2), while steps (1) and (3) remain the same for all algorithms.

2.1   Costs Generation

In this step, the cost volume is constructed. We follow [9] and choose the matching measure to be a mixture of truncated color difference $M()$ and gradient difference $G()$ to compute each cost value. The costs $C(p, d)$ for matching pixel p at disparity d are defined as:

$$C(p, d) = \alpha \cdot \min\left(\tau_c, M(p, d)\right) + (1 - \alpha) \cdot \min\left(\tau_g, G(p, d)\right). \qquad (1)$$

Here, α balances the color and gradient terms and τ_c, τ_g are color and gradient truncation values respectively.

2.2 Weighted Costs Aggregation

The performance of the ASW local stereo methods depends to a large degree on the support weights that are used in the aggregation step. The aggregated weighted costs value at pixel p and disparity d is defined as follows:

$$C'(p, d) = \sum_{q \in w_p} W_{p,q}(I_{ref}).C(q, d). \qquad (2)$$

Here, $C'(p, d)$ denotes the aggregated weighted matching costs inside the support window w_p centered at pixel p. The weights $W_{p,q}$ are computed depending on image I_{ref}, which is the reference image. The weighting function $W_{p,q}()$ is the subject of our study. In the following we give a brief review of the techniques that are used in our evaluation as well as their abbreviations used in the remainder of this paper.

Bilateral Support Weights (BL). The bilateral support weights [15] are defined as follows:

$$W(p, q) = \exp\left(-\left(\frac{Col(p, q)}{\gamma_c} + \frac{Dist(p, q)}{\gamma_d}\right)\right). \qquad (3)$$

Here, $Col(p, q)$ and $Dist(p, q)$ are functions to measure the color similarity and spatial distance, respectively, of pixels inside the support window with respect to the window's center pixel. γ_c and γ_d are color and distance constants that can be tuned by the algorithm. Intuitively, γ_c controls the amount of smoothing, while γ_d controls the degree of edge-preservation.

Geodesic Support Weights (Geo). The geodesic weights are computed as inversely proportional to the geodesic distance between pixels inside the support window and the window's center pixel. The geodesic support weights, according to [6], are computed as follows:

$$W(p, q) = \exp\left(-\frac{GeoDist(p, q)}{\gamma}\right). \qquad (4)$$

Here, γ is a user-defined parameter that controls the strength of the resulting color-segmentation (inside the window) and $GeoDist(p, q)$ is a function to compute the geodesic distance between pixel q inside the support window and the window's center pixel p. In our evaluation we follow [6] in the way of implementing the function $GeoDist(p, q)$.

Guided Image Support Weights (GI). Originally, the "guided image" is a novel type of explicit image filter that was recently proposed in [4]. The filter weights, which are derived from a color *guidance* image, are defined as follows:

$$W(p,q) = \frac{1}{|\omega|^2} \sum_{k:(p,q)\in\omega_k} (1 + (I_p - \mu_k)^T (\Sigma_k + \epsilon U)^{-1}(I_q - \mu_k)). \tag{5}$$

Here, I is the reference image and Σ_k and μ_k are the covariance matrix and mean vector of I in the window ω_k centered at pixel k, respectively. The number of pixels in this window is $|\omega|$ and ϵ is a smoothness parameter. I_p, I_q and μ_k are 3×1 (color) vectors, and the covariance matrix Σ_k and identity matrix U are of size 3×3. The most important property of the guided image support weights is that the weights do not have to be computed explicitly in the aggregation process. Instead, some linear operations are applied which rely exclusively on box filters and can be computed in $O(N)$ time, where N is the number of image pixels. For more details about the guided image filtering, the reader is referred to [4].

Weighted Median Support Weights (WM). We have also tested the weighted median support weights. Instead of a weighted summation of the pixels in a window, the result is the weighted median of pixels, which helps to prevent outlier pixels from distorting the result as suggested in [2]. For computing the weighted median of a window, we sort all its pixels to derive a vector $\{p_1, p_2, \cdots, p_n\}$ for which $C(p_1, d) \leq C(p_2, d) \leq \cdots \leq C(p_n, d)$, where n is the number of pixels inside the window. Let $S(p_i)$ be a partial sum in this sorted array computed by $S(p_i) = \sum_{j=1}^{j=i} W_j$, with the weights W being defined in eq. 3. We then search the pixel p_m for which $S(p_m) \leq \frac{S(p_n)}{2}$ and $S(p_{m+1}) > \frac{S(p_n)}{2}$. The weighted median of the window is then given by: $C'(p, d) = C(p_m, d)$. This method shares similarity with the disparity map post-processing procedure of [9].

Segmentation-Based Support Weights. The segmentation-based support weights as described in [12] are defined as follows:

$$W(p,q) = \begin{cases} 1.0 & \text{if } q \in S_p \\ \exp\left(-\frac{Col(p,q)}{\gamma_c}\right) & \text{otherwise} \end{cases} \tag{6}$$

Here, S_p represents the segment on which pixel p is lying and $Col(p, q)$ and γ_c are defined as in eq. 3. This weighting function means that all pixels lying on the same segment as the center pixel have the same influence (weight = 1.0). For all other pixels outside the segment of the window's center pixel, the weights are computed depending only on the color distance and independent of their spatial distance to the central pixel. In our evaluation we study the segmentation-based weighting function with the aforementioned support weights methods[2]. Formally,

---

[2] Except for the GI method, because the weights in this case are not computed explicitly.

$W(p, q)$ is defined as:

$$W(p, q) = \begin{cases} 1.0 & \text{if } q \in S_p \\ W & \text{otherwise} \end{cases} \tag{7}$$

with:

$$W = \begin{cases} \exp\left(-\dfrac{Col(p,q)}{\gamma_c}\right) & \text{for BL and WM} \\ \exp\left(-\dfrac{GeoDist(p,q)}{\gamma}\right) & \text{for Geo} \end{cases} \tag{8}$$

Here, $GeoDist(p, q)$ is defined as in eq. 4. Throughout the paper we will denote the segmentation-based support weights with a "Seg" tailing abbreviation.

2.3   Disparity Assignment

Once the matching costs are aggregated over the support region, the disparity level with the minimum cost is selected as the output for each pixel by applying the local minimization method of Winner-Takes-All (WTA):

$$f_p = \operatorname*{argmin}_{d \in \mathcal{D}} C'(p, d) \tag{9}$$

where $\mathcal{D}$ represents the set of all allowed disparities.

3   Experiments and Discussion

In this evaluation study, all stereo algorithms are tested using a 2.4 GHZ PC. We implemented all algorithms on a GPU using a GeForce GTX480 graphics card with 1.5 GB of memory along with the CUDA technique of NVIDIA [1]. Besides the ASW techniques discussed in section 2.2, we also include the dual-cross-bilateral grid method of [10] and the constant-time, $O(1)$, bilateral weights approximation technique based on [14] in our evaluation. These two methods are denoted by "DCBGrid" and "BLO(1)" in our evaluation table. For "DCBGrid", we used the GPU code provided online by the authors, while all other algorithms were implemented by ourselves.

In order to evaluate the accuracy of the different ASW techniques, we chose to use all 35 stereo data sets that are provided by Middlebury [11][3]. Throughout our test runs, each algorithm's parameters were set to constant values for all stereo image pairs. Each ASW strategy has its own constants, which were tuned to give best results for all data sets[4].

---

[3] These data sets have different challenges and should therefore be well suited to discriminate the performance of different support weights computation methods.

[4] We tuned the parameters to give the smallest average error percentage in non-occluded regions for all 35 image pairs.

Table 1. Quantitative performance of the investigated support weights computation methods. The red subscripts represent the rank of the method in the table.

Support Weights	Avg. Error (%)	Avg. Rank	MDE/s
BL	6.20_2	2.80_1	141.80_5
BLSeg	6.62_5	3.80_4	307.25_2
BLO(1)	6.72_6	4.06_5	163.38_4
DCBGrid [10]	15.71_9	8.91_9	124.30_7
Geo	6.31_3	3.63_3	125.71_6
GeoSeg	6.55_4	4.74_6	175.72_3
WM	9.13_7	7.03_7	1.36_9
WMSeg	9.82_8	7.04_8	1.51_8
GI	5.84_1	3.00_2	343.90_1

3.1   Accuracy Evaluation

To measure the matching accuracy, two error metrics are computed. In the first metric, we compute the percentage of wrong pixels that have an absolute disparity error larger than one pixel in non-occluded regions. In the second metric, for each test pair, we rank the ASW methods according to their error percentages, so that the ASW method with the lowest error percentage takes rank 1, while the worst-performing one is given rank 9. We compute the average errors and average ranks over all 35 test image pairs (all Middlebury data sets) and plot the corresponding values in Table 1.

From the Avg. Error (see Table 1), the GI support weights show the best performance, followed by the BL method. The listing according to the Avg. Rank confirms that GI and BL are the two best performing ASW methods. In figure 1, we show the results of these two weighting functions at different locations in the Middlebury images. As can be seen from this figure, for both methods, the edges of the color image are well-preserved in the weight masks. The edge-preservation characteristic is the main reason for getting high-quality results.

The Geo weights strategy is the 3rd best performing method according to both errors metrics. The lower ranks in Table 1 are taken by the DCBGrid method, for which we used an available implementation, and the WM technique. The table also shows that the two error metrics are largely consistent. Comparison with the literature reveals a contradiction between the 3rd rank we found for the Geo weights, and the result reported earlier by [6]. In that former publication, the geodesic support weights have a better performance than the bilateral weights of [15]. We believe that this inconsistency can be attributed to two reasons: First, in the earlier evaluation based on the Middlebury ranking, only a subset of four images was used. Second, the cost function used in our study is different from the one that was employed in the original paper of geodesic support weights by [6][5].

---

[5] The cost function used in [6] is based on mutual information.

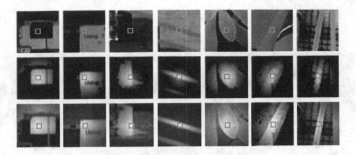

Fig. 1. Weights masks computed using the BL and GI weighting functions. The first row shows image crops. The second and third rows show the BL and GI weights computed for the marked pixels of the first row. Bright pixels represent high weights.

Regarding the segmentation-based support weights, we found for all three algorithms (BL, Geo, and WM) that the segmentation-based variant worsened the accuracy results. For example, according to the Avg. Rank metric, BLSeg lies at rank 4 while BL takes rank 1. This finding is contradicting with the reported results of [12], who mention that using segmentation improves the disparity calculation. The same arguments as above of the different amount of test images and choice of the cost function would provide an explanation.

For a visual comparison, we show disparity and error maps for four selected stereo image pairs generated by the top three ranked methods in figure 2. The error maps are derived by plotting pixels whose absolute disparity error is larger than one pixel. These pixels are shown in black.

3.2 Efficiency Evaluation

In order to evaluate the computational efficiency of each evaluated ASW method, the average Million Disparity Estimations per second (MDE/s) metric is computed. For any stereo image pair, the MDE/s is computed as follows:

$$\text{MDE/s} = (imgW \times imgH \times \mathcal{D} \times \text{FPS})/10^6. \tag{10}$$

Here, imgW and imgH are the image width and height, respectively, in pixels. $\mathcal{D}$ is the number of disparity levels and FPS represents the number of frames per second computed for each stereo image pair. The average MDE/s (computed for all 35 image pairs) for the studied ASW methods are shown in the rightmost column of Table 1. All figures refer to a GPU implementation, and the MDE/s values are measured at the same parameters settings as used for the rankings in the other columns of Table 1.

The results in Table 1 demonstrate that excellent computational efficiency can be achieved by using the GI method. It exhibits the largest MDE/s value (faster) and, hence, is ranked 1st in the table. The second competitor is the BLSeg method. However, it should be noted that this method is a segmentation-based ASW method which means that extra runtime, which is not included in this

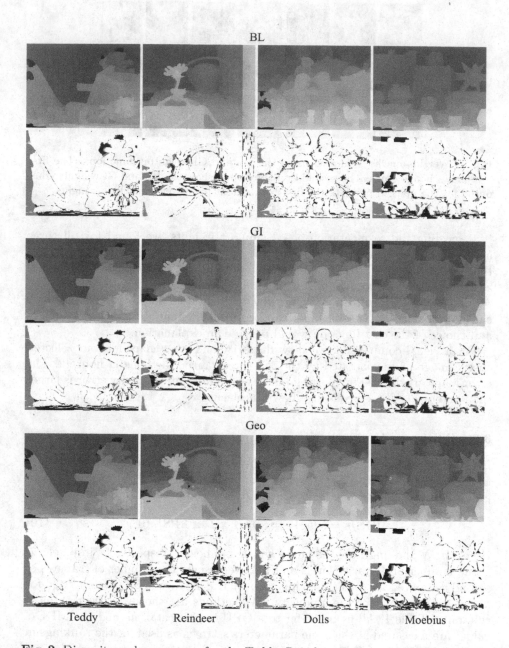

Fig. 2. Disparity and error maps for the Teddy, Reindeer, Dolls and Moebius images. We show the results of the three top-performers of table 1, i.e., GI, BL and Geo. In the error maps, pixels that have a disparity error larger than one pixel are shown in black. Gray pixels represent errors in occluded areas.

table, is needed for carrying out the segmentation process. This indicates that the GI method is the top performing method in terms of speed and is suitable for real-time applications.

In another experiment, we have tested the performance of the studied ASW methods in terms of average MDE/s measured with varying the support window size[6]. The results of this experiment are shown in figure 3[7]. From this figure it is seen that there are three methods which have a runtime independent of the support window size (GI, DCBGrid and BLO(1) methods). The runtime of the other methods is increasing sharply with increasing the support window size [8].

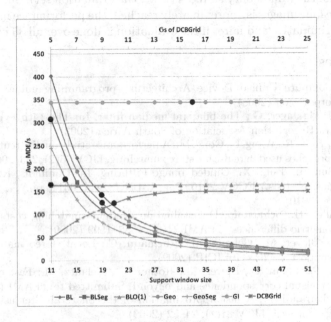

Fig. 3. Efficiency comparison of different weighting functions used in our study. Here the average MDE/s is plotted versus the support window size. The optimal window size (adjusted to get smallest average error percentage for each method individually) is marked by a black circle.

---

[6] In the DCBGrid [10] method there is no explicit form for the support window size. Instead, we measure the performance with varying the values of σ_s (spatial sampling rate), since this parameter affects the amount of smoothing during the costs aggregation process, which is considered as filtering process. As this method relies on the bilateral grid approximation, the number of grid cells is inversely proportional to σ_s: larger values for σ_s result in smaller numbers of the grid cells and, consequently, require less memory giving faster run times. This is why the average MDE/s measured for this method increases with increasing values for σ_s.

[7] This is an extension of a similar figure shown in [7] for a subset of algorithms.

[8] In this plot we excluded the evaluation of WM methods since the runtime of these methods increases tremendously with increasing window sizes. See values of MDE/s in table 1.

4   Conclusions

This paper investigates the effects of different strategies for computing adaptive support weights in local stereo matching on the accuracy of the final disparity maps and the efficiency of recovering them. Our results show that the guided image filter technique is the overall top performer in terms of both quality and computational speed. If real-time performance is needed, it will be the first candidate method.

An interesting finding is that it is not sufficient to measure the performance of a suggested support weights computation function on only the four most frequently used images of the Middlebury stereo set (i.e., the evaluation set). Since the solution for those four images is approximately reached, the performance measure will be more discriminative and fairer if the evaluation is done over all 35 image pairs.

References

1. CUDA: Compute Unified Device Architecture programming guide. Tech. rep., Nvidia Corporation (2008)
2. Francis, J., de Jager, G.: The bilateral median filter. In: The 14th Symposium of the Pattern Recognition Association of South Africa (2003)
3. Gong, M., Yang, R., Wang, L., Gong, M.: A performance study on different cost aggregation approaches used in real-time stereo matching. IJCV 75(2), 283–296 (2007)
4. He, K., Sun, J., Tang, X.: Guided Image Filtering. In: Daniilidis, K., Maragos, P., Paragios, N. (eds.) ECCV 2010, Part I. LNCS, vol. 6311, pp. 1–14. Springer, Heidelberg (2010)
5. Hirschmüller, H., Scharstein, D.: Evaluation of stereo matching costs on images with radiometric differences. TPAMI 31(9), 1582–1599 (2009)
6. Hosni, A., Bleyer, M., Gelautz, M., Rhemann, C.: Local stereo matching using geodesic support weights. In: ICIP (2009)
7. Hosni, A., Rhemann, C., Bleyer, M., Rother, C., Gelautz, M.: Fast cost-volume filtering for visual correspondence and beyond. Submitted to TPAMI (2012)
8. Paris, S., Durandi, F.: A fast approximation of the bilateral filter using a signal processing approach. IJCV 81(1), 24–52 (2009)
9. Rhemann, C., Hosni, A., Bleyer, M., Rother, C., Gelautz, M.: Fast cost-volume filtering for visual correspondence and beyond. In: CVPR (2011)
10. Richardt, C., Orr, D., Davies, I., Criminisi, A., Dodgson, N.A.: Real-time Spatiotemporal Stereo Matching Using the Dual-Cross-Bilateral Grid. In: Daniilidis, K., Maragos, P., Paragios, N. (eds.) ECCV 2010, Part III. LNCS, vol. 6313, pp. 510–523. Springer, Heidelberg (2010)
11. Scharstein, D., Szeliski, R.: A taxonomy and evaluation of dense two-frame stereo correspondence algorithms. IJCV 47 47(1/2/3), 7–42 (2002), http://www.middlebury.edu/stereo/
12. Tombari, F., Mattoccia, S., Di Stefano, L.: Segmentation-Based Adaptive Support for Accurate Stereo Correspondence. In: Mery, D., Rueda, L. (eds.) PSIVT 2007. LNCS, vol. 4872, pp. 427–438. Springer, Heidelberg (2007)
13. Tombari, F., Mattoccia, S., Di Stefano, L., Addimanda, E.: Classification and evaluation of cost aggregation methods for stereo correspondence. In: CVPR (2008)
14. Yang, Q., Tan, K., Ahuja, N.: Real-time O(1) bilateral filtering. In: CVPR (2009)
15. Yoon, K., Kweon, S.: Adaptive support-weight approach for correspondence search. TPAMI 28(4), 650–656 (2006)

Groupwise Shape Registration
Based on Entropy Minimization

Youngwook Kee[1,2], Daniel Cremers[2], and Junmo Kim[1]

[1] Department of Electrical Engineering, KAIST, South Korea
[2] Department of Computer Science, TUM, Germany

Abstract. In this paper, we propose a unified framework for global-to-local groupwise shape registration based on an unbiased diffeomorphic shape atlas. We introduce the information-theoretic concept of *entropy* as the energy functional for shape registration. To this end, for given example shapes, we estimate the underlying shape distribution on the space of signed distance functions in a nonparametric way. We then perform global-to-local shape registration by minimizing the shape entropy estimate and entropy of displacement vector field. In addition, the gradient flow for the shape entropy is derived explicitly using the $\mathcal{L}_2$-distance in Hilbert space for a template shape estimation. Diffeomorphisms which are estimated by rigid/nonrigid registrations obviously establish dense correspondences between an example shape and the template shape. In addition, the composition rule gives a way to establish consistent correspondences by guaranteeing another diffeomorphism.

1   Introduction

Many frameworks for rigid/nonrigid image registration have been studied mainly in medical image analysis applications such as motion compensation, multimodal fusion and segmentation. On the other hand, only a few works have been done in shape registration literatures, in particular many problems have still remained unsolved in regard to groupwise shape registration. For example, if we simply extend a pairwise framework to the groupwise registration by choosing arbitrary shape as a reference coordinate to which all the given shapes are registered, it can cause a certain bias on the registration result. Besides, for a test shape, computational load to establish correspondences with all the given example shapes increases combinatorially as the data set increases.

Recently, an atlas based registration frameworks have been proposed in computational anatomy contexts to analyze inter/intra population variability, where they typically construct a diffeomorphic atals. For example, shape averaging method has been studied in the framework of elasticity theory for groupwise registration [7]. In our work, we follow similar procedures, i.e. we construct a representative shape and then estimate diffeomorphisms between the given example shapes. However, our method differs from previous works in that it is based on the information-theoretic framework and an implicit shape representation using the level set method, allowing an easy extension to 3-D shape registrations.

A. Pinz et al. (Eds.): DAGM/OAGM 2012, LNCS 7476, pp. 347–356, 2012.
© Springer-Verlag Berlin Heidelberg 2012

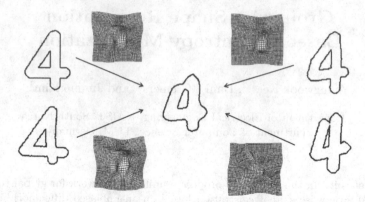

Fig. 1. We propose a groupwise shape registration by constructing a diffeomorphic atlas. For the given example shapes (digit 4), we estimate the template shape (center) by minimizing the entropy of the shape distribution. The correspondences are established by diffeomorphisms (warping fields) which are estimated by the global-to-local registration procedure.

1.1   Contributions

We propose one of the information-theoretic quantities, *entropy* as an energy functional to construct an unbiased diffeomorphic shape atlas. Thereby we solve the groupwise shape registration and correspondence problem simultaneously. To this end, we follow the global-to-local way of framework which has recently been proposed in shape registration context in [4]. However, our method differs from it in two ways. First, we estimate shape distribution in a nonparametric way to deal with various shapes which are typically known for having non-Gaussian distributions. Second, we cover groupwise registration in terms of the entropy minimization. As for the global registration proposed by [9], although they deal with groupwise alignment from variational point of view, their method mainly tries to maximize overlap between transformed shapes with a heuristic modifier that prevents a trivial solution of shrinking all the shapes to a single point.

From statistical point of view, since our framework is based on a nonparametric density estimation technique, it covers various shape distributions not limited to a parametric form of distributions such as Gaussian distribution. In addition, our method can be easily extended by incorporating a new shape metric, since the nonparametric shape density estimate and the corresponding shape entropy is formulated in terms of a generic shape distance metric. Regrading the nonrigid local registration, although we use the cubic B-spline parametrization with one of the typical regularizers which are widely used for optical flow estimation for penalizing displacement vector field so that it is not to be diffeomorphism, we unify it in terms of entropy minimization. In addition, by introducing a template shape which is also derived from the same framework, our method has additional benefit in a computational cost aspect in that we do not need to calculate all the $\binom{n}{2}$ warping fields. All we have to calculate is just n warping fields between the template shape and all the example shapes, and we consider the composition rule between diffeomorphisms.

2 Entropy for Groupwise Shape Registration

2.1 Entropy-Based Energy Functional

Let $\mathcal{C}$ be a random shape with probability distribution $p_{\mathcal{C}}(C)$, then the entropy of the random shape is defined as a functional of its probability distribution [2]:

$$h(\mathcal{C}) = -\mathbb{E}[\log p_{\mathcal{C}}(C)] = -\int_{\mathcal{S}} p_{\mathcal{C}}(C) \log p_{\mathcal{C}}(C)\, dC, \tag{1}$$

where the support of integral is the shape space $\mathcal{S}$. We describe the shape C and its transformation $\tilde{C}$ as $\tilde{C} = T[\mathbf{p}, \Theta]\{C\}$, , where $\mathbf{p}$ and Θ are global (rigid, similarity or affine) and local (nonrigid) transformation parameters, respectively. In our work, since we use signed distance functions to describe shapes, $\tilde{C}$ is represented as the zero level set of its signed distance function, i.e. $\tilde{\phi}(\mathbf{x}) = T[\mathbf{p}, \Theta]\{\phi(\mathbf{x})\}$, where $\mathbf{x} \in \mathbb{R}^n$ ($n=2$ for a curve and $n=3$ for a surface) and $\mathcal{S}$ is the space of signed distance functions. From now on, we omit the argument of the signed distance function if there is no ambiguity.

Meanwhile, since we do not assume any parametric form of the example shape distribution, we estimate the above shape probability distribution with the kernel density estimator in a nonparametric sense as in [3]. Thus the differential entropy of given example shapes is estimated as follows:

$$h(\Phi) \approx -\frac{1}{N} \sum_{i=1}^{N} \log p_{\Phi}(\phi_i) \tag{2}$$

$$\approx -\frac{1}{N} \sum_{i=1}^{N} \log \left(\frac{1}{N} \sum_{j=1}^{N} k_\sigma(d_{\mathcal{S}}(\phi_i, \phi_j)) \right), \tag{3}$$

where (2) comes from weak law of large numbers and (3) is result from the kernel density estimation using intrinsic distance metric $d_{\mathcal{S}}(\cdot, \cdot) : \mathcal{S} \times \mathcal{S} \to \mathbb{R}$ on the the space of signed distance functions (metric space). Here the composition of the 1-dimensional kernel function k_σ and the distance metric $d_{\mathcal{S}}$ plays a role of an infinite dimensional kernel function for the space of shapes. In addition, this entropy estimator is a well known consistent estimator in a mean square error sense [1].

From variational framework, the transformation parameters $\mathbf{p}_k$ and Θ_k, for all $k = 1, \ldots, N$, can be estimated by solving the following optimization problem:

$$\{(\mathbf{p}_1, \Theta_1), \ldots, (\mathbf{p}_N, \Theta_N)\} = \operatorname*{argmin}_{(\mathbf{p}_1, \Theta_1), \ldots, (\mathbf{p}_N, \Theta_N)} E((\mathbf{p}_1, \Theta_1), \ldots, (\mathbf{p}_N, \Theta_N)), \tag{4}$$

where the above energy functional is given by

$$E((\mathbf{p}_1, \Theta_1), \ldots, (\mathbf{p}_N, \Theta_N)) = -\frac{1}{N} \sum_{i=1}^{N} \log \left(\frac{1}{N} \sum_{j=1}^{N} k_\sigma(d_{\mathcal{S}}(\tilde{\phi}_i, \tilde{\phi}_j)) \right). \tag{5}$$

This energy functional can deal with groupwise shape registration in a global-to-local manner without being biased, which can be caused by choosing a particular shape as a reference shape. From an information-theoretic point of view, this framework finds the transformation parameters $\{(\mathbf{p}_k, \Theta_k)\}_{k=1}^{N}$ minimizing an uncertainty of the given shapes.

To solve the (4) directly using gradient descent method we need to derive a gradient of the energy functional (5) taken with respect to transformation parameters $\{(\mathbf{p}_k, \Theta_k)\}_{k=1}^{N}$. Since the global and local transformation parameters are related to each other in the above energy functional, there is no guarantee that the solution is unique in this way. In our work, therefore, we deal with the registration problem in a global-to-local manner incorporating the template shape which is discussed in Section 4. Consequently, we minimize (5) with respect to $\mathbf{p}_k$ for each $k = 1, \ldots, N$ in the beginning. The partial derivative with respect to $\mathbf{p}_k$ is given by

$$\nabla_{\mathbf{p}_k} E(\mathbf{p}_1, \ldots, \mathbf{p}_N) = -\frac{1}{N^2} \sum_{\substack{i=1 \\ i \neq k}}^{N} \frac{1}{\hat{p}(\tilde{\phi}_i)} k_\sigma(d_{\mathcal{S}}(\tilde{\phi}_i, \tilde{\phi}_k)) \nabla_{\mathbf{p}_k} \left(\frac{d_{\mathcal{S}}^2(\tilde{\phi}_i, \tilde{\phi}_k)}{-2\sigma^2} \right)$$

$$-\frac{1}{N^2} \frac{1}{\hat{p}(\tilde{\phi}_k)} \sum_{j=1}^{N} k_\sigma(d_{\mathcal{S}}(\tilde{\phi}_k, \tilde{\phi}_j)) \nabla_{\mathbf{p}_k} \left(\frac{d_{\mathcal{S}}^2(\tilde{\phi}_k, \tilde{\phi}_j)}{-2\sigma^2} \right), \tag{6}$$

where $k_\sigma(d_{\mathcal{S}}(\tilde{\phi}_i, \tilde{\phi}_k)) = \frac{1}{\sqrt{2\pi\sigma^2}} \exp(\frac{d_{\mathcal{S}}^2(\tilde{\phi}_i, \tilde{\phi}_k)}{-2\sigma^2})$ and the derivative of the kernel is given by $\nabla_{\mathbf{p}_k} k_\sigma(d_{\mathcal{S}}(\tilde{\phi}_i, \tilde{\phi}_k)) = k_\sigma(d_{\mathcal{S}}(\tilde{\phi}_i, \tilde{\phi}_k)) \nabla_{\mathbf{p}_k} \left(\frac{d_{\mathcal{S}}^2(\tilde{\phi}_i, \tilde{\phi}_k)}{-2\sigma^2} \right)$. As we can see, to expand this formula more, we need to know explicitly how the intrinsic metric is defined on $\mathcal{S}$.

2.2   Approximation of the Intrinsic Distance

In the energy functional (3), there is an issue of how to define the intrinsic metric on the shape space $\mathcal{S}$. Since we simply know that the space of the signed distance functions is not Euclidean space (curvature $\kappa = 0$), we should use a distance metric containing the space curvature information. However, this problem is beyond the scope of this work, accordingly we approximate the intrinsic distance metric to other mathematically tractable distance function based on some reasonable assumptions in [5] along with an iterative back projection strategy; back project $\phi + \delta$ which is off the shape manifold onto the shape manifold $\mathcal{S}$ itself during optimization process whenever it is needed.

The space of signed distance functions $\mathcal{S}$ is a subset of the infinite dimensional Hilbert space $\mathcal{L}_2$, which is defined as the collection of all square integrable functions from image space Ω to $\mathbb{R}$, i.e. $\mathcal{S} \subset \{\psi \mid \psi : \Omega \to \mathbb{R}, \ \|\psi\| = \sqrt{\frac{1}{|\Omega|} \int_\Omega |\psi(\mathbf{x})|^2 \, d\mathbf{x}} < \infty\}$, where the norm is induced from the inner product which is defined by:

$$\left\langle \tilde{\phi}_k, \tilde{\phi}_j \right\rangle_{\mathcal{L}_2} = \frac{1}{|\Omega|} \int_\Omega \tilde{\phi}_k(\mathbf{x}) \tilde{\phi}_j(\mathbf{x}) d\mathbf{x}. \tag{7}$$

Except the scaling factor in front of the integration, this is one of the general inner products for the typical Hilbert space. However, we introduce normalizing factor to remove dependency on the size of images, which has been discussed in [5]. Hence, the $\mathcal{L}_2$-distance is induced from this inner product as follows:

$$d_{\mathcal{L}_2}(\tilde{\phi}_k, \tilde{\phi}_j) = \sqrt{\left\langle \tilde{\phi}_k - \tilde{\phi}_j, \tilde{\phi}_k - \tilde{\phi}_j \right\rangle_{\mathcal{L}_2}} = \sqrt{\frac{1}{|\Omega|} \int_{\Omega} (\tilde{\phi}_k(\mathbf{x}) - \tilde{\phi}_j(\mathbf{x}))^2 d\mathbf{x}}. \quad (8)$$

In our work, we use (8) to approximate the intrinsic distance metric on shape manifold $\mathcal{S}$. During minimization we back-project $\phi + \delta$ onto the space of signed distance functions by solving eikonal equation:

$$|\nabla \phi| = 1 \quad (9)$$

using the Tsitsiklis algorithm [10].

3   Global Registration

3.1   Similarity Transformation Model

We consider two equivalent planar shapes with different poses, $\phi(\mathbf{x})$ and $\tilde{\phi}(\mathbf{x})$. These shapes are identical if there exists a similarity transformation $T[\mathbf{p}]$ such that $\tilde{\phi}(\mathbf{x}) = T[\mathbf{p}]\phi(\mathbf{x})$. Since the similarity transformation is linear, $T[\mathbf{p}]$ parameterized by $\mathbf{p} = (a\ b\ \theta\ h)^\top$ is given by

$$T[\mathbf{p}] = R(\theta) \circ H(h) \circ M(a, b), \quad (10)$$

where a, b are x-axis and y-axis translation, θ is a counterclockwise rotation angle and h is an isotropic scaling parameter, respectively. Thus, the mapping from (x, y) to $(\tilde{x}, \tilde{y}) = T[\mathbf{p}](x, y)$ by $T[\mathbf{p}]$ is explicitly given by

$$\begin{aligned}
\left(\tilde{x}\ \tilde{y}\ 1\right)^\top &= T[\mathbf{p}] \left(x\ y\ 1\right)^\top \\
&= \underbrace{\begin{pmatrix} \cos\theta & \sin\theta & 0 \\ -\sin\theta & \cos\theta & 0 \\ 0 & 0 & 1 \end{pmatrix}}_{R(\theta)} \underbrace{\begin{pmatrix} h & 0 & 0 \\ 0 & h & 0 \\ 0 & 0 & 1 \end{pmatrix}}_{H(h)} \underbrace{\begin{pmatrix} 1 & 0 & a \\ 0 & 1 & b \\ 0 & 0 & 1 \end{pmatrix}}_{M(a,b)} \begin{pmatrix} x \\ y \\ 1 \end{pmatrix} \\
&= \underbrace{R(\theta) \circ H(h) \circ M(a, b)}_{T[\mathbf{p}]} \left(x\ y\ 1\right)^\top.
\end{aligned} \quad (11)$$

The above is formulated a bit differently from [9] in order to emphasize the fact that the order of operation is important. Thus, two same shapes having differen pose parameters are related by

$$\tilde{\phi}(T[\mathbf{p}](x, y)) = \phi(x, y), \qquad (x, y) \in \Omega, \quad (12)$$

equivalently

$$\tilde{\phi}(\tilde{x}, \tilde{y}) = \phi(T^{-1}[\mathbf{p}](\tilde{x}, \tilde{y})), \qquad (\tilde{x}, \tilde{y}) \in \Omega, \qquad (13)$$

where

$$T^{-1}[\mathbf{p}] = M^{-1}(a, b) \circ H^{-1}(h) \circ R^{-1}(\theta) = M(-a, -b) H(\frac{1}{h}) R(-\theta). \qquad (14)$$

Note that as for the isotropic scaling (12) and (13) are not satisfied, i.e. h is related as $\tilde{\phi}(h(x, y)) = \frac{1}{h}\phi(x, y)$. However, since the back-projection scheme is turned on every iteration, the equalities are consistent under this treatment.

3.2   Gradient for the Global Registration

Based on the assumption in Section 2.2, we replace $d_{\mathcal{S}}(\cdot, \cdot)$ by $d_{\mathcal{L}_2}(\cdot, \cdot)$. Then gradient of the proposed energy functional (6) becomes:

$$\nabla_{\mathbf{p}_k} E(\mathbf{p}_1, \ldots, \mathbf{p}_N) = -\frac{1}{N^2} \sum_{\substack{i=1 \\ i \neq k}}^{N} \frac{1}{\hat{p}(\tilde{\phi}_i)} k_\sigma(d_{\mathcal{L}_2}(\tilde{\phi}_i, \tilde{\phi}_k)) \nabla_{\mathbf{p}_k} \left(\frac{d_{\mathcal{L}_2}^2(\tilde{\phi}_i, \tilde{\phi}_k)}{-2\sigma^2} \right)$$

$$\qquad (15)$$

$$- \frac{1}{N^2} \frac{1}{\hat{p}(\tilde{\phi}_k)} \sum_{j=1}^{N} k_\sigma(d_{\mathcal{L}_2}(\tilde{\phi}_k, \tilde{\phi}_j)) \nabla_{\mathbf{p}_k} \left(\frac{d_{\mathcal{L}_2}^2(\tilde{\phi}_k, \tilde{\phi}_j)}{-2\sigma^2} \right),$$

where

$$\nabla_{\mathbf{p}_k} \left(\frac{d_{\mathcal{L}_2}^2(\tilde{\phi}_k, \tilde{\phi}_j)}{-2\sigma^2} \right) = -\frac{1}{\sigma^2} \frac{1}{|\Omega|} \int_\Omega (\tilde{\phi}_k(\mathbf{x}) - \tilde{\phi}_j(\mathbf{x})) \nabla_{\mathbf{p}_k} \tilde{\phi}_k d\mathbf{x}, \qquad (16)$$

and from the relation (13), we can derive $\nabla_{\mathbf{p}} \tilde{\phi}_k$ as follows:

$$\nabla_{\mathbf{p}} \tilde{\phi}_k = \nabla_{\mathbf{p}} (\phi_k \circ T^{-1}[\mathbf{p_k}])(\tilde{x}, \tilde{y})|_{\mathbf{p}=\mathbf{p_0}} = \begin{pmatrix} \frac{\partial \phi_k(T^{-1}[\mathbf{p_k}](\tilde{x}, \tilde{y}))}{\partial p_1^k} \\ \frac{\partial \phi_k(T^{-1}[\mathbf{p_k}](\tilde{x}, \tilde{y}))}{\partial p_2^k} \\ \frac{\partial \phi_k(T^{-1}[\mathbf{p_k}](\tilde{x}, \tilde{y}))}{\partial p_3^k} \\ \frac{\partial \phi_k(T^{-1}[\mathbf{p_k}](\tilde{x}, \tilde{y}))}{\partial p_4^k} \end{pmatrix}^{\mathsf{T}}_{\mathbf{p}=\mathbf{p_0}}, \qquad (17)$$

where each component (17) is given by:

$$\frac{\partial \phi_k(T^{-1}[\mathbf{p}](\tilde{x}, \tilde{y}))}{\partial p_l^k} = \nabla \phi(x, y)|_{(x,y)=T^{-1}[\mathbf{p}](\tilde{x}, \tilde{y})} \frac{\partial T^{-1}[\mathbf{p}]}{\partial p_l^k}|_{\mathbf{p}=\mathbf{p_0}} \begin{pmatrix} \tilde{x} \\ \tilde{y} \\ 1 \end{pmatrix} \qquad (18)$$

where $\nabla \phi(x, y)|_{(x,y)=T^{-1}[\mathbf{p}](\tilde{x}, \tilde{y})} = \begin{pmatrix} \frac{\partial \phi}{\partial x} & \frac{\partial \phi}{\partial y} & 0 \end{pmatrix}|_{(x,y)=T^{-1}[\mathbf{p}](\tilde{x}, \tilde{y})}$ and $p_1^k = a$, $p_2^k = b$, $p_3^k = \theta$, $p_4^k = h$. The partial derivatives of inverse transformation is given by matrix derivative with respect to the pose parameters.

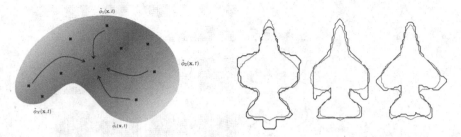

Fig. 2. Entropy minimizing paths of example shapes on the space of signed distance functions via the gradient flow (left) and overlay of aircraft shapes with the template shape (right). Left is a schematic figure representing the nonlinear shape manifold embedded in Hilbert space, where all the points and paths (which are back-projected trajectories) are lying on the manifold.

4   Gradient Flow for the Template Shape

Once the example shapes are globally aligned by the similarity transformation, we consider the problem of building a representative shape; specifically we focuss on the gradient flow for the entropy estimate. Then, the level set method is used to implement the curve evolution via the gradient vector field; all the example shapes are evolved simultaneously under this vector field until they are converged. Let us consider the entropy estimate of the globally aligned shapes with time dependency as follows:

$$E(\tilde{\phi}_1(\mathbf{x},t),\ldots,\tilde{\phi}_N(\mathbf{x},t)) = -\frac{1}{N}\sum_{i=1}^{N}\log\left(\frac{1}{N}\sum_{j=1}^{N}k_\sigma(d_{\mathcal{L}_2}(\tilde{\phi}_i(\mathbf{x},t),\tilde{\phi}_j(\mathbf{x},t)))\right) \ . \quad (19)$$

Generally, we should take a functional derivative using the variational calculus to derive the gradient flow of (19). However, as we discussed in Section 2.2, the $\mathcal{L}_2$-distance which is defined by the inner product in Hilbert space is represented by region integral of squared difference between two signed distance functions on image domain Ω. Therefore, the gradient flow can be derived straightforwardly using the region integral technique in [8]. For space limitation, we omit the derivation process but state the final result as follows:

$$\frac{\partial\tilde{\phi}_k(\mathbf{x},t)}{\partial t} = \frac{1}{\sigma^2}\frac{1}{N^2}\sum_{\substack{i=1\\i\neq k}}^{N}\frac{1}{\hat{p}(\tilde{\phi}_i(\mathbf{x}))}k_\sigma(d_{\mathcal{L}_2}(\tilde{\phi}_i(\mathbf{x}),\tilde{\phi}_k(\mathbf{x},t)))(\tilde{\phi}_i(\mathbf{x})-\tilde{\phi}_k(\mathbf{x},t))$$

$$+\frac{1}{\sigma^2}\frac{1}{N^2}\frac{1}{\hat{p}(\tilde{\phi}_k(\mathbf{x},t))}\sum_{j=1}^{N}k_\sigma(d_{\mathcal{L}_2}(\tilde{\phi}_j(\mathbf{x}),\tilde{\phi}_k(\mathbf{x},t)))(\tilde{\phi}_j(\mathbf{x})-\tilde{\phi}_k(\mathbf{x},t)).$$

$$(20)$$

Note that all the globally aligned shapes become similar to each other during the curve evolution process. This means that entropy goes to negative infinity

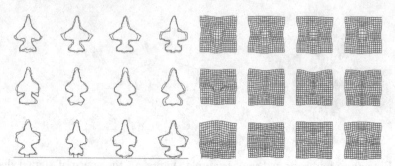

Fig. 3. Local registration from globally aligned shapes (black) to the template shape (red) using the free form deformation. The dense correspondences are established by estimating their warping fields. Along with the template shape, these construct an atlas for the given example shapes.

as the kernel size of the density estimate goes to 0. Since this typically implies that some normalization or regularization is missing, in order to resolve this unboundedness characteristic of the shape entropy, we introduce the following hard constraint not to let density estimate converge to the Dirac delta function:

$$\sigma(t) \geq \epsilon, \quad \text{for all } t. \tag{21}$$

Although this guarantees that the entropy is bounded, it is just a heuristic constraint. Thus, future work is focussed on identifying more principled solutions to the above problem. The curve evolution process on the space of signed distance functions is depicted in Fig. 2.

5   Local Registration

Based on the globally registered shapes $\{\tilde{\phi}_k(\mathbf{x})\}_{k=1}^{N}$ and the estimated template shape $\bar{\phi}(\mathbf{x})$, the pairwise nonrigid local registration is performed to establish dense correspondences between example shapes and the template shape. To this end, we use cubic B-spline parametrization which uses a lattice of control points and interpolates other points in between them with the cubic B spline basis functions [6]. We use this algorithm along with the smoothness regularizer for displacement vector field, which is typically used for optical flow estimation as follows:

$$E(\mathbf{\Theta_k}) = d_{\mathcal{L}_2}(\bar{\phi}(\mathbf{x}), \tilde{\phi}(T^{-1}[\mathbf{\Theta_k}](\mathbf{x}))) + \lambda \int_{\Omega} ||\nabla\Theta_k||^2 d\mathbf{x}, \quad \text{for all } k, \tag{22}$$

where $\mathbf{\Theta_k} : \Omega \to \mathbb{R}^2$ is a displacement field of k-th image.

The smoothness regularization term can be expressed in terms of an entropy, so the minimization of (22) is interpreted as the entropy minimization framework as follows: If we consider $h(\nabla\Theta_k)$ and the displacement vector field whose associating distribution is assumed to be Gaussian, then the entropy becomes

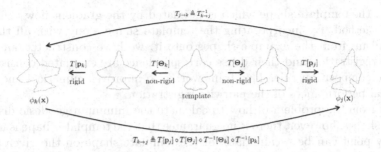

$$T_{j \to k} \triangleq T_{k \to j}^{-1}$$

$$T_{k \to j} \triangleq T[\mathbf{p}_j] \circ T[\Theta_j] \circ T^{-1}[\Theta_k] \circ T^{-1}[\mathbf{p}_k]$$

Fig. 4. Matching two aircraft shapes (leftmost to the rightmost, or vice versa) passing through the template shape (middle). The correspondences between two shapes are established via composition of the diffeomorphisms which are estimated by the global and local registrations. Since the estimated transformations are diffeomorphic, the correspondences are not changed regardless of the composition order, i.e. its result is the same from the leftmost to the rightmost or vice versa.

proportional to $\log \mathrm{Var}(\nabla \Theta_k)$. In other words, the regularization term is proportional to $e^{h(\nabla \Theta_k)}$, so minimizing the regularization term means minimizing the entropy of the rate of change of displacement field. The local deformation result and their diffeomorphisms (warping fields) are depicted in Fig. 3.

6 Shape Atlas Construction

Now, for each example shape we have their diffeomorphisms onto the template shape, i.e. composition of the similarity transformation and local deformation field. Thus, along with the template shape we construct a consistent diffeomorphic shape atlas; any two shapes within the atlas coordinate are related in the one-to-one correspondence sense, where the template shape plays a significant role such as a regularization not to make the warping fields folded. For any two shapes $\phi_k(\mathbf{x})$ and $\phi_j(\mathbf{x})$, we have the consistent transformation $T_{k \to j}$ such that $\phi_j(\mathbf{x}) = T_{k \to j}\{\phi_k(\mathbf{x})\}$, where $T_{k \to j} \triangleq T^{-1}[\mathbf{p}_j] \circ T^{-1}[\Theta_j] \circ T[\Theta_k] \circ T[\mathbf{p}_k]$ and $T_{j \to k} \triangleq T_{k \to j}^{-1}$. If we regard $T_{k \to j}$ as a map from Ω_k to Ω_j, therefore, the one-to-one correspondences between the two shapes are naturally defined by:

$$\phi_j(T_{k \to j}(\mathbf{x})) = \phi_k(\mathbf{x}), \quad \mathbf{x} \in \Omega_k, \tag{23}$$

equivalently

$$\phi_j(\mathbf{x}) = \phi_k(T_{j \to k}(\mathbf{x})), \quad \mathbf{x} \in \Omega_j. \tag{24}$$

This composition and correspondences establishment are illustrated in Fig. 4.

7 Discussion and Conclusion

In this paper, we have proposed a variational framework for groupwise shape registration using nonparametric shape distribution. In addition, we have established dense correspondences among the example shapes by deforming all the shapes to the template shape which is estimated by the gradient flow using the level set method. By incorporating the template shape along with all the diffeomorphisms from the example shapes onto it, we have constructed an atlas. Pairwise registration and their dense correspondence are evaluated consistently using the composition rule. This framework also improves numerical and computational performances of the pairwise registration.

Apart from the problem of how to calculate the minimum geodesic distance between shapes, however, there is no guarantee that the template shape is unique since any point can be a candidate for the template shape on the given shape space. In other words, if all the example shapes are deformed to arbitrary shape in a certain way, it is the minimizer of the entropy functional the value of which goes to $-\infty$. In our work, the template shape has a meaning that it is the point where all the shapes meet when they are moving in a way that decreases the entropy functional most rapidly.

References

1. Ahmad, I., Lin, P.: A nonparametric estimation of the entropy for absolutely continuous distributions (corresp.). IEEE Transactions on Information Theory 22(3), 372–375 (1976)
2. Cover, T.M., Thomas, J.A.: Elements of Information Theory. Wiley (2006)
3. Cremers, D., Osher, S.J., Soatto, S.: Kernel density estimation and intrinsic alignment for shape priors in level set segmentation. International Journal of Computer Vision 69(3), 335–351 (2006)
4. Huang, X., Paragios, N., Metaxas, D.: Shape registration in implicit spaces using information theory and free form deformations. IEEE Transactions on Pattern Analysis and Machine Intelligence 28(8), 1303–1318 (2006)
5. Kim, J., Cetin, M., Willsky, A.: Nonparametric shape priors for active contour-based image segmentation. Signal Processing 87(12), 3021–3044 (2007)
6. Rueckert, D., Sonoda, L., Hayes, C., Hill, D., Leach, M., Hawkes, D.: Nonrigid registration using free-form deformations: application to breast mr images. IEEE Transactions on Medical Imaging 18(8), 712–721 (1999)
7. Rumpf, M., Wirth, B.: A nonlinear elastic shape averaging approach. SIAM Journal on Imaging Sciences 2(3), 800–833 (2009)
8. Tsai, A., Yezzi Jr., A., Willsky, A.: Curve evolution implementation of the mumford-shah functional for image segmentation, denoising, interpolation, and magnification. IEEE Transactions on Image Processing 10(8), 1169–1186 (2001)
9. Tsai, A., Yezzi Jr., A., Wells, W., Tempany, C., Tucker, D., Fan, A., Grimson, W., Willsky, A.: A shape-based approach to the segmentation of medical imagery using level sets. IEEE Transactions on Medical Imaging 22(2), 137–154 (2003)
10. Tsitsiklis, J.: Efficient algorithms for globally optimal trajectories. IEEE Transactions on Automatic Control 40(9), 1528–1538 (1995)

Adaptive Multi-cue 3D Tracking
of Arbitrary Objects

Germán Martín García, Dominik Alexander Klein, Jörg Stückler,
Simone Frintrop, and Armin B. Cremers

Department of Computer Science III
Rheinische Friedrich-Wilhelms-Universität Bonn

Abstract. We present a general method for RGB-D data that is able to
track arbitrary objects in real-time in challenging real-world scenarios.
The method is based on the Condensation algorithm. The observation
model consists of a target/background classifier that is boosted from a
pool of grayscale, color, and depth features. The training set of the observation model is updated with new examples from tracking and the
classifier is re-trained to cope with the new appearances of the target.
A mechanism maintains a small set of specialized candidate features in
the pool, thus decreasing the computational time, while keeping the performance stable. Depth measurements are integrated into the prediction
of the 3D state of the particles. We evaluate our approach with a new
benchmark for RGB-D tracking algorithms; the results prove our method
to be robust under real-world settings, being able to keep track of the
targets over 96% of the time.

1 Introduction

Visual object tracking is the task of estimating the state of a target of interest
among consecutive images. Its applications are well known and among them we
find automatic surveillance [18], sports events video analysis [11], or autonomous
navigation [4]; in the robotics community it is also a key ability in tasks such as
visual servoing [12]. Visual tracking is a difficult task, since trackers usually have
to deal with the problem that the target's appearance and dimensions change
constantly, illumination varies in the scene, etc. A recent survey [23] gives a good
overview and taxonomy of solutions. More recently, visual tracking has also been
surveyed from the point of view of the robotics community in chapter 3 of [17].

Some of the proposed solutions are focused on a specific task or a type of
object. Wu and Nevatia [22] proposed a system that is able to detect parts of
humans independently and merge them to form solid hypotheses and thus deal
with partial occlusions. Giebel et al. [8] use a set of training data to learn a
representation of the object in the form of Dynamic Point Distribution Models
before the tracking starts. Three visual cues, shape, texture, and stereo disparity
measurements are integrated in the observation model of a particle filter. Our
approach to the tracking problem, however, is not specific to a task, nor to any
specific type of object.

A. Pinz et al. (Eds.): DAGM/OAGM 2012, LNCS 7476, pp. 357–366, 2012.
© Springer-Verlag Berlin Heidelberg 2012

When no previous knowledge of the object is available, the representation of the target needs to be updated to be able to cope with new appearances. The adaptation of the model brings along the drifting problem: the tracker can adapt to an object that is not the target. Using several cues is a common way to improve the robustness of the tracker. From the field of visual attention, a component-based tracker was introduced [7]; high contrast components in intensity and color channels are found and integrated in a descriptor. This descriptor is then used as part of the observation model of a particle filter. Recently, the tracking-by-detection paradigm has attracted more attention. Santner et al. [20] propose a combination of three trackers that adapt at increasing rates: template-based, on-line random forest, and optical flow. To solve the drifting problem, the trackers are disposed on a cascade so that updates can be inhibited. Avidan [2] treats tracking as a binary classification problem. An ensemble of weak classifiers is calculated using AdaBoost and is adapted to new appearances of the object. Grabner et al. [9] also used Adaboost to form a strong classifier of weak classifiers that are trained on-line with incoming frames. They propose a feature pool update mechanism where the worst weak classifiers are removed and new ones are sampled. We followed this idea to keep a reduced set of candidate features as well as specialized to the object modalities. Very related is the work of Klein et al. [14,15]: Haar-like [15] and Gradient features [14] are boosted into a strong classifier. It keeps a training set of examples that is updated over time, on which the classifier is re-trained to cope with new appearances of target and background. This adaptive observation model is integrated in a particle filter [13].

The present work follows that of Klein et al. [14,15]. We make use of the Kinect sensor as a source of RGB and depth data instead of a monocular camera. Therefore, the variety of objects that can be tracked is only limited by the measurement principle of the sensor. To improve the robustness of the algorithm, we propose the use of several cues: not only grayscale but also color and depth features. To deal with the increasing size of the feature space, we define a mechanism that keeps its cardinality low, thus saving computational time, as well as specialized to the target appearance modalities: the feature space is now composed of three different kinds in number proportional to their discriminative power. Furthermore, depth information allows us to improve the accuracy of the predictions of the particle filter, through the definition of a 3D state space for the particles. To test the convenience of the proposed improvements we developed an RGB-D tracking benchmark, where the benefit of each of the contributions is evaluated with respect to the old approach. The success of the applicable enhancements is also evaluated in two existing RGB benchmarks and compared with other state of the art algorithms.

2   Adaptive Tracking

The tracking system is based on the Condensation algorithm [13]: a set of N weighted particles $S_t = \{\pi_i, x_i\}_{i=1}^{N}$, where π_i is the weight and x_i is the state of the ith particle, approximates the conditional pdf of the state given the measurements $p(x_t|z_{1:t})$ at time t, and thus, estimates the location and appearance of the target over time. In the original tracker, the state space of the particles is two-dimensional: $x_{2d,t} = \{p_u, p_v, \dot{p}_u, \dot{p}_v, w, h\}$. Particles have position p_u, p_v, velocity $\dot{p}_u, \dot{p}_v$, and dimensions w, h defined in the image plane. The observation model is constructed by boosting a strong classifier of center surround Haar-like [15] or grayscale gradient features [14]. The feature space, or feature pool, consists of features of different sizes and positions that cover the entire object sub-window. The Gentle Boost algorithm [6] builds a strong classifier c as the combination of M features/classifiers weak that best discriminates the target from the background: $c(x) = \frac{1}{M} \sum_{i=1}^{M} weak_i(x)$. A key aspect of the tracker is that the observation model is continuously adapted to the new appearances of the target and background. At every frame, to prevent from drifting, if the confidence on the estimate is high enough and the particles have enough overlap, the update is performed: the target estimate of the particle with the highest weight is added to the training set as a new positive example, and new negative examples are randomly drawn from the current background; finally the classifier is re-trained on the new training set. The weights of the particles are set by exponentiating the result of the classifier; more details can be found in [15,14].

2.1   3D State Space

As opposed to the previous approach, where the particles "live" in the image plane, we define the particles' state space by the position r_t and velocity v_t of a bounding cylinder around the object in 3D world coordinates: $x_{3d,t} = \{r_t, v_t\}$. The pose of the cylinder is assumed to be upright with respect to the camera axis. Its height H and diameter D are fixed in the initialization of the tracking process. This is different from the previous approach, where the width and height were adapted. A first order autoregressive motion model is applied to the particles. Every time step, the positions are updated with the velocities and the value of the time interval. The velocities are also updated by adding Gaussian white noise with a variance of $550 \, \mathrm{mm^2/s^2}$. Equation 1 summarizes this step:

$$r'_t = r_{t-1} + v_{t-1} \, \Delta t, \qquad\qquad v'_t = v_{t-1} + \mathcal{N}(0; \Sigma), \qquad (1)$$

The state of the particles is now corrected by incorporating the depth information of the sensor. At the predicted position of the particle r'_t, its projection onto the image plane is found. The projection is a rectangle in the image plane; the average of depth measurements is computed in an inner rectangle defined by 10% of the projection's dimensions. This depth is used to correct the particles' positions as well as the speeds, Equation 2.

$$r_t = \phi(r'_t), \qquad\qquad v_t = v'_t + \frac{r_t - r'_t}{\Delta t}. \qquad (2)$$

where ϕ finds the corrected position as discussed above. By making this correction we ensure that the particles' positions are restricted to existing points in the point cloud. At the corrected position we project the particle onto the image plane to apply the observation model. Since the bounding cylinder is assumed to

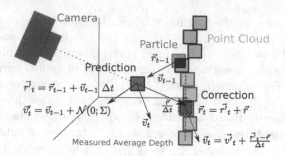

Fig. 1. At time $t - 1$, a particle at position r_{t-1} moving with velocity v_{t-1}. Based on the motion model, the predicted position is r'_t and the velocity v'_t. They are corrected according to the sensor data giving r_t and v_t.

be upright with respect to the camera axis, its image projection is a rectangle. The process of prediction and correction is represented in Figure 1.

As a side effect of using a 3D state of the particles, the generation of negative examples for the observation model improves. Having the dimensions of the target in 3D, we are able to determine the size that a negative example should have at a given position in the image with a given depth measurement. This improves the accuracy of the observation model, since we are generating negative examples of the sizes that the target would have in the image if it occupied that position in 3D space.

2.2   Feature Kinds

In [14], the features are intensity gradients defined over rectangular regions. The features are computed in constant time with the help of integral images [21]. The weak classifier consists of a central bin that captures weak gradients and outer bins that incorporate strong gradients. It interpolates the gradient feature responses to the training examples, to the closest bins according to their orientation and magnitude. The gradient magnitude multiplied by the weight coming from the boosting algorithm is stored. When binning is finished, a log-normal distribution is fitted over the training examples. The prediction of a weak classifier is given by the ratio of maximum-likelihood estimators for the positive and negative example distributions: $\frac{p}{p+n}$. For further details about the weak classifier one can refer to the original paper [14]. Here, we extend the previous work based on gray value intensity gradients work by additionally using depth gradients and color averages. They are represented in Figure 2.

Depth Gradient Features. The grayscale scalable gradient features of [14] can be applied to the depth layer. In the classifier, depicted in Figure 3, the thresholds that define the center and outer bins need to be adjusted to a meaningful value in the depth layer. We considered gradient values below 5 cm to correspond entirely to the center bin. Values between 5 and 20 cm are interpolated between center and outer bins, and those stronger than 20 cm fall entirely into the outer bins.

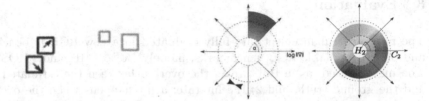

Fig. 2. Left: depth gradient features. Right: color average features

Fig. 3. Left: depth feature classifier. Right: color feature classifier

Color Features. Color averages are measured over rectangular regions in the image. An approximation of the HSV color space [10] is used to allow for real-time processing. The V value, corresponding to brightness, is here discarded since it is already captured by the grayscale features. The feature computation happens as follows. Given the RGB image, the HSV Cartesian representation approximation, given by $\alpha = \frac{1}{2}(2R - G - B)$ and $\beta = \frac{\sqrt{3}}{2}(G - B)$, is calculated.

Integral images [21] let us compute α and β averages over feature regions in constant time. The Cartesian averages can then be transformed to the polar representation of $H_2 = atan2(\beta, \alpha)$ and $C_2 = \sqrt{(\alpha^2 + \beta^2)}$. The color feature result is formed by the tuple (H_2, C_2). The features compute color averages represented by two-dimensional vectors. To classify them, we use the same strategy of binning and regression of the gradient features classifier. The inner and outer bin thresholds were adjusted empirically to 1 and 3 respectively.

2.3 Feature Sampling and Dynamic Feature Pool

We define two mechanisms to reduce the number of candidate features in the pool, as well as to let them adapt to the object modalities. First, for each feature kind, 50 dynamic features are added to the pool. For the color ones, the positions are drawn from a truncated Gaussian distribution in the interval $[0, 1] \times [0, 1]$ with mean at $(0.5, 0.5)$, the center of the object window, and covariance a diagonal matrix with elements 0.15^2. This is done to position the color features closer to the center of the object window where the target is more likely to be contained. The depth and grayscale gradient features' positions are uniformly randomly sampled. Additionally, the pool contains a small fixed set of equally distributed static features[1]. Second, to adapt to the object modalities the dynamic feature pool set is updated concurrently with the observation model: at each iteration one feature kind is chosen for removal and one for addition; this decision is taken proportionally to the mean training error of the feature kinds. Of the kind chosen for removal, the feature with the highest error is removed; of the kind chosen for addition, a new feature is sampled using the strategy defined before. The pool update does not affect the fixed set of static features.

---

[1] Features are here three times less densely sampled as in the previous approach [14], the actual number depends on the size of the object in the image. The ratio of dynamic:static features was between 1:1.5 and 1:2 in the tests performed.

3   Evaluation

The proposed enhancements are fully evaluated in a new RGB-D benchmark, and on two available RGB benchmarks, namely BoBoT [16] and PROST [20]. The metrics used, as in [15], are 1) the overlap between the estimated target and the ground truth, and 2) the hit rate; a hit happens when the overlap in one frame is bigger than $\frac{1}{3}$. In each sequence of the benchmarks, we run our algorithm ten times and compute the average metrics.

3.1   RGB Benchmarks

On the following two benchmarks, we evaluate the performance of the color features and the new feature pool mechanisms. The same parameters were used throughout the tests, namely: 2000 particles, 32 classifiers and 140 training examples. These parameters let the tracker run at a rate of 25 fps[2]. Four sets of tests were performed; in all of them the 2D state space was used:

- Test 1.1: grayscale and color features; new sampling approach, dynamic pool behavior enabled
- Test 1.2: grayscale and color features; new sampling approach, dynamic pool behavior disabled
- Test 1.3: grayscale and color features; old feature sampling approach
- Test 1.4 (as in [14] approach):grayscale features; old feature sampling approach

Table 1. BoBoT Benchmark Results: overlap and hit rate for test sequences A to L. The column *cpu* shows the average time in ms consumed for each frame. The best result is displayed in bold; the second best is underlined.

	A Over.	A Hit	B Over.	B Hit	C Over.	C Hit	D Over.	D Hit	E Over.	E Hit	F Over.	F Hit	G Over.	G Hit
1.1	<u>76.29</u>	99.95	80.55	100.0	92.33	100.0	**81.07**	100.0	**87.26**	100.0	65.19	**91.85**	73.68	100.0
1.2	75.06	**99.98**	80.22	100.0	91.85	100.0	<u>80.48</u>	100.0	87.08	100.0	**65.47**	91.74	72.60	100.0
1.3	**76.78**	99.8	<u>81.59</u>	100.0	92.95	100.0	<u>80.48</u>	100.0	87.03	100.0	<u>65.40</u>	91.83	72.64	100.0
1.4	62.09	94.0	**81.71**	100.0	**93.20**	100.0	79.94	100.0	**87.26**	100.0	65.00	91.78	**76.01**	100.0

	H Over.	H Hit	I Over.	I Hit	Ja Over.	Ja Hit	Jb Over.	Jb Hit	K Over.	K Hit	L Over.	L Hit	cpu	Averages Over.	Averages Hit
1.1	**97.25**	100.0	86.96	96.12	<u>83.75</u>	**98.61**	80.20	96.92	**85.84**	100.0	**68.76**	**90.83**	30.89	<u>80.00</u>	**97.51**
1.2	96.52	100.0	87.91	96.58	82.74	98.53	**82.16**	**98.05**	85.20	100.0	<u>62.86</u>	<u>78.85</u>	31.13	**80.01**	<u>97.44</u>
1.3	96.12	100.0	<u>87.99</u>	**97.02**	82.71	98.53	78.14	<u>97.46</u>	85.37	100.0	48.33	62.58	37.80	78.70	94.93
1.4	95.80	100.0	**88.02**	<u>97.01</u>	**83.91**	98.61	62.38	80.75	<u>85.37</u>	100.0	57.36	84.66	<u>31.12</u>	77.74	94.37

BoBoT Benchmark. The BoBoT benchmark [16] contains thirteen RGB sequences suitable for evaluating tracking algorithms. As it was shown in [15], the algorithm of [15] proved to be superior to the particle filter based approaches of [19] and [7]. The results, in Table 1, show that the use of color features together

---

[2] The experiments were executed on an Intel ® Xeon(R) CPU W3565 @ 3.20GHz x 4.

Table 2. Pascal score and mean distance error for the PROST Benchmark [20]. The cpu column shows the average time in ms consumed for each frame. The best result is displayed in bold; the second best is underlined.

	board		box		lemming		liquor		Averages		
	pascal	distance	pascal	distance	pascal	distance	pascal	distance	cpu	pascal	distance
GRAD [14]	**94.3**	**14.7**	91.8	13.2	78.0	28.4	91.4	11.9		**88.9**	17.05
PROST	75.0	37.0	91.4	**12.1**	70.5	25.4	83.7	21.6	-	80.15	24.02
MILTrack [3]	67.9	51.2	24.5	104.6	**83.6**	14.9	20.6	165.5	-	49.15	84.05
FragTrack [1]	67.9	90.1	61.4	57.4	54.9	82.8	79.9	30.7	-	66.02	65.25
Test 1.1	81.25	26.78	89.54	12.95	77.38	**12.57**	<u>95.20</u>	8.57	36.65	85.84	<u>15.22</u>
Test 1.2	78.43	28.85	86.52	14.10	79.92	12.62	95.76	8.83	37.40	85.16	16.10
Test 1.3	78.03	22.88	**92.33**	<u>12.15</u>	<u>83.21</u>	<u>12.71</u>	**96.49**	**7.60**	42.02	<u>87.52</u>	**13.84**
Test 1.4 [3]	<u>87.86</u>	21.59	92.62	12.49	67.16	60.95	92.83	12.06	41.30	85.12	26.77

with the new feature pool improves both overlap and hit rates without significant additional cost in computational time. In sequences A and Jb the use of color features gives a considerable benefit.

PROST Benchmark. PROST [20] introduced an RGB benchmark of four sequences and compared their results with other state-of-the-art tracking approaches. The metrics used are the percentage of frames correctly tracked (based on the PASCAL score [5]) and the mean distance error to the ground truth. The results, in Table 2, show that our approach is on average better than three other state-of-the-art tracking algorithms.

3.2   BoBoT-D Benchmark

The new benchmark consists of five RGB-D video sequences recorded with the Kinect sensor; it is also available at [16]. The ground truth data was manually labeled for each of them as the smallest rectangle that contains the target at each frame. Figure 4 shows a preview of the sequences. Sequence 1 shows a breakfast table. The target is a milk tetra-pack that is lifted, opened and from which some milk is poured into a coffee cup. This sequence attempts to test the performance of the algorithm on object rotations around the view point axis. In sequence 2, we find two persons passing a ball that is the target of the sequence. A radio control tank is the target of sequence 3; it moves around a scenario with batteries and a carton bridge. The next sequence contains a person walking down a corridor; the recording platform moves along while several people get in the way producing occlusions. The last of the sequences shows a white lunch box carried in front of an untextured background. The results are depicted in Table 3; videos with the results are included as supplemental material. For the following experiments, 2000 particles and 23 classifiers were used:

- Test 2.1: 3D state space; three feature kinds; new sampling of features and pool update mechanism.

---

[3] The results of the first line are those reported in [14]. They slightly differ to the ones we obtained with the current configuration in the last entry of the table (Test 1.4). Ours were obtained with a real-time configuration and the same set of parameters for arbitrary RGB sequences.

Fig. 4. BoBoT-D Benchmark: RGB and depth data for the five sequences: 'Milk', 'Ball', 'Tank', 'Person', and 'Lunch Box'.

- Test 2.2: 3D state space; three feature kinds; new sampling of features but no update of the feature pool.
- Test 2.3: 3D state space; three feature kinds; old feature pool.
- Test 2.4: 2D state space; three feature kinds; old feature pool.
- Test 2.5: 2D state space, grayscale features and old feature pool.

Sequence 1 (Milk). The results were similar in the five experiments,with an overlap above 70% and hit rate around 95% in tests 2.1, 2.2, and 2.3.

Sequence 2 (Ball). The use of color features is crucial to the success of this experiment. This can be seen when comparing test 2.4 with 2.5: only by adding the new features, the hit rate raised from 19.07% to 83.68%. When the 3D model was used, the hit rate went up to over 95%.

Sequence 3 (Tank). The 3D state space played an important role in this sequence, with hit rates higher than 93%. The relatively low score of the overlap average, around 55% with the 3D model, can be explained by the fact that once the dimensions of the bounding cylinder are learned from the first frame they are never updated. The tank's appearance is learned from a side view in the first frame, and since the dimensions of the bounding cylinder are fixed, when it moves to a frontal view less overlap occurs.

Sequence 4 (Person). The use of the 3D state space didn't result as crucial in this sequence because the size of the target remains almost constant. The occlusions occurring in this sequence can be observed in the three down peaks of the overlap plot of Figure 5.

Table 3. BoBoT-D Benchmark Results: overlap and hit rate for test sequences 'Milk', 'Ball', 'Tank', 'Person', and 'Lunch Box'. The cpu column shows the average time in ms consumed for each frame. The best result is displayed in bold; the second best is underlined.

	1 (Milk)		2 (Ball)		3 (Tank)		4 (Person)		5 (Box)		Averages		
	Over.	Hit	Over.	Hit	Over.	Hit	Over.	Hit	Over.	Hit	cpu	Over.	Hit
T. 2.1	<u>73.47</u>	**96.77**	**69.80**	96.91	**55.33**	94.09	70.67	<u>95.32</u>	73.10	99.81	<u>30.69</u>	<u>68.47</u>	**96.58**
T. 2.2	**74.61**	95.29	66.39	95.31	55.01	**94.27**	70.55	95.31	<u>75.20</u>	**100.00**	31.4	68.35	96.04
T. 2.3	73.21	<u>96.39</u>	<u>68.63</u>	**96.94**	<u>54.46</u>	<u>93.80</u>	**71.92**	95.17	**75.57**	**100.00**	33.52	**68.76**	<u>96.46</u>
T. 2.4	73.45	94.48	55.60	83.68	32.23	40.72	<u>70.72</u>	**95.92**	70.88	99.76	36.97	60.58	82.91
T. 2.5	69.01	89.14	14.08	19.07	28.92	32.30	67.07	91.70	47.42	70.66	**27.90**	45.3	60.57

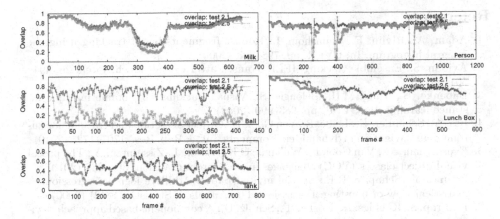

Fig. 5. Overlap plots in sequences 'Ball', 'Tank', 'Person', and 'Lunch Box'.

Sequence 5 (Lunch Box). The first three experiments gave very close results. The depth features were essential in this sequence: comparing 2.4 and 2.5, there is a considerable difference in both metrics; and not that much between 2.4 and the tests with the 3D state space.

Figure 5 compares the overlap of the tracker with all the improvements against the old approach. The results show that the 3D state space and the two new feature kinds give a considerable improvement on the performance of the tracking algorithm. Both metrics, overlap and hit rate, are significantly higher as compared to the old approach (Test 2.5). As reflected in Test 1.1: the hit rate of 96.58% on average, shows that targets were very successfully tracked; the overlap average of 68.47% shows an adequate estimation of the position and dimensions of the target. In sequences 2 and 3, the old approach could not keep track of the target. The speed gain can be seen when comparing the results of tests 2.1 and 2.2 against 2.3; having similar overlap and hit rates, the time consumed differs on about 10% in favor of the reduced feature pool.

4   Conclusion

We have presented several improvements to the existing tracking algorithm of [14]. First, we use a Kinect sensor that provides RGB-D data. To achieve robustness we propose the use of several cues instead of one: intensity, color and depth. The precision of the predictions is increased by extending the particles' state space to 3D world coordinates, and by integrating depth measurements in it. We proposed a mechanism that reduces the size of the feature space and specializes the content to the object modalities, reducing execution time. We compared our approach with several other state of the art trackers in three different benchmarks. When depth measurements are available, the tracker is highly robust and precise, being able to track the targets over 96% of the frames in difficult real world scenarios.

References

1. Adam, A., Rivlin, E., Shimshoni, I.: Robust fragments-based tracking using the integral histogram. In: CVPR, pp. 798–805 (2006)
2. Avidan, S.: Ensemble tracking. IEEE Trans. Pattern Anal. Mach. Intell. 29, 494–501 (2007)
3. Babenko, B., Yang, M.H., Belongie, S.: Visual tracking with online multiple instance learning. In: CVPR, pp. 983–990 (2009)
4. Ess, A., Schindler, K., Leibe, B., Van Gool, L.: Object detection and tracking for autonomous navigation in dynamic environments. Int. J. Rob. Res., 1707–1725 (2010)
5. Everingham, M., Van Gool, L., Williams, C.K., Winn, J., Zisserman, A.: The pascal visual object classes (VOC) challenge. Int. J. Comput. Vision, 303–338 (2010)
6. Freund, Y., Schapire, R.E.: Special invited paper. Additive logistic regression: A statistical view of boosting: Discussion. The Annals of Statistics 28(2) (2000)
7. Frintrop, S., Koenigs, A., Hoeller, F., Schulz, D.: A component-based approach to visual person tracking from a mobile platform. Int. J. of Social Robotics, 4531–4536 (2010)
8. Giebel, J., Gavrila, D.M., Schnörr, C.: A Bayesian Framework for Multi-cue 3D Object Tracking. In: Pajdla, T., Matas, J. (eds.) ECCV 2004, Part IV. LNCS, vol. 3024, pp. 241–252. Springer, Heidelberg (2004)
9. Grabner, H., Grabner, M., Bischof, H.: Real-time tracking via on-line boosting. In: Proc. BMVC, pp. 6.1–6.10 (2006)
10. Hanbury, A.: Constructing cylindrical coordinate colour spaces. Pattern Recogn. Lett. 29(4), 494–500 (2008)
11. Hess, R., Fern, A.: Discriminatively trained particle filters for complex multi-object tracking. In: CVPR 2009, pp. 240–247. IEEE (2009)
12. Hutchinson, S., Hager, G., Corke, P.: A tutorial on visual servo control. IEEE Transactions on Robotics and Automation, 651–670 (1996)
13. Isard, M., Blake, A.: Condensation-conditional density propagation for visual tracking. Int. J. of Computer Vision 29, 5–28 (1998)
14. Klein, D.A., Cremers, A.B.: Boosting scalable gradient features for adaptive real-time tracking. In: ICRA, pp. 4411–4416 (2011)
15. Klein, D.A., Schulz, D., Frintrop, S., Cremers, A.B.: Adaptive real-time video-tracking for arbitrary objects. In: IROS, pp. 772–777 (2010)
16. Klein, D.A.: BoBoT - Bonn Benchmark on Tracking,
    http://www.iai.uni-bonn.de/~kleind/tracking/index.html
17. Kragic, D., Vincze, M.: Vision for robotics. Foundations and Trends in Robotics (2009)
18. Liem, M., Gavrila, D.M.: Multi-person Localization and Track Assignment in Overlapping Camera Views. In: Mester, R., Felsberg, M. (eds.) DAGM 2011. LNCS, vol. 6835, pp. 173–183. Springer, Heidelberg (2011)
19. Pérez, P., Hue, C., Vermaak, J., Gangnet, M.: Color-Based Probabilistic Tracking. In: Heyden, A., Sparr, G., Nielsen, M., Johansen, P. (eds.) ECCV 2002, Part I. LNCS, vol. 2350, pp. 661–675. Springer, Heidelberg (2002)
20. Santner, J., Leistner, C., Saffari, A., Pock, T., Bischof, H.: Prost: Parallel robust online simple tracking. In: CVPR, pp. 723–730 (2010)
21. Viola, P., Jones, M.: Robust real-time object detection. Int. J. of Computer Vision (2001)
22. Wu, B., Nevatia, R.: Detection and tracking of multiple, partially occluded humans by bayesian combination of edgelet based part detectors. Int. J. Comput. Vision, 247–266 (2007)
23. Yilmaz, A., Javed, O., Shah, M.: Object tracking: A survey. ACM Comput. Surv. (2006)

Training of Classifiers for Quality Control of On-Line Laser Brazing Processes with Highly Imbalanced Datasets

Daniel Fecker, Volker Märgner, and Tim Fingscheidt

Institute for Communications Technology
Technische Universität Braunschweig
Schleinitzstr.22, 38106 Braunschweig, Germany
{fecker,maergner,fingscheidt}@ifn.ing.tu-bs.de

Abstract. This paper investigates on the training of classifiers with highly imbalanced datasets for industrial quality control. The application is on-line process monitoring of laser brazing processes and only a limited amount of data of an imperfection class is available for training. Bayesian adaptation is used to derive a model of the imperfection class from a well sampled model of the class representing a high grade joint surface. For this application, we are able to show that with the sparse training data a performance comparable to a training with a balanced dataset is achievable and even a moderate increase of training data quickly yields a performance gain.

1 Introduction

Laser brazing is a well established joining process in the automotive industry. The quality requirements for the brazed joints are usually very high. Especially in regions of a vehicle which are easily observable by the customers (e.g., the boot lid), it is mandatory that the joints do not contain any imperfections which degrade the visual appearance of the coated surface. For providing a high grade standard, a brazed work piece is conventionally inspected in several test stations. In the past years, new systems have been developed which enable to measure the quality on-line during the brazing process [4,1,16,8,6]. This type of quality control monitoring is already known from the application of laser welding [12].

Our paper focuses on a detection system for the on-line detection of imperfections under the constraint that only a highly imbalanced dataset for the training of a classifier is available. Like in many other production processes, it is difficult to get enough data of sporadic product imperfections. Even though, in this application the data was obtained in an experimental assembly, it was difficult to generate certain types of imperfections artificially (e.g., small pores[1]). To achieve this, the process parameters had to be adjusted in such a way that the process often became unstable. Even if a continuous joint was generated, it was

---

[1] Pores are holes in the joint caused by air inclusion.

A. Pinz et al. (Eds.): DAGM/OAGM 2012, LNCS 7476, pp. 367–376, 2012.
© Springer-Verlag Berlin Heidelberg 2012

not in the same quality condition like the ones generated by a stable process. In a real assembly line this problem would be getting even worse because of the high costs which would be caused by generating imperfections on purpose. So in general only a lot of data showing brazed joints with a high grade surface and, if at all, only data of a few imperfections is available. This means an automatic imperfection detection system should be able to handle this highly imbalanced training datasets with a fraction of less than 1% imperfection data.

In the literature a lot of approaches exist which handle the problem of imbalanced training datasets in classification systems. Some approaches try to compensate the imbalance on the data level, e.g. by undersampling [9] or oversampling [2] the training data. Other approaches are working on an algorithmic level. For instance, a possible approach for our application is to train a model which fits the well-known target class of the high grade joint surfaces and dismiss all data as anomalies or outliers which do not correspond to this model. These so-called novelty detection [13] or one-class classification [14] systems utilize different strategies. On the one hand there exist approaches which try to model the probability density function of the known target class [13]. The classification decision is carried out with a threshold on the determined probability value of an unknown data. On the other hand there are approaches which try to find a minimal enclosing volume around the known class [11,15]. These approaches apply a threshold on the distance of the unknown data which is often measured in a kernel space in order to be able to describe complex structures [14]. A few of the one class classifiers are capable of including known outlier data in the training stage for optimizing the target model, e.g. the support vector data description (SVDD) [15].

Our proposal follows a different strategy by emulating a model for the sparse imperfection data. For this, an approach is utilized which originates from speech processing, more specifically, speaker verification. We train a probability density model from the data of the target class and generate a new model with the sparse imperfection data by Bayesian adaptation [10]. These models are used for hypothesis testing with the Bayesian decision rule [5]. We will show to what extent we even benefit from these sparse imperfection data and how the results will change when an increasing knowledge about the imperfection class is available.

The paper is organized as follows: The next section specifies the experimental setup used for the on-line monitoring of laser brazing. Section 3 provides information about the feature extraction. In Section 4 the theoretical framework of our classification system is presented. Section 5 describes the datasets which were used in our experiments and achieved results are discussed in Section 6. Finally, conclusions are comprised in Section 7.

2   Hardware Setup

The setup for monitoring a brazing process is shown in Figure 1. In this setup two cameras are integrated coaxially into the laser beam path of a laser optic. These cameras are providing synchronous images in the visual (VIS) and near-infrared

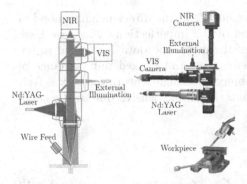

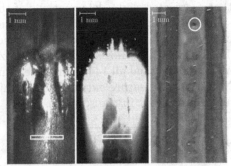

Fig. 1. Experimental setup of the monitoring system [16]. Schematic design (left) and realized system (right) incorporating a near-infrared (NIR) and a visual (VIS) camera.

Fig. 2. Brazing process in VIS image (left) and NIR image (center). Rectangles mark sections where features are extracted. Processed joint containing an imperfection (pore) marked with a circle (right).

(NIR) spectral range. They have a resolution of 1024 × 440 pixels (8 bit) in the VIS and 320 × 148 pixels (14 bit) in the NIR image which yield in conjunction with the optical setup a process resolution of about 8 μm/pixel and 26 μm/pixel in the VIS and NIR image, respectively. The high speed cameras allow a detailed observation of the process with up to 300 frames/s per camera. Example images of both cameras are shown in Figure 2. Also included is a picture of a resulting joint taken after the process. An imperfection, a small pore, is displayed in the upper part of the joint marked by a circle. Further details of this monitoring system are presented in [4] and [16].

3   Feature Extraction

Features of the joint in the images are extracted in slit sections at a fixed position directly behind the position of the laser beam (see the rectangles in Figure 2 left and center). This allows to monitor fluctuations of the inner heat emissions in the NIR images because the generated joint is always inspected a fixed time after the brazing process, assuming a constant process velocity. The fact that the captured images are highly overlapping, due to the high frame rate of the cameras, is utilized to delimit the size of the sections. A brazing velocity set to 1.3 m/min lets new sections of the generated joint appear with a size of about 9-10 and 3-4 lines in the VIS and NIR image, respectively. For fusion purposes, the position of the section in the VIS image corresponds to the one in the NIR image. This is achieved off-line by calibrating both cameras with the help of a test pattern. Some advantages of this approach are that no parts of the joint are missed and small imperfections can be successfully detected. First order statistics of each image section and its gradient image are used as features, in total seven features per image type. These global features have the advantage that associated slight deformations of the surface in the direct neighborhood of small imperfections support the detection of the imperfections. Since we have cameras operating in two different spectral ranges, the data has to be fused. Thus, the data is normalized to have zero mean and a fixed unit variance of maximum one and all 14 features are combined in a single feature vector $\mathbf{x} \in \mathbb{R}^{14}$. Note that the feature extraction is computational inexpensive due to the small amount of pixels in the sections.

4   Classification Framework

For the training of the classifier a dataset $\mathcal{X} = (\mathbf{x}_{0,1}, .., \mathbf{x}_{0,N}, \mathbf{x}_{1,1}, .., \mathbf{x}_{1,M})$ with $N >> M$ is available. The first index $i = 0$ represents the class of joint sections with a high grade surface C_0, and index $i = 1$ represents the class of sparse joint sections with imperfections C_1. The task is to determine to which of these two classes a given feature vector $\mathbf{x}$ belongs.

Let $D(\mathbf{x}) = i$ imply the decision for choosing C_i, $i = 0, 1$. This two-category hypothesis test can be decided by the Bayesian decision rule [5]

$$D(\mathbf{x}) = 0, \;\; \text{if} \;\; \frac{p(\mathbf{x}|C_0)}{p(\mathbf{x}|C_1)} > \frac{\lambda_{01} - \lambda_{11}}{\lambda_{10} - \lambda_{00}} \cdot \frac{P(C_1)}{P(C_0)} = \Theta \tag{1}$$

where $p(\mathbf{x}|C_i)$, $i = 0, 1$ are the probability density functions for each class C_i, $\lambda_{ij} = \lambda(D(\mathbf{x}) = i|C_j)$, $i, j = 0, 1$, is the loss associated with deciding for C_i if the true state of nature is C_j, and $P(C_i)$, $i = 0, 1$, are discrete *a priori* probabilities for each class. We assume that the small, unknown *a priori* probability for a sporadic imperfection is outweighed by the high costs for a missed imperfection which leads to the combined decision threshold Θ [6].

As probability density functions, Gaussian mixture models (GMMs) are used because of their ability to approximate arbitrary probability density functions [3]. By having multidimensional feature vectors, the mixtures consist of multivariate Gaussian distributions in the form

$$\mathcal{N}(\mathbf{x}; \boldsymbol{\mu}, \boldsymbol{\Sigma}) = \frac{1}{(2\pi)^{\frac{d}{2}}|\boldsymbol{\Sigma}|^{\frac{1}{2}}} e^{-\frac{d}{2}(\mathbf{x}-\boldsymbol{\mu})^{\mathsf{T}}\boldsymbol{\Sigma}^{-1}(\mathbf{x}-\boldsymbol{\mu})} \tag{2}$$

where $\boldsymbol{\mu}$ is a d-dimensional mean vector, $\boldsymbol{\Sigma}$ is a $d \times d$ covariance matrix and $|\boldsymbol{\Sigma}|$ is the determinant of $\boldsymbol{\Sigma}$. In the following we are using only the main diagonal matrix values $\boldsymbol{\sigma}^2 = \text{diag}(\boldsymbol{\Sigma})$, assuming features being independent from each other. Because of the sufficiently available data of joint sections without imperfections, the GMM for C_0 can be generated by supervised training using the expectation maximization (EM) algorithm. This yields the probability density function

$$p(\mathbf{x}|C_0) = \sum_{k=1}^{K} c_{0,k} \cdot p_k(\mathbf{x}|C_0) = \sum_{k=1}^{K} c_{0,k} \cdot \mathcal{N}(\mathbf{x}; \boldsymbol{\mu}_{0,k}, \boldsymbol{\sigma}^2_{0,k}) \tag{3}$$

with variable $\mathbf{x}$, K being the number of assumed Gaussian distributions and c being a weighting factor.

For training the imperfection class C_1 the Bayesian adaptation [10] approach is used. This approach is quite similar to the EM algorithm, but it allows to approximate the GMM only with sparse data. Given the known model $p(\mathbf{x}|C_0)$ and the sparse training set $\boldsymbol{\mathcal{X}}_{i=1} = (\mathbf{x}_{1,1}, .., \mathbf{x}_{1,M})$ for the imperfections, the first step is that the probabilistic alignment of the imperfection training set with the high grade joint surface model for each associated mixture j is computed

$$P(j|\boldsymbol{\mathcal{X}}_{i=1}, C_0) = \frac{c_{0,j} p_j(\boldsymbol{\mathcal{X}}_{i=1}|C_0)}{\sum\limits_{k=1}^{K} c_{0,k} p_k(\boldsymbol{\mathcal{X}}_{i=1}|C_0)}. \tag{4}$$

These mixture-dependent probabilities are used to determine local statistics for the imperfection class [7]:

$$b_j = \sum_{m=1}^{M} P(j|\mathbf{x}_{1,m}, C_0) \tag{5}$$

$$\tilde{c}_{1,j} = \frac{b_j}{M} \tag{6}$$

$$\tilde{\boldsymbol{\mu}}_{1,j} = \frac{1}{b_j} \sum_{m=1}^{M} P(j|\mathbf{x}_{1,m}, C_0)\mathbf{x}_{1,m} \tag{7}$$

$$\tilde{\boldsymbol{\sigma}}^2_{1,j} = \frac{1}{b_j} \sum_{m=1}^{M} P(j|\mathbf{x}_{1,m}, C_0)\mathbf{x}^2_{1,m}. \tag{8}$$

Here and in the following, the operation $\mathbf{x}^2$ is a shorthand for $\mathrm{diag}(\mathbf{xx}^\mathbf{T})$. The calculated local statistics are combined with the parameters of the high grade joint surface model to generate the adapted model by:

$$\hat{c}_{1,j} = [\alpha_j \tilde{c}_{1,j} + (1 - \alpha_j)c_{0,j}]\gamma \tag{9}$$

$$\hat{\boldsymbol{\mu}}_{1,j} = \alpha_j \tilde{\boldsymbol{\mu}}_{1,j} + (1 - \alpha_j)\boldsymbol{\mu}_{0,j} \tag{10}$$

$$\hat{\boldsymbol{\sigma}}^2_{1,j} = \alpha_j \tilde{\boldsymbol{\sigma}}^2_{1,j} + (1 - \alpha_j)(\boldsymbol{\sigma}^2_{0,j} + \boldsymbol{\mu}^2_{0,j}) - \hat{\boldsymbol{\mu}}^2_{1,j}. \tag{11}$$

The parameter γ is a normalization factor to ensure that the sum of the adapted weights equals one. α_i is a mixing coefficient which balances the global and local statistics of the mixtures dependent on the amount of adaptation data

$$\alpha_j = \frac{b_j}{b_j + r}. \tag{12}$$

The parameter r is a fixed relevance factor. The smaller this relevance factor is the more influence small data sizes have on the adapted model. The final adapted GMM which is used for the hypothesis testing in (1) is

$$\hat{p}(\mathbf{x}|C_1) = \sum_{k=1}^{K} \hat{c}_{1,k} \cdot \mathcal{N}(\mathbf{x}; \hat{\boldsymbol{\mu}}_{1,k}, \hat{\boldsymbol{\sigma}}_{1,k}). \tag{13}$$

5   Experimental Setup

The proposed method is tested with data generated by the presented monitoring system in a laboratory assembly. Video sequences were captured which are showing brazing processes of test pattern joints. The used workpieces have a length of about 15 cm and two different brazing geometry types were used, flanged and fillet. In addition, two different process head units were used in the experiments. One is a free running and the other a tactile-guided head unit which is also capable of brazing 3D joints. Both systems generate slightly different images in terms of process resolution, sharpness and luminance. Thats why the data from the different systems and brazing geometries are distributed in several independent datasets. In each dataset the captured video sequences are results from a series of experiments with fixed illumination power, lens sizes and exposure times. The main difficulty was to artificially create sporadic joint imperfections. For this, several experimental series were needed. We are using four imperfection categories, small, medium and large pores and wetting failures. They have in common that all of them are holes in the joint with different sizes. The smallest pores have a size of about 50μm. To enable a binary classification, all imperfections types are combined in a single imperfection class. This class is coherent but partly overlapping with the class for the high grade surface. In the overlapping area mostly the small pores are situated, making them the most demanding imperfections.

Table 1. Overview on the datasets. Imperfection data is divided in imperfect sections (Sec.) and total number of imperfections (Im.). * denotes that no data is available.

Dataset	High Grade Sec.	Small Pores Sec.	Im.	Medium Pores Sec.	Im.	Large Pores Sec.	Im.	Wetting Failures Sec.	Im.
Flanged	10684	313	104	831	146	2212	90	4770	34
Tactile	9170	230	64	174	32	338	22	*	*
Fillet	2981	59	20	160	20	269	24	1223	34

An overview on the datasets is given in Table 1. Please note that one imperfection consists of several sections. The datasets were generated from 25 process sequences for the flanged, 11 for the tactile and 18 for the fillet dataset. Because of the unstable process conditions solely joint sections with an apparent high grade surface were regarded as imperfection-free. Cross validation is used as a jack knife method to separate a dataset in a training and a test set. The data is divided into three parts. Two parts are used for training and the other for testing. To achieve that the imperfection categories are evenly distributed in the training and test datasets, single imperfections with their corresponding sections were randomly drawn without replacement.

6   Experimental Results

The results of our experiments are expressed with detection error trade-off (DET) curves for the joint sections[2] (Figure 3). In this curves the correlation of both kinds of possible classification errors, false alarm and miss, are depicted, showing the theoretically achievable performance. We obtained these curves by varying the decision threshold in (1). The EM algorithm is initialized by the K-means algorithm. For analyzing the influence of the available amount of data of the imperfections on the classification results, we use as adaptation data only one imperfection and than increase the number step by step. To achieve better statistically independent results, for each step the imperfections are drawn several times randomly, dependent on the total amount of available imperfections. This is also done for each imperfection subclass independently, for separately examining their contribution. The used cases are one, two, four, eight and all imperfections of the subclass. As an additional case all available training data of all imperfections are used for adaptation. This represents a nearly balanced training case[3]. A relevance factor in (12) of $r = 4$ and a set number of Gaussians of $K = 4$ worked well in our experiments[4]. To compress the results, the equal error rate (EER) and the area under curve (AUC) of the DET curves are calculated.

Table 2 shows the overall results for the datasets. The best results are achieved with the flanged dataset. With one to two known imperfections of any kind, nearly error rates comparable to the training with the whole imperfection set are obtained. This means that the fraction of the imperfection data in the training dataset is less than 0.1%. Similar results are accomplished for the tactile dataset. The EER and AUC are in general slightly higher, but here also the use of only two small pores achieve a remarkable performance. Comparing the general results for the small pores with the results for the large pores another effect is observable: training with solely small pores leads to better results than training with a dataset containing solely large pores. Further experiments showed that adapting two different models for the small and large imperfections, respectively, can improve the results.

The results for the fillet dataset are slightly worse[5]. But indeed, the effect of increasing the adaptation dataset is clearly observable in the DET curves (Figure 3a). The results for the small pores in the tactile dataset and the small and medium pores in the fillet dataset are showing that with just an increase of one known imperfection the performance nearly is twice as good as solely for one known imperfection.

---

[2] For simplicity reasons, we focus only on the number of joint sections rather than imperfections.

[3] The results are also closely similar to the training of two separate GMMs with the EM algorithm for both classes.

[4] A too small or large r can worsen the results for the cases of sparse adaptation data.

[5] The fillet dataset is the most difficult one.

Table 2. EER and AUC results (in %) for experiments with increasing the adaptation dataset. DS is shorthand for dataset and * denotes that no data is available.

		Small Pores		Medium Pores		Large Pores		Wetting Failures	
		EER	AUC	EER	AUC	EER	AUC	EER	AUC
Flanged DS	1 Im.	0.070	4.7e-03	0.076	7.1e-03	0.074	7.3e-03	0.094	48.0e-03
	2 Im.	0.067	4.9e-03	0.073	7.0e-03	0.077	11.9e-03	0.071	23.2e-03
	4 Im.	0.065	5.0e-03	0.074	8.2e-03	0.075	13.9e-03	0.060	16.5e-03
	8 Im.	0.063	5.0e-03	0.069	8.0e-03	0.071	12.1e-03	0.061	15.4e-03
	Max. Im.	0.059	5.5e-03	0.071	7.7e-03	0.071	5.8e-03	0.060	8.1e-03
	All Im.	0.059	4.9e-03	0.059	4.9e-03	0.059	4.9e-03	0.059	4.9e-03
Tactile DS	1 Im.	1.09	0.14	0.66	0.12	0.82	0.30	*	*
	2 Im.	0.65	0.10	0.66	0.12	0.87	0.47	*	*
	4 Im.	0.61	0.12	0.72	0.14	0.95	0.51	*	*
	8 Im.	0.62	0.14	0.71	0.22	0.98	0.47	*	*
	Max. Im.	0.63	0.21	0.72	0.35	0.94	0.45	*	*
	All Im.	0.79	0.36	0.79	0.36	0.79	0.36	*	*
Fillet DS	1 Im.	3.02	0.65	2.48	0.70	1.26	0.35	1.20	0.28
	2 Im.	1.38	0.32	1.33	0.24	1.23	0.33	1.22	0.25
	4 Im.	1.19	0.22	1.19	0.24	1.21	0.24	1.14	0.17
	8 Im.	1.11	0.20	1.13	0.26	1.15	0.21	1.07	0.14
	Max. Im.	1.18	0.19	1.19	0.28	1.08	0.16	1.04	0.14
	All Im.	1.04	0.14	1.04	0.14	1.04	0.14	1.04	0.14

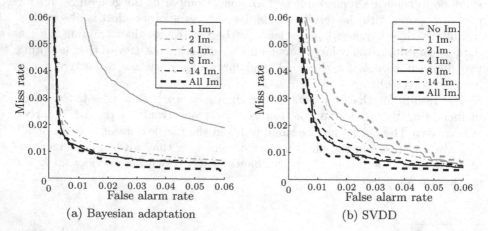

(a) Bayesian adaptation   (b) SVDD

Fig. 3. DET curves of classified joint sections for the Bayesian adaptation and the SVDD algorithm, both on the fillet dataset using solely small pores. The curves are showing results for different amounts of training data. In the case "No Im." no imperfection and in the case "All Im." all available imperfections of all types are used for training.

For comparison, we used the SVDD algorithm [15] which is also capable of including known outlier data for training. Because of the large computing time, we solely used the fillet dataset for testing, and manually optimized the parameters of the SVDD with a grid search[6]. We used the same test cases as for the Bayesian adaptation with an additional case for no known imperfections. Figure 3a shows the obtained results for the training with solely small pores. The performance with no and one known imperfection outperforms the Bayesian adaptation approach but for the other cases the Bayesian adaptation achieves better results. For larger imperfections the results for the Bayesian adaptation are generally superior. This means that only for very sparse training data the SVDD could be a better choice (without regarding the long training time for larger datasets).

7   Conclusions and Future Work

In this paper we have presented the results of our experiments with highly imbalanced datasets from the application of on-line quality control of laser brazing. We used a modeling approach and experimented with the Bayesian adaptation algorithm for creating an imperfection model with only sparse training data. We showed how well this algorithm works with different amounts of adaptation data. The experimental results are showing that for this application with sparse training data a performance comparable to a training with a balanced dataset is achievable. For some cases a moderate increase of training data quickly yields a performance gain. This approach could help to establish a quality control system in a production assembly with only a few known examples of imperfections. If after a time more imperfections are available the imperfection model can be updated in an active learning manner.

Future work will target tests with other datasets (e.g., from UCI Machine Learning Repository) and detailed comparisons with other algorithms and techniques for imbalanced datasets to generalize our findings. A special focus will be set on the optimization of the decision threshold for the Bayesian decision rule.

Acknowledgments. The German Federal Ministry of Economics and Technology (BMWI, Project: IN7023-EQOS) is gratefully acknowledged for financial support. Furthermore, we want to thank our reseach colleagues at Fraunhofer Institute for Production Technology IPT and Fraunhofer Institute for Laser Technology ILT, both in Aachen, Germany, for providing the data.

References

1. Grimm, A., Schmidt, M.: Possibilities for online process monitoring at laser brazing based on two dimensional detector systems. In: Proc. 28th Int. Congr. on Applications of Laser & Electro Optics, Orlando, FL, USA (2009)

---

[6] The used parameters are $\sigma = 10$ for a RBF-kernel and a fraction reject of 0.01 for both classes.

2. Akbani, R., Kwek, S., Japkowicz, N.: Applying Support Vector Machines to Imbalanced Datasets. In: Boulicaut, J.-F., Esposito, F., Giannotti, F., Pedreschi, D. (eds.) ECML 2004. LNCS (LNAI), vol. 3201, pp. 39–50. Springer, Heidelberg (2004)
3. Bishop, C.: Pattern Recognition and Machine Learning. Inf. Science and Statistics. Springer (2006)
4. Donst, D., Abels, P., Ungers, M., Klocke, F., Kaierle, S.: On-line quality control system for laser brazing. In: Proc. of 28th Int. Congr. on Applications of Laser & Electro Optics, Orlando, FL, USA (2009)
5. Duda, R., Hart, P., Stork, D.: Pattern Classification, 2nd edn. Wiley-Interscience (2001)
6. Fecker, D., Maergner, V., Fingscheidt, T.: Online detection of imperfections in laser brazed joints. In: Proc. of the 12th IAPR Conference on Machine Vision Applications (MVA), Nara, Japan, pp. 223–227 (2011)
7. Fierrez-Aguilar, J., Garcia-Romero, D., Ortega-Garcia, J., Gonzalez-Rodriguez, J.: Bayesian adaptation for user-dependent multimodal biometric authentication. Pattern Recognition 38(8), 1317–1319 (2005)
8. Kaierle, S., Ungers, M., Franz, C., Mann, S., Abels, P.: Understanding the laser process. Laser Technik Journal 7(7), 49–52 (2010)
9. Kubat, M., Matwin, S.: Addressing the curse of imbalanced training sets: One-sided selection. In: Proc. of the Fourteenth International Conference on Machine Learning, pp. 179–186. Morgan Kaufmann, San Francisco (1997)
10. Reynolds, D., Quatieri, T., Dunn, R.: Speaker verification using adapted gaussian mixture models. Digital Signal Processing 10, 19–42 (2000)
11. Schölkopf, B., Platt, J.C., Shawe-Taylor, J., Smola, A.J., Williamson, R.C.: Estimating the support of a high-dimensional distribution. Neural Computation 13(7) (2001)
12. Shao, J., Yan, Y.: Review of techniques for on-line monitoring and inspection of laser welding. Journal of Physics: Conference Series 15, 101–107 (1995)
13. Tarassenko, L., Hayton, P., Cerneaz, N., Brady, M.: Novelty detection for the identification of masses in mammograms. In: Proc. of IEEE Conference on Artifical Neural Networks, Paris, France, pp. 442–447 (1995)
14. Tax, D.: One-class Classification. Phd thesis, Delft University of Technology, Delft (June 2001)
15. Tax, D., Duin, R.P.W.: Support vector data description. Machine Learning 54(1), 45–66 (2004)
16. Ungers, M., Fecker, D., Frank, S., Donst, D., Maergner, V., Abels, P., Kaierle, S.: In-situ quality monitoring during laser brazing. In: Proc. of Laser Assisted Net Shape Engineering 6, Erlangen, Germany, pp. 493–503 (2010)

PCA-Enhanced Stochastic Optimization Methods

Alina Kuznetsova, Gerard Pons-Moll, and Bodo Rosenhahn*

Institute for Information Processing (TNT),
Leibniz University Hanover, Germany
{kuznetso,pons,rosenhahn}@tnt.uni-hannover.de

Abstract. In this paper, we propose to enhance particle-based stochastic optimization methods (SO) by using Principal Component Analysis (PCA) to build an approximation of the cost function in a neighborhood of particles during optimization. Then we use it to shift the samples in the direction of maximum cost change. We provide theoretical basis and experimental results showing that such enhancement improves the performance of existing SO methods significantly. In particular, we demonstrate the usefulness of our method when combined with standard Random Sampling, Simulated Annealing and Particle Filter.

1 Introduction

A large number of computer vision problems requires to optimize a cost function that depends on a high number of parameters. When the cost function is convex, the global optimum can be found reliably. Unfortunately, many problems are hard or even impossible to formulate in convex form. It is well known that in such cases typical gradient-based local optimization methods easily get trapped in local minima and therefore stochastic optimization algorithms must be employed. In general terms, stochastic optimization algorithms consist of generating random proposals, or particles, to find regions of parameter space with low costs. However, the number of particles needed to reach the global minimum with high probability grows exponentially with the dimension of parameter space. To improve sampling efficiency in high-dimensional spaces a common strategy is to follow the cost function gradient of good samples. Unfortunately, this has two major limitations. Firstly, for many cost functions used in computer vision there is no analytic expression for the gradient and approximating it by finite differences is computationally expensive. Secondly, the gradient is a very local measure of the cost function landscape that ignores the underlying global shape. Hence, this approach is susceptible to get the particles trapped in local minimum. Inspired by methods based on Hamiltonian Monte Carlo (HMC) [14], we introduce PCA-based Stochastic Optimization (PCA-SO). We propose

---

* This work has been partially funded by the ERC within the starting grant Dynamic MinVIP

A. Pinz et al. (Eds.): DAGM/OAGM 2012, LNCS 7476, pp. 377–386, 2012.
© Springer-Verlag Berlin Heidelberg 2012

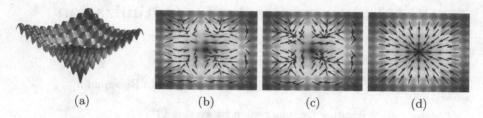

Fig. 1. Shift directions: (a) Ackley function with many local minimum, (b) directions of maximal function decrease - oppositely directed to the gradient of the function, (c) shift direction computed from a small neighborhood and (d) shift direction computed from a bigger neighborhood. As it can be observed, for small neighborhoods (c) our method computes directions that are parallel to the local gradients and for bigger neighborhoods (d) the computed directions capture more global properties of landscape.

to improve the particles in terms of cost function based on the landscape geometry, constructed from already computed neighboring samples. In that sense, our method is related to particle swarm optimization methods [10]. Specifically, we approximate the cost function in a neighborhood by a hyperplane, efficiently computed using PCA. This results in the direction of the maximum cost function variance in a bigger neighborhood, while for a small enough neighborhood this direction coincides with the local gradient. Then, the step size is chosen in the direction of the maximal cost function change in the parameter space. In several experiments, we show that this modified stochastic search scheme results in faster convergence and reduced variance of final solution.

2   Previous Work

Perhaps one of the most widely used stochastic inference methods in vision is the Particle Filter (PF) [9], which can be seen as one instance of importance sampling. For many applications however, the dimension of parameter space is too high and a huge number of samples are needed to approximate the posterior or even to find a good maximum a posteriori (MAP) approximation. An example of such application, for instance, is human pose estimation from video in which the number of parameters to estimate ranges from 20 to 60. One way to make the search more efficient is to use annealing schemes. The traditional Simulated Annealing (SA) [11] starts from a set of hypotheses and decides to move the system to a new state with an acceptance probability that depends on the optimization gain and the temperature T of the system. During the selection of random neighboring states, the temperature is gradually decreased during the iterations. The idea is that the choice between the previous and current solution is almost random (at the beginning) when T is large, but it increasingly selects closer located "downhill" samples as T approaches zero [5,6]. Although in principle such schemes explore the search space more efficiently, very often all samples concentrate around a single local optimum. Another commonly used strategy is to follow the gradient of good samples during stochastic search [3,16,2], this has been shown to reduce the effect of volume wastage which occurs when a large number of particles are rejected. When the gradient cannot be computed covariance matrix adaptation can be very effective [8,7]. Closely related are HMC methods [14,4]. The basic idea behind HMC is to construct a Hamiltonian in which the potential energy is proportional to the cost function and the position corresponds to the variables of interest. Then a momentum is added artificially to the particles. Intuitively, this can speed up convergence and increase robustness to local minimum because the momentum of the particles allows them to go downhill faster and continue when they encounter uprising slopes. In HMC methods the momentum is calculated independently for every particle and is closely related to following the gradient direction [4]. By contrast, we compute the particle shift based on local neighborhood of a particle. This allows to better capture the underlying landscape of the cost function, smoothing out local irregularities. Other approaches combining PCA and Stochastic optimization perform sampling in PCA space instead of performing sampling in the original space [12], which is completely different to our approach.

2.1 Contributions

In this work, we propose a simple but very effective modification for stochastic optimization that adds robustness to local minimum and speeds up convergence. One of the main advantages of the proposed method is that it can be easily integrated to any stochastic optimization technique. We demonstrate the benefits of PCA-SO in three different methods, namely plain Random Sampling (RS), Simulated Annealing (SA) and Particle Filter (PF), applied to typical vision problems, such as image registration and tracking.

3   Stochastic Optimization

In this section, we briefly describe the basic ingredients of a global stochastic optimization algorithm. Most stochastic search algorithms consist of three steps, namely *weighting*, *selection* and *mutation*. In the weighting step, the cost function is evaluated and the particles are given a proportional weight. This is usually the most time consuming step. In the selection step, the weighted particles are accepted or rejected with some probability that can depend on their weight, optimization gain and temperature, if an annealing schedule is used. In the mutation step new candidate locations are generated from the current particles. A commonly used heuristic is that particles give offspring proportional to their current weights so that more computational resources are allocated for promising candidate locations. One of the main advantages of PCA-SO is that it can be easily integrated in the mutation step of any stochastic optimization algorithm.

4 PCA-Based Stochastic Optimization

Let $f : \mathbb{R}^d \mapsto \mathbb{R}$ be a multivariate cost function where d is the dimension of the parameter space. Optimization entails finding the parameter vector $\boldsymbol{x} = (x_1, \ldots, x_d)$ that minimizes the function f:

$$\boldsymbol{x}^* = \arg \min_{x_1, \ldots x_d} f(x_1, \ldots, x_d). \tag{1}$$

The function f defines a hyper-surface in $\mathcal{S} \subset \mathbb{R}^{d+1}$, whose points are $\boldsymbol{y} = (x_1, \ldots, x_d, z)$ with $z = f(x_1, \ldots, x_d)$. Equivalently, we can represent the points in the hyper-surface as the zero level-set of the function $F(x_1, \ldots, x_d, z) = f(x_1, \ldots, x_d) - z$. The gradient of F is trivially related to the gradient of the original cost function f gradient by

$$\nabla_{\boldsymbol{y}} F = \left(\frac{\partial F}{\partial x_1}, \ldots, \frac{\partial F}{\partial x_d}, \frac{\partial F}{\partial z} \right) = (\nabla_{\boldsymbol{x}} f, -1). \tag{2}$$

Obviously, since the gradient must be orthogonal to the level sets of the function $F(x_1, \ldots, x_d, z) = 0$, $\nabla_{\boldsymbol{y}} F$ is perpendicular to the hyper-surface defined by $f(\boldsymbol{x})$. The gradient of the cost function $\nabla_{\boldsymbol{x}} f$ provides the direction of local maximum increase of the cost function f. In principle, this direction can be used to shift the particles which can speed up convergence in many situations. However, this approach is susceptible to get the particles trapped in local minima, because particles falling into local minima will not be shifted since the gradient vanishes at those points.

Therefore, we propose to compute the direction of maximum increase (or decrease, depending on the optimization direction) of the cost function in a bigger neighborhood. Specifically, for every particle $\boldsymbol{y}^i = (\boldsymbol{x}^i, z^i)$ we take all the samples inside a ball of radius r, $\mathcal{N}_i[\boldsymbol{y}^i] \triangleq \{\boldsymbol{y} \in \mathcal{S} \mid d(\boldsymbol{x}^i, \boldsymbol{x}) \leq r\}$. PCA provides means to compute the orthogonal directions in which the variance of the sample set is maximized. Conceptually, it is desirable to shift the particle in the direction $\delta \boldsymbol{x} \in \mathbb{R}^d$ of parameter space that maximizes the cost function change. Given the center of the neighborhood $\boldsymbol{\mu}^i = \frac{1}{N} \sum_{\boldsymbol{y}_n \in \mathcal{N}_i} \boldsymbol{y}_n$, the directions provided by PCA are the eigenvectors $(\boldsymbol{\varphi}_1^i, \ldots, \boldsymbol{\varphi}_{d+1}^i)$ of the sample covariance matrix $\boldsymbol{\Sigma}^i = \sum_{\boldsymbol{y}_n \in \mathcal{N}_i} (\boldsymbol{y}_n - \boldsymbol{\mu}^i)(\boldsymbol{y}_n - \boldsymbol{\mu}^i)^T$ with eigenvalues $\sigma_1^i > \sigma_2^i, \ldots > \sigma_{d+1}^i$ corresponding to the variance of the sample set, projected into the principal directions. It can be shown that the direction $\boldsymbol{\varphi}_{d+1}^i$ of the smallest variance for a small enough neighborhood of a differentiable function is parallel to the normal $\hat{\boldsymbol{n}}^i$ to the surface at the point $\boldsymbol{y}^i$:

$$\hat{\boldsymbol{n}}^i = \left. \frac{\nabla_{\boldsymbol{y}} F^T}{\|\nabla_{\boldsymbol{y}} F\|} \right|_{\boldsymbol{y}^i} = \gamma \frac{\boldsymbol{\varphi}_{d+1}^i}{\|\boldsymbol{\varphi}_{d+1}^i\|}, \qquad \gamma = \pm 1 \tag{3}$$

Therefore, the linear space spanned by $(\boldsymbol{\varphi}_1^i, \ldots, \boldsymbol{\varphi}_d^i)$ forms the tangential hyper-plane to the surface $\mathcal{S}$ at the point $\boldsymbol{y}^i$, based on the neighborhood $\mathcal{N}_i[\boldsymbol{y}^i]$. Thereby, at the k-th iteration particle $\boldsymbol{y}^i$ is shifted by $\delta \boldsymbol{x}^i$

$$\boldsymbol{x}_{k+1}^i := \boldsymbol{x}_k^i - \lambda \delta \boldsymbol{x}_k^i \qquad \delta \boldsymbol{x}_k^i := \frac{\pi_{d+1}(\boldsymbol{\varphi}_{d+1}^i)}{\|\pi_{d+1}(\boldsymbol{\varphi}_{d+1}^i)\|} \tag{4}$$

where $\pi(\cdot)_j$ is the projection operator that drops the j-th component of a vector and λ is a step size parameter. For a small enough neighborhood radius r, δx is parallel to the cost function gradient $\nabla_x f$. Therefore, methods that combine stochastic search with gradient descent [13,3,4,16,2] are special cases of PCA-SO. As the ball radius r increases, Eq. 3 does not hold anymore and the shift vector reflects the direction of maximum function change in a bigger neighborhood. Notably, this provides a direction that is robust enough to make a particle jump over spurious local minimum, see Fig 1.

To summarize, the PCA-SO algorithm consists of the following steps:

1. Sample an initial set of particles randomly and evaluate the cost function.
2. Sample one or more new particles, find the already evaluated particles in their neighborhood, compute shift directions and shift steps (see (4)), using the already evaluated particles.
3. Shift the particles in the found directions and evaluate the cost function at the new locations.
4. Accept the particles with improved cost function values and add to the initial set of particles
5. Go to step 2.

A time-consuming step of our approach can be finding the neighborhood of every particle. If necessary, K-D trees can be used [1], since they allow finding neighbors in $\log(N)$ time. Since the shift direction and the step varies smoothly for neighboring particles, a more efficient alternative is to cluster the particles and give the same shift to every particle within the same cluster.

5   Experiments

In this section, we show the benefits of PCA-SO integrated in three different stochastic optimization/sampling methods, namely random sampling (RS), simulated annealing (SA) and particle filtering (PF). We apply our technique to two different vision applications: image registration and target tracking. To evaluate the effectiveness of a given optimization method we report two measures: (i) the number of iterations needed to reach a good approximation of the solution, and (ii) the value of the cost function after a fixed number of iterations.

5.1   Image Registration Using Random Sampling

We tested our approach for image registration using random sampling (RS). In Fig. 2a the images used for registration are presented. They are histology images of heart tissue cross-sections that need to be registered to generate 3D models. Assuming an affine transformation between images

$$T = \begin{pmatrix} s_x \cos(\theta) & s_x \sin(\theta) & t_x \\ -s_y \sin(\theta) & s_y \cos(\theta) & t_y \\ 0 & 0 & 1 \end{pmatrix}, \tag{5}$$

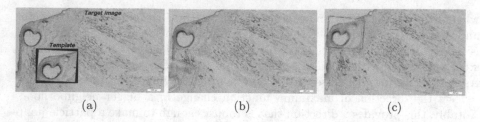

(a)   (b)   (c)

Fig. 2. Image registration results: (a) target image and template; (b) standard RS registration; (c) PCA-SO RS registration

Table 1. Comparison between standard random sampling and its enhancement using PCA-SO; cost function values are in $[9.50, 20.30]$; results are aggregated from 50 independent runs of optimization till the termination criteria

termination criteria	without PCA (mean, ± std)	with PCA (mean, ± std)
number of iterations		
value reached ($J \leq 13$)	22 ± 15	17 ± 11
value reached ($J \leq 12$)	43 ± 13	37.66 ± 15
minimum cost function value		
# of iteration ($N = 10$)	13.04 ± 0.83	12.88 ± 0.81
# of iteration ($N = 200$)	11.53 ± 0.56	10.92 ± 0.40

we need to estimate rotation angle θ, scaling s_x, s_y and translation t_x, t_y parameters. Let $I(\boldsymbol{p})$ denote the target image value at point $\boldsymbol{p}$ and $I_t(\boldsymbol{p})$ denote the template image value at point $\boldsymbol{p}$. Rectangle $\mathcal{R}$ defines the region to be matched. Here $|\mathcal{R}|$ denotes the number of pixels in the rectangle. The cost function $J(I_t, I)$ is defined as following:

$$J(I_t, I) = \frac{1}{|\mathcal{R}|} \sum_{\boldsymbol{p} \in \mathcal{R}} (I(\boldsymbol{p}) - I_t(\boldsymbol{T}\boldsymbol{p}))^2 \qquad (6)$$

As can be seen, no analytical expression for derivatives of J exists. Integration of our enhancement is straightforward: sample small number of particles; for each new sample use the already evaluated particles to build local neighborhood and improve it with respect to the cost function; accept it if the cost function value improved. As it can be seen in Table 1, PCA-SO reduces both the number of required iterations to reach a good fit and the quality of the fit after the fixed number of iterations. In Fig. 2b,2c we show the registration results of 5 different runs of the algorithm, with 200 particles sampled during each run. As it can be observed, the quality of the RS result, shown in Fig. 2b, heavily depends on the particular run of the method in contrast to PCA-SO (results are shown in Fig. 2c), that consistently converges to the same solution.

5.2   PCA-Enhanced Simulated Annealing

To show the flexibility of PCA enhancement we integrate it in another SO technique - Simulated Annealing (SA). Here, we optimize the famous non convex

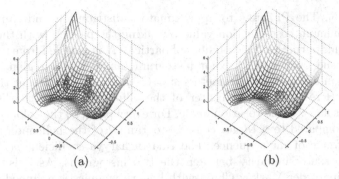

(a)   (b)

Fig. 3. (a) standard SA experiment (b) SA experiment enhanced by PCA-SO; as can be seen, much less samples are needed to achieve desired function value

Table 2. Comparison between standard simulated annealing and its enhancement; minimum function value is -1.03

termination criteria	without PCA-SO	with PCA-SO
number of iterations		
value reached ($f \leq -0.4$)	492 ± 2291	22 ± 15
value reached ($f \leq -1$)	115 ± 54	55 ± 28
minimum cost function value		
# of iteration ($N = 200$)	-0.66 ± 0.43	-1.00 ± 0.03
# of iteration ($N = 1000$)	-0.96 ± 0.13	-1.00 ± 0.02

six-hump camelback function $f(x)$; for analyzing the proposed algorithm and used the open source implementation of SA available at [17]. Our method is applied as following: for each new simulated particle, PCA tangential hyperplane is build based on (already evaluated) particles that are in the neighborhood of the new particle; particle is shifted in the direction of the cost function improvement; then the particle is processed as in standard SA method. The results for 50 independent optimization runs of SA and SA+PCA-SO with random initialization are shown in Table 2. It can be observed that the number of iterations required by SA to reach a good approximation of the global optimum is several orders of magnitude larger compared to PCA-SO. Notably, to reach a cost function value lower than -0.4 the average number of iterations needed by PCA-SO is only 22 ± 15 which is a remarkable improvement compared to the iterations needed by SA alone 492 ± 2291. Fig 3 illustrates results of one optimization run of each method and shows significant difference in the number of particle needed to reach the value, close to minimum. We attribute such good performance to the fact that PCA-SO shifts the particles in the direction of the minimum, allowing them to travel longer distances and therefore reduce random walk behavior.

5.3 Tracking with Particle Filter

In the last experiment, we also used our approach to improve object tracking accuracy with a Particle Filter (PF). Here, we used an open source tracking algorithm [15]. The PF aims to approximate a distribution and can be used to obtain minimum cost function value by taking the particle with the highest weight. For this purpose, a fixed number of particles N is sampled from a specified distribution and evaluated. A color histogram sampled in a region, which is bounded by an ellipse with parameters $\boldsymbol{x} = (x, y, a, b, \theta)^T$, represent the object appearance. Here (x, y) is the center of the ellipse, (a, b) are the lengths of principal axis and θ is the rotation angle. For every particle, the color histogram $\mathcal{Q}^i$ is then compared to a target color histogram $\mathcal{P}$ of the helicopter obtained in the first frame of the sequence. The Bhattacharyya coefficient $\rho(\mathcal{P}, \mathcal{Q})$ [15] is used to measure similarity between the two histograms. As it is usual for tracking, a first order Markov Chain with linear dynamics is assumed. The full state vector is given by $\boldsymbol{s} = [x, y, \dot{x}, \dot{y}, a, b, \theta]^T$, where $(\dot{x}, \dot{y})$ is the velocity of the center of the ellipse. The Bhattacharyya coefficients, i.e. the cost function values, are mapped to probabilities w_t^i using the exponential function:

$$w_t^i = \frac{\hat{w}_t^i}{\sum_{i=1}^N \hat{w}_t^i}, \qquad \hat{w}_t^i = \exp\left(-\frac{1 - \rho(\mathcal{Q}_t^i(\boldsymbol{x}), \mathcal{P})}{2\sigma^2}\right) \qquad (7)$$

After weighting, the particles are resampled (selection) and propagated over time with the linear dynamical model: $\boldsymbol{S}_{t+1} = \boldsymbol{A}\boldsymbol{S}_t + \boldsymbol{\varepsilon}$ (mutation) where $\boldsymbol{\varepsilon}$ is noise, A is a constant motion matrix defined in [15], $\boldsymbol{S}_t = [\boldsymbol{s}_t^1 \dots \boldsymbol{s}_t^N] \in \mathbb{R}^{d \times N}$. We apply our enhancemnent directly after the dynamic step. In PF, several particles are generated at the same time. Only the particles with high weights are optimized, since optimization of all the particles will lead to the degradation of weight distribution due to normalization. As before, we build hyper-planes, based on the particles generated in the current time step. Note, that the cost function $f(\boldsymbol{x}) = \rho(\mathcal{P}, \mathcal{Q}(\boldsymbol{x}))$ depends only on the ellipse parameters and therefore PCA space is build only for $\boldsymbol{x}$. Improved particles are then resampled according to their weights.

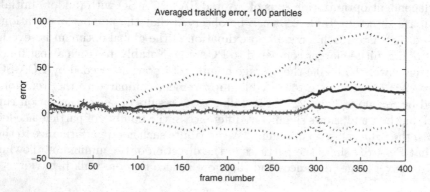

Fig. 4. Comparison of the tracking error for the standard Particle Filter (blue) and the improved PCA-SO Particle Filter (red); solid lines show mean tracking error over 30 independent runs; dotted lines show tracking error variance.

(a) Frame: 270   (b) Frame: 280   (c) Frame: 290   (d) Frame: 300   (e) Frame: 310

(f) Frame: 270   (g) Frame: 280   (h) Frame: 290   (i) Frame: 300   (j) Frame: 310

Fig. 5. Tracking results obtained with PF (top row) and with proposed PCA-SO (bottom row). The PF method loses track of the object due to occlusions starting from the frame 290, while the proposed method is able to correctly follow the object after the occlusion.

To compare the two methods, we use the standard Euclidean distance between the ground truth object coordinates and the results produced by the given tracking algorithm as an error measure. Fig. 4 shows once more, that PCA-SO reduces the mean tracking error as well as the variance. PCA-SO can track the object after a heavy occlusion occurring between frames 270 and 310 in contrast to standard PF that looses track of the object; this can be observed both quantitatively, see Fig. 4, and qualitatively, see Fig. 5. It should be noted that a sufficient number of samples, e.g. more than $70 - 80$, are needed in order for PCA-SO to work well, because the PCA-based approximation is more reliable with denser neighborhood samples.

6   Conclusions

In this paper, we presented PCA-SO, a method to improve global stochastic optimization algorithms by improving the samples. The direction is given by the PCA component with smallest eigenvalue computed in a local neighborhood around the sample. We have shown that this yields the gradient of the cost function for small neighborhoods whereas for larger neighborhoods the direction reflects more global properties of the cost function landscape. Therefore, methods that combine stochastic search with local methods are a special case of our algorithm. The main advantages of PCA-SO methodology are its effectiveness and easy integration into stochastic optimization methods. In several experiments, we have shown improvement in both accuracy and convergence rates using Random Sampling, Simulated Annealing and Particle Filter.

References

1. Bentley, J.L.: Multidimensional binary search trees used for associative searching. Commun. ACM 18(9), 509–517 (1975)
2. Bray, M., Koller-Meier, E., Van Gool, L.: Smart particle filtering for 3D hand tracking. In: Proceedings of Sixth IEEE International Conference on Automatic Face and Gesture Recognition, pp. 675–680. IEEE (2004)
3. Cham, T., Rehg, J.M.: A multiple hypothesis approach to figure tracking. In: CVPR (1999)
4. Choo, K., Fleet, D.J.: People tracking using hybrid monte carlo filtering. In: International Conference on Computer Vision, vol. 2, pp. 321–328 (2001)
5. Deutscher, J., Reid, I.: Articulated body motion capture by stochastic search. IJCV 61(2), 185–205 (2005)
6. Gall, J., Potthoff, J., Schnorr, C., Rosenhahn, B., Seidel, H.: Interacting and annealing particle filters: Mathematics and a recipe for applications. Journal of Mathematical Imaging and Vision 28, 1–18 (2007)
7. Hansen, N., Ostermeier, A.: Adapting arbitrary normal mutation distributions in evolution strategies: The covariance matrix adaptation. In: Proceedings of IEEE International Conference on Evolutionary Computation, pp. 312–317. IEEE (1996)
8. Igel, C., Hansen, N., Roth, S.: Covariance matrix adaptation for multi-objective optimization. Evolutionary Computation 15(1), 1–28 (2007)
9. Isard, M., Blake, A.: Condensation - conditional density propagation for visual tracking. International Journal of Computer Vision 29, 5–28 (1998)
10. Kennedy, J., Eberhart, R.: Particle swarm optimization. In: Proceedings of IEEE International Conference on Neural Networks, vol. 4, pp. 1942–1948 (November/December 1995)
11. Kirkpatrick, S., Gelatt Jr., C.D., Vecchi, M.P.: Optimization by simulated annealing. Science 220, 671–680 (1983)
12. Kreinin, A., Merkoulovitch, L., Rosen, D., Zerbs, M.: Principal component analysis in quasi monte carlo simulation. Algo Research Quarterly 1(2), 21–30 (1998)
13. Martin, O., Otto, S.W., Felten, E.W.: Large-step Markov chains for the traveling salesman problem (1991)
14. Neal, R.M.: Mcmc using hamiltonian dynamics. In: Handbook of Markov Chain Monte Carlo, vol. 54, pp. 113–162 (2010)
15. Nummiaro, K., Koller-Meier, E., Van Gool, L.: An adaptive color-based particle filter. Image and Vision Computing 21(1), 99–110 (2003)
16. Sminchisescu, C., Triggs, B.: Covariance scaled sampling for monocular 3D body tracking. In: CVPR, vol. 1 (2001)
17. Vandekerckhove, J.: General simulated annealing algorithm (2006), http://www.mathworks.de/matlabcentral/fileexchange/10548

A Real-Time MRF Based Approach
for Binary Segmentation

Dmitrij Schlesinger

Dresden University of Technology

Abstract. We present an MRF based approach for binary segmentation that is able to work in real time. As we are interested in processing of live video streams, fully unsupervised learning schemes are necessary. Therefore, we use generative models. Unlike many existing methods that use Energy Minimization techniques, we employ max-marginal decision. It leads to sampling algorithms that can be implemented for the proposed model in a very efficient manner.

1 Introduction

In this work we deal with segmentation – perhaps one of the most popular tasks in computer vision. In our opinion, the actually most successful methods are based on Energy Minimization techniques. Both modelling aspects (especially for segmentation) and efficient algorithms were extensively studied and elaborated in the past. However, there are still many open questions in this context. The first one is that simple pairwise energies are rarely able to produce satisfactory results in practice without further enhancement and/or learning. Simple and more or less general models (like e.g. [3]) give satisfactory results only in quite easy situations, for example if the colour distributions for segments are known and do not essentially overlap. Usually, either user interaction [8] or very elaborated energy functions (e.g. [2,4,6]) are necessary to improve the results. Unfortunately, very often the Energy Minimization tasks to be solved occur to be quite hard. It leads to inference algorithms, which are typically not very efficient.

In this paper we follow another strategy which is becoming increasingly popular for MRF-based approaches, namely the Maximum Marginal decision. It was already shown, that the marginal based decision strategies give at least competitive results for example for image denoising and deblurring [11,12] and stereo reconstruction [9]. For segmentation however, this option seems to remain unexplored so far. In our opinion, the main challenge for a comprehensive comparison is the lack of algorithms for marginal based inference, which are both accurate and computationally efficient enough for typical computer vision tasks. Therefore, for complex models the marginal based inference usually does not perform well in practice. In this work we address this problem in a straightforward way – we show, how to reach good (in our case real-time) performance using reasonable assumptions and a careful implementation.

Another important question is learning. Modern models usually use Conditional Random Fields (CRF) in order to incorporate as many additional aspects

A. Pinz et al. (Eds.): DAGM/OAGM 2012, LNCS 7476, pp. 387–396, 2012.
© Springer-Verlag Berlin Heidelberg 2012

as possible. The CRF framework is very convenient in this respect, because it allows to incorporate almost everything in a sound theoretical way. Elaborated general methods can be used for learning, for example the framework of Structural SVM-s (see e.g. [7] and references therein). CRF-s have, however, their price. The most crucial question is the generalization ability. The more complex the model, the more effort is needed to provide statistically sound guarantees for the results. The next problem is that the semi-supervised learning becomes extremely difficult. Furthermore, fully unsupervised learning is not possible at all. Especially this aspect becomes crucial in situations where there is no chance to have completely labelled data for training. One such situation is the segmentation of live video streams, which we address in this work. In dealing with learning we heavily exploit the fact, that the same quantities are necessary for both inference and learning. Therefore the latter can be easily included with almost no additional computational cost.

2 Model

The presented approach is based mainly on [5,10] except for the appearance model and the shape parametrization. In this section we recall the main ideas and discuss different model parts.

Let R be a set of image pixels. They are considered as vertices of a graph $G = (R, E)$, where the edges $\{r, r'\} \in E$ connect neighbouring pixels (in particular we use 4-neighbourhood). The image $x : R \to C$ is a mapping that assigns a colour value $c \in C$ to each pixel $r \in R$. The colour value in a pixel r is denoted by x_r. In binary segmentation a label $k \in \{0, 1\}$ (background/foreground) should be assigned to each position r forming a labelling $y : R \to \{0, 1\}$. A label chosen by the segmentation in a pixel r is denoted by y_r. As we are interested in segmentation of a live video stream, we cannot expect a reasonable user interaction, i.e. the learning of unknown parameters should be performed in a fully unsupervised manner. Therefore, we advocate a generative model that consists of the prior probability distribution of labellings $p(y)$ and a conditionally independent probability distribution $p(x|y) = \prod_r p(x_r|y_r)$ for observations. For the prior we use the Ising model enhanced by a shape prior. To summarize, the probability distribution for pairs (x, y) reads

$$p(x, y; \phi, \theta) = \frac{1}{Z(\phi, \theta)} \exp\big[E(x, y; \phi, \theta)\big], \tag{1}$$

with the energy

$$E(x, y; \phi, \theta) = \alpha \sum_{rr'} \mathbb{1}(y_r = y_{r'}) + \lambda \sum_r y_r \phi(r) + \sum_r q(x_r, y_r; \theta) \tag{2}$$

and the normalizing constant $Z(\phi, \theta)$[1]. The coefficients α and λ weight the importance of the Potts prior and the shape prior respectively. Unfortunately,

---

[1] The parameters to be learned are separated from the random variables by semicolon.

their learning is very time consuming (especially in an unsupervised manner) and actually can not be performed in real time. Hence, we consider them to be known. Other parameters of the probability distribution are the shape function $\phi : R \to \mathbb{R}$ and the unknown parameters θ of the appearance model.

The second energy term is the shape prior, that assigns additional unary terms $\phi(r)$ for the foreground label in each pixel r. We use simple quadratic shape, parametrized in a Gaussian like manner as

$$\phi(r) = \phi_0 - \frac{(r_x - z_x)^2}{2\sigma_x^2} - \frac{(r_y - z_y)^2}{2\sigma_y^2}. \tag{3}$$

(subscripts x and y correspond to the horizontal and vertical directions, respectively). The parameters of the shape function are the centre z, variances σ and a bias ϕ_0. The function has the following influence on the prior probability distribution. Foreground labels $y_r=1$ at positions close to the centre z are supported by an additional positive energy $\phi(r)$. The centre z has thereby the maximal possible support of ϕ_0. Positions far from the centre are suppressed accordingly. Zero level set is an orthogonal ellipse with the half-axes $\sigma_x\sqrt{2\phi_0}$ and $\sigma_y\sqrt{2\phi_0}$.

The data-terms $q(x_r, y_r; \theta)$ in (2) are logarithms of conditional colour probabilities $p(x_r|y_r; \theta)$. A common choice for the appearance model is a multivariate Gaussian mixture for each segment (see e.g. [8]). Taking into account that the model should be as simple as possible for computation and can be learnt quickly, we modify the standard Gaussian mixture model in the following way. First of all we use orthogonal isotropic Gaussians instead of the multivariate ones, i.e. the i-th Gaussian is given by[2]

$$\mathcal{N}(c; \mu_i, \sigma) \sim \frac{1}{\sigma^{3/2}} \exp\left[-\frac{\|c - \mu_i\|^2}{2\sigma^2}\right]. \tag{4}$$

The variance σ is thereby common for all Gaussians. This simplification is obviously computationally more efficient because it is not necessary to compute matrix products. However, it has its price, namely more Gaussians are needed in order to adequately represent the target probability distributions of colours. In the next section we give some hints how to cope with this problem using appropriate computational schemes.

The second modification is that we use a common set of Gaussians for both segmentation labels, i.e. the probability of a colour c for a label k is

$$p(c|k) = \sum_{i=1}^{n} w_{ki}\mathcal{N}(c; \mu_i, \sigma). \tag{5}$$

Hence, the appearance models for labels differ only by the mixture coefficients w_{ki}. This modification has numerous advantages compared to the standard case, where distinct Gaussian sets are used for different segmentation labels. The main one is with respect to learning. In video processing it is often the case that the

---

[2] Colours c are three-dimensional vectors e.g. in the RGB colour space.

appearance model should be re-learnt very quickly. Let us consider the situation, when a new object appears in the video stream. If distinct sets of Gaussians are used for different labels, this object is labelled as foreground or background mainly based on its colouring. In the proposed modification instead, both labels "have a chance" to occupy the object. Hence, other model aspects can influence the final decision about it. Besides, it is easy to see that the case of separate Gaussian sets for each segment is a special case of the proposed "common pool", if particular weights of the latter are set to zero. Therefore we do not see the necessity to additionally restrict the appearance model.

3   Inference and Learning

The segmentation is formulated as a Bayesian decision task with the Hamming distance between two labellings $H(y, y') = \sum_r \mathbb{I}(y_r \neq y'_r)$ as the cost function. It leads to the maximum marginal decision

$$y_r^* = \arg \max_k p(y_r = k | x; \phi, \theta). \tag{6}$$

The posterior marginal probabilities of states are computed approximately using Gibbs Sampling. In the next section we give some additional technical details for its efficient implementation.

The most interesting part is the estimation of the shape function. We consider it as an unknown parameter of the prior probability distribution of labellings and follow the Maximum Likelihood principle. The goal is to maximize

$$F = \ln \sum_y p(x, y; \phi) = \ln \sum_y \exp\left[E(x, y; \phi)\right] - \ln Z(\phi) \to \max_\phi. \tag{7}$$

(in doing so we assume that the appearance parameters θ are known and omit them here for readability). We use the Expectation Maximization algorithm. In the n-th E-step the marginal label probabilities – this time both posterior $p(y_r = 1 | x; \phi^{(n)})$ and prior $p(y_r = 1; \phi^{(n)})$ ones – should be estimated for the current shape $\phi^{(n)}$. The gradient of the function to be maximized in the M-step is then

$$\frac{\partial F}{\partial \cdot} = \sum_r p(y_r = 1 | x; \phi^{(n)}) \frac{\partial \phi(r; \cdot)}{\partial \cdot} - \sum_r p(y_r = 1; \phi^{(n)}) \frac{\partial \phi(r; \cdot)}{\partial \cdot}, \tag{8}$$

where $(\cdot)$ stands for the parameter to be estimated (e.g. ϕ_0, z or σ).

In practice we often observe (for reasonable values of the energy weights α and λ), that the prior label probabilities for the foreground are almost 1 inside and almost 0 outside the zero level set of ϕ. Therefore a good approximation for the second term in (8) can be computed explicitly. In particular it is zero for the differentiation with respect to the shape centre z, i.e. under the above assumption the normalizing constant in (1) does not depend on z at all. To summarize, the above assumption leads to the simple system of equations

$$\frac{\partial F}{\partial z} \sim \sum_r p(y_r{=}1|x; \phi^{(n)}) \cdot (r - z) = 0$$

$$\frac{\partial F}{\partial \sigma_x} \sim \sum_r p(y_r{=}1|x; \phi^{(n)}) \cdot (r_x - z_x)^2 - \pi \phi_0^2 \sigma_x^3 \sigma_y = 0$$

(likewise for σ_y)

$$\frac{\partial F}{\partial \phi_0} = \sum_r p(y_r{=}1|x; \phi^{(n)}) - 2\pi \phi_0^2 \sigma_x \sigma_y = 0, \tag{9}$$

that can be easily solved for z, σ and ϕ_0.

Let us remember that the marginals are calculated approximately by sampling. An important question is, how many samples are necessary in order to reliably approximate marginals. The parameters of interest here are "of global nature" – these are just five real numbers that influence (and are influenced by) the whole pixel domain. Hence, it is reasonable to assume that statistics accumulated over the whole set of labellings do not deviate essentially from the statistics that are accumulated just over one labelling, sampled according to the given probability distribution. This leads to the following updating schema. First, a labelling $\bar{y}$ is sampled according to the posterior probability distribution with current parameters. The posterior label probabilities in (9) are replaced by 0/1 depending on the sampled label $\bar{y}_r$ in each pixel r. Then the system (9) is solved for the unknown parameters. Finally, the actual shape parameters are moved towards the found "optimal" ones by a step $\eta < 1$.

We omit the detailed considerations for learning of the appearance model $p(c|k)$. In short, we follow a similar scheme. According to the Maximum Likelihood principle the corresponding Expectation Maximization schema is derived. Then the necessary statistics are replaced by the ones accumulated for one generated labelling.

4   Implementation Details

To start with, we consider Gibbs Sampling for labellings y. In each pixel r a label is sampled according to the posterior label probabilities conditioned on the current labels in the neighbouring pixels (we denote them by $N(r)$ and the corresponding restriction of y by $y_{N(r)}$):

$$p(k|x, y_{N(r)}) \sim \exp\left[q(x_r, k) + \phi(r) \cdot k + \alpha \sum_{r' \in N(r)} \mathbb{I}(k{=}y_{r'})\right]. \tag{10}$$

As these probabilities are normalized to sum to 1, it is not necessary to compute the above expression for both background and foreground. Only a difference of energies (expression in the square brackets) should be computed:

$$\Delta e = q(x_r, k{=}1) - q(x_r, k{=}0) + \phi(r) + \alpha \sum_{r' \in N(r)} (2y_{r'} - 1) \tag{11}$$

(here for "foreground–background"). Let ξ be a random number sampled in the range $[0 \ldots 1]$. Then the foreground label should be chosen if

$$\xi > \frac{1}{1 + \exp(\Delta e)} \tag{12}$$

holds. The expression on the right-hand side is a simple function of the energy difference Δe, which can be precomputed in advance and stored in a look-up table. In summary, it is only necessary to compute (11) in order to sample a new label in a pixel. It is indeed a very simple expression and can be computed very fast, provided that q and ϕ are known.

The most time consuming part is the computation of the data energies q, which are logarithms of the observation probabilities (5). To accelerate it we make use of the observation that the Gaussian number i in (5) can be seen as an additional random variable i_r for each pixel – i.e. the probabilities $p(x_r|y_r)$ are obtained by marginalization over i_r. Therefore the summation over i_r can be replaced by its sampling. Note, that in this case the values of q in (11) are just Gaussian weights, i.e. $q(x_r, k) = \ln w_{ki_r}$, which makes the computation of (11) even faster. We tested different sampling techniques for generation of i_r and finally decided for Metropolis Sampling that gave the best results (taking into account both quality and efficiency). In one sampling step only two "proposals" are considered – the current Gaussian and a new one chosen randomly. The sampling is performed based on difference of their energies. Since we use isotropic Gaussians of the same variance, this difference is a linear function of colour values. Its coefficients can be pre-computed in advance (after each learning step) that makes computations in each pixel extremely fast. For the exponent the corresponding look-up table can be used in a similar way as for the Gibbs Sampling considered above.

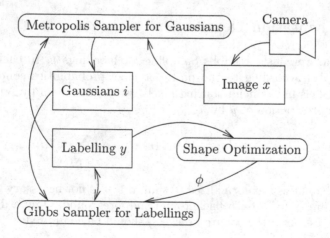

Fig. 1. System architecture

The last question we would like to discuss is the possibility to run different parts of the model in parallel. It is often useful to provide sampling procedures with an initial labelling of high probability in the target probability distribution in order to reduce the so-called "burn-in" phase. In the case of video processing it is reasonable to take as an initialization the last generated labelling, sampled for the previous frame. Consequently, nothing additional should be done in the sampling procedure during the transition from frame to frame, i.e. the procedure should just continue to generate. Moreover it needs not "to know" that the frame was changed. To summarize, the overall system structure is presented in Fig. 1. Common data blocks are shown by rectangles. Rounded rectangles represent procedures, which work asynchronously. Arrows depict data flows. In addition, a fourth procedure is necessary for frame capturing and visualisation. Hence, the system fits very well into modern quad-core architectures.

In this section we described only the most important aspects that allow to implement the needed inference and learning procedures in a very efficient manner. More technical details will be given in a technical report in the near future. The complete source code can be found in [1].

5   Experiments

The first question we would like to discuss in this section is the quality of obtained segmentations[3]. We would like to note from the very beginning that our system of course does not outperform state-of-the-art methods, mainly because of its simplicity. In our opinion, the main advantage of the proposed approach is a closed and compact form that gives satisfactory results, it includes unsupervised learning and works in real time. Therefore we prefer just to give qualitative results together with discussions about the system capabilities and limitations.

The model consists of three main parts: the Potts prior, the shape prior and the appearance model. Hence, an important question is, what is, for example, the influence of the shape prior and would the results be considerably worse without it. The impact of different model parts is illustrated in Fig. 2. In the top row two examples are presented. In the first one (fish) the colours are highly ambiguous which makes the segmentation quite difficult. In the second example (flower) the colours are discriminative enough. However, the shape differs considerably from an ellipse. In the second row results are presented that were obtained by the model without the Potts prior (i.e. $\alpha = 0$). The zero level set of the found shape is shown in red. A higher density of foreground pixels can be clearly observed close to its centre. However, the results are very noisy and obviously far from satisfactory. In the third row results are shown that were obtained without the shape prior (i.e. $\lambda = 0$). This clearly illustrates, that in this case the unsupervised learning of the appearance model often goes into a completely wrong direction – although the results are not noisy as before, the foreground segment does not represent a compact "object".

---

[3] Here we present results for still images only. Examples of the live video segmentation are given in [1].

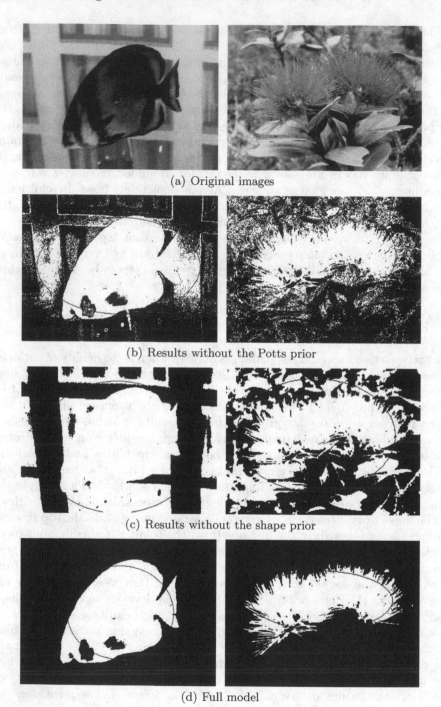

(a) Original images

(b) Results without the Potts prior

(c) Results without the shape prior

(d) Full model

Fig. 2. Influence of different model parts

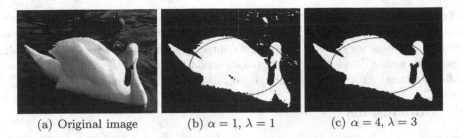

(a) Original image   (b) $\alpha = 1$, $\lambda = 1$ (c) $\alpha = 4$, $\lambda = 3$

Fig. 3. Influence of the model parameters

Table 1. Performance indicator for different environments

Intel Core i7-2620M	4×2.7 GHz	Ubuntu	2062
Intel Xeon 54XX v7.0	8×2.8 GHz	MacOS	2020
Intel Core2 Quad Q6600	4×2.4 GHz	WindowsXP	1970
Intel Core2 Duo T5750	2×2.0 GHz	Ubuntu	735
AMD Athlon X2	2×2.2 GHz	Windows7	473

In the next experiment we would like to illustrate the influence of the model parameters, which are not learned, i.e. the Potts strength α and the weight λ for the shape. This is shown in Fig. 3. In Fig. 3(b) the results are given for values, which we consider as most appropriate for the real-time video processing. It is easy to see, that they lead to non-satisfactory results due to both colour ambiguities and deviation from the elliptical shape. In order to obtain better results (see Fig. 3(c)) it is necessary to make the prior model stronger (in particular to use higher Potts strength). Unfortunately, a high Potts parameter leads to the long burn-in phase of Gibbs Sampling – i.e. more iterations are necessary to sample a good segmentation for the current frame starting with the last generated labelling for the previous one. Therefore a strong prior model can be used for real-time set-up only with video streams of low resolution or for a relatively slow motion.

Finally, we discuss the computational speed of the method. Unfortunately, the notation "real-time" is not well defined as such, because it highly depends on the particular environment. Therefore we prefer to give some concrete data, obtained for different architectures. Most of our experiments were performed on an Intel Core i7-2620M, 2.70GHz (64 bit, quad-core) for frame resolution 320×240 at 30 frames per second under Linux. The Metropolis Sampling for Gaussians was able to perform about 11 sampling iterations[4] per frame, the Gibbs Sampling for labellings – about 13 iterations per frame and the shape optimization was done about 45 times per frame. We measure the overall performance of a particular environment just by counting all activities (sampling iterations or optimization steps) per second. For example, in the above configuration there were about 2060 activities per

---

[4] One iteration is a scan over the whole image.

second. This performance indicator for different environments for 320×240 frame resolution is summarized in Table 1. In higher resolution (e.g. 640×480) the system gives satisfactory results as well. Of course, in comparison with low resolution the performance drops accordingly (to about 530 for the first environment), that influences the quality of the results, especially for fast motion.

6   Conclusions

In this work we presented an approach for binary segmentation that (i) is simple and therefore more or less general, (ii) includes fully unsupervised learning, (iii) is able to work in real-time and (iv) gives satisfactory results.

As our model is very simple, there are numerous ways for improvements. The main one is to use more elaborated shape priors. In our current implementation it is oversimplified and does not represent a "shape" in a common sense, but rather a "region of interest" that regularizes the learning. We hope however that more complex shapes can also be implemented in a similar manner, because our assumption about prior marginal probabilities in (9) seems to hold for other shape models as well.

References

1. http://www1.inf.tu-dresden.de/~ds24/rtsegm/rtsegm.html
2. Bleyer, M., Rother, C., Kohli, P., Scharstein, D., Sinha, S.: Object stereo – joint stereo matching and object segmentation. In: CVPR, pp. 3081–3088 (2011)
3. Boykov, Y., Jolly, M.P.: Interactive graph cuts for optimal boundary & region segmentation of objects in n-d images. In: ICCV, vol. 1, pp. 105–112 (2001)
4. Delong, A., Gorelick, L., Schmidt, F., Veksler, O., Boykov, Y.: Interactive Segmentation with Super-Labels. In: Boykov, Y., Kahl, F., Lempitsky, V., Schmidt, F.R. (eds.) EMMCVPR 2011. LNCS, vol. 6819, pp. 147–162. Springer, Heidelberg (2011)
5. Flach, B., Schlesinger, D.: Combining Shape Priors and MRF-Segmentation. In: da Vitoria Lobo, N., Kasparis, T., Roli, F., Kwok, J.T., Georgiopoulos, M., Anagnostopoulos, G.C., Loog, M. (eds.) S+SSPR 2008. LNCS, vol. 5342, pp. 177–186. Springer, Heidelberg (2008)
6. Gulshan, V., Rother, C., Criminisi, A., Blake, A., Zisserman, A.: Geodesic star convexity for interactive image segmentation. In: CVPR (2010)
7. Nowozin, S., Lampert, C.: Structured Learning and Prediction in Computer Vision. Foundations and Trends in Computer Graphics and Vision 6 (2010)
8. Rother, C., Kolmogorov, V., Blake, A.: "GrabCut": interactive foreground extraction using iterated graph cuts. ACM Trans. Graph. 23(3), 309–314 (2004)
9. Schlesinger, D.: Gibbs Probability Distributions for Stereo Reconstruction. In: Michaelis, B., Krell, G. (eds.) DAGM 2003. LNCS, vol. 2781, pp. 394–401. Springer, Heidelberg (2003)
10. Schlesinger, D., Flach, B.: A Probabilistic Segmentation Scheme. In: Rigoll, G. (ed.) DAGM 2008. LNCS, vol. 5096, pp. 183–192. Springer, Heidelberg (2008)
11. Schmidt, U., Gao, Q., Roth, S.: A generative perspective on MRFs in low-level vision. In: CVPR (June 2010)
12. Schmidt, U., Schelten, K., Roth, S.: Bayesian deblurring with integrated noise estimation. In: CVPR (June 2011)

Pottics – The Potts Topic Model
for Semantic Image Segmentation

Christoph Dann[1], Peter Gehler[2], Stefan Roth[1], and Sebastian Nowozin[3]

[1] Technische Universität Darmstadt
[2] Max Planck Institute for Intelligent Systems
[3] Microsoft Research Cambridge

Abstract. We present a novel conditional random field (CRF) for semantic segmentation that extends the common Potts model of spatial coherency with latent
topics, which capture higher-order spatial relations of segment labels. Specifically, we show how recent approaches for producing sets of figure-ground segmentations can be leveraged to construct a suitable graph representation for this
task. The CRF model incorporates such proposal segmentations as topics, modelling the joint occurrence or absence of object classes. The resulting model is
trained using a structured large margin approach with latent variables. Experimental results on the challenging VOC'10 dataset demonstrate significant performance improvements over simpler models with less spatial structure.

1 Introduction

Semantic segmentation of natural images aims to partition the image into semantically
meaningful regions. Depending on the task, each region represents high-level information such as individual object instances or object parts, types of surfaces, or object class
labels. Semantic segmentation is a challenging research problem in computer vision;
major progress has been made in the last decade, originating from three developments:
First, larger benchmark data sets with thousands of annotated training images are now
common [6]. Second, conditional random fields (CRFs), estimated from training data,
have become a standard tool for modeling the spatial relations of segment labels. Algorithmic advances in inference and estimation for these models, as well as insights in
how to build these models efficiently has enabled further performance gains [11,15,20].
Third, segmentation and object detection priors that are independent of the object class
have been developed [1,5]. Incorporating such priors into a segmentation model has
proven to yield large performance gains.

In this paper we build on these recent developments and present a simple, but effective model for the task of semantic scene segmentation. The model is a conditional
random field with two groups of random variables: segments and regions. *Segments* are
large overlapping parts of the image, which we extract using constrained parametric
min-cuts [5]. Each segment is more likely to be homogeneous with respect to the semantic labeling of the image, but because different segments overlap there may exist
multiple contradicting segments. *Regions* are smaller entities that partition the image;
we use superpixels to define these regions. Since regions are small, we can assume that
they are pure in the semantic labeling. Yet, regions are typically too small to cover an

A. Pinz et al. (Eds.): DAGM/OAGM 2012, LNCS 7476, pp. 397–407, 2012.
© Springer-Verlag Berlin Heidelberg 2012

entire semantic instance such as an object. Therefore they provide only limited evidence for a semantic class. Regions and segments represent two complementary levels of groupings of image pixels. This is illustrated in Fig. 1.

Our CRF model combines the two primitives into one coherent semantic segmentation model. To that end, segments represent latent topics and regions represent the actual consistent image labeling. The two components are coupled by an interaction term that associates semantic labels of regions with latent segment-level topics. The topics thus describe how region labels are spatially arranged. By learning the interaction terms from training data we jointly discover latent topics and their relation to the region-level class label.

Our contributions are the following: (1) A novel semantic segmentation model that integrates latent segment-level topics with a consistent image labeling, and (2) an efficient latent structural SVM training method for the model. Experiments on the challenging PASCAL VOC 2010 challenge demonstrate significant accuracy gains over various baselines, including Potts-based label smoothing.

2   Related Work

Our approach integrates a segmentation prior into a random field model. This follows a range of previous work, which has remained limited in various ways. Superpixel segmentations [17], small coherent regions in the image that are likely to belong a single object class, build the foundation of several recent semantic labeling approaches. It is a standard practise to define a structured model, such as a CRF, on top of superpixel segmentations [2,16,13,8,7], because the superpixels provide computational benefits and regularization. These previous approaches differ in the way they incorporate spatial consistency between superpixels.

Flat CRF models, such as [16,7,2], are formulated on class assignments of superpixels and penalize different labels of neighbors by a pairwise smoothing term. In case of [2], the spatial relation is estimated from training data. [7] additionally considers image features on superpixels and their direct neighbors. These features are then classified, leading to spatially robust decisions. All these methods use a flat neighborhood relation to formulate spatial consistency.

Hierarchical CRFs in contrast, promote spatial label consistency using higher-level entities to couple pixel classes. [14] uses a tree-structured CRF on iteratively refined superpixels that allows efficient parameter learning. Recent extensions [8,13] augment this hierarchical CRF with higher-order potentials to incorporate image-level information and promote smoothness among many pixels.

Another class of methods [3,16] first performs an intelligent oversegmentation of the image into likely objects, and then processes the "segment soup" to find objects. By combining the found objects, a single segmentation of the input is produced. The approach of [3] performs very well but is algorithmic, therefore has no explicit model that can be estimated from data. In [16] a manually tuned CRF is used to fuse multiple oversegmentations. Multiple attempts keep the flavour (and performance) of [3] while providing a principled probabilistic model have been made recently. In [4] and its extensions [9,10], a pairwise graph is constructed by adding an edge between each

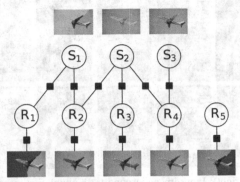

Fig. 1. CRF factor graph structure: CPMC segments (top row) represent latent topics, the regions from the corresponding decomposition of the image (bottom row) yield the semantic labels. A region is connected to a segment if it is fully contained in it; image evidence enters through unaries. Simplified example with 3 segments and 5 regions.

overlapping pair of segments. By solving a maximal clique problem on the graph a coherent segmentation of the image is obtained. While principled, the approach is limited, because it only considers pairwise terms between segments; in contrast our approach uses latent variables that can act on all regions within a segment.

3 Pottics Model

Our proposed CRF for semantic segmentation builds on three main components: *(i)* Segmentation proposals from [3], which yield the regions via a superpixelization of the input image as well as the graph structure; *(ii)* the CRF model itself including the potentials, which model bottom-up image evidence and the segment-region relations; and *(iii)* structured max-margin training with latent variables for the learning part [21]. For learning we assume that we are given a set of N training images $I^i, i = 1, \ldots, N$ along with ground truth pixel-wise class labelings $Y^i, i = 1, \ldots, N$. We now describe the model components in turn.

3.1 CPMC Segmentation Proposals

We build upon the Constrained-Parametric-Min-Cuts (CPMC) method [5] that generates a set of plausible figure-ground segmentations. The main idea behind this algorithm for the use of semantic segmentation is to pre-generate a number of plausible segmentations, from which, in a separate step, a segment is chosen as the final prediction. This largely reduces the state space and also reduces the problem of semantic segmentation to a ranking problem, which allows efficient ranking algorithms to be used. This method consistently performed with top scores on the PASCAL VOC segmentation challenges [6].

The complete CPMC algorithm is rather involved; we can thus only present a brief summary and refer to [5] for details. CPMC operates in three steps to generate a set of binary foreground-background segmentations. First a graph-cut problem is solved

Fig. 2. *Top row* (left to right): Input image, ground truth annotation, example of seeds used for min-cut, top-four segments with their score. *Bottom row* (left to right): segments 5–10, resulting region segmentation from pairwise intersection of segments.

multiple times with different pixels in the images being forced to become foreground. Figure 2 (top row, 3rd from left) illustrates this: By forcing different pixels (green) to be foreground and solving the graph-cut problem, CPMC produces different binary segmentation masks. Parts of the image borders may be chosen as foreground in order to allow for partially occluded objects. This first step generates a large number of plausible segmentation hypotheses, but many of these segmentations are almost identical. The second step of the CPMC algorithm filters the set of segments based on a score computed from their overlap. In addition, segments that are deemed too small are removed. On average, about 300–400 segmentation masks per image are retained after this filtering procedure. In the third and last step, the segments are scored in order to predict how "object-like" they are. To this end 34 different features derived from segment shape, gestalt, and graph properties are used. For illustration, we show the ten highest scored segments for an example image in Fig. 2.

For every input image we generate a set of *segments* $S_i, i = 1, \ldots, N_S$ using the CPMC procedure. From these segments we compute the set of all their intersections. We refer to these as the *regions* $R_i, i = 1, \ldots, N_R$ of the image. By construction all the regions are disjoint, $R_i \cap R_j = \emptyset, \forall i, j$. For the running example in Fig. 2 the output of this step is depicted on the bottom right. Here, the image is partitioned into 1550 different regions.

3.2   CRF Formulation

We use the multiple segmentations from CPMC to construct a random field model as follows (see Fig. 1 for an example): Assume that the image has been segmented into N_R regions and N_S segments, where the values N_R, N_S can vary from image to image. In order to maintain a simple notation we will ignore this. Each region i can take values in $R_i \in \{1, \ldots, C\}$, where C denotes the number of semantic classes. The segments j are modeled as taking values in $S_j \in \{1, \ldots, T\}$, where T is the number of latent topics, to be determined by model selection. With bold letters we will refer to the concatenation of variables, i.e. $\mathbf{R} = (R_1, \ldots, R_{N_R})$. We connect all regions with the segments they are contained in and place a pairwise potential function on them. Furthermore we connect the region variables with image evidence by using unary potentials. The full CRF joint probability is now given as $p(\mathbf{R}, \mathbf{S}) \propto \exp(-E(\mathbf{R}, \mathbf{S}))$ with

$$E(\mathbf{R}, \mathbf{S}) = -\langle w, \phi(\mathbf{R}, \mathbf{S}, I)\rangle = -\sum_{i=1}^{N_R} \langle w_u, \phi_u(R_i, I)\rangle - \sum_{i=1}^{N_R} \sum_{j\sim i} \langle w_p, \phi_p(R_i, S_j, I)\rangle.$$

(1)

We use $j \sim i$ to denote that region i is contained in segment j, that is, whether the variables R_i and S_j share a common edge in the graph. We make a simple choice for the pairwise features, namely $\phi_p(R, S)$ being a binary vector of size $C \cdot T$, with a 1 at the entry that corresponds to (R, S) and 0 otherwise. This allows the parameters w_p to be represented a vector of size $C \cdot T$. For the unary features we use standard, pre-computed image descriptors; more details are given in Sec. 4.

3.3 Learning

The undirected bi-partite graph structure of the model renders computation of the normalization function intractable. Therefore, maximum likelihood learning of the model is intractable as well, and one would have to resort to approximate versions or different estimators, such as contrastive divergence or the pseudo-likelihood. We here follow a different route and use a max-margin approach.

Specifically, we learn the parameters of the CRF in Eq. (1) using a structured SVM with latent variables [21]. The optimization problem can be written as

$$\min_{w,\xi} \frac{1}{2}\|w\|^2 + C\xi$$

(2)

$$\text{sb.t.} \sum_i \left(\max_{\bar{\mathbf{R}}} \left[\max_{\bar{\mathbf{S}}} \langle w, \phi(\bar{\mathbf{R}}, \bar{\mathbf{S}}, I^i)\rangle + \Delta(\bar{\mathbf{R}}, Y^i) \right] - \max_{\mathbf{S}} \langle w, \phi(\mathbf{R}^i, \mathbf{S}, I^i)\rangle \right) \le \xi$$

This non-convex problem is solved with the cutting plane algorithm as implemented in the latentSVM^{struct} software package.[1] With $\Delta : \mathcal{Y} \times \mathcal{Y} \to \mathbb{R}_+$ we denote the loss function that measures the quality of our prediction.

In order to optimize Eq. (2), the following *loss-augmented inference problem* needs to be solved:

$$\bar{\mathbf{R}} = \operatorname*{argmax}_{\tilde{\mathbf{R}}} \left[\max_{\mathbf{S}} \langle w, \phi(\tilde{\mathbf{R}}, \mathbf{S}, I)\rangle + \Delta(\tilde{\mathbf{R}}, Y) \right].$$

(3)

To make a prediction on a novel test image, we need to solve the energy minimization problem

$$\mathbf{R}^* = \operatorname*{argmax}_{\mathbf{R}} \max_{\mathbf{S}} \langle w, \phi(\mathbf{R}, \mathbf{S}, I)\rangle.$$

(4)

Different loss functions Δ have been used for semantic scene segmentation. The authors of the PASCAL VOC challenge [6] implement the following criterion to cope with the unbalanced number of pixels per class

$$\Delta(\bar{Y}, Y) = \frac{1}{C} \sum_{k=1}^{C} \frac{|Y_k \cup \bar{Y}_k|}{|Y_k \cap \bar{Y}_k|}.$$

(5)

---

[1] http://www.cs.cornell.edu/people/tj/svm_light/svm_struct.html

With Y_k we denote the binary segmentation mask with 1's where Y is of class k, 0 otherwise. However, this loss is hard to incorporate during training because it does not decompose over individual regions due to the normalizing denominator. In other words, optimally predicting segmentations for one test image alone is not possible, and all test images need to be predicted jointly. In [19] this issue is addressed by recognizing it to be a problem of inference with a higher order potential. An exact inference algorithm that empirically scales with $N \log N$ is given. We take an easier approach and circumvent this problem by substituting the loss function during training time with the Hamming loss as a proxy

$$\Delta_H(\bar{Y}, Y) = \frac{1}{|Y|} \sum_{i=1}^{|Y|} [Y(i) \neq \bar{Y}(i)], \tag{6}$$

where $[\cdot]$ denotes the Iverson bracket and $Y(i)$ the ith pixel of the segmentation Y. This renders Eq. (3) to be decomposable per image, and furthermore even per region in the image. The loss-augmented inference for image-label pair (I, Y) then reduces to

$$\operatorname*{argmax}_{\bar{\mathbf{R}}} \max_{\mathbf{S}} \sum_{i=1}^{N_R} \langle w_u, \phi_u(\bar{R}_i, I) \rangle + \sum_{i=1}^{N_R} \sum_{j \sim i} \langle w_p, \phi_p(\bar{R}_i, S_j, I) \rangle + \sum_{i=1}^{N_R} \Delta_H(\bar{R}_i, Y). \tag{7}$$

Hence the loss can be seen as just another unary factor applied to the regions.

To approximately solve the inference problems in Eqs. (4) and (7), we apply Iterated Conditional Modes (ICM). With fixed region variables, we update the segment variables, then for fixed segment variables we update the region variables. Since the graph is bi-partite all regions and segments can be updated in parallel. Convergence is typically reached in about 3 iterations per image.

4   Experiments

We test our model[2] on the very challenging PASCAL VOC 2010 semantic segmentation dataset. Since the test set is not publicly available, we train on the *train* split while testing using the *val* split (964 images each).

The main objective of this work is to utilize proposal segmentations and CRFs to improve over unary or region-wise prediction methods. Therefore, we use a single, competitive unary [12] from the literature as a baseline, which has been pre-trained on the training portion of VOC'10 and is publicly available[3]. The unary potentials are based on TextonBoost [18] augmented by color, pixel location, histogram of gradients (HOG) information, as well as the outputs of bounding box object detectors. While unary feature functions can be learned jointly with the pairwise components, this is not the main motivation here. Since, moreover, piecewise training has been shown to be a competitive speed-up (e.g. [14]) we fix the pre-trained unaries as our unary feature ϕ_u and train only a scaling factor w_u as well as the pairwise potentials.

---

[2] Part of the code used in our experiments is available at
http://github.com/chrodan/pottics
[3] http://graphics.stanford.edu/projects/densecrf/unary/

4.1 Baseline Methods

We test against various baseline methods: First, we use the unary potential function to predict pixel class membership directly (UO). Next, pixel-predictions are accumulated over regions and all pixels within a region are assigned to the maximal class score (RP). A third method makes use of the CPMC segments. To that end, all segments accumulate the pixel-predictions of the unary factor and the highest scoring class is chosen as the "segment-label". Since a pixel may be contained in multiple segments, its class is predicted to be the majority vote of all segment labels of segments that it is contained in. We call this method segment-prediction (SP).

Besides these simple voting strategies, we evaluate the classic Potts model as another baseline. That is we connect all neighboring regions (in the sense of a pixel being in a 4-connected neighbourhood relationship with another region) with a pairwise factor of the simple form $\phi_p(R_i, R_j) = \alpha[R_i = R_j]$. We choose α by model selection, but found that any value $\alpha \neq 0$ deteriorates the performance. We still include this method (Potts) with $\alpha = 0.5$. Last, we consider our model with the number of topics T being set to 1 as a generalized form of the Potts model that makes use of the special graph structure that we are building. This model (1T) is also trained using the max-margin learning. All methods use the same set of $N_S = 100$ segments and the resulting region decomposition. We found that fewer segments cannot represent details in images well enough and additional segments deteriorate performance because of their low quality.

4.2 Empirical Results

The empirical results are summarized in Table 1. We report both accuracy using the Hamming loss (left, Eq. (6)) and the VOC loss (right, Eq. (5)). Here the Pottics model has been trained with the number of topics set to $T = 50$ (we tested with setting $T \in \{25, 100\}$ and found qualitatively the same results). We make the following observations: The Pottics model outperforms the other baselines on most classes, and in the class-averaged total score. This confirms our intuition that the CPMC segments provide valuable information on how to connect different regions in the image. We also note that turning this additional information into better performance is not immediate. All other baseline methods that use the constructed graph (SP, Potts, 1T) perform worse than the simple UO baseline. Against our intuition, Potts performs worse as well. We suspect that the unary pixel prediction is sufficiently strong to already incorporate neighbourhood information, hence a simple class smoothing performs worse.

The gain of Pottics over UO is quite substantial with an 5.2% increase in average VOC performance. In Fig. 3 we show images where the improvement in terms of accuracy using the Hamming loss is highest, and in Fig. 4 example images where performance drops compared to UO.

We note that other approaches obtain higher absolute scores (e.g. [12]), but they are computationally more involved and also include elaborate feature tuning and stacking. We restrict ourselves to a simple, efficient base method to show the desired effects, but expect similar improvements when the Pottics model is used in combination with more advanced approaches.

404   C. Dann et al.

Table 1. Performance on the VOC 2010 validation set: *(left)* accuracy using Hamming loss, *(right)* VOC accuracy. The different methods are described in the text.

Hamm. %	UO	RP	SP	Potts	1T	Pottics
background	96.1	96.8	97.1	95.0	**96.8**	92.5
plane	29.2	28.5	13.0	26.0	10.2	**45.9**
bicycle	0.7	0.6	0.0	0.6	0.1	**4.8**
bird	14.4	13.7	2.5	12.4	3.0	**35.6**
boat	17.0	16.8	4.9	15.7	4.8	**27.0**
bottle	16.2	15.6	2.3	12.8	3.9	**27.9**
bus	36.4	35.9	31.3	36.3	23.2	**59.5**
car	47.0	47.1	40.6	47.9	32.3	**62.5**
cat	49.6	50.1	43.3	50.2	**72.1**	70.9
chair	6.7	6.8	0.3	6.4	2.8	**8.7**
cow	11.5	11.1	2.2	9.0	2.6	**23.3**
table	6.5	5.5	1.0	5.3	2.9	**20.2**
dog	16.0	15.7	8.0	14.7	4.9	**16.0**
horse	19.4	19.1	3.9	16.2	6.5	**21.7**
motorbike	33.6	34.1	24.2	32.2	17.8	**42.2**
person	48.3	48.0	41.4	50.4	33.4	**51.6**
plant	11.5	10.7	9.0	10.5	5.9	**19.8**
sheep	**24.8**	25.1	10.4	21.6	11.3	23.4
sofa	**14.9**	14.7	6.0	13.9	7.9	14.4
train	33.1	33.0	20.4	31.1	19.0	**46.4**
tv	26.5	24.6	8.2	22.2	4.2	**33.8**
average	26.6	26.4	17.6	25.3	17.4	**35.6**
total	79.2	**79.7**	77.6	78.2	77.3	78.9

VOC %	UO	RP	SP	Potts	1T	Pottics
background	80.3	80.5	77.5	78.8	78.7	**80.8**
plane	27.6	27.4	12.8	22.4	10.1	**41.0**
bicycle	0.6	0.6	0.0	0.6	0.1	**3.9**
bird	11.9	11.9	2.3	10.7	2.8	**22.1**
boat	16.0	16.1	4.8	13.7	4.8	**25.3**
bottle	15.2	14.9	2.3	12.7	3.8	**24.2**
bus	33.0	33.1	29.0	32.2	22.4	**41.3**
car	43.3	44.2	37.3	43.2	31.4	**52.8**
cat	28.8	**30.4**	25.4	26.5	25.0	25.3
chair	5.2	5.5	3.4	5.4	2.5	**6.4**
cow	10.7	10.5	2.2	7.8	2.5	**20.2**
table	5.4	4.7	1.0	4.5	2.7	**12.5**
dog	12.2	**12.3**	7.3	11.9	4.5	11.5
horse	16.1	16.3	3.7	13.4	6.1	**18.6**
motorbike	28.4	29.4	20.9	26.9	16.5	**34.7**
person	34.6	35.7	33.2	35.2	28.4	**37.1**
plant	11.0	10.3	8.4	9.7	5.7	**16.2**
sheep	20.0	20.9	9.9	17.4	10.8	**21.0**
sofa	12.8	**12.9**	5.7	11.7	7.4	12.3
train	30.1	30.3	19.1	28.8	18.2	**39.9**
tv	23.2	22.0	8.0	20.9	4.2	**27.6**
total	22.2	22.4	14.8	20.7	13.8	**27.4**

Training of the Pottics model takes about 3 hours with $T = 50$ on the 964 training images. ICM typically converges in 3 iterations, which in our implementation requires about 5 seconds per image. Most time is spent in generating the CPMC segments, about 5-10 minutes for a single image using the public implementation[4] of the authors of [5].

4.3   Effect of Segment Topics

In Fig. 6 we show the learned parameters of the Pottics model when using $T = 50$ topics per segment. High values correspond to less probable combinations, e.g. topic #15 has low values for *bus* (class 6) and *car* (7), since those are likely to appear together, while at the same time making joint occurrence with classes such as *cat, table, dog, horse* a unlikely and thus down-weighting their score.

The class *table* is one that performs better under the Pottics model, with an increase of 7.1% in VOC accuracy. In Fig. 5 we show two examples of this class. The topic #21 is dominant, its value having the effect of placing higher scores on the labels *table*. Most probably this accounts for the effect of tables not being segmented well by the CPMC algorithm, which the Pottics model can address. In the right example of Fig. 5 a *table* segment emerges, since the topic has a positive effect on the two objects *bottle* and *table* appearing jointly. The *table* is not present in the ground truth annotation though, hence this example deteriorates performance.

---

[4] http://sminchisescu.ins.uni-bonn.de/code/cpmc/ [Version 1.0]

Fig. 3. Example segmentations for which the Pottics model improves most. From left to right: UO output, Pottics prediction, ground truth. In the second row, the monitor is almost perfectly recovered. In the airplane example the Pottics model corrects the boat class (blue) to be an airplane.

Fig. 4. Example segmentations for which the performance deteriorates. Same ordering as in Fig. 3. In the lower left, the person segment is wrongly joined with the horse segment. In the lower right example, the table is mistaken for a chair.

Fig. 5. Two examples for the topic impact of tables. From left to right: UO prediction, Pottics prediction, ground truth. Classes *person*, *table* and *bottle*.

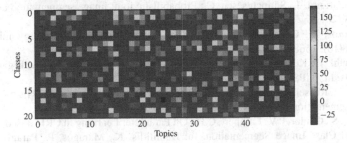

Fig. 6. Learned parameters w_p. The value of the unary parameter is $w_u = -156.6$. High values correspond to less probable combinations. The class ordering corresponds to the listing in Table 1.

5   Conclusion

We introduced a novel CRF model for semantic image segmentation that goes beyond Potts-like spatial smoothing using latent topics. The model is inspired by the success of methods that generate class-independent figure-ground proposal segmentations, which are used to define the graph structure between regions to be labeled and segments, which represent the latent topics. Training relied on a structured max-margin formulation with latent variables. We evaluated our model on the challenging VOC'10 dataset and found it to significantly improve performance over non-spatial as well as simple spatial baselines.

This paper focused on showing the effect of incorporating segmentation information into the prediction. There are many different ways on how the proposed Pottics model can be extended. First, the unary potential function of the regions could be jointly trained with the entire model. The segment variables could further be made image-dependent and equipped with unary factors. While we find that both the Hamming and VOC accuracy are positively correlated, prediction remains sub-optimal when the inference is done using the Hamming loss.

References

1. Alexe, B., Deselaers, T., Ferrari, V.: What is an object? In: CVPR (2010)
2. Batra, D., Sukthankar, R., Chen, T.: Learning class-specific affinities for image labelling. In: CVPR (2008)
3. Carreira, J., Li, F., Sminchisescu, C.: Object Recognition by Sequential Figure-Ground Ranking. IJCV (August 2011)
4. Carreira, J., Ion, A., Sminchisescu, C.: Image segmentation by discounted cumulative ranking on maximal cliques. arXiv CoRR abs/1009.4823 (2010)
5. Carreira, J., Sminchisescu, C.: Constrained parametric min-cuts for automatic object segmentation. In: CVPR, pp. 3241–3248 (2010)
6. Everingham, M., Van Gool, L., Williams, C.K.I., Winn, J., Zisserman, A.: The Pascal Visual Object Classes (VOC) Challenge. IJCV 88(2), 303–338 (2009)
7. Fulkerson, B., Vedaldi, A., Soatto, S.: Class segmentation and object localization with superpixel neighborhoods. In: ICCV (2009)
8. Gonfaus, J., Boix, X., van de Weijer, J., Bagdanov, A., Serrat, J., Gonzalez, J.: Harmony potentials for joint classification and segmentation. In: CVPR (2010)
9. Ion, A., Carreira, J., Sminchisescu, C.: Image segmentation by figure-ground composition into maximal cliques. In: ICCV (2011)
10. Ion, A., Carreira, J., Sminchisescu, C.: Probabilistic joint image segmentation and labeling. In: NIPS (2011)
11. Kolmogorov, V.: Convergent tree-reweighted message passing for energy minimization. PAMI 28(10), 1568–1583 (2006)
12. Krähenbühl, P., Koltun, V.: Efficient inference in fully connected crfs with gaussian edge potentials. In: NIPS (2011)
13. Ladicky, L., Russell, C., Kohli, P., Torr, P.H.S.: Associative hierarchical CRFs for object class image segmentation. In: ICCV. IEEE (September 2009)
14. Nowozin, S., Gehler, P.V., Lampert, C.H.: On Parameter Learning in CRF-Based Approaches to Object Class Image Segmentation. In: Daniilidis, K., Maragos, P., Paragios, N. (eds.) ECCV 2010, Part VI. LNCS, vol. 6316, pp. 98–111. Springer, Heidelberg (2010)

15. Nowozin, S., Lampert, C.: Structured Learning and Prediction in Computer Vision. Foundations and Trends in Computer Graphics and Vision 6(3-4), 185–365 (2011)
16. Pantofaru, C., Schmid, C., Hebert, M.: Object Recognition by Integrating Multiple Image Segmentations. In: Forsyth, D., Torr, P., Zisserman, A. (eds.) ECCV 2008, Part III. LNCS, vol. 5304, pp. 481–494. Springer, Heidelberg (2008)
17. Ren, X., Malik, J., Division, C.S.: Learning a classification model for segmentation. In: ICCV (2003)
18. Shotton, J., Winn, J., Rother, C., Criminisi, A.: Textonboost for image understanding: Multi-class object recognition and segmentation by jointly modeling texture, layout, and context. IJCV (2007)
19. Tarlow, D., Zemel, R.: Big and tall: Large margin learning with high order losses. In: CVPR Ws. on Inference in Graphical Models with Structured Potentials (2011)
20. Vishwanathan, S.V.N., Schraudolph, N.N., Schmidt, M.W., Murphy, K.P.: Accelerated training of conditional random fields with stochastic gradient methods. In: ICML (2006)
21. Yu, C.N., Joachims, T.: Learning structural svms with latent variables. In: ICML (2009)

Decision Tree Ensembles
in Biomedical Time-Series Classification

Alan Jović, Karla Brkić, and Nikola Bogunović

Faculty of Electrical Engineering and Computing, University of Zagreb,
Unska 3, 10000 Zagreb, Croatia
{alan.jovic,karla.brkic,nikola.bogunovic}@fer.hr

Abstract. There are numerous classification methods developed in the field of machine learning. Some of these methods, such as artificial neural networks and support vector machines, are used extensively in biomedical time-series classification. Other methods have been used less often for no apparent reason. The aim of this work is to examine the applicability of decision tree ensembles as strong and practical classification algorithms in biomedical domain. We consider four common decision tree ensembles: AdaBoost.M1+C4.5, Multi-Boost+C4.5, random forest, and rotation forest. The decision tree ensembles are compared with SMO-based support vector machines classifiers (linear, squared polynomial, and radial kernel) on three distinct biomedical time-series datasets. For evaluation purposes, 10x10-fold cross-validation is used and the classifiers are measured in terms of sensitivity, specificity, and speed of model construction. The classifiers are compared in terms of statistically significant wins-losses-ties on the three datasets. We show that the overall results favor decision tree ensembles over SMO-based support vector machines. Preliminary results suggest that AdaBoost.M1 and MultiBoost are the best of the examined classifiers, with no statistically significant difference between them. These results should encourage the use of decision tree ensembles in biomedical time-series datasets where optimal model accuracy is sought.

1   Introduction

Biomedical time-series (BTS) are series of measurements taken from a complex biological system with the basic purpose of diagnosis and treatment of the disorders present in the system. The most common types of BTS measured today are: heart rhythm, electrocardiogram (ECG), electroencephalogram (EEG), electromyogram (EMG), pulse oxymetry, and others [1]. Any analysis of BTS needs to include specific measures (features) that describe it in a way that is the most suitable for discerning different disorder patterns. The cardinality of the feature space of almost any type of BTS is infinite. A "good" set of selected features is the one that would allow the researcher to differentiate the patterns present in the series with ease. Obtaining such a set is highly dependent on the following: type of BTS, types of analyzed patterns, noise present in the BTS, and availability of patient data. In general, the researchers do not agree on the optimal set of features for a specific disorder, and clinical guidelines provide only limited recommendations about the use of particular features [2].

A. Pinz et al. (Eds.): DAGM/OAGM 2012, LNCS 7476, pp. 408–417, 2012.
© Springer-Verlag Berlin Heidelberg 2012

Arguably, the most common type of BTS analysis is classification, wherein the researcher seeks a model that would allow him to accurately classify two or more disorders present in the BTS. Many approaches to classification of BTS have been presented in literature. Some of the more common ones include various types of artificial neural networks (ANN) [3,4] and support vector machines (SVM) [5,6]. Other methods such as Bayesian networks [7] and decision trees (CART) [8] are used occasionally. From the perspective of both the algorithm's accuracy and speed, it is mostly unclear why various forms of decision trees are not used more often for classification of BTS. One of the possible reasons may be that the researchers regard only a single decision tree such as C4.5 or CART (due to interpretability), which is not strong enough to compare to the classification results of ANN or SVM. Another reason is that ANN and SVM are theoretically more well-founded. Nevertheless, the researchers in the field of BTS analysis might not be aware of more recent development in decision tree based classifiers.

In this work, we focus on ensembles of decision trees classifiers and compare them with the SVM classifiers. Some of the known ensembles include AdaBoost, Multi-Boost, random forest, and rotation forest. Decision tree ensembles tend to produce very accurate results on a variety of datasets due to the reduction in both bias and variance component of the generalization error of the base classifier [9]. Previous work indicated that some of the decision tree ensembles (AdaBoost.M1+C4.5 and random forest) may have advantages over ANN and SVM classifiers in classification of heart rhythm time-series in terms of speed and accuracy [10]. SVM classifiers are known to have some advantages over ANN, particularly in terms of accuracy and overfitting avoidance [11]. Therefore, in this paper, we focus on SVM and reserve the consideration of ANN algorithms for future work. This paper aims to determine: 1) whether decision tree ensembles are comparable to or better than SVM algorithms in terms of accuracy and speed of BTS classification models, and 2) which of the inspected decision tree ensembles gives the best results for BTS classification.

We will restrict the work presented in this paper to multiclass classification of a single output class categorical attribute (disorder type), with input attributes being BTS features of either categorical or numerical type. This covers most of the BTS classification datasets. Also, the restriction is on classification methods that have models with no clear interpretation, with the aim of maximum model accuracy. The analysis will be empirical, as the algorithms will be compared on three distinct datasets. The first one is the well-known "Arrhythmia" dataset from UCI repository [12] that contains 16 categories of patient disorders. The dataset is mostly based on ECG time-series with some additional patient information. The second and third datasets are based only on features of heart rate variability extracted from freely available PhysioNet databases [13] with different classification goals.

The structure of this paper is as follows. In Section 2, we describe the employed machine learning algorithms. An overview of the datasets and the classification procedure are given in Section 3. The results of the comparison between the constructed classifiers are presented and discussed in Section 4. Conclusion is given in Section 5.

2   Classification Methods

2.1   AdaBoost.M1+C4.5

AdaBoost.M1 (AB) is a well-known algorithm for boosting weak classifiers [14]. AB is a member of a broader family of iterative machine learning algorithms that build the final classifier through a finite series of improvements to the classifier. The idea of the AB algorithm is to penalize the instances in the training set that are correctly classified by the classifier. The penalized instances then have a smaller chance to be re-selected for the training set. The algorithm focuses on the more problematic instances in each successive step.

Let K be the number of successive steps of the AB algorithm. In the first step, the algorithm selects N (N is the number of instances in the training set) instances to form the first training set by randomly taking instances with equal chance from the initial set with replacement (bootstrap method). Each instance may be selected more than once or may not be selected at all. The algorithm then trains the base classifier and classifies the instances. The instances that are correctly classified receive the penalty to their weight for the next step:

$$w_j^{i+1} := w_j^i \frac{e_i}{1-e_i}, \quad e_i = \sum_{j=1}^r w_j^i e(x_j), \quad e(x_j) = \begin{cases} 1, f_i^{Alg}(x_j) = y_j \\ 0, f_i^{Alg}(x_j) \neq y_j \end{cases}, \quad (1)$$

where $f_i^{Alg}(x_j)$ denotes the i-th classifier built by the classification algorithm Alg (e.g. C4.5). Additional modifications of the weights are possible in cases where error exceeds 50% or drops to 0. The algorithm terminates after a number of successive steps K is reached. A weight is contributed to each constructed classifier. In the testing phase, each classifier in row gives a prognosis for the target class. Each time a target class is selected, its weight is increased depending on the weight of the classifiers. Finally, voting is performed that selects the target class with the highest weight.

The reason why AB is so successful is because it significantly lowers both the classifier variance and bias errors [9]. High variance error is typical for most of the decision tree algorithms, including C4.5. Originally, AdaBoost.M1 used a very simple decision tree, decision stump, as base classifier. Some researchers noticed that better classification results might be obtained if C4.5 is used as the base classifier instead of the stump. C4.5 can deal with weights associated to instances. AB has been shown to significantly improve the results of the basic C4.5 algorithm on a variety of datasets, including biomedical data [9,15].

2.2   MultiBoost+C4.5

MultiBoost (MB) is regarded as an extension to AdaBoost that combines the AB algorithm with the wagging procedure, which is itself extension of the basic bagging method [16]. Instead of K single classifiers used by the AB algorithm, MB constructs a number of sub-committees consisting of a number of trees. Each sub-committee has its own specific iteration $I_k \leq K, \sum_k I_k = K$ in which it terminates. Sub-committee is formed by AB using wagging instead of bootstrap. Wagging works by setting random weights of instances to those drawn from an approximation of the continuous Poisson distribution. After the weights are assigned, the vector of weights is always standardized to sum to N. All instances in the training set are used to train the base classifier using the designated weights. The weights are corrected in each subsequent step of constructing the sub-committee by using (1). All other steps of MB are equal to the AB algorithm, including the testing phase. Using C4.5 as the base classifier for MB is straightforward, as C4.5 handles weights associated to instances. Wagging is shown to be particularly successful in reducing the variance error. Therefore, the combination of wagging and AB can, in principle, lead to better results. MB can also be parallelized at the sub-committee level.

2.3   Random Forest

Random forest (RF) is a decision tree ensemble learner developed by Breiman [17]. RF supports classification, regression, feature selection, prototyping, and other data mining methods. Decision trees that compose the forest are constructed by choosing their splitting attributes from a random subset of k attributes at each internal node. The best split is taken among these randomly chosen attributes and the trees are built without pruning, as opposed to C4.5. The quality of the split at an attribute   is determined by its Gini impurity index. RF avoids overfitting due to two sources of randomness - the aforementioned random attribute subset selection and bootstrap training set sampling. Breiman has shown that if one constructs the forest consisting of a large enough number of such decision trees, the overall classification error will be minimized and the accuracy will reach a plateau. RF is widely used in various classification problems, especially in domains with larger numbers of attributes and instances, because of its high speed and accuracy [17].

2.4   Rotation Forest

Rotation forest (RTF) is a more recent decision tree ensemble method proposed by Rodriguez et al. [18]. The ensemble is capable of both classification and regression, depending on the base classifier. In most applications, C4.5 algorithm is used as the base learner. Algorithm focuses on presenting transformed data to the classifier by using a projection filter. The most common projection filter and the one that has been shown to be the main factor for the success of the ensemble is the principal component filter [19].

Let the number of base classifiers be given as K. In order to create the training set for each base classifier, the instances are first sampled using the bootstrap method. Next, the feature set is randomly split into M subsets and principal component analysis is applied to each subset. All of the eigenvectors are retained as the new features in order to preserve the variance in the data. The idea why these M data transformations are performed is to encourage simultaneously individual accuracy and diversity of classifiers within the ensemble, as this is the most important precondition for a successful ensemble [17]. Diversity is achieved through random splitting of the feature set, and accuracy is sought by retaining all the principal components.

2.5   Support Vector Machines

Support vector machines (SVM) is a kernel based machine learning family of methods that are used to accurately classify both linearly separable and linearly inseparable data [20]. The basic idea when the data is not linearly separable is to transform them to a higher dimensional space by using a transformation kernel function. In this new space the samples can usually be classified with higher accuracy. Many types of kernel functions have been developed, with the most used ones being polynomial and radial-based.

In this work, three types of SVM are considered: linear SVM, squared polynomial SVM, and radial-based SVM. As the learning method, sequential minimal optimization (SMO) type algorithm will be used. The proposed algorithm efficiently resolves quadratic programming optimization problem that arises when determining the maximum margin hyperplane of the support vector machines classifier. Original work on SMO by Platt was later optimized by Keerthi et al. [21], and this optimization, which is implemented in Weka platform [22], will be used. We also considered the LIBSVM [23] implementation of C-SVC in Java as proposed by Fan et al. [24]; however training times were an order of magnitude higher than the Keerthi's method with no improvement in accuracy of the models.

Because SMO is a binary classification algorithm, for multiclass classification purposes it is adapted such that it performs $n*(n-1)/2$ binary classifications. The SVM algorithm is parametric and deterministic. The most significant parameters are the cost of the margin and the radial kernel parameter gamma (γ).

3   Datasets and Evaluation Specifics

3.1   Datasets

The first considered dataset is the "Arrhythmia" dataset from UCI repository [14]. Arrhythmia dataset contains a total of 452 instances of 12-lead ECG measurements. 275 features are extracted from each ECG and additional four patient features are taken into consideration (age, sex, height, weight) to a total of 279 predictive attributes. ECG features include mostly morphological characteristics of observed ECG waves and wave to wave interval durations. Most features are numerical (206), and the rest are categorical or binary (73). There is a single output attribute (ECG class), with 16 possible types, out of which 13 are actually present in the dataset. The majority of the dataset is covered by examples of normal ECGs. Due to the lack of data for some of the ECG disorders, this dataset is considered by some to be difficult for classification, with reported results achieving only 62% total classification accuracy [25].

The second dataset is obtained by extracting features from heart rate variability (HRV) records from two MIT-BIH databases (Arrhythmia and Supraventricular Arrhythmia), available from PhysioNet [13]. For feature extraction, we used the HRVFrame framework of Jović and Bogunović [26]. We extracted a total of 230 numerical features from 125 patient records from both databases. The features included linear time domain, frequency domain, time-frequency, and a large number of nonlinear features. A total of 8843 instances were obtained for time-segments of 20 s, which is known to be near-optimal segment duration for arrhythmia detection [6,10]. The goal was to classify 9 types of commonly occurring heart rhythm patterns found in the databases. To our knowledge, there exists no previously published research that used these two databases.

The third dataset is obtained by extracting HRV features from six MIT-BIH databases, which include: MIT-BIH Normal Sinus Rhythm, Normal Sinus Rhythm RR Interval, MIT-BIH Arrhythmia, MIT-BIH Supraventricular Arrhythmia, BIDMC Congestive Heart Failure, and Congestive Heart Failure RR-interval [13]. A total of 3317 instances from 237 records were obtained for time segments of 5 min with intention of finding potentially accurate models for distinction of the three patient groups: healthy persons, arrhythmic patients, and congestive heart failure (CHF, of different severity level). For feature extraction, we also employed the HRVFrame framework of Jović and Bogunović [26] and extracted a total of 237 numerical features. The features included linear time domain, frequency domain, time-frequency, and a large number of nonlinear features. Previously reported accuracy on this dataset for four-class classification (supraventricular arrhythmia was considered as a separate class of arrhythmia) was 72% [27]. Distribution of instances for all three datasets is shown in Table 1. More on these disorders can be found in [28].

3.2   Evaluation Specifics

For evaluation of the classifiers on each dataset, we use 10x10-fold cross-validation. Evaluation measures used are standard in BTS analyses: sensitivity (SENS), and specificity (SPEC):

$$SENS = \frac{TP}{TP+FN}, \quad SPEC = \frac{TN}{TN+FP}, \tag{2}$$

where TP, TN, FP, and FN are the numbers of: true positives, true negatives, false positives, and false negatives, respectively. For multiclass case, these measures can be obtained from the confusion matrix by comparing numbers of instances for each class in the matrix against instances of all the other classes. The reported values have been weighted and averaged among classes.

Parameters of the algorithms were modified in order to obtain the best possible result using systematic approach on the first 10-fold iteration. The other nine 10-fold

Table 1. Distribution of disorders/rhythm patterns in the two analyzed datasets

Dataset (instance count)	Disorder (instance count)
Arrhythmia (452)	Normal (245), CAD (44), Old anterior MI (15), Old inferior MI (15), Tachycardia (13), Bradycardia (25), PVC (3), PAC (2), LBBB (9), RBBB (50), LV hypertrophy (4), AFIB or AFL (5), Other (22)
HRV (8843)	NSR (4121), PAC (1065), PVC (1466), AFIB (749), VBI (375), VTR (299), ABI (272), ATR(178), PACE(318)
CHF (3317)	Healthy (1182), Arrhythmic (1328), Congestive heart failure (827)

iterations are used for obtaining classification results. Possible combinations of parameters were evaluated by increasing their values step-wise in Weka until an optimal setting (with respect to maximum model sensitivity) on the first 10-fold iteration was found. The searching set for each parameter differed, thus, e.g. number of iterations of AB started from 10 and continued to 100 with the step of 10, while cost parameter C for SVM started at 0.01 and continued to 2048 but with a nonlinear step increase.

For the analyzed datasets, only the best parameters for the SVM classifiers differed. For other classifiers, the optimal parameters on all three datasets were: AB: 40 iter., C4.5 pruning conf. = 0.4; MB: 40 iter., 5 sub-committees, C4.5 pruning conf. = 0.4; RF: 100 trees, max. depth = 20; RTF: 30 iter., 8 max. and 8 min. group members. SVM: Arrhythmia dataset (SVM lin.: C=1; SVM sq.: C=0.03, included first order, SVM rad.: C=5, γ=0.15), HRV dataset (SVM lin.: C=1; SVM sq.: C=0.03, included first order, SVM rad.: C=128, γ=0.01), CHF dataset (SVM lin.: C=10; SVM sq.: C=0.15, included first order, SVM rad.: C=512, γ=0.15). Variations in parameter values would probably be greater if the datasets had more diverse feature counts (around 200 features were present in all three datasets).

4   Results

The algorithms were compared by their mean values and standard deviations for each evaluation measure obtained on nine 10-fold cross-validation iterations. Results for the three datasets are shown in Fig. 1. It is noticeable that the boosting algorithms perform favorably to the other algorithms. Also, if one disregards the apparent failure of RF on the first dataset (probably because of too few examples for the random trees to learn from), all decision tree ensembles compare favorably to SVM algorithms, both for sensitivity and for specificity. To confirm this result statistically, win-loss-tie comparison of the algorithms based on sensitivity is presented in Table 2. Statistically significant wins and losses were obtained using two-sided paired Student t-test on the mean results for the nine 10-fold iterations, with significance level $\alpha = 0.05$. Apparently, SVM algorithms lose to decision tree ensembles on all three datasets (except to RF on the Arrhythmia dataset). Arguably, radial SVM gave the best results among the SVM SMO classifiers. RF and RTF seem to have similar results on average, and they lose to both AB and MB. There are no significant differences between the two best ensembles.

The failure of SVM may be surprising, but it is probably due to the characteristics of the datasets that are common in this domain. All three datasets are multiclass and the samples are not linearly separable. Extending SVM to multiclass case is not straightforward [29], and the implemented SMO algorithms used pair-wise classification. It would be interesting to see if one-vs.-all strategy would lead to better results.

In Table 3, average times needed for classifier construction for the three datasets are shown. Random forest is the fastest algorithm overall. AdaBoost.M1+C4.5 and MultiBoost+C4.5 have reasonably satisfactory model construction times, although slower than most of the other algorithms.

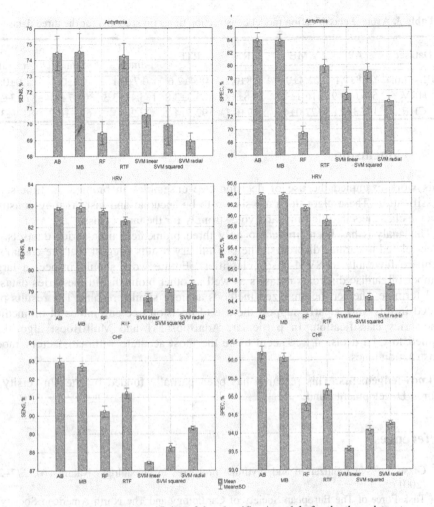

Fig. 1. Sensitivity and specificity of the classifiers' models for the three datasets

Table 2. Win/loss/tie comparison of the algorithms based on sensitivity for the three datasets, Student's paired t-test, $\alpha = 0.05$

vs.	AB	MB	RF	RTF	SVM linear	SVM squared	SVM radial
AB	-	0/0/3	2/0/1	2/0/1	3/0/0	3/0/0	3/0/0
MB	0/0/3	-	2/0/1	2/0/1	3/0/0	3/0/0	3/0/0
RF	0/2/1	0/2/1	-	1/1/1	2/1/0	2/0/1	2/0/1
RTF	0/2/1	0/2/1	1/1/1	-	3/0/0	3/0/0	3/0/0
SVM linear	0/3/0	0/3/0	1/2/0	0/3/0	-	1/2/0	1/1/1
SVM squared	0/3/0	0/3/0	0/2/1	0/3/0	2/1/0	-	0/1/2
SVM radial	0/3/0	0/3/0	0/2/1	0/3/0	1/1/1	1/0/2	-

Table 3. Average classification model construction times (in seconds) for the three datasets

Dataset	AB	MB	RF	RTF	SVM linear	SVM squared	SVM radial
Arrhythmia	21.8±0.1	22.4±0.3	2.8±0.2	48.4±2.6	0.7±0.1	1.0±0.1	1.0±0.1
HRV	675.6±8.9	616.1±1.8	29.8±1.0	825.3±3.8	135.4±13.3	301.7±4.4	370.3±3.0
CHF	177.3±2.8	177.0±4.2	8.7±0.1	192.5±4.2	77.2±3.4	63.3±0.2	81.9±3.6

5   Conclusion

This work examined the use of decision tree ensembles in biomedical time-series classification. These algorithms are shown to be accurate and fast, as they construct diverse classifiers in little time, and vote strongly for the target class.

The analysis has been limited to only three biomedical time-series datasets, all three related to cardiac disorders. The preliminary results suggest that the ensembles compare favorably to SVM-based classifiers. Future work should inspect a larger number of cardiac disorders datasets as well as other biomedical time-series datasets to determine whether the analyzed methods achieve similar results. The results presented in this work clearly support the use of decision tree ensembles in biomedical time-series classification. In particular, AdaBoost.M1 and MultiBoost algorithms applied to C4.5 decision tree seem to be the most accurate with satisfactory model construction times.

Acknowledgements. This research has been partially funded by the University of Zagreb Development Fund.

References

1. Glass, L.: Synchronization and rhythmic processes in physiology. Nature 410, 277–284 (2001)
2. Task Force of The European Society of Cardiology and The North American Society of Pacing and Electrophysiology: Heart rate variability guidelines: Standards of measurement, physiological interpretation, and clinical use. Eur. Heart J. 17, 354–381 (1996)
3. Acharya, R.U., Kumar, A., Bhat, P.S., Lim, C.M., Lyengar, S.S., Kannathal, N., Krishnan, S.M.: Classification of cardiac abnormalities using heart rate signals. Med. Biol. Eng. Comput. 42, 288–293 (2004)
4. Manis, G., Nikolopoulos, S., Alexandridi, A., Davos, C.: Assessment of the classification capability of prediction and approximation methods for HRV analysis. Comp. Biol. Med. 37, 642–654 (2007)
5. Osowski, S., Hoai, L.T., Markiewicz, T.: Support vector machine-based expert system for reliable heartbeat recognition. IEEE Trans. Biomed. Eng. 51, 582–589 (2004)
6. Asl, B.M., Setarehdan, S.K., Mohebbi, M.: Support vector machine-based arrhythmia classification using reduced features of heart rate variability signal. Artif. Intell. Med. 44(1), 51–64 (2008)
7. Soman, T., Bobbie, P.O.: Classification of Arrhythmia Using Machine Learning Techniques. WSEAS Trans. Comp. 4(6), 548–552 (2005)

8. Pecchia, L., Melillo, P., Sansone, M., Bracale, M.: Discrimination power of short-term heart rate variability measures for CHF assessment. IEEE Trans. Inf. Technol. Biomed. 15(1), 40–46 (2011)
9. Schapire, R.E., Freund, Y., Bartlett, P., Lee, W.S.: Boosting the margin: A new explanation for the effectiveness of voting methods. In: 14th Int. Conf. Mach. Learn., pp. 322–330. Morgan Kaufmann, San Francisco (1997)
10. Jović, A., Bogunović, N.: Evaluating and comparing performance of feature combinations of heart rate variability measures for cardiac rhythm classification. Biomed. Signal Process. Control (in press), doi:10.1016/j.bspc.2011.10.001
11. Lisboa, P.J., Vellido, A., Wong, H.: Bias reduction in skewed binary classification with Bayesian neural networks. Neural Networks 13, 407–410 (2000)
12. Blake, C.L., Merz, C.J.: UCI repository of machine learning databases, http://www.ics.uci.edu/~mlearn/MLRepository.html
13. PhysioNet: Physiologic signal archives for biomedical research, http://www.physionet.org
14. Freund, Y., Schapire, R.E.: A Decision-Theoretic Generalization of on-Line Learning and an Application to Boosting. In: Vitányi, P.M.B. (ed.) EuroCOLT 1995. LNCS, vol. 904, pp. 23–37. Springer, Heidelberg (1995)
15. Pramanik, S., Chowdhury, U.N., Pramanik, B.K., Huda, N.: A Comparative Study of Bagging, Boosting and C4.5: The Recent Improvements in Decision Tree Learning Algorithm. Asian J. Inf. Tech. 9(6), 300–306 (2010)
16. Webb, G.I.: MultiBoosting: A Technique for Combining Boosting and Wagging. Mach. Learn. 40, 159–239 (2000)
17. Breiman, L.: Random forests. Mach. Learn. 45, 5–32 (2001)
18. Rodriguez, J.J., Kuncheva, L.I., Alonso, C.J.: Rotation Forest: A New Ensemble Method. Pattern Anal. Mach. Intell. 28(10), 1619–1630 (2006)
19. Kuncheva, L.I., Rodríguez, J.J.: An Experimental Study on Rotation Forest Ensembles. In: Haindl, M., Kittler, J., Roli, F. (eds.) MCS 2007. LNCS, vol. 4472, pp. 459–468. Springer, Heidelberg (2007)
20. Vapnik, V.: The nature of statistical learning theory. Springer, New York (1995)
21. Keerthi, S.S., Shevade, S.K., Bhattacharyya, C., Murthy, K.R.K.: Improvements to Platt's SMO Algorithm for SVM Classifier Design. Neural Computation 13(3), 637–649 (2001)
22. Witten, I.H., Frank, E., Hall, M.: Data Mining: Practical Machine Learning Tools and Techniques, 3rd edn. Morgan Kaufmann, Burlington (2011)
23. Fan, R.-E., Chen, P.-H., Lin, C.-J.: Working set selection using second order information for training SVM. J. Mach. Learn. Res. 6, 1889–1918 (2005)
24. Chang, C.-C., Lin, C.-J.: LIBSVM: a library for support vector machines. ACM Trans. Intell. Syst. Tech. 2(27), 1–27 (2011)
25. Guvenir, H.A., Acar, B., Demiroz, G., Cekin, A.: A supervised machine learning algorithm for arrhythmia analysis. In: Computers in Cardiology Conference CINC 1997, pp. 433–436. IEEE Press, New York (1997)
26. Jovic, A., Bogunovic, N.: HRVFrame: Java-Based Framework for Feature Extraction from Cardiac Rhythm. In: Peleg, M., Lavrač, N., Combi, C. (eds.) AIME 2011. LNCS, vol. 6747, pp. 96–100. Springer, Heidelberg (2011)
27. Jovic, A., Bogunovic, N.: Random Forest-Based Classification of Heart Rate Variability Signals by Using Combinations of Linear and Nonlinear Features. In: Bamidis, P.D., Pallikarakis, N. (eds.) MEDICON 2010. IFMBE, vol. 29, pp. 29–32. Springer, Berlin (2010)
28. Garcia, T.B., Holtz, N.E.: 12-Lead ECG: The Art of Interpretation. Jones and Bartlett Publishers, Sudbury (2001)
29. Criminisi, A., Shotton, J., Konukoglu, E.: Decision Forests for Classification, Regression, Density Estimation, Manifold Learning and Semi-Supervised Learning. Microsoft Research Technical Report TR-2011-114 (2011)

Spatio-temporally Coherent Interactive Video Object Segmentation via Efficient Filtering

Nicole Brosch*, Asmaa Hosni**, Christoph Rhemann***, and Margrit Gelautz

Institute of Software Technology and Interactive Systems
Vienna University of Technology, Austria

Abstract. In this paper we propose a fast, interactive object segmentation and matting framework for videos that allows users to extract objects from a video using only a few foreground scribbles. Our approach is based on recent work [12] that obtains high-quality image segmentations by smoothing the likelihood of a color model with a fast edge-preserving filter. The previous approach was originally intended for single static images and does not achieve temporally coherent segmentations for videos. Our main contribution is to extend the approach of [12] to the temporal domain. Our results are spatially and temporally coherent segmentations, in which the borders of the foreground object are aligned with spatio-temporal color edges in the video. The obtained binary segmentation can be further refined in a temporally coherent and equally efficient alpha matting step. Quantitative and qualitative evaluations show that our extension significantly reduces flickering in the video segmentations.

1 Introduction

This paper presents a fast, interactive segmentation and matting framework for videos. Given a video in which some frames have been annotated with sparse user input in the form of scribbles (e.g., [2,15]) or pre-segmentations (e.g., [1,9]), interactive video segmentation aims to partition the scene into fore- and background regions. To account for transparencies at object borders that originate from, e.g., hair, the binary segmentation can be refined in an alpha matting step.

Interactive video segmentation has to deal with two types of challenges: those related to user interaction and those related to the segmentation process. Ideally, the segmentation can be performed based on minimal user interaction that avoids time-consuming annotations of entire frames or frequent corrections. Key challenges concerning the segmentation process involve the generation of spatially and temporally coherent results (i.e., no noise, no flickering). Another crucial

---

* Supported by the Doctoral College on Computational Perception at TU Vienna and by the Vienna Science and Technology Fund (WWTF) through project ICT08-019.

** Supported by the Vienna PhD School of Informatics.

*** Has been funded by the Vienna Science and Technology Fund (WWTF) through project ICT08-019.

A. Pinz et al. (Eds.): DAGM/OAGM 2012, LNCS 7476, pp. 418–427, 2012.
© Springer-Verlag Berlin Heidelberg 2012

point is the scalability of a segmentation algorithm. For practical applicability the large number of pixels in a video often has to be processed in real-time.

In this paper, we propose an efficient interactive video segmentation and matting framework that addresses both types of challenges. Our framework offers a scribble-based user interface (UI), where the user marks the foreground object. Drawing a scribble triggers a local optimization process that assigns pixels in all frames of a video to either the foreground or the background in real-time. The optimization is based on spatio-temporal cost-volume filtering. This means that we exploit temporal information implicitly. Hence we do not need to perform a challenging and costly optical flow estimation. The obtained binary segmentation can be refined in a temporally coherent and likewise efficient alpha matting step.

Earlier work most closely related to ours are [7] and [12]. Rhemann et al. [12] proposed a cost filtering scheme that can be applied to a variety of computer vision tasks, including image segmentation. Based on color models, initialized through user-scribbles, they generate a cost map that contains each pixel's probability of belonging to the foreground. Smoothing the cost map with an edge-preserving filter [6] yields a spatially smooth labeling. However, this scheme lacks temporal aggregation of costs. When being applied to our task of video segmentation, which calls for a labeling that is smooth *temporally* as well as spatially, their approach can cause flickering. Accordingly, the main contribution of our work is to extend the single image segmentation approach in [12] to the temporal domain. We achieve temporally coherent segmentations by additionally aggregating the costs across frames. This is similar to [4] and [7], where spatio-temporal filtering was used in the domains of stereo matching, optical flow estimation, and depth propagation. Our framework is concerned with a different application, namely interactive video segmentation.

While interactive image segmentation and matting is a widely treated problem (e.g., [2,3,12,14]), fewer approaches are concerned with the problem's extension to videos (e.g., [1,2,5,9,11,15]). Related methods that focus on video segmentation include [2]. In [2] the segmentation is based on the geodesic distance of a pixel to the fore- and background scribbles. The geodesic distance is computed as the weight of the shortest path in a cost-volume that was generated from color models. This approach requires the cost-volume to be accurate. Noise and variations can lead to errors at object boundaries. In contrast, our approach smoothes the cost-volume under guidance of the input video and yields spatially and temporally coherent segmentations, in which label changes coincide with spatio-temporal edges in the input video. Bai et al. [1] propose a framework that is able to process scenes that contain similar colors in the foreground and the background. However, it relies on accurate manual segmentation of keyframes. Furthermore, the method is based on different components that add to the complexity and to the computational cost, such as motion estimation. In contrast, our real-time segmentation framework does not require optical flow estimation, because spatio-temporal filtering implicitly includes the spatio-temporal neighborhood. Since our framework requires sparse and less accurate user input in the form of scribbles, our approach additionally saves annotation time.

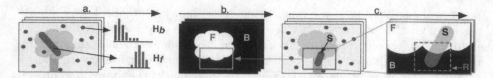

Fig. 1. Progressive labeling (after [10]). First foreground scribble (a.): The foreground model (H_f) is based on the marked pixels (*red scribble*). The background model (H_b) is based on randomly chosen pixels (*blue dots*). Obtained segmentation (b.): Foreground (F) white, background (B) black. Second scribble (c.): Scribble (S). H_f is based on newly marked pixels ($B \cap S$) and local foreground pixels ($R \cap F$) in a bounding box (R)

Another class of video object segmentation approaches relies on global optimization (e.g., [9,15]). Although these methods can potentially leverage the totality of video pixels in support of computing a segmentation, processing them at the same time leads to high computational cost. Wang et al. [15] reduce the runtime by jointly processing groups of pixels. However, the requisite pre-processing step is itself costly (e.g., $720 \times 480 \times 175$ video: 39 minutes [15]). In contrast, our local approach achieves run times of 250 frames (620×360) per second.

2   Algorithm Description

The proposed video object segmentation and matting framework comprises three components. First, to enable a user to extract objects from a video, a scribble-based UI is implemented (Section 2.1). Users draw on frames, indicating that the marked pixels belong to the foreground (or background). After drawing a scribble, a fast optimization (Section 2.2) based on spatio-temporal cost-volume filtering is triggered. The filtered cost-volume is then thresholded to get the binary segmentation. Finally, an optional matting step can account for mixed pixels at object borders. Below, we discuss these components in detail.

2.1   Scribble-Based User Interface

Our framework offers a scribble-based UI that supports local and progressive editing. The user draws scribbles on a frame and color[1] models are built from the user-marked pixels. These color models are then used as data cost in our segmentation algorithm (Section 2.2). As color models we use color histograms that sum up to one. Our UI follows three main concepts: foreground selection, progressive labeling and local editing. The concepts were presented in [10] and we transfer them to the temporal domain. In the following we discuss these concepts.

Foreground Selection. In general, only foreground scribbles are necessary to extract a foreground object.[2] This is more intuitive and reduces the amount of

---

[1] Note that other features (e.g., motion vectors [2]) could be additionally used.

[2] It is possible to add background scribbles by reversing the roles of fore- and background.

Fig. 2. Local editing. Frame and foreground scribble (*red*) (*a.*). Segmentation maps which accept all (*b.*) and only local changes (*c.*). Foreground: white; Background: black

user interaction (i.e., fewer scribbles, no need to change the scribble label). Given a foreground scribble, the foreground color histogram H_f is built from the marked pixels (Fig. 1, *a.*, *red scribble*). The background color histogram H_b is built from a number of random background samples (i.e., 1200) from the same frame (Fig. 1, *a.*, *blue dots*). Although these samples might not all be true background samples, the model is further refined with subsequent user interactions.

Progressive Labeling. Based on the foreground and background histogram a segmentation is computed (Fig. 1, *b.*). This segmentation, with foreground F and background B, can be expanded by adding new scribbles in any frame of the video (Fig. 1, *c.*). When a new scribble S is drawn, the histograms are updated. H_f is re-built from the newly marked foreground pixels $B \cap S$ and local foreground pixels, which are available from the previous interaction. Given a bounding box[3] R around $B \cap S$, local foreground pixels are defined as $R \cap F$. To avoid that the local foreground pixels' colors are dominant in H_f, we lower their contribution in H_f based on their spatial distance to S. Next we update the background histogram H_b. This is done by replacing those samples which were assigned to F by the previous segmentation result (Fig. 1, *b.*). The progressive labeling preserves the segmentation from previous interactions by only expanding either the foreground or the background. Specifically, when adding a foreground scribble, the previous result is updated by switching only labels of background pixels.

Local Editing. Based on the observation that users most often want to change the segmentation only locally, we try to avoid unwanted changes far away from local user input. We implement the concept of local editing in two ways: Firstly, we build the foreground color histograms locally. We do this because color re-occurs quite frequently in a video and hence global color models would be ambiguous. In contrast, the color information is more unique in a small spatio-temporal window. Secondly, a scribble can only affect the selection locally. In particular, if a scribble generates a selection with disconnected regions from the scribble, we remove the disconnected regions. This is illustrated in Fig. 2, where the user marks the dog's head with a foreground scribble (Fig. 2, *a.*). Due to color ambiguities, regions of the background are erroneously assigned to the foreground (Fig. 2, *b.*). However, removing regions from the resulting binary segmentation which are not spatio-temporally connected to the scribble, leads to a better result (Fig. 2, *c.*).

---

[3] We additionally expand the bounding box by 40 pixels in the spatial domain and two frames in the temporal domain.

Fig. 3. Temporally coherent cost-volume filtering. Frame from guidance video *"Who"* (*a.*) with scribble (*red*), corresponding xy-slice from cost-volume (*b.*) and from spatio-temporally filtered cost-volume (*c.*). yt-slice at position of the *green arrow* from video (*d.*), per-frame filtered (*e.*) and spatio-temporally filtered cost-volume (*f.*)

2.2   Spatio-temporal Video Segmentation

Given the foreground color model H_f and the background color model H_b, we assign all pixels of a video to either the fore- or the background. The assignment should ideally be spatio-temporally coherent (no noise or flickering) and fast. To achieve these goals, we follow three steps: (i) to build a cost-volume, (ii) to filter the cost-volume and (iii) to assign labels according to the cost-volume.

Cost-Volume Generation. In the context of video object segmentation, a spatio-temporal cost-volume (Fig. 3, *b.* shows an xy-slice for fixed t) contains the cost p_i that a pixel $i = (x, y, t)$ belongs to the foreground (or the background $1 - p_i$). This cost is based on the comparison of the frequencies of i's bin in H_f and H_b:

$$p_i = 1 - \frac{H_f(i)}{(H_f(i) + H_b(i))}. \tag{1}$$

Previously marked pixels have already been assigned by the user and are accordingly set to 0 or 1. The result of this procedure — the cost-volume — is itself a segmentation cue (e.g., Fig. 3, *b.*). However, naively using this cost-volume for extracting the foreground using thresholding ($p_i > 0.5$) would result in a segmentation that is spatially and temporally not coherent. This is due primarily to color ambiguities, missing colors in the color models or noise (e.g., Fig. 3, *b.*). To account for these problems, a smoothness assumption is commonly implemented to propagate costs to neighbor pixels that are similar in terms of color.

Spatio-temporal Filtering. For smoothing we use an efficient, edge-preserving filtering technique to locally smooth the costs of similar neighbor pixels. When filtering the cost-volume in a frame-to-frame manner [12], holes are smoothed — the segmentation is spatially more coherent — and edges in the cost-volume are aligned with spatial edges in the input video (Fig. 3, *c.*). However, filtering frames independently from each other does not prevent flickering (Fig. 3, *d.-f.*). To obtain a spatially and temporally coherent result, we use a temporally extended version of the guided filter [4,7]. This three-dimensional filter kernel additionally smoothes temporally close-by pixels of the cost-volume which are similar in a guidance video (i.e., the input video). This means cost-edges that

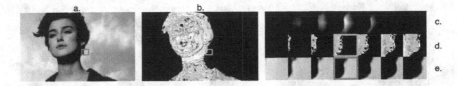

Fig. 4. Filter kernel. Frame from guidance video *"Girl"* (*a.*) and corresponding xy-slice from cost-volume (*b.*). Zoom-in on the marked windows and their temporal extent (*d., e.*). Corresponding filter weights (*c.*) with $r_s = 15$, $r_t = 3$ and *eps* $= 0.002$.

coincide with spatio-temporal video edges are preserved. The described behavior is realized by a weighted average whose weights are given by:

$$W_{i,j} = \frac{1}{|\omega|^2} \sum_{k:(i,j)\in\omega_k} (1 + (I_i - \mu_k)^T (\Sigma_k + \epsilon U)^{-1}(I_j - \mu_k)). \qquad (2)$$

Here, ω_k is a spatio-temporal window, with spatial radius r_s and temporal radius r_t, that is centered around a pixel k. i and j are pixels in ω_k. $|\omega|$ is the number of pixels in ω_k. μ_k (3×1) is the mean color vector in ω_k and Σ_k (3×3) is the corresponding covariance matrix. U is the 3×3 identity matrix. The filter's sensitivity can be controlled by ϵ (a higher ϵ leads to smoother videos). Fig. 4 illustrates a filter kernel for guided video filtering. It can be seen that pixels that are similar to the central pixel have high weights. Pixels on the other side of the spatio-temporal edge have low weights. It has been shown that the spatio-temporal guided filter can be implemented in linear time using a sliding window technique (see [7] for details). We additionally experimented with a temporal weighting [13] of a kernel's time slices, meaning that we give higher weights to frames near the kernel's central frame than to frames at window borders.

Fore- and Background Assignment. Finally, we apply a threshold (> 0.5) to the filtered cost-volume. This yields an assignment of each pixel to either the fore- or the background. To obtain a soft segmentation, which accounts for mixed pixels at object borders, an additional, temporally coherent matting step can be performed. It has been shown that the spatial guided image filter approximates a matting algorithm [6], when being applied to binary segmentations. We apply a spatio-temporal guided filter to the previously obtained binary segmentation volume. To be more precise, the thresholded cost-volume is filtered with guidance of the input video. This leads to temporally smooth matting results.

3 Experimental Results

Our interactive segmentation algorithm was implemented and tested on a 2.4 GHz Intel Core 2 Quad PC with a GeForce GTX40 graphics card. We used CUDA for the GPU implementation. Our implementation requires 4 milliseconds to segment a frame with a resolution of 620×360 pixels. Throughout our tests,

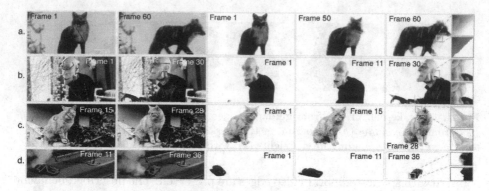

Fig. 5. Experimental results. Frames and user input (*first two columns*): foreground scribbles (*red*); Corresponding soft segmentation (*last three columns*). The zoom-ins show the results before (*bottom*) and after (*top*) matting. All user inputs are shown

Fig. 6. Result based only on data cost (without smoothing). Frames and user input (*first two columns*): foreground scribbles (*red*); Soft segmentation (*last three columns*). The zoom-ins show the results before (*bottom*) and after (*top*) matting

we use the following constant filter parameters to obtain a binary segmentation: $r_s = 11$, $r_t = 2$, $eps = 0.002$. The color histograms use 32 bins per channel. Fig. 5 and the supplementary material show segmentation and matting results generated by our algorithm. The videos consist of 60 (*a.*), 31 (*b.*), 30 (*c.*) and 41 (*d.*) frames, respectively. In each video only two frames had to be annotated (Fig. 5, *first two columns*) to obtain the results shown (Fig. 5, *last three columns*). On average, eight scribbles were placed in a video of 41 frames. Note that we used only foreground scribbles. We obtained spatially and temporally coherent segmentations, in which temporal and spatial edges coincide with edges in the corresponding input video volume. As can be seen in the zoom-ins (Fig. 5, *right*), the additional matting step further refines our segmentations by capturing fine details and transparencies. The test videos include examples with similar colors in the fore- and background (e.g., Fig. 5, *b.*), which would have led to errors when only using the data cost without smoothing (Fig. 6). We observed limitations in scenes with weak boundaries between fore- and background regions. Fig. 7 shows an example where the color of a ground patch matches the color of the bison's horn, which causes it to be erroneously assigned to the foreground.

Comparison to Per-Frame Filtering [12]. We compare our proposed method, which aggregates costs spatially as well as across frames, with the per-frame cost-volume filtering method of [12] that uses a two dimensional (spatial) kernel. For both methods we use the same user input and color models, which

Fig. 7. Failure case. Frames and user input (*first two columns*): foreground scribbles (*red*); Soft segmentation (*last three columns*); Zoom-ins: result (*top*), input (*bottom*)

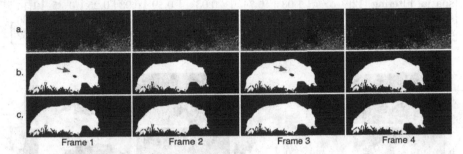

Fig. 8. Comparison of per-frame cost-volume filtering [12] (*b.*) and spatio-temporal cost-volume filtering (*c.*). Frames from *"Bear"* (*a.*); Binary segmentation maps (*b.*, *c.*)

result in the same cost-volume. Except for the additional temporal extension, we use the same parameters (i.e., $r_s = 11$, $eps = 0.002$) as for the filter in [12]. We observe that the filtered cost-volume and, more importantly, the segmentation results are temporally more coherent when using our proposed method. Fig. 8 gives an example for this case. Please also see the video supplied as additional material. It can be seen that our approach achieves a largely flicker-free segmentation (Fig. 8, *c.*). This is not the case for the per-frame method [12] (Fig. 8, *b.*).

We quantitatively compare the resulting binary segmentation maps (e.g., Fig. 8, *b.* and *c.*) using a measure for temporal coherence presented in [8], which we refer to as Flickering Error (FE):

$$FE_i(t) = \frac{|a_i - a_j|}{|I_i - I_j| + 1}. \tag{3}$$

This measure detects label changes ($a \in \{0, 1\}$, 0 background, 1 foreground) of temporally neighboring pixels i and j. The error for such a label change is given by the pixels' color similarity I_i, I_j. Accordingly, the error for label changes at similar pixels is higher than for label changes that go along with color changes. It can be seen (Table 1, Fig. 8, video supplied as supplementary material) that filtering the cost-volume with our spatio-temporal method significantly reduces the error (e.g., for *"Bear"* reduction of 56 percent from *"spatial filtering"* to *"spatio-temporal"*), which indicates temporally more coherent results.[4] An additional temporal weighting (Table 1, *"spatio-temporal + weights"*) can lead to improvements over the approach without weighting.

---

[4] We observed similar error rates when comparing the matting results.

Table 1. Averaged Flickering Error [8] for the binary segmentation of eight videos. From top to bottom: The segmentations were computed by thresholding the unfiltered cost-volume, the per-frame filtered cost-volume and the spatio-temporally filtered cost-volume without and with weighting. The numbers are scaled by 1000

Averaged Flickering Error	Bear	Board	Temple	Who	Girl	Surf	Arms	Fish
no filtering	3.23	5.67	0.12	1.18	3.64	3.23	4.43	4.23
spatial filtering [12]	1.03	0.74	0.03	0.19	0.93	0.25	1.35	1.14
spatio-temporal	0.45	0.32	0.02	0.10	0.64	0.17	0.52	0.66
spatio-temporal + weights	0.43	0.31	0.02	0.09	0.61	0.17	0.47	0.62

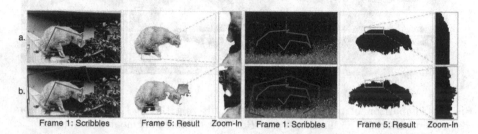

Frame 1: Scribbles   Frame 5: Result Zoom-In   Frame 1: Scribbles   Frame 5: Result   Zoom-In

Fig. 9. Comparison to geodesic segmentation [2] on two videos. Frame and user input (*left*) and binary segmentation of a frame (*right*). User input and results for the proposed method (*a.*) and for [2] (*b.*). The user input differs only in the additional background scribble (*blue*) for [2]. The comparison uses the same foreground scribble (*red*)

Comparison to Geodesic Segmentation [2]. Due to the lack of segmentation ground truth, we visually compare the result of our binary segmentation to those of a geodesic segmentation framework (Fig. 9). We use our re-implementation of [2] to generate the shown binary segmentations. Our algorithm outperforms the geodesic segmentation algorithm using the same foreground scribble as input. While our background model is based on randomly chosen samples, in [2] users initialize it with an additional background scribble. As can be seen in Fig. 9, our segmentation results adapt better to the scenes than those of [2]. In contrast to the results obtained by the re-implemented geodesic algorithm (Fig. 9, *b.*), in our results (Fig. 9, *a.*) label changes coincide with spatio-temporal edges in the input video. This is, in fact, a result of guided filtering, which smoothes costs in homogenous regions in the input video.

4   Conclusion

We proposed an interactive segmentation and matting framework for videos that obtains spatio-temporally coherent segmentations in real-time. Our main contribution was to extend an interactive single image segmentation approach, which is based on spatial cost-volume filtering, to the temporal domain. We qualitatively and quantitatively showed that additional aggregation of costs across frames significantly reduces flickering in the segmentation results. We further show that our proposed approach outperforms previous video segmentation methods that have similar runtime capabilities as ours. Our user interface allows performing the segmentation based on minimal user interaction (i.e., few foreground scribbles).

References

1. Bai, X., Wang, J., Simons, D., Sapiro, G.: Video SnapCut: Robust video object cutout using localized classifiers. In: SIGGRAPH 2009, pp. 70:1–70:11 (2009)
2. Bai, X., Sapiro, G.: Geodesic matting: A framework for fast interactive image and video segmentation and matting. IJCV 82(2), 113–132 (2009)
3. Boykov, Y., Jolly, M.P.: Interactive graph cuts for optimal boundary and region segmentation of objects in N-D images. In: ICCV 2001, vol. 1, pp. 105–112 (2001)
4. Brosch, N., Rhemann, C., Gelautz, M.: Segmentation-based depth propagation in videos. In: ÖAGM/AAPR 2011, pp. 1–8 (2011)
5. Criminisi, A., Cross, G., Blake, A., Kolmogorov, V.: Bilayer segmentation of live video. In: CVPR 2006, pp. 53–60 (2006)
6. He, K., Sun, J., Tang, X.: Guided Image Filtering. In: Daniilidis, K., Maragos, P., Paragios, N. (eds.) ECCV 2010, Part I. LNCS, vol. 6311, pp. 1–14. Springer, Heidelberg (2010)
7. Hosni, A., Rhemann, C., Bleyer, M., Gelautz, M.: Temporally Consistent Disparity and Optical Flow via Efficient Spatio-temporal Filtering. In: Ho, Y.-S. (ed.) PSIVT 2011, Part I. LNCS, vol. 7087, pp. 165–177. Springer, Heidelberg (2011)
8. Lee, S.Y., Yoon, J.C., Lee, I.K.: Temporally coherent video matting. Graphical Models 72(3), 25–33 (2010)
9. Li, Y., Sun, J., Shum, H.Y.: Video object cut and paste. In: SIGGRAPH 2005, pp. 595–600 (2005)
10. Liu, J., Sun, J., Shum, H.Y.: Paint selection. In: SIGGRAPH 2009, pp. 69:1–69:7 (2009)
11. Price, B., Morse, B., Cohen, S.: LIVEcut: Learning-based interactive video segmentation by evaluation of multiple propagated cues. In: ICCV 2009, pp. 779–786 (2009)
12. Rhemann, C., Hosni, A., Bleyer, M., Rother, C., Gelautz, M.: Fast cost-volume filtering for visual correspondence and beyond. In: CVPR 2011, pp. 3017–3024 (2011)
13. Richardt, C., Orr, D., Davies, I., Criminisi, A., Dodgson, N.A.: Real-time Spatiotemporal Stereo Matching Using the Dual-Cross-Bilateral Grid. In: Daniilidis, K. (ed.) ECCV 2010, Part III. LNCS, vol. 6313, pp. 510–523. Springer, Heidelberg (2010)
14. Rother, C., Kolmogorov, V., Blake, A.: "GrabCut": Interactive foreground extraction using iterated graph cuts. In: SIGGRAPH 2004. pp. 309–314 (2004)
15. Wang, J., Bhat, P., Colburn, R., Agrawala, M., Cohen, M.: Interactive video cutout. Trans. Graph. 24(3), 585–594 (2005)

Discrepancy Norm as Fitness Function for Defect Detection on Regularly Textured Surfaces

Gernot Stübl[1], Jean-Luc Bouchot[2], Peter Haslinger[1], and Bernhard Moser[1]

[1] Software Competence Center Hagenberg,
Softwarepark 21, A-4232 Hagenberg, Austria
[2] Department of Knowledge-based Mathematical Systems,
Altenbergerstr. 69, A-4040 Linz, Austria

Abstract. This paper addresses the problem of quality inspection of regular textured surfaces as, e.g., encountered in industrial woven fabrics. The motivation for developing a novel approach is to utilize the template matching principle for defect detection in a way that does not need any particular statistical, structural or spectral features to be calculated during the checking phase. It is shown that in this context template matching becomes both feasible and effective by exploiting the so-called discrepancy measure as fitness function, leading to a defect detection method that shows advantages in terms of easy configuration and low maintenance efforts.

1 Introduction

This paper is motivated by the demand for performant, highly discriminative and still easy to configure visual defect detection algorithms.

In literature one can find statistical, structural, model-based or filtering approaches for optical quality inspection. See, e.g., Xie[29] or Kumar[17] for a survey. Statistical approaches rely on histograms and first or second order statistics of the intensity image. Features like mean, variance, median, entropy, inertia or contrast can be computed from such statistics. See, e.g., Haralick[13], Ng[25]. Structural approaches, see, e.g., Mirmehdi et al.[20], are based on the principle of defining a structural element and finding its spatial distribution applying morphological operations. Fractal-based methods [10] exploit the concept of fractal dimension as characteristic of textures. Markov Random Fields [9] rely on probabilistic models of the spatial dependencies of the intensity values. Filtering methods aim at characterizing textures by informative spatial or spectral features. Typical examples are approaches based on wavelets [7] or Gabor filters [4]. Approaches based on TEXEM models [30] consider textures as superposition of texture elements in order to represent the texture under consideration.

As a further approach we introduce and study template matching in the context of quality inspection of regular textured surfaces as for instance encountered in industrial woven fabrics (sieves, airbag hose, textiles for automotive interior etc.). The goal is to utilize the template matching principle for defect detection in a way that does not need any particular statistical, structural or spectral

A. Pinz et al. (Eds.): DAGM/OAGM 2012, LNCS 7476, pp. 428–437, 2012.
© Springer-Verlag Berlin Heidelberg 2012

features to be calculated. It will be shown that this goal can be achieved by exploiting the so-called discrepancy measure as fitness function.

This paper is structured as follows. Section 2 discusses whether template matching is an appropriate approach for detecting defects in regular textures. In this context the following three aspects are addressed: a) choice of appropriate dissimilarity measure in Section 3, b) design of an algorithm for matching test patches with a reference in Section 4, and c) specification of a discriminative rule for detecting defect candidates in Section 5. This Section proposes a RANSAC inspired algorithm for realizing this template matching concept. The next Section contains experimental evaluations on woven fabrics to show the stability and performance of the algorithm. The conclusion, Section 7, outlines future research potentials.

2   Template Matching for Texture Analysis

In quality inspection a sensed image I is scanned by a sliding window with varying center (i,j). This sliding window crops a test image patch $T_{(i,j)} \subseteq I$ that has to be analysed whether it indicates a defect or not. Template matching requires a notion of (dis-)similarity d that measures to which extent the test patch, $T_{(i,j)}$, matches a given reference image, R. We call the resulting map $\Theta_d(i,j) = d(T_{(i,j)}, R|_{T_{(i,j)}})$ the (dis-)similarity map induced by the (dis-)similarity measure d, $R|_{T_{(i,j)}}$ denotes the restriction of R to the set of pixels of $T_{(i,j)}$.

One way to define a (dis-)similarity map is based on applying a distance measure to extracted features as for example interest points which are widely used in Computer Vision [1,19]. In this case the dissimilarity measure is defined as a metric in the corresponding feature vector space. The question whether feature-based (dis-)similarity concepts for template matching are reliable or not depends on the number and the distinctiveness of the available feature points. Particularly, for textures, standard methods for template matching usually fail because of the lack of sufficiently distinctive and reproducible feature points. Therefore, generally speaking, the usage of feature points for texture analysis is not recommendable.

Measuring the (dis-)similarity directly by applying a (dis-)similarity measure d to the images as sets of (ordered) intensity values is an alternative to the feature-based similarity approach. Such a (dis-)similarity based approach requires a) to choose an appropriate dissimilarity measure (Section 3), b) to choose the size of the test patch, c) to define a matching concept (Section 4), and d) to specify a rule how to distinguish defect from defect-free samples (Section 5).

The choice of the test patch size is crucial for the inspection of periodic and quasi-periodic textures. A too small size might cause undesired registration artefacts whereas a too large size causes unnecessary processing time. The optimal size is closely related to the estimation of the length of the repetitive pattern. However window size estimation is not the topic of this paper and therefore the window size is always calculated with an existing software tool which is based on a modified algorithm of Lizarraga-Morales et al.[18].

The main question is whether and under which circumstances a (dis-)similarity based template matching approach is appropriate to allow a discriminative analysis of defects. The reason why this approach might lead to serious problems is not clearly analysed in the literature so far. This paper contributes to giving an answer to this analysis and, at the same time, to opening up a new approach that mitigates problems inherently induced by commonly used (dis-)similarity measures.

3   Choice of Appropriate Dissimilarity Measure

This section focusses on the adequateness of similarity measures in the context of defect detection. First of all, let us point out that commonly used (dis-)similarity measures induce the occurrence of local extrema as artefacts. Particularly it can be shown that commonly used (dis-)similarity measures like L_2 norm, mutual information, cross-correlation, Bhattacharyya measure[3] or Kullback-Leibler divergence measure[16] are likely to lead to artefacts in terms of local extrema that corrupt the resulting (dis-)similarity map Θ_d. For details see Moser et al.[23]. As an alternative measure we suggest to exploit Weyl's concept of discrepancy [28], which was introduced in order to measure irregularities of distributions [2,15]. Due to Moser[22] let us propose

$$\|I\|_D := \max \left\{ \max_{0 \le k \le n, 0 \le l \le m} \left\{ \sum_{i=0}^{k} \sum_{j=0}^{l} I_{(i,j)} \right\}, \max_{0 \le k \le n, 0 \le l \le m} \left\{ \sum_{i=0}^{k} \sum_{j=0}^{l} I_{(n-i,j)} \right\}, \quad (1)$$
$$\max_{0 \le k \le n, 0 \le l \le m} \left\{ \sum_{i=0}^{k} \sum_{j=0}^{l} I_{(i,n-j)} \right\}, \max_{0 \le k \le n, 0 \le l \le m} \left\{ \sum_{i=0}^{k} \sum_{j=0}^{l} I_{(n-i,n-j)} \right\} \right\},$$

$(I_{(0,0)} := 0)$ as an extension of Weyl's discrepancy measure to image data with an image I of the width n and the height m. The indexed variables k and l indicate the current partial sum. Note that (1) can be efficiently computed in $O(n \cdot m)$ by using integral images, see Moser[22].

The interesting point about this is that based on Weyl's discrepancy concept distance measures can be constructed that guarantee desirable registration properties: (R1) the measure vanishes if and only if the lag vanishes, (R2) the measure increases monotonically with an increasing lag, and (R3) the measure obeys a Lipschitz condition that guarantees smooth changes also for patterns with high frequencies.

4   Template Matching by Registration

This section discusses a recently outlined template matching algorithm [5]. It is state-of-the art to process a test image by specifying a so-called sliding window for consecutively cropping image patches and comparing them to reference data. Usually the reference image data are chosen to have the same size as the sliding window.

In this paper we concentrate on textures with regular or nearly regular patterns. Examples for this kind of regular textures are woven fabrics as e.g. for automotive interiors, industrial sieves, air-bag hoses, etc. Different localizations of the sliding window yield patches having different offsets with respect to the repetitive pattern. By this the resulting patches are varying in their appearance, although they refer to the same reference pattern. This effect can be interpreted in terms of translational misalignment. As discussed in Section 3 such a misalignment might lead to undesirable artefacts when applying commonly used similarity measures.

The basic idea of Bouchot et al.[5] is to make the usual reference-test image matching more flexible by allowing registration on a larger reference image that covers multiple periods of the repetitive pattern. To avoid the before mentioned artefacts the approach introduces the discrepancy norm as similarity measure and, thereby, fitness function for the registration. At the same time the enlarged reference image size can be chosen also to capture variations in appearance due to other effects like changes in illumination or admissible variations in production.

Mathematically speaking, given a test patch T the registration step aims at identifying optimal transformation parameters $\xi = (\xi_1^*, \ldots, \xi_k^*)$ that minimize the match given by

$$d_T(\xi) = d\left(H_\xi(T), R|_{H_\xi(T)}\right) \tag{2}$$

where d denotes an appropriate dissimilarity measure, R represents the chosen defect-free reference, T the actual patch of a test image, H is a parametrized transformation model (in our case translations) and $R|_{H_\xi(T)}$ denotes the sub-region of the reference which is specified by the pixel coordinates of the transformed test patch $H_\xi(T)$. To allow only translational transformations is no restriction for usage in an in-line inspection system of endless material where the camera position is fixed and no rotations and scale variations occur. However with a more complex transformation model also other variations can be covered. In this context it has to be noticed that discrepancy norm is also able to cope with small rotations as demonstrated in Moser[22].

Two drawbacks keep the algorithm of Bouchot et al.[5] from industrial usage. Firstly the window size has to be manually chosen, which is now done with a modified algorithm of Lizarraga-Morales et al.[18]. Secondly although the computational costs are below exhaustive transformation parameters search, they are still too high for usage in an in-line inspection system. To improve speed, this paper adds a statistical level set analysis of the (dis-)similarity map Θ_d, gathered on the defect free reference image as a preprocessing step. Through this a threshold for a RANSAC like global optimization algorithm can be estimated, which accelerates the decision if a patch is defect free or not drastically (from minutes to fractions of a second, on Matlab with a standard PC). This is in strong contrast to the brute-force registration principle used in Bouchot et al.[5].

5   Discriminative Rule for Detecting Defect Candidates

A defect can be excluded if registration parameters ξ can be found that reduce the dissimilarity (2) between the test image T with a defect-free reference patch from R below some threshold θ.

The threshold θ can be determined from the cumulative distribution function of dissimilarity values generated by applying defect-free patches to the reference. For example θ can be defined as q-quantile. The lower q the more sensitive the detection, but also the higher the expected rate of pseudo-defects. Its optimal choice depends on the texture characteristics and the type of defects under consideration.

In order to turn this principle into a computational rule for detecting defect candidates let us consider a RANSAC like algorithm. Randomized Sampling Consensus (RANSAC)[12] is a common method to fit models into noisy data by constructing candidate models out of random samples and choosing the model with the best fit. Given a test patch T the problem is to find a position $\xi \in R$ for which $d_T(\xi) \leq \theta$. The key idea of the proposed approach is to randomly compare the test patch to different positions on the reference image and choose the best position to start a local optimization. Suppose that T is defect-free, and let denote $\mathcal{F}$ the set of defect-free patches. The probability $\alpha_\theta = P(d_T(\xi) \leq \theta \,|\, T \in \mathcal{F})$ to randomly choose a position $\xi \in R$ with $d_T(\xi) \leq \theta$ can be estimated as ratio between the area of the level set $\lambda_\theta = \{\xi \in R | d_T(\xi) \leq \theta\}$ and the area of the reference image R.

Let denote $\{\xi_1, \ldots, \xi_k\}$ a sequence of k independent random trials and consider the conditional error probability $\varepsilon = \varepsilon_{\{\xi_i\},\theta} = P\left(\min_{i=1}^k d_{\xi_i} > \theta \,|\, T \in \mathcal{F}\right)$ that all trials yield positions outside λ_θ. Then, we obtain $\varepsilon_{\{\xi_i\},\theta} = (1 - \alpha_\theta)^k$. Starting with a probability $p_s = 1 - \varepsilon$, e.g., $p_s = 0.995$, the estimated number k of trials amounts to

$$k = \ln(1 - p_s) / \ln(1 - \alpha_\theta). \qquad (3)$$

Therefore, we obtain the rule:

"If a position $\xi \in R$ with match dissimilarity $d_T(\xi) \leq \theta$ is found with at most k trials given by (3), then the test patch T is considered defect-free, otherwise a defect candidate."

This rule can be modified by taking a maximal number of local optimization iterations into account in order to accelerate the evaluation. Computational experiments showed that the quasi-Newton BFGS method is a reasonable choice for the local optimizer[6].

6   Evaluation

The applicability of the proposed approach is demonstrated on the basis of defect samples of regular textures taken from the TILDA database and industrial applications of the involved research institutes.

Figure 1 depicts three types of defects: a) high contrast structural defects spreading over many repetitive pattern units, see Figures 1(a) and 1(c), b) more challenging contrast structural defects spreading over many repetitive pattern units in Figures 1(e), 1(g), 1(i) and 1(k), and low contrast defects affecting only a small number of repetitive pattern units in Figure 1(m), 1(o), 1(q) and 1(s). Each image is shown in two versions, the test image and the output of the algorithm, which was not thresholded. The reference images which hold about four to five periods of the original pattern are not depicted. The structure in the output images indicates the number of steps in the search for the best matches due to the coarse-to-fine approach outlined above. For example, Figures 1(a) and 1(c) took less steps than in the other images. What also can be observed is that the defect positions are not always precise. This effect originates from the block processing working principle of the algorithm: if a defect is not fully covered by a single block, the position cannot be located precisely. In future versions this misalignment can be compensated by an additional registration.

These examples of various defect types may demonstrate the potential of the proposed approach also to detect low contrast defects. With a MATLAB implementation on a standard PC the evaluation on one test image of size 756×512 took fractions of a second. This shows that the proposed approach is computationally feasible.

Stability. Stability analysis is performed on a set of 20 test images. For each test image the algorithm output is split into blocks with window size equal to the length of the period. This is also the finest scale of the coarse-to-fine approach. We choose $p_s = 0.9999$ and $\theta = 1.5\sigma + \mu$, where μ and σ denote the mean and standard deviation of the discrepancy values computed from dissimilarity maps of 10 randomly chosen patches from the according reference image. For this configuration we observe an average α_θ of 0.2 which lead to a range of $[26, 88]$ for k pattern comparisons. A block is marked as belonging to a defective region if more than 50 % of its pixels are defective according to the rule of Section 5.

Since the aim of the stability analysis is to show the repeatability of the results, every image is processed 100 times and a defect probability p_i is calculated for each block. In the worst case this probability is 0.5, which means that no clear decision can be made whether the block is defective or not. Therefore as measurement of the stability the entropy $H_i = p_i(1 - p_i)$ is calculated on each block. For the whole test set of 20 images and 7735 blocks this leads to a mean entropy of 0.0036 bit, which demonstrates the high stability of the algorithm despite the random working principle.

Performance. In the current state of development the proposed algorithm is not supposed to outperform any state-of-the art textile defect detection algorithm. It is rather thought as demonstration on how a novel dissimilarity measure can open up new possibilities in this application context. Nevertheless a comparison with current state-of-the art algorithms in the application field of textile defect detection was done. The evaluation is based on the work of Tolba et al.[27]. These authors directly compare several state-of-the art algorithms by calculating a performance measure called Percentage of Correct Detection (PCD)

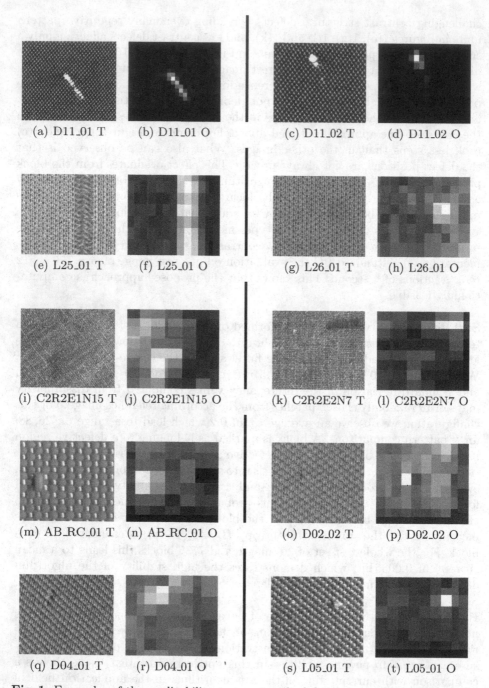

Fig. 1. Examples of the applicability test on textile defect images. For each example the test image (T) as well as the output (O) of the algorithm is shown. Reference images are not shown. The algorithm output is for illustration purposes not thresholded.

Table 1. Performance comparison of texture characterization approaches using Percentage of Correct Detection (*PCD*), for details see Tolba et al.[27]. The original Table contains multiple entries per reference, here only the best performing ones are listed. Furthermore the top performing method of Murino et al.[24] is skipped because it is a pure classification algorithm without detection. The discrepancy norm based algorithm can be compared with the class of Grey-Level Co-occurrence Matrices (GLCM) and filter (Gabor, wavelet) based feature extraction algorithms.

Method	PCD (%)	Reference
Decision Fusion	98.64	[27]
GLCM	97.09	[21]
GLCM + Gabor + wavelet packets (selected from 219 features)	96.90	[14]
Selected from Gabor and GLCM	96.90	[11]
Discrepancy Norm Based Template Matching	**96.10**	-
Clustering	91.60	[8]
Wavelet97	88.15	[7]
Local Binary Patterns	85.83	[26]

$$PCD = (1 - (FAR + FRR)) \times 100 \qquad (4)$$

out of the False Acceptance Rate (*FAR*) and False Rejection Rate (*FRR*) reported in papers of the algorithm designers. The performance for our algorithm is evaluated on the above mentioned test set of 20 images using hand-labelled ground truths and the same decision rule as in the stability analysis. This leads to a *PCD* of 96.1 %. Table 1 summarizes the best performing algorithms listed in Tolba et al.[27] together with our method. It shows up that the performance is in the same class as a combination of Grey-Level Co-occurrence Matrices (GLCM) and filter (Gabor, wavelet) based feature extraction algorithms. However in contrast to the work of Drimbarean and Whelan[11], who use a neural network classifier, the proposed approach does not need any training, but only relies on one sample image. Another issue with state-of-the art methods is the sometimes expensive computation of features, as can be found in Karoui et al.[14], Monadjemi[21] and Tolba et al.[27]. The latter even suggest to outsource the feature generation on FPGAs. Our proposed approach does not have the computational complexity problem. Nevertheless it does not reach the detection performance of other methods since the failure location is due to the block processing nature not always precise. Therefore it cannot compete with highly tuned state-of-the-art methods. To solve the location problem is a future research topic. Furthermore it has to be mentioned that our approach is limited to regular or near regular textures. Despite that the algorithm performs surprisingly good, having in mind that it is a not yet optimized straight forward approach with only one sensitivity configuration parameter for the coarse-to-fine working principle.

7   Conclusion

The template matching principle in the context of quality inspection of regular textures has been addressed. The motivation was to come up with a method that effectively can be implemented, shows distinctiveness also for low contrast defects and still is easy to configure. The approach outlined only requires the configuration of a sensitivity parameter which reduces the efforts of configuration. Experimental results indicate its usefulness and motivate further research to improve the defect localization. The approach outlined in this paper can also be combined with other methods e.g. Decision Fusion [27] which remains future research.

Acknowledgements. This work was supported in part by the Austrian Science Fund (FWF) under grant no. P21496 N23, and by the European Fund for Regional Development under Regionale Wettbewerbsfähigkeit OÖ 2007-2013. We also want to thank the reviewers for their comments and suggestions.

References

1. Bay, H., Ess, A., Tuytelaars, T., Gool, L.V.: SURF: Speeded up robust features. Computer Vision and Image Understanding 110, 346–359 (2008)
2. Beck, J., Chen, W.W.L.: Irregularities of distribution. Cambridge University Press, New York (2009)
3. Bhattacharyya, A.: On a measure of divergence between two statistical populations defined by probability distributions. Bull. Calcutta Math. 35, 99–109 (1943)
4. Bodnarova, A., Bennamoun, M., Latham, S.: Optimal Gabor filters for textile flaw detection. Pattern Recognition 35, 2973–2991 (2002)
5. Bouchot, J.L., Stübl, G., Moser, B.: A template matching approach based on the discrepancy norm for defect detection on regularly textured surfaces. In: Proceedings of the SPIE 10th International Conference on Quality Control by Artificial Vision. SPIE, Saint Etienne (2011)
6. Broyden, C.G.: The convergence of a class of double-rank minimization algorithms 1. General considerations. IMA Journal of Applied Mathematics 6(1), 76–90 (1970)
7. Chen, C.M., Chen, C.C., Chen, C.C.: A comparison of texture features based on SVM and SOM. In: Proceedings of the 18th International Conference on Pattern Recognition, ICPR 2006, vol. 02, pp. 630–633. IEEE Computer Society, Washington, DC (2006)
8. Cheng, H.D., Sun, Y.: A hierarchical approach to color image segmentation using homogeneity. IEEE Transactions on Image Processing 9(12), 2071–2082 (2000)
9. Cohen, F., Fan, Z., Attali, S.: Automated inspection of textile fabrics using textural models. IEEE Transactions on Pattern Analysis and Machine Intelligence 13, 803–808 (1991)
10. Conci, A., Proença, C.B.: A fractal image analysis system for fabric inspection based on a box-counting method. Computer Networks and ISDN Systems 30, 1887–1895 (1998)
11. Drimbarean, A., Whelan, P.F.: Experiments in colour texture analysis. Pattern Recognition Letters 22(10), 1161–1167 (2001)
12. Fischler, M.A., Bolles, R.C.: Random sample consensus: a paradigm for model fitting with applications to image analysis and automated cartography. Communications of the ACM 24(6), 381–395 (1981)
13. Haralick, R.M., Shanmugam, K., Dinstein, I.: Textural features for image classification. IEEE Transactions on Systems, Man, and Cybernetics 3, 610–621 (1973)

14. Karoui, I., Fablet, R., Boucher, J.M., Pieczynski, W.: Fusion of textural statistics using a similarity measure: application to texture recognition and segmentation. Pattern Analysis and Applications 11(3-4), 425–434 (2008)
15. Kuipers, L., Niederreiter, H.: Uniform distribution of sequences. Dover Publications, New York (2005)
16. Kullback, S., Leibler, R.A.: On information and sufficiency. The Annals of Mathematical Statisitcs 22(1), 79–86 (1951)
17. Kumar, A.: Computer-vision-based fabric defect detection: A survey. IEEE Transactions on Industrial Electronics 55, 348–363 (2008)
18. Lizarraga-Morales, R.A., Sanchez-Yanez, R.E., Ayala-Ramirez, V.: Homogeneity Cues for Texel Size Estimation of Periodic and Near-Periodic Textures. In: Martínez-Trinidad, J.F., Carrasco-Ochoa, J.A., Ben-Youssef Brants, C., Hancock, E.R. (eds.) MCPR 2011. LNCS, vol. 6718, pp. 220–229. Springer, Heidelberg (2011)
19. Lowe, D.G.: Distinctive image features from scale-invariant keypoints. International Journal on Computer Vision 60, 91–110
20. Mirmehdi, M., Marik, R., Petrou, M., Kittler, J.: Iterative morphology for fault detection in stochastic textures. Electronic Letters 32, 443–444 (1996)
21. Monadjemi, A.: Towards efficient texture classification and abnormality detection. Ph.D. thesis, University of Bristol, UK (2004)
22. Moser, B.: Similarity measure for image and volumetric data based on Hermann Weyl's discrepancy measure. IEEE Transactions on Pattern Analysis and Machine Intelligence 33(11), 2321–2329 (2011)
23. Moser, B., Stübl, G., Bouchot, J.-L.: On a Non-monotonicity Effect of Similarity Measures. In: Pelillo, M., Hancock, E.R. (eds.) SIMBAD 2011. LNCS, vol. 7005, pp. 46–60. Springer, Heidelberg (2011)
24. Murino, V., Bicego, M., Rossi, I.A.: Statistical classification of raw textile defects. In: 17th International Conference on Proceedings of the Pattern Recognition (ICPR 2004), vol. 4, pp. 311–314. IEEE Computer Society, Washington, DC (2004)
25. Ng, H.F.: Automatic thresholding for defect detection. Pattern Recognition Letters 27, 1644–1649 (2007)
26. Pietikäinen, M., Ojala, T.: Nonparametric texture analysis with simple spatial operator. Spectrum (1999)
27. Tolba, A.S., Khan, H.A., Mutawa, A.M., Alsaleem, S.M.: Decision fusion for visual inspection of textiles. Textile Research Journal 80 (2010)
28. Weyl, H.: Über die Gleichverteilung von Zahlen mod. Eins. Mathematische Annalen 77, 313–352 (1916)
29. Xie, X.: A review of recent advances in surface defect detection using texture analysis techniques. Electr. Letters on Computer Vision and Image Analysis 3, 1–22 (2008)
30. Xie, X., Mirmehdi, M.: TEXEMS: Texture exemplars for defect detection on random textured surfaces. IEEE Transactions on Pattern Analysis and Machine Intelligence 29, 1454–1464 (2007)

Video Compression with 3-D Pose Tracking, PDE-Based Image Coding, and Electrostatic Halftoning

Christian Schmaltz and Joachim Weickert

Mathematical Image Analysis Group, Faculty of Mathematics and Computer Science,
Building E1 7, Saarland University, 66041 Saarbrücken, Germany
{schmaltz,weickert}@mia.uni-saarland.de

Abstract. Recent video compression algorithms such as the members of the MPEG or H.26x family use image transformations to store individual frames, and motion compensation between these frames. In contrast, the video codec presented here is a model-based approach that encodes fore- and background independently. It is well-suited for applications with static backgrounds, i.e. for applications such as traffic or security surveillance, or video conferencing. Our video compression algorithm tracks moving foreground objects and stores the obtained poses. Furthermore, a compressed version of the background image and some other information such as 3-D object models are encoded. In a second step, recent halftoning and PDE-based image compression algorithms are employed to compress the encoding error. Experiments show that the stored videos can have a significantly better quality than state-of-the-art algorithms such as MPEG-4.

1 Introduction

Due to the huge amount and increasing resolution of videos that are created and viewed each day, video compression remains a topic of ongoing research. Most popular video compression algorithms such as the ones from the MPEG and H.26x family calculate the motion of pixel blocks to estimate the appearance of these blocks from nearby frames. In addition to the estimated displacement, an approximation of the reconstruction error is stored. In the decoding phase, this information is used to reconstruct individual frames. For a detailed introduction to general video codecs, we refer to the survey by Sullivan and Wiegand [19], or the overview of Abomhara *et al.* [1].

Apart from general purpose video compression algorithms, there are also video compression codecs using *model-based* coding schemes. The idea behind these schemes is to compress fore- and background independently. This concept is fundamentally different from standard video compression algorithms, and thus has different advantages and drawbacks. For example, model-based coding typically requires previous knowledge to distinguish fore- and background region. Furthermore, the video sequence must have a fairly static background. However,

A. Pinz et al. (Eds.): DAGM/OAGM 2012, LNCS 7476, pp. 438–447, 2012.
© Springer-Verlag Berlin Heidelberg 2012

several views of the same scene can often be encoded very efficiently, and generating intermediate frames is often much easier. Examples in which these conditions are fulfilled include traffic or security surveillance, or video conferencing.

Since the seminal work by Forchheimer and Fahlander [6], different approaches to model-based video coding have been pursued. We will give a short summary of the ideas presented in this context, but refer to [14] and [23] for a more detailed overview of the field.

In [20], Toelg and Poggio propose an approach that uses a small set of example images containing a human face with different facial expressions. With the help of a pose estimation algorithm, a novel view or facial expression is constructed from these example images. Vieux *et al.* employ a similar approach for their "Orthonormal Basis Coding" in [21].

These approaches are based on 2-D example images, but there are also methods that utilise full 3-D models. In [10], a partial description of a model-based coding which builds upon the MPEG-4 standard is presented. However, this method requires manual interaction, and it is not specified how the necessary texture is stored. Although these questions are answered in the work by Granai *et al.* [7], both methods only explain how to compress the foreground, and ignore the background. In [2], motion compensated temporal interpolation is used to estimate the background onto which the 3-D object model is projected. Various extensions to model-based coding have been proposed, e.g. for varying illumination conditions [5] or for different facial expressions [4,13]. The latter was even included into MPEG-4 as facial animation parameters [12].

The model-based video compression codec we propose differs fairly much from these existing approaches. It combines three state-of-the-art algorithms from apparently unrelated fields, namely 3-D pose tracking, PDE-based image compression, and halftoning. As illustrated in Section 4, their combination makes it possible to beat the results of MPEG-1, and even of MPEG-4. In contrast to many other model-based coding algorithms, our approach is not specialised to faces or other specific objects. Thus, it is applicable for different kinds of videos.

Our paper is structured as follows: Section 2 explains our baseline video compression algorithm (*MB*), which is extended to an algorithm with residual coding (*MB+DH*) in Section 3. We continue with an evaluation of both approaches in Section 4 and conclude the paper with a summary in Section 5.

2 Our Baseline Codec (MB)

Before we explain the steps of our codec in detail, lets us give an overview of our algorithm: First, we track the moving objects in the video. As a second step, the tracking results are used to estimate the colour of each vertex of the object model. Thirdly, the background is reconstructed, if necessary, and compressed. Finally, all data is saved and compressed using PAQ [11], a general purpose entropy coder. To reconstruct a frame of the video, the object model is simply projected onto the loaded background image using the pose tracked while encoding. We denote this *model based* codec by *MB*.

For the first step of our codec, we employ the 3-D pose tracking algorithm explained in [16], as it reports one of the best tracking results in the HumanEva-II benchmark [18]. Assuming that the necessary data (a projection matrix of each view, an (uncoloured) 3-D object model, and a pose initialisation in the first frame) are known, we find the pose of the free-form surface consisting of rigid parts interconnected by n predefined joints as minimiser of the cost function

$$E(\chi) = - \sum_{i=0}^{\ell} \int_{\Omega} \Big(Pv_{i,\chi}(\boldsymbol{x}) \log p_{i,\chi}(\boldsymbol{x}) \Big) \mathrm{d}\boldsymbol{x} \ . \tag{1}$$

Thereby, the pose $\chi \in \mathbb{R}^{6+n}$ consists of the 3-D position and orientation of the object model, as well as of the n joint angles (or other internal parameters) searched for. The index i runs over the background ($i = 0$) and all ℓ model components. The set Ω denotes the 2-D image domain, while the function $p_{i,\chi}(\boldsymbol{x})$ models the appearance of the i-th component. These appearances are estimated and adapted while tracking. The indicator function $Pv_{i,\chi}(\boldsymbol{x})$, which is 1 if the i-th model component is visible at the image point $\boldsymbol{x}$ and 0 otherwise, ensures that occlusions are taken into account in an adequate way. Even if model components belong to different object models, all occlusions are automatically handled correctly. Thus, even tracking multiple mutually occluding object is possible. This is favourable for our codec in case of multiple moving foreground objects.

Equation 1 is minimised with a modified gradient descent: The object model is projected onto the image plane, and the resulting silhouette points are displaced depending on to which region they fit better. This displacement is then transferred to the 3-D pose of the object. These steps are repeated until convergence, and the pose initialisation of the next frame is obtained by extrapolation.

In the second step of the *MB* codec, we estimate the appearance of the object model. As the tracking algorithm requires an (uncoloured) object model, we already know to which image point each vertex of the object is projected in each frame. Thus, to estimate the colour of each vertex, we simply average the colour at the projected vertex position over all frames in which this vertex is visible. This simple estimation is far from being perfect, though. Consequently, the obtained video quality should improve significantly if a better estimation is used.

In the third step, we reconstruct the background image, if necessary. This step is easy in our setting as we know which parts of the background are occluded after the tracking step.

Then, we employ the PDE-based image compression algorithm from [17] to encode the background image. We chose this algorithm as is reports better a compression quality than JPEG 2000. Moreover, it is related to the approach to store the residual image introduced in the next section.

The basic idea behind the algorithm from [17] is to store only a small subset of all image points, while the remaining points are reconstructed using edge-enhancing anisotropic diffusion (EED) [22], i.e. by computing the steady-state $\inf_{t \to \infty} u(\boldsymbol{x}, t)$ of the evolution equation

$$\partial_t u = \text{div}(g(\boldsymbol{\nabla} u_\sigma \boldsymbol{\nabla} u_\sigma^\top)\boldsymbol{\nabla} u) \ . \tag{2}$$

Here, $u = u(\boldsymbol{x}, t)$ is the image value of the point $\boldsymbol{x}$ at time t, $u_\sigma := K_\sigma * u$ denotes the image convolved with a Gaussian K_σ with standard deviation σ, and g is the Charbonnier diffusivity function $g(s^2) := \frac{\lambda}{\sqrt{\lambda^2 + s^2}}$ with contrast parameter λ. The diffusion tensor $g(\boldsymbol{\nabla} u_\sigma \boldsymbol{\nabla} u_\sigma^\top)$ is a symmetric 2×2 matrix with eigenvectors parallel and orthogonal to $\boldsymbol{\nabla} u_\sigma$, and corresponding eigenvalues $g(|\boldsymbol{\nabla} u_\sigma|^2)$ and 1. Since EED smoothes along edges, while reducing smoothing across them, this diffusion process is able to create sharp edges.

This concludes the description of our baseline codec, which is often sufficient to yield a reasonable reconstruction. However, tracking failures or model inaccuracies can sometimes result in a bad video quality. Thus, we introduce an algorithm that can correct such problems in the next section.

3   Video Codec with Residual Coding (*MB+DH*)

Our enhanced codec explained in this section is an extension of the *MB* codec. It additionally encodes the residual images, i.e. the error of each frame compressed by our baseline codec. This residual image is stored as set of pixels between which inpainting with homogeneous diffusion is performed. Therefore, we compute the steady-state of the linear diffusion equation [8]

$$\partial_t u = \Delta u = \text{div}(\boldsymbol{\nabla} u) \ . \tag{3}$$

Let us start by considering only the first frame of a grey-valued video. When inpainting with homogeneous diffusion, we know that the interpolation points should be distributed according to the magnitude of the Laplacian of a smoothed version of the image [3]. Thus, we can employ a dithering algorithm to obtain the inpainting mask. In [3], the Floyd-Steinberg algorithm was used for dithering, while we compare the performance of four different dithering algorithm. Two representative results are shown in Figure 1. In these experiment, we use 500 mask points, but results are similar for other numbers: Independent of the image and the amount of presmoothing, the electrostatic halftoning algorithm from [15] performs best. Thus, we chose this algorithm in our codec.

The basic idea behind the electrostatic halftoning algorithm is to model black dots as negatively charged particles, while the pixels are positively charged [15]. Consequently, particles repel each other, but are attracted to dark image areas. Let us denote the grey value at position $\boldsymbol{x}$ by $u(\boldsymbol{x}) \in [0,1]$. Then, the charge of the pixel $\boldsymbol{x}$ is equal to $1 - u(\boldsymbol{x})$. When choosing the charge of the particles is such a way that the total amount of positive and negative charges is equal, the particles are automatically bound to the image domain. The final halftoning result is then obtained as the steady-state of this particle system. Adding all forces acting on each particle results in the update equation

$$p_n^{k+1} = p_n^k + \tau \Big(\sum_{\substack{\boldsymbol{x} \in \Omega \\ \boldsymbol{x} \neq p_n}} \frac{1 - u(\boldsymbol{x})}{|\boldsymbol{x} - p_n^k|} e_{n,x} - \sum_{\substack{m \in \mathcal{P} \\ m \neq n}} \frac{1}{|p_m^k - p_n^k|} e_{n,m} \Big), \tag{4}$$

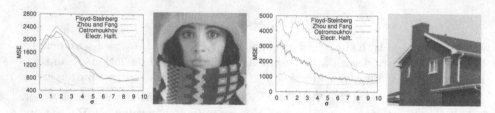

Fig. 1. Evaluation of dithering algorithms in the context of image interpolation. The mask points are obtained by dithering the (scaled) absolute value of the Laplacian of the smoothed input image, where a Gaussian with standard deviation σ is used for smoothing. The graphs show the results for the two images "trui" and "house".

where p_n^k is the position of the n-th particle at time k, $\tau = 0.1$ serves as an artificial time step parameter, and $\mathcal{P}$ denotes the set of all particles. The two vectors $e_{n,m}$ and $e_{n,x}$ denote unit vectors between the n-th and m-th particle, and between the n-th particle and the pixel x, respectively.

The optimal standard deviation σ of the Gaussian used to smooth the residual image before dithering varies with the image and the number of mask points. Thus, we try different standard deviations in our codec and take the σ for which the best approximation is obtained. As σ is not needed to decompress the video, this does not increase the final file size. Furthermore, we restrict the domain of the dithering algorithm to a region containing the foreground region and points close to it, as inaccuracies in the background region are easier solved by storing an improved version of the background image.

We store the position of the points in the inpainting mask K using the JBIG file format [9], which is a lossless compression algorithm for binary images. The grey-values of the mask points are quantised uniformly before entropy coding.

For colour videos, we compute a grey-valued variant of the difference image to find the inpainting mask. Thereby, different colour models are possible. According to our experiments, the results are very similar, though. Thus, we simply average the red, green, and blue colour channels to get a grey-valued variant of the difference image.

In the remaining frames, we initialise the dithering process with the inpainting mask from the previous frame. This requires much fewer iterations of electrostatic halftoning. In addition to speeding up the computations, this allows to store the particle movements relative to the last frame instead of the particle positions. This reduces the amount of data that must be encoded if the number of particles is reasonable. While it is trivial to obtain the particle motion when using electrostatic halftoning, this is a difficult or even impossible problem with other dithering algorithms. This is another reason why it is advantageous to use the electrostatic halftoning algorithm as dithering step in our codec.

Finally, all data is compressed with the same entropy coder as in the baseline codec. We denote this *model-based* codec which stores the *d*ifference image by *h*alftoning as *MB+DH*.

To reconstruct the video, we first execute the steps explained for our baseline codec. Afterwards, the inpainting mask is loaded (first frame) or reconstructed

Table 1. Overview over the frame and file sizes, as well as the mean square errors (MSE) of results with MPEG-1, MPEG-4, and the proposed algorithms. The numbers in parenthesis state the number of additional points stored per frame. In line 4, this number was chosen in such a way that the file size is similar to MPEG-4. Note that the codecs from the MPG-family cropped some of the video material.

Codec	HumanEva-II S4			Cart		
	frame size	file size	MSE	frame size	file size	MSE
MPEG-1	656 × 480	2019733	187.25	496 × 368	202847	48.53
MPEG-4	656 × 490	537404	210.58	500/496 × 380	112182	31.52
MB	656 × 490	161223	102.57	500 × 380	68721	52.38
MB+DH (400/200)	656 × 490	494246	48.09	500 × 380	109137	41.55
MB+DH (100)	656 × 490	194513	76.53	500 × 380	83355	47.04
MB+DH (500)	656 × 490	612452	43.66	500 × 380	196465	32.77
MB+DH (1000)	656 × 490	1256973	30.27	500 × 380	353026	26.64

using the stored particle motion and the particle locations in the preceding frame. The loaded values of the error image are interpolated and added to the frame. Thereby, we use Dirichlet boundary conditions to ensure that the difference image is zero at the boundary.

4   Experiments

In this section, we compare the performance of our codecs against MPEG-1 and MPEG-4. We created the MPEG-1 videos with the program "mpeg_encode" using three P-frames between successive I-frames, and three B-frames between other frames, i.e. the pattern "IBBBPBBBPBBBPBBB". This is a common pattern which typically allows a strong compression. The quantisation levels for all types of frames were set to the lowest possible value (31) to obtain a compression ratio which is as close as possible to the one of our approach. To create the MPEG-4 videos, we used the Linux program "mencoder", the codec "msmpeg4v2", the AVI container format, and the smallest possible variable bit rate (4000 bits per second). Nevertheless, we could neither create MPEG-1 nor MPEG-4 videos which are as small as the ones from our baseline codec MB (see Table 1). Note that MPEG-1 cropped the original frames, while MPEG-4 replaced a part of the frames in one sequence by a black boundary.

In our first experiment, we encode the sequence S4 of the HumanEva-II tracking benchmark [18]. Figure 2 illustrates an example frame from the resulting videos, as well as a graph showing the mean square error (MSE) each method obtained per frame. The video created with our approach is considerably smaller than those of the other methods. Nevertheless, its error is always below that of MPEG-1 and MPEG-4, even though the result of the tracking approach is inaccurate in some frames.

Figure 3 shows magnifications of the results depicted in Figure 2. We see that our *MB* codec creates sharp boundaries, while the approaches from the MPG family generate blocky results. Due to the rather poor performance of our simple

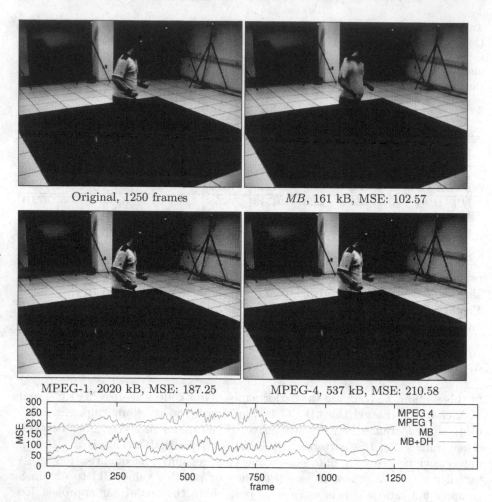

Original, 1250 frames   *MB*, 161 kB, MSE: 102.57

MPEG-1, 2020 kB, MSE: 187.25   MPEG-4, 537 kB, MSE: 210.58

Fig. 2. Comparison of our *MB* codec against MPEG-1 and MPEG-4 using the HumanEva-II sequence S4. In the graph showing the mean square error in each frame, the result of our *MB+DH* codec with 400 point per frame is shown as comparison. The corresponding files sizes are denoted below the images, which show frame 500.

Original   *MB*   MPEG-1   MPEG-4   *MB+DH*

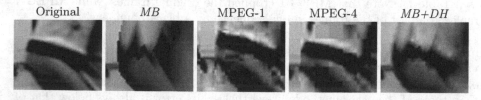

Fig. 3. Magnifications of the experiment from Figure 2. Note the block artifacts when using MPEG-1 or MPEG-4. One can see that our approach has sharp boundaries in object and background region, and that our simple model colouring algorithm is far from being perfect. The better result of our algorithm *MB+DH* with 400 additional points, which tries to reduce this problem, is shown on the right.

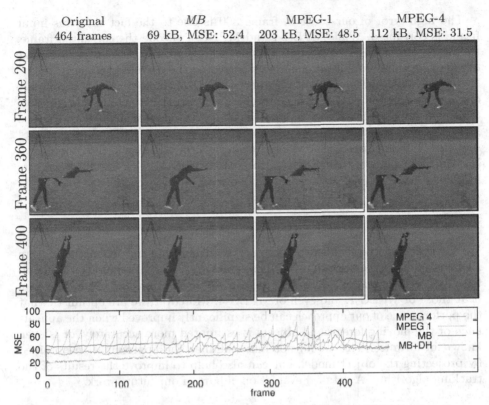

Fig. 4. Comparison of our method *MB* against MPEG-1 and MPEG-4 using the sequence "Cart". The jump with MPEG-4 in frame 250 and the sawtooth pattern with MPEG-4 are due to the different frame types. While our codec *MB* ignores the corruption in frame 360, MPEG-1 and MPEG-4 encode the original frame.

model colouring approach from in Section 2, the *MB* codec yields suboptimal results at the sleeves, though. As shown on the right, this is improved by the additional information stored. A more accurate representation of the object model should significantly boost the performance of our algorithm, though.

Furthermore, we encode the sequence "Cart", in which a person performs a cart wheel; see Figure 4. This sequence is much more challenging than the first video for our codec due to several reasons: First of all, the background is very noisy, which deteriorates the results of the diffusion-based image compression approach. Moreover, the object model is often not able to represent the complex movement performed by the actor, e.g. due to muscle contractions or missing joint angles. Additionally, the lower side of the feet are visible in many frames. Since the feet are not included in the object model, the human is partly seen from the inside, which results in wrong colours. Finally, this sequence is shorter than the HumanEva-II sequence, resulting in a larger overhead for object model and background. Due to these reasons, the *MB* algorithm is worse than MPEG-4 for this sequence; see Figure 4. However, we still beat MPEG-1 in most frames even though the file created with our approach is significantly smaller.

The high error of our codec in frame 360 is due to the fact that this input frame is corrupted. While MPEG-1 and MPEG-4 encode the corrupted frame, the codec *MB* stores a "corrected" version. This may even be seen as advantage of our algorithm, since it automatically corrected the corrupted frame.

Table 1 also shows results of the codec *MB+DH*. In particular, we compare our codec against MPEG-4 with similar file sizes. For the HumanEva-II sequence S4, this results in 400 additional particles, while 200 additional particles are used for the "Cart" sequence. We are still slightly worse than MPEG-4 in the "Cart" sequence, but one can see that we clearly outperform MPEG-4 in the HumanEva-II sequence S4: Even though the video created with MPEG-4 is 8% larger, its MSE is about 4.4 times as large as the one with our approach.

5   Summary

We have demonstrated how to combine recent state-of-the-art methods from PDE-based image compression, 3-D pose tracking, and halftoning into a model-based video compression codec. Our algorithms show promising results that can beat those of MPEG-1, and even of MPEG-4. Moreover, we are optimistic that the performance of our approach can be significantly improved when the appearance of the moving foreground objects is estimated more accurately, or is even known in advance. This would not only enhance the approximation obtained by projecting the object model, but can also help to improve the results of the tracking algorithm. A detailed evaluation is part of our future work.

References

1. Abomhara, M., Khalifa, O.O., Zakaria, O., Zaidan, A., Zaidan, B., Rame, A.: Video compression techniques: An overview. Journal of Applied Sciences 10(16), 1834–1840 (2010)
2. Artigas, X., Torres, L.: A model-based enhanced approach to distributed video coding. In: Workshop on Image Analysis for Multimedia Interactive Services (WIAMIS 2005), Article No. 1127 (2005)
3. Belhachmi, Z., Bucur, D., Burgeth, B., Weickert, J.: How to choose interpolation data in images. SIAM Journal on Applied Mathematics 70(1), 333–352 (2009)
4. Eisert, P., Girod, B.: Facial expression analysis for model-based coding of video sequences. In: Proc. Picture Coding Symposium, Berlin, pp. 33–38 (1997)
5. Eisert, P., Girod, B.: Model-based coding of facial image sequences at varying illumination conditions. In: Proc. 10th Image and Multidimensional Digital Signal Processing Workshop, Alpbach, pp. 119–122 (1998)
6. Forchheimer, R., Fahlander, O.: Low bit-rate coding through animation. In: Proceedings of Picture Coding Symposium, pp. 113–114 (March 1983)
7. Granai, L., Vlachos, T., Hamouz, M., Tena, J.R., Davies, T.: Model-based coding of 3D head sequences. In: Proc. 3DTV Conference. IEEE Computer Society Press (2007)
8. Iijima, T.: Basic theory on normalization of pattern (in case of typical one-dimensional pattern). Bulletin of the Electrotechnical Laboratory 26, 368–388 (1962) (in Japanese)

9. ISO/IEC: Information technology – lossy/lossless coding of bi-level images (2001), ISO/IEC 14492. Latest corrections in 2004 (2004)
10. Javůrek, R.: Model based facial video sequences coding. In: Radioelektronika 2003 – Conference Proceedings, pp. 115–118 (2003)
11. Mahoney, M.: Data compression programs (2009), http://mattmahoney.net/dc/ (last visited November 30, 2009)
12. Pandzic, I.S., Forchheimer, R. (eds.): MPEG-4 Facial Animation: The Standard, Implementation and Applications. Wiley, New York (2003)
13. Pardàs, M., Bonafonte, A.: Facial animation parameters extraction and expression detection using hidden markov models. In: Signal Processing: Image Communication, vol. 17, pp. 675–688 (2002)
14. Pearson, D.E.: Developments in model-based video coding. Proceedings of the IEEE 83(6), 892–906 (1995)
15. Schmaltz, C., Gwosdek, P., Bruhn, A., Weickert, J.: Electrostatic halftoning. Computer Graphics Forum 29(8), 2313–2327 (2010)
16. Schmaltz, C., Rosenhahn, B., Brox, T., Weickert, J.: Localised Mixture Models in Region-Based Tracking. In: Denzler, J., Notni, G., Süße, H. (eds.) DAGM 2009. LNCS, vol. 5748, pp. 21–30. Springer, Heidelberg (2009)
17. Schmaltz, C., Weickert, J., Bruhn, A.: Beating the Quality of JPEG 2000 with Anisotropic Diffusion. In: Denzler, J., Notni, G., Süße, H. (eds.) DAGM 2009. LNCS, vol. 5748, pp. 452–461. Springer, Heidelberg (2009)
18. Sigal, L., Balan, A.O., Black, M.J.: HUMANEVA: Synchronized video and motion capture dataset and baseline algorithm for evaluation of articulated human motion. International Journal of Computer Vision 87(1/2), 4–27 (2010)
19. Sullivan, G.J., Wiegand, T.: Video compression – from concepts to the H.264/AVC standard. Proceedings of the IEEE 93(1), 18–31 (2005)
20. Toelg, S., Poggio, T.: Towards an example-based image compression architecture for video-conferencing. Tech. Rep. AIM-1494, Massachusetts Institute of Technology, Cambridge, MA, USA (1994)
21. Vieux, W.E., Schwerdt, K., Crowley, J.L.: Face-Tracking and Coding for Video Compression. In: Christensen, H.I. (ed.) ICVS 1999. LNCS, vol. 1542, pp. 151–161. Springer, Heidelberg (1998)
22. Weickert, J.: Theoretical foundations of anisotropic diffusion in image processing. Computing Supplement 11, 221–236 (1996)
23. Yao, Z.: Model-based Coding – Initialization, Parameters Extraction and Evaluation. Ph.D. thesis, Department of Applied Physics and Electronics, Umeå University, Sweden (January 2005)

Image Completion Optimised for Realistic Simulations of Wound Development

Michael Schneeberger, Martina Uray, and Heinz Mayer

Institute for Information and Communication Technologies
Joanneum Research, Graz, Austria
{michael.schneeberger,martina.uray,heinz.mayer}@joanneum.at

Abstract. Treatment costs for chronic wound healing disturbances have a strong impact on the health care system. In order to motivate patients and thus reduce treatment times there was the need to visualize possible wound developments based on the current situation of the affected body part. Known disease patterns were used to build a model for simulating the healing as well as the worsening process. The key point for the construction of possible wound stages was the creation of a nicely fitting texture including all representative tissue types. Since wounds are mostly circularly shaped, as first step of the healing an image completion based on radial texture synthesis of small patches from the healthy tissue surrounding the wound was developed. The radial information of the wound border was used to optimize the overlap between individual patches. In a similar way complete layers of all other appearing tissue types were constructed and superimposed using masks representing trained possible appearances. Results show that the developed texture synthesis together with the trained knowledge is perfectly suited to construct realistic wound images for different stages of the disease.

1 Motivation

In the German-speaking world currently several million people suffer from chronic wound healing disturbances mainly caused by diabetes, peripheral arterial occlusive disease, chronic venous disorder, decubitus wounds or postoperative healing disorders. In order to ensure an optimal healing, besides the medical treatment, an active involvement of the patient is necessary. That is, the better the compliance of a patient, the faster a healing is possible. Due to the fact, that for many patients this is hard to see there was the need to simulate possible developments of such a wound. Actually, not any wound but the one of the own body. Furthermore, to emphasize the urgency not only the healing has to be predicted and visualized but the worsening as well. Thus, the goal was to develop an easy to use software tool which is able to predict various possible wound developments based on the current situation. Not only the healing and the worsening are relevant but also an estimation of the development period directly related to influences like wound care/neglect, healthy/unhealthy lifestyle, inconsistent therapy, etc. These simulations had to be embedded into a tool directly

A. Pinz et al. (Eds.): DAGM/OAGM 2012, LNCS 7476, pp. 448–457, 2012.
© Springer-Verlag Berlin Heidelberg 2012

comparing the optimal predicted wound development with the estimated development depended on the mentioned influences. The outcome of this awareness strategy should be a higher motivation of the patients to follow the doctors instructions and consequently a reduction of the treatment costs (currently under evaluation). The main technical challenge was the extraction and combination of suited features from the image data, the development of a learning algorithm and the corresponding texture synthesis simulating the healing or worsening process addressing several possible patients influences (determined by involved experts) over time. That is, given a collection of images, the disease, the contour of the wounds and the relevant influences, several features such as colour, texture, size, etc. were extracted and correlations between those information were established. The generation of the predicted wound development is based on a suited order of the different possible synthesised tissue layers (varying for the different diagnoses) for different stadiums of the disease. At this place the main contribution of this paper comes in. That is, the introduction of a new image completion method for the construction of the healthy tissue as basis wound layer. Then, the trained progression of disease and extracted representative wound patches from the training data are used to estimated various scenarios on any new image (depicting the current situation). A combination of masks, scaling, thresholding and morphological operations finally results in the desired videos visualizing healing and worsening respectively.

The remainder of the paper is organized as follows. In Section 2, we give an overview of standard image based tools in wound management and an outline of actual image completion techniques. Section 3 describes the details of the complete framework and then focuses on the developed image completion method and wound layer concept as main contribution, reinforced by the results in Section 4. Finally, the conclusion is drawn in Section 5.

2   Related Work

Although there already exists some work and even products employing image handling in the wound context (see e.g. [1,6,9,16]) they all focus on the documentation and assessment of wounds during the period of treatment. Some of those applications store only the images and corresponding details of the diagnosis. Others include basic image processing functionalities like semi-automatic or even automatic measuring of wound size and/or tissue classification (necrosis, granulation, fibrin, epithelium). But currently there is no tool predicting possible wound developments by synthesis of texture. Consequently the approach of automatic feature extraction and associated training algorithms for the prediction of possible clinical courses is an absolutely new concept. To the best of the author's knowledge there exists no software forecasting possible appearances of wounds employing machine vision methods on images together with diagnostic data. Learning methods for the estimation of appearances were only considered at single moments, that is, in a statistical context [3,10,13,21]. Existing simulations, e.g. virtual assisting systems in wound surgery [20], refer to optimum primary care only, not handling defects in wound healing with long-term treatments. Our approach tackles the field of image completion, where a variety of research has been done during the last years. Criminisi et. al. [7] developed an algorithm that combines simultaneous propagation of texture and structure information, in order to deal with unpleasant linear structures and contours crossing or reaching into a region to be filled. To avoid the misplacing of patches leading to artefacts in conventional greedy algorithms, Komodakis and Tziritas [11] posed the task as a discrete global optimisation problem and solved it by means of an improved belief propagation method. While Barnes at al. [2] increased the speed of the time-consuming search of proper patches for image completion by improving their PatchMatch algorithm, Mansfield et. al. [15] developed a technique to increase the variety of available source patches in an image by incorporating transformations like scale, rotation and brightness changes. None of these methods focus on circular shaped image completion which showed to be a good approach in case of wound images.

3   Methodology

An important requirement for the simulation tool to be developed was to keep the effort for usage to a minimum. The final procedure includes taking a photo of the affected body part, choosing relevant influences and segmenting the wound from the surrounding tissue (an automatic segmentation was not requested for the first step). Based on these three manual steps all wound developments regarding healing and worsening are generated fully automatically.

Image Acquisition: In order to solve the requirements on synthesis a proper acquisition and pre-processing of the data is essential. For that reason the wound label (a white cardboard strip with a printed rectangle of specified dimension) used in everyday clinical practice was replaced by a more sophisticated label additionally containing 24 colour fields. Given these information a normalization of size and colour appearance, to ensure comparability of different wounds, was possible. Furthermore, all images were taken with the same camera equipped with an annular flash and two linear polarization filters, 90° twisted against each other, to reduce the influence of reflections (wounds are often wet). In this way time series of the healing process of three illnesses, which are diabetic foot disease (DFS), peripheral arterial occlusive disease (PAOD) and venous leg ulcer, were collected and assigned to four different stages of disease (classification determined together with experts). Note that, due to given treatments data for the worsening process was not available and thus, based on the experience of attending physicians, was roughly considered to visually develop in the opposite direction but temporally much faster. Each of the covered medical advices not complied, additionally slows the healing and accelerates the worsening according a given scheme.

Wound Analysis: Besides geometrical features like diameter, circumference, covered area or solidity-measures there exist several other image based ways to describe a wound, e.g. via colour based features. Depending on the stadium of disease a wound physiologically consists of different tissues which differ in colour. The main types are epithelising, granulation, fibrous and necrotic tissue. On the one hand these types are clearly distinguishable since epithelising tissue possesses pink shades, granulation tissue has red shades, fibrous tissue is yellow and sometimes slightly green- or blue-tinted if special bacteria like pseudomonas are involved and necrotic tissue is normally black sometimes brown or grey but mostly dark coloured. On the other hand the colour based approach entails some potential sources of error. Fresh blood for instance looks like granulating tissue and dried blood has a similar dark appearance to necrotic tissue. Therefore, and to avoid other misclassifications due to wound dressings and ointments, it is necessary to clean the wound before taking an image. Furthermore some wounds especially those of DFS sometimes exhibit cavities, which indicates an advanced stage of disease, also may be confused with necrotic tissue. To circumvent this problem the cavities are automatically detected and the affected wound subregions are excluded from colour segmentation. The cavity detection was implemented by using Statistical Region Merging [17] followed by a local minimum search in order to identify wound areas with lower intensity values than their neighbours. Taking all these aspects into account the final colour based wound segmentation was implemented using a Support Vector Machine (SVM, [5]). The SVM was trained using a radial basis function kernel on about 600 RGB samples from different tissues in 50 colour normalized wound images. The RGB colour space was chosen due to its good discriminative properties regarding wound tissues, compared to HSV, L*a*b* and others, observed in our experiments. To describe the textures of the individual wound tissues Local Binary Patterns (LBP, [19,18]) as well as the feature point descriptor Binary Robust Independent Elementary Features (BRIEF, [4]) were analysed for their fitness. In our tests the refined uniform LBP in combination with a contrast measure clearly outperformed BRIEF, suggesting that this method is not appropriate for the task described herein. Based on the selected geometric, colour and texture features a cluster analysis was conducted to investigate their applicability for automatic wound classification. Due to the limited dataset available the thus constructed feature space was too sparse to receive reliable clusters. Therefore, for each diagnosis a decision tree was developed for classification into the four stages of disease. The trees considered the following features: total wound area, the percentage of necrotic, fibrous and granulating tissue and in case of DFS the binary information whether a cavity in the wound was detected or not.

Wound Synthesis and Simulation: The synthetic wound is mainly created by automatically stacking and blending synthetic wound tissues (Figure 1). The textures representing necrotic, fibrin and granulation tissue are generated in a pre-processing step by means of example based texture synthesis picking up ideas from [8,14]. The sample patches were taken from wound images containing the specific tissue type. The so created textures, several from each type, were stored in a database for further use in wound synthesis. The skin layer is created for each wound separately, using our new image completion method as described in Section 3. The automated creation steps of a particular synthetic wound, using

Fig. 1. Concept for combination of layers

the example of PAOD, are as follows: For each type of wound tissue a proper texture was taken from the database. To improve the visual similarity between a texture and its corresponding tissue in the initial wound, the luminance of the former was moderately adjusted within a limited range between -20 and +15 per cent. In the next step the different layers were merged one by one, beginning with the granulation layer (Figure 2a), then fibrin layer (Figure 2b) and finally the necrosis layer (Figure 2c). The fusion was done by means of blending and by usage of special filter masks, one for each layer. After adding a synthetic wound border by darken the wound edges (Figure 2d) an additional shading filter mask was applied to attenuate wound regions close to the contour of the body. This causes a realistic 3D-like effect of the wound and prevents the wound from protruding the affected body part (Figure 2e). Finally, the generated wound tissue is merged with the skin layer (Figure 2f). The original wound (before colour normalisation) can be seen in Figure 2g and the final result of the wound synthesis at an advanced stage of disease is presented in Figure 2h. In addition to the described synthesis there were more features implemented to increase the realistic visual impression of the created wound. In case of DFS a deformation field was calculated in order to simulate the swelling of the affected foot, which typically comes along with the worsening process. For this purpose an image transformation based on Thin Plate Splines was conducted. Another feature was the creation of synthetic cavities in the wound. Therefore, the affected wound area was attenuated by a filter mask based on the distance transformation. To simulate inflammation, the periwound skin region was tinted red by increasing the red and slightly attenuating the intensity of the green and blue channel using a Gaussian filter. The final simulation of a wound development is done by altering the already mentioned tissue masks. These is realised by applying scaling, thresholding and morphological operations steps to the masks, according to the parameters previously learned from the training image sequences and also according to the given personal circumstances of the patient. The so created videos of growing or shrinking wounds are generated and depicted in a GUI.

Image Completion: Since the healthy human skin exhibits no contours, edges or other elongate macro structures, there was no need to deploy complex image completion algorithms that were designed to cope with such structures, like that

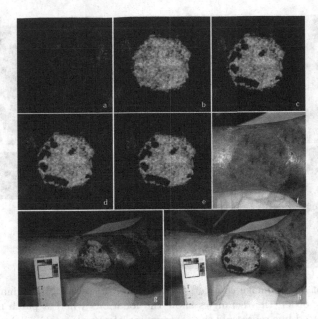

Fig. 2. Concept of wound synthesis: (a-e) Stepwise fusion of tissue layers, (f) skin layer after removing the original wound via image completion, (g) original wound image, (h) final synthesis result in an advanced stage of disease.

of [7]. Knowing, that our wound images are scale and colour normalised, there was also no necessity to involve methods described in [15]. Thus we created a new optimized solution for the given application. As can be seen below, our algorithm is based on circular image completion which is a quite intuitive approach. In order to receive satisfying results without wound border artefacts, it is necessary to completely remove the wound and its directly adjacent tissue, which differ from intact skin in colour and texture. Therefore the given wound mask is morphologically eroded by a disk-shaped structuring element. During our experiments we recognised that the best fitting patches were located nearby the wound (presumed that the wound border is removed as described). Therefore a Search-Mask allowing us to limit and optimise the search space, was introduced. Since we know the contour of the body and the wound label, all non skin regions can be excluded from the search space, too. Additionally to the pseudo code, some details of the algorithm should be declared. After a proper patch is found, it is merged to the output image, accordingly to Figure 3f, whereas the upper left patch depicts the rectangular site of the image to be filled (superimposed by a seam mask), and the upper right patch shows the best matching patch (superimposed by the inverted seam mask). Adding these two patches results in a final patch (depicted underneath the two patches) that can be directly inserted into the output image. By the way, the mentioned seam mask is constructed due to smoothing the binary mask of the overlapping region using a Gaussian filter kernel. Furthermore the in-painting of the remaining gaps after the last iteration as depicted in Figure 3d is done by the same patch matching and blending steps as described before.

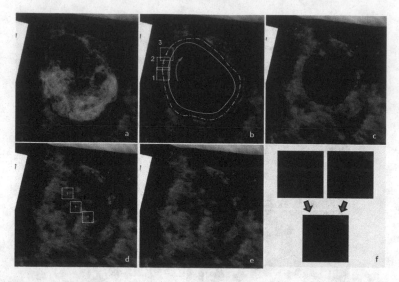

Fig. 3. Concept of our image completion technique: (a) section of original image, (b) clockwise filling order; the rectangles show the locations where a patch is fitted; the orange dash-dotted line represents the contour line of actual iteration, along which the overlap between patch and filled area is 30 per cent; the white solid line represents the contour along which the image is cropped after each iteration, (c) result after two iterations, (d) remaining gaps after the last iteration, that were filled using the same blending technique as for the other patches; the rectangles depicts the window for the matching, (e) final result, (f) shows blending step

Pseudo code of image completion algorithm

```
01  Img        ... RGB input image that has to be completed
02  FillMask    ... binary mask indicating vacant pixels in InputImg
03  SearchMask ... binary mask defining locations from where DstPatch may be matched
04  PatchSize  ... initial PatchSize e.g. [81, 81]
05
06  MeanFilterKernel <- ones(PatchSize)
07  NumVacantPix <- sum of set bits in FillMask
08  NSSDArray <- []
09
10  while true
11      FiltFillMask <- filter(FillMask, MeanFilterKernel)
12      ThresholdMask <- threshold(FiltFillMask, 0.3)
13      ContourLineSet <- extractcontours(ThresholdMask)
14      if ContourLineSet is empty
15          if sum of set bits in FillMask == 0
16              break
17          else
18              inpaint remaining small unfilled regions
19              break
20      for each ContourLine in ContourLineSet do
21          NumRefPoints <- numel(ContourLine) * 1.5 / min(vPatchSize)
22          RefPointSet <- extract NumRefPoints equidistant points from ContourLine
23          for each RefPoint in RefPointSet do
24              extract RefPatch from Img centered @ RefPoint
25              for each SeachPosition in SearchMask do
26                  CandidatePatch <- extract Patch centered @ SeachPosition in Img
27                  NSSD <- calc_normalized_SSD_of_overlapping_region(RefPatch, CandidatePatch)
28                  append NSSD to NSSDArray
29              IndexArray <- sort(NSSDArray, ascending)
30              IndexOfChosenPatch <- pick randomly one of the first 1 per cent of elements in IndexArray
31              ChoosenPatch <- getPatch(IndexOfChosenPatch)
32              insert ChoosenPatch into Img centered @ RefPoint by blending
33              set all pixels of FillMask to false according to the covered region of the new inserted Patch
34          FiltFillMask <- filter(FillMask, MeanFilterKernel)
35          clear Img where FiltFillMask > 0.5
36          clear FillMask where FiltFillMask > 0.5
37          NumVacantPix <- sum of set bits in FillMask
38  OuputImg <- Img
```

4   Experiments

Figure 4 presents our image completion results compared to those of Komodakis and Tziritas [11]. It can clearly be seen that for our specific application we can compete with quite complex state of the art techniques.

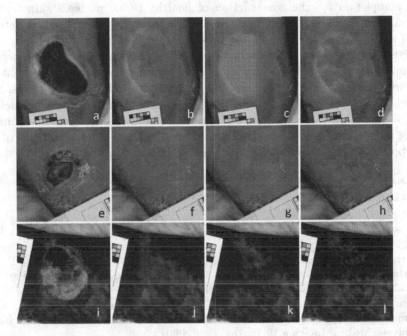

Fig. 4. Image completion results: The first column (a, e, i) shows the original images, the second (b, f, j) depicts the results of [11] using the whole image for search space and the third column (c, g, k) gives the results of [11] on a reduced search space. Column four (d, h, l) presents our result, also based on a reduced (and optimized!) search space.

The algorithm used for the comparison experiments comes from [12]. The first column of the image shows a section of the original images comprising the wound region, and the second as well as the third column depicts the results of [11], the second column using the whole image and the third solely the actual image section for search space (which is fairer for comparison, since our algorithm also uses masks to ensure appropriate patches for selection). The last column shows our result, also based on the reduced search space. As one can see, it is essential to reduce the search space to a close surrounding of the wound in order to ensure the sampling of fitting patches. A larger search space (comprising the whole image) does not come along with an appreciable image completion. Despite the fact that some results from [11] using the local search space are quite appropriate there are often examples where only our radial approach can correctly handle the patch selection (Figure 4).

5   Conclusion

In this paper we presented how to build a model for simulating the healing as well as the worsening process of chronic wounds based on known disease patterns. The key point for the construction of possible wound stages was the creation of a nicely fitting texture including all representative tissue types. The radial image completion for the construction of healthy tissue as basis skin texture layer builds the key contribution of our work. The overlap of individual patches as well as the creation of masks for superimposing different tissue types were optimized. In addition to the detailed description of our tissue creation method we compared the results to another approach that does not take into account the radial information. Furthermore, several created wound images were presented in order to back up our claim on realistic simulations. Further work will include an absolute comparison of the prediction to real wound developments. Finally, putting more effort in the training process including even more knowledge of the development process will improve the realistic impression of our results.

References

1. Akestes GmbH: WundManager (2001), http://www.akestes.de/ (accessed June 20, 2012)
2. Barnes, C., Shechtman, E., Goldman, D.B., Finkelstein, A.: The Generalized Patch-Match Correspondence Algorithm. In: Daniilidis, K. (ed.) ECCV 2010, Part III. LNCS, vol. 6313, pp. 29–43. Springer, Heidelberg (2010)
3. Bon, F.X., Briand, E., Guichard, S., Couturaud, B., Revol, M., Servant, J.M., Dubertret, L.: Quantitative and kinetic evolution of wound healing through image analysis. Medical Imaging 19(7), 767–772 (2000)
4. Calonder, M., Lepetit, V., Strecha, C., Fua, P.: BRIEF: Binary Robust Independent Elementary Features. In: Daniilidis, K., Maragos, P., Paragios, N. (eds.) ECCV 2010, Part IV. LNCS, vol. 6314, pp. 778–792. Springer, Heidelberg (2010)
5. Chang, C.C., Lin, C.J.: LIBSVM: A library for support vector machines. ACM Trans. on Intelligent Systems and Technology 2, 27:1–27:27 (2011)
6. Coloplast GmbH: Wunddokumentation, http://www.coloplast.de/wundversorgung/wundeverstehen/wundmanagement/ (accessed June 20, 2012)
7. Criminisi, A., Pérez, P., Toyama, K.: Region filling and object removal by exemplar-based image inpainting. Image Processing 13, 1200–1212 (2004)
8. Efros, A.A., Freeman, W.T.: Image quilting for texture synthesis and transfer. In: SIGGRAPH, pp. 341–346 (2001)
9. Jalomed GmbH: JalomedWD, http://www.jalomed.de/de/ (accessed June 20, 2012)
10. Kolesnik, M., Fexa, A.: Multi-dimensional Color Histograms for Segmentation of Wounds in Images. In: Kamel, M.S., Campilho, A.C. (eds.) ICIAR 2005. LNCS, vol. 3656, pp. 1014–1022. Springer, Heidelberg (2005)
11. Komodakis, N., Tziritas, G.: Image completion using efficient belief propagation via priority scheduling and dynamic pruning. Image Processing 16(11), 2649–2661 (2007)

12. Lafreniere, D.: An implementation of Komodakis' and Tziritas' Image Completion Using Efficient Belief Propagation Via Priority Scheduling and Dynamic Pruning, http://lafarren.com/image-completer/, (accessed June 20, 2012)
13. Lashkia, G.V., Anthony, L.: An inductive learning method for medical diagnosis. Pattern Recognition Letters 24(1-3), 273–282 (2003)
14. Liang, L., Liu, C., Xu, Y., Guo, B., Yeung Shum, H.: Real-time texture synthesis by patch-based sampling. ACM Trans. on Graphics 20, 127–150 (2001)
15. Mansfield, A., Prasad, M., Rother, C., Sharp, T., Kohli, P., Gool, L.V.: Transforming image completion. In: BMVC, pp. 121.1–121.11 (2011)
16. Medizinische Universität Wien: W.H.A.T. (Wound Healing Analysing Tool), http://cemsiis.meduniwien.ac.at/mbm/wf/projekte/what/ (accessed June 20, 2012)
17. Nock, R., Nielsen, F.: Statistical region merging. PAMI 26, 1452–1458 (2004)
18. Ojala, T., Pietikaeinen, M., Maeenpaeae, T.: Multiresolution gray-scale and rotation invariant texture classification with local binary patterns. PAMI 24(7), 971–987 (2002)
19. Ojala, T., Pietikäinen, M., Mäenpää, T.: A Generalized Local Binary Pattern Operator for Multiresolution Gray Scale and Rotation Invariant Texture Classification. In: Singh, S., Murshed, N., Kropatsch, W.G. (eds.) ICAPR 2001. LNCS, vol. 2013, pp. 397–406. Springer, Heidelberg (2001)
20. Seevinck, J., Scerbo, M.W., Belfore, L.A., Weireter, L.J., Crouch, J.R., Shen, Y., McKenzie, F.D., Garcia, H.M., Girtelschmid, S., Baydogan, E., Schmidt, E.A.: A Simulation-Based Training System for Surgical Wound Debridement. Studies in Health Technology and Informatics 119, 491–496 (2006)
21. Treuillet, S., Albouy, B., Lucas, Y.: Three-dimensional assessment of skin wounds using a standard digital camera. Medical Imgaging 28(5), 752–762 (2009)

Automatic Model Selection
in Archetype Analysis

Sandhya Prabhakaran, Sudhir Raman, Julia E. Vogt, and Volker Roth

Department of Mathematics and Computer Science, University of Basel,
Bernoullistrasse 16, CH-4056 Basel, Switzerland
{sandhya.prabhakaran,sudhir.raman,julia.vogt,volker.roth}@unibas.ch

Abstract. Archetype analysis involves the identification of representative objects from amongst a set of multivariate data such that the data can be expressed as a convex combination of these representative objects. Existing methods for archetype analysis assume a fixed number of archetypes a priori. Multiple runs of these methods for different choices of archetypes are required for model selection. Not only is this computationally infeasible for larger datasets, in heavy-noise settings model selection becomes cumbersome. In this paper, we present a novel extension to these existing methods with the specific focus of relaxing the need to provide a fixed number of archetypes beforehand. Our fast iterative optimization algorithm is devised to automatically select the right model using BIC scores and can easily be scaled to noisy, large datasets. These benefits are achieved by introducing a Group-Lasso component popular for sparse linear regression. The usefulness of the approach is demonstrated through simulations and on a real world application of document analysis for identifying topics.

1 Introduction

Archetypes are defined as an original model or type based on which similar things are patterned. Archetype analysis as developed in [3] is an approach which summarizes data using a small number of archetypes or "pure" data samples. This summary is based on the precept that the data can be well represented as convex mixtures of these archetypes. Archetype analysis can also be interpreted as a dimensionality reduction approach and has been applied to various domains. Examples include analysis of galaxy spectra studies [2], image analysis [1], analysis of the human genotope [5] and text mining [7]. Although conventional low-rank approximation methods like principal component analysis (PCA) also deal with compressed data representation, interpreting the resulting compression can become tedious. The key benefit of archetype analysis is that since the archetypes are connotations of the data itself, they are able to render a more meaningful interpretation of the data.

Given a data matrix $X_{n \times d}$ with n observations $\{x_1, x_2, \ldots, x_n\}$, where $x_i \in \mathbb{R}^d$, the goal of archetype analysis is to find a sparse set of archetypes or "pure" samples $Z_{p \times d}$ with p archetypes $\{z_1, z_2, \ldots, z_p\}$ where $p \ll n$ and $z_i \in \mathbb{R}^d$.

A. Pinz et al. (Eds.): DAGM/OAGM 2012, LNCS 7476, pp. 458–467, 2012.
© Springer-Verlag Berlin Heidelberg 2012

The archetypes are such that the observations x_i are noisy convex combinations of these archetypes:

$$x_i = Z^t a_i + \epsilon_i, \qquad \text{for} \quad i = 1 \dots n, \qquad (1)$$

where $\epsilon_i \sim \mathcal{N}_d(0, \mathbf{I})$ represents the stochastic nature of x_i and a_i is a composition vector such that $a_{ij} \geq 0$ and $\sum_{j=1}^{p} a_{ij} = 1$. The archetypes themselves are defined to be convex mixtures of the data points. Hence archetypes are chosen to be a small number of points (typically smaller than n) residing in close proximity to this convex hull. The optimization procedure in archetype analysis involves finding a small set of archetypes such that the error in approximation of the data points as convex mixtures of the archetypes is minimized.

Based on this formulation, an iterative optimization algorithm was introduced in [3]. This version is still not computationally feasible for large datasets. A more scalable version was introduced in [1]. The scalability relied on choosing archetype candidates as points lying close to the convex hull. Another approach was introduced in [7] that was based on kernelizing the data prior to extracting the archetypes. All these methods assume in advance a fixed number of archetypes p and then attempt to find these archetypes. Since these methods do not have any internal built-in criteria for model selection, multiple reruns of these algorithms are required corresponding to different values of p. This can prove to be computationally infeasible especially in the cases of very large datasets. Moreover in high-noise settings, as is with most real datasets, it is hard to perform model selection as done in [3] and [7].

The primary focus in this paper is that of permitting automatic model selection meaning p does not have to be assumed a priori. The archetypes and their number are learnt during the optimization process. Our work is based on the idea of enforcing sparsity on a set of composition vectors using the Group-Lasso formulation which is defined in [11] for enforcing grouped sparsity. Since there are efficient methods available for computing the solution path of the Group-Lasso, multiple reruns of our algorithm are not necessary to assess the best model thus making our method computationally feasible even on noisier and larger datasets.

2 Conventional Archetype Analysis - Model Description

We start with a description of the conventional archetype analysis. The data is present as a $n \times d$ matrix X with n observations $\{x_1, x_2, \dots, x_n\}$ where each x_i^T is a row of X representing a d-dimensional observation. Given these n observations, the goal of archetype analysis is to identify the fixed number p of d-dimensional archetypes which can be represented in the form of a $p \times d$ matrix Z having p archetypes $\{z_1, z_2, \dots, z_p\}$ with $p \ll n$.

We split the identification of the archetypes into multiple steps as in [1]. Given a set of archetypes Z, the compositions for all the data points can be estimated based on the optimization problem:

$$\hat{A} = \operatorname{argmin}_A \sum_{i=1}^{n} \left\| x_i - \sum_{j=1}^{p} a_{ij} z_j \right\|^2, \qquad (2)$$

where $\| \cdot \|$ denotes the ℓ_2 norm of a vector and A is a $n \times p$ composition vector matrix which comprises of composition vectors $\{a_1, a_2, \cdots, a_n\}$. Since a_i are composition vectors, additional constraints are imposed to ensure that each data point is a meaningful combination of the archetypes and that the data points are represented as mixtures of the archetypes:

$$a_{ij} \geq 0 \quad \text{and} \quad \sum_{j=1}^{p} a_{ij} = 1. \qquad \text{for} \quad i = 1 \ldots n. \tag{3}$$

Further, we assume that the archetypes lie within close proximity to the convex hull of the given observations. Hence, each z_i can be expressed as a convex combination of the data points:

$$z_i = \sum_{j=1}^{n} b_{ij} x_j, \tag{4}$$

with the coefficients $b_{ij} \geq 0$ and $\sum_{j=1}^{n} b_{ij} = 1$. The coefficient vectors b_i's are represented as a $p \times n$ matrix B, with the rows comprising of composition vectors $\{b_1, b_2, \cdots, b_p\}$. This choice of b_i's assures that the archetypes resemble the data and that they are a convex mixture of the data.

In matrix form, with $X \in \mathbb{R}^{n \times d}$, $Z \in \mathbb{R}^{p \times d}$, $A \in \mathbb{R}^{n \times p}$ and $B \in \mathbb{R}^{p \times n}$, a suitable choice of archetypes will minimize the residual sum of squares problem:

$$(\hat{A}, \hat{B}) = \text{argmin}_{A,B} \|X - AZ\|^2 = \|X - ABX\|^2$$

$$\text{s.t.} \quad b_{ij} \geq 0, \quad \sum_{j=1}^{n} b_{ij} = 1, \quad a_{ij} \geq 0, \quad \sum_{j=1}^{p} a_{ij} = 1. \tag{5}$$

Thus the overall problem of finding a fixed predetermined number of archetypes for a given set of observations translates into a constrained optimization problem involving two sets of coefficients $\{a_{ij}\}$ and $\{b_{ij}\}$. Such an optimization-based formulation is solved using an alternating least squares procedure detailed in [1].

Complexity Analysis for Conventional Methods. The complexity of one iteration of the algorithm in [3] is given by $\mathcal{O}(n^2 p)$. The approach in [1] resort to preselecting the archetypes candidates by subsampling a set of n' points ($n' \ll n$) that reside on the convex hulls obtained from random 2D projections, thereby reducing the complexity to $\mathcal{O}(n'^2 p)$. Despite this preprocessing, the resulting dataset can still have relatively high n' and p values. To enable model selection, multiple runs of these algorithms are necessary for different values of p which can become computationally inefficient for large n and p. To accentuate further the problem with model selection, when the data are noisy, the RSS decay curves (refer Fig. 1) do not exhibit a prominent *knee region* that can be relied on for model selection. Hence model selection for archetype analysis using these methods becomes difficult in very large and noisy datasets.

3   Automatic Detection of the Number of Archetypes

To overcome the aforementioned problems with the conventional methods, we look at the modified problem of not requiring a fixed number of archetypes beforehand, but rather being able to select a sparse set of archetypes based on the given data. To achieve this, we make use of a Group-Lasso component to automatically identify a sparse set of archetypes. The fact that we can also efficiently sample the solution path of the Group-Lasso offers a computationally-efficient model selection procedure.

3.1   Sparse Archetype Selection Using the Group-Lasso

We start with a $n \times d$ data matrix X as before. Since n is the maximum number of archetypes that would be needed to represent data, we consider a $n \times d$ matrix Z (instead of $p \times d$ as referred in Section 2) which assumes that atmost n archetypes are required to represent data. Our goal is to formulate an optimization problem for identifying a sparse set of archetypes which translates to obtaining a sparse matrix Z where most of the rows are zero. Hence the non-zero rows of Z will culminate as the selected archetypes of the data.

This type of a sparsity attainment can be related to the Group-Lasso formulation (as defined in [11]) which involves solving a linear regression problem with the goal of achieving grouped sparsity in the regression coefficients. The solution path of the Group-Lasso is efficiently computed using a fast active-set algorithm defined in [8]. As in the Group-Lasso, we use similar constraints on the matrix Z to impose grouped sparsity where the groups are the rows of the matrix and the aim is to obtain sparsity at a group level. This is achieved by imposing a $\ell_{1,2}$ norm constraint on the rows of the matrix Z. The modified optimization problem with $X \in \mathbb{R}^{n \times d}$, $Z \in \mathbb{R}^{n \times d}$, $A \in \mathbb{R}^{n \times n}$ and $B \in \mathbb{R}^{n \times n}$, is now:

$$(\hat{A}, \hat{B}) = \mathrm{argmin}_{A,B} \|X - AZ\|^2 = \|X - ABX\|^2$$

$$\text{s.t.} \quad b_{ij} \geq 0, \quad \sum_{j=1}^{n} b_{ij} = 1, \quad a_{ij} \geq 0, \quad \sum_{j=1}^{n} a_{ij} = 1 \tag{6}$$

$$\text{s.t.} \quad \sum_{j=1}^{n} \|z_j\| \leq \kappa.$$

To solve this optimization problem we use the same alternating least squares idea used in previous methods, however with several algorithmic changes. To compute the optimized set of coefficients $\{a_{ij}\}$ and $\{b_{ij}\}$ using Eq. 6, we use MIFSR (refer Section 3.3). We also have a modified step to compute the intermediate archetypes. Instead of solving $\hat{Z} = \mathrm{argmin}_Z \|X - AZ\|^2$ using ordinary least squares *(OLS)*, we now introduce the Group-Lasso optimization step:

$$\hat{z}^{GL} = \mathrm{argmin}_{z^{GL}} \|x^{GL} - \mathcal{A} z^{GL}\|^2 \quad \text{s.t.} \quad \sum_{j=1}^{n} \|z_j^{GL}\| \leq \kappa, \tag{7}$$

where in terms of the standard Group-Lasso formulation, $\mathcal{A} \in \mathbb{R}^{nd \times nd}$, $x^{GL} \in \mathbb{R}^{nd}$, and $z^{GL} \in \mathbb{R}^{nd}$ i.e.

$$
\mathcal{A} = \begin{pmatrix} a_1 & 0_n & \cdots & 0_n & a_d & 0_n & \cdots & 0_n \\ 0_n & a_1 & 0_n & \cdots & & 0_n & a_d & 0_n & \cdots \\ & \ddots & & & \cdots & & & \ddots \\ 0_n & 0_n & \cdots & a_1 & & 0_n & 0_n & \cdots & a_d \end{pmatrix}, \quad x^{GL} = \begin{pmatrix} x_1 \\ \vdots \\ x_n \end{pmatrix} \quad \text{and} \quad z^{GL} = \begin{pmatrix} z_1 \\ \vdots \\ z_n \end{pmatrix}.
$$

Eq. 7 is solved using the fast active-set algorithm defined in [8]. The details of our method are given in Alg. 1.

Algorithm 1. Group-Lasso extension for archetype analysis

A : Initialize Z

begin

    B : Determine coefficients a_{ij} by minimizing $\|x_i - Z^T a_i\|^2$ s.t. $a_{ij} \geq 0$ and $\sum_{j=1}^{n} a_{ij} = 1$ for $i = (1, \ldots, n)$ using MIFSR in [4] (see Section 3.3).

    C : Solve Eq. (7) for z^{GL} to obtain $\hat{z}^{GL}$ using the active-set algorithm in [8].

    D : Determine coefficients b_{ij} by minimizing $\|\hat{z}_j - X^T b_j\|^2$ s.t. $b_{ij} \geq 0$ and $\sum_{j=1}^{n} b_{ij} = 1$ for $i = (1, \ldots, n)$ using MIFSR in [4] (see Section 3.3).

    E : Update the archetypes by setting $Z = BX$.

end

3.2   Model Selection

For selecting a sparse set of archetypes according to Eq. 7, however involves tuning the parameter κ which controls the level of sparsity in the solution. Since different κ return different parsimonious models, model selection is required to select one amongst these models. Although cross-validation is generally used for model selection, it can tend to be computationally expensive.

We use the Bayesian Information Criterion (BIC) scoring mechanism for Group-Lasso as detailed in [11] for model selection. The BIC score is given as:

$$
\text{BIC}(\hat{\mu} \equiv \hat{\mathcal{A}} \hat{z}^{GL}) = \frac{\|x^{GL} - \hat{\mu}\|}{n\sigma^2} + \frac{\log(n)}{n} \cdot \widehat{df}(\hat{\mu}) \tag{8}
$$

with

$$
\widehat{df}(\hat{\mu}) = \sum_{j}^{J} \mathbb{I}(\|\hat{\mathcal{A}}_j\| > 0) + \sum_{j}^{J} \frac{\|\hat{\mathcal{A}}_j\|}{\|\hat{\mathcal{A}}_j^{LS}\|} (n_j - 1), \tag{9}
$$

where $\mathbb{I}(\cdot)$ is the indicator function, $\hat{\mathcal{A}}$ and $\hat{z}^{GL}$ are the estimated values of $\mathcal{A}$ and z^{GL} based on a particular κ value, n_j is the number of non-zero coefficients of $\hat{A}_j$ of the jth group, $\|\hat{A}_j\|$ is the ℓ_2 norm of $\hat{A}_j$ and $\|\hat{A}_j^{LS}\|$ is the ℓ_2 norm of the least-square estimate of $\hat{A}_j$. We use this BIC score to evaluate the models obtained with different κ values.

Our model relies on the virtue that the active-set algorithm [8] used to solve the Group-Lasso optimization problem (Eq. 7) permits sampling of the solution path at discrete sets of κ, thereby allowing stepwise BIC score computation. Since no additional costs are involved in computing the BIC scores over the entire solution path, it renders our method to be computationally efficient. This proves advantageous in that there is no need to restart the entire algorithm for a fixed number of archetypes as opposed to the multiple algorithm reruns required for the conventional methods.

3.3 MIFSR

To obtain the constrained optimized set of coefficients $\{a_{ij}\}$ and $\{b_{ij}\}$ using Eq. 6 (and steps B and D respectively in Alg. 1), we implement the monotone incremental forward stage-wise regression (MIFSR) as introduced in [4]. We use this heuristic for closely approximating Eq. 6 to reduce the computational complexity further rather than directly solving the quadratic program.

For instance, the respective optimization problem in terms of the MIFSR for step B can be written as:

$$\min_{a_i} \|x_i - Z^T a_i\|^2 \quad \text{s.t } a_{ij} \geq 0 \ \forall j \quad \text{and} \quad \sum_{j=1}^{n} a_{ij} \leq 1 \quad \text{for } i = 1 \ldots n . \quad (10)$$

Alg. 2 depicts MIFSR for step B that involves the optimization of a_i. Step D involves the similar optimization for b_j.

Algorithm 2. MIFSR algorithm for step B

1: Start with $r = x_i - mean(x_i)$, $a_{ij} = 0 \ \forall j$.
2: Find predictor $\tilde{z}_j$ most positively correlated with r.
3: Update $a_{ij} \leftarrow a_{ij} + \epsilon$
4: Update $r \leftarrow r - \epsilon \tilde{z}_j$ and repeat steps 2 and 3 until no predictor has any correlation with r.

By construction, Alg. 2 terminates after κ/ϵ steps meaning that there is a fixed number of iterations that neither depend on n or p but only on κ and ϵ which are constant in this setting. The only cost involved then would be that of the correlation (Step 2 of Alg. 2) that scales according to the dimension of the concerned column and this would be $\mathcal{O}(np)$.

3.4 Further Acceleration of our Algorithm

To further accelerate our already-efficient archetype analysis model, we utilize preprocessing steps as described below.

Dimensionality Reduction with Robust PCA. The first aspect of preprocessing involves dimensionality reduction which aims at reducing d. Real-world
datasets are usually of high dimensions which call for the use of dimensionality
reduction techniques such as PCA that project the data to a low-dimensional
manifold. It becomes relevant to use PCA in finding such low-rank projections
in the context of archetype analysis. This is due to the fact that a set of convex
mixtures of p archetypes cannot lie on a subspace greater than p and since convex
sets are linear manifolds, the search for these linear manifolds is justified using
PCA-based projections. However, PCA is highly susceptible to outliers and thus
it becomes essential to filter out the outliers before performing PCA. We resort
to a robust version of PCA as given in [10] that deals with Outlier Pursuit.

This method involves decomposing the data matrix X as $X = X_L + X_C$
where X_L is the low-rank matrix comprising the true subspace of the non-outlier
points and X_C the column-sparse matrix denoting presence of outliers. Through
robust PCA, we estimate X_L that represents the uncorrupted data. Details of
the method are given in [10].

Preselecting the Archetype Candidates. After obtaining the outlier-free
data matrix with reduced dimensionality, we focus our attention on reducing
the number of possible archetypes from n to a lower number for computational
gains. The driving force of this reduction is the fact that archetypes are located
on the convex hull obtained from random 2D projections of the data points
(proved in [3]). The representative archetypes are therefore sparse mixtures of
those data points x_i residing in the vicinity of the convex hull of X and not
inside the hull.

For preselecting the archetype candidates we use the approach as in [1]. Calculating the convex hull in 2D is easier since the combinatorial complexity of
calculating the hull for n points in d dimensions dramatically increases with d
as $\mathcal{O}(n^{\lfloor d/2 \rfloor + 1})$ [9]. If the dataset consisted of only 2 archetypes, these would lie
on the first principal component (PC) of the data. Thus by considering many
such 2D projections, one arrives at the set of all possible archetypes. With this
reasoning, we look at many pairwise 2D PC projections, compute the convex
hull for every pair and consolidate points that constitute these convex hulls to
arrive at the set of all possible archetype candidates.

4   Experiments

Simulation Examples. We generate two datasets, one with high noise using
a Student-t distribution (known to confuse traditional PCA but not the robust
PCA) and another with low Gaussian noise. Each dataset consists of $n = 10000$
observations in $\mathbb{R}^{100}$ and $p = 15$ archetypes. The datasets are subject to preprocessing as described in Section 3.4: first for dimensionality reduction using
robust PCA followed by reducing the number of archetype candidates to those
points residing near the convex hull of the data.

For comparison, we run our algorithm and the algorithm in [1] for archetype
detection. For [1], we compute the percentage decay in the residual sum of

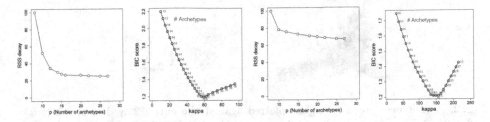

Fig. 1. Comparison of our method with that of [1]. RSS decay curves for [1] and BIC curves for our method are shown. **Left to right**: RSS decay curves plotted against p archetypes for a low-Gaussian noise dataset, BIC score versus κ for the low-Gaussian noise dataset, RSS decay curves plotted against p archetypes for a high Student-t noise dataset and BIC score versus κ for the high Student-t noise dataset. Both datasets were generated using 15 archetypes. It is obvious that with the RSS curves model selection will be cumbersome since the *knee region* in these curves signals the wrong number of archetypes and for 15 archetypes and more the RSS curves are flatter. On the other hand, our Group-Lasso based model automatically identifies 15 archetypes as shown clearly by the prominent *knee regions* in the BIC curves

squares (RSS) error against the number of archetypes found in both datasets. Refer 1st and 3rd plots in Fig. 1. For our method, we plot the BIC curves computed at discrete steps of κ versus the κ values (2nd and 4th plots in Fig. 1). As is evident, the visual inspection of RSS decay curves is not very informative for model selection in noisy datasets. On the other hand, the BIC curves show a clear demarcation of the *knee region* that serves to determine the right p. Thus with our Group-Lasso based method, a reasonable model is automatically selected. Model selection using the algorithm in [1] required multiple runs for different p whereas for our method following the solution path of the Group-Lasso in steps of κ was sufficient.

Text Categorization Using Reuters Corpus Volume 1. As a real-world example, we apply our archetype analysis model for categorizing texts where the focus is to obtain automatic annotations of the text corpus leading to potential new categories as opposed to manually-provided categories. Since the term frequency (TF) of a document can be described as an ideal convex mixture of words, in archetype analysis the pursuit would be to find those archetype documents that can be meaningfully interpreted as a convex combination of legitimate words comprising one of the main categories.

We use the Reuters Corpus Volume 1 (RCV1), an archive of news documents manually categorized and made available through [6]. The four categories reflecting the content of the corpus are *CCAT*: Corporate/Industrial, *ECAT*: Economics, *GCAT*: Government/Social and *MCAT*: Markets. The dataset we use consists of 23149 TF-IDF normalized documents with their corresponding labels and 57180 words. We compute the Gram matrix of this dataset and apply kernel-PCA that results in the dataset having 23149 documents and a reduced dimensionality of 200 words.

Fig. 2. Archetypes (green triangles) plotted against the entire 23K documents (left) and against documents, categorically annotated of the RCV1 corpus (right). The archetype landscape is clearly distributed across all four categories

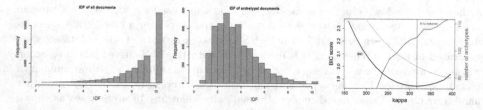

Fig. 3. Inverse Document Frequency (IDF) of all documents (left) and archetype documents (centre). The archetype documents successfully capture the high-frequency terms present in the RCV1 corpus. BIC scores and number of archetypes plotted against different models obtained for various κ values (right)

We apply our Group-Lasso based method on this corpus and retrieve 88 archetype documents as shown in Fig. 2. Analyzing the archetypes identified, it is obvious that all 88 archetypes are spread out across all the four core categories. Another interesting result is that the archetypes also capture all the high-frequency terms denoting rare words present in the corpus (see Fig. 3 (left and centre)). Thus the identified archetypes can be seen as those apex documents in the corpus meaningfully representing the core categories.

Next, we plot the BIC scores using Eq. 8 for the different parsimonious models obtained for various values of κ as shown in Fig. 3 (right). The BIC scores are computed by following the solution path of the Group-Lasso in successive steps of κ. The scores of each model along with the corresponding number of archetypes supporting that model are shown. We also plot the RSS curves obtained at these stepwise intervals of κ. From the plot, it is clear that the RSS curve cannot be used for reliable model selection since there is no prominent *knee* in the curve. On the other hand the BIC curve clearly shows a *knee region* emphasizing that automatic model selection using the active-set algorithm of Group-Lasso works well in reclaiming the a priori unknown number of archetype documents.

5   Conclusion

We have presented an efficient archetype analysis algorithm that in addition to finding the sparse set of archetypes also automatically identifies their number using a Group-Lasso based formulation. Conventional archetype analysis methods require that the number of archetypes be known a priori. Thus for model selection, these have to be restarted for every choice of archetypes which is computationally demanding for larger datasets. Further, for noisy data, model selection based on examining the decay curves of the residual sum of squares (RSS) becomes practically impossible due to the flattening of these curves. We have overcome these problems by enabling automatic model selection that avoids multiple restarts of our algorithm altogether. This in-built mechanism of model selection is achieved by computing the BIC scores at subsequent steps of the solution path of the Group-Lasso. Model selection is attained by observing the pronounced minimum in the BIC curve. We have demonstrated that our method of model selection for archetype analysis works well on both simulations and real-world RCV1 text corpus and can also be scaled to noisy and large datasets.

References

1. Bauckhage, C., Thurau, C.: Making Archetypal Analysis Practical. In: Denzler, J., Notni, G., Süße, H. (eds.) DAGM 2009. LNCS, vol. 5748, pp. 272–281. Springer, Heidelberg (2009)
2. Chan, B.H.P., Mitchell, D.A., Cram, L.E.: Archetypal analysis of galaxy spectra. Monthly Notices of the Royal Astronomical Society 338(3), 790–795 (2003)
3. Cutler, A., Breiman, L.: Archetypal analysis. Technometrics, 338–347 (1994)
4. Hastie, T., Taylor, J., Tibshirani, R., Walther, G.: Forward stagewise regression and the monotone Lasso. Electronic Journal of Statistics 1, 2007 (2006)
5. Huggins, P., Pachter, L., Sturmfels, B.: Toward the human genotope. Bulletin of Mathematical Biology 69, 2723–2735 (2007)
6. Lewis, D.D., Yang, Y., Rose, T.G., Li, F., Dietterich, G., Li, F.: RCV1: A new benchmark collection for text categorization research. Journal of Machine Learning Research 5, 361–397 (2004)
7. Morup, M., Hansen, L.K.: Archetypal analysis for machine learning and data mining. Neurocomputing 80, 54–63 (2012)
8. Roth, V., Fischer, B.: The Group-Lasso for generalized linear models: uniqueness of solutions and efficient algorithms. In: ICML 2008, pp. 848–855. ACM (2008)
9. Skiena, S.S.: The Algorithm Design Manual. Springer, New York (1997)
10. Xu, H., Caramanis, C., Sanghavi, S.: Robust PCA via outlier pursuit. In: Lafferty, J., Williams, C.K.I., Shawe-Taylor, J., Zemel, R.S., Culotta, A. (eds.) Advances in Neural Information Processing Systems 23, pp. 2496–2504 (2010)
11. Yuan, M., Lin, Y.: Model selection and estimation in regression with grouped variables. J. Roy. Stat. Soc. B, 49–67 (2006)

Stereo Fusion from Multiple Viewpoints

Christian Unger[1,2], Eric Wahl[2], Peter Sturm[3], and Slobodan Ilic[1]

[1] Technische Universität München, Germany
Slobodan.Ilic@in.tum.de
[2] BMW Group, München, Germany
{Christian.Unger,Eric.Wahl}@bmw.de
[3] INRIA Rhône-Alpes and Laboratoire Jean Kuntzmann, France
Peter.Sturm@inrialpes.fr

Abstract. Advanced driver assistance using cameras is a first important step towards autonomous driving tasks. However, the computational power in automobiles is highly limited and hardware platforms with enormous processing resources such as GPUs are not available in serial production vehicles. In our paper we address the need for a highly efficient fusion method that is well suited for standard CPUs.

We assume that a number of pairwise disparity maps are available, which we project to a reference view pair and fuse them efficiently to improve the accuracy of the reference disparity map. We estimate a probability density function of disparities in the reference image using projection uncertainties. In the end the most probable disparity map is selected from the probability distribution.

We carried out extensive quantitative evaluations on challenging stereo data sets and real world images. These results clearly show that our method is able to recover very accurate disparity maps in real-time.

1 Introduction

Dense real-time multi-view stereo allows for a wide spectrum of useful applications including automotive driver assistance or robotics. Although a large amount of research has been devoted to the stereo problem using image pairs [1,3,5,7,6,8,14,17] and using multiple cameras [2,10,12,13,15,16], obtaining dense high-quality disparity maps in real-time is still a challenging problem. Traditional real-time stereo methods [6,17] still lack accuracy compared to methods which do not impose time constraints. A few multi-view stereo methods [11,18] may achieve real-time performance, but only by using the enormous processing power of graphics cards. However, such hardware is usually not available on mobile platforms and therefore it is absolutely necessary that all calculations can be performed in real-time on a standard mobile CPU at video frame rate.

Another important problem based on traditional pairwise stereo methods is *motion-stereo*. In Fig. 1 we show an example of our automotive driver assistance application where the camera is mounted laterally on a vehicle. The disparity maps can be computed from consecutive image frames over time while the vehicle is moving. From these disparity maps, we build a model of the environment, in

A. Pinz et al. (Eds.): DAGM/OAGM 2012, LNCS 7476, pp. 468–477, 2012.
© Springer-Verlag Berlin Heidelberg 2012

(a)   (b)   (c)   (d)

Fig. 1. Real-time motion-stereo for automotive driver assistance. When the vehicle moves, depth is inferred via motion-stereo. (a) A camera on the side of the vehicle observes the lateral space. (b) One frame captured by the side camera. (c) Disparity map obtained by pairwise real-time stereo matching. (d) Result of our proposal.

order to mitigate collisions or to find lateral parking spaces. Even at higher velocities, the disparity maps obtained over time exhibit a large overlap and thus depth information is highly redundant. At the same time, due to the real-time stereo method used, disparities are very error prone. The question is how to fuse all those disparity maps to improve the accuracy of the disparity map defined by a reference image pair, for example, the last two images in case of motion-stereo.

In our paper we assume that a set of disparity maps is available and that they were computed using any available short baseline stereo technique. Then, given any other reference view pair, we propose a novel *stereo fusion* method to produce an accurate disparity map of the given reference view pair by fusing all available disparity maps. In our approach, we first project all disparity maps to the reference view pair. After maintaining visibility constraints, we estimate a probability density function over all valid disparities in the reference view using uncertainties of these reprojections. Finally, this allows us to select the most probable disparity map from this distribution.

We tested our method on the challenging datasets of Middlebury [14] and compared it to the fusion methods of [11] and [19]. The experiments show that our technique is very robust and that the quality is significantly improved, especially at object boundaries. We also show results on real-world sequences acquired from a camera attached to a vehicle. A very important fact is that our method allows real-time operation on CPU without dedicated hardware.

In the remainder of the paper we will first review related work, then present our method and finally show an exhaustive experimental evaluation.

1.1   Related Work

In recent years, traditional stereo and multi-view stereo methods have been extensively studied and tested using the available Middlebury datasets [15]. While resulting in a large amount of excellent results, little attention has been spent on computational performance. However, when that was the case and real-time stereo methods were proposed [6,17], the reconstruction quality was significantly decreasing. While multi-view stereo approaches introduce assumptions on shape priors and use robust photo-consistency measures, there are others which aim to produce consistent disparity maps [4,10,11,16,19,20]. In many cases disparity maps are produced locally using a number of overlapping views and are later fused into either a global disparity video [19] or a full 3D model [11,18]. Again, the vast majority of works aim at high quality reconstructions of single objects and only very few try to minimize the computational overhead.

Since the main motivation of our work comes from motion-stereo we tend to fuse locally overlapping disparity maps and do not aim to produce full 3D models. Works of Merrell et al. [11] and Zhang et al. [19], which explicitly deal with fusion of the disparity maps are thus directly related to our approach.

Merrell et al. [11] compute depth maps between neighboring views and fuse this information based on the *stability* of every depth. In order to keep track of occlusions, the stability is determined for every depth hypothesis and is defined by counting occlusions in the reference and other views. A valid depth is defined as the first depth hypothesis which is stable. However outliers affect the stability and such hard decisions may produce incorrect depth estimates. Further, the computational complexity grows quadratically with the number of disparity maps and in practice real-time operation is only possible with GPU hardware. In our paper, we overcome these problems. Our probabilistic approach employs reprojection uncertainties, handles outliers robustly and depth-accuracy gets improved compared to this approach.

Zhang et al. [19] impressively generalized the fusion problem by formulating it as an energy minimization problem. In their *bundle optimization* framework all disparity maps are optimized iteratively using belief propagation. In contrast to Merrell et al. [11] they do not model occlusions or visibility constraints explicitly. In their work these constraints are handled by the simultaneous use of *geometric coherence* and *color-similarity* as well as the regularization of belief propagation. The minimization of the energy functional is in practice very time consuming and thus, this method is not an option for mobile real-time applications.

Koch et al. [9] introduced the efficient *correspondence linking algorithm*: by *chaining* correspondences across many views outliers are rejected and accuracy is improved. However, no solution was provided for multiple disparity maps per view and disparities in occluded regions or outliers near the beginning of the chain are problematic. Zach [18] fuses multiple depth maps to obtain a full volumetric 3D reconstruction. It was formulated as a relatively efficient method using the GPU and produces very good results. However, the hardware requirements are too high and the volumetric representation is problematic for our application.

Compared to other fusion methods, our work focuses on both real-time performance and high quality depth maps. In our exhaustive experimentation we obtained better depth maps, especially in occluded and discontinuity areas.

2   Method

The major problem in motion and multi-view stereo are occlusions and discontinuities. Here we consider a reference view pair (RVP) in which we want to improve disparities, especially in occluded and discontinuity areas by bringing the information from other view pairs to the RVP. For this, we propose to compute a probability density function (pdf) estimating the probabilities of the disparities in the RVP. It is done by the reprojection of all available disparity maps to this RVP. This allows us to construct a global pdf which is sampled from a relatively large number of measurements coming from all disparity maps reprojected to the RVP.

2.1   Reprojection

Our goal is to compute an improved disparity map $\hat{\mathcal{D}} = \hat{\mathcal{D}}_{R_1,R_2}$ for a specific RVP $(\mathcal{I}_{R_1}, \mathcal{I}_{R_2})$. To do this we transfer the disparity maps from all input view pairs (e.g. $\mathcal{D}_{0,1}$, $\mathcal{D}_{2,3}$) to the RVP $(\mathcal{I}_{R_1}, \mathcal{I}_{R_2})$. A simple triangulation and projection is sufficient [19] to perform this transfer. Independent from the transfer method used, we refer to it using the transfer function $\Theta_k^{A,B} : (\mathbf{x}_A, d_{A,B}) \mapsto \mathbf{x}_k$, which transfers the point $\mathbf{x}_A$ using input disparity $d_{A,B} = \mathcal{D}_{A,B}(\mathbf{x}_A)$ into view $\mathcal{I}_k$. So, we use functions $\Theta_{R_1}^{A,B}$ and $\Theta_{R_2}^{A,B}$ to compute a *reprojected* disparity map $\tilde{\mathcal{D}}_{A,B}$ by applying the transfer to every disparity in $\mathcal{D}_{A,B}$: $\tilde{\mathcal{D}}_{A,B}(\mathbf{x}_{R_1}) = \Theta_{R_1}^{A,B}(x_A, \mathcal{D}_{A,B}(x_A)) - \Theta_{R_2}^{A,B}(x_A, \mathcal{D}_{A,B}(x_A)) = \mathbf{x}_{R_1} - \mathbf{x}_{R_2}$. In practice, all available disparity maps are transferred to the RVP and they are used to compute the pdf of the disparities in the RVP.

2.2   Visibility Model

There are in general zero, one or even multiple disparity estimates for every pixel of a reprojected disparity map depending on the occlusions and discontinuities in $\mathcal{D}_{A,B}$. In an ideal world, the case with only one disparity occurs when cameras of the reference and input views observe only non-occluded scene points. Multiple disparities occur due to depth discontinuities where several input disparities of different scene surfaces reproject to the same location in the reference view with different disparities. In these cases we pick the closest depth estimate (i.e. the occluding surface) to maintain correct visibility. Zero disparities occur mainly due to occlusions and thus, no disparity information is available.

The Reliable Area: We must ensure that every reprojected disparity comes from a surface observable in both, reference and input view pair. If that is not the case, it means that the point corresponding to this disparity is potentially occluded or not visible in the RVP. To check this we verify if a point on the surface defined by the maximum disparity is outside the frustum of $\mathcal{I}_A$ and $\mathcal{I}_B$. In practice, for every point $\mathbf{x}_{R_1} \in \mathcal{I}_{R_1}$ we compute $\mathbf{x}_k = \Theta_k^{R_1,R_2}(\mathbf{x}_{R_1}, d_{\max})$ and check if $\mathbf{x}_k \in \mathcal{I}_k$ for $k \in \{A, B\}$. If $\mathbf{x}_k \notin \mathcal{I}_k$, then the disparity at $\mathbf{x}_{R_1}$ is invalidated, meaning that either it is occluded in the RVP or it is not visible in the input views. Here, $d_{\max}$ is the maximum disparity of view pair $\mathcal{I}_{R_1}$ and $\mathcal{I}_{R_2}$.

2.3   Probability Density Function of Disparity

We reproject all input disparities to the RVP and use them as measurements to compute a probability density function of the disparities in the reference image.

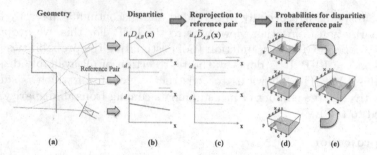

Fig. 2. The pdf estimation: (a) The 2D-geometry is observed from three different stereo cameras. (b) Disparity maps from input stereo pairs are determined. (c) The reprojected disparity maps to the reference view pair lead to (d) three pdfs for each reprojected disparity map which are finally (e) combined in one pdf.

Later, we draw from this pdf the most probable disparity at every pixel location of the reference view as illustrated in Fig. 2.

First we build the set S of reprojected disparity maps by reprojecting all N input disparity maps to the RVP. Now we use these disparity maps as measurements to sample the pdf of disparity d at every given pixel location $\mathbf{x}$ in the reference image. The unknown pdf p can be modeled as:

$$p(\mathbf{x}, d) = \sum_{\tilde{\mathbf{x}} \in \mathcal{I}_{R_1}} \sum_{\tilde{d} \in S(\tilde{\mathbf{x}})} p(\mathbf{x}, d \mid \tilde{\mathbf{x}}, \tilde{d})\, p(\tilde{\mathbf{x}})\, p(\tilde{d}) \tag{1}$$

where $p(\mathbf{x}, d|\tilde{\mathbf{x}}, \tilde{d})$ is the joint probability of disparity d at pixel location $\mathbf{x}$ given a measurement $\tilde{d} \in S(\mathbf{x})$ at measured location $\tilde{\mathbf{x}}$ of a reprojected disparity map in S. We assume that all the measurements of locations and disparities are equally probable. Therefore we consider them constant and write after marginalization:

$$p(\mathbf{x}, d) \sim \sum_{\tilde{\mathbf{x}} \in \mathcal{I}_{R_1}} \sum_{\tilde{d} \in S(\tilde{\mathbf{x}})} p(\mathbf{x}, d \mid \tilde{\mathbf{x}}, \tilde{d}) \tag{2}$$

The probability $p(d, \mathbf{x} \mid \tilde{\mathbf{x}}, \tilde{d})$ depends on the reprojection uncertainty defined by the probability $p_L(\mathbf{x}, d \mid \tilde{\mathbf{x}}, \tilde{d})$ that the scene point $\mathbf{X}(\tilde{\mathbf{x}}, \tilde{d})$ (computed from the uncertain correspondence $\mathbf{x}_A \leftrightarrow \mathbf{x}_B$ before reprojection) projects to the location $\mathbf{x}$ in the image $\mathcal{I}_{R_1}$. It further depends also on the probability $p_D(\mathbf{x}, d \mid \tilde{\mathbf{x}}, \tilde{d})$ that the disparity of $\mathbf{X}$ is d in the RVP. So we write it as:

$$p(\mathbf{x}, d \mid \tilde{\mathbf{x}}, \tilde{d}) = p_L(\mathbf{x}, d \mid \tilde{\mathbf{x}}, \tilde{d}) \cdot p_D(\mathbf{x}, d \mid \tilde{\mathbf{x}}, \tilde{d}) \tag{3}$$

These uncertainties are naturally coming from the input image pairs and can be directly estimated there. In the following, we use the transfer function Θ to relate the uncertainties to the RVP. The location uncertainty at pixel position $\mathbf{x}$ is measured by the discrepancy between the true location $\mathbf{x}_A = \Theta_A^{R_1, R_2}(\mathbf{x}, d)$ and the measured location $\tilde{\mathbf{x}}_A = \Theta_A^{R_1, R_2}(\tilde{\mathbf{x}}, \tilde{d})$ in the input image obtained by back-projections of the true $\mathbf{x}$ and measured $\tilde{\mathbf{x}}$ locations from the reference image. Thus, p_L has its maximum value when the true $\mathbf{x}_A$ and measured $\tilde{\mathbf{x}}_A$ back-projections coincide and it decreases with increasing distance. So we use:

$$p_L(\mathbf{x}, d | \tilde{\mathbf{x}}, \tilde{d}) \sim \exp\left(-\frac{1}{2\sigma_x^2} \left\| \Theta_A^{R_1, R_2}(\mathbf{x}, d) - \Theta_A^{R_1, R_2}(\tilde{\mathbf{x}}, \tilde{d}) \right\|_2^2\right) \qquad (4)$$

Similarly, p_D is maximal at $\tilde{d}$ and decreases for differing depths:

$$p_D(\mathbf{x}, d | \tilde{\mathbf{x}}, \tilde{d}) \sim \exp\left(-\frac{1}{2\sigma_d^2} \left\| (\Theta_B(\tilde{\mathbf{x}}, \tilde{d}) - \Theta_A(\tilde{\mathbf{x}}, \tilde{d})) - (\Theta_B(\mathbf{x}, d) - \Theta_A(\mathbf{x}, d)) \right\|_2^2\right)$$
$$(5)$$

where $\Theta_A = \Theta_A^{R_1, R_2}$, $\Theta_B = \Theta_B^{R_1, R_2}$ and σ_x is the location uncertainty defined by pixelwise sampling and σ_d is the accuracy of the disparity estimation. Note that $\tilde{\mathbf{x}}$ and $\tilde{d}$ are taken from the set of reprojected disparity maps. If the disparities d and $\tilde{d}$ are the same, the point defined by $(\mathbf{x}, d)$ will project to exactly the same input locations $\tilde{\mathbf{x}}_A$ and $\tilde{\mathbf{x}}_B$ and define the same disparity in the input view, which will result in the maximum value. Otherwise, points with different disparities or locations will back-project to locations away from the measurement $(\tilde{\mathbf{x}}, \tilde{d})$ and get lower values.

2.4 Disparity Estimation

Finally we estimate the most probable disparity map from the estimated pdf. From $p(\mathbf{x}, d) = p(d|\mathbf{x})p(\mathbf{x})$ and assuming that image positions $\mathbf{x}$ are equiprobable we get: $\hat{d} = \mathrm{argmax}_d\, p(d|\mathbf{x}) = \mathrm{argmax}_d\, p(\mathbf{x}, d)$.

3 Results

We evaluated our method using classical stereo datasets with ground truth [14] and real world data. In our experiments we used $\sigma_d = 1$ and $\sigma_x = 1$. The standard two-frame stereo datasets from Middlebury [14] contain up to 9 images from which we computed 72 (*Venus, Teddy, Cones*) or 42 (*Art, Moebius, Aloe*) disparity maps from all possible image combinations. After that, we fused these disparity maps to the standard reference view pair (e.g. (2, 6) for *Teddy*) and computed the percentage of erroneous pixels (disparities that differ by more than 1). For stereo processing we used Geodesic Support Weights [8] (GSW). We used constant parameters for stereo among all baselines and datasets.

3.1 Comparison to Other Fusion Methods

We compare our method to other fusion algorithms, in particular the stability-based algorithm of Merrell et al. [11] using our own implementation running on CPU and the bundle optimization of Zhang et al. [19] using their implementation (without their stereo-matching and without final bundle adjustment). We used

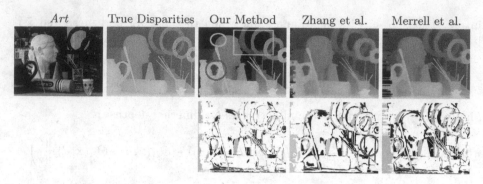

Fig. 3. The disparities and bad pixels of different fusion methods for the dataset *Art*.

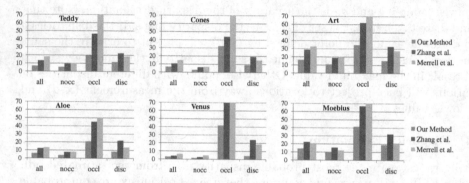

Fig. 4. The performance of different fusion methods. Disparity maps were computed using GSW [8]. Error bars show percentages of disparities that differ by more than 1 from the ground truth in the whole image (all), non-occluded (nocc) or occluded pixels (occl) and regions near discontinuities (disc). We fused up to 72 disparity maps.

the same input data (i.e. disparity maps) for all fusion methods. The method of [19] seems to be optimized for short baselines (the video sequences of [19] have much smaller baselines than the datasets of [14]). Our method works better with larger baselines, which is our target application. The error bars in Fig. 4 show that our method performs very well. It is also visible in Fig. 3 and Fig. 5 where our method preserved sharp object boundaries and thin structures.

Analysis: In Merrell, visibility-constraints are enforced using their expensive definition of stability (having a complexity of $\mathcal{O}(N^2)$ – please note that the computation of $\mathcal{S}$ is $\mathcal{O}(N)$ and that for every disparity of $\mathcal{S}$, $N-1$ projections are performed). However, visibility can be maintained more efficiently using our reprojection and the reliable area (having $\mathcal{O}(N)$, because at every entry of $\mathcal{S}$ we only update the global pdf by summation). This also has the big advantage that projection uncertainties can be used later, whereas in Merrell it is not possible. Moreover, for optimal stability calculation it is important that the number of outliers having a negative stability is equal to the number of outliers

Left Image   True Disparities   Our method   Zhang et al.   Merrell et al.

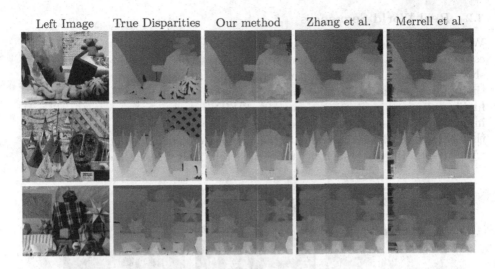

Fig. 5. The disparity maps of different fusion methods for the datasets *Teddy* (first row), *Cones* (second row) and *Meobius* (bottom row).

with positive stability. Our experiments suggest that this assumption is often violated in occluded regions, where usually many outliers are present.

In Zhang's method, the correct disparity is supported by the **simultaneous** combination of *geometric coherence* and *color similarity*. Geometric coherence alone supports also background disparities of surfaces occluded by foreground objects in the reference view, because visibility is not determined and this is problematic in cases where fore- and background objects are of similar color. The optimization using belief propagation ensures smoothness in these ambiguous situations, but seems to perform suboptimally in regions near discontinuities. Due to the results we obtained during our evaluation (our method does not use any kind of optimization), we believe that our pdf will also bring a huge advantage in comparison to the method of Zhang, especially near discontinuities and for wide-baseline sequences. We would like to stress that we explicitly compute visibility to disambiguate depth hypotheses at an early stage and model projection uncertainties.

Execution Times: For the dataset *Teddy* (72 disparity maps) our method took 8.7 s (not optimized), the method of [11] took 40.7 s and the method of [19] 175 minutes (i.e. 146 s/disparity map). These times do not include stereo matching and were measured on an Intel E8200 dual-core with 2.66 GHz (for our method and [11]) or an Intel E5405 quad-core Xeon CPU with 2.00 GHz (for [19]). For our real-time implementation, we use SIMD-instructions of the SSE2 instruction set and simplified the reprojection for motion-stereo. Using pre-computed kernels, we are able to fuse 16 disparity maps in just 30 ms on a mobile CPU (2 GHz; 320x240 pixels; 60 disparity levels).

3.2   Real World Sequences

We tested our method on real world sequences from a moving vehicle and we estimate the the transfer function from sensors attached to the vehicle. Fig. 6 shows a rectified camera frame, one input disparity map (computed using a real-time stereo method [17]) and one fused disparity map. For fusion we used a highly optimized implementation (using SIMD instructions) to fuse 16 adjacent input disparity maps. Due to the monocular camera system, it must be noted that objects which move parallel to the image plane might be determined with a wrong depth. However, such situations arise relatively seldom in our application.

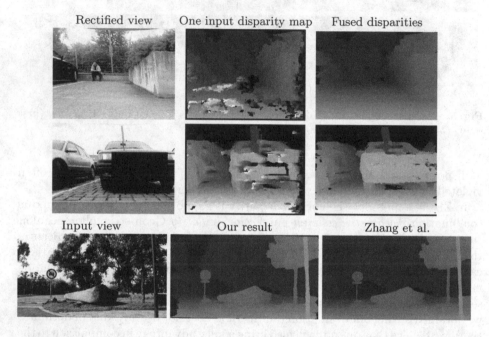

Fig. 6. First two rows: Our method applied to sequences from our vehicle using real-time stereo [17]. Last row: results for the sequence *Road* provided by [19].

Fig. 6 shows fused disparities of a sequence provided by [19], along with the camera frame and their fusion result. For stereo matching we used GSW [8] and ensured a minimal and maximal baseline of 5 and 7 frames (the baseline of adjacent frames was too small for robust matching with GSW). We fused disparity maps of only 20 adjacent frames and this explains why some disparities which are outside of the field of view are missing (black regions).

4   Conclusion

In this paper, we propose a novel probabilistic method for fusing disparity maps in classical stereo or motion-stereo setups. We achieve this by computing a probability density function from all provided disparity maps. From this distribution, we determine the most probable disparity map for a given reference view pair.

We introduced a generic probabilistic model that uses projection uncertainties for robustness against outliers and reprojection using the reliable area for efficient and explicit visibility determination.

Acknowledgements. We want to thank Guofeng Zhang for running his method on the datasets. This work is supported by the BMW Group.

References

1. Boykov, Y., Veksler, O., Zabih, R.: Fast approximate energy minimization via graph cuts. In: ICCV, pp. 377–384 (1999)
2. Collins, R.T.: A space-sweep approach to true multi-image matching. In: CVPR, p. 358 (1996)
3. Felzenszwalb, P.F., Huttenlocher, D.P.: Efficient belief propagation for early vision. IJCV 70(1), 41–54 (2006)
4. Gargallo, P., Sturm, P.: Bayesian 3D modeling from images using multiple depth maps. In: CVPR, pp. 885–891 (2005)
5. Hirschmüller, H.: Accurate and efficient stereo processing by semi-global matching and mutual information. In: CVPR, pp. 807–814 (2005)
6. Hirschmüller, H., Innocent, P.R., Garibaldi, J.: Real-time correlation-based stereo vision with reduced border errors. IJCV 47(1-3), 229–246 (2002)
7. Hirschmuüller, H.: Stereo vision in structured environments by consistent semi-global matching. In: CVPR, pp. 2386–2393 (2006)
8. Hosni, A., Bleyer, M., Gelautz, M., Rhemann, C.: Local stereo matching using geodesic support weights. In: ICIP (2009)
9. Koch, R., Pollefeys, M., Van Gool, L.: Multi Viewpoint Stereo from Uncalibrated Video Sequences. In: Burkhardt, H.-J., Neumann, B. (eds.) ECCV 1998. LNCS, vol. 1406, pp. 55–71. Springer, Heidelberg (1998)
10. Kolmogorov, V., Zabih, R.: Multi-camera Scene Reconstruction via Graph Cuts. In: Heyden, A., Sparr, G., Nielsen, M., Johansen, P. (eds.) ECCV 2002, Part III. LNCS, vol. 2352, pp. 82–96. Springer, Heidelberg (2002)
11. Merrell, P., Akbarzadeh, A., Wang, L., Frahm, J.M., Yang, R., Nistér, D.: Real-time visibility-based fusion of depth maps. In: ICCV, pp. 1–8 (2007)
12. Okutomi, M., Kanade, T.: A multiple-baseline stereo. PAMI 15(1), 353–363 (1993)
13. Sato, T., Kanbara, M., Yokoya, N., Takemura, H.: Dense 3-D reconstruction of an outdoor scene by hundreds-baseline stereo using a hand-held video camera. IJCV 47, 119–129 (2002)
14. Scharstein, D., Szeliski, R., Zabih, R.: A taxonomy and evaluation of dense two-frame stereo correspondence algorithms. IJCV 47, 7–42 (2002)
15. Seitz, S.M., Curless, B., Diebel, J., Scharstein, D., Szeliski, R.: A comparison and evaluation of multi-view stereo reconstruction algorithms. In: CVPR (2006)
16. Szeliski, R.: A multi-view approach to motion and stereo. In: CVPR, p. 1157 (1999)
17. Unger, C., Benhimane, S., Wahl, E., Navab, N.: Efficient disparity computation without maximum disparity for real-time stereo vision. In: BMVC (2009)
18. Zach, C.: Fast and high quality fusion of depth maps. In: 3DPVT (2008)
19. Zhang, G., Jia, J., Wong, T.T., Bao, H.: Consistent depth maps recovery from a video sequence. PAMI 31(6), 974–988 (2009)
20. Zitnick, L.C., Kang, S.B., Uyttendaele, M., Winder, S., Szeliski, R.: High-quality video view interpolation using a layered representation. In: SIGGRAPH (2004)

Confidence Measurements for Adaptive Bayes Decision Classifier Cascades and Their Application to US Speed Limit Detection

Armin Staudenmaier[1,2,3], Ulrich Klauck[1], Ulrich Kreßel[2], Frank Lindner[2], and Christian Wöhler[3]

[1] Hochschule Aalen, Beethovenstraße 1, 73430 Aalen, Germany
[2] Daimler AG, Group Research, P.O. Box 2360, 89013 Ulm, Germany
[3] Technische Universität Dortmund, Otto-Hahn-Str. 4, 44221 Dortmund, Germany

Abstract. This article presents an adaptive Bayes model for the decision logic of cascade classifier structures. The proposed method is fast and robust with respect to multimodal and overlapping distributions and can be applied to arbitrary stage classifiers with continuous outputs. The method consists of an adaptive computation of thresholds and probability density functions which outperform the threshold based decision. It furthermore guarantees high detection rates independent of the number of stage classifiers. Based on this Bayes model different confidence measures are proposed and evaluated statistically and used for merging detection windows. The algorithm is applied to the detection of US speed limit signs under typical driving conditions. Results show that on a single CPU with 3.3 GHz the proposed method yields single image detection rates of 97 % with 0.2 false positives per image running at 13 Hz, and for a different setup a detection rate of 93 % with 0.2 false positives per image performing with 43 Hz for scanning the whole image (752x480 pixels).

1 Introduction

Robust and fast object detection is applicable to a very large set of computer vision based applications. This paper presents a machine learning method for the detection of US speed limit signs. This is a challenging task since strong consistent features like circles or thick edges are missing, in contrast to circular signs. Even aspect ratios and digit types vary.

Most systems for US traffic sign recognition build on the work of Viola and Jones [12, 11] who use strong classifiers composed of weak classifiers boosted [14] in a classifier cascade with an implicit iterative method for setting thresholds. The performance of each stage classifier has influence on all subsequent stage classifiers and is therefore essential for a good overall performance. Most authors therefore try to reduce the number of stage classifiers. Overett et al. [10] argue that each stage likely reduces the detection rate and thus use only three to five stages. Rasolzadeh et al. [3] present a method for the computation of thresholds

A. Pinz et al. (Eds.): DAGM/OAGM 2012, LNCS 7476, pp. 478–487, 2012.
© Springer-Verlag Berlin Heidelberg 2012

and a histogram based method for a single stage classifier and the RealBoost Algorithm.

This paper focuses on the cascaded structure and presents a novel modular approach for an adaptive Bayesian Classifier Cascade. It is shown how the optimal decision values and thresholds of these stage classifiers can be computed with low effort independently of the number and type of stage classifiers while maintaining high detection rates with low false positive rates. Zaragoza et al. [4] present an overview of existing confidence measures with probability based confidences yielding remarkable performance. The proposal is therefore for three different methods of confidence measures based on the Bayesian approach for binary classification problems which can be extracted with little effort by fusion of the confidence values of each stage classifier. The best performing confidence measure is used for merging different detections into one by means of linear combination.

This paper is organized as follows. Section 2 explains the algorithm for the Bayes decision for cascaded classifier structures and propose a confidence measure depending on the stage classifiers. Different settings of the cascaded Bayes decision algorithm are evaluated with respect to their detection and run-time performances in Section 3.1. Additional confidence values are introduced and compared in Section 3.2.

2 Bayes Decision for Cascaded Classifier Structures

In principle, a cascade classifier is a series of ordered stage classifiers. According to [11] the decision function of a cascade classifier h_C containing $h_1, \ldots, h_T$ stage classifiers is as follows:

$$
h_C^T = (h_1, \ldots, h_T) = \begin{cases} \omega_0 & \text{if } h_j = \omega_0, \text{ for } 1 \leq j \leq T \\ \omega_1 & \text{else} \end{cases} \tag{1}
$$

where ω_1 is the class for objects and ω_0 is the background class. An object is detected only if it is accepted by each stage classifier. A stage classifier typically extracts specific features from the region to be detected and then applies a classification function to obtain a decision. Only samples which are not rejected are passed to the next stage, such that each stage classifier changes the prior probabilities of successive stages. Due to the structure of the discrete decision of the cascade the detection rates of each classifier are multiplicative and therefore adding more classifiers without adaptation of decision functions results in a degradation of the detection performance. By using a Bayesian approach, the prior probabilities of object and background classes can be tracked and the stage classifier detection rates are maintained for the cascade classifier. The prior probability for classes ω_i induced by a classifier h with output $o(x)$ and and its probability density function p is:

$$
P_h(\omega_i) = \frac{1}{|\Omega^i|} \int_{x \in \Omega^i \wedge h(x) = \omega_1} p(o(x)|\omega_i) \, do \tag{2}
$$

with $i \in \{0, 1\}$ and with the set Ω^1 for objects and Ω^0 for background. For each sample in Ω^i the output is accumulated in a frequency table over the output and then normalized and stored which allows estimating $p(o(x)|\omega_i)$ and calculating P_h with a sum. The rule for updating the prior probabilities $P_j(\omega_i)$ after the classification with stage classifier h_j is:

$$P_{j+1}(\omega_i) = P_{h_j}(\omega_i)P_j(\omega_i) \tag{3}$$

where $\Omega^1_j = \Omega^1$ and $\Omega^0_j = \{x \in \Omega^0 | h_C(x) = \omega_1\}$ are classified as objects in stage j, therefore the complexity factors for samples are increasing at each stage. The priors used in Eq. (3) correspond to the detection and false positive rates [5] which is shown in Fig. 1(a). A more accurate but also computationally more expensive way is to use Eq. (2) with the actual cascade h^j_C. Initial prior probabilities are set to one since optical transfer is identical for each sample. To prevent vanishing prior probabilities, $P(\omega_0) = \max(P(\omega_0), P_{min})$ with $P_{min} \simeq 10^{-9}$. The final Bayes decision function is then given by:

$$h_j(x) = \begin{cases} \omega_1 & \text{if } p_j(o(x)|\omega_1)P_j(\omega_1) - p_j(o(x)|\omega_0)P_j(\omega_0) \geq 0 \\ \omega_0 & \text{else} \end{cases} \tag{4}$$

where $o(x)$ is the output value and $p_j(o(x)|\omega_i)$ is obtained from the frequency table (see Eq. (2) above). Fig. 1(b) shows the feature extraction part followed

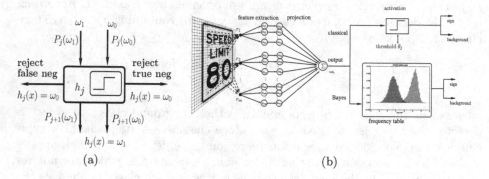

(a)   (b)

Fig. 1. 1(a): Change of prior probability induced by a stage classifier. 1(b): Extraction of features and decision for a stage classifier. The upper row shows the decision with a classical threshold perceptron while the lower row shows a frequency table used for the decision and tracking of probabilities.

by the decision part which is the classical threshold decision function in the upper row and the Bayes decision function modeled with a frequency table in the lower row as described above. The feature extraction scheme and feature types used are a combination of intensity based and structure tensor features in combination with linear perceptrons [13] as described in [1]. The weights of the perceptron are computed based on Fisher LDA [6, 8] in combination with a sequential forward selection of features [2] using the training set $\{\Omega_j^0, \Omega_j^1\}$ since no external parameters are involved and the training procedure requires about 50 ms on average. Besides, it can be shown that it is directly related to a minimum squared error procedure [7]. This training procedure is repeated for each new stage j and stage classifiers are added until the prior probability of a negative $P_{h_j}(\omega_0)$ approaches a value of 0.95. If this threshold is lowered, the training will stop earlier resulting in a higher overall false positive rate.

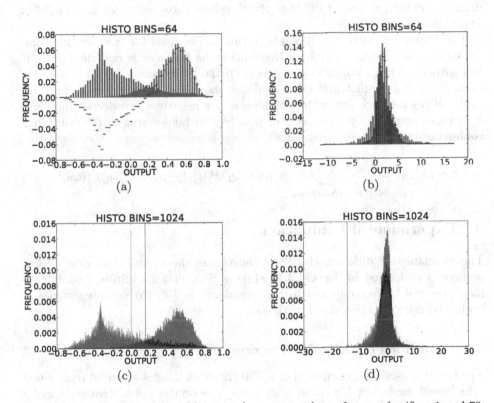

Fig. 2. First row: Frequency tables over the output values of stage classifiers 1 and 79 (see 2(a), 2(b)) out of $T = 211$ with 64 bins. The blue bars are the calculated decision values for a positive decision and black bars for a negative decision for each bin. Second row: Frequency tables over the output of classical threshold perceptron classifier 1 and 65 (see 2(c),2(d)) out of $T = 81$. The threshold is marked as a blue line. To enable more precise positioning, 1024 bins are used. Green bars correspond to output belonging to objects, red bars to output associated with background patches.

Fig. 2 shows frequency tables of stage classifiers. Green bars model the pdf of positives and red bars model the pdf of negatives. In the first row blue bars correspond to detected objects and black bars which are less than zero are rejections (see Fig. 2(a) and 2(b)). Due to the modified prior probabilities the black bars are close to zero in Fig. 2(b). The lower row shows the threshold decision method. The blue line marks the computed threshold and all values to the right of it are classified as objects. The two peaks in Fig. 2(a) and 2(c) near the output 0.0 are due to homogeneous patches (e.g. sky) which are mapped to zero. To determine the threshold, the frequencies are multiplied by their prior probabilities and the threshold is placed at the point of minimum error. Comparing Fig. 2(b) and 2(d), which correspond to stage classifiers 79 and 65, one can see the advantage of the histogram-based decision which contains three positive decision regions (two small additional regions near output 9.5 and 12.0) and four negative, yielding a lower FPR than the threshold classifier which has a FPR of approximately 99 %.

The Bayes approach described above can also be used for the effective computation of confidences. For high frequencies the classifier is confident since it has gathered a large number of evidences. If the frequencies of both classes are high, there is a conflict and the confidence should be low. By using the prior probabilities for each stage the confidences for negatives are decreasing since it is increasingly likely to encounter positives in higher stages, resulting in a confidence value:

$$\gamma_1(h_c^T, x) = \frac{1}{T} \sum_{j=1\,,\,h_j(x)=\omega_1}^{T} |p_j(o(x)|\omega_1)P_j(\omega_1) - p_j(o(x)|\omega_0)P_j(\omega_0)| \quad (5)$$

3   Experimental Evaluation

The evaluation of different classifiers concerning the overall detection performances is performed in Section 3.1, while in Section 3.2 additional confidence measures which are compared to the confidence in Eq. (5) are suggested and evaluated using two statistical methods.

3.1   Evaluation of Detection Performances

The training uses a set composed of 10000 grayscale images acquired from a test vehicle and displaying US speed limit signs. The images show strongly varying lighting conditions, the presence of cast shadows, as well as structures resulting from the Bayer pattern of the utilized camera. Some typical examples are shown in Fig. 3. The two-digit block with a small border and base widths ranging from 24 to 60 pixels are cut out and used for training, since the positioning of other attributes like the words "speed" or "limit" are variable and additional plate information is integrated into some signs. As training examples for the negative background class ω_0, the images containing signs are scanned and all windows ranging from 24 to 60 pixels which do not overlap any sign are collected, yielding set sizes of 10815 positives and 5×10^8 negatives. For the stage classifiers the complexity of negative training samples increases since there are two digit combinations, for example on road signs or billboards which can hardly be distinguished from the digits of a speed limit sign. Fig. 3 shows some typical examples

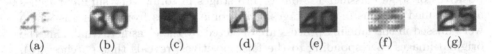

(a) (b) (c) (d) (e) (f) (g)

Fig. 3. Speed limit signs acquired under difficult illumination conditions. The two–digit block is used for the detector. The squared structure is induced by the Bayer pattern of the camera.

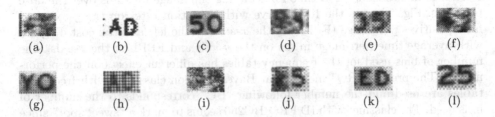

(a) (b) (c) (d) (e) (f)

(g) (h) (i) (j) (k) (l)

Fig. 4. Normalized false positives for stage classifier 113 out of 118. The patches 4(c), 4(e) and 4(l) originate from images with two signs (left and right) where one has been missed in the labeling process. The patch 4(k) represents the letters "E D" from "S P E E D".

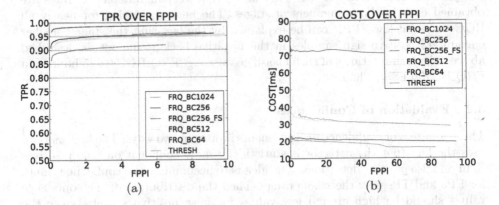

(a) (b)

Fig. 5. ROC curves with detection rates (TPR) on the y-axis and false positives per image (FPPI) on the x-axis. The cascades starting with FRQ contain frequency tables with different numbers of bins. The cascade with ID FRQ_BC256_FS e.g. contains 256 bins and uses a finer sampling method. The threshold perceptron cascade with ID THRESH terminates at 5 false positives per image.

displaying difficult illumination conditions whereas Fig. 4 shows normalized false positives of stage classifier 113 out of 118 stages in total. Very similar patches are classified as signs in high stages, even some patches from real signs which were missed in the labeling process are detected by the classifier. Analyzing the original images corresponding to the false positives, reveals that patches 4(c), 4(e) and 4(l) originate from images with two signs located at each side of the street where one has been missed in the labeling process.

Different classifiers with Bayes decision functions differing in their number of bins for the frequency tables have been trained. For evaluation, Receiver Operating Characteristics (ROC) curves are constructed by successively removing stage classifiers. We also determine the average computational burden of the detection in milliseconds CPU time for scanning the image for signs over the false positives. Fig. 5 shows the ROC curve with detection rates on the y-axis and false positives per image (FPPI) on the x-axis on the left and the cost diagram with average time per image in ms on the y-axis and FPPI on the x-axis. The number of bins used for the frequency tables has different effects on the performance. The prefix "FRQ" means that Bayes decision classifiers with frequency tables are used and the number following "BC" corresponds to the number of bins used. The classifier with ID FRQ_BC256 seems to mark a "sweet spot" since the system performs at 43 Hz and the single image detection rates yield 93 % and 0.2 FPPI scanning the whole image (752x480 pixels) on a single processor with 3.3 GHz. Using a finer sampling, detection rates of of 97 % and 0.2 FPPI are achieved running at 13 Hz (see FRQ_BC256_FS). The classical threshold classifier has high detection rates but training stopped at 5 FPPI since the error of the stage classifier was too high. The total number of classifiers used are: FRQ_BC1024=87, FRQ_BC512=159, FRQ_BC256=118, FRQ_BC256_FS=168, FRQ_BC64=211, THRESH=81. This shows that very high detection rates are obtained even for large numbers of stages. The bend appearing for nearly all ROC-curves at low FPPIs can be explained by the fact that the stage classifier encounters positive sign samples in the negative background set as described above. The training times of each classifier vary, e.g. FRQ_BC256=25 hours and FRQ_BC256_FS=29 hours.

3.2   Evaluation of Confidences

The evaluation of confidence measurements is done in two ways. The first method uses the fact that the detector is statistically more confident on true positives than on false positive detections. The idea is to accumulate the confidence values for FPs and TPs over the whole range. Then the distribution of the confidence values should be high around low values for false positive samples since the detection is not correct and it should be high for large values for true positive samples since the classifier should then be confident about its decision. To obtain the statistics, around 6000 FPs and about 6000 TPs are gathered from the detector, the confidences are accumulated and the resulting histogram is equalized. For comparison we introduce further confidence values:

$$\gamma_2(h_c^T, x) = \frac{1}{T} \sum_{j=1, h_j=\omega_1}^{T} \frac{|p_j(o(x)|\omega_1)P_j(\omega_1) - p_j(o(x)|\omega_0)P_j(\omega_0)|}{p_j(o(x)|\omega_1)P_j(\omega_1) + p_j(o(x)|\omega_0)P_j(\omega_0)} \tag{6}$$

$$\gamma_3(h_c^T, x) = \frac{1}{T} \sum_{j=1, h_j=\omega_1}^{T} |o(x) - \theta| \tag{7}$$

and their corresponding statistics are shown in Fig. 6. There it can be seen clearly that the decision-based confidence according to Eq. (5) outperforms those computed by a distance to the threshold (Eq. (7)) and the normalized version (Eq. (6)) since the overlap between the distributions is smaller. The second evaluation method is based on a statistically exact measurement of confidence values [9] which states that for K classifiers trained on disjoint data sets an exact confidence measure can be obtained by averaging the classifiers decisions. For training of the cascades 10 disjoint sets consisting of 1300 images each were used. To generate more diverse classifiers, four classifiers with different parame-

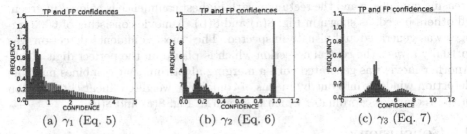

(a) γ_1 (Eq. 5)   (b) γ_2 (Eq. 6)   (c) γ_3 (Eq. 7)

Fig. 6. Accumulated confidence values for true positives (green bars) and false positives (red bars)

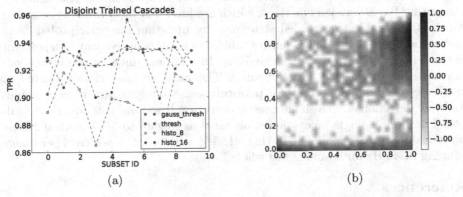

(a)   (b)

Fig. 7. 7(a): Detection rates of 40 classifiers trained on 10 disjoint training sets consisting of 1300 images each. Each point corresponds to a cascade classifier. The x-axis denotes the subsets. 7(b): Statistical confidence values on the x-axis vs. the proposed confidence measure according to (Eq. 5) on the y-axis using a logarithmic scale.

  (a)   (b)   (c)   (d)

Fig. 8. Visualization of confidence values. 8(a) and 8(b): Detections are visualized as rectangles and their confidences are shown as vertical bars, sorted by decreasing order. The most confident rectangle is colored green, all others are colored red. 8(c) and 8(d): Merged windows obtained by linear combinations of confidence values.

ters were trained per set. Then for a set of 6000 test signs the confidence values obtained by averaging the 40 classifier decisions for each classification were compared to the confidence γ_1 from Eq. (5) generated by the single cascade with ID FRQ_BC256_FS from Fig. 5 with a logarithmic plot shown in Fig. 7(b). The result shows that one cluster appears for positive and negative decisions, respectively. Fig. 7(a) shows the detection performance of each single cascade trained with the corresponding subset. The last evaluation is a visual inspection of the confidence values of detected signs. Each detection of a sign is visualized as a rectangle and its confidence value as a vertical bar. The bars are sorted by decreasing confidence and the rectangle with highest confidence is colored in green, all others in red, as shown in Fig. 8(a) and 8(b). A movie consisting of 6000 images was generated and visually inspected. The "most confident" detection was virtually always the central detection which is placed on the perfect digit block. Another movie was generated with a merging algorithm that combines multiple detection windows into one by means of confidence weighted linear combination of the rectangles coordinates which is shown in Fig. 8(c) and 8(d).

4   Conclusion

This article presents a modular approach for an adaptive Bayesian classifier cascade which was used in the real world detection of US speed limits. A method for computing Bayes decision functions, which are known to be optimal, is proposed which is applicable to cascaded structures by updating the prior probabilities and modeling the probability density functions in an adaptive way independent of the number and type of stage classifiers. In addition, different confidence values have been suggested and compared. The measure most closely related to the Bayes decision, yields the best performance. A merging algorithm combines multiple detections into a single precise detection based on their confidence values. The overall single image detection rates aggregate to 97 % with 0.2 false positives per image running at 13 Hz and 93 % with 0.2 false positives per image running at 43 Hz for scanning the whole image.

References

1. Staudenmaier, A., Klauck, U., Lindner, F., Kreßel, U., Wöhler, C.: Resource Optimized Cascaded Perceptron Classifiers using Structure Tensor Features for US Speed Limit Detection. In: 8th International Workshop on Intelligent Transportation, WIT 2011 (2011)

2. Whitney, A.W.: A direct method of nonparametric measurement selection. IEEE Trans. Computers 20, 1100–1103 (1971)
3. Rasolzadeh, B., Petersson, L., Pettersson, N.: Response Binning: Improved Weak Classifiers for Boosting. In: Intelligent Vehicles Symposium, IEEE IV, pp. 344–349 (2006)
4. Zaragoza, H., d'Alché-Buc, F.: Confidence Measures for Neural Network Classifiers. In: Proceedings of the Seventh Int. Conf. Information Processing and Management of Uncertainty in Knowlegde Based Systems (1998)
5. Toth, N., Pataki, B.: On Classification Confidence and Ranking Using Decision Trees. In: Intelligent Engineering Systems, INES 2007, pp. 133–138 (June-July 2007)
6. Fisher, R.A.: The Statistical Utilization of Multiple Measurements. Annals of Eugenics 8, 376–386 (1938)
7. Duda, R.O., Hart, P.E., Stork, D.G.: Pattern Classification, 2nd edn. Wiley-Interscience (2001)
8. Alessandro, S.-J.K., Magnani, A., Boyd, S.P.: Robust Fisher Discriminant Analysis. In: Advances in Neural Information Processing Systems, pp. 659–666 (2006)
9. Cui, T., Grumpe, A., Hillebrand, M., Kreßel, U., Kummert, F., Wöhler, C.: Analytically tractable sample-specific confidence measures for semi-supervised learning. In: Proc. Workshop Computational Intelligence, pp. 171–186 (2011)
10. Overett, G., Petersson, L.: Large Scale Sign Detection using HOG Feature Variants. In: Intelligent Vehicles Symposium, IEEE IV, Baden-Baden, Germany, pp. 1–6 (June 2011)
11. Viola, P., Jones, M.: Rapid object detection using a boosted cascade of simple features. In: Proceedings of the 2001 IEEE Computer Society Conference on Computer Vision and Pattern Recognition, CVPR 2001, vol. 1(C), pp. I 511 I–518 (2001)
12. Viola, P., Jones, M.: Robust Real Time Object Detection. In: IEEE ICCV Workshop Statistical and Computational Theories of Vision, vol. 57(2), pp. 137–154 (July 2001)
13. Rosenblatt, F.: The Perceptron: A Probabilistic Model for Information Storage and Organization in the Brain. Psychological Review 65(6), 386–408 (1958)
14. Freund, Y., Schapire, R.E.: A Decision-Theoretic Generalization of On-Line Learning and an Application to Boosting. In: Vitányi, P. (ed.) EuroCOLT 1995. LNCS, vol. 904, pp. 23–37. Springer, Heidelberg (1995)

A Bottom-Up Approach for Learning Visual Object Detection Models from Unreliable Sources

Fabian Nasse and Gernot A. Fink

TU Dortmund, Department of Computer Science, Dortmund, Germany
{fabian.nasse,gernot.fink}@udo.edu

Abstract. The ability to learn models of computational vision from sample data has significantly advanced the field. Obtaining suitable training image sets, however, remains a challenging problem. In this paper we propose a bottom-up approach for learning object detection models from weakly annotated samples, i.e., only category labels are given per image. By combining visual saliency and distinctiveness of local image features regions of interest are extracted in a completely automatic way without requiring detailed annotations. Using a bag-of-features representation of these regions, object recognition models can be trained for the given object categories. As weakly labeled sample images can easily be obtained from image search engines, our approach does not require any manual annotation effort. Experiments on data from the Visual Object Classes Challenge 2011 show that promising object detection results can be achieved by our proposed method.

1 Introduction

Most successful approaches in the field of computer vision today apply machine learning techniques for acquiring the relevant information about the task considered. Consequently, the methods do not require explicit encoding of expert knowledge but their parameters can rather automatically be estimated from annotated sample images. For example, in object recognition the characteristic visual properties of objects are automatically extracted from sample images that show examples of the object categories to be recognized. Though being able to learn from examples is the major advantage of machine learning approaches, it is at the same time their most severe limitation. The acquisition of a substantial amount of annotated image data requires considerable effort by human annotators for the detailed labeling of example images – for the purpose of object recognition wrt. the category and position of the objects within the images.

Crowd sourcing can offer a way to alleviate the labeling problem as shown by Russel and colleagues in the *LabelMe* project [14]. The approach there is to share annotated images via the Internet. The access to the database is free and everyone is asked to contribute annotations. Another possibility for acquiring annotated image data pioneered by Fergus *et al.* [7] is to make use of web-based

A. Pinz et al. (Eds.): DAGM/OAGM 2012, LNCS 7476, pp. 488–497, 2012.
© Springer-Verlag Berlin Heidelberg 2012

image search engines. However, as image search engines automatically retrieve labels for images from the hyper-textual context these are embedded in, such label information will necessarily be unreliable. Furthermore, such an approach is unable to obtain any further more detailed annotation information, such as the localization of an object within an image, as the automatically derived labels apply to images as a whole.

In this paper we propose an approach which builds on the idea of sample acquisition by using image-search engines and extends it with a completely automatic bottom-up procedure for localizing objects within the images they are tentatively shown on. Thus detectors for different object categories can be trained without any manual annotation effort. The unreliable category labels are obtained via Google Image Search. Subsequently, candidate regions of interest (ROI) are extracted from the retrieved images combining two different bottom-up cues, namely visual saliency and the presence of distinctive local features. For the interesting ROIs determined such a bag-of-features type representation is computed combining local feature statistics and global information from color histograms. This representation is then used to train random forest classifiers. When applying the same process to an unknown image, objects can be detected by classifying the ROIs identified within the image.

As our proposed method uses only unreliable high-level annotations we refer to this type of learning approach as *weakly supervised*. In contrast to traditional supervised learning of object detectors our approach does not require the specification of the localization of objects within images, e.g., by specifying appropriate bounding boxes. The approach is also different from semi-supervised learning as for all samples used in training the same type of unreliable high-level annotations are available. Furthermore, in contrast to related work on web-based object learning as detailed in the next section, our approach produces *explicit* localization and segmentation hypotheses in a bottom-up process and does not *implicitly* infer the localization of objects from a top-down object recognition model.

2   Related Work

Our method is related to techniques of visual attention for which one of the most widely used computational models was proposed in [8]. We build on the assumption that there is a strong link between salient and interesting image content [4]. A method to find salient objects in images was proposed in [11]. The authors used spatial color distribution analysis and center-surround histograms for defining a model of visual saliency. The basic difference to our approach is that they expect a large object centrally located within the image. We propose a more general approach which is also capable of finding multiple objects in more complex scenes which is useful, e.g., for scene recognition.

The idea of using web-based image search engines for acquiring large weakly labeled image collections from the Internet was first proposed in [7] for training object recognition models. Since then this idea has been used for approaching other data intensive computational vision problems, e.g., for the learning of color information [16] or for large-scale scene recognition [15].

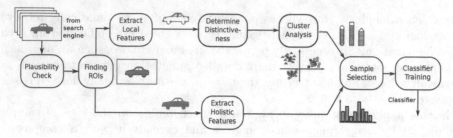

Fig. 1. Architectural overview of our approach

When trying to use weakly labeled images acquired from the web for object learning the problem of localizing object information within the training images has to be addressed. In [7] the localization is implicitly obtained from bag-of-features models for the object categories considered. Therefore, this can be considered a top-down approach for deriving the localization information as a task model is required. The approaches in [3,6] employ more complex object models for recognition that are also trained in a weakly supervised manner. The process for obtaining the localization of objects in images remains the same, however, as it is implicitly given by the final recognition result. A model for explicitly detecting ROIs for interesting objects from a large unannotated image set, which was also crawled from the web, was proposed in [10]. Though the method does not require any label information to be available, it implicitly assumes that a small set of relevant objects are dominantly shown in most of the images within the collection considered.

3   Bottom-Up Learning of Object Detectors

This section gives an overview of our proposed method for learning object de-tection models from weakly annotated data. The overall process is illustrated in Figure 1. Our method explicitly locates and segments objects. We start by searching for interesting regions inside the images that we obtained from an im-age search query. Our approach is based on the idea of salience detection. The assumption is that image regions that can be clearly distinguished from their vicinity are most likely relevant [4]. We locate interesting regions by means of local feature detection, namely SIFT features [13], and a region based saliency approach [2] in combination with active contour segmentation [9]. After some interesting regions were detected we extract feature descriptors from them. For our method we rely on both, local features as well as holistic features. For the former we extract SIFT features, for the latter we use color histograms that are computed over the whole region. The idea is that the right features must be found in the right area in order to identify an object. We extract one holistic feature for each detected region and an unspecified number of local features. The number depends on how many feature points are found within the region. Due to the uncertain source of our images and the lack of annotation data we expect a considerable amount of noise within the feature set. What we do next is to search for the local features that are suitable to describe the object class. Our approach is to search for features that are repetitive among the interesting regions but uncommon among arbitrary images. We assume that some types of features are more common among natural images than others. Hence, we delete local features that are too common. This is done by comparing each feature to a large set of features extracted from arbitrary images. Next, we perform a cluster analysis on the remaining features. We delete features that are too far away from any of the detected clusters. If a region loses all local features in this selection process the entire region will be deleted. The result is a set of local key features with corresponding holistic features that can be used for classifier training. For this, we rely on the Random Forest classifier [1].

The actual object detection works along the lines of the learning process. We search for interesting regions and extract the features in the same way. The features are then analyzed by the classifier to decide whether the region shows the object in question or not.

4   Creating Image Sets

Our aim is to collect images of a specific topic from the Internet that can be used for classifier training. Several web services that link textual information with image content come into consideration. In this paper we concentrate on web search engines like Google and Microsoft Bing. Although those services are not highly reliable, they fulfill our requirements. We take into account that some of the images might not be related to the search query. Our focus is on object detection, thus for our experiments we select search words that clearly describe a certain type of object such as 'house', 'tree' or 'cat'. In some cases additional words prevent ambiguities. For example, the use of the word 'fruit' in combination with 'apple' avoids confusion with the company of the same name. By means of empirical rules the search engine will deliver the images in descending order with respect to their significance. Therefore, we limit the number of images that we add to the image set. Furthermore, we apply a plausibility check. We measure the entropy and determine distribution of colors to sort out images with poor information content.

5   Locating the Interesting Regions

Now, that we have collected our image set as described in the previous section, we are next searching for the relevant regions inside the images. The way we do this is straight forward and illustrated in figure 2. We are looking for salient parts that include local features. We determine a saliency map by using the region based saliency approach proposed in [2]. The map is determined by means of global contrast differences and spatial coherence (fig. 2 (2)). Next, we detect appropriate feature points. For this task we use the well known and widely recognized SIFT method [13]. Afterwards, the located feature points are bundled to groups. We start at a random feature point and look for other neighboring

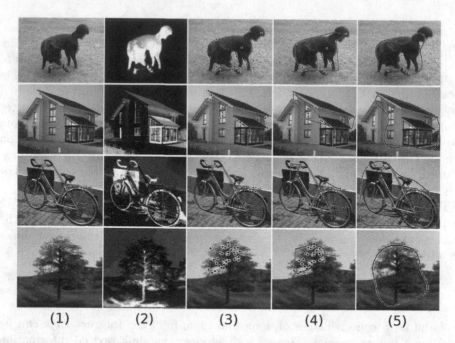

(1)   (2)   (3)   (4)   (5)

Fig. 2. Detection of interesting regions: (1) Original images. (2) Saliency maps determined by means of global contrast differences and spatial coherence (3) Detection of SIFT features. (4) Coarse outlines by connecting outermost features. (5) Results for the active contour approach.

points that are within a certain maximum distance. The process is recursively repeated for all feature points. As result we have several groups of connected feature groups. Next, we determine the outlines of each group. A coarse solution is determined by traversing clockwise around the outermost features (fig. 2 (4)). The solution is then refined using the saliency map combined with an active contour approach [9]. Saliency is used to define gradient forces that will move the initial contour. Additional parameters, e.g. the elasticity, define how the contour reacts to the forces. The contour will be stretched and bent until it converges to the boundaries of the object (fig. 2 (5)). If regions overlap, they will be merged to one region. For our method it is important that the contour covers a larger part of the object to describe the wider vicinity around the local features. Finding the object boundaries is not necessary but a nice plus. However, we give the contour the tendency to grow when parts of the contour don't converge. This way we avoid that the resulting region becomes too small. Furthermore, we give the contour some stiffness so that it will keep a relative simple form. This is done, because we assume that due to physical and practical reasons most man-made as well as natural objects have a more or less compact shape from a distant view.

6   Processing the Interesting Regions

So far we have extracted interesting regions from a set of images and for each region we obtained a set of feature points. Now we continue by analyzing the SIFT-descriptors for all the feature points. Obviously, many of the detected features are not suitable to describe the desired object class. In fact, any region could have a content that is totally unrelated to the topic. But even if a feature belongs to the right object doesn't mean that it is distinctive and characteristical. To decide whether a feature is suitable for describing the considered object class we check for the following two conditions: (1) The feature must be repetitive among object instances. (2) The feature mustn't be repetitive among other image content. First, we concentrate on the second condition. In general we assume that some feature types are more common among natural images than others. We want to sort out common features and keep the distinctive ones. We use the absolute distance measure as indicator to rate the resemblance of two feature descriptors. In order to determine the distinctiveness of a feature we use a statistical approach. For a set of 0.5 million random features taken from around 10,000 arbitrary images, we compute all pairwise absolute distances and build a distance distribution from that. Not surprisingly, it turns out that the distances follow a normal distribution as figure 3 shows.

P_5 and P_{95} are the 5th and 95th percentile for all pairwise distances. That means 5% of the pairwise distances are less than P_5 and 95% are less than P_{95}. The distinctiveness D of a feature f is then estimated by

$$D(f) = \frac{1}{N} \sum_{n=1}^{N} d(|f - f_n|). \tag{1}$$

where N is the number of random features, f_n is the n-th random feature and d is defined as

$$d(a) = \begin{cases} 1, & a > P_{95} \\ -1, a < P_5 \\ 0, & \text{otherwise} \end{cases} . \tag{2}$$

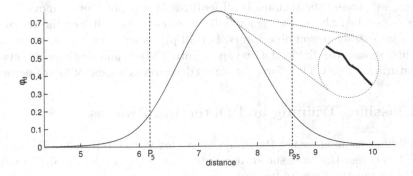

Fig. 3. Distribution of pairwise absolute distances

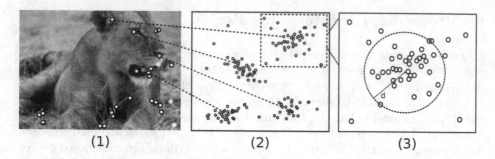

(1)   (2)   (3)

Fig. 4. Cluster analysis. (1) Sample with repetitive features. (2) Clusters in feature space. (3) Selection of features within distance d.

This gives a value between -1 and 1 where a big value means that the feature is highly distinctive. We keep only a small fraction (e.g. 20%) of the most distinctive features.

Next, we have to check whether the remaining features are also characteristical for the considered object class. As illustrated in figure 4, we perform a cluster analysis to find repetitive features and pool them to feature classes. We want our detector to learn only a small number of feature classes, so we search for a small number of center points (e.g. 4). We found that the simple k-means approach is sufficient to obtain the desired results. The next important step is to remove the clutter features that are too distant from any center point. We don't use a hard threshold but optimize a function to balance the number of features that are kept for classifier training,

$$\arg\max_{d_i} \frac{\alpha N(d_i)}{d_i^2}, \tag{3}$$

where α is a constant and $N(d_i)$ is the Number of features that lie within the distance d_i to the center point. In this way, we remove features that are too far away from the center, but we also make sure that a sufficient number of features remain for training.

Next, we process the regions. If all features of a region were removed in the process described above, the region will be removed as well. For the remaining regions we extract region descriptors. For all pixels within a region we create a color histogram. We divide the hue space into 32 bins and distinguish between four saturation levels. Therefore, the region descriptors consist of 128 dimensions.

7   Classifier Training and Detection Process

For classifier training we use Random Forest classifiers [1]. Random Forest is an efficient classifier that was shown to produce accurate results on SIFT features [12]. For our method we use two independently trained classifiers, one to classify feature descriptors and one to classify region descriptors. The detection process

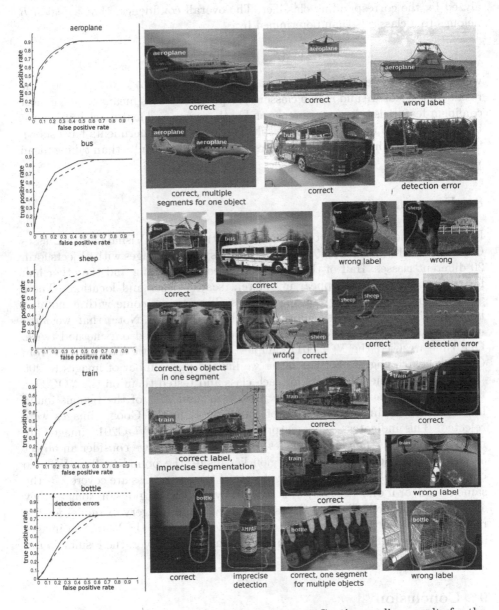

Fig. 5. Exemplary results for the VOC2011 image set. Continuous line: results for the detector trained with the VOC2011 training images. Dashed line: results using images from the search engine.

starts by identifying the interesting regions as described in section 5. For each region the feature descriptors and the region descriptor are extracted and analyzed by the corresponding classifier. The overall confidence, that a region R belongs to a class c is than determined by

$$\min\{\max\{p_{f,c}|\forall f \in F_R\}, p_{R,c}\}, \tag{4}$$

where F_R is the set of features that lie inside R and $p_{f,c}$ and $p_{R,c}$ are the results of the feature and region classifier, respectively. This means that the most confident feature is taken as reference and both, region and feature classifier must be positive for an overall positive result. Our practical experiments have shown that taking the min- and max-operators produce better results than taking mean values instead.

8   Experiments

In order to validate our method, we used the data set of the Visual Object Classes Challenge 2011 (VOC2011) [5]. The set contains 11, 540 images with objects form 20 different classes. Half of the images are used for training and the other half for testing. The objects appear in different scales, poses and locations. There are also images that show multiple objects. The images come with annotated bounding boxes and coarse information about the pose. Note, that we *don't* use those annotations for our learning process. We applied our method twice. One time we used the VOC2011 samples and one time we used images from Google's search engine. For the latter we limited the number of images to 400 per class. We trained detectors for each class and tested them on the VOC2011 test images. In the feature selection process around 15% of the regions found in the VOC2011 images and 20% of those found in the Google images were rejected. This indicates — not surprisingly — that the VOC2011 images are more reliable than the Google images. For the evaluation we consider an object as located, if at least half of the region lies inside the bounding box. We also count as correct, if multiple close-by objects of the same class are covered by the same region, or if one large object is covered by multiple regions, as long as they are correctly labeled. Figure 5 shows ROC curves and imagery examples for the results for some of the classes. In most cases the results for the VOC2011 images are slightly better than those for the Google images. However, the results do not differ significantly.

9   Conclusion

We proposed an automatic bottom-up process for object detection that performs explicit localization and learns fully automated without using manually annotated image data. Experiments with the VOC2011 dataset showed good results for localization and recognition. Also multiple objects in the same image could be successfully located in many cases. One aspect of this paper was the use of unreliable sources, namely image search engines. Experiments with images obtained from Google's search engine have shown results almost as well as those with the VOC2011 training images. Therefore, the use of an image search engine can be seen as an useful alternative to explicitly collected datasets.

References

1. Breiman, L.: Random forests. Machine Learning, 5–32 (2001)
2. Cheng, M.M., Zhang, G.X., Mitra, N.J., Huang, X., Hu, S.M.: Global contrast based salient region detection. In: IEEE CVPR, pp. 409–416 (2011)
3. Crandall, D.J., Huttenlocher, D.P.: Weakly Supervised Learning of Part-Based Spatial Models for Visual Object Recognition. In: Leonardis, A., Bischof, H., Pinz, A. (eds.) ECCV 2006, Part I. LNCS, vol. 3951, pp. 16–29. Springer, Heidelberg (2006)
4. Elazary, L., Itti, L.: Interesting objects are visually salient. Journal of Vision 8(3), 1–15 (2008)
5. Everingham, M., Van Gool, L., Williams, C.K.I., Winn, J., Zisserman, A.: The PASCAL Visual Object Classes Challenge 2011 (VOC 2011) Results (2011), http://www.pascal-network.org/challenges/VOC/voc2011/workshop/index.html
6. Fergus, R., Perona, P., Zisserman, A.: Weakly supervised scale-invariant learning of models for visual recognition. Int. J. Comput. Vision 71(3), 273–303 (2007)
7. Fergus, R., Li, F.F., Perona, P., Zisserman, A.: Learning object categories from Google's image search. In: Proc. Int. Conf. Computer Vision (2005)
8. Itti, L., Koch, C., Niebur, E.: A model of saliency-based visual attention for rapid scene analysis. IEEE Transactions on Pattern Analysis and Machine Intelligence 20(11), 1254–1259 (1998)
9. Kass, M., Witkin, A., Terzopoulos, D.: Snakes: Active contour models. International Journal of Computer Vision 1(4), 321–331 (1988)
10. Kim, G., Torralba, A.: Unsupervised detection of regions of interest using iterative link analysis. In: Annual Conference on Neural Information Processing Systems, NIPS 2009, Vancouver, Canada (2009)
11. Liu, T., Yuan, Z., Sun, J., Wang, J., Zheng, N., Tang, X., Shum, H.Y.: Learning to detect a salient object. IEEE Trans. on Pattern Analysis and Machine Intelligence 33(2), 353–367 (2011)
12. Liu, Z., Xiong, H.: Object detection and localization using random forest. In: International Conference on Intelligent System Design and Engineering Application, pp. 1074–1078 (2012)
13. Lowe, D.G.: Distinctive image features from scale-invariant keypoints. Int. J. Comput. Vision 60(2), 91–110 (2004)
14. Russell, B., Torralba, A., Murphy, K., Freeman, W.: Labelme: A database and web-based tool for image annotation. International Journal of Computer Vision 77, 157–173 (2008)
15. Torralba, A., Fergus, R., Freeman, W.T.: 80 million tiny images: A large data set for nonparametric object and scene recognition. IEEE Trans. on Pattern Analysis and Machine Intelligence 30(11), 1958–1970 (2008)
16. van de Weijer, J., Schmid, C., Verbeek, J.: Learning color names from real-world images. In: Proc. IEEE Comp. Soc. Conf. on Computer Vision and Pattern Recognition, Los Alamitos, CA, USA, pp. 1–8 (2007)

Active Learning of Ensemble Classifiers
for Gesture Recognition

J. Schumacher[1], D. Sakič[1], A. Grumpe[2], Gernot A. Fink[1],
and Christian Wöhler[2]

[1] Lehrstuhl Informatik XII, Technische Universität Dortmund, Germany
[2] Image Analysis Group, Technische Universität Dortmund, Germany

Abstract. In this study we consider the classification of emblematic gestures based on ensemble methods. In contrast to HMM-based approaches processing a gesture as a whole, we classify trajectory segments comprising a fixed number of sampling points. We propose a multi-view approach in order to increase the diversity of the classifiers across the ensemble by applying different methods for data normalisation and dimensionality reduction and by employing different classifier types. A genetic search algorithm is used to select the most successful ensemble configurations from the large variety of possible combinations. In addition to supervised learning, we make use of both labelled and unlabelled data in an active learning framework in order to reduce the effort required for manual labelling. In the supervised learning scenario, recognition rates per moment in time of more than 86% are obtained, which is comparable to the recognition rates obtained by a HMM approach for complete gestures. The active learning scenario yields recognition rates in excess of 80% even when only a fraction of 20% of all training samples are used.

1 Introduction

It is undisputed that gestures constitute an important modality in human-human and human-machine interaction. Therefore, a multitude of approaches for recognising different types of gestural expressions – ranging from hand-arm gestures to full-body motion – have been proposed in the literature [11].

In this study we focus on the aspect of mapping the motion parameters of the relevant body parts (e.g. the gesturing hand or the upper body including head and arms) to a gesture or action category, assuming that body motion has already been captured successfully and has been converted to a stream of 3D trajectory data. In contrast to related approaches, we make use of classifier ensembles for recognition as these are known to usually improve recognition performance in a wide range of pattern recognition tasks [8]. Additionally, we rely on both labelled and unlabelled data in an active learning framework for classifier training in order to reduce the manual labelling effort.

In order to be able to use a sufficiently diverse set of classifier types we decided not to consider gesture recognition as a problem of recognising variable length trajectories, which is usually solved by applying hidden Markov models (HMMs)

A. Pinz et al. (Eds.): DAGM/OAGM 2012, LNCS 7476, pp. 498–507, 2012.
© Springer-Verlag Berlin Heidelberg 2012

[11] or dynamic Bayesian networks [20]. Rather, we address the problem by classifiying trajectory segments comprising a fixed number of sampling points.

For both active learning and for building powerful classifier ensembles, considering different views on the data or the classification problem is highly beneficial. Considering the issue of diversity on two levels of abstraction, we first create different feature representations of the trajectory data obtained by applying different subspace transforms. Second, different classifier types are used for constructing heterogeneous ensemble classifiers, as the diversity of homogeneous classifier ensembles usually comes at the cost of a large number of base classifiers, which in turn requires that many different views on the data can be obtained by sampling in feature or sample space [10]. In combination, by considering different feature representations, different classifier types, and different parameterisations of the two, a considerable variety of classification approaches is available for combination within an ensemble. Eventually, the most promising configurations are selected by applying a genetic search algorithm.

2   Related Work

The field of gesture recognition in general deals with the problem of recognising meaningful expressions conveyed by human motion [11]. Many approaches focus on either the recognition of hand-arm gestures or on the interpretation of full-body motion, usually referred to as "action recognition" [14]. The recognition of hand-arm gestures, which is mostly considered for artificially crafted gesture alphabets such as sign languages [12], involves first the capturing of the dynamic movement of the relevant body parts and second the analysis of the resulting temporal trajectories. Capturing dynamic motion of human body parts constitutes a challenging computer vision problem (cf. e.g. [15]), which may be simplified using visual markers or depth cameras [19].

For analysing time-series data in general and such obtained from human gestural expressions in particular, HMMs are most widely used today [11]. Other common approaches include dynamic Bayesian networks [20] and conditional random fields [22]. Interestingly, to the authors' best knowledge the problem of dynamic gesture recognition has not been addressed yet using learning approaches based on ensemble classifiers.

The combination of multiple base classifiers within a classifier ensemble has been shown to improve classification performance for a wide range of pattern recognition problems [8,16]. In order to build a successful classifier ensemble, a set of base classifiers has to be created that is as diverse as possible while achieving satisfactory individual performances. Then the decisions of the base classifiers have to be combined into a final classification decision of the ensemble.

Classical ensemble creation techniques like bagging and boosting combine base classifiers of the same type but with different parameterisations by using different subsets or differently weighted versions of the training data for parameter estimation [10]. Random subspace sampling applies a similar strategy to the original feature space by randomly selecting different feature subsets [6]. The quite popular random-forest technique combines dataset sampling known from bagging with the use of decision trees as base classifiers [2].

In order to obtain the final decision of a classifier ensemble from the individual classifier outputs, a variety of techniques can be applied [24], such as majority voting or boosting, where classifier outputs are usually combined as a weighted average. The most general combination method is generalised stacking, where the problem of combining classifier outputs is considered as another classification problem [23].

As fully supervised learning of gestures requires a large amount of labelled training data, it is favourable to reduce the labelling effort by employing active learning techniques. In the concept of active learning it is assumed that the classifier is trained initially based on a relatively small amount of labelled training data. It then selects from a large set of unlabelled data the most informative samples and requests their labels from the user ("oracle") by performing a query. A broad overview of active learning approaches is given in [18]. For single classifiers, the strategy to select samples close to the decision boundary, for which the classification result is uncertain, is shown to be optimal in [13]. This concept is thus termed "uncertainty sampling" [18]. For a combination of several classifiers, such as the ensemble classifiers regarded in this study, the "query by committee" algorithm is introduced in [5], which selects those samples from the unlabelled data for which the results of the individual classifiers are most dissimilar [18]. In this study we will rely on a selection strategy which combines these two approaches.

3   Ensemble Classifiers for Gesture Recognition

The classifier ensemble used for gesture recognition in this study combines different classifier types with different views on the data, i.e. different sets of features, in order to obtain a high degree of diversity within the ensemble.

The 3D positions of the head and the hands of the gesturing person were obtained from multiocular image sequences as described in detail in [15]. According to [15], various features such as the coordinates of the hand positions relative to the head, velocity values, or trajectory curvatures are extracted. As the recognition result is desired to be independent of the position and orientation of the person in 3D space, additional variants of all features based on their changes over time ("delta features") are determined. These extraction steps result in an overall number of 90 features.

Based on the extracted features, we compute different views on the data by a combination of different preprocessing steps. The feature values are normalised to the same order of magnitude using as a first approach the transformation to the interval $[-1, +1]$ based on the corresponding minimum and maximum values and as a second approach the division of each feature by its mean absolute value. The dimensionality of the feature vectors is reduced by two methods: principal component analysis (PCA) [17] and independent component analysis (ICA) [7].

For the classifier ensembles, three types of classifiers are used: a linear, quadratic, or cubic polynomial classifier (PC) [17], a multi-layer perceptron

(MLP) [10], and a support vector regression (SVR) [1]. The MLP is used with only one hidden layer, where the number of hidden neurons is chosen such that the number of network parameters does not exceed 20% of the number of training samples and also remains smaller than one-half of the dimension of the input data. The SVR is used rather than the more commonly applied support vector machine (SVM) as it allows to compute the confidence bands of the estimated class-specific probabilities, which are much less straightforward to obtain for the SVM due to its discrete decision function. For a polynomial kernel and a RBF kernel of the SVR, the γ parameter according to [1] is chosen as the inverse average scalar product between the training samples [3] and as the inverse squared average mutual RMS distance between the training samples, respectively.

In the context of ensemble learning, it is generally assumed that using classifiers with dissimilar behaviour within an ensemble leads to an increased recognition performance [16]. In this study we quantify the diversity of the classifiers based on the cross-correlation measure and the rate of double faults as defined in [9], which both consider the respective class assignments of the individual samples and decrease with increasing diversity. These diversity measures can only be computed for pairs of classifiers. For more than two combined classifiers, we estimate the overall diversity by the average of the pairwise diversities.

The selection of the most promising ensemble configurations is based on a multi-criteria optimisation using a genetic search algorithm [4], considering the correlation coefficient, the rate of double faults, and the average classification error. This optimisation results in a three-dimensional Pareto front which comprises all Pareto-optimal solutions, where a solution is Pareto-optimal if no other solution exists for which all three criteria obtain a smaller value. Classifier ensembles consisting of L base classifiers are selected from those comprised by the Pareto front based on three criteria:

1. Select the classifier ensemble with the smallest average classification error under the constraint that its cross-correlation coefficient does not exceed the minimum value by more than 5%.
2. Select the classifier ensemble with the smallest average classification error under the constraint that its rate of double faults does not exceed the minimum value by more than 5%.
3. Select the classifier ensemble with the smallest rate of double faults under the constraint that its cross-correlation coefficient does not exceed the minimum value by more than 10%.

In order to keep the computational effort of the classifier ensembles in a reasonable range, only ensembles consisting of $L = 3$, 5, and 7 base classifiers are regarded. For each number L three classifier ensembles are selected according to the above criteria.

It is assumed that each of the L base classifiers determines a class assignment y_l and a decision vector $d_l = (d_{l1}, d_{l2}, \ldots, d_{lK})$ with $\sum_{j=1}^{K} d_{lj} = 1$. Five methods to determine the overall ensemble decision are applied to the selected classifier ensembles:

1. Majority voting.
2. Sum of decision values. The class assignment is given by the maximum of the vector $\boldsymbol{d}_{\text{ens}} = \sum_{l=1}^{L} \boldsymbol{d}_l$.
3. Weighted sum of decision values. The class assignment is given by the maximum of the vector $\boldsymbol{d}_{\text{ens}} = \sum_{l=1}^{L} \boldsymbol{w}_l^T \boldsymbol{d}_l$. The elements of the weight vector $\boldsymbol{w}_l$ are given by $w_{li} = 1/\sigma_{li}$ with σ_{li} as the renormalised confidence as defined in [3] of the i-th decision value of the l-th classifier.
4. Master classifier for decision values. The class assignment is obtained by generalised stacking, relying on the output of a "master classifier" which combines the decision values of the base classifiers. We always use a first-order PC as the master classifier, leading to $\boldsymbol{d}_{\text{ens}} = A\boldsymbol{d}_L^*$ with A as the coefficient matrix of the PC and $\boldsymbol{d}_L^* = \begin{bmatrix} \boldsymbol{d}_1^T & \boldsymbol{d}_2^T & \dots & \boldsymbol{d}_L^T \end{bmatrix}^T$ as the concatenated decision vectors of the base classifiers.
5. Master classifier for decision values and renormalised confidences. The master classifier determines the ensemble decision $\boldsymbol{d}_{\text{ens}}$ based on the decision values and the renormalised confidences of the base classifiers, such that $\boldsymbol{d}_{\text{ens}} = A\boldsymbol{d}_{\sigma L}^*$ with $\boldsymbol{d}_{\sigma L}^* = \begin{bmatrix} \boldsymbol{d}_1^T & \boldsymbol{\sigma}_1^T & \dots & \boldsymbol{d}_L^T & \boldsymbol{\sigma}_L^T \end{bmatrix}^T$.

4   Active Learning of Gestures

As a first step, a supervised training of the ensemble classifier is performed based on the initial labelled training set. During active learning, a sample is selected from the set of unlabelled samples and its label is queried if at least one of the four following conditions is fulfilled:

1. The maximum decision values of all L base classifiers are below a given threshold θ_1.
2. The differences between the highest and the second-highest decision value of all L base classifiers are below a given threshold θ_2.
3. The renormalised confidence values [3] of all L base classifiers exceed a given threshold θ_3.
4. The class assignment is different for all L base classifiers.

Condition 1 corresponds to the approach of uncertainty sampling. Condition 2 also selects unlabelled samples for which no clear class assignment can be obtained. Condition 3 relies on the renormalised confidence values, which have been found in [3] to denote how closely a new sample resembles the samples already used during the training process. Condition 4 selects unlabelled samples with a high degree of dissimilarity among the class assignments of the base classifiers and is thus a variant of the query by committee approach [5,18].

5   Experimental Evaluation

The 3D trajectory data used in this study were extracted from enblematic gestures in a multi-camera framework. The labelled data set was adopted from [15],

Fig. 1. Examples of the gesture classes (from left to right) "circle", "come here", "down", "go away", "point", "stop", "up", "horizontal wave", and "vertical wave". The extracted 3D trajectories have been reprojected into the image (from [15]).

Table 1. Number of instances and samples per gesture class

	Circle	Come here	Down	Go away	Point	Stop	Up	Hor. wave	Vert. wave
# instances	95	92	92	96	86	83	88	89	79
# samples	4000	2015	2056	1941	1573	1549	1651	3497	5617

where a detailed description is provided and the data are utilised for the classification of gestures using HMMs.[1] The gestures considered are performed by 16 different persons. According to [15], the raw 3D trajectories are smoothed using impulse-based resampling, which leads to a curvature-dependent distance between the resampled trajectory points obtaining low values when the local curvature of the trajectory is high. Table 1 lists the nine different classes, the number of instances (performed gestures) per class, and the number of samples (feature vectors corresponding to overlapping windows) per class.

Based on a series of tests of a variety of classifier configurations, the most appropriate window length corresponds to 8 subsequent resampled points. For the training data, the offset between two subsequent samples amounts to 1 step, while 4 steps are used for the test data. A number of 22 favourable base classifiers defined by the utilised normalisation technique, dimensionality reduction method, and classifier type were identified. In this context, the number of PCA components was chosen such that the reconstruction error corresponds to 0.1 and 0.01, respectively. The number of ICA components was set manually [7], where the "virtual dimensionality" [21] was used as an upper limit. The degree of the PC was set to 1, 2, and 3, where higher degrees were restricted to manageable sizes of the weight matrix. The SVR approach was used with polynomial kernels of degree 2 and 3 and with RBF kernel, and the number of hidden neurons of the MLP was determined automatically (cf. Section 3).

For all three selection criteria according to Section 3, the recognition rates of ensembles of size 5 are generally better than those of ensembles of size 3 and comparable to those of ensembles of size 7. The best ensembles of size 5 obtained with the genetic search algorithm are listed in Table 2.

For the evaluation of the ensemble classifiers, an 8-fold cross-validation was performed, where for each run the samples associated with 14 persons were used

---

[1] The trajectory data set is accessible at http://patrec.cs.tu-dortmund.de.

Table 2. Determined ensembles of size 5. "BC" stands for "base classifier". The numbers after "PCA" and "ICA" denote the reduced number of dimensions. The digits after "PC" and "Poly" denote the polynomial degree.

Selection criterion (cf. Section 3)	Base classifiers			
	ID	Normalisation	Dim. red.	Classifier type
Cross-correlation (1)	BC1	Division by mean	PCA59	PC2
	BC2	Min-max interval	ICA59	PC2
	BC3	Division by mean	ICA59	PC2
	BC4	Min-max interval	PCA150	SVR Poly2
	BC5	Division by mean	PCA240	MLP
Rate of double faults (2)	BC1	Min-max	PCA120	SVR RBF
	BC2	Min-max interval	ICA569	SVR RBF
	BC3	None	ICA471	SVR RBF
	BC4	Min-max interval	ICA569	SVR Poly3
	BC5	Min-max interval	PCA150	SVR Poly2
Combination (3)	BC1	Division by mean	PCA200	SVR RBF
	BC2	None	ICA471	SVR RBF
	BC3	Min-max interval	ICA59	PC2
	BC4	Division by mean	ICA59	PC2
	BC5	Min-max interval	PCA150	SVR Poly2

for training and the samples associated with the remaining 2 persons for testing. The recognition rates obtained are shown as box plots in Fig. 2. For all configurations considered, the median recognition rate of the best ensemble classifier is higher than that of the best base classifier. However, the difference is always smaller than the uncertainty intervals of the recognition rates. The master classifier which takes into account the base classifier decision values and renormalised confidence values yields the highest recognition rate for ensemble selection methods 1 and 3 and the second highest for ensemble selection method 2. The median recognition rates of the best ensemble classifiers are higher than 86%. Note that all recognition rates are per moment in time and not per trajectory.

5.1   Active Learning Scenario

For active learning, the data set is divided into an initial training set comprising 5% of all training samples associated with 3 different persons, a larger set of unlabelled samples associated with 11 persons used for active learning, and an independent test set consisting of samples associated with 2 persons. These data sets are permuted 8 times in order to facilitate an 8-fold cross validation.

We found that for the small training sets encountered during active learning the most favourable ensemble classifier consists of a SVR with RBF kernel, a SVR with polynomial kernel of degree 2, and a quadratic PC, combined by a weighted sum of their decision values with the inverse renormalised confidence values as weights (method 3 according to Section 3). The feature values were normalised to the interval $[-1, 1]$ based on their minimum and maximum values. Using PCA, the dimensionality of the samples was reduced to 120 and 80 for the

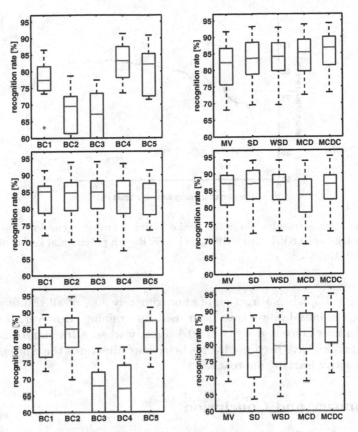

Fig. 2. Box plots of the recognition rates of the base classifiers (left column) and the ensemble decisions using different combination methods (right column) for (from top to bottom) selection criteria 1, 2, and 3. The ensembles correspond to those listed in Table 2. BC: base classifier; MV: majority voting; SD: sum of base classifier decision values; WSD: sum of base classifier decision values weighted by inverse renormalised confidence values; MCD: master classifier for decision values; MCDC: master classifier for decision values and renormalised confidence values.

SVR with quadratic polynomial kernel and with RBF kernel, respectively. For the quadratic PC, the number of PCA components was adapted dynamically to the increasing number of training samples in order to ensure that the coefficient matrix did not become underdetermined for small sample set sizes, where the maximum number of PCA components was set to 59. For sample selection from the set of unlabelled samples according to the conditions listed in Section 4, the threshold values were set to $\theta_1 = 0.5$, $\theta_2 = 0.1$, and $\theta_3 = 2$. Each time when 500 samples had been queried, the ensemble classifier was re-trained.

The results of the active learning scenario are shown in Fig. 3, where the solid curve denotes the median recognition rate and the dotted curves the 25% and 75% quantiles, respectively. The recognition rate saturates at a value of

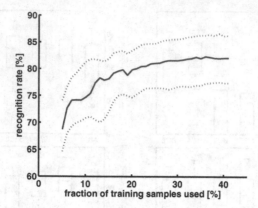

Fig. 3. Recognition results obtained in the active learning scenario. The ensemble classifier consists of a SVR with RBF kernel, a SVR with polynomial kernel of degree 2, and a quadratic PC.

about $82\% \pm 4\%$, when a fraction of approximately 30% of all training samples (including the initial ones) have been used for training. However, the median recognition rate exceeds a value of 80% already when a fraction of 20% of all training samples have been used. This behaviour illustrates the efficiency of the employed active learning approach.

6   Summary and Conclusion

We have investigated the classification of gestures based on ensemble methods by classifying trajectory segments comprising a fixed number of sampling points. We have presented a multi-view approach in order to increase the diversity of the classifiers across the ensemble. In addition to supervised learning, an active learning framework has been employed in order to reduce the manual labelling effort. In the supervised scenario, we have obtained median recognition rates per moment in time of more than 86%. Similar recognition rates in between 84% and 90% are observed for the HMM-based approach in [15] for complete gestures. A median recognition rate of about 80% has been obtained in the active learning scenario, using an initial training set of 5% of all training samples. An amount of further 15% has been selected according to four criteria specifying those samples for which the class assignment of the ensemble classifier is most uncertain. The recognition rate saturates at a value of about $82\% \pm 4\%$. The recognition performance observed in the supervised and in the active learning scenario illustrates that gesture recognition based on the classification of trajectory segments using ensemble methods is a promising approach that may be applied in various areas, such as human-robot interaction or non-obtrusive user interfaces.

References

1. Bishop, C.M.: Pattern Recognition and Machine Learning. Springer (2007)
2. Breiman, L.: Random forests. Machine Learning 45, 5–32 (2001)
3. Cui, T., Grumpe, A., Hillebrand, M., Kreßel, U., Kummert, F., Wöhler, C.: Analytically tractable sample-specific confidence measures for semi-supervised learning. In: Proc. Workshop Computational Intelligence, pp. 171–186 (2011)
4. Deb, K.: Multi-Objective Optimization Using Evolutionary Algorithms. Wiley (2001)
5. Freund, Y., Seung, H.S., Shamir, E., Tishby, N.: Selective sampling using the query by committee algorithm. Machine Learning 28, 133–168 (1997)
6. Ho, T.K.: The random subspace method for constructing decision forests. IEEE Trans. on Pattern Analysis and Machine Intelligence 20(8), 832–844 (1998)
7. Hyvärinen, A., Karhunen, J., Oja, E.: Independent Component Analysis. Wiley (2001)
8. Kuncheva, L.I.: Combining pattern classifiers: methods and algorithms. Wiley (2004)
9. Kuncheva, L.I., Whitaker, C.J.: Measures of diversity in classifier ensembles and their relationship with the ensemble accuracy. Machine Learning 51, 181–207 (2003)
10. Marsland, S.: Machine Learning: An Algorithmic Perspective. CRC Press (2009)
11. Mitra, S., Acharya, T.: Gesture recognition: A survey. IEEE Trans. on Systems, Man, and Cybernetics, Part C 37(3), 311–324 (2007)
12. Ong, S., Ranganath, S.: Automatic sign language analysis: A survey and the future beyond lexical meaning. IEEE Trans. on Pattern Analysis and Machine Intelligence 27(6), 873–891 (2005)
13. Park, J.M., Hu, Y.: Online learning for active pattern recognition. IEEE Signal Processing Letters 3(11), 301–303 (1996)
14. Poppe, R.: A survey on vision-based human action recognition. Image and Vision Computing 28, 976–990 (2010)
15. Richarz, J., Fink, G.A.: Visual recognition of 3D emblematic gestures in an HMM framework. J. of Ambient Intelligence and Smart Environments 3(3), 193–211 (2011)
16. Rokach, L.: Pattern classification using ensemble methods. World Scientific (2010)
17. Schürmann, J.: Pattern Classification. Wiley-Interscience (1996)
18. Settles, B.: Active learning literature survey. Computer Sciences Technical Report 1648, University of Wisconsin–Madison (2009)
19. Shotton, J., Fitzgibbon, A., Cook, M., Sharp, T., Finocchio, M., Moore, R., Kipman, A., Blake, A.: Real-time human pose recognition in parts from single depth images. In: Proc. IEEE Conf. on Computer Vision and Pattern Recognition (2011)
20. Suk, H.I., Sin, B.K., Lee, S.W.: Hand gesture recognition based on dynamic bayesian network framework. Pattern Recognition 43(9), 3059–3072 (2010)
21. Wang, J., Chang, C.I.: Independent component analysis based dimensionality reduction with applications in hyperspectral image analysis. IEEE Trans. on Geoscience and Remote Sensing 44, 1586–1600 (2006)
22. Wang, S.B., Quattoni, A., Morency, L.P., Demirdjian, D.: Hidden conditional random fields for gesture recognition. In: Proc. IEEE Conf. on Computer Vision and Pattern Recognition, vol. 2, pp. 1521–1527 (2006)
23. Wolpert, D.H.: Stacked generalization. Neural Networks 5, 241–259 (1992)
24. Xu, L., Krzyzak, A., Suen, C.: Methods of combining multiple classifiers and their applications to handwriting recognition. IEEE Trans. on Systems, Man and Cybernetics 22(3), 418–435 (1992)

Author Index

Ackermann, Jens 287
Aktaş, Mehmet Ali 307
Aldoma, Aitor 113
Angelopoulou, Elli 185

Ballester, Coloma 31
Beinrucker, A. 256
Beljan, Mate 287
Bilen, Hakan 134
Bischof, Horst 195
Blanchard, G. 256
Bleyer, Michael 337
Böer, Gordon 155
Bogunović, Nikola 408
Bouchot, Jean-Luc 428
Bräuer-Burchardt, Christian 276
Brkić, Karla 408
Brosch, Nicole 418
Brox, Thomas 21, 103
Bruhn, Andrés 73
Buchholz, Dirk 93

Caselles, Vicent 31
Cremers, Armin B. 357
Cremers, Daniel 347

Dann, Christoph 397
Demetz, Oliver 73
Denzler, Joachim 1
Dogan, Ü. 256
Dragon, Ralf 123

Ebert, Sandra 327
Elhayek, A. 266
Enzberg, Sebastian von 175

Fecker, Daniel 367
Fenzi, Michele 123
Fingscheidt, Tim 367
Fink, Gernot A. 488, 498
Fleischmann, Oliver 297
Franzel, Thorsten 144
Frintrop, Simone 246, 357
Fritz, Mario 327

Fröhlich, Björn 1
Fugl, Andreas Rune 165

Gao, Qi 62
García, Germán Martín 357
Garrido, Lluis 31
Gehler, Peter 397
Gelautz, Margrit 337, 418
Goesele, Michael 287
Grumpe, A. 498

Hahmann, Ferdinand 155
Haslinger, Peter 428
Haxhimusa, Yll 11
Hosni, Asmaa 337, 418
Huerta, Ramón 216

Ilic, Slobodan 468
Ion, Adrian 11

Jordt, Andreas 165
Jović, Alan 408

Kee, Youngwook 347
Keuper, Margret 83
Kim, Junmo 347
Kim, K.I. 266
Klauck, Ulrich 478
Klein, Dominik Alexander 246, 357
Koch, Reinhard 165, 236
Kohli, Pushmeet 41
Köstinger, Martin 195
Kreßel, Ulrich 478
Kühmstedt, Peter 276
Kuznetsova, Alina 377

Lampert, Christoph H. 205
Lazcano, Vanel 31
Leal-Taixé, Laura 123
Lindner, Frank 478
Liu, Kun 21

Märgner, Volker 367
Mayer, Heinz 448
Michaelis, Bernd 175

Moser, Bernhard   428
Muezzinoglu, Mehmet K.   216
Müller, Andreas C.   205

Nagaraja, Naveen Shankar   21
Namboodiri, Vinay P.   134
Nasse, Fabian   488
Notni, Gunther   276
Nowozin, Sebastian   205, 397

Ochs, Peter   21
Ostermann, Jörn   123

Palme, Klaus   83
Pasternak, Taras   83
Petersen, Henrik Gordon   165
Pons-Moll, Gerard   377
Prabhakaran, Sandhya   458

Raman, Sudhir   317, 458
Rhemann, Christoph   418
Riess, Christian   185
Rilk, Markus   93
Rodner, Erik   1
Ronneberger, Olaf   83
Rosenhahn, Bodo   123, 377
Roth, Peter M.   195
Roth, Stefan   52, 62, 144, 397
Roth, Volker   317, 458
Rother, Carsten   41
Ruppertshofen, Heike   155
Rusu, Radu Bogdan   113

Sakič, D.   498
Schelten, Kevin   52
Schiele, Bernt   327
Schlesinger, Dmitrij   387
Schmaltz, Christian   438
Schmidt, Thorsten   83
Schmidt, Uwe   144
Schneeberger, Michael   448

Schramm, Hauke   155
Schroers, Christopher   73
Schumacher, J.   498
Seidel, H.-P.   266
Shekhovtsov, Alexander   41
Sommer, Gerald   297
Spehr, Jens   93
Stannarius, Ralf   155
Staudenmaier, Armin   478
Stoll, C.   266
Stübl, Gernot   428
Stückler, Jörg   357
Sturm, Peter   468

Theobalt, C.   266
Tombari, Federico   113

Ummenhofer, Benjamin   103
Unger, Christian   468
Uray, Martina   448

Valgaerts, Levi   73
Van Gool, Luc J.   134
Vembu, Shankar   216
Vergara, Alexander   216
Vincze, Markus   113
Vogt, Julia E.   458

Wahl, Eric   468
Wahl, Friedrich M.   93
Weickert, Joachim   73, 438
Willatzen, Morten   165
Winkelbach, Simon   93
Wöhler, Christian   478, 498

Zach, Fabian   185
Zankl, Georg   11
Zdunek, Rafał   226
Zhang, Lilian   236
Zimmer, Henning   73
Žunić, Joviša   307